T0204528

West Indian Societies

by the same author

George Perkins Marsh: Versatile Vermonter (Columbia University Press, 1958)
The West Indies Federation: Perspectives on a New Nation (Columbia University Press, 1961; Oxford University Press, 1962)

edited by David Lowenthal

Man and Nature (Harvard University Press, 1965)
Environmental Perception and Behavior (University of Chicago, 1967)

DAVID LOWENTHAL

West Indian Societies

Published for the
Institute of Race Relations, London
in collaboration with the American Geographical Society, New York

OXFORD UNIVERSITY PRESS
NEW YORK   LONDON   TORONTO
1972

American Geographical Society Research Series
Number 26

Printed in the United States of America

Foreword

This book is part of a plan, of which the embryo was conceived many years ago. The purpose, which in 1952 seemed less obvious and perhaps less naïve than today, was to compare with each other a wide range of societies within which there were ethnic or physical differences carrying some social significance, to consider in each the degree of social importance attached to physical characteristics, and to consider what other factors might be responsible for the differences in social structures that emerged. Studies of Brazil and of the Caribbean were essential to the scheme because it was then often claimed that colour of skin and other racial characteristics were in these regions not only of much less social significance than in the United States or South Africa, but were actually of almost negligible effect. It was said that these societies had 'solved' a problem that was getting worse elsewhere. If this was an exaggeration, was there anything in it? Was there really a lesson for anyone else, not only in what distinguished the Caribbean from the rest of the world, but in what distinguished the islands from each other? The Caribbean, it was often said, was a natural laboratory. The numerical proportions of the races, the history of conquest, the differing cultures and religions of the colonial powers, economic factors, and terrain—all these made differences which would illuminate the subject.

It was some years before the general concept of a group of books on different areas, with a comparative survey of the results, focused with sufficient clarity to make it possible to apply to the Ford Foundation for funds. The Institute of Race Relations was fortunate to find in the Ford Foundation the sympathetic imagination of Joseph Slater, who encouraged the project and helped to frame it. And, in the next stage, the Institute was again fortunate in finding in David Lowenthal a scholar steeped in knowledge of the Caribbean who was prepared to undertake—and, what is more, has completed—a study of so many aspects of so many societies. Finally, the Institute was fortunate in the co-operation of the American Geographical Society.

What has emerged is not, of course, exactly what was expected. The enterprise would be disappointing, indeed, if it merely confirmed existing hypotheses; in any case, at the moment of writing this foreword, nearly ten years have passed since the Foundation made the grant, and they have been years of rapid change. There has been change in the structure of the island societies themselves, but even more important have been changes in attitudes and reactions throughout the world to race as a social phenomenon. To these I shall return, but first let us emphasize one point which has emerged from this whole series and is confirmed by David Lowenthal's analysis. This is the uniqueness of each situation and its firm roots in the past.

It had been hoped that the differences between the way race is regarded in, say, Barbados and Trinidad, might be attributable to factors, such as numerical proportion, which could be isolated, and whose effect could be measured, almost as the elements in a chemical compound can be separated and measured. Further, it was hoped that, again almost as in chemistry, these results could be applied to large regions, say Brazil and the Southern States. This is really not so. Of course, the differences between social structure in Barbados and Trinidad, which were so marked ten years ago, *were* due to such factors as the exclusively British history of Barbados, contrasted with Trinidad's French and Spanish past; to the presence of East Indians in Trinidad; to the difference in size of the islands, and the nature of the country. But it is the *combination* of these and other factors that gives each society its peculiar flavour; no one can take one factor, such as numerical proportion, and draw a smooth curve, illustrating its effect on social relations, which will hold good for Brazil, the Southern States, South Africa, and various Caribbean societies. For example, the attitude to freed slaves and people of mixed blood, as between these four regions, does not accord solely with the demographic proportions. If the proportions of white to black were the ruling factor, one would expect to find the Southern States at one end of a scale which ran through Brazil and South Africa to the Caribbean. In attitudes and social structure, the Southern States and Brazil would resemble each other, while South Africa would resemble the Caribbean. But of course this is not at all the case. South Africa resembles the Southern States in holding that any share of black blood contaminates, not, as traditionally in the Caribbean and Brazil, that white blood raises the social status. To explain the reactions of the White South to freed slaves, one has to look for other factors—such as religion, attitude to work, the external challenge to the society, and the kind of social structure assumed to be normal. And one might generalize that the more egalitarian in outlook the free society is within itself, the less likely it is to welcome or even tolerate a freed slave. Since there is no place for him except an equal place, he cannot have a place at all. But where free society is frankly hierarchical, the freed slave or the man of mixed blood is much less of a challenge. He can start at the bottom.

But though each of the island societies is unique, there is a strong resemblance between them. Indeed, progressively closer study of them seems first to underline their differences and later to reassert their underlying resemblance. As in one of the attempts at definition for a biological species, they resemble each other more than they resemble anything else. There is something in these West Indian societies which can be called a standard Creole structure. It is a pyramid, based on a past history of slavery and a present legacy of colour, or more precisely of shade, as one indication of status among several. It is a pyramid composed sometimes of visible terraces or steps, as in the architecture of Mexico, rather than smoothly graded as in the pyramid of Cheops. But there has until recently been some movement from step to step, particularly in the higher tiers, which has been partly due to the emigration of the most able or the most successful. Today, the pyramid of standard Creole structure has been turned upside down in the political dimension, but in the social and economic dimensions it is very little changed. And of course this already complex situation is further complicated where a territory also contains sizeable elements—usually East Indian—who are outside the Creole structure.

The Caribbean presents in microcosm, sharply exaggerated, the most acute dilemmas of the last third of the twentieth century. One of these is presented by the intersection at this stage of history of two contradictory tendencies. At a time when Britain was becoming aware of the need to join Europe, Anguilla with six thousand inhabitants asserted that it was so important to preserve her identity—to do her own thing—that she must be sovereign and independent. And later, she reluctantly accepted colonial status so long as she was separate from St. Kitts. Only large blocks of population can in general afford such immensely expensive modern necessities as hospitals and universities, not to mention motorways, state medical care, and paid holidays. Everyone wants these things, but the price is some surrender of unfettered national freedom. Yet there is such a passion for self-expression that, all over the world, the tiniest groups clamour for a separate and independent sovereignty. The centralizing tendency lies in the economic, the centrifugal in the cultural dimension—but this is a distinction for the study not for the hustings. Caribbean societies, already impoverished, condemn themselves by their separatism to further impoverishment; Welsh, Basque, and Breton nationalists are eager to share their fate.

There is another intersection of trends which the Caribbean societies underline. Modern scientific techniques have created wants which demand an increasingly tight administrative system; the loose traditional *laissez-faire* administration of the colonial past is felt by all to be insufficient. The state intrudes into spheres of life which it would not have touched in the Victorian era. At the same time, there is a break-down in the hierarchy of unequal social status into which all Europeans were born—and in this the Caribbean societies *are* European. Ad-ministration grows tighter and more pervasive and is in the hands of a technocracy which cuts across the old pattern of ascriptive status; new tensions are born. Where the old pyramid has been stood—politically—on its head, the tension is likely to grow acute. Not only are there new masters, but personal freedom is actually diminished at the moment when a new freedom seems to be proclaimed. And it seems likely that the smaller the unit, the more intolerable the assertion of a centralized modern system of government will be. In a vast continental territory, the successful technocrat will leave the village where he is known for a distant capital. Not so in a small island. The animosities that would be aroused by a more socialist tone of government in any Caribbean society would be of a most intimate and enduring kind; the local resentment at the intrusions of the centre are likely to become more acute.

There is one more aspect of the present situation which has always been a difficulty for small societies—for the Basques, the Bretons, the Welsh—but which is far more severe for the Creole societies. The path to success has been by education in the language and culture of the metropolitan society. This kind of success has meant escape from the narrow world of the provincial society, to which it has been doubly damaging. It has meant the erosion of the apex of the pyramid, loss by assimilation to the greater society of the ablest and most enterprising native sons. But this has been the least of the damage. It has also meant that success has been measured in the smaller society by the degree of assimilation to the greater. The native son could make good only by renouncing his birthright. In the premiership of Lloyd George—who had reached the pinnacle of success in the larger society—a point was reached when this tide began to turn for the Welsh and it became increasingly fashionable for the successful native son to proclaim his Welshness. In the politics of the Caribbean, this stage was reached a generation later, in the nineteen-fifties.

But while in the dimension of politics the Caribbean leader had to show that he *was* truly a son of his island, and often to identify himself with 'the barefoot party', he still had to show himself master of essenti-ally European (or mainland American) procedures if he wanted to raise a loan or appear at ease at a smart party. And he was faced with a difficulty far more acute than the Basque or the Welshman. They had a language and the remains of a culture, which had been repressed, certainly, and in some areas extinguished. But there *was* a living language, there were traditions at least of a culture that had been their own. But none of this is true of the Creole societies in the Caribbean. The former slaves had been robbed of their language, forcibly dispossessed of their marriage customs and their whole social background; what is more, they had been prevented from acquiring the customs of their enslavers.

They had come into contact only with a debased backwater from the mainstream of European culture; the owners of the larger estates were usually absentees and their representatives, the agents and lesser planters, were in general socially, educationally, and morally below the standards of people in the metropolitan society who held comparable positions. Even from this muddy creek the slaves were excluded; marriage and education were alike discouraged. The consequence was that, when emancipation came, the former slaves had nothing of their own; they were conscious of no means of escape from poverty and ignorance but by becoming more like Europeans. As Lowenthal makes clear, the tradition followed by the majority of the 'folk', that is the mass of the former field hands, was one of hostility to the Government and its laws. But it is surprising, considering the models for imitation which were often presented to them, that there should have developed also, at first no doubt largely among freedmen, house slaves, and those of mixed descent, the contrary tradition of conformity to Victorian ideals—the Protestant ethic of work and respectability. But it was an ideal that there was no possibility of attaining except by self-delusion; they could not become physically European.

The Caribbean was the most colonial of all colonial societies; here the deepest wrong was done. The mass of the people—whether they followed the tradition of rejection or of imitation—had no target to aim at, no ideal vision, that was not self-defeating. Lowenthal quotes Fanon's story of his childhood. His mother would say to him: 'Stop acting like a nigger.' Then how was he to act? Like a white man? But in that case, he must despise himself. He had no solution but the impossible fantasy that he was somehow an exception, that he was really white, though no one perceived it.

Thus the search for a cultural pedigree, the desire for roots in a past that is not derived from the former masters, is stronger here than anywhere else in the world. It has led sometimes to a nihilism which denies value to all intellectual achievement, to scientific discovery, to art, to the creative imagination; it has led also to fictitious pedigrees, bogus history, nostalgia for a romantic Africa which never existed. Less explicitly, it leads often to self-distrust which is manifested as over-confidence, to a dogmatic refusal to compromise, to a rejection of any classification of persons, plans, or ideas but the most extreme, a polarization of all relations into hostility or support.

It is against this psychological background that one must see the obvious dilemma of the Caribbean in respect of food, population, and resources. The islands are tiny territories; to combine would indeed be difficult but they have decisively rejected the attempt. They are over-populated and generally suited to producing goods of which the world has enough. Outlets by emigration are closing in a world which grows more parochial as communications improve. Emancipation awakened expectations that were never fulfilled; independence has served merely to remove a scapegoat. The populations of the islands are now vividly alive to the way the developed nations live; they resent their poverty and there is no solution for it in sight.

In the United States, polarization has become the cry; the hope that black and white could live peacefully together is out of fashion. The view that there can be no common ground becomes increasingly popular. In a world of such stark confrontation, what—some may ask—is the use of a patient and sensitive assembly of information about the social structure of West Indian societies? But, in the first place, to learn more of any society in whose structure ideas about race play a part is to learn something about every other. In particular, the Caribbean has much to tell about the distinction between notional race and biological race—that is, between the idea of race as a social signal and the facts of physical and genetic difference. West Indians, as David Lowenthal says, believe in integration—and at least to the limited extent of making no absolute distinctions, they practise it. But to me—having read this book at three different stages—the first richly and rewardingly amorphous, the third pruned and disciplined—the outstanding impression is of the many dimensions in which man lives as a social animal. 'I will buy with you, sell with you, talk with you, walk with you . . . but I will not eat with you, drink with you nor pray with you', says Shylock and I heard an even longer and more explicit catalogue of the same kind the first day I spent in Barbados. And surely it is on the lines of cultural diversity within an economic unity that a solution lies for minorities such as the East Indians or the Basques. The art of politics is to reconcile these dimensions. The fact remains that, if West Indians have something to teach the world in this respect, there remain for them problems of food and population to which there can be no solution that is not in part international. If any attempt to deal with these problems internationally is ever made, David Lowenthal's book will surely be prescribed reading for the planners.

PHILIP MASON

Acknowledgements

For permission to quote excerpts, I am indebted to

Guy Lasserre, for *La Guadeloupe: étude géographique*, Union Française d'Impression, 1961, Vol. I, p. 322;

Annemarie de Waal Malefijt, for *The Javanese of Surinam: Segment of a Plural Society*, Van Gorcum, 1963, p. 29;

Mervyn Morris, for 'To An Expatriate Friend', from *Jamaica Journal*, Vol. 3, No. 4, December 1969;

Allen S. Ehrlich, for 'East Indian Cane Workers in Jamaica', Ph.D. thesis in Anthropology, University of Michigan, 1969, p. 82;

Andre Deutsch, Ltd., for *The Mystic Masseur*, 1957, pp. 201–4, and *The Middle Passage*, 1962, pp. 196–8, both by V. S. Naipaul;

Alfred A. Knopf, Inc., for Melville J. Herskovits, *Life in a Haitian Valley*, p. 39 (copyright, Alfred A. Knopf, 1937);

Inter-Varsity Fellowship, for Joyce Gladwell, *Brown Face, Big Master*, pp. 23–5 (copyright, Inter-Varsity Press, 1969);

Oxford University Press, for Edward Brathwaite, *Rights of Passage*, p. 42, published by Oxford University Press, 1967.

Preface

The West Indies were long treated simply as pawns of imperial rivalries, as imperfect replicas of European countries, or as exotic refuges from civilized life. Only within the past few decades have they attracted much scrutiny in their own right.

Islanded among continental giants are eleven million West Indians in some fifty societies, each distinct from the others, yet all different from the Anglo-American and Latin American leviathans that frame the Caribbean. This book chronicles the likenesses and differences of these societies, their insularities and common bonds, and their citizens' efforts, in the wake of the hemisphere's longest history of slavery and colonialism, to transform vitality, elan, and creativity into a viable sense of identity. 'We strive to be ourselves,' notes a West Indian university head, 'not Englishmen or Africans or Indians or Chinese, but West Indians.'[1] The distinctive quality lies less in what is uniquely local, however, than in the West Indian amalgam.

Of general information about the West Indies there is a plethora. They have been more surveyed than any other area of similar size. One bibliography of the non-Hispanic Caribbean, excluding Haiti, contains seven thousand items from the twentieth century alone. Historical and geographical studies, social and economic analyses, anthropological and psychological investigations, and literary expressions of West Indian states of mind all abound. In addition, an abundant polemical literature flows from local universities, political parties, labour unions, and all manner of social and religious agencies. Public memoirs, novels, short stories, and poems afford additional insights into West Indian affairs. Other printed sources—newspapers, government reports, pamphlets, broadsides—are of staggering quantity and variety. Unpublished letters, account books, estate inventories, court and parish records, wills and deeds, and legislative debates are voluminous and accessible in official archives and private collections in the Caribbean,

[1] W. Arthur Lewis, 'On Being Different', graduation address, UWI, Barbados, reprinted in *Dominica Star*, 20 February 1971, pp. 6–7.

Europe, and America. Merely to list local archival resources in Barbados, the Windwards, and the Leewards requires three substantial volumes.[1]

Yet most Caribbean studies are sharply restricted in time, place, or subject matter. Scholarly surveys of individual territories are numerous, but except for Eric Williams's *From Columbus to Castro* and J. H. Parry and P. M. Sherlock's *A Short History of the West Indies*, only travellers and littérateurs have tried to paint the whole Caribbean canvas. The quality of what is known about any West Indian territory depends partly on its size. Several of the smaller islands—Carriacou, San Andrés, St. Barthélemy, Saba—have been comprehensively studied. But no comparable syntheses exist for such larger territories as Jamaica, Martinique, or Surinam, though scores of observers have looked at communities and investigated specific problems there. What Trinidad is like is less agreed upon than is the case, say, for Tortola, not only because Trinidad is a larger and more complex island, but also because it is seen from a broader range of perspectives. And because certain areas and some issues are more thoroughly studied than others, generalizations inevitably reflect the wealth or paucity of data.

British, French, Dutch, and American suzerainty, past or present, make strict comparisons impossible. Differences in local styles of life are compounded by metropolitan policy and prejudice, law and custom, even scholarly idiosyncrasies. The way British anthropologists study Jamaica, French geographers Guadeloupe, or Dutch sociologists Curaçao, affects the questions they ask, the answers they get, and the data they choose to emphasize. And these studies in turn influence local behaviour and self-images.

Similar caveats apply also to first-hand observations. In seventeen years my itinerary has taken me to most Caribbean territories, but I have stayed longer in the Guianas and the former British West Indies—notably Dominica, Montserrat, Barbados, and Jamaica—than in the French and Netherlands Antilles. The Commonwealth territories make up three-fourths of all Caribbean societies and, excluding Haiti, contain two-thirds of all West Indians. But I have tried to incorporate enough from the rest of the Caribbean to point up both similarities and differences.

In the West Indies, as in many other former colonies, nationalism and the search for identity today seem to require local, not foreign, interpreters. Some feel that only West Indians ought to write about the West Indies. The work of metropolitan social scientists may be dis-

[1] Lambros Comitas, *Caribbeana 1900–1965*, 1968; M. J. Chandler, *A Guide to Records in Barbados*, Oxford, Blackwell for UWI, 1965; E. C. Baker, *A Guide to Records in the Windward Islands*, Oxford, Blackwell for UWI, 1968; idem, *A Guide to Records in the Leeward Islands*, Oxford, Blackwell for UWI, 1965.

missed as irrelevant even when it is not condemned as imperialist.
Scholarly convergence is said to be a virtue limited to 'those who belong
to the Caribbean'.[1] Colour complicates the issue. A West Indian
resenting an American article about Trinidad inveighs against 'yet
another dissection . . . by people who, being used to some sort of racial
strife, tend to see it lurking in our society.'[2] Interpretations of the West
Indies in this book necessarily reflect external preoccupations, not least
the current American racial crisis.

In the West Indies, as elsewhere, there are indeed things only an
insider can know, approaches only an insider can take, errors only an
outsider is prone to make. But parochialism on the other hand limits
the West Indian; and the committed insider is apt to be intensely
partisan. One cannot safely rely on either approach exclusively; both
are essential. 'Every people must interpret its own history in the light
of its own traditions and experience', writes an American in the context
of minority affairs. 'At the same time, the history of every people must
be written from without, if only to provide a necessary perspective;
sooner or later the history of every people must flow from the clash of
viewpoints and sensibilities.' In America 'there is simply no way of
learning about either blacks or whites without learning about the
other.'[3] These strictures apply no less to the Caribbean, where
distinctions of race and colour shade into those of class. The West
Indian social order, however stressful, displays no rigid polarities but
rather a continuum within which individuals occupy a variety of
shifting positions.

Whatever the virtues or drawbacks of being an insider, Caribbean
diversity finally constrains most West Indians to be outsiders as well.
Haitians, Anguillans, Barbadians, and Surinamese are all equally West
Indian, but each sees things in a different way. The variegated perspectives of individuals of every background throughout the entire archipelago, and beyond, comprise essential parts of the whole West Indian
scene.

In trying to understand and delineate that scene, I have had the support
of many friends and colleagues. For their enduring insight, encouragement, and hospitality in the Caribbean I am deeply indebted to
David T. Edwards, Marjorie Lumsden, Eric Murray, Philip Nassief,
Jean Mathivet, Philip Sherlock, Michael G. Smith, and their families.

[1] Raymond T. Smith, 'Social Stratification, Cultural Pluralism and Integration in
West Indian Societies', in S. Lewis and T. G. Mathews, *Caribbean Integration*, 1967,
pp. 226–58, ref. p. 227.

[2] Elma Reyes, 'Trinidad Rebuttal', *New York Times*, 24 December 1967, Travel
Section, p. 29.

[3] Eugene D. Genovese, 'American Slaves and Their History', *New York Review of
Books*, 3 December 1970, pp. 34–42, ref. p. 34.

In Britain and America Colin G. Clarke, Lambros Comitas, Sidney M. Greenfield, and Vera Rubin have been stimulating collaborators and advisers.

For countless acts of kindness and for access to people, places, and data in various Caribbean lands, my thanks go to Peter Abrahams, Keith Alleyne, Phyllis Allfrey, Kenneth Blackburne, Lloyd Braithwaite, William Bramble, Michael Chandler, Liliane Chauleau, Yves Collart, Bertram Collins, Leslie Cummings, Gloria and George Cumper, Frank Dowdy, Betty Drayton, Charlesworth Edwards, Barry Floyd, William Gocking, Shirley Gordon, Elsa Goveia, Douglas Hall, Wilson Harris, John Hearne, Dudley Huggins, Frank C. Hutson, H. P. Jacobs, Norman Manley, Elisabeth Mueller, Robert Le Page, Vernon Leslie, H. L. Lindo, Rex Nettleford, A. J. A. Quintus-Bosz, S. S. Ramphal, Wilfred Redhead, Venetta Ross, Hugh Springer, and Raymond T. Smith.

In North America, I have benefited from the sympathetic criticism of John P. Augelli, Haywood Burns, Daniel J. Crowley, Carl N. Degler, Eugene D. Genovese, Richard A. Howard, Donald Q. Innis, Harold R. Isaacs, Annemarie de Waal Malefijt, Gordon Merrill, Ivar Oxaal, James J. Parsons, Carl O. Sauer, Constance Sutton, and Elisabeth Wallace.

I owe special gratitude to S. Resa Ahsan for material on East Indians in Guyana and Trinidad; to Edith Clarke for access to family correspondence and to newspaper files; to Allen Ehrlich for data on East Indians in Jamaica; to Harmannus Hoetink for material on Surinam and the Netherlands Antilles; to Edith Kovats-Beaudoux for access to her unpublished dissertation on the white Creoles of Martinique; to Carl S. Matthews for Marcus Garvey letters; to Charles C. Moskos for interview data on the ranking of 'influential' West Indians; and to H. Orlando Patterson for papers on Jamaican society. Additional data from archives and personal research were generously made available by Eva Abraham-van der Mark, Mervin Alleyne, Valerie Bloomfield, Lawrence D. Carrington, William V. Davidson, Silvia de Groot, Danayand Maharaj, Frank J. McDonald, Cyril A. Rogers, and Beate Salz.

Drafts of individual chapters were scrutinized by Colin G. Clarke, David Brion Davis, Sidney W. Mintz, Hugh Tinker, and Pierre van den Berghe. I am grateful to them, and still more to Lambros Comitas, Philip Mason, Eric Murray, Philip Sherlock, and Michael G. Smith, who read the bulk of the manuscript at various stages.

The American Geographical Society has provided both general support and individual assistance. For three years, Marquita Riel helped to reorganize the data for and the structure of this book, and I owe much to her searching questions and analytic acuity. In and beyond my Augean library, Erica Kelly located and corrected every quotation and footnote reference, and compiled the bibliography. Naomi Burns contributed an informed and sensitive editorial judgement. Mary Alice Lamberty worked with me through many drafts of the text, making and enforcing countless grammatical and other decisions. Betty O'Connell and Joan Nolan assisted far beyond the monumental task of typing, retyping, and proof-reading. Miklos Pinther and Christy Miller drew the map.

I am indebted to the staff of the Institute of Race Relations for many kindnesses, in particular to Janet Evanson and A. Sivanandan for help in the early years and to Simon Abbott and Dale Gunthorp for their patient support in seeing the book through to production. The Research Institute for the Study of Man generously provided ancillary support for research and data gathering.

My deepest gratitude goes to Philip Mason, who gave me the opportunity to write the book, offered constructive advice at every stage, and never lost faith during the years it remained unfinished; and to Michael G. Smith, on whose inspiration and guidance this work is essentially founded.

DAVID LOWENTHAL

Abbreviations for Bibliography and Footnotes

AA   *American Anthropologist*
CERAG   *Cahiers du C.E.R.A.G.* (Centre d'Études Régionales Antilles-
              Guyane)
CO-M   *Cahiers d'Outre-Mer*
CQ   *Caribbean Quarterly*
CS   *Caribbean Studies*
GR   *Geographical Review*
ICS   Institute of Caribbean Studies (University of Puerto Rico)
ISER   Institute of Social and Economic Research (University of the
              West Indies)
JHR   *Jamaican Historical Review*
JJ   *Jamaica Journal*
NWQ   *New World Quarterly*
SES   *Social and Economic Studies*
WIE   *West Indian Economist*
UWI
UCWI } University (College) of the West Indies

Contents

West Indian Societies

CHAPTER I

Introduction

This book is about West Indians: black, white, and brown; French, Dutch, and English; African and Chinese; East Indian and Amerindian —and West Indian. The terms themselves imply questions that need answers. Who are 'West Indians'? What is West Indian society, and how is it organized? What bonds keep West Indians together, and what tensions pull them apart? What personal traits stem from the circumstances of West Indian life, and what attitudes toward self and toward others? Is there a 'West Indian personality'? If so, how and why does it differ from any other? What relevance have these questions for paramount West Indian problems—making a living, raising a family, running a government, establishing a sense of identity? And finally, what light can the answers throw on people and problems elsewhere?

More explicitly, I aim to explain how the West Indies and their people became what they are, to show what makes them unique or ordinary, and to describe how they get on with one another and with the world outside.

One focus most of these themes share is the transcendent issue of race and colour. Within the West Indies, to be sure, racial stress is only one of many major problems. But there are few aspects of West Indian life that race and colour do not significantly touch. As a form of identification, racial classification is perhaps unavoidable. 'The desire to distinguish races', says one apologist, 'is nothing more than the desire to be specific, to replace literary abstractions by a concrete sense of the endless variety of life and nature, to introduce local color, even to show sympathy with what is alien to one's customs and prejudices.'[1] To be aware of difference is not automatically to discriminate; whereas to be (or profess to be) colour-blind may signal grave anxiety or conceal latent hostility. But racial distinctions are usually *meant* to be invidious: they carry an implication that one group is not just different from, but better than, another. And because individual effort can never wholly eliminate racial barriers, stratification by race and colour impedes

[1] Jacques Barzun, *Race: A Study in Modern Superstition*, 1938, pp. 112–13.

economic and cultural development, depresses enterprise, and restricts personal opportunities.

Racial and ethnic situations vary markedly in type and intensity. In South Africa prejudice is deliberately employed to bolster apartheid and white dominance over a black majority; in the United States ghetto life for a black minority belies egalitarian social premises; in Brazil colour ascription is almost universal but formal segregation is rare. Black–white confrontations are not the only divisive issues: the Chinese in South-East Asia struggle for mastery or for community survival; the French and the English in Canada contend on political and linguistic fronts; the presence of Indians in Kenya poses dilemmas for Africans and for Britons.

West Indian societies exhibit analogues of all these situations except the South African; for West Indians have experienced as wide a range of racial circumstances as exists any place. Each Caribbean territory is unique, but each discloses instances of difficulties confronted elsewhere. In a racial sense, West Indians are a global microcosm. They have in one way or another faced, and to some extent resolved, many issues that still divide larger nations and torment mankind.

The West Indian social hierarchy is generally arrayed by colour from white through mixed to black. But colour is neither so clear nor so rigid an indicator of status as in South Africa, the United States, or Britain; and segregation is officially proscribed and in many realms of life practically vestigial. In much of the Caribbean, colour is less consequential than in Brazil, where it is crucial for economic, political, and social opportunity. The fact that black and coloured West Indians have long been an overwhelming majority, not a minority group, is one outstanding difference. But demographic predominance is no panacea; problems of colour continue to affect West Indian society, culture, and personality.

Caribbean attitudes, racial and other, do not exist in a vacuum; they occur within the context of specifically West Indian social and cultural institutions. But before describing West Indian ways of life, let us see what and where the West Indies are.

In the strict physical sense, the West Indies are an archipelago curving 2,500 miles from Florida in the north to Venezuela in the south, facing Central America on the west, and on the east separating the Atlantic Ocean from the Caribbean Sea (Map, pp. 6–7). The main links of the island arc are to the west the Greater Antilles (Cuba, Hispaniola, Jamaica, Puerto Rico), outliers of an ancient Central American mountain chain; and to the east the Lesser Antilles, a chain of smaller volcanic and limestone islands stretching from the Virgin Islands in the north through Grenada in the south. On the continental fringes of these island groups lie the Bahamas, Trinidad and Tobago, and numerous islands off the Venezuelan and Central American coasts.

The term 'West Indian' as generally understood, however, is both more and less extensive than this. It excludes countries—or more specifically the inhabitants—of Spanish background and culture, notably Cuba, Puerto Rico, and the Dominican Republic. These islands are neither identical to Central and South American countries nor wholly unlike their island neighbours, but their main affinities lie with Latin America and outside the West Indian orbit.

Certain continental realms, by contrast, have close West Indian ties and lack strong Latin attachments. British Honduras in Central America and the three Guianas—French Guiana, Surinam (Netherlands), and Guyana (formerly British)—in north-eastern South America are socially and culturally 'West Indian'. Because 'British Guiana is a mainland colony,' a local writer a generation ago felt that it was 'not to be classed with "a mere string of little islands in the Caribbean."'[1] Yet like the West Indies proper, the Guianas are really insular; virtually unpopulated swamp, savanna, and rain-forest interiors isolate their inhabited coastal fringes from Brazil and Venezuela. Although much larger than the islands, the mainland territories are far less populous, containing just over a million people in 471,000 square kilometres, in contrast with ten million people in 57,000 square kilometres on the islands. Altogether there are about as many West Indians as there are Australians, Algerians, Ceylonese, or Venezuelans.

Alike in not being Iberian, the West Indies are not North American either, nor indeed do they fit any ordinary regional pattern. Not so much undeveloped as overdeveloped, exotic without being traditional, they are part of the Third World yet ardent emulators of the West. Even from a statistical purview they lie outside, or are marginal to, standard national categories.[2]

Yet the West Indies differ widely among themselves in geography, government, and culture. Five territories—Haiti, Jamaica, Trinidad and Tobago, Barbados, and Guyana—are independent nations; it is no accident that these, Barbados excepted, are the most populous lands. The rest remain formally linked to an external power. Allied with Great Britain as internally self-governing 'Associated States' are most of the Windward and Leeward islands in the Lesser Antilles, while British Honduras, Montserrat, the Bahamas, the Caymans, the Turks and Caicos, and the British Virgin Islands are British colonies. French

[1] Edgar Mittelholzer, 'Color, Class and Letters', *Nation*, 17 January 1959 (New York), p. 56. By contrast, the Prime Minister of independent Guyana declares that 'the Caribbean is a country. Places like Guyana are part of that country' (*News from Guyana*, Ministry of Information, No. 40, 18–24 October 1970, p. 3).

[2] Bruce M. Russett, *International Regions and the International System: A Study in Political Ecology*, 1967, pp. 32–5.

overseas *départements*, sharing the formal status of mainland France, are Martinique, Guadeloupe with its small dependencies, and coastal French Guiana; the Guianese interior (the *arrondissement* of l'Inini) is administered separately as a colony. There are two self-governing Netherlands Caribbean states, dependent on The Hague only for foreign affairs and defence: Surinam (Dutch Guiana) and the Netherlands Antilles, which comprises the Netherlands Leewards (Curaçao, Aruba, Bonaire) off the coast of Venezuela and the smaller Netherlands Windwards (Saba, St. Eustatius, half of St. Maarten) mingled among the British Leewards. The American Virgin Islands (St. Croix, St. Thomas, and St. John), the Colombian *intendéncias* of San Andrés and Providencia, and the Bay Islands of Honduras complete the list of inhabited West Indian colonial remnants. The Colombian and Honduran islands are no more 'Latin' than the others; for they are peopled by English-speaking Protestants of British West Indian origin. Similar West Indian communities dominate much of the Caribbean littoral of Central America.

Language and culture reflect West Indian colonial history, to which present political status is a more fallible guide. French and its derivatives are dominant not only in the three French Caribbean *départements* (except for English-speaking St. Martin, a dependency of Guadeloupe) but also in Haiti; a French patois is the mother-tongue in British-associated St. Lucia and Dominica, and remnants of patois and French custom persist also in Grenada and Trinidad. The other British-connected territories and Commonwealth states are English in speech and British in culture and institutions, save for relics of French speech and Spanish custom in Trinidad and of Dutch law in Guyana. Variants of English are also the *lingua franca* in the Netherlands Windwards, San Andrés and Providencia, the Bay Islands, and to some extent Surinam. Dutch is the formal tongue of the educated minority in Surinam and Curaçao.

More than most former colonies, the independent West Indies remain intimately associated with Europe. A variety of euphemisms describes these connections, but the actual circumstances are everywhere semi-colonial. Haiti was one of the first sovereign nations of the western hemisphere, but awareness of Haitian post-revolutionary disasters delayed the advent of self-government elsewhere in the Caribbean. Jamaica, Trinidad and Tobago, Barbados, and Guyana strove for nationhood less than they were compelled to accept it following the break-up of the West Indies Federation in 1962. 'The idea of independence was left on the shore, as a sort of ideological driftwood, [but] the senior politicians . . . look at it much as Laocoon looked at the Wooden Horse.'[1] To the despair of local nationalists, the colonial condition

[1] 'Politics for 1962', *WIE*, Vol. 4, No. 6, December 1961, pp. 4–5.

permeates West Indian ways of thought. 'Colonialism, however important, was an incident in the history of Nigeria and Ghana, Kenya or Uganda; but it is the whole history of the West Indies, and . . . it has a deeper meaning for the West Indian than for the African'.[1]

The West Indies also remain attached to the western orbit by their patterns of production, marketing, and consumption. This aspect of life is so familiar that many West Indians imagine no alternative and consider export agriculture their only surety against starvation. Yet every major West Indian export crop is grown more cheaply and on a larger scale somewhere else, and without European and American subsidies these commodities would cease to be exported at all. This eventuality is unthinkable to West Indians in a position of economic power; they are the world's keenest protectionists. But protection subsumes bondage to a distant metropolis for manufactured goods, credit, and entrepreneurial capital and skills. The smaller the territory or the greater the predominance of export agriculture, the less adequate the supply of local foodstuffs and the greater the dependence on imports. And the cost of metropolitan products is further inflated by charges for financing, brokerage, shipping, warehousing, agents' fees.

If Europe dominates West Indian political and economic life, in terms of culture the West Indies are also Old World appendages. No other ex-colonies are so convinced they are British or French or cling more keenly to their European heritage. Local loyalties or pan-Caribbean feelings notwithstanding, Englishness, Frenchness, and even Dutchness and Americanness permeate all aspects of West Indian life. Contrasts are illuminating: in India English is the *lingua franca* of the elite, but local Indian tongues are the sole languages of the vast majority; in the West Indies English and French (with their Caribbean variants) are the historic languages of all. In post-colonial Africa and Asia, village or tribal ways antedating European suzerainty are the common mode of life and the touchstones even of the westernized elite; in the Caribbean, European culture and institutions, artifacts and ideas, are the only generally recognized heritage.

These physical and cultural alignments account for many West Indian continuities and resemblances. But the main theatre of Antillean activity is neither the area as a whole nor any territorial grouping; it is the particular land that is home. Although most of the islands are within sight of others, insularity is a basic fact of West Indian life. Economic and political affairs generally occur in an island context; social institutions are structured in an island framework. To be sure, West Indians are also members of families, residents of villages and towns, inhabitants of valleys and peninsulas, parishes and counties. And at times they function in the context of island clusters, of cultural or economic

[1] Philip Sherlock, *West Indies*, 1966, pp. 12–13.

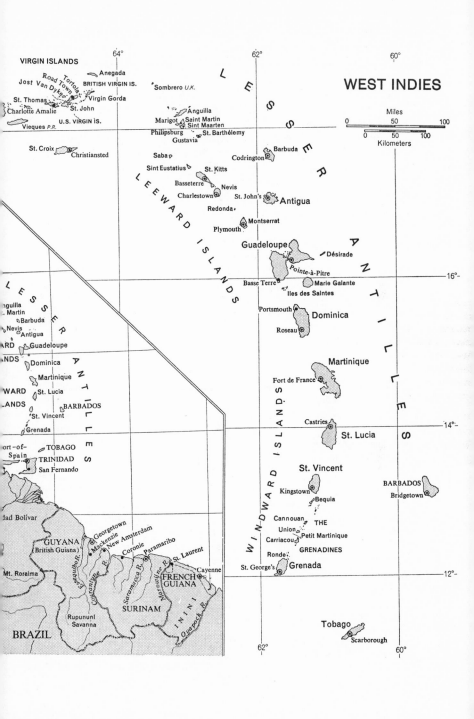

WEST INDIES

VIRGIN ISLANDS

Anegada

Road Town
Jost Van Dyke
Tortola
BRITISH VIRGIN IS.

Sombrero *U.K.*

Virgin Gorda

St. Thomas
St. John
Charlotte Amalie
U.S. VIRGIN IS.

Vieques *P.R.*

Ânguilla
Marigot
Saint Martin
Sint Maarten
Philipsburg
Gustavia
St. Barthélemy

St. Croix
Christiansted

Barbuda

Saba
Codrington

Sint Eustatius
St. Kitts

Basseterre
Nevis
Charlestown
St. John's
Antigua

Redonda
Montserrat
Plymouth

Guadeloupe
Désirade

Pointe-à-Pitre
Basse Terre
Marie Galante
Iles des Saintes

Portsmouth
Dominica
Roseau

Martinique
Fort de France

Castries
St. Lucia

St. Vincent
Kingstown
Bequia

BARBADOS
Bridgetown

Cannouan
THE
Union
Carriacou
Petit Martinique
GRENADINES
Ronde
St. George's
Grenada

Miles
0   50   100
0   50   100
Kilometers

L E S S E R

A N T I L L E S

L E E W A R D   I S L A N D S

W I N D W A R D   I S L A N D S

nguilla
. Martin
Barbuda
Nevis
Antigua
Guadeloupe
Dominica
Martinique
St. Lucia
BARBADOS
St. Vincent
Grenada
TOBAGO
TRINIDAD
San Fernando

L E S S E R   A N T I L L E S

ort-of-
Spain

ARD

NDS

WARD
LANDS

dad Bolívar

GUYANA
(British Guiana)

Georgetown
Mackenzie
New Amsterdam
Coronie
Paramaribo
St. Laurent
Cayenne

Mt. Roraima

**FRENCH
GUIANA**

Rupununi
Savanna

SURINAM

BRAZIL

Tobago
Scarborough

64°   62°   60°

16°

14°

12°

62°   60°

affiliations up and down the archipelago, and of national or sentimental attachments with European states. But it is at the island level that West Indians mainly identify.

A West Indian island really is a world. Polynesians and Melanesians, more at home with the ocean, make it a highway instead of a barrier, but the Caribbean Sea more often constrains and attenuates the social network. A man who says, 'I am a Jamaican', or 'I am a Barbadian', is usually expressing the broadest allegiance he cares about. West Indian social organization consequently differs profoundly from that, say, of the Caroline Islands, where interdependence based on the exchange of both goods and lineage patterns binds inhabitants of several islands into one society.[1]

Each West Indian island has its special features, a unique self-image, and a particular view of the others. Large and small islands are equally conscious of individuality. Jamaican and Anguillan parochialisms are much alike, though one is a country of two million people and the other of six thousand. Whatever the size of an island, physical insularity intensifies the sense of belonging. Jamaicans in the Blue Mountains are different from inhabitants of the Cockpit Country, and Kingston residents have little in common with those on Frome sugar estate. But such differences do not divide Jamaica into a hundred separate Anguillas, nor even into two or three.

Communities and neighbourhoods are generally ill-defined and seldom self-sufficient. They are more significant in some territories than others, not always depending on size. Despite fairly rigid class barriers, Barbados, with 250,000 people, is practically one geographical community, owing to its historic cultural homogeneity and an efficient road network. On the other hand Dominica's 70,000 people evince great local self-consciousness because of the early collapse of the island-wide plantation economy, and because villages are isolated by difficult topography and poor communications. In Jamaica and Trinidad, physical and social distance notwithstanding, national feeling tends to prevail over local interests, partly because island radio and newspapers, government and politics, are omnipresent. Unifying forces are weaker in the Grenadine island of Bequia: one can walk round Bequia in a day, but its 3,000 people inhabit three mutually exclusive communities. By contrast, the web of kinship brings most of the 6,000 folk of nearby Carriacou into close association.

Administrative alignment is no gauge to the local state of mind. Trinidad controls Tobago, St. Kitts dominates Nevis, Antigua rules

[1] William H. Alkire, *Lamotrek Atoll and Inter-Island Socioeconomic Ties*, 1965, pp. 170–2. The Trinidadian Samuel Selvon's novel, *An Island Is a World*, 1955, exemplifies the point. The theme is developed in my 'The Range and Variation of Caribbean Societies', *Annals New York Academy of Sciences*, Vol. 83, 1960, pp. 786–95.

Barbuda, Grenada and St. Vincent share the Grenadines, St. Barthélemy owes allegiance to Guadeloupe, and Saba to Curaçao. These unions are mainly adventitious, however; a man from Tobago thinks of himself as Tobagonian, not Trinidadian. St. Kitts and Nevis are only two miles apart and economically interdependent, but their inhabitants traditionally disagree. Dependent Carriacou has little in common with Grenada save mutual suspicion; but Carriacou and its own tiny dependency, Petit Martinique, are also dissimilar; the five hundred Petit Martinicans consider themselves neither Carriacouans nor Grenadians. Autonomy further impels each territory to congratulate 'itself on being so fully and quirkily itself'.[1] Lesser Antillean feeling, in one scholar's phrase, is 'a case of insular psychology gone mad'.[2]

The ill-fated West Indies Federation attests to the strength of this feeling: 'These Islands are afflicted with such rugged individuality that they . . . decided, after a brief trial period of three years, not to live together in unity with people who had the same historical background, spoke the same language, had similar economies and had a wide community of interests.' But the insular jealousies and rivalries seldom erupt into open conflict. As the Prime Minister of Barbados concluded, 'We live together very well, but we don't like to live together together.'[3]

Even the smallest and the most tourist-filled islands possess an overriding sense of individuality. Thus American Virgin Islanders are said to be convinced that 'the sun actually shines just a little brighter in the Virgins than any other place else in the world', that local folk are 'born knowing how to do' whatever they set their minds to, and that their problems are the United States Congress's sole concern. But these traits are generic West Indian expressions 'of small-island pride, of the heliocentric image that all of the islanders hold of themselves.'[4] West Indians who do not think their particular territory specially blessed are apt to find it specially cursed. Distinctions drawn locally cannot always be taken at face value; features claimed as unique may in fact be common to many territories. But the real differences, whether or not locally perceived, are none the less profound and enduring.

[1] Donald Davie, 'Enjoy the African Night', *New Statesman*, 10 December 1965, p. 936.

[2] R. H. Whitbeck, 'The Lesser Antilles—Past and Present', *Annals Association of American Geographers*, Vol. 23, 1933, pp. 21–6, ref. p. 25. Evidence of, and reasons for, particularism are elaborated in my 'Levels of West Indian Government', *SES*, Vol. 11, 1962, pp. 363–91.

[3] Errol Barrow, 'A Role for Canada in the West Indies', *International Journal*, Vol. XIX, 1964, pp. 172–87, ref. p. 181. West Indian interpretations of the federation's collapse are given in Hugh W. Springer, *Reflections on the Failure of the First West Indian Federation*, 1962; John Mordecai, *The West Indies: The Federal Negotiations*, 1968; and Sir Arthur Lewis, *The Agony of the Eight* [1965].

[4] Gordon K. Lewis, 'An Introductory Note to the Study of the Virgin Islands', *CS*, Vol. 8, No. 2, July 1968, pp. 5–21, ref. p. 19.

Because the West Indies are small, unimportant in world affairs, and peopled mainly by folk of African descent, American and European observers are apt to be unaware of these differences or to dismiss them as trivial, and to think of West Indians as everywhere alike. 'The characteristics of the people are the same in all the Antilles, and could be studied' in any island, asserted a celebrated British historian a century ago.[1] 'We might as well be told that because the nations of Europe are generally white', a West Indian retorted, 'they could be studied one by the light derived by acquaintance with another.' To the contrary, he noted, nearly every island was markedly dissimilar. 'In speech, character, and deportment, a coloured native of Trinidad differs as much from one of Barbados as a North American black does from either'.[2]

Islanders insist on these differences as a matter of local pride and also to express solidarity against outsiders. Martinique boasts of being more civilized than Guadeloupe, Guadeloupe more independent-minded than Martinique. It is said that 'Jamaica has a difficulty for every solution: Trinidad a solution for every difficulty: Barbados has no difficulties'.[3] As this implies, self-esteem is epitomized in Barbados. 'Barbadians', a former governor said, 'consider that they and their institutions are perfect.'[4] Of countless illustrative legends one must suffice: 'At the beginning of the last war (whichever war that happened to be) Barbados sent a telegram to England, saying "Go in England, Barbados is behind you". . . . Hitler, on being informed of this message, sent a signal to Barbados, saying, "If you stay out, we will give you Trinidad". As everyone knows, Barbados supported England and Hitler was defeated.'[5]

Anguilla offers a recent instance of insular self-esteem in action. On this sliver of limestone, fifteen miles long and two miles wide, some 6,000 people poke a precarious living out of saltpans and a sandy soil, build an occasional boat, send their young men to the sea and to jobs in other islands and abroad, and eke out subsistence and remittances with smuggling. Anguilla had no paved roads, no telephones, no electricity, and but one doctor. Yet in the spring of 1967 Anguillans rejected a

[1] James Anthony Froude, *The English in the West Indies: or The Bow of Ulysses*, 1888, p. 51.

[2] J. J. Thomas, *Froudacity* [1889], p. 74.

[3] O. R. Marshall, 'Legal Education for the West Indies', in *Law in the West Indies: Some Recent Trends*, 1966, pp. 137–52, ref. p. 152.

[4] Sanford Freeling to Lord Carnarvon, 9 August 1875, quoted in Bruce Hamilton, *Barbados & the Confederation Question 1871–1885*, 1956, p. 1. Barbadian idiosyncrasies are detailed in my 'The West Indies Chooses a Capital', *GR*, Vol. 48, 1958, pp. 336–64, ref. pp. 352–6.

[5] Hugh W. Springer, 'Barbados as a Sovereign State', *Journal of the Royal Society of Arts*, Vol. CXV, 1967, pp. 627–41, ref. p. 629.

constitution that bound them to the new Associated State of St. Kitts–
Nevis, repelled a Kittician police force, guarded their airstrip and
coastline against invasion, and declared their independence after a
plebiscite vote of 1,813 to 5. Aid and comfort were sought from, and
denied by, the United Kingdom, Canada, other West Indies, and the
United States—Anguilla's then leader could not understand 'how the
United States can send the flower of its youth to die for freedom in
Vietnam and yet not acknowledge Anguilla's independence in the
Caribbean.'[1] The island was blockaded; mail and money and medicine
were impounded in St. Kitts; Premier Bradshaw of St. Kitts threatened
to 'turn Anguilla into a desert. They will find salt in their coffee, bones
in their rice, and sand in their sugar. . . . They will have to suck each
other's bones.'[2] But Anguilla managed to argue its case before the
United Nations and world public opinion; it instituted its own mail
service, printed its own stamps, found its own doctors and teachers. It
even survived a host of friends, from quixotic well-wishers attached to
the virtues of self-sufficiency to glib promoters and paradise-hunters
who, as an island leader put it, 'just seem interested in how lax our laws
are on abortion, divorce, alcohol, and wife-swapping'.[3] Anguilla could
not prevent a British paratroop takeover of 1969 but in 1971 gained
separate status as a colony detached from St. Kitts.

Anguillan cohesiveness is a matter of historical record. As early as
1825 Anguilla objected to the transfer of legislative powers to St. Kitts:
'Laws enacted . . . for this community . . . by a body of men living in a
distinct and remote Island, possessing no property of any kind here and
having no connexion or relation whatever', were unlikely to 'be made
with much regard' for Anguillans.[4] In 1873 an Anguillan petition to
the Colonial Office described Kitticians as 'utter Strangers to us,
ignorant of the community, careless of their wants, and therefore
unequal to discharge . . . the important duties of Legislation for us.'[5]
West Indians have long memories, especially for interisland disputes.

The Anguillan case is by no means unique. Similar expressions of
local feeling could be gleaned from many small West Indian islands.
Early in 1968 the impoverished Turks and Caicos rejected closer connection with the Bahamas, fearing relegation to the status of 'farthest
out of the Out Islands'. One Turks leader explained, 'What we want is
a national identity.'[6]

[1] Peter Adams, quoted in *Washington Post*, 21 July 1967, p. 12.

[2] Robert L. Bradshaw, quoted in the *Sunday Times*, 23 March 1969, p. 14.

[3] Peter Adams, quoted in *Washington Post*, 21 July 1967, p. A–1.

[4] Address from the inhabitants of Anguilla to Governor Maxwell, 10 March 1825,
Maxwell to Bathurst, 18 June 1825, C.O. 239/12, No. 171, P.R.O.

[5] 23 August 1873, C.O. 71/192, No. 192, P.R.O.

[6] Quoted in Homer Bigart, 'Tiny Colony in the Caribbean Is Asking Britain for
"A Little More Say"', *New York Times*, 29 January 1968, p. 14. Some West Indians

The world-as-island is a recurrent West Indian theme, but the island is not the only world. And diverse as the West Indies are, they are in many ways highly similar. Resemblances from island to island are substantial and durable: West Indian social structure and ways of life vary from place to place, but their basic forms persist throughout the Caribbean and distinguish the West Indies from Latin America and Anglo-America. These broad similarities are apparent to, and valued by, West Indians themselves, however distant or superficially unalike they may be. 'West Indians recognize each other as such' even when they are with Africans or American Negroes, asserts a Jamaican familiar with the whole area. 'The West Indian walks differently, laughs differently, dresses differently, and uses different gestures. . . . Despite the differences between islands . . . there is such a thing as a "West Indian personality"'.[1]

Race and colour are crucial to the larger West Indian identity; the Caribbean is a visibly Negro—that is, black and coloured—world. But it is not a world West Indians feel they own, in the sense that black Africans do theirs. The West Indies were early and thoroughly Europeanized, and the European colonial heritage (including slavery) transcends territorial boundaries. As a result, West Indians today are ambivalent about national autonomy, economic and social viability, and individual identity. Though fundamental change is slow, an expectation of—even a demand for—change suffuses the social order. A gulf between expectation and actuality, a disposition to dreams impossible of realization, characterizes West Indians from every territory.

These common traits seldom impel West Indians to practical cooperation or joint action. But awareness of a shared past and of similar plights today ensures that news and rumours from Haiti or Grenada will strike chords of recognition in Barbados and Surinam, Trinidad and Martinique. Important West Indian events have analogues throughout the archipelago. And West Indians who travel to another territory or communicate through a common literature draw strength from their mutual heritage. Some may read too much of the past into the present or assume that contemporary problems are everywhere alike and require the same solutions, but they merely exaggerate the truth. For many circumstances are extraordinarily similar throughout the Caribbean.

These circumstances stand in sharp contrast with the typical tourist image of 'primitive', 'natural', fun-loving West Indians, too happy-go-lucky to bother about race and colour, class and nationality. The stereotype is as prevalent as it is notoriously false; that it survives in

viewed Anguilla's 'unilateral declaration of independence [as] an important landmark in Caribbean history' (*NWQ*, Vol. 3, No. 4, Cropover 1967, p. 2); but in 1971 Caribbean rulers saw Britain's legalization of Anguillan secession as a threat to stability.
[1] Mordecai, *The West Indies*, pp. 383–4.

defiance of the facts is itself a major problem for West Indians, a problem that exacerbates relations with the outside world and that intensifies the crisis of identity at home.

The image of the West Indies as 'Eden without apples', spiced with exotic African sex, is a staple Caribbean appeal to tourists from the cold, repressed north. It 'is today perpetuated in its crassest form . . . in the [New York] *Times* Sunday travel section and the meretricious *New Yorker* advertisements.'[1] But these advertisements are largely paid for and distributed by West Indians themselves. It is the local tourist boards that most assiduously purvey the promise of paradise.

The durable popularity of white sands, turquoise waters, smiling bow-tied waiters, and 'native' talent shows in luxury hotels suggests that for tourists the myth is real. But the better the myth succeeds the more must other realities be concealed: tourist enclaves screen out intrusions by 'real' West Indians. The visitor who leaves his immaculate palm-fringed beach for any ramshackle, garbage-strewn West Indian city finds a contrast in behaviour too: the welcoming smile of Montego Bay gives way to sullen hostility—'What's your business here, white man?'—of the unemployed poor of Kingston.[2] 'It is impossible to walk or even drive through West Kingston without being challenged or cat-called from every corner', found a recent visitor from Britain, noting 'a verbal hostility towards whites unparalleled in the day-to-day life of any US ghetto'.[3]

Colour conflict, a frequent focus of these differences, also corrodes attempts to achieve harmony. To curb mounting hostility towards tourists, the Jamaica Tourist Board perennially promotes 'Tourism Matters to You' campaigns; outside the hotel belt, this has little appeal to Jamaicans whose friends and relations in Britain simultaneously confront slogans like 'Keep Britain White' and 'Niggers Go Home'.

The paradisiacal image also arouses bitter tensions because it resembles a portrait drawn by masters of slaves—a condescending rather than a complimentary likeness. Far from promoting progress, it seems to relegate the West Indies to perpetual backwardness.

The myth of West Indian tropical felicity originated with Columbus, who lured Europeans to the islands by extolling their secure harbours, beautiful scenery, luxuriant vegetation, fertile plains, and native Indians who were 'generous with all they possess'.[4] After generosity

[1] Richard M. Morse, 'The Caribbean: Geopolitics and Geohistory', in S. Lewis and T. G. Mathews, eds., *Caribbean Integration: Papers on Social, Political, and Economic Integration*, 1967, pp. 155–73, ref. p. 164.

[2] Henry Giniger, 'Problems of Jamaica', *New York Times*, 25 February 1967.

[3] Colin McGlashan, 'The Two Jamaicas', *Sunday Observer Review*, 23 November 1969, p. 25.

[4] 'Letter of Columbus on the First Voyage' [1493], in Cecil Jane, ed., *Select Documents Illustrating the Four Voyages of Columbus*, 1930, Vol. I, pp. 2–19, ref. p. 8.

proved fatal to the Indians, African slaves succeeded to the role of simple denizens in an effortless paradise. The vision was apotheosized by Froude in the 1880s:

The curse is taken off from nature, and like Adam again they [the Negroes] are under the covenant of innocence. Morals in the technical sense they have none, but they cannot be said to sin, because they have no knowledge of a law. . . . They are naked and not ashamed. . . . They are perfectly happy. . . . They have no aspirations to make them restless.[1]

Let us look more closely at the principal components of this mock paradise, to use Aimé Césaire's term; that is, environmental delectability, effortless subsistence, carefree dispositions, devotion to sensual pleasures (music, dance, sex), and easy racial intermingling.

The West Indies share the reputation of tropical islands everywhere for beauty and physical comfort. Images of Eden kept alive in medieval gardens and embellished by travellers from the Orient aroused expectations for the Caribbean that Columbus and his followers were happy to confirm. And the islands did conform to preconceptions of paradise. A sunny and equable climate, a profusion of colourful trees and flowers, the virtual absence of dangerous beasts, picturesque landforms large enough to promise rich treasures, small enough to be circumnavigated with ease—these features delighted sixteenth-century European visitors, as they attract the tourist today. And there is no gainsaying their value to West Indians themselves. No plaint is more persistently voiced by islanders in New York or Montreal, London or Liverpool, than the unendurability of the dismal northern winters, and their homesickness for the sun and spaciousness of life back home. Ignored or forgotten are less attractive aspects of West Indian nature—the occasional hurricane and earthquake, the frequent flood and drought, the inescapable heat, the persistent dampness.

The myth of tropical plenitude stems in part from geographical misconception. Who can imagine working in paradise? Where nature is so agreeable, houses are seen more as luxuries than as necessities, and the most modest accommodation will do. From this standpoint, West Indian slums and shacks seem like picturesque improvidence rather than evidence of misery and penury.

This 'Kodachrome syndrome' made Grenada, for example, look to a recent visitor 'so pretty, so lush, so quaint, so balmy, so *easy*going—so goddam picturesque—that life *had* to be sweet there. . . . In this beatific setting man must find the idyll of his heart, the Eden of his spirit.'[2] The distorting lens of the picturesque long dominated Caribbean literature. Lush, verdant nature was the focus, human misery was ignored. Even

[1] Froude, *The English in the West Indies*, pp. 49–50.
[2] Frank Trippett, 'Grenada: The Nowhere Island', *Look*, 10 March 1970, p. 28.

local writers adopted the exotic tone, always seeing the Antilles from a European point of view, as a place of passage, of vacation, of lazy retreat, *Eden aux vertes eaux*, 'never thinking of the leprosy, the yaws, the malaria, the tuberculosis, the alcoholism, . . . all the follies which poison this land.'[1]

Additional errors bolster West Indian *dolce far niente*. The variety and exuberance of plant life persuaded countless observers that the islands were fruitful enough to supply all human needs. The myth is tellingly refuted by the Amazon rain forest, which supports the world's most abundant vegetation but cannot yield food for two persons per square mile. The West Indies are richer than Amazonia, but their infertile, dry, or poorly drained soils, precipitous slopes, and long history of soil erosion and depletion contrast sharply with the stereotype of lush tropical gardens that will bear fruit if one just pokes a stick in the ground.

This impression derived initially from European misconceptions about Indian agriculture. The Indians intermixed root crops with seed plants on lands seldom cleared of other vegetation. Europeans were used to broadcasting grain on cleared fields, to harvesting with draft animals, to clearly demarcated field boundaries, and to permanent and visibly distinctive agricultural landscapes. By contrast with Old World field and pasture, meadow and woodlot, Indian cultivation made so little dent on the landscape that it seemed slovenly and lazy.

Underestimating the labour and expertise that Indian productivity required, the Spanish withdrew manpower from agriculture into gold mining. Within a generation food output dropped so drastically that the Indian population starved to death.[2] But the myth survived, attached next to Africans brought in to replace Indians. And the fortunes later made out of West Indian sugar plantations confirmed beliefs that West Indian soils were naturally fecund.

Sugar-growing required a high degree of organization, a lot of capital equipment, and plentiful unskilled labour. Productivity depended on a large, resident working force. These needs were thought to justify slavery; freed Negroes, the argument ran, would at once abandon hard plantation labour for a life of slothful ease. A man could support himself in comfort even in the rugged interior, Europeans believed, by a few weeks' labour out of a year. The indolent African lazing the day away under his pumpkin tree was a stereotype made

---

[1] Jack Corzani, *Splendeur et misère: l'exotisme littéraire aux Antilles*, 1969; Corzani quotes on p. 42, Daniel Thaly, *Jardin des tropiques* (1911), and on p. 12, Edouard Glissant, *La lézarde* (1958). See also Edward Brathwaite, 'Creative Literature of the British West Indies during the Period of Slavery', *Savacou*, Vol. 1, No. 1, June 1970, pp. 46–74.

[2] See Carl Ortwin Sauer, *The Early Spanish Main*, 1966, pp. 51–69, 200–6.

vivid by Carlyle and Froude.[1] It remains current to this day, despite the malnutrition, poverty, and rural despair apparent in West Indian territories, and against the testimony of hard work and careful planning needed to eke a bare living from small plots of land on steep, eroded island slopes.

The myth of tropical exuberance accompanied the notion that Africans were primitive and simple people with minimal wants, content to live at a level far below the European. Only force could compel them to harvest abundant West Indian resources. With his few wants supplied by the slave-owner or employer, he had no need to plan for the morrow. The West Indian today, lacking material goods, is still typically seen as cheerful, contented, and carefree. The Haitian peasant, for example, is said to 'find himself perfectly happy with a life that many would find miserable'[2] despite the hemisphere's worst nutrition and sanitation, marked deficiencies in weight and height, endemic infectious diarrhoea, and recurrent starvation. 'The shortage of calories is undoubtedly a major factor in the impression of laziness or lethargy. . . . Haitian laborers . . . simply aren't getting enough food to be productive.'[3]

The problem is not confined to Haiti; malnutrition and gastro-enteritis among children under five account for 57 per cent of all deaths in St. Vincent.[4] Even in more prosperous Trinidad, a radical leader wonders 'why in a majority black society . . . must black people be as poor as they are, depressed as they are, unhappy as they are'.[5] Yet a foreign observer describes Trinidadians as extraordinarily 'happy and friendly' because 'life is the thing. Rioting, burgeoning, bursting life . . . , laughter and music'.[6]

This myth, which ignores both the slave provision-ground and the coloured middle-class zeal for conspicuous consumption, is a simple rationalization of West Indian penury. It derives in part from the ascription of a 'Sambo' mentality to the 'good' slave who smiled, flattered, and accommodated, unlike the 'bad' slave who disobeyed,

---

[1] Thomas Carlyle, 'Occasional Discourse on the Nigger Question', *Fraser's*, Vol. XL, 1849, pp. 667–79; Froude, *The English in the West Indies*. See also Sydney Olivier, 'Thomas Carlyle on "Niggers"', in his *The Myth of Governor Eyre*, 1933, Ch. 2, pp. 19–36; and Bernard Semmel, 'The Issue of "Race" in the British Reaction to the Morant Bay Uprising of 1865', *CS*, Vol. 2, No. 3, October 1962, pp. 3–15.

[2] Roger Houzel, *La situation économique de la république d'Haïti*, (1934), p. 21, quoted in Paul Moral, *Le paysan haïtien: Étude sur la vie rurale en Haïti*, 1961, p. 215. Moral refutes the statement.

[3] Kendall W. King, 'Nutrition Research in Haiti', in Richard P. Shaedel, ed., *Papers of the Conference on Research and Resources of Haiti*, 1969, pp. 347–70, ref. on pp. 349–54.

[4] *The Development Problem in St. Vincent: A Report by a University of the West Indies Development Mission* [1969], pp. 4–5.

[5] James Millette, 'Leading Politically', *Moko*, No. 24, 20 March 1970, p. 3.

[6] Robin Bryans, *Trinidad and Tobago: Isles of the Immortelles*, 1967, p. 13.

malingered, ran away, or rebelled. Both types converge in the contemporary stereotype of the essentially cheerful, feckless, lazy West Indian, prone, however, to occasional 'childish' outbursts, throwing off civilized restraints and reverting to savagery.

Uninhibited sexuality, a supposed concomitant of tropical climate and black virility, looms large in the Caribbean tourist stereotype. To this image some West Indians cheerfully pander. 'I was what those people come to see', realizes an islander in a recent short story. 'I was a Barbadian, a man of the tropics, wild, untamed, supple, POTENT—what every northern woman wishes for. It was a generally accepted idea among us men on the island that the only thing that women from Canada, England, and the States came down to the West Indies for was to sleep with the Natives.'[1] West Indians abroad gain a similar impression. 'The English, Scottish and Irish women who date coloured West Indians want only to test the mythical Negro virility', concluded a Jamaican student in Britain, 'and should be given at the earliest opportunity the chance to do so.'[2] As performed in America, a West Indian play depicts 'a mythical world where unbridled virility brings no unwanted children, freedom from the drudgery of work brings no starvation, and uninhibited vitality no tragic violence. . . . The Trinidadian peasants become the reassuringly "charming" and harmless people every good American dreams of'.[3]

Central to the image of felicity is the impression that West Indians enjoy harmony and practise tolerance among manifold races, colours, and creeds. By outsiders, Caribbean race relations are often termed exemplary. An American clergyman describes Jamaica as 'a graphic example of racial harmony'.[4] The unimportance of racial distinctions struck a British Colonial Secretary as something 'which you in the West Indies have much to teach the rest of the world.'[5] A coloured novelist writes that Jamaicans 'have gone farther toward working out the problems of how people of different colors can live together in harmony and dignity and respect than any other place and any other people I know'; he lives there because 'Jamaica represents, in terms of race and color, the antithesis of my own native South Africa'.[6]

[1] Paul Layne, 'Sunny Barbados', *Bim*, Vol. 13, No. 49, July–December 1969, pp. 46–51, ref. p. 48.

[2] Mervyn Morris, 'Feeling, Affection, Respect', in Henri Tajfel and John L. Dawson, eds., *Disappointed Guests: Essays by African, Asian, and West Indian Students*, 1965, pp. 5–26, ref. p. 19.

[3] Louis James, review of Errol Hill, 'Man Better Man', in *CQ*, Vol. 12, No. 2, June 1966, p. 54.

[4] The Rev. Terence Finlay, reported in *Jamaica Daily Gleaner*, 13 March 1970, p. 18.

[5] Ian MacLeod, quoted in *Jamaica Daily Gleaner*, 1 June 1961.

[6] Peter Abrahams, 'We Can Learn to Be Color-Blind', *New York Times Magazine*, 11 April 1965, pp. 38, 102–6, ref. p. 38.

This interracial image has local as well as outside roots. It is industriously promoted by West Indian governments eager to attract foreign investments, to emphasize social progress, and to vaunt national achievements. Guyana, formerly the 'Land of Six Peoples', now proclaims it is 'One People, One Nation'; Trinidad's coat of arms reads 'Together We Aspire, Together We Achieve', her national anthem asserts 'Here ev'ry race and creed find an equal place', and the ruling party's slogan is 'All o' we is one'; Jamaica proclaims 'Out of Many, One People', and in 1963 stated that 'racial integration, in our society, is not merely an ideal: it is in fact a part of life'. 'Nowhere in the world', said Jamaica's Premier, 'has more progress been made in developing a non-racial society in which colour is not . . . psychologically significant.' A West Indian journalist emphatically denied 'the legend that it is race that divides us.' High and low, rich and poor, 'are no longer separated by race, but by the distinction of their ability to better themselves'.[1]

West Indians are apt to blame local occurrences of discrimination on visitors 'who bring with them prejudices they acquired in societies less tolerant';[2] to many Jamaicans the tourist industry is a 'symbol of something that we want to forget—white exclusivity.'[3] Racial attitudes in the United States are seen as a particular threat to West Indian harmony. 'Americans pour millions into the bellies of undernourished countries,' cautioned a small-island editor in 1968, but 'they also take their odious habit of colour prejudice with them wherever they go.' A correspondent echoed his warnings against tourist development, 'since the majority of white Americans are prejudiced'. Americans had brought 'Dixie-style race hate' to their war-time bases in Trinidad, St. Lucia, and Antigua, and 'there is no reason why they should not attempt it here.'[4]

Left to themselves, all this implies, West Indians maintain friendly relationships regardless of race. Some Jamaicans claim to be 'a mixture of races living in perfect harmony and as such provide a useful lesson

[1] Jamaica, Ministry of Development and Welfare, Central Planning Unit, *Five Year Independence Plan, 1963–68: A Long Term Development Programme for Jamaica*, 1963, p. 3; Norman W. Manley, address to the National Press Club, Washington, D.C., 19 April 1961, quoted in *Congressional Record*, Vol. 107, p. 7306; Orford St. John, 'A New Horizon', *Public Opinion*, 30 September 1961, p. 3.

[2] Jamaica Government, Report to the United Nations on Racial Discrimination, quoted in *Jamaica Daily Gleaner*, 4 October 1964. For examples of these problems see Edwin Chapman, 'Problems of Tourism in Jamaica', in *Tourism in the Caribbean: Essays on Problems in Connection with Its Promotion*, 1964, pp. 126–7; for similar problems in Martinique see François Gresle and Jean-Luc Morel, 'Les touristes en Martinique', *CERAG*, No. 14, 1968.

[3] Tony Abrahams, 'Corner Stones of Jamaica's Tourism Future', *Jamaica Architect*, Vol. 2, No. 2, 1969, p. 21.

[4] *Dominica Herald*, 2 January 1968, p. 2; Joseph Peltier, letter in ibid., 6 April 1968, p. 10; 'Editor's Note', ibid., 10 February 1968, p. 10.

to a world torn apart by race prejudice.'[1] Even in Barbados, by common agreement the most colour-conscious island, the Social Welfare Department sponsored formal debates on the issue 'that the main contribution of the [then] Federated West Indies to world culture is the solving of the colour problem'.[2]

By contrast with the rigidity of South Africa or the United States, race relations in the West Indies are indeed free and pleasant. As the majority group, non-white West Indians often contrast their lot *vis-à-vis* whites favourably with that of Negro Americans. 'However black and dispossessed' West Indians may have been, explains a Barbadian, they never 'felt the experience of being in a minority.' They suffer neither the ghettoization nor the sense of isolation and anomie, helplessness and powerlessness, that afflicts many black Americans. Yet small as it is, the West Indian white minority is omnipresent, and 'the West Indian has learnt, by sheer habit, to take that white presence for granted.'[3]

The rosy image of multi-racial harmony, however, grossly distorts both the actual facts and the way they are locally seen. A generation ago an official survey showed colour prejudice increasing and racial feelings growing more intense.[4] Race and colour antagonisms are still more manifest today: a local panel in Jamaica concludes that 'colour and class prejudice are rampant'.[5] Scholarly inquiries have confirmed local misgivings. A UNESCO study of social relations in Martinique and Guadeloupe reported antagonism between white entrepreneurs and coloured labourers and racial categories that parallel those of class. A sociological description of Trinidad depicted a society at odds with the popular picture of easy-going interracial mingling. The light-coloured elite of Grenada, wholly remote from the black peasantry, are measurably stratified by shade and ancestry.[6]

Nowhere in the West Indies has racial discrimination legal sanction, and social exclusion based on colour, once the rule, is now much moderated. But colour distinctions continue to correlate with class differences and dominate most personal associations. If prejudice is less blatant it is still visible. 'The colour discrimination which still persists in this island is not of any real importance', a Barbados editorial

---

[1] Rex Nettleford, 'National Identity and Attitudes to Race in Jamaica', *Race*, Vol. VII, 1965–6, pp. 59–72, ref. p. 62.

[2] Barbados, Social Welfare Department, *Eighth Annual Report*, 1958, p. 10.

[3] George Lamming, 'The Pleasures of Exile', *Tamarack Review*, No. 14, Winter 1960, pp. 32–56, ref. p. 40.

[4] *West India Royal Commission Report*, Cmd. 6607, 1945, p. 59.

[5] Christian Action Group meeting reported in *Abeng*, 8 February 1969, p. 1.

[6] Michel Leiris, *Contacts de civilisations en Martinique et en Guadeloupe*, 1955; Lloyd Braithwaite, 'Social Stratification in Trinidad: A Preliminary Analysis', *SES*, Vol. 2, Nos. 2 and 3, October 1953, pp. 5–175, especially pp. 38–61; M. G. Smith, *Stratification in Grenada*, 1965.

concluded, 'but it is embarrassing.'[1] Social clubs there still exclude dark people, and a black legislator accused the Government itself of bias at entertainments where 'you see a sprinkling of the population that looks like myself, and then you see a whole mass of the [white] minority.'[2] An editorial claim 'that in the last 15 years the colour bar in this island has all but disappeared' was followed a week later by a charge that prejudice was rife in almost every sector of Barbadian life.[3]

In Jamaica, by contrast with Barbados, it is said that 'the practice of discrimination precipitates a row.'[4] But a local university lecturer regards colour as 'the single most important factor in Jamaican society today',[5] and in most realms of Jamaican life black and white are far from equal. 'There are still upper class whites who talk and think about damned niggers, and throw their children out of the house for marrying people with a touch of colour', observed a local columnist only a decade ago.[6] And an editorial contends that 'many people in Jamaica still boast that they have never entertained a negroid person in their homes.'[7]

In Trinidad too, business continues to discriminate; job advertisements requiring photographs suggest that 'ethnic origin or complexion . . . is the yardstick' for hiring. The Prime Minister himself adjures local establishments to clean house; 'we do not deceive ourselves that we have eliminated all traces of racial discrimination or there is no cause for concern.' Styling racial harmony 'a misleading and empty boast', one observer praises black Trinidadians for their 'freedom from racial intolerance and antipathy in the face of many provocative situations', but a more severe critic denounces 'the rampant discriminatory practices we deceitfully tolerate . . . in this cesspit of hypocrisy which we call happy cosmopolitan Trinidad'.[8]

Even the cricket field, famous for interracial fellowship, has a long history of discrimination. Introduced from England about 1850, cricket soon became a universally popular West Indian sport. Coloured clubs played against whites in the 1880s, but territorial teams remained white; in 1893 Barbados and British Guiana threatened to call off an

[1] 'Colour Bar Should Be Swept Away', *Barbados Advocate*, 13 February 1962.

[2] F. L. Walcott in the House of Assembly, quoted in *Barbados Advocate*, 14 February 1962.

[3] *Barbados Advocate*, 13 and 19 February 1962.

[4] Mitchie Hewitt, 'Yes, She's as Subtle as a Serpent', *Barbados Advocate*, 19 February 1962.

[5] Aubrey Phillips, quoted in McGlashan, 'The Two Jamaicas', p. 25.

[6] Thomas Wright, 'Candidly Yours', *Jamaica Daily Gleaner*, 25 April 1961.

[7] *Jamaica Daily Gleaner*, 6 May 1964.

[8] R. John, letter in *Trinidad Express*, 30 March 1970, p. 4; Eric Williams, quoted in *Trinidad Guardian*, 21 March 1970, p. 1; R. K. Richardson, '"Majority Power" Would Be Better', *Trinidad Guardian*, 26 March 1970, p. 10; Jomo Wahtuse, 'Letter to the Editor', *Moko*, No. 12, 11 April 1969, p. 4.

intercolonial match if Trinidad included coloured players. A generation later West Indian cricket teams were predominantly coloured, but clubs were still racially homogeneous; Trinidad maintained white, near-white, brown, dark brown, and black cricket clubs; British Guiana had Portuguese, East Indian, and Chinese clubs as well. Non-whites always occupied inferior positions on colony teams; the working principle was that 'the white men batted and the black men bowled.'[1] Until the late 1950s, when a disastrous Australian tour under an ageing Barbadian white led the press to intensify campaigns for reform, the West Indies team was racially stratified, with 'black or brown men under a white captain. The more brilliantly the black men played, the more [the audience would think] . . . "funny, isn't it, they cannot be responsible for themselves—they must always have a white man to lead them."'[2]

Meanwhile, island cricket clubs remain almost as exclusive as before, audiences at cricket matches divide sharply by race and class (white and light in the pavilion, black in the bleachers), and feelings run so high that fear of losing to England has precipitated several riots. Cricket 'is the game we love for it is the only game we can play well', writes a Jamaican sociologist. 'But it is the game, deep down, which we must hate—the game of the master'.[3] That is why victory is so important. It is hard to gainsay C. L. R. James's conclusion that 'there was racialism in cricket, there is racialism in cricket, there will always be racialism in cricket.'[4]

Existing racial problems in the West Indies seem more or less grave depending on the locale, the observer, and the context. 'The glory of being West Indians,' one of them writes, 'is that we have exploded the myth of racial superiority'; another feels that West Indian society 'multi-racial though it is, is very "race"-conscious and therefore is racial'; a third finds 'more race prejudice in the West Indies than anywhere in the world'; a fourth detects 'an amazing degree of ambivalence . . . at all levels of the society.'[5] Individual ambivalence is also striking; the same person may express diametrically opposite views. 'People . . . will tell you that there is none of this "racial superiority" in Dominica',

[1] Garfield Sobers and J. S. Barker, eds., *Cricket in the Sun: A History of West Indies Cricket*, 1967, pp. 7–11, 44, 51–2, 66–8.

[2] C. L. R. James, *Beyond a Boundary*, 1963, p. 225.

[3] H. Orlando Patterson, 'The Ritual of Cricket', *Jamaica Journal*, Vol. 3, No. 1, March 1969, pp. 23–5.

[4] James, *Beyond a Boundary*, p. 64.

[5] Philip Sherlock, quoted in Morris, 'Feeling, Affection, Respect', p. 8; Neville Maxwell, *The Power of Negro Action*, 1965, p. 47; Ivor Leila, 'The Changing Attitude to Mixed Marriages', *Flamingo*, No. 2, October 1961, p. 36; Elliott Bastien, 'The Weary Road to Whiteness and the Hasty Retreat into Nationalism', in Tajfel and Dawson, eds., *Disappointed Guests*, pp. 38–54, ref. p. 39.

commented a local editor in 1968. 'But they are living in a fool's paradise, a never-never land'; race prejudice 'may not be as explosive as it is in the United States . . . but it is right here just the same.' Yet only seven months later the same editor asserted as 'a well-known fact that . . . Dominica is not afflicted with the malady of race prejudice. It just does not exist here.'[1]

With such confusion in so small a society, it is no wonder that larger places defy generalization. A Prime Minister who had once termed Jamaica's social structure 'very simple' later admitted that 'I was wrong. Jamaica has a very complex, intimate social structure which very few people understand. . . . We are only beginning to unify it.' A decade later, Trinidad's Prime Minister doubted that much progress had been made: 'We are not a nation but a bunch of transients.'[2]

Such assessments depend on the vantage-point of the viewer. 'Living in the Caribbean can offer a rare and liberating experience of racial sanity', writes a West Indian who had spent years abroad. 'Living as I now do in Guyana', replies a not unsympathetic critic, 'this sentence reads to me like complete nonsense.'[3] West Indians who have been away and remain in touch with world affairs examine their own society from a special perspective. 'When we talked about the racial situation in the world', recalls a Jamaican in England, 'the West Indies was an area of hope; when we talked about the West Indies in isolation it was a hot-bed of racial neuroses.'[4] In the light of global racism some West Indians think their own neuroses of small moment. But they also perceive how home issues link with wider problems; West Indians today confront difficulties that transcend local solutions. As a Trinidadian puts it, 'The Caribbean is a part of the world where racialism is growing. Each act of racial discrimination of England or the United States shakes the foundations of racial harmony in the West Indies.'[5]

The harshest critics of West Indian multi-racialism are those who grew up in its shadow but rebelled against the system that nurtured both myth and opposite fact. One of 'the greatest lies of our society' is that 'anywhere in these islands we have achieved racial harmony', judges C. L. R. James.[6] 'That the Caribbean is an area where all groups live together in harmony and blissful togetherness . . . [is] the

[1] 'Breaking Down Racial Superiority', *Dominica Herald*, 20 April 1968, p. 4; 'Deportation Threat to Foreigners', ibid., 23 November 1968, p. 1.

[2] Norman W. Manley, quoted in *Jamaica Daily Gleaner*, 18 July 1961, p. 2; Eric Williams, quoted in *Trinidad Express*, 5 July 1970.

[3] 'Introduction', in Louis James, ed., *The Islands in Between: Essays on West Indian Literature*, 1968, pp. 1–49, ref. p. 4; Kathleen Drayton, review in *CS*, Vol. 9, No. 2, July 1969, pp. 84–91, ref. p. 86.

[4] Morris, 'Feeling, Affection, Respect', p. 19.

[5] Louis James, *The Islands in Between*, p. 4.

[6] C. L. R. James, *Party Politics in the West Indies* [1962], p. 140.

first myth that has to be exploded', says a Barbadian in London.[1] The gulf is apparent even to outsiders. 'Quaint' and 'exotic' at first, Trinidad at length struck one British observer as 'a sociologist's nightmare' where 'nerve-jangling suspicion and distrust . . . can be felt all the time'.[2]

The disparity between myth and reality magnifies the tensions. 'For years Jamaicans have regarded Jamaica as the world's finest instance of multiracial harmony'. Consequently the 1960 Kingston riots, the fruit of both racial unrest and economic travail, took middle-class Jamaicans by surprise.[3] And each successive outburst, similarly unexpected, enhances the sense of national crisis. 'In both Trinidad and Jamaica the ruling *élites* love to stress the cosmopolitan, multi-racial character of their communities', comments a local sociologist; 'protests against racial discrimination are frequently attributed to personal immaturity or a pre-occupation and obsession with race.'[4] Thus an inquiry into charges of racial discrimination against American Negroes at the Trinidad Country Club took place 'against the background of Trinidad and Tobago's international reputation for interracial harmony' and concluded that the incidents had not 'seriously tarnished' that reputation.[5]

When black-power demonstrations disrupted Trinidad in 1970 it was the threat to reputation that most disturbed some government and business leaders. 'I can only hope', said the president of Trinidad Manufacturers Association, 'that our image as a stable, multi-racial and democratic society has not been impaired.' The Minister of West Indian Affairs was unhappy that those who once 'saw Trinidad and Tobago as an example of peaceful co-existence and progress, now think of the nation as a place of unrest. . . . The damage to the country's image is priceless.' Neither considered that the image 'may be false. . . . Most Trinidadians . . . are too taken up with "image"'.[6]

Meanwhile Trinidad continued to advertise its 'rendezvous of cultures [as] a happy blend of African, Chinese, East Indian, Spanish, French, you name it.'[7] Foreigners 'who have heard only of our coconut trees and beaches, believe that we listen to drums all day and fornicate

---

[1] Maxwell, *The Power of Negro Action*, p. 46.

[2] Derek Bickerton, *The Murders of Boysie Singh*, 1962, pp. 10–11.

[3] M. G. Smith, 'Race and Politics in Jamaica', typescript, p. 2.

[4] Lloyd Braithwaite, 'Race Relations and Industrialisation in the Caribbean', in Guy Hunter, ed., *Industrialisation and Race Relations: A Symposium*, 1965, pp. 30–45, ref. pp. 40, 42.

[5] Trinidad Government, *Report of the Commission Appointed by His Excellency the Governor-General to Investigate Allegations of Discriminatory Practices by the Management of the Trinidad Country Club*, 1969, pp. 5, 31.

[6] Colin Stewart, quoted in *Trinidad Express*, 20 March 1970, p. 1; Kamaluddin Mohammed, quoted in *Trinidad Guardian*, 11 March 1970, p. 1; 'Our Opinion', *Trinidad Express*, 21 March 1970, p. 4.

[7] Advertisement in *New York Times Magazine*, March 1970.

under the trees and on the beaches for twenty-four hours, with rum punches being served by girls in grass skirts.' But locals too 'like to feel that the "image" of Trinidad is exactly what is written on the colourful tourist brochures. . . . They live in a world of make believe.'[1] And an editorialist agreed that 'the promise we sing about in the national anthem is a lie and a subterfuge. . . . This is a time of poverty, unemployment and discrimination.'[2] Conditions may not have worsened; the problem is that despite all the promises they are not better. 'In 1938 Jamaicans were born into a society which professed no ideals,' explains a local analyst; 'since 1938 they have been born into a society which has professed high ideals and the gap between these ideals and realities has become intolerable.'[3]

Social reform is difficult because the need for it cannot be openly admitted if the myth of racial harmony is to be maintained. Thus West Indians tend to focus not on civil rights but on economic and political palliatives. Fanon expressed the consequent frustration: the West Indian 'needs a challenge to his humanity, he wants a conflict, a riot. . . . He wants the white man to turn on him and shout: "Damn nigger." . . . But it is too late. . . . The white man tells him "Brother, there is no difference between us." . . . In the United States, the Negro battles and is battled.'[4] By avoiding such head-on confrontations, West Indians seldom experience the 'liberating, self-creative expression' of black Americans.[5]

Black West Indians perhaps have less need of such expression; never a racial minority, they have not suffered the ghetto experience of black Americans. But 'whiteness is only half the enemy', one West Indian adds. 'Like the American Negro, the West-Indian is dispossessed. Unlike the American Negro, he has never faced that terrible white power-structure that has made black definition there possible', and as a result 'he cannot relate himself to himself.'[6] The West Indian obsession with differences in shade sustains an atmosphere that, if less polarizing, perpetuates other serious problems of identity and action, problems for white, coloured, and minority groups as well as for black West Indians.

West Indian nationalism today fosters both the expression of multiracial harmony and the need to believe in it. Social and cultural

[1] Dennis Mahabir, 'What Is This Thing Called "Image"?' *Trinidad Express*, 19 March 1970, p. 9.

[2] 'Please, Dr. Williams, Don't Say It', *Trinidad Express*, 23 March 1970, p. 4.

[3] Vernon Arnett, 'Jamaica—Dictatorship or Democracy?' *Moko*, No. 4, 13 December 1968, p. 2.

[4] Frantz Fanon, *Black Skin, White Masks*, 1967, p. 221.

[5] Edward Brathwaite, 'Jazz and the West Indian Novel', *Bim*, Vol. 11, No. 44, January–June 1967, pp. 275–84, ref. p. 278.

[6] Winston Hackett, 'Identity in the Poetry of Walcott', *Moko*, No. 8, 14 February 1969, p. 2.

inequities are officially ascribed to class differences rather than to racial prejudices. Yet to act on this assumption, whatever its initial validity, is to help create a climate conducive to change; for class distinctions are more malleable than those of race. The West Indian experience could be a harbinger of racial harmony, perhaps of integration. 'Integration in the United States must be primarily an act of the white majority', writes a recent visitor to the islands; 'in the Caribbean, where the majority is black, integration feels closer.'[1] One reviewer dismisses Trinidad as 'a dim, corrupt little society, bedevilled by racialism; an accidental potpourri of nationality, caste, and color, on the forgotten edge of the world.'[2] But just such a backwater may none the less 'offer a chance of skipping several nightmare chapters of race relations'.[3] That West Indians have not skipped many of these chapters so much as rewritten them is perhaps the principal lesson Caribbean history teaches.

[1] John Updike, 'Letter from Anguilla', *New Yorker*, 22 June 1968, pp. 70–80, ref. p. 79.
[2] J. H. Elliott, 'Triste Trinidad', *New York Review of Books*, 21 May 1970, pp. 25–6.
[3] Updike, 'Letter from Anguilla', p. 79.

CHAPTER II

History

Racial distinctions have mattered longer in the West Indies than any-where else in America. A West Indian scholar sees the Caribbean as the first area to have experienced the 'modern problem of race relations and the contact between so-called "advanced" and "backward" peoples.'[1] The former were British, French, Dutch, Danish, and American; the latter mainly Amerindian, African, and Asian. They were separately categorized from the start, with European masters over non-European labourers; for 'both prejudices and laws . . . presume that every black man is, or ought to be, a slave.'[2]

Attitude and action alike set the West Indies apart from Latin America. Although apologists exaggerate the differences, Spanish and Portuguese ideas about race, slavery, freedom, and equality differed from those of other New World Europeans. Slavery in colonial Latin America did not play the pervasive role it did in the British, French, and Dutch Caribbean, where slaves preponderated.

The geography of West Indian sugar and slavery was created by European rivalries. The Iberian conquest of America brought Europe untold wealth, but the Spanish never really prospered in the West Indies and neglected the islands for lucrative mainland spoils. Cinchona bark and indigo, cacao and coffee, sugar and tobacco, leather and cabinet woods, above all precious metals from Mexican and Peruvian mines, swelled the coffers of Castile. The West Indies, first and last ports of call, meanwhile served Spanish colonists and treasure fleets as harbours and provisioning grounds.

The Netherlands, France, and England feared Spanish power and envied her American wealth. Their raids in the Spanish Main culminated with Hawkins's and Drake's captures of Spanish treasure. To secure bases for piracy was one motive for Dutch, French, and English

[1] Eric Williams, *The Historical Background of Race Relations in the Caribbean*, 1955, p. 3.
[2] W. Dickson, *Mitigation of Slavery*, 1814, Part II (Letters To Thomas Clarkson), p. 512, quoted in Douglas G. Hall, 'Slaves and Slavery in the British West Indies', *SES*, Vol. 11, 1962, pp. 305–18, ref. p. 314.

colonization of the eastern Caribbean islands and the Guiana coast, areas disdained by Spain and Portugal.

Permanent agricultural settlements followed these early trading and raiding posts. The 1620s and 1630s saw Guiana, Barbados, St. Kitts, Antigua, and Martinique colonized. Financed by governments and joint stock companies, proprietors and tenants divided the land into family-sized farms, cleared the jungle, and raised produce for export to Europe. Only high-value commodities repaid shipping costs; tobacco was favoured, along with dye-stuffs like indigo, annotto, and logwood, and lesser amounts of ginger, sugar, and cotton. But within two generations most of these territories were transformed into sugar plantations. Tobacco, grown more abundantly and cheaply in Virginia, became less profitable; cotton flourished better in a drier climate and on lighter soil; and Europe consumed too little dye and ginger to sustain Caribbean production.

Sugar, by contrast, was in enormous demand and was well suited to West Indian soils and climate, and sugar capital and technology were newly available to West Indian planters through Dutch merchants who had pioneered large-scale sugar estates in north-eastern Brazil in the 1620s. In the 1640s the Dutch extended their operations to Barbados, then throughout the Caribbean. Closer to Europe, Caribbean transport costs were far lower than Brazil's, planters in Barbados bought slaves for half the Pernambuco price, and initial soil fertility made West Indian sugar production a bonanza for local planters, slave-traders, and Amsterdam refiners and financiers. Dutch planters and Jewish refugees expelled from Brazil when Portugal recaptured Pernambuco in 1654 further sped West Indian conversion to sugar.[1]

Sugar brought a social as well as an agricultural revolution. Tobacco and other previous crops required intensive cultivation but only small outlays for processing and labour; a family could economically run a farm with a few indentured servants. By contrast, sugar could be grown extensively with little expertise but was perishable and had to be processed immediately. A sugar factory required a heavy investment in buildings, machinery, and labour and continuous substantial supplies of raw cane; thus sugar estates were much larger than the earlier farms. Within a few years the diversified smallholdings of Barbados, St. Kitts, and Martinique were swallowed up by great estates growing little but sugar.

Sugar was a rich man's crop: it took a lot of money to acquire the necessary land, equipment, and labour. Few entrepreneurs had such

[1] Matthew Edel, 'The Brazilian Sugar Cycle of the Seventeenth Century and the Rise of West Indian Competition', CS, Vol. 9, No. 1, April 1969, pp. 24–44; A. J. R. Russell-Wood, 'Class, Creed and Colour in Colonial Bahia: A Study in Prejudice', Race, Vol. IX, 1967–8, pp. 134–57, ref. pp. 143–5.

capital themselves; they relied on European bankers and merchants. Control and often possession of West Indian sugar properties were soon vested in Amsterdam, London, and Paris mercantile houses, which advanced loans to build the factories and to operate the estates, monopolized traffic in slaves and supplies, and gleaned most of the profits.

With sugar came slavery. There had been slaves in the West Indies since the Discovery; Columbus himself enslaved Indians, and Africans were sold in Cuba and Hispaniola before 1500. But slavery was on a small scale in the Spanish islands until sugar production there was modernized in the nineteenth century. In the English, French, and Dutch colonies, indentured servants, deported criminals, political prisoners, religious refugees, and a few Indians initially supplied enough labour for tobacco and other tasks; but for sugar these did not suffice. Moreover, cane cultivation was arduous and, unlike small-scale agriculture, offered European labourers little opportunity to acquire property and to climb the social ladder. So capitalists and planters turned to Africa. African slaves were not only cheaper than indentured servants, but they and their offspring were bound for life and were presumably already habituated to hard tropical labour. Slaves were needed in quantity; a West Indian sugar plantation of 500 to 1,000 acres might require 250 hands in field and factory.

The best estate land was devoted to sugar, some of it to freshly planted cane, the rest to ratoons grown from cane stalks cut in previous years. On the remainder draft animals were pastured, slaves' provisions grown, and trees cut for building materials and for fuel to run the factory. The cluster of stone factory buildings—mill, boiling house, curing house, and often a rum distillery—was often substantial. Their remnants, together with ruins of aqueducts and windmills, still evoke the characteristic West Indian plantation landscape. Round about were wooden workshops, storage sheds with cane trash and supplies, slave huts, and, usually at some distance, the planter's residence, or 'Great House'.

Cane did not entirely supplant other crops; coffee, cacao, and cotton were grown for export. But given capital and suitable climate and terrain, the West Indian planters preferred sugar. And by the end of the eighteenth century sugar plantations with large-scale African slavery had spread to every Caribbean land that North European enterprise could capture and colonize.

Elsewhere in America from Brazil to Maryland plantation slavery also flourished, but its impact was nowhere so pervasive as in the Caribbean. West Indian physical landscapes, social structures, and ways of life are in large measure plantation by-products. Sugar not only caused Caribbean territories to resemble one another, it substantially unified them. This fact is obscured by the kaleidoscope of European rivalry—

thus St. Lucia changed hands seven times in the space of half a century. But imperial interchanges actually enhanced Caribbean homogeneity. Agricultural affairs usually continued with little reference to, or inter-ference from, naval conquest and diplomatic barter.

When a West Indian territory exchanged one European master for another, its planters and slaves, merchants, and even officials, often carried on regardless. The eighteenth-century English conquests of Dominica, St. Lucia, and Trinidad, for example, left most of the French landowners undisturbed. An English settler in Trinidad complained that of the 'medley of inhabitants: English, Scotch, Irish, Welch, Spaniards, Germans, Swiss, Italians, Americans and French', Picton, the English governor, 'has encouraged all denominations to settle in preference to the British'.[1] 'Foreign' planters here and there suffered civil or religious disabilities, as the French did in Grenada and sub-sequently in Trinidad. But because white planters were in scarce supply, West Indian governments welcomed almost any European entrepreneur. Thus Catholics gained civil rights in the British West Indies long before they did in England, and dissenting Protestants were more tolerated in the French Antilles than in France. Père Labat, in need of a sugar refiner for the Dominican Order's factory in Martinique, was happy to hire a Lutheran; 'it is indifferent to me whether his sugar is Lutheran or Catholic provided it is good and white'.[2] Pan-European in origin, West Indian planters were equally at home in any territory.

Moreover, they frequently moved about the Caribbean. Many held or managed property in two or more territories, constantly travelling from one to another. Planters often changed islands in search of richer soils or cheaper labour. Technicians and overseers, merchants and money lenders, accompanied sugar-cane from Surinam, Barbados, and St. Kitts to all the other islands. Slave uprisings impelled other migra-tions: French planters fleeing the Haitian revolution in the 1790s settled throughout the eastern Caribbean from Guadeloupe to Surinam, as well as in Jamaica and the United States.

Other Europeans—indentured servants, yeoman farmers, 'poor whites' generally—were likewise West Indianized by sugar. Small-holders and indentured servants forced out by sugar-estate engrossment were often unemployable. Lacking means of sustenance, 30,000

[1] Pierre F. M'Callum, *Travels in Trinidad, during the Months of February, March, and April, 1803*, 1805, p. 23. In St. Vincent, too, Governor Valentine Morris 'admired the French settlers because they were hard-working and looked upon their estates as their homes' (Ivor Waters, *The Unfortunate Valentine Morris*, 1964, p. 35, see also pp. 55–8).

[2] Jean-Baptiste Labat, *Voyage du Père Labat, aux isles de l'Amerique*, 1724, Vol. III, pp. 382–3. See also Liliane Chauleau, *La société à la Martinique au XVIIe siècle (1635–1713)*, 1966, p. 178; and Elsa V. Goveia, *Slave Society in the British Leeward Islands at the End of the Eighteenth Century*, 1965, pp. 98, 211–12.

Europeans streamed out of Barbados alone during the latter half of the seventeenth century. A few returned to Europe, more went to the Carolinas and Georgia, but the majority remained in the Caribbean, relocating over and over again in Jamaica, Guiana, the Windwards, and Trinidad.[1] In the British expeditionary force that took Jamaica in 1655, recruits from Barbados and St. Kitts preponderated, subsequently settling as small farmers, overseers, artisans, and militiamen. Later European colonists were similarly peripatetic. 'If a white settler could not succeed in one island, he simply moved to another, carrying with him . . . the "colonial patent of nobility"—his white skin—and began claiming and exercising his privileges all over again.'[2] Intermarriage and political and commercial ties have sustained and amplified these trans-Caribbean connections; it would be hard to find a native-born white in Guyana, St. Vincent, or Trinidad without Barbadian relatives, or one in Guadeloupe without ancestors in Martinique.

Pan-Caribbean connections were by no means exclusively white. Slaves moved between territories involuntarily as chattels or to elude capture as runaways; there were continual escapes from one island to another. Traffic in rum and molasses, fruit and vegetables, timber and rice, involved merchants and mariners of many races. Communication among various local folk languages gave rise to a Caribbean-wide linguistic community, and some sense of regional familiarity penetrated the remotest country districts. Colonial administrations, schools, and churches also shunted personnel from territory to territory. These transfers of officials and technicians, doctors and teachers, increasingly came to include non-whites. West Indians turned naturally to other Caribbean territories for emigration opportunities: British West Indian settlements in Aruba and Curaçao, Dominicans and St. Lucians in French Guiana, St. Barthois in St. Thomas, are living testimony to intermingling throughout the region. Some West Indians have been too peripatetic to put roots down anywhere. Prototypical is the St. Thomas resident who was 'born in Santo Domingo, but his mother returned to Anguilla, his father to Guadeloupe, he has a brother in Curaçao, a sister in England, a wife in St. Vincent'.[3]

Along with the continuous flux of people goes a general community of culture, ideas, and institutions. This likewise stems from slavery and

[1] For the Barbados exodus, see G. W. Roberts, 'Emigration from the Island of Barbados', *SES*, Vol. 4, 1955, pp. 242–88; V. T. Harlow, *A History of Barbados 1625–1685*, 1926, p. 310; and A. D. Chandler, 'The Expansion of Barbados', *Journal of the Barbados Museum and Historical Society*, Vol. XIII, 1946, pp. 106–36.

[2] James Millette, 'The Civil Commission of 1802: An Account and an Explanation of an Issue in the Early Constitutional and Political History of Trinidad', *JHR*, Vol. VI, Nos. 1 and 2, 1966, pp. 29–111, ref. p. 99.

[3] H. B. M. Murphy and H. M. Sampath, 'Mental Illness in a Caribbean Community: A Mental Health Study of St. Thomas, V.I.', 1967, p. 48.

sugar. Planters and agents throughout the Caribbean collaborated in every aspect of the economy, from importing labour and equipment to marketing produce and developing cane varieties. Cane breeding and technology still depend on pooled research; territories join in packaging and selling a wide range of commodities.

The attitudes of planters and of the local governments they dominated were everywhere markedly alike, and the spread of information bolstered the similarities. Threats of slave uprisings, natural disasters, or outside competition could arouse concerted action. Although formal interterritorial organization was rudimentary, transnational values played a major role in West Indian affairs: thus British islands took in royalist refugees from Guadeloupe during the French Revolution, and Dutch and English planters in Guiana made common cause against runaway slaves. Legislative decrees broadcast throughout the Caribbean gained support from, and buttressed the authority of, local elites.

There were keen territorial rivalries, to be sure, and there remains much local ignorance about Caribbean neighbours. But linkages of persons, things, and ideas have persisted throughout West Indian history and lend the whole realm a special unity. The connections are truly Caribbean in character: they link all these territories and extend beyond them only where West Indians have settled *en masse*.

Another quality that West Indian societies share is a sense of artificiality, of owing less to natural growth than to deliberate manufacture. This feeling stems from two historical circumstances: the early eradication of practically all the indigenes and the absence of any deep attachment among newcomers.

When Columbus reached the West Indies they were peopled chiefly by two Indian groups, Arawak and Carib. Both derived from northern South America and had cultural affinities with Amazonian forest tribes; both practised agriculture supplemented by fishing and hunting. The Arawaks, more populous, sedentary, and technologically advanced, inhabited the Greater Antilles; the Caribs, more mobile, aggressive, and relative newcomers, dominated the Lesser Antilles and were then pushing westward from the Virgin Islands into Puerto Rico. More than elsewhere in the New World, Europeans met native Indians only to annihilate them—the Spanish 'falling first upon their knees, and then upon the Indians', and other Europeans bypassing the first fall. Columbus and his followers combed the Indies for labour to work the mines and to grow food for the miners. 'The political geography of the West Indies is starkly simple: the French, English, and Dutch colonies of the seventeenth century occupied islands that had been emptied of their natives early in the sixteenth century in order to keep Española going.'[1]

[1] Carl Ortwin Sauer, *The Early Spanish Main*, 1966, p. 194.

Indians were not in fact entirely extinct; Carib assaults long kept French and English settlers in the Lesser Antilles at bay, and a few Indians were enslaved in Barbados and elsewhere. The Indians were not all local, however; aborigines captured in North America were sent to the West Indies as slaves in exchange for Caribs and Negroes—for settlers in both places sought to discourage Indian tribal reprisals.[1] By the end of the eighteenth century the Arawaks of the larger islands were extinct, and the small-island Caribs were reduced to a few hundred intermixed with runaway African slaves in mountain fastnesses. Today a few score Caribs remain in the islands, principally Dominica, but beyond appearance little about them is distinctively Indian. In the Guianas a small remnant of the pre-Columbian population retains a recognizable Indian culture, but one increasingly attenuated by wage labour, Christian missions, and nationalist assimilation. The Indian canoe and hammock, cassava and other foods, poisons and medicaments, and a few place names and folk tales, are integral to the West Indian scene but hardly constitute an indigenous cultural tradition.

Since the Indians left little impress, the only remembered West Indian past is that of the newcomers. This circumstance is not unique; the same is true of New England, for example. But New Englanders developed a sense of tradition and a view of themselves as 'natives'. No less aboriginal, West Indians after three centuries still identify themselves, if not as strangers, at best as 'Creoles'—an expression of condition rather than of nationality.

'Creole' highlights the essentially alien quality felt to characterize much of West Indian life. A word of Spanish origin, it originally denoted Negro slaves born in the New World, as distinct from the African-born. 'Creole' soon came to refer to anyone, black or white, born in the West Indies. It was then extended to things, habits, and ideas; plants grown, goods manufactured, and opinions expressed in the West Indies were all 'Creole'. Recently the term has reverted to its earlier association, and in some areas 'Creole' is now a euphemism for coloured or black. But its meaning varies locally. In Jamaica 'Creole' designates anyone of Jamaican parentage except East Indians, Chinese, and Maroons (back-country descendents of runaway slaves, who are considered 'African'). In Trinidad and Guyana it excludes Amerindians and East Indians; in Surinam it denotes the 'civilized' coloured population, as apart from tribes of rebel-slave descent called Bush Negroes. In the French Antilles 'Creole' refers more to local-born whites than to coloured or black persons; in French Guiana, by contrast, it is used

[1] Jerome S. Handler, 'The Amerindian Slave Population of Barbados in the Seventeenth and Early Eighteenth Centuries', *CS*, Vol. 8, No. 4, January 1969, pp. 38–64; Almon Wheeler Lauber, *Indian Slavery in Colonial Times within the Present Limits of the United States*, 1913, pp. 68, 124–7, 188.

exclusively for non-whites.[1] In the Commonwealth Caribbean, where independence and black power now favour national and ethnic appellations, the term 'Creole' is today considered old-fashioned, self-conscious, or 'arty'. But it is still common in French-speaking territories, and English-speakers use 'Creole' to describe those of French descent or tradition in the older generation. As a generic term to distinguish white, coloured, and black West Indians from all others, however, there is no substitute for 'Creole', and I shall employ it in that sense throughout this book.

The Caribbean developed no indigenous tradition not only for lack of Indians but also because most settlers came not to live but merely to make a living—or to enrich others. 'The flora, the fauna, the economy, and the people were all at various times imported into empty islands and spread out there like butter on waiting slices of bread.'[2] The masters felt almost as alien as their slaves; 'Europeans have always been doubly "European" in the West Indies, not only out of nostalgia, but in order to preserve their identity in an alien land.'[3]

North European settlers acquired the Spanish practice of viewing these locales not as dwelling places but only as sources of fortune. Few forged lasting bonds with land or peoples. The ties between Spanish and Indian in Mexico, and the familial obligations of slave-holders on Latin American *haciendas*, had few Caribbean counterparts. This was partly because the Dutch, French, and English were more energetic and economically successful in their enterprises than the Spanish. Instead of gold the North Europeans produced sugar; for Indian labour they substituted African. Sugar and slaves became a smoothly functioning machine capable of almost indefinite continuation.

The European planter was also a machine for making money. The wealthy West Indian was a stock figure of the eighteenth century, but

[1] F. G. Cassidy and R. B. Le Page, *Dictionary of Jamaican English*, 1967, p. 130; Wally Thompson, 'Creoles and Pidgins, East and West', *NWQ*, Vol. 2, No. 4, Crop-over, 1966, pp. 11–16, ref. p. 11; André Nègre, 'Origines et signification du mot "créole"', *Bulletin de la Société d'Histoire de la Guadeloupe*, Nos. 5–6, 1966, pp. 38–42. These attributions all differ from Louisiana, where 'Creole' refers to whites of French or Spanish descent and culture. The West Indian range of uses is closer to that in Sierra Leone, where the descendants of Africans repatriated from London, Nova Scotia, Jamaica, and captured slave vessels styled themselves 'Creole', as distinct from tribal Africans; Europeanized Africans of any ancestry have since adopted the term. For Sierra Leone, see Arthur T. Porter, *Creoledom: A Study of the Development of Freetown Society*, 1963, pp. 51–2; John Peterson, 'The Sierra Leone Creole: A Re-appraisal', in Christopher Fyfe and Eldred Jones, eds., *Freetown: A Symposium*, 1968, pp. 100–17, ref. pp. 114–15.

[2] A. P. Thornton, 'Aspects of West Indian Society', *International Journal*, Vol. XV, 1960, pp. 113–21, ref. p. 116.

[3] 'Introduction', in Louis James, ed., *The Islands in Between: Essays on West Indian Literature*, 1968, pp. 1–49, ref. p. 23.

the money he made flowed back to London, Paris, and Amsterdam. He spent lavishly in Europe, not in the West Indies. 'There never was any hard cash knocking about the colonies'; planters received goods as advances against the next sugar crop from metropolitan agents who had liens on the estates. 'No money was ever sent out to the colonies if it could be avoided. . . . Everybody had to live on a single credit pyramid.'[1] With few exceptions, plantation 'Great Houses' were great only by contrast with the slave huts and barracks; European visitors found them bleak barns, barely adorned, poorly furnished, and subject to swift decay. Spanish and French Caribbean settlement might display 'some generosity of imaginative endowment', but one authority sums up the Dutch and British material legacy as little more than 'warehouses . . . [and] ugly, barely functional cities'.[2]

Many affluent estate owners never set foot in the Caribbean; those who succeeded there lost no time returning to Europe. Even in the heyday of sugar prosperity, absentee proprietors owned most of the property and slaves in Jamaica; a century later, with slavery ended, sugar prices down, and mortgages foreclosed, two-thirds of Grenada's sugar estates, four-fifths of those in St. Vincent and Tobago, and nine-tenths of the cultivated land in Jamaica were held by absentees.[3]

Resident planters differed from absentees mainly in envying them. 'Their "home" was not in the West Indies, their degree of identification with colonial life and society was small and they hoped it would be fleeting.'[4] A Governor of Martinique observed that colonists 'thought continually of their return to France and kept everything in readiness to leave at a moment's notice';[5] in British islands, 'except a few regular Creoles . . . everyone regards the colony as a temporary lodging place, where they must sojourn in sugar and molasses till their mortgages will

[1] Christopher Nicole, *The Self Lovers*, 1968, p. 59.

[2] W. I. Carr, 'Roger Mais: Design from a Legend', *CQ*, Vol. 13, No. 1, March 1967, pp. 3–28, ref. p. 13. For the degrees of absenteeism exhibited by various European types of colonies, see 'Attitudes to Slavery in the New World', in Anthony de Rueck and Julie Knight, eds., *Caste and Race: Comparative Approaches*, 1967, pp. 208–9.

[3] Edward Long, *History of Jamaica, or, General Survey of the Antient and Modern State of That Island*, 1754, Vol. I, Book II, Chapter II, especially pp. 386–91; John Bigelow, *Jamaica in 1850, or, The Effects of Sixteen Years of Freedom on a Slave Colony*, 1851, p. 79; W. K. Marshall, 'Social and Economic Problems in the Windward Islands 1838–65', in F. M. Andic and T. G. Mathews, eds., *The Caribbean in Transition: Papers on Social, Political, and Economic Development*, 1965, pp. 234–57, ref. p. 239.

[4] Douglas G. Hall, 'Absentee-Proprietorship in the British West Indies to about 1850', *JHR*, Vol. IV, 1964, pp. 15–35, ref. p. 27. See Philip D. Curtin, *Two Jamaicas: The Role of Ideas in a Tropical Colony, 1830–1865*, 1955, pp. 42–60; Richard Pares, 'Merchants and Planters', *Economic History Review*, Supplement 4, 1960, pp. 42–44; Lowell Joseph Ragatz, 'Absentee Landlordism in the British Caribbean, 1750–1833', *Agricultural History*, Vol. V, 1931, pp. 7–24.

[5] Jean-Charles de Baas to Ministre, 26 December 1669, quoted in Chauleau, *La société à la Martinique au XVIIe siècle*, p. 104.

let them live elsewhere.'[1] A colonial official in the 1830s doubted that
there was 'a white man in the Island of Jamaica who does not regard
England as his home and the Colony as a place of Exile.'[2] A prominent
twentieth-century resident discerned 'no time in the history of Jamaica
when the wealthier classes . . . did not prefer to pass most of their life in
England', and added that 'the same preference exists today'.[3]

Colonial planters sent their sons and daughters across the Atlantic
for schooling and marriage. Three hundred children a year, three-
fourths of the elite legitimate offspring, went from mid-eighteenth-
century Jamaica to England; eighty-nine Jamaicans had been to
Oxford, ninety-seven to Cambridge by 1820. Fewer than two out of
three ever came back,[4] and many who did return regretted it. 'Disappointed and vexed [by] the houses, servants, and society, the dull
routine of life,' one young Jamaican bemoaned the 'many dull and
cheerless moments I am doomed to lead in the absence of those dear
amusements which have so enchanted me on the other side of the
Atlantic'.[5] Education abroad, felt a chronicler of St. Domingue (Haiti),

made most of the Colonists alien to the land where they were born. . . . Those
who came back brought with them tastes that could not be satisfied there. . . .
Hence, our aversion toward our birthplace and the boredom that makes us
see ourselves only as transients in a country where we are sometimes forced
to stay for our whole life. Hence, our unconcern for the well-being and prosperity of a country from which we expect only the means of living elsewhere.[6]

West Indian whites were not totally unconcerned; a parish vestry
complained to the Jamaican Assembly in 1805 that 'inefficient' local
schools obliged 'many children . . . to be sent to Europe, while others,
for want of means, remain uneducated'. The Government supported
several free schools, including by 1813 one for free coloured children;

[1] Henry Nelson Coleridge, *Six Months in the West Indies in 1825*, 1832, p. 131.

[2] James Stephen, 'Answer to the Objections to the Proposed Order in Council
Respecting Slavery', Memorandum of October 1831 (Howick Papers), in Kenneth
N. Bell and W. P. Morrell, eds., *Select Documents on British Colonial Policy, 1830–1860*,
1928, pp. 372–82, ref. p. 373.

[3] H. G. de Lisser, *Twentieth Century Jamaica*, 1913, p. 189.

[4] Edward Long, *History of Jamaica*, Vol. I, pp. 438, 511; Ragatz, 'Absentee Landlordism in the British Caribbean, 1750–1833', pp. 9–10; Edward Brathwaite, 'Jamaican Slave Society, A Review', *Race*, Vol. IX, 1967–8, pp. 331–42, ref. p. 335.

[5] Letter signed 'Melissa', *Jamaica Magazine*, Vol. 4, 1813, quoted in H. Orlando
Patterson, *The Sociology of Slavery*, 1967, pp. 38–40.

[6] Médéric-Louis-Élie Moreau de Saint-Méry, *Description topographique, physique,
civile politique et historique de la partie française de l'isle Saint-Domingue* [1797], Vol. I,
pp. 30–1. See also Lowell Joseph Ragatz, *The Fall of the Planter Class in the British
Caribbean, 1763–1833: A Study in Social and Economic History* [1928], pp. 21–3. For an
analogous situation in the Southern United States see Frederick Law Olmsted, *The
Slave States before the Civil War*, excerpted from *The Cotton Kingdom* [1861], pp. 249–51.

two years later the Assembly paid £3,000 in school costs.[1] A few clubs kept small libraries; there was a handful of local historians and litté-rateurs. But among most planters 'the Office of a Teacher is look'd upon as contemptible, and no Gentleman keeps Company with one of that Character; to read, write, and cast up Accounts, is all the Education they desire, and even these are but scurvily taught. A Man of any Parts or Learning would be despised and starve.'[2] And without teachers and students the West Indies lacked a general sense of culture. 'No civilized Society, on earth', judged a former sojourner there, was 'so entirely destitute of learned leisure, of literary and scientific intercourse and even of liberal recreations.'[3]

Because men of substance and taste found the Caribbean unfit to live in, the territories failed to acquire a true elite. 'In British West Indian colonial society a man became a member of the elite only when he qualified as a potential absentee.... "Colonial elite" was a contradiction in terms [to men] . . . whose means permitted them to be elite rather than colonial.'[4] Since most whites of intelligence and enterprise went 'home', the inadequacies of those who remained were the more apparent. 'Gens presque tous fort ignorans, souvent très injustes, mais toujours entestés d'une vanité insuportable' was how the Governor of Martinique saw members of his *Conseil Souverain* in 1712.[5] 'A sad set indeed', a Jamaican Governor in 1834 termed his local Council. 'Their poverty and inefficiency is a matter of public notoriety, they have no influence, they enjoy no respect'.[6] The Speaker of the Jamaican House of Assembly in 1855 was appalled to find a session chaired by a member who 'could neither read nor write'.[7] Late nineteenth-century Mont-serrat was governed by 'hungry and illiterate "white" adventurers', wrote a local citizen. 'Our Council is composed of an imbecile in the last stage of his dotage; a Constitutional idiot; two wily Esculapians "whose whole souls are money and place"; and a hypocrite without the slightest vested interest in this island nor any sympathy with its inhabi-

[1] Edward Brathwaite, 'Jamaican Slave Society, A Review', pp. 335–6.

[2] Charles Leslie, *History of Jamaica*, 1740, pp. 28, 30, 31, 35–9, quoted in Frank Wesley Pitman, *The Development of the British West Indies, 1700–1763* [1917], pp. 24–5.

[3] Stephen, 'Answer to the Objections to the Proposed Order in Council Respecting Slavery', p. 373.

[4] Hall, 'Absentee-Proprietorship in the British West Indies to about 1850', pp. 27, 29.

[5] Phélypeaux to Ministre, 8 January 1712, quoted in Chauleau, *La société à la Martinique au XVIIe siècle*, p. 88.

[6] Marquis of Sligo, Sligo Papers (Institute of Jamaica), quoted in Patterson, *The Sociology of Slavery*, p. 38.

[7] Choppin to Eyre, 22 June, in Colebrooke to Russell, 3 July 1855, C. O. 260/83, quoted in W. P. Morrell, *British Colonial Policy in the Mid-Victorian Age: South Africa, New Zealand, The West Indies*, 1969, pp. 379–80.

tants.'[1] White skins were usually the sole qualification for office. West Indian societies were in effect socially truncated. Their natural leaders were either in Europe or proscribed by colour; educated non-whites were barred from the elite, at first by law, later by prejudice. White rule was, increasingly, rule by poor whites, fearful, embattled, and intransigent.

The elite steadily withdrew its stake as well as itself. After four generations on the island of Nevis, the Pinney family sold out entirely. They resumed residence in their native Dorset, wrote the family biographer, 'as if they had never been out of the country.'[2] But a West Indian adds: 'That is the picture seen through British eyes. Seen through West Indian eyes, against the background of the derelict island today, it is as if they had never been in Nevis.' Whites who stayed on increasingly isolated themselves from other local connections.[3]

Only in Barbados and Martinique, and for a time, in Curaçao and Antigua, did endogamy sustain a durable white elite. Elsewhere ruling whites were more apt to be Europeans than Creoles. They were no better equipped for leadership, however, than the residual native whites. For many expatriates the islands existed only to be exploited. Officials, lawyers, doctors, and ministers appointed to West Indian posts regularly farmed them out to substitutes. Caribbean societies were dominated by remittance men to whom oligarchy was the sole compensation for exile.

Not all expatriates were inferior, but attrition, as among the planters, continuously lowered the general level. 'The best go away . . . not being able to justify profiting from daily injustice or simply out of pride'. For colonies in general, as Memmi shows, the double defection of intelligent natives and worthy newcomers is a lasting catastrophe, 'the mediocre ones remain, and for their whole life. . . . It is the mediocre citizens who set the general tone of the colony.'[4] So in Trinidad, the English colonists were at first

distinguished . . . by their intellectual liveliness, . . . a carryover from the metropolis. In the slave society, where self-fulfillment came so easily, this liveliness began to be perverted and then to fade, and the English saw their pre-eminence, more simply, as a type of racial magic. . . . The emigration of the ambitious was a further intellectual depletion. . . . The quality of controversy declined, and the stature of men. What remained was a colony.[5]

Creolization subjugated colonial masters no less than slaves. 'Englishmen arriving in the Colony are easily initiated into the habits and

---

[1] 'Montserrat, Thy Day Is Come', letter signed 'Pro Bono Publico', *Dominica Guardian*, 8 and 15 January 1896.

[2] Richard Pares, *A West-India Fortune*, 1950, p. 332.

[3] Eric Williams, *British Historians and The West Indies*, 1964, p. 34.

[4] Albert Memmi, *The Colonizer and the Colonized* [1957], pp. 48, 50.

[5] V. S. Naipaul, *The Loss of El Dorado: A History*, 1969, p. 316.

customs they meet,' commented a small islander at the turn of this century. 'At home he would die for liberty; abroad he preaches slavery in some form. . . . In England his justice to his fellow men . . . is prover-bial, in the Colonies he metes out justice with a very stinted hand'.[1] As Aimé Césaire put it, 'la colonisation travaille à *déciviliser* le colonisateur, à *l'abrutir* au sens propre du mot, . . . à le convoitise, à la violence, à la haine raciale, au relativisme morale'.[2]

Antillean absenteeism left rural whites little alternative except slave modes of life. Isolated from other whites, with daily contacts limited to slaves and free coloured servants, the Creole woman in particular took on folk speech, diet, and customs, 'gobbling pepper-pot, seated on the floor, with her sable hand-maids around her. . . . Her ideas are narrowed to . . . the business of the plantation, the tittle-tattle of the parish; the tricks, superstitions, diversions, and profligate discourses, of black servants'.[3] A resident of St. Domingue penned a similar description of plantation tedium:

Have pity for an existence which must be eked out far from the world of our own people. We here number five whites, my father, my mother, my two brothers, and myself, surrounded by more than two hundred slaves. . . . From morning to night, wherever we turn, their faces meet our eyes. No matter how early we awaken, they are at our bedsides. . . . Our conversation has almost entirely to do with the health of our slaves, their needs which must be cared for, the manner in which they are to be distributed about the estate, or their attempts at revolt, . . . our entire life is so closely identified with that of these unfortunates that, in the end, it is the same as theirs.[4]

The discrepancy between the slave-master's authority and his circumstances was for him a source of aggravation and shame. He found himself dependent on his slaves at every point—for livelihood, for safety, for comfort, even for companionship. Power encouraged a taste for tyranny: the typical planter was 'a petty monarch, as capri-cious as he is despotic'.[5] Yet the galling recognition of dependency on a despised inferior helps to explain why whites often described their own lives in terms of slavery. Thus in Littleton's *Groans of the Plantations*[6] it is the planters who are groaning, not the slaves.

[1] 'Open Letter No. 4', *Montserrat Herald*, 5 February 1903.

[2] Aimé Césaire, *Discours sur le colonialisme*, 1955, p. 11.

[3] Edward Long, *History of Jamaica*, Vol. II, p. 279.

[4] Letter, in Pierre de Vaissière, *Saint-Domingue (1629–1789): la société et la vie créoles sous l'ancien régime*, 1909, pp. 280–1, quoted in Melville J. Herskovits, *Life in a Haitian Valley*, 1937, p. 39.

[5] J. G. Stedman, *Narrative, of a Five Years' Expedition, Against the Revolted Negroes of Surinam, in Guiana, on the Wild Coast of South America; from the year 1772, to 1777*, 1806, Vol. II, p. 60.

[6] Edward Littleton, *Groans of the Plantations*, 1689, p. 34, cited in Pitman, *The Development of the British West Indies, 1700–1763*, pp. 31–2.

Africans and their descendants have outnumbered all other West Indians since the 1650s. Their story, one of them writes, is 'one prolonged agony of dispossession, enslavement, and colonisation.'[1] Brought to the West Indies by force and forcibly held there, they felt it as a prison. However little they recalled of Africa, it remained their homeland.

Succeeding generations of slaves remembered less of Africa, and Creoles learned to scorn slaves born there, but they gained no local attachments to replace the ancestral one. 'How strange is the race of creole Negroes—of Negroes, that is, born out of Africa', exclaimed Trollope, who visited the West Indies in 1860. 'They have no country of their own, yet they have not hitherto any country of their adoption. . . . They have no idea of country, and no pride of race'.[2]

It was little wonder they lacked racial pride; for their race had been denied even personality. Whites considered themselves the only West Indian inhabitants. Even those who baptized, punished, or slept with their slaves viewed them more as property than as persons. Slave status was the lot of the overwhelming West Indian mass. In no other western society have there been so few free men and so many slaves; nowhere else but in South Africa has a racially differentiated majority so long endured degradation. Most West Indian slaves had individual legal status only for purposes of discipline and defence; planters were required to provide white militiamen in proportion to the number of their slaves. 'In so far as the slave is allowed personality before the law', concludes a student of West Indian slave codes, 'he is regarded chiefly, almost solely, as a potential criminal.'[3]

Slave conditions and treatment varied with the nationality and religion of the owner, the nature of the local economy, and the numerical balance between slave and free, black and white. Legal codes differed substantially in both nature and administration. Spanish law, derived from ancient Roman practices codified in the thirteenth-century *Siete Partidas*, treated slaves as members of families and beings with moral personalities. The French *Code Noir* of 1685, likewise based on Roman and canon law but designed with specific reference to West Indian servitude, elaborated slave routines, duties, and punishments, and the obligations of masters. British colonies lacked a comprehensive code, and their planter-inspired local laws tended to be harsher and more minatory than the French and Spanish codes, minimizing public

[1] H. Orlando Patterson, 'Without History', *New Statesman*, 8 March 1968, p. 304. For the provenance of Caribbean slaves, see R. B. Le Page and David De Camp, *Jamaican Creole*, 1960, pp. 21–76, and Philip D. Curtin, *The Atlantic Slave Trade: A Census*, 1969, pp. 123–30, 163–70, 182–203, 220–30, 251–64.

[2] Anthony Trollope, *The West Indies and the Spanish Main*, 1860, p. 55.

[3] Elsa V. Goveia, 'The West Indian Slave Laws of the Eighteenth Century', *Revista de Ciencias Sociales*, Vol. IV, 1960, pp. 75–105, ref. p. 86.

interposition between master and slave. But actual treatment was often at variance with laws governing slave usage. The *Code Noir* as promulgated from Paris seemed excessively liberal to planters in the Antilles, where its protective aspects were progressively eroded. British colonial slave laws, often formally disallowed in London, for all practical purposes remained locally in force. Local realities required principle to yield to custom, usually in a fashion adverse to slave 'rights'.

Popular stereotypes about slave treatment focused on supposed national and religious traits. The Dutch were reputed crueller masters than the French, Protestants than Catholics, coloured than white. Writers were usually eager to exonerate their own nations. 'No nation . . . feeds its slaves as badly as the English,' concluded a French traveller in seventeenth-century Barbados,[1] whereas an English Governor of previously Dutch Surinam related, 'I have spent 21 years in the West Indies and in each colony I heard that it was a severe punishment for a negro to be sold to a planter in Surinam and I now find that this is true.'[2] Yet slave circumstances were perhaps easiest in Dutch Curaçao, where aridity impeded plantation agriculture, and most onerous in French St. Domingue. But the commingling of European backgrounds renders all such comparisons suspect. In Trinidad, for example, slavery was relatively mild, but it is hard to estimate how much amelioration owed to Spanish law, English rule, French-planter mores, the early growth of a free-coloured class, or to Trinidad's late agricultural development.

Geography made more difference than nationality. Slavery was harsh in the Guianas owing to the high ratio of slaves to whites and to the ease of escape into the interior, and less onerous in entrepôts like St. Eustatius. But barbarities occurred in every West Indian territory, large and small, of whatever European nationality and religion, ratio of slave to free, mode of slave employment, and opportunities for escape. Most variations in slave treatment were trivial or inconsistent. The West Indian slave suffered much the same fate everywhere; differences reflect the character or circumstances of slave-owners more than any territorial distinctions. The ex-slave Equiano found servitude almost the same in fifteen islands, 'so nearly, indeed, that the history of an island or even a plantation . . . might serve for a history of the whole.'[3]

[1] Antoine Biet, *Voyage de la France equinoxiale en l'isle de Cayenne enterpris par les françois en l'année M. DC. LII*, 1664, p. 290.

[2] Pinson Bonham to Bathurst, 8 June 1813, quoted in R. A. J. van Lier, 'Negro Slavery in Surinam', *Caribbean Historical Review*, Nos. III–IV, December 1954, pp. 108–48, ref. p. 112. See also John Augustine Waller, *A Voyage in the West Indies*, 1820, pp. 90–4. The gulf between theory and practice, and the role of the Catholic clergy in slavery, are surveyed in Antoine Gisler, *L'esclavage aux Antilles françaises (XVIIe– XIXe siècle) : contribution au problème de l'esclavage*, 1965.

[3] Olaudah Equiano, *Equiano's Travels* [1789], pp. 72–3.

Comparisons of slave systems are legion and generally defective. American scholars long believed that Latin American slavery was more benign than Anglo-American. Tannenbaum argues that Roman Catholicism, Latin legal codes, and a long tradition of racial mixing eased conditions in Brazil; Elkins hypothesizes that capitalism made American slavery peculiarly harsh; and Klein compares seventeenth-century Virginia unfavourably with nineteenth-century Cuba. Davis and Sio cast doubt on these hypotheses, and Degler demonstrates that the slave's lot in Brazil was no better than in the American South. Whatever the formal differences, van den Berghe is 'struck by astonishing similarities between the slave plantation regimes of the Americas in terms of modes of production, life style of masters and slaves, distinctions between house and field slaves, institutionalized concubinage and miscegenation, etiquette and rules of social distance, forms of violence, slave revolts, and many other characteristics.'[1] Caribbean slavery raises further doubts about the traditional comparisons; for in the West Indies Catholics no less than Protestants denied their slaves Christianity, Englishmen were often more casual than Brazilians about their slave liaisons, and other contradictions qualify or invalidate the usual generalizations.

The whole debate concerning the relative severity of different systems of slavery is 'a waste of time', Harris suggests, since beyond a certain point of brutality and dehumanization, differences of degree hardly matter to an oppressed population.[2] Yet certain features distinguish the Caribbean as a whole from other American slave systems.

[1] Frank Tannenbaum, *Slave and Citizen: The Negro in the Americas* [1946]; Stanley M. Elkins, *Slavery: A Problem in American Institutional and Intellectual Life*, 2nd ed., 1968; Herbert S. Klein, *Slavery in the Americas: A Comparative Study of Virginia and Cuba*, 1967; David Brion Davis, *The Problem of Slavery in Western Culture*, 1966; Arnold A. Sio, 'Interpretations of Slavery: The Slave Status in the Americas', *Comparative Studies in Society and History*, Vol. VII, 1965, pp. 289–308; Carl N. Degler, 'Slavery in Brazil and the United States: An Essay in Comparative History', *American Historical Review*, Vol. LXXV, 1970, pp. 1004–28; Pierre L. van den Berghe, 'The African Diaspora in Mexico, Brazil, and the United States' [1970], p. 10. C. R. Boxer, *Race Relations in the Portuguese Colonial Empire, 1415–1825*, 1963, and *The Golden Age of Brazil: 1695–1750: Growing Pains of a Colonial Society*, 1963, explodes the myth of Portuguese racial tolerance, but the old stereotypes endure, even among scholars who find racial discrimination in Brazil today more pervasive than in the United States: 'The Portuguese colonizer of Brazil['s] . . . treatment of the slaves was almost humane, if compared with the tortures administered to the Negro slaves in the English, Dutch, and especially the French colonies' (Jean-Claude Garcia-Zamor, 'Social Mobility of Negroes in Brazil', *Journal of Inter-American Studies and World Affairs*, Vol. XII, 1970, pp. 242–54, ref. p. 243).

[2] 'There is no conceivable way in which we can now be certain that they were indeed treated better in one place than the other. . . . Better to dispute the number of angels on a pinhead than to argue that one country's slavery is superior to another's' (Marvin Harris, *Patterns of Race in the Americas*, 1964, pp. 71, 74).

West Indian slavery was more than a way of life, it was *the* way of life, the only one that mattered there. Virtually no whites, or for that matter non-slaves of any colour, were not intimately connected with slavery or utterly dependent on it. This helps to explain why slave-holders elsewhere almost universally adjudged West Indian slavery the most severe. Virginians considered it a condign punishment: George Washington sold a slave into the West Indies only because 'this fellow is both a rogue and a runaway.'[1] Another Southern slave-holder thought that the 'Slave Trade, the horrors of the Middle Passage, and West India slavery were enough to rouse the most torpid philanthropy', and American slavery was by contrast 'a benign and protective institution'.[2]

North American planters denounced West Indian slave-masters, to be sure, the better to justify their own system of bondage. But West Indian slave conditions *were* appalling. Conditions of work, nourishment, confinement, and punishment were probably the worst in the New World. The paucity of whites made repression of rebellion more savage than in Brazil or the American South; the West Indian slave regimes generally became more severe as the ratio of Negro to white increased. Caribbean sugar plantations rapidly used up slaves and continuously imported fresh ones. Americans encouraged slaves to bear and raise children; West Indian planters considered slave-breeding unrealistically humanitarian. Purchases, unlike births, supplied labour where wanted and without delay. Even the Society for the Propagation of the Gospel in Foreign Parts, which endeavoured to run an eighteenth-century Barbados estate in humane fashion, considered offspring inadequate recompense for the loss of their mothers' labour and the cost of rearing: half the children died before the age of five. Yet half the replacements from Africa perished during the first three years.[3] Jamaican overseers explicitly aimed 'to work the Slaves out, and trust for supplies from Africa'. Death was no deterrent; 'though I have killed 30 or 40 Negroes per year more', one explained, 'I have made my employer 20, 30, 40 more hogsheads per year than any of my predecessors ever did'.[4] From the Middle Passage to infrequent old age, slave mortality in the West

---

[1] Mazyck, *George Washington and the Negro*, quoted in W. E. B. DuBois, *Black Reconstruction in America* [1935], p. 45.

[2] George Fitzhugh, *Cannibals All! or, Slaves Without Masters* [1857], p. 201.

[3] J. Harry Bennett, Jr., *Bondsmen and Bishops: Slavery and Apprenticeship on the Codrington Plantations of Barbados, 1710–1838*, 1958. The preference for importing rather than breeding slaves, with its concomitant cruelties, was similarly characteristic of Brazil. See Stanley Stein, *Vassouras: A Brazilian Coffee County, 1850–1900*, 1957, p. 155; Degler, 'Slavery in Brazil and the United States', pp. 1017–20.

[4] Henry Coor, testimony before 'A Committee of the House of Commons . . . Respecting the African Slave Trade (1790–1791), *Parliamentary Papers before 1801*, Vol. 38, p. 90.

Indies was daunting. Almost four million Africans were sold into the British, French, and Dutch Caribbean; yet when slavery ended in these territories, the West Indian population of African descent was no more than a million and a half.

A comparison with American rates of survival underscores the harshness of West Indian conditions. When the slaves were emancipated, the Caribbean contained scarcely one-third the number imported; the United States had eleven times the number brought in. The effects of the difference are enduring. The United States imported less than 5 per cent of the slaves brought to the Americas but in 1950 had 33 per cent of the Afro-American population. At the other extreme, the Caribbean islands imported more than 40 per cent but in 1950 had only 20 per cent of the hemisphere's Afro-Americans.[1]

High mortality encouraged West Indian planters to treat slaves callously. They had small interest in easing the lot of workers after they ceased to be productive. It was not uncommon for Jamaican planters to bring false accusations against their sick and lame slaves; for when slaves were executed as criminals, the Government compensated their owners.[2] The typical West Indian estate employed many more slaves than the average Southern plantation, and relatively fewer attachments developed between master and slave. In any case the West Indian master was often simply not there. Absenteeism promoted harsh treatment; managers and overseers thinking of short-run returns were apt to be more demanding—and more penurious—than resident owners. Slave rations were most meagre and runaways most frequent on absentee-owned estates. Many estate owners returned after long absences to find soils exhausted and slaves brutalized by fear and hunger.

Much slave mistreatment was a consequence of Caribbean circumstances—mercantilism, planter absenteeism, the predominance of sugar, the high ratio of slave to free. These conditions generally lay beyond individual European control or influence. But they created environments favourable to cruelty and inhumanity and attracted planters and officials who could enjoy or endure them.

Throughout the West Indies slaves had fewer rights than elsewhere in the New World. French Antillean slaves were consistently underfed; statutory clothing allowances seldom reached slaves in Barbados and

[1] Philip D. Curtin, *The Atlantic Slave Trade: A Census*, 1969, pp. 88–9, 92, 268. The average length of life for a Guyanese slave in the early nineteenth century was under twenty-three years (G. W. Roberts, 'A Life Table for a West Indian Slave Population', *Population Studies*, Vol. V, 1951–2, pp. 238–43). See also George W. Roberts, *The Population of Jamaica*, 1957, pp. 165–75, 219–47; Philip D. Curtin, 'Epidemiology and the Slave Trade', *Political Science Quarterly*, Vol. LXXXIII, 1968, pp. 190–216.

[2] George Metcalf, *Royal Government and Political Conflict in Jamaica, 1729–1783*, 1965, pp. 5–6.

the Leeward Islands; slaves in Jamaica and the Guianas seldom had enough time to cultivate the 'garden plots' allotted them in lieu of food rations. In times of crisis when prices fell or when hurricanes demolished provision grounds, slaves were the first to suffer.

The high incidence of West Indian slave rebellion suggests the harshness of that regime or, alternatively, may reflect a less demoralizing subjugation. Scarcely a decade passed without an organized uprising somewhere in the Caribbean. Runaways were also frequent, partly because slaves greatly outnumbered whites, making detection and recapture difficult, especially in the Guianas and the larger mountainous islands. Maroons, or runaway slaves, eluded capture in island interiors more or less continuously into the nineteenth century. Also conducive to rebellion was the high proportion of African-born to Creole slaves; for many revolts were tribally exclusive, and most were African-led. Only after the slave trade ended and Africans ceased to enter the Caribbean did Creoles, seeking more to ameliorate than to escape the plantation system, dominate slave uprisings.[1]

West Indians who remained in bondage, like those in the American South, both adjusted to slavery and resisted by malingering, by work slow-downs, by self-mutilation, and even by suicide. Elkins's hypothesis that slavery engendered a passive, obedient, brain-washed 'Sambo' personality, resembling that of concentration-camp inmates, no doubt oversimplifies or exaggerates; many slaves refused to accommodate, others fashioned techniques of psychic defence against spiritual destruction. Yet bondage affected even the strongest-willed. After escaping from North Carolina to New York City, J. W. C. Pennington remarked, 'It was four years before I had thrown off the crouching aspect of slavery'.[2] Such traits were perhaps less pronounced in the Caribbean. 'The cowering humility, the expressions of servile respect with which the negro approaches a white man' in the United States were frequently compared with Edward Long's assertion that West Indian slaves addressed their master with 'freedom and confidence', and with a House of Commons Committee report of 'frankness and

[1] Eric Williams, *Capitalism and Slavery*, 1944, pp. 203–8; Gabriel Debien, 'Le marronage aux Antilles françaises au XVIIᵉ siècle', *CS*, Vol. 6, No. 3, October 1966, pp. 3–43; Monica Schuler, 'Akan Slave Rebellions in the British Caribbean', *Savacou*, Vol. 1, No. 1, June 1970, pp. 8–31. Gabriel Debien, 'La nourriture des esclaves sur les plantations des Antilles françaises aux XVIIᵉ et XVIIIᵉ siècles', *CS*, Vol. 4, No. 2, July 1964, pp. 3–27, presents evidence of widespread malnutrition. The causes and consequences of the most successful West Indian slave revolt are graphically related in C. L. R. James, *The Black Jacobins: Toussaint L'Ouverture and the San Domingo Revolution* [1938].

[2] J. W. C. Pennington, quoted in Gilbert Osofsky, *The Burden of Race: A Documentary History of Negro–White Relations in America*, 1967, p. 3. For an acknowledgement of similar traumatic effects in the West Indies, see Elsa Goveia, 'Introduction', *Savacou*, Vol. 1, No. 1, June 1970, pp. 3–7, ref. p. 4.

boldness'.[1] To this day British West Indians in the United States stereotype American Negroes as descendants of slaves, in contrast with their own presumed legacy of freedom.[2]

Just as slave-owners tried to show that slavery in their own country was milder than elsewhere, so some slave descendants view their own ancestral history as especially rugged. West Indian slave stamina is an article of local faith; only those whose spirits were broken, it is said, were shipped to North America. A comparison of folk songs suggests that adjustment may in fact have been more the norm in the Southern states. American slave ditties characteristically emphasize duty, obedience, and other Christian virtues. Jamaican and Trinidadian chants focus on the oppression, cruelty, and degradation of slavery, and sometimes on avenging them. 'Pain 'ou ca mange', a popular Trinidad folk song, parodies Communion in celebrating an 1807 plot to kill Europeans: 'The bread you eat is the white man's flesh,/The wine you drink is the white man's blood,/Hey San Domingo, remember San Domingo'.[3]

In one respect West Indian slavery was less onerous than in America: the ease of manumission and opportunities for economic advance. West Indian slaves could and did gain freedom more often and more rapidly than slaves in the Southern states could. West Indian whites tolerated free coloured persons, for whom American society found no place; the West Indies needed coloured men in occupational niches that whites pre-empted in the United States. Perhaps a worse feature of American slavery than its cruelty, Elkins suggests, was the closing off of channels for talent, energy, ambition. Because initiative and self-reliance—prime values of nineteenth-century American society—were denied to blacks during slavery, proportionately fewer Negro American freedmen made their mark than in the West Indies.[4]

[1] William Law Mathieson, *British Slave Emancipation 1838–1849* [1932], p. 100. But American slave folklore 'affirms the existence of a large number of vital, tough-minded human beings who, though severely limited and abused by slavery, had found a way both to endure and preserve their humanity' (Sterling Stuckey, 'Through the Prism of Folklore: The Black Ethos in Slavery', *Massachusetts Review*, Vol. 9, 1968, pp. 417–37, ref. p. 437).

[2] John Jasper Spurling, *Social Relationships between American Negroes and West Indian Negroes in a Long Island Community*, 1969, pp. 49, 60.

[3] Edric Connor, *Songs from Trinidad*, 1958, pp. 46–7. The folk-song comparison made by Patterson (*Sociology of Slavery*, pp. 254–7) is open to question, however; for American compilers may have deliberately excluded the more aggressive and vengeful songs (Norman E. Whitten, Jr., and John F. Szwed, 'Introduction', in their *Afro-American Anthropology: Contemporary Perspectives*, 1970, pp. 23–60, ref. p. 31). For the view that the more submissive slaves were sent from the Caribbean to North America, see interview with Malcolm X, *Jamaica Daily Gleaner*, 12 July 1964, quoted in Amy Jacques Garvey, 'The Source and Course of Black Power in America', in her *Black Power in America*, 1968, pp. 4–12, ref. p. 6.

[4] Stanley M. Elkins, *Slavery*, 2nd ed., p. 243. For the advantages of recognized white ancestry, early freedom, and mulatto status among American Negroes, see Horace

Between the millions of slaves and the thousands of whites, the intermediate group of 'free coloured'—manumitted slaves and their descendants—occupied an increasingly prominent position in the West Indies. In the late eighteenth century from 5 to 25 per cent of West Indian populations were free coloured or black; by the time of emancipation they outnumbered whites.

Free coloured people were distinguishable from slaves not only by freedom but by colour. Many of them had in fact been freed by white fathers or grandfathers. Some free persons were black and some slaves were coloured—indeed, half or more of all coloured persons were slaves. But a preponderance of mixed ancestry (mulatto, quadroon, octoroon) among free non-whites, and of unmixed African descent among slaves, shaped a tendency to designate free persons as 'coloured' and slaves as 'black'. West Indian whites, unlike Americans, regarded the free coloured as superior both to slaves and to free blacks and accorded them special privileges. In Surinam, for example, free men of colour and free-born blacks could vote, but freed blacks could not.[1] Among the free coloured, status and fortune depended on closeness to European features and white ancestors.

In the United States, as in the West Indies, light-coloured folk generally felt superior to dark Negroes. 'The faintest admixture of white blood', Fanny Kemble noted, seemed 'by common consent of their own race, to raise them in the scale of humanity.'[2] However, coloured as distinct from black men failed to establish a separate identity in the American social hierarchy. The crucial difference lay in the relative proportion of white and black. West Indian slaves so outnumbered whites that the latter viewed free coloured people as allies against slave insurrection—indeed, many slave-owners were coloured. Caribbean slaves were intermittently freed and armed in time of war. In 1763 Martinican whites were so eager for free-coloured assistance against a threatened English attack that they pretended to sell slaves into other islands and had them return as free men.[3] But whites in the United States, everywhere numerous, saw free coloured men more as leaders of slave revolts than as buffers against rebellion or external attack. In the West Indies the absence of white artisans

Mann Bond, cited in Andrew Billingsley, *Black Families in White America*, 1968, pp. 108–9, 117.

[1] R. A. J. van Lier, 'Social and Political Conditions in Suriname and the Netherlands Antilles: Introduction', in *Developments towards Self-Government in the Caribbean: A Symposium*, 1955, pp. 125–33, ref. p. 129.

[2] Frances Anne Kemble, *A Journal of a Residence on a Georgian Plantation, 1838–1839*, 1863, p. 194.

[3] *Code de la Martinique*, Vol. II, p. 557, n. 389, cited in E. Hayot, 'Les gens de couleur libres du Fort-Royal, 1679–1823', *Revue Française d'Histoire d'Outre-Mer*, Vol. LVI, No. 203, 1969, p. 13.

encouraged free coloured men to take up skilled occupations, but in the United States free-coloured access to similar jobs was bitterly opposed by white labourers.

The greater prominence of coloured people induced West Indian whites to make colour distinctions meaningless to Americans. And the scarcity of whites inclined them to accept a wide range of intimate associations with free coloured people. Moreover, as Europeans, white West Indians took a socially stratified order for granted and viewed the separate identity and special privileges of the free coloured as a means of consolidating their own hegemony. By contrast, the American egalitarian mystique made free coloured people an embarrassment even to whites who detested slavery; there was no room for colour compromise in a social order where all free *white* men were equal. The very existence of mulattoes struck white Americans as an enormity of nature. They considered all non-whites, slave or free, black or coloured, equally inferior.[1]

In the West Indies, interracial sexual liaisons were openly countenanced, especially where white women were few. Whites customarily had coloured mistresses, and white fathers regularly placed coloured daughters as concubines; so few coloured girls were exempt from this system that brown men were said to have 'no other recourse than black women.'[2] The practice came under heavy criticism; visitors and local luminaries alike deplored its evil consequences, ranging as they saw it from personal defilement to extinction of the white race. But they inveighed in vain against the well-nigh universal custom, perpetuated in a moral climate that discouraged European women from West Indian residence. When a candidate for Lieutenant-Governor of Jamaica was said to be unsuitable because he 'frequently Lyes with Black Women', his supporters rejoined that 'the same could be said of virtually every planter on the Island'.[3] As late as 1870 a clergyman

[1] Winthrop D. Jordan, *White over Black: American Attitudes towards the Negro, 1550–1812*, 1968, pp. 167–70; Goveia, *Slave Society in the British Leeward Islands*, pp. 232–3, 258–9, 315–17. For the role of the free coloured in the United States see Winthrop D. Jordan, 'American Chiaroscuro: The Status and Definition of Mulattoes in the British Colonies', *William and Mary Quarterly*, 2nd ser., Vol. 19, 1962, pp. 183–200; Charles S. Sydnor, *Slavery in Mississippi*, 1966, p. 203; Leon F. Litwack, *North of Slavery: The Negro in the Free States, 1790–1860*, 1961; and Richard C. Wade, *Slavery in the Cities: The South 1820–1860*, 1964, especially pp. 249–52. Champions of slavery thought it 'cruel and unwise . . . not to extend the *blessings of slavery* to the free negroes' (George Fitzhugh, 'What Shall Be Done with the Free Negroes?' [1854], quoted in Osofsky, *The Burden of Race*, p. 57). Only in New Orleans, with a Creole society, did whites flout rigid legal barriers and consort openly with a flourishing free coloured population in the West Indian manner (Roger A. Fischer, 'Racial Segregation in Ante Bellum New Orleans', *American Historical Review*, Vol. LXXIV, 1969, pp. 926–37).

[2] M. G. Lewis, *Journal of a West India Proprietor, 1815–17*, 1929, p. 144.

[3] Metcalf, *Royal Government and Political Conflict in Jamaica*, p. 100.

agreed that 'it is unreasonable to expect white young men to lead moral lives in such a community as this'.[1] An equivalent system of *plaçage* spread from French St. Domingue to Creole New Orleans and to Charleston, but elsewhere in the South relationships between white men and coloured women were usually clandestine.

Well-to-do West Indian whites not only recognized their coloured offspring but often educated them in Europe and left them large properties. Some coloured families rivalled elite whites in wealth and style of life. In Trinidad, where they outnumbered whites more than two to one as early as 1802, the free coloured, together with slave artisans, in a sense already ran things because 'there's no one else to: Planter no bother, sailor and soldier not stay long, white trash too stupid, black slave is chained. That leave we.'[2] The future was clearly theirs; for unlike most whites the free coloured were not mere sojourners but permanent residents. 'They were in their time the true West Indians,' one historian has said, 'and they knew it.'[3]

Prominent coloured West Indians could sometimes exempt themselves from the usual disabilities of colour. In the late eighteenth and early nineteenth centuries the Jamaican legislature passed hundreds of bills granting well-educated and well-to-do coloured individuals the perquisites of whites. And in the French Antilles, highly-placed men of colour and whites married to coloured women could buy birth certificates proving Carib ancestry so as to disavow African.[4]

Passing for white was important in the West Indies, but the mechanism and social context differed from the American phenomenon. In the United States, a Negro who sought to pass would move to a remote milieu where his background was unknown. In the West Indies, the small size of the society and the limited number of white families, all genealogically well known, put such a procedure out of the question. West Indian 'passing' was not the achievement of the stranger whose African ancestry no one could know; it was accomplished by the prominent figure who was accepted as white despite what everyone surmised of his ancestry.

The lot of most West Indian free coloured and black people was far less agreeably 'white', however. More than three-fourths of the free

[1] The Rev. Henry Clarke to the Hon. Edward Rushworth, 10 February 1870, *Letterbook 9*, No. 5, Edith Clarke Papers. See also Davis, *The Problem of Slavery in Western Culture*, pp. 276–7.

[2] Colin MacInnes, *Westward to Laughter*, 1969, p. 29.

[3] Millette, 'The Civil Commission of 1802', p. 38. See also Charles H. Wesley, 'The Free Colored Population in the British Empire', *Journal of Negro History*, Vol. XIX, 1934, pp. 137–70.

[4] Sheila J. Duncker, 'The Free Coloured and Their Fight for Civil Rights in Jamaica, 1800–1830', 1961, pp. 39–48; Hayot, 'Les gens de couleur libres du Fort-Royal, 1679–1823', p. 127.

coloured of Jamaica in the 1820s, for example, were reputed 'absolutely poor'.[1] They were barred from many types of employment, their residence, travel, dress, and diet were sharply restricted, and they suffered indignities from whites of all classes. White paupers got more money than coloured ones. Coloured men were always subordinate to whites in the militia and other organizations. Every joint function was hierarchically organized, though the lines were always shifting. Thus free-coloured pews in churches were increased as the need grew, but church-going did not offset distinctions of colour. Church bells tolled longer for whites than for coloured folk in Jamaica; in Antigua a smaller bell was used to announce a coloured demise.[2]

Free black and coloured people were moreover constantly at the risk of re-enslavement. Slave escapes or rebellion led to a general hue and cry in which non-whites had to prove their free status by written certificate; for 'every person of that Complexion is to be Supposed a Slave,' as the Antiguan legislature ruled, 'till authentic, legal Proofs to the Contrary are produced.'[3] And no document was adequate defence against unscrupulous whites. 'Hitherto I had thought only slavery dreadful,' observed Equiano after several harrowing escapes. 'But the state of a free negro appeared to me now equally so at least, and in some respects even worse, for they live in constant alarm for their liberty; and even this is but nominal, for they are universally insulted and plundered without the possibility of redress'. Those in bondage might well 'prefer even the misery of slavery to such a mockery of freedom'; Equiano could never feel 'entirely free' in the West Indies.[4]

Growing numbers and affluence often strained free-coloured relations with whites. In Trinidad they were suspected of republican sympathies and harassed by countless special regulations. White settlers in the French Antilles resented free-coloured privileges and wealth and imposed restrictions on their modes of life and work. In St. Domingue white–coloured rivalry became so fierce that the embattled groups ignored portents of the slave revolt that overwhelmed them both. The Haitian débâcle induced post-revolutionary reaction in Martinique and Guadeloupe, where free coloured people came under strict surveillance

[1] Douglas G. Hall, 'The Social and Economic Background to Sugar in Slave Days (with Special Reference to Jamaica)', *Caribbean Historical Review*, Nos. III–IV, December 1954, pp. 149–69, ref. p. 157; Wesley, 'The Emancipation of the Free Colored Population in the British Empire', p. 140.

[2] Duncker, 'The Free Coloured and Their Fight for Civil Rights in Jamaica', pp. 117–20, 126. For comparable conditions in the French Antilles, see Yvan Debbasch, *Couleur et liberté: le jeu du critère ethnique dans un ordre juridique esclavagiste*, Vol. I: *l'affranchi dans les possessions françaises de la Caraïbe (1635–1833)*, 1967.

[3] Antigua Council Minutes, 31 July and 24 September 1783, C.O. 9/28, quoted in Goveia, *Slave Society in the British Leeward Islands*, p. 221; see also pp. 181, 222.

[4] Equiano, *Equiano's Travels*, pp. 84–5.

by Creole whites. Refugees from St. Domingue were especially fearful of free-coloured numbers and privileges. But official restrictions conflicted with the personal habits of white planters who continued to manumit their concubines and advance their coloured offspring, while deploring free-coloured strength in general. Several free-coloured uprisings were quashed with great severity. White–coloured conflict in Martinique engendered such lasting bitterness that one historian maintains 'emancipation in 1848 had less profound and less lasting repercussions.'[1] In 1830 France abolished legal distinctions of colour among free persons, but white Creole planters continued to exclude coloured people from the suffrage through high property requirements. Still disaffected, the free coloured joined the slaves and metropolitan anti-slavery leaders in their drive for emancipation.

In the British and Dutch territories barriers between white and coloured remained high; for colour itself was crucial to the stability of the social hierarchy. Whites believed that colour distinctions among the free were essential to maintain control over slaves. Free-coloured equality would destroy 'the ascendancy which the white population holds over the blacks'.

The Dominion which we hold over the Blacks, arises from an acknowledged Superiority of the Whites, rather than from their fleets or armies. Destroy this opinion by a degrading association with an inferior class (whom they despise, and are jealous of) and you break down the only barrier between us and insurrection.[2]

Up to the eve of emancipation, law as well as custom discriminated against the free coloured, who were precluded from participation in government. When civil rights were at last accorded, they were designed to ally coloured with white against free black and the mass of blacks soon to be freed. But the free coloured remained, like the slaves, an inferior social order. And the small white minority exercised absolute power over social institutions that everywhere discriminated against non-whites, slave and free.

Yet within two generations, between 1791 and 1863, all West Indian slaves were freed and legal disabilities on grounds of colour were terminated. In Haiti, where slave and free coloured had suffered the most, revolution reversed the power structure; surviving whites were forbidden to own land, and mulattoes were harried by blacks. In the Danish Virgin Islands, slave revolts led to general emancipation on St.

[1] Hayot, 'Les gens de couleur libres du Fort-Royal', p. 19. See also Debbasch, *Couleur et liberté*, pp. 260–86.

[2] 'Report of Meeting of Planters Merchants and Others interested in the Island of Dominica held at the City of London, 4 February 1822', in J. Colquhoun to R. Wilmot, 22 February 1822, C.O. 71/59; Alex Robinson to John Blackburn, 15 December 1822, C.O. 71/59, P.R.O.

John and St. Thomas. In Guadeloupe and French Guiana, Negroes freed by the French Revolution were re-enslaved a decade later and, like Martinicans, remained in bondage until 1848. In the British West Indies, abolition of the slave trade led to slave-law reforms and finally to emancipation in the 1830s.

How did this come about? Few masters willingly relinquished their slaves. Individuals were manumitted, to be sure, but occasional release by favour or self-purchase betokened no general abandonment of slave property. In no Caribbean colony did slave-holders give up slavery of their own accord. Most did so only with extreme reluctance under outside pressure.

The pressure stemmed from two principal causes: one was economic self-interest, the other was humanitarian reform. It is hard to weigh the significance of non-economic ideas and forces, but 'the rights of man' helped to inspire the revolution that freed 450,000 slaves in Haiti, and evangelical fervour was immediately responsible for releasing 650,000 slaves in the British Caribbean. And eventual freedom for 180,000 French Antillean and 50,000 Netherlands Caribbean slaves reflected the broad acceptance of reformist ideas in Europe.

Yet the anti-slavery impulse also went hand in hand with *laissez-faire* capitalism. Assailing slavery in 1774, John Wesley disdained material considerations, but Adam Smith's *Wealth of Nations* immeasurably strengthened the abolitionist cause. 'The experience of all ages and nations', according to Smith, showed that 'the work done by freemen comes cheaper in the end than that performed by slaves.'[1] European reformers generally attended to economic common sense. 'Slavery costs more to maintain than it would cost to destroy', claimed Schoelcher,[2] citing militia expenses required to defend Antillean planters against rebellion.

Morality allied with economic interest animated the anti-slavery impulse on both sides of the Atlantic; many leading abolitionists in Philadelphia and New York, as in London and Manchester, were Quaker merchants. But in the United States the growth of the cotton industry and sectional divisions gave slavery issues a sharper edge. Abolitionism became more morally insistent; Garrison and like-minded American crusaders eschewed politics on principle in order to make no compromise with evil. British reform rhetoric and passion sometimes matched Garrison's own. But as practical statesmen, British anti-slavery advocates were more gradualist in approach. They amassed and assessed data, they attacked specific aspects of slavery

[1] Adam Smith, *An Inquiry into the Nature and Causes of the Wealth of Nations*, 1793, Vol. I, p. 123.

[2] Victor Schoelcher, *Esclavage et colonisation*, quoted in Michel Leiris, *Contacts de civilisations en Martinique et en Guadeloupe*, 1955, p. 26.

rather than merely condemning it as a whole, they favoured emancipation by degrees, they tried to persuade colonial interests to take the lead in West Indian slave reform, and finally they stipulated a period of apprenticeship before final freedom.[1]

Piecemeal as British reform was, its leaders never concealed their intention to do away with slavery. The abolition of the slave trade in 1807 was designed to encourage planters to treat slaves considerately. 'Few will continue so insane as to maltreat and work out their stock,' Brougham believed, 'when they can no longer fill up the blanks occasioned by their cruelty, or their inhuman and shortsighted policy. . . . In a very few years all the Negroes in the West Indies will be Creoles, and all the masters will treat them with kind indulgence for their own sakes'.[2] Despite efforts to flout the embargo, by the late 1820s more than two-thirds of the slaves were Creole-born; even the field gangs were English-speaking and Creole in outlook.

To improve slave conditions was more difficult. Parliamentary slave registration acts, bitterly opposed in the Caribbean, were ignored or contravened in practice. Laws of 1823 forbade the flogging of women, debarred officials from owning slaves, and removed local hindrances to manumission. These reforms were accepted by West Indian interests in London but met vehement opposition in the Caribbean; planters feared that even talk of reform would incite slave revolts. Britain did not insist; after all, the laws would not be workable without local co-operation. In crown-ruled Trinidad alone were the amelioration acts enforced, to show how harmless and efficacious they were and to encourage emulation by colonial legislatures.

The example was ignored until 1829, when local officials were ordered to obey the imperial mandate. West Indian governments then accepted amelioration mainly to stave off a greater evil—emancipation itself. But the reformers' patience was exhausted, and Buxton's Emancipation Act passed the House of Commons on 1 August 1833. Even then, freedom was neither confiscatory nor immediate. West Indian planters were awarded £17 million compensation for slave property and were permitted to hold that property for up to four years longer. Except in

---

[1] David Brion Davis, 'The Emergence of Immediatism in British and American Antislavery Thought', *Mississippi Valley Historical Review*, Vol. XLIX, 1962–3, pp. 209–30; Stanley M. Elkins and Eric McKitrick, 'Institutions and the Law of Slavery: The Dynamics of Unopposed Capitalism', *American Quarterly*, Vol. IX, 1957, pp. 3–21. A Southern slave-owner believed that 'if the north had directed its strength against the evils of slavery instead of assailing it as a sin *per se*, it could not have survived to the present day' (*A South-Side View of Slavery; or, Three Months at the South, in 1854*, 1855, p. 157, quoted in Elkins, *Slavery*, p. 193).

[2] Henry Brougham, *A Concise Statement of the Question Regarding the Abolition of the Slave Trade*, 1804, quoted in D. J. Murray, *The West Indies and the Development of Colonial Government, 1801–1834*, 1965, pp. 92–3.

Antigua and Bermuda an apprenticeship scheme bound ex-slaves to work forty hours a week for their former owners; only overtime was compensated with wages.[1]

French West Indian slaves contended against similar planter intransigence, compounded by a legacy of betrayal. After a decade of freedom, Napoleon in 1802 reimposed slavery in Guadeloupe and French Guiana. Planters hunted down their former slaves with packs of dogs and brought them back in chains; 'thousands of "former free citizens" were led back to their old hutments . . . beneath a rain of sticks and ropes' ends.'[2] Well-to-do coloured people, born free or set free long before the Revolution, but fearing 'mistakes' or retribution, sold or abandoned their Antillean properties and fled to Trinidad, New Orleans, and Paris.

French Antillean planters learned little from British experience. They set at nought slave amelioration acts passed in France during the 1830s. They defended slavery as economically and socially essential in view of Negro 'laziness'. When anti-slavery forces urged parliamentary emancipation in 1838, Creole planters asserted that many freed slaves had become vagrants and warned that full freedom would bring havoc and ruin. Slavery ended in 1848 after the July revolution; slave-owners were compensated; former slaves became free men with the full rights of citizens. In the Virgin Islands, Denmark followed suit, ratifying a local emancipation decree forced by a general strike, but without compensating slave-owners.

Slave revolts in the Netherlands Caribbean were touched off by both the British and the French emancipation acts. The St. Maarten slaves were in effect free after 1848 when they could simply move from the Dutch to the French half of the island. Surinam slaves likewise escaped into neighbouring British and French Guiana. In Curaçao and Bonaire, an 1857 amelioration edict distressed masters without satisfying slaves. In 1862 planters in Surinam and the remaining slave islands accepted emancipation with compensation, but indentures for able-bodied slaves delayed final freedom until 1873.

Caribbean slavery ended partly because men of great influence condemned it as morally wrong. 'Slavery such as it is in the West Indies,' wrote James Stephen in 1827, was 'a practice which God has forbidden and from which, therefore, man should desist, be the expense or risk what it may.'[3] Well into the twentieth century the British esteemed

---

[1] The compensation total is given in Hume Wrong, *Government of the West Indies*, 1923, p. 55. W. L. Burn, *Emancipation and Apprenticeship in the British West Indies*, 1937, is the standard work on the period of semi-freedom.

[2] Alejo Carpentier, *Explosion in a Cathedral*, 1962, p. 319.

[3] James Stephen to Henry Taylor, 29 June 1827, Bodleian MS, quoted in Murray, *The West Indies and the Development of Colonial Government*, p. 149.

West Indian emancipation an act of pure virtue. 'The conscience of all England was awakened', wrote one historian in this vein; 'the slave system was abolished not because it was good policy or good business to abolish it . . . but simply because of its iniquity.'[1] A West Indian remarks that it was 'as if Britain had introduced Negro slavery solely for the satisfaction of abolishing it.'[2] But abolitionist views were not initially shared by popular opinion. If moral zeal sparked the impulse, slaves were freed only when European governments and local slave-owners found freedom expedient. A passion for liberty and equality animated French revolutionaries to declare slavery illegal in 1794, but other motives persuaded the French in the West Indies to promulgate the decree, and even, in St. Domingue, to anticipate it. 'In Haiti they did it to get the Spaniards off their backs, in Guadeloupe to make sure of chasing out the English,' and in French Guiana, a novelist comments, 'to give a death blow to the rich land-owners. . . . Colonial politics—that's all!'[3] In any event, the circumstances of emancipation clearly differed from one territory to another.

To Britain emancipation became imperative only when economic needs buttressed social morality. 'If the British West Indian sugar industry had not been in severe economic difficulties', Goveia concludes, it is 'unlikely that the humanitarians could have succeeded in abolishing either the British slave trade or British colonial slavery. For they failed in their demands for effective reform whenever these demands were supported only by appeal to humanitarian principles, and they succeeded only when their humane objectives coincided with practical political and economic circumstances'.[4]

Among these circumstances was the diminishing value of the West Indies to British interests. In the heyday of the old colonial system, the sugar islands created wealth that sparked the Industrial Revolution, but that revolution then made the West Indian sugar monopoly a drag on free enterprise. British Caribbean planters, once hard-pressed to supply the demand for sugar, now competed in markets glutted by

[1] Reginald Coupland, 'The Memory of Wilberforce', in his *The Empire These Days: An Interpretation*, 1935, pp. 262–74, ref. p. 268.

[2] Williams, *British Historians and the West Indies*, p. 233. Williams relates that when he sought to publish his *Capitalism and Slavery*, which refuted this 'general British view, . . . Britain's most revolutionary publisher, Warburg, . . . told me: "Mr. Williams, are you trying to tell me that the slave trade and slavery were abolished for economic and not for humanitarian reasons? I would never publish such a book, for it would be contrary to the British tradition" ' (Eric Williams, *Inward Hunger: The Education of a Prime Minister*, 1969, pp. 50–3).

[3] Carpentier, *Explosion in a Cathedral*, p. 230. Danton announced the suppression of slavery as an act which would ruin England (Hayot, 'Les gens de couleur libres du Fort-Royal, 1679–1823', p. 134n). See also Gaston-Martin, *Histoire de l'esclavage dans les colonies françaises*, 1948, pp. 224–35.

[4] Goveia, *Slave Society in the British Leeward Islands*, pp. 335–6.

cheaper producers—first St. Domingue, then Mauritius, Brazil, Cuba —and, finally, by beet sugar; only monopoly prices enabled them to survive.

More galling to British interests than the high cost of West Indian sugar were the accompanying export restrictions. West Indian territories, once the chief focus of English trade, had become relatively small customers of manufactured goods. The West Indian share of all British exports fell from one-ninth to one-seventeenth between 1821 and 1832. The Caribbean could not match the new large markets opened up by imperial expansion.

British exports to the world could be paid for only in raw materials—the cotton of the United States, the cotton, coffee, and sugar of Brazil, the sugar of Cuba, the sugar and cotton of India. . . . The British West Indian monopoly, prohibiting the importation of non-British-plantation sugar for home consumption, stood in the way. . . . Every important vested interest . . . joined in the attack on West Indian slavery.[1]

The slave trade and slavery were abolished in part to weaken the West Indian sugar interest and shake off the monopoly. It was, as a Member of Parliament put it, a 'lucrative humanity'.[2] Many who favoured British Caribbean emancipation supported slavery in Brazil, Cuba, and the Southern United States, where free trade assured cheap raw materials.

Economic arguments for emancipation failed to convince British Caribbean planters because economic interests were transcended by others. The habit of despotism, as much as the hope of gain, led planters to cling to slavery. Jamaicans were 'too reluctant to part with their power over the Slaves', the Governor asserted.[3] In the final reckoning, what slave-holders valued most was not property but authority. 'The love of power of these planters over the poor Negroes,' the Governor of Barbados explained, 'has found as great an obstacle to freedom as the love of their labour'.[4] Still more, the planters viewed slavery as the foundation stone of the whole West Indian society; without it, as Haiti demonstrated, anarchy and bloodshed would ensue. But in the end

[1] Williams, *Capitalism and Slavery*, pp. 153, 154. Between 8 and 10 per cent of Britain's income came from the West Indies in the eighteenth century (R. B. Sheridan, 'The Wealth of Jamaica in the Eighteenth Century', *Economic History Review*, Vol. 18, 1965, pp. 292–311, ref. p. 306).

[2] William Hutt, 22 February 1848, in *Hansard's Parliamentary Debates, Third Series*, Vol. XCVI, p. 1096.

[3] Manchester to Bathurst, 6 September 1823, private, C.O. 137/154, quoted in A. E. Furness, 'George Hibbert and the Defense of Slavery in the West Indies', *JHR*, Vol. V, No. 1, May 1965, pp. 56–70, ref. p. 66.

[4] Smith to Stanley, 13 July 1833, C.O. 28/111, quoted in Williams, *Capitalism and Slavery*, p. 201.

even the planters came to see that slavery was inexpedient. Emancipation might ruin the estates and wreck society, but it posed a danger less grave than the probable alternative, a protracted struggle against British authority and slave insurrection. Recognition of their weak position saved white Creoles from the horrors and the consequences of civil war.

Not surprisingly, slave freedom proved incomplete. The emancipated found their rights curtailed, equality an empty term, prejudice and discrimination the order of the day. The injustices of slavery concerned humanitarians more than the welfare of the freed slaves. Emancipation achieved, many reformers assumed their work was done. Few of them had any first-hand knowledge of slavery or appreciated its long-term debilitating effects; most expected ex-slaves to be eternally grateful and well behaved. 'You must be orderly and industrious, and do your duty honestly and faithfully', a Governor told Barbadian slaves. 'England is to pay twenty millions of pounds sterling for your gradual freedom. You can only deserve or understand this blessing by a course of good conduct, by obeying the laws, and being dutiful to all those entitled to your services'.[1] The colonies, it was assumed, could now be left to themselves.

Black freedom certainly did not imply black power. Most reformers looked to continued white colonial control, with a small and gradual infusion of coloured representation. A few naïve optimists hoped that West Indian whites would accept the freed blacks as fellow citizens and share the direction of affairs with them. But many, perhaps most, considered Negroes by nature inferior and hence requiring white rule for a long time, if not forever. Emancipation zeal fired evangelical paternalism, especially in Britain. The anti-slavery crusade 'engendered an idea that the African was a being to be helped rather than exploited, and by exemplifying British moral superiority' justified British rule.[2] 'The conscience of the British people', an apologist claimed, had acquired 'a tradition of humanity and of responsibility towards the weak and backward black peoples whose fate lay in their hands.'[3]

Those who thought Negroes inherently inferior saw much to bolster their prejudice in the post-emancipation West Indies. To be sure, the riots and chaos that planters had foretold did not materialize, nor did

[1] 'Proclamation of the Governor of Barbados', 22 January 1834, quoted in F. R. Augier and Shirley C. Gordon, *Sources of West Indian History*, 1962, p. 196. See also Murray, *The West Indies and the Development of Colonial Government*, pp. 214–18.

[2] H. Alan C. Cairns, *Prelude to Imperialism: British Reactions to Central African Society, 1840–1890*, 1965, p. 76. See also Philip D. Curtin, *The Image of Africa: British Ideas and Action, 1780–1850*, 1964, pp. 227, 239–40.

[3] Reginald Coupland, *Wilberforce* [1923], p. 424.

the sugar industry at once collapse.[1] Production on some estates in fact increased; slave compensation payments enabled many planters to clear debts and encouraged a few to modernize production. But ex-slaves took issue with planters over wages and rents, and many quit the estates; resident plantation labourers in Jamaica declined from 42,000 to 14,000 between 1832 and 1846. Sugar production dropped by as much as 40 per cent even before Britain equalized sugar duties in 1846, and hundreds of planters were driven into bankruptcy. Not for another decade did production in British Guiana and Trinidad offset declines in the older sugar islands. But provision crops flourished where exports faltered. The estimated total value of Jamaican agricultural output fell by one-third between 1832 and 1850, yet production for home consumption rose from less than one-third to more than one-half the total, and peasant proprietors improved their lot.[2]

West Indian estates growing sugar and other export commodities were hurt by free trade and by unwillingness or inability to give wages and working conditions competitive with small farming. Earlier, only tariff protection and the periodic acquisition of new fertile lands had averted disaster. But habituation to slavery had blinded planters to the diseconomies of the plantation system; emancipation made a better scapegoat than economics. Planters and foreign observers alike commonly attributed the decline to ex-slave laziness. 'The dismal results are before us,' asserted an American pro-slavery advocate in 1860, 'constitutional [Negro] indolence has converted the most beautiful islands of the sea into a howling waste.'[3]

British humanitarians, like American abolitionists after the Civil War, were often disheartened by Negro 'failure' to fulfil expectations based on middle-class goals and values. On or off the plantations, ex-slaves seemed less diligent, obedient, virtuous, and grateful than the reformers had expected. Now that blacks were no longer coerced as slaves, whites ascribed their 'defects' to racial inferiority, innate and ineradicable.

[1] 'The opponents of Abolition had declared that . . . enfranchisement would lead to disorder, drunkenness, insubordination, and a general refusal to do any more work. None of this came true. When at midnight on July 31, 1834, the historic moment came, there were celebrations and rejoicings, but the ex-slaves behaved with decency and order. . . . There was nothing like a general "strike". The output of sugar between 1834 and 1838 fell from the average level of the previous six years by less than ten per cent' (Reginald Coupland, *The British Anti-Slavery Movement* [1933], pp. 142–3).

[2] Gisela Eisner, *Jamaica, 1830–1930: A Study in Economic Growth*, 1961, pp. 121, 168–72, 189–95.

[3] B. M. Palmer, *Slavery a Divine Trust: The Duty of the South to Preserve and Perpetuate the Institution*, 1861, p. 9. For opposing American viewpoints see James M. McPherson, 'Was West Indian Emancipation a Success? The Abolition Argument during the American Civil War', *CS*, Vol. 4, No. 2, July 1964, pp. 28–34.

West Indian emancipation was a blunder of swindling philanthropy. People were told that the negroes, after emancipation, would work harder, work for less, and be more of slaves than before. . . . But philanthropy . . . forgot the few wants and indolent habits of the negro. . . . The negro *is really free*, and luxuriates in sloth, ignorance, and liberty, as none but a negro can. The mistake and the failure consisted in setting him really free, instead of nominally so.[1]

This picture of West Indian freedom was grossly overdrawn, but the exegesis of reformer—and planter—intentions was close to the mark. A Jamaican complained that his former slaves considered themselves free. 'They turn out to work when they like, do what they choose, take what days they like—in fact, do as they think proper.'[2] In the post-emancipation West Indies, as was observed of the American South, 'the whites esteem the blacks their property by natural right'. Although they no longer owned slaves as individuals, 'they still have an ingrained feeling that the blacks at large belong to the whites' collectively.[3]

Where emancipation made slaves really free, those who had owned them were appalled. But for most emancipation was partial and incomplete. The freed slaves remained in economic bondage, political subservience, and social limbo.

Crucial to the planter and the Government was the post-emancipation relationship of employer to employed. West Indian plantations were imperilled by competition without and turmoil within; unless the estates could be rehabilitated, the Caribbean territories would remain millstones around imperial necks.

Planter well-being was advocated less as an economic necessity than as a *sine qua non* of West Indian social stability. The success of emancipation was gauged by whether sugar production rose or fell, by whether ex-slaves laboured regularly, in short by whether things went on as before. Planters asserted, and imperial rulers agreed, that the very survival of West Indian society hinged on estate perpetuation; without sugar and the white planter, freed Negroes would degenerate into

---

[1] Fitzhugh, *Cannibals All!* p. 185. See also Goveia, *Slave Society in the British Leeward Islands*, p. 309.

[2] 'Evidence before Committee of House of Assembly Jamaica, to Enquire into the Working of the New System of Labour, 31 October 1834', in Augier and Gordon, *Sources of West Indian History*, p. 207. The 'wicked plantocracy under which the ex-slaves were bullied and browbeaten into submission and the acceptance of starvation wages' was a myth, at least in Jamaica; 'in slavery they [the planters] had held the whip, but in freedom they had to bargain, and . . . it was the labourers who held the upper hand in wage negotiations' (Douglas G. Hall, *Free Jamaica 1838–1865: An Economic History*, 1959, pp. 43–4).

[3] Samuel Thomas, assistant commissioner of the Freedmen's Bureau in Mississippi, Document No. 27, in 'Report of Carl Schurz on the States of South Carolina, Georgia, Alabama, Mississippi, and Louisiana', 39th Congress, 1st sess., *Senate Executive Document No. 2* (1865), p. 81.

barbarism, as in Haiti. This belief was self-serving but none the less sincerely held. Thus the Virgin Islands regime used 'stringent measures to compel the labourers on the estates to work', since it was thought 'better that the laborers suffer a temporary evil, than that they should be given up to their ways, to their own serious and permanent injury, and the serious injury, if not destruction, of the social order.'[1]

Planters and governments throughout the Caribbean curtailed the freedom of labourers and bound them to estate work. They denounced as 'vagrants' and 'idlers' those who preferred such alternatives as small farming, urban trades, or emigration. This bias long dominated the West Indian agricultural scene and endures to this day in local reluctance to relinquish the sugar industry. It was rooted in three suppositions:

(1) White self-interest was understood to require white estate monopoly. Even those ruined by their plantations resisted Negro acquisition. Only in British Guiana did ex-slaves acquire substantial plantation land, by grouping together to buy estates from bankrupt owners. On the islands land was available only in the hills or on poor soil outside the plantation belts. To this day sugar occupies the best land and is white-owned where sugar most matters: by British firms in Guyana and Trinidad, by white Creoles in Martinique and Barbados, by expatriates and local whites in Jamaica. Where other crops—cotton, coconuts, coffee, cacao, bananas—outlasted or replaced sugar, whites were less successful in preventing non-white acquisition. Coloured estate ownership is today widespread in the non-sugar islands, notably the British Windwards, the more mountainous of the Leewards, parts of Trinidad and Guadeloupe, and, of course, Haiti.

(2) Whites considered non-whites incapable of agricultural enterprise. White ownership therefore seemed to them essential for the well-being of all. 'The white races govern the tropics on the ground that the native is unfitted to govern himself', wrote a presumed authority as late as 1914, 'and the same consideration applies with equal force to agriculture.'[2] State rule and estate management were not merely analogous, they were symbiotic; the function of West Indian government was to secure order and plantation profits. This view discouraged non-whites from agricultural training, since even those who acquired it were relegated to subordinate positions. Black and coloured West Indians seldom enrolled at Trinidad's Imperial College of Tropical Agriculture; through the 1950s most I.C.T.A. graduates were whites, and Trinidad's Prime Minister declared that it remains 'grossly under-utilized' as the University Faculty of Agriculture; 'we cannot get young people with the requisite academic background to apply for agricultural training.'[3]

[1] John P. Knox, *A Historical Account of St. Thomas, W.I.*, 1852, p. 122.
[2] J. C. Willis, *Agriculture in the Tropics*, 1914, p. 146.
[3] Eric Williams, quoted in the *Trinidad Sunday Guardian*, 29 March 1970, p. 10.

Non-whites eschew agriculture because they associate it with plantation slavery. But their distaste also reflects current reality; for few coloured West Indians could breach the white monopoly of agricultural place and power. Plantation agriculture is reminiscent of slavery both because of past servitude and because of present discrimination.

(3) Planters thought punitive force essential to regular work. They were too used to slavery to believe that men would willingly labour without the whip.

Accustomed to see the negro work only from coercion, the idea that he will do so from any other motive never enters [the planter's] head, coercion in his mind becomes identified with labour and when . . . coercion is by degrees lessened and other stimulants used he considers that you are undermining the very groundwork of labour.[1]

Old habits, more than financial need, induced planter-dominated legislatures to bind the Negroes to work for low wages on pain of hunger, eviction, or imprisonment.

The impact of these constraints depended on the alternatives available to ex-slaves. In densely settled Barbados, St. Kitts, and Antigua, where sugar plantations took up all cultivable land and a substantial body of whites ran local regimes, freed men had virtually no choice but to remain on the estates. 'Masters and Servants' acts required tenants to work at low fixed wages and bound them to plantations even when owners could not employ them. Not until 1938 was this form of serfdom relaxed in Barbados, though a peasant proprietory body had emerged earlier with the return of labourers from Panama and Cuba who could afford to buy lots carved out of estates in chancery.[2]

Elsewhere, though the plantation system endured, many former slaves forsook the estates for smallholdings—often extensions of slave garden plots—on abandoned lands or in the hills. Many bought or simply squatted on unused private or Crown lands. Co-operative groups, sometimes church- or mission-aided, established many free villages in Jamaica, Antigua, and British Guiana. Direct imperial rule prevented Guianese and Trinidadian planters, unlike others, from enacting vagrancy and located labourers' laws binding ex-slaves to the estates. The Colonial Office is credited with being more concerned, at least in Guiana, 'with the establishment of personal and political free-

---

[1] Stipendiary Magistrate Polson, May 1838, in McGregor to Glenelg, 31 July 1838, C.O. 260/57, quoted in Marshall, 'Social and Economic Problems in the Windward Islands', p. 247.

[2] Sidney M. Greenfield, *English Rustics in Black Skin: A Study of Modern Family Forms in a Pre-Industrialized Society*, 1966, pp. 56–8, 146–7; Bruce Hamilton, *Barbados and the Confederation Question, 1871–1885*, 1956, pp. 4–6; David Callender, 'The Relationship between the Social Structure and Public Reaction to the Sugar Depression of 1884–1914 in Barbados and Trinidad', pp. 12, 85.

dom for the emancipated class than with the preservation of economic prosperity'.[1]

Where sugar gave way entirely to other crops, or plantation agriculture as a whole became moribund, as in Surinam, the Windwards, Montserrat, and the Virgin Islands, former slaves rented land and worked it as sharecroppers. White planters in Montserrat alternated sharecropping with wage labour until the 1900s, when beet sugar forced the island out of cane production. Some estates then converted to Sea Island cotton, with the same labour systems; elsewhere bankruptcy or climatic unsuitability led to estate abandonment, and the resident blacks became freeholders almost by default.[2]

'Emancipation changed radically the whole basis of social organization', a Jamaican asserts, 'by making the slave a free man, with the power to sell or withhold his labour, to remain on the estate or to move away from the estate. His labour had to be bought, and for this labour the planter had to pay cash.'[3] Efforts to compel work led West Indians to seek other opportunities all the more eagerly. They could hardly 'reconcile their state of freedom with the coercive necessity to labour continuously on the estates as they had done throughout slavery', concludes an historian; 'the relatively new attraction and inducement of a money wage could not fully compensate for the limitation of their freedom of action'.[4]

To keep wages down and ensure a steady labour supply, sugar growers sought new manpower sources outside the Caribbean. Recruitment bounties, usually government supported, induced hundreds of thousands to cross the Atlantic and become indentured West Indian

[1] William A. Green, Jr., 'The Apprenticeship in British Guiana, 1834–1838', *CS*, Vol. 9, No. 2, July 1969, pp. 44–66, ref. p. 65. For ex-slave village settlements, see Hugh Paget, 'The Free Village System in Jamaica', *CQ*, Vol. I, No. 4 [1951], pp. 7–19; Sidney W. Mintz, 'Historical Sociology of the Jamaican Church-Founded Free Village System', *West-Indische Gids*, Vol. 38, 1958, pp. 46–70; Inez Knibb Sibley, *The Baptists of Jamaica*, 1965, pp. 13–15; Rawle Farley, 'The Rise of the Village Settlements of British Guiana', *CQ*, Vol. 3, No. 2, September 1953, pp. 101–8; idem, 'The Rise of the Peasantry in British Guiana', *SES*, Vol. 2, No. 4, March 1954, pp. 76–103; Allan Young, *Approaches to Local Self-Government in British Guiana*, 1958, pp. 9–23.

[2] *Montserrat Cotton Industry Enquiry* [1953]; David Lowenthal, 'Montserrat: Autonomy in Microcosm', 1961, pp. 17–20, 73. For labour arrangements elsewhere see Woodville K. Marshall, 'Notes on Peasant Development in the West Indies since 1838', *SES*, Vol. 17, 1968, pp. 252–63; and idem, 'Metayage in the Sugar Industry of the British Windward Islands, 1838–1865', *JHR*, Vol. V, No. 1, May 1965, pp. 28–55; for the sugar industry see S. B. Saul, 'The British West Indies in Depression 1880–1914', *Inter-American Economic Affairs*, Vol. XII, No. 3, Winter 1958, pp. 3–25; and R. W. Beachey, *The British West Indies Sugar Industry in the Late 19th Century*, 1957.

[3] Philip Sherlock, *West Indies*, 1966, p. 70.

[4] Marshall, 'Social and Economic Problems in the Windward Islands', p. 250.

labourers during the century after 1840.[1] Chinese and Madeiran immigrants at the outset suffered heavy mortality, and the survivors soon left agriculture to take up peddling and retail shopkeeping. But most of the 600,000 East Indians and Javanese who came to the West Indies on two- to five-year (and later up to ten-year) plantation contracts remained on the land, either as estate workers or subsequently as small farmers. In Jamaica, Martinique, and Guadeloupe a modest influx from India gave the remaining planters enough labour to enable most of them to weather ex-slave 'defections', free trade, and beet-sugar competition, meanwhile retrenching and rationalizing factory processes. The demand for plantation labour was far greater, however, in Trinidad, British Guiana, and Surinam, where sugar acreage and productive capacity were still expanding, and here Asians transformed the scene.

Indian indentured labourers endured conditions reminiscent of slavery if not worse. Self-interest alone had animated some planter concern for slave welfare, but from East Indians many estate managers sought simply to extract maximum returns during the indenture period. Whereas African slaves were selected in part for strength and endurance, Indian recruiters did no such pruning, nor was the voyage so lethal as the Middle Passage. As a result, many Indians who reached the Caribbean were aged, infirm, or otherwise unsuited to agricultural labour. Some planters were purposely cruel to the East Indian 'coolies': those who malingered, left estates without written permission, or otherwise broke their contracts had to undergo additional years of indenture and might be kept in indefinite servitude. The planters viewed them, like the slaves, simply as sugar-producing machines. Criticized for the woeful condition of his Indian barracks, a Trinidad sugar planter replied in 1889: 'The people ought to be in the field all day. I do not build cottages for idlers.' The care of children and pregnant women did not concern him either: 'I want two years of good crops and good prices, and then I will sell my estates and go to live in Europe.'[2]

Similar conditions prevailed throughout the Caribbean. A compassionate Jamaican termed indenture 'more unjust and inhuman than slavery; . . . Coolies were cheated and starved and flogged and mur-

[1] G. W. Roberts and J. Byrne, 'Summary Statistics on Indenture and Associated Migration Affecting the West Indies, 1834–1918', *Population Studies*, Vol. XX, 1966–7, pp. 125–34.

[2] Lochmere Guppy, evidence at the Royal Commission of the Franchise in 1889, quoted in Eric Williams, *Massa Day Done: A Masterpiece of Political and Sociological Analysis*, 1961, p. 8. See also Eric Williams, *History of the People of Trinidad and Tobago*, 1962, pp. 103–22 and 212–13; D. W. D. Comins, *Note on Emigration from India to Trinidad*, 1893; I. M. Cumpston, *Indians Overseas in British Territories 1834–1854*, 1953.

dered'.[1] The Indians got little sympathy from black and coloured West Indians, who resented them for keeping wages down or spurned them as drudges. Where East Indians were numerous, Negroes moved off the sugar estates into the towns or on to smallholdings, shunning plantation work as fit only for slaves.

Most ex-slaves participated in local affairs only marginally more than the East Indians. For a century, non-white exclusion from political power paralleled their economic subordination. Emancipation removed civil barriers of race, but in every West Indian territory political equality was a legal fiction. Universal suffrage in the French Caribbean was meaningless: up to 1870 the *Conseils Généraux* were entirely nominated, and after that centralization in Paris emasculated local governments. In the British Caribbean white rule was successfully challenged only in Dominica, where a group of coloured families, known as the 'Mulatto Ascendancy', kept control of the legislature for two generations after emancipation, inducing at least one white overseer to leave for another island with the comment that he hoped 'niggers will not be quite so saucy as they are here. . . . The day is not far distant when this miserable place will be a miniature San Domingo'.[2] Elsewhere whites controlled local legislatures together with a handful of 'qualified' (rich, educated, or accommodating) men of colour; only a few subordinate government posts went to non-whites.

To the freed slaves, voting did not suggest political power; it symbolized social participation. Baptist congregations in post-emancipation Jamaica banded together to buy freeholds to qualify individuals for the franchise. But lack of property kept the vast majority of freed slaves from voting, let alone office-holding. In a quarter century, fewer than two thousand new names were added to the Jamaican electoral roll, and by 1865 only ten of the forty-seven members of the Assembly were coloured. In Barbados before 1884 only 1,300 exercised the franchise in a population of 180,000; in Trinidad, as recently as 1938, income qualifications allowed fewer than 7 per cent of the population to vote. The hierarchical habit was so ingrained that few West Indians thought of a broad suffrage; they viewed the ballot as a special privilege, not a natural right as in the United States.[3]

[1] Henry Clarke to Hugh W. Austin, 28 October 1862, Letterbook 2, No. 49, Edith Clarke Papers.
[2] 'Amicus', in *Dominica Colonist*, 11 July 1863. For the Dominica story, see also Joseph Alfred Boromé, 'George Charles Falconer', *CQ*, Vol. 6, No. 1, 1959–60, pp. 11–17; idem, 'How Crown Colony Government Came to Dominica by 1898', *CS*, Vol. 9, No. 3, October 1969, pp. 26–67.
[3] For the United States, see Frederick Douglass, 'What the Black Man Wants', n *The Equality of All Men before the Law* [1865], pp. 36–9, quoted in Osofsky, *The Burden of Race*, p. 148. For West Indian suffrage see Curtin, *Two Jamaicas*, pp. 178–91, 263; John H. Hinton, *Memoir of William Knibb, Missionary in Jamaica*, 1847, p. 428;

Still, the smallest inroads alarmed West Indian whites. As their own numbers diminished, every new coloured elector became a harbinger of ultimate white eclipse. 'The African race must ultimately become dominant in the West Indies', one Jamaican predicted. He foresaw 'the European landholder continuing to cultivate his estate, and enjoy[ing] the profits of it in security, . . . though the great majority of those filling superior positions' would ultimately be 'descendants of the African.' But it would require great wisdom, he realized, to bring about the revolution 'gradually and benefically'.[1]

Most West Indian whites had no intention of accepting that revolution at all. The spectre of Haiti reinforced their reluctance to yield any power or perquisites. 'I know what the black man is,' declared an Englishman long resident in Haiti; 'he is incapable of the art of government, and . . . to entrust him with framing and working the laws for our islands is to condemn them to inevitable ruin.'[2] Only after British insistence did the Jamaica Assembly, in 1846, consent to seat an elected former slave.[3] But nothing in the old representative regime could prevent the numerically dominant African descendents from ultimately ruling the West Indies. Confronting hopeless demographic odds, West Indian whites more or less willingly relinquished local control for direct imperial rule. During the last third of the nineteenth century every British Caribbean territory except Barbados (which had a white population large enough to assert authority) regressed from self-government to Colonial Office rule.

In Jamaica, Crown Colony government followed the Morant Bay uprising of 1865, in which a local protest against poverty and injustice led to a score of deaths; in the ensuing 'pacification', militiamen killed 580 Jamaicans, and the Governor had George William Gordon, a coloured reform leader in the Assembly, executed for 'complicity'.[4] But Morant Bay was less the cause than a justification for ceding legislative control. Under pressure from Britain the same process was already in train in less disturbed territories. 'Those of European descent are most fitted to understand and enjoy the blessings of the English Constitution', a Governor of Dominica explained in a despatch; under the island's Mulatto Ascendancy 'civilization is retrograding, confidence is destroyed, and the

Hamilton, *Barbados and the Confederation Question*, p. 111; F. A. Hoyos, *The Road to Responsible Government*, p. 41; Hewan Craig, *The Legislative Council of Trinidad and Tobago*, 1952; H. O. B. Wooding, 'The Constitutional History of Trinidad and Tobago', *CQ*, Vol. 6, Nos. 2 and 3, May 1960, pp. 143–59, ref. pp. 153–7.

[1] T. H. Milner, *The Present and Future State of Jamaica Considered*, 1839, pp. 26–7.
[2] Spenser St. John, *Hayti, or, The Black Republic*, 1889, p. xi.
[3] Anton V. Long, *Jamaica and the New Order, 1827–1847*, 1956, p. 90.
[4] Sydney Olivier, *The Myth of Governor Eyre*, 1933; Bernard Semmel, *The Governor Eyre Controversy*, 1962; Roy Augier, 'The Consequences of Morant Bay: Before and After 1865', *NWQ*, Vol. 2, No. 2, Croptime 1966, pp. 21–42.

natural order of society is being . . . subverted.'[1] The prospect that men
of African descent might dominate Caribbean lands was as repugnant
to many in the Imperial Government as it was to West Indian whites.

This repugnance was not the only motive for the transfer of power.
Some Englishmen favoured Crown Colony rule to protect blacks
against local white oligarchies. 'Constituted as the popular branch of
the legislature now is,' asserted Governor Lionel Smith of Jamaica in
1839, '*no governor will be permitted to do justice to the negro population.*'[2] Many
non-whites likewise felt that imperial control afforded them better
protection. 'Without the protection of [Her Majesty's] Government our
fellow colonists would not allow us to enjoy the breath we breathe',
asserted coloured freeholders who opposed the re-establishment of an
elected legislature.[3]

But if Britain had the interest of the West Indian majority at heart, it
never conceived that interest as self-rule. Crown Colony government
substantially reduced the number of coloured and black office-holders,
because white Creoles carried more weight with expatriate officials, and
because it was settled policy not to name non-whites to positions of
responsibility. In the absence of local whites Europeans were appointed
regardless of the availability of qualified non-whites. A British Government guided by land-owners, as a Jamaican legislator confidently
predicted, would 'never allow the island to be placed in the hands of
those who have no property rights.'[4] Colonial officials concurred with
Froude that coloured men were unfit for place or power. The Registrar
and Provost Marshal of Trinidad asked the Governor in 1894 to
appoint a supernumerary 'with as little coloured blood as possible, and
if practicable with no coloured blood at all, as these have given considerable trouble in the Department within the past two years'.[5] The
Leeward Islands' Governor a decade later urged the promotion of a
young white treasury clerk in Montserrat as 'indispensable in the case
of the absence or illness of the Commissioner, who is the only executive
officer of pure European descent in the island.'[6]

[1] Lieutenant-Governor Samuel W. Blackall to Henry Taylor, 31 December 1854,
and confidential, 5 February 1854, C.O. 71/117.

[2] Lionel Smith quoted in William Law Mathieson, *British Slavery and Its Abolition
1823–1838*, 1926, p. 313.

[3] Statement on behalf of Negroes to Royal Commission of 1882–3, *Parliamentary
Papers*, 1884, C. 3820, pp. 163–5, quoted in Ronald V. Sires, 'The Jamaica Constitution of 1884', *SES*, Vol. 3, 1954, pp. 64–81, ref. p. 71.

[4] H. A. Whitelock, in Jamaica House of Assembly, 14 December 1865, quoted in
Curtin, *Two Jamaicas*, p. 202. This view seems to have been in essential accord with
that of Henry Taylor, the Colonial Office architect of Crown Colony government
(Morrell, *British Colonial Policy in the Mid-Victorian Age*, p. 28).

[5] Cecil F. Monier-Williams to Napier Broome, quoted in 'Colour Prejudice',
Dominica Guardian, 18 July 1894.

[6] Governor Strickland to Colonial Office, 6 April 1903, No. 157, C.O. 152/278.

As long 'as we are governed by the Colonial Office, and the Colonial Office is governed . . . by the West Indian merchant,' wrote a clergyman in 1878, 'I have no faith whatever that the Jamaican government will honestly undertake any measure for the benefit of the Jamaican people'.[1] Little had changed since Governor Smith's criticism of self-government a generation before. The same forces dominated; black and coloured West Indians had merely exchanged direct for indirect subordination to white Creole minorities, and political emancipation was retarded by half a century. The suffrage gradually expanded and more non-whites sat in local legislatures, but votes and seats meant little when appointed officials were all-powerful. Powerless to impel substantive change, an elected representative could only make noise. Even if initially zealous, he eventually relaxed into vain protest or was bought off by the administration. His legislative function was strictly ceremonial and emblematic. Men elected under this system were seldom representative even of the small minority who could vote. Indeed, most elections went uncontested.

Kept from economic and political power, West Indian non-whites likewise obtained a meagre share of social goods and benefits. Health, education, and welfare allocations remained rudimentary for a century after emancipation; few West Indians received either schooling or medical care.

One reason was that these were not generally available anywhere; most countries have recognized education and health as public responsibilities only in the past century. In the West Indies the few doctors and schools were privately provided. Those who could afford them were mostly white, and governments seldom exerted themselves on behalf of non-whites. Medical neglect was a special hardship for many blacks, who often lacked access to elementary precautions and remedies, were unused to coping with illness, and were ill-equipped to manage community health and sanitation. The effects were most grievous in the Guianas, where organization was essential to maintain the drainage and irrigation channels interlacing the cultivated coastal zone. Freed slaves who had bought estate lands lacked funds and skills, pumps fell into disrepair, debris clogged the canals, drinking water became polluted, and malarial mosquitoes proliferated in the undrained swamps and water courses.[2]

Education was also inequitably dispensed. West Indian whites, like Europeans, thought schooling suitable only for the elite; in the West

---

[1] The Rev. Henry Clarke to Edmund Sturge, 8 January 1878, Letterbook 11, No. 435, Edith Clarke Papers.

[2] Anton V. Long, *Jamaica and the New Order, 1827–1847*, pp. 88–9; K. O. Laurence, 'The Development of Medical Services in British Guiana and Trinidad 1841–1873', *JHR*, Vol. IV, 1964, pp. 59–67. See also Curtin, *Two Jamaicas*, pp. 160–1.

Indies that elite went 'home' to be educated, and the territories were left with scarcely the rudiments of a school system. Emancipationists had spoken of the need to train former slaves for life in a free society, but little was done. Small educational grants came from the metropolitan governments and from churches, smaller sums from local legislatures. But most schools established under local patronage were elite institutions. At first they catered to whites alone; middle-class coloured children later gained admission. Higher education remained an elite process, based on European models rather than local conditions and designed to turn out gentlemen and administrators.

Schooling conceived in this spirit was felt undesirable for the masses, in whom it would only confirm distaste for the life of hard physical labour that they were doomed to lead. Primary schooling spread slowly and touched most folk superficially. Even after basic education was in theory compulsory it was far from universal; as late as the 1940s one West Indian in three could not read or write, one child in four never went to school, half the remainder attended only irregularly, and most received fewer than four years of schooling.[1]

Formal freedom thus availed most West Indians little in the face of customary discrimination. Indeed, emancipation increased racial prejudice; with slavery gone, colour criteria took on greater importance in West Indian society, not less. Failure to create an instant utopia and the supposed decline of the West Indian economy were cited as evidence of Negro inferiority, unfitness for self-rule, and hereditary ineducability. White Creoles undercut black freedom with vagrancy laws, contracts tying tenancy to plantation duties, and state-subsidized indentured immigration that kept down estate wages. And coloured West Indians occupied an uneasy middle position, emphasizing the conflicts as much as the continuities of the structure.

'A race has been freed, but a society has not been formed', a colonial official reminded Britain in 1848.[2] For most Europeans, West Indian 'society' did not include the freed slaves. British magnanimity was exhausted in compensating the slave-holders; they allotted less than 1 per cent of that sum to school former slaves for freedom. 'Is education what going to release this village, this island, from the tyrannies o'

---

[1] Conditions of course varied from territory to territory. For the background, see Shirley C. Gordon, *A Century of West Indian Education: A Source Book*, 1963; Carl Campbell, 'Towards an Imperial Policy for the Education of Negroes in the West Indies after Emancipation', *JHR*, Vol. VII, Nos. 1 and 2, 1967, pp. 68–102; Vincent Roy D'Oyley, *Jamaica: Development of Teacher Training through the Agency of the Lady Mico Charity from 1835 to 1914*, 1964; Klébert Viélot, 'L'enseignement primaire en Haïti', in Richard P. Schaedel, ed., *Papers of the Conference on Research and Resources of Haiti*, 1969, pp. 281–346.

[2] Harris to Grey, Trinidad, 19 June 1848, *Parliamentary Papers*, 1847–8, xlvi, in Bell and Morrell, *Select Documents on British Colonial Policy*, p. 432.

slavery', remarks a Barbadian in a novel. 'But slavery abolished, long time!' says his friend. Not so, the first replies. 'One kind they abolish, but they forget to abolish the next kind'.[1] Nowhere was emancipation complete. 'The planters still kept and intended to keep the majority of the Negroes in subordinate social, political and economic positions. The possibility of an alternative society . . . was not recognized; or, if it was recognized, it was ignored.'[2]

The century following emancipation bore witness to great changes, to be sure. The West Indian majority exchanged slavery for formal freedom; ex-slaves acquired land and a peasantry emerged; immigrant labourers from Asia profoundly affected many territories; black and coloured numbers increased everywhere, whereas whites diminished; sugar ceased to be the economic touchstone and in some areas vanished entirely; local autonomy gave way to stronger metropolitan control; and middle-class coloured and working-class black began to enter some institutional realms hitherto exclusively white.

Yet these changes fundamentally altered neither the structure of society nor most relationships between ruler and ruled, white and black, landowner and labourer. West Indian ways of life, social circumstances, and prevalent viewpoints remained substantially those of a hundred years before. Countless observers have expressed amazement at how things stayed the same. In other countries travellers look assiduously for traces of the past; in the Caribbean the past is a living presence. It is easy to match previous descriptions of people, places, and prospects with the contemporary scene. *Plus ça change, plus c'est la même chose* is the common *leit-motiv* of West Indian commissions of inquiry. A 1963 UNESCO mission in British Guiana disinterred an old suggestion that schools should relate to the local environment and use local textbooks; 'what should be said on the curriculum', the UNESCO team commented acidly, 'was said a hundred years ago.'[3] To leaf through old reports is to be struck by the uncanny similarity of past and present problems, of forces impeding reform, and of solutions ineffectually proposed.

Voices of protest everywhere continue to lament the lack of change. It was 'a shabby and a cruel anomaly', a junior official felt in 1954, 'that the conditions in our loyal and ancient Caribbean colonies are . . . worse than they were eighty or one hundred years ago'.[4] A Trinidadian asserts that until the mid-1950s nothing had changed but 'the legal position of the slave as a slave. The same type of people remained in

[1] Austin C. Clarke, *The Survivors of the Crossing*, 1964, p. 24.

[2] Marshall, 'Social and Economic Problems in the Windward Islands, 1838–65', p. 257.

[3] *Report of the UNESCO Educational Survey of British Guiana*, 1962–3, WS/0663.22, p. 45.

[4] James Pope-Hennessy, *The Baths of Absalom: A Footnote to Froude*, 1954, p. 64.

charge. . . . The administrative attitudes were the same. The same crops were grown. The same basic plantation system remained.' And despite subsequent independence 'a greater area of our land is now under the slave crop than ever before. The same people own it, the same people ship it, the same people refine it.' Jamaica, too, has seen 'no fundamental change in human relationships. . . . The hostilities built into the society three hundred years ago still exist. . . . The expatriates have merely been replaced by local overseers working for the same bosses.' A Dominican notes the prevailing poverty, the stagnation of custom and thought. 'Looking at our Society today', he asks, 'can we really say that slavery is not still with us?' A St. Vincent survey finds that most of the people on the island are 'living in a way which, in terms of material and environmental conditions, could scarcely be far removed from . . . slavery'.[1]

One reason the West Indian scene has been so durable was the orderly transition out of legal slavery. In most territories emancipation came without riot, bloodshed, or disorder, despite the planters' fears and failure to plan for the future. By contrast, civil war and great turmoil accompanied emancipation in the United States. Yet American slave-owners formed a minority of the whites, whereas the whole structure of West Indian society was slave-based. West Indian social structure was indeed the product of slavery, but slavery proved not essential to its continuance. For the planter emerged after emancipation with his prerogatives fairly intact. This helps to explain the absence of other change. In the American South emancipation imperilled the plantation system, undermined planter power, and vitiated planter values; in the West Indies the plantocracy retained system, power, and values. Many estates failed, changed hands, or were consolidated, and imperial rule replaced Creole. But although some of the faces were new, the shape and implicit aims of the system were none the less substantially unaltered.

Most of the former free coloured and newly freed slaves remained mute or resigned to that continuance. Many thousand workers abandoned the estates for subsistence farming, many hundred coloured professionals were discouraged by white discrimination, many missionaries and magistrates deplored planter coercion and legislative social neglect. Yet such desertions, disappointments, and protests seldom led to rebellion and never to anarchy; by and large West Indians in all walks of life accepted things as they were.

[1] Elton Richardson, 'Only Social Upheaval Will Bring Change', *Trinidad Express*, 1 April 1970, p. 9; Vernon Arnett, 'Jamaica—Dictatorship or Democracy?' *Moko*, No. 4, 13 December 1968, p. 2; Julian N. Johnson, 'Reflections of August Monday', *Dominica Herald*, 5 August 1967, p. 8; *The Development Problem in St. Vincent: A Report by a University of the West Indies Development Mission* [1969], pp. 8–9.

Although hierarchical in structure and European in focus, West Indian society is locally ameliorative and encourages some social mobility. As the whites departed and non-white suffrage broadened, as local education expanded and discriminatory barriers relaxed, coloured and later black West Indians gradually moved into positions of power and prestige, in the process emulating white outlooks and attitudes. Indeed, to gain success one had to adopt colonial values. Coloured middle-class accession to white elite perquisites involved no fundamental change in the hierarchical structure nor in its sustaining values. Quite to the contrary, middle-class West Indians opposed structural change as a threat to the status they had gained or coveted.

Success, the world over, frequently weakens middle-class reform and compromises their ideals. West Indian history is unique in that middle-class achievers rarely intend fundamental change; firm believers in the system, they seek mainly to inherit white places. Social reform inspires many young West Indians, to be sure; the memoirs of most West Indian men of affairs relate how they tried to banish misery and poverty. But until recently such sentiments seldom lasted much beyond student days abroad. Once back home, radical change seemed chimerical or mischievous, and reformers became careerists.

Most West Indian leaders during the century after emancipation were men of profoundly conservative temper, at home with imperial control and at ease with imperial values—including a hierarchy based on colour. Black and coloured legislators, civil servants, judges, and doctors were increasingly numerous, but their values were correspondingly white. In this context it is easy to understand West Indian reluctance to throw off European bonds. White and non-white alike viewed the imperial connection not as a shackle but as a support; independence would threaten their view of the world and their place in it.

A close parallel to the West Indian situation is found in Sierra Leone, where the English-speaking urban Creole professionals privately deplored the 'independence' that ended their hegemony over the tribal majority. The Sierra Leone elite was substantially of West Indian origin, and like Europeanized West Indians at home viewed Africans as savages.[1]

Conflicts of loyalty have similarly weakened Negro-American unity. Whites traditionally view as 'black leaders' those who affirm white values or deliver black votes; perennially disillusioned, blacks express anger at their betrayal by these so-called spokesmen. 'To characterize those blacks who joined the establishment as "selling out"' may be unfair, as Whitney Young recently claimed; but his Harlem audience

[1] See E. R. Braithwaite, *A Kind of Homecoming*, 1963, pp. 108–9.

shouted back, 'it still happens.'[1] West Indian disappointment is less coherent and less hostile; leaders are not rejected because they fail to deliver, nor blamed for selling out. Few expect them to behave otherwise, for anyone in power is expected to be culturally 'white'. Whereas blacks who succeed in white America alienate other blacks, coloured and black West Indians who achieve prominence are praised as exemplars, no matter how remote their way of life and tenor of thought from that of the masses.

Although the West Indian social hierarchy persists, its altered colour composition has engendered new values. Most radically altered are prescriptions for co-existence in a stratified society. Separation by colour, still a cardinal fact of West Indian life, lost first its philosophic rationale and then its respectability; racial mixing became the general West Indian ideal; most recently an egalitarianism of under-privilege has emphasized the narrower goals of the black majority.

Under slavery the difference between bond and free dominated every aspect of society. Since all slaves were black or coloured and all whites were free, racial distinctions were taken for granted and required that free black and coloured people be set apart from both free white and slave black. Emancipation destroyed the legal but strengthened the pragmatic justification for colour distinctions. Awakening 'after the drunken joy of finding myself free,' a French West Indian is imagined finding that 'the hard reality that stared me in the face was that nothing had changed. . . . Like all the other Negroes, I was still here in this accursed country; the *békés* [white Creoles] still owned the land, all the land in the place, and we went right on working for them as before.'[2] But colour, not condition, now determined servitude. And although colour distinctions were less absolute, the distances and grievances between white, brown, and black widened after emancipation.

Whites who had formerly wooed free-coloured support now rebuffed them, intolerant of coloured equality, let alone hegemony. In Jamaica white–coloured factionalism helped to trigger the Morant Bay revolt. In Dominica white praise for coloured loyalty turned to bitter hostility in 1837 when coloured leaders, cheated of promised spoils, founded their own party. In Martinique, which whites exclusively controlled, the end of the empire in 1870 brought dramatic change: 'coloured men now swarm in all the public offices. . . . Wherever you turn you meet with individuals of African descent filling almost all the

[1] David Bird, 'Young Deplores "Sell-Out" Gibes', *New York Times*, 27 October 1969, p. 46. For black American suspicions of their 'leaders', see Nathan Hare, *The Black Anglo-Saxons*, 1970.

[2] Joseph Zobel, *La rue cases-nègres*, 1950, pp. 60–1, quoted in Daniel Guérin, *The West Indies and Their Future*, 1961, p. 14.

posts of honour. This elevation of the hated race has been too sudden not to be extremely galling to the whites.'[1]

West Indian whites typically saw in those of mixed race an incapacitating hereditary taint. Even those 'so fair, that no new arrival in the West Indies would guess that they were not what is called white' proved on closer acquaintance to 'retain some of the predominant characteristics of the negro race'—that is, in the writer's view, temper, vanity, and avarice.[2] But coloured West Indians were also conceded a share of white genetic virtues. 'Coffee and tobacco need higher cultivation than the more thriftless class of negroes usually care to bestow upon them,' asserts the author of a late nineteenth-century Jamaican short story, 'but Clemmy [the white protagonist's mulatto 'housekeeper'] was a brown girl, and she worked as became the descendant of so many strenuous white ancestors.' And Clemmy claimed the white man for herself on grounds of colour: 'You doan't can go an' sleep wit' all dem common negur dah.'[3]

Coloured efforts to gain white favour, however unsuccessful, aroused black animus. 'I was a black man and therefore had absolutely no right to lead', Garvey found in Jamaica in 1914; 'in the opinion of the "coloured" element, leadership should have been in the hands of a yellow or a very light man. . . . There is more bitterness among us negroes because of the caste of color than there is between any other peoples'.[4]

In time black as well as coloured men gained positions of leadership. But high appointive posts, when not held by whites, until quite recently remained a light-coloured domain. The coloured middle class, which an ex-Jamaican Governor half a century ago saw as a force for West Indian cultural homogeneity, has struck other observers as a divisive element more apt to perpetuate than to eliminate colour prejudice.[5]

[1] 'Politics in Martinique', *The Dominican*, 20 November 1872.

[2] Charles William Day, *Five Years Residence in the West Indies*, 1852, Vol. II, p. 229.

[3] Grant Allen, 'Ivan Greet's Masterpiece', in his *The Jaws of Death*, 1897, pp. 174–5.

[4] Marcus Garvey, 'The Negro's Greatest Enemy', *Current History*, Vol. XVIII, 1923, pp. 951–7, ref. p. 954.

[5] 'The mixed race . . . is a valuable and indispensable part of any West Indian community. . . . A colony of black, coloured, and whites has far more organic efficiency and far more promise in it than a colony of black and white alone. A community of white and black alone is in far greater danger of remaining . . . a community of employers and serfs, concessionaires and tributaries. . . . The graded mixed class in Jamaica helps to make an organic whole of the community and saves it from this distinct cleavage' (Sydney Olivier, *White Capital and Coloured Labour*, 1910, pp. 38–9). Frederick Douglass, as American Minister and Consul-General in Haiti, came to the opposite conclusion: 'The blacks hate the mulattoes and the mulattoes look down upon the blacks. Many of the whites have colored wives and black men have white wives, and in the face of all this mixture, fools indulge in prejudice and turn up their noses' (Frederick Douglass to Rosetta Douglass Sprague, 5 February 1890, in Benja-

Social structures varied with post-emancipation economic and demographic circumstances. Where sugar estates circumscribed livelihoods, labourers were rigidly subordinated. As late as 1949 Antigua's future Chief Minister assailed the island's sugar combine as 'a relic of slavery':

This industry has been owned for centuries by Europeans, whose arrogant superiority is bolstered by the predominant position of their race. . . . The coloured man is made to feel that he is an inferior being. . . . The people were cowed by the fact that the owners of the sugar factory and the plantations were as a rule from the same country as the governors and the administrators, and . . . saw little to distinguish the one from the other. The workers have thus always regarded the employers as rulers to be obeyed.[1]

Where ex-slaves found a living off the estate, distance diminished interracial intercourse. 'The black Jamaicans tended to withdraw from the estates and to found the free peasant communities . . .; the brown Jamaicans tended to consolidate their positions as a professional-commercial class based on the towns; the whites either abandoned the island altogether or tried [to] maintain a separate social existence,' a Jamaican summarized the process. 'There was far less daily contact between the mass of the black majority and the white or coloured minority', and cultural differences became accentuated. In time, the peasantry developed its own patterns of behaviour and belief.[2]

Throughout the West Indies 'the communicative network hardly changed. The Negro masses . . . did not participate. . . . Two worlds existed with an abysmal gulf separating them and preventing any real contact except the surviving one of employer-employed.'[3] Sexual connections too became more clandestine: emancipation diminished the availability of non-white women to white men, and Victorian morality, reinforced by resident European women, constrained planter mores.

min Quarles, 'Frederick Douglass: Letters from the Haitian Legation', *CQ*, Vol. 4, No. 1, January 1955, pp. 75–81, ref. p. 77). By contrast with the 'abyss of hate between the three classes in Haiti', mulattoes in Spanish Santo Domingo 'began by calling themselves white and, in the absence of any injurious objections, ended by considering themselves such', thus contributing to social cohesion (G. d'Alaux [pseudonym for M. Raybaud], *L'empereur Soulouque et son empire*, 1856, quoted in Harmannus Hoetink, 'The Dominican Republic in the Nineteenth Century: Some Notes on Stratification, Immigration, and Race', in Magnus Mörner, ed., *Race and Class in Latin America*, 1970, pp. 96–121, ref. p. 115).

[1] Vere C. Bird, 'Minority Report', in *Report of the Commission Appointed to Enquire into the Organization of the Sugar Industry of Antigua*, 1949, p. 118. For the background see Novelle H. Richards, *The Struggle and the Conquest; Twentyfive Years of Social Democracy in Antigua* [ca. 1964], especially pp. 11–31; Andrew Peter Phillips, 'The Development of a Modern Labor Force in Antigua', 1964, espec. pp. 39–40.

[2] John Hearne, 'European Heritage and Asian Influence', in Hearne and Rex Nettleford, *Our Heritage*, pp. 7–34, ref. p. 30.

[3] Mervin C. Alleyne, 'Communication between the Elite and the Masses', in Andic and Mathews, *The Caribbean in Transition*, pp. 14–19, ref. p. 14.

Social segregation characterizes French Antillean whites to this day, even where white and non-white economic and cultural circumstances are similar. In the British and Dutch Caribbean, however, local demography and metropolitan pressures have made apartheid impossible. Segregated schools had almost everywhere disappeared by the end of the nineteenth century; racially exclusive social clubs survive only covertly today. Both elite and 'poor' whites in Jamaica, Barbados, St. Vincent, and Saba increasingly intermingle with black and coloured folk.

Deliberate segregation re-appeared in the West Indies with Asian contract labourers. Housed by themselves in estate barracks, East Indians and Javanese were kept apart from the Creoles. Those who quit the estates to farm for themselves tended to remain in closed ethnic communities. Many Guyanese villages are still almost entirely East Indian, and in Surinam the Government lent formal support to homogeneous rural communities of Javanese, Hindustanis, and Negroes. But Asian exclusiveness is more cultural than racial, and ethnic segregation is everywhere publicly deplored.

Integration, the goal of free coloured West Indians, became the ambition of most slave descendants. But integration had different connotations for coloured, black, and white. To the free coloured it meant the emulation of European standards and social acceptance by white Creoles. To the emancipated blacks it meant self-esteem and a fair share of material and social goods. The exemplar for both was the white West Indian, hospitable and tyrannical, greedy and improvident, extravagant and overbearing, energetic but disliking manual labour. And for most non-white West Indians, achievement in terms of European standards is still a prime goal, notwithstanding the new significance of black Africa.

This was not the white ideal of integration. Whites wanted the black or coloured West Indian to pattern himself after a docile, tractable, hard-working European peasant—to be 'an English rustic in a black skin', as one observer characterized nineteenth-century Barbadians.[1] Emulation by non-whites, as whites saw it, ought to stop short of such goals as social equality and high status. Several generations have not entirely obliterated this presumption, though West Indian whites who remain unpersuaded of coloured and black rights to equality no longer voice their doubts in public.

In the past generation, however, the accelerated pace of change has in many ways made the Caribbean a new world. The transition from colonial status to autonomy and equality has already been sketched. The tempo of internal change is no less rapid. In 1940 whites dominated

[1] J. Graham Cruickshank, *Black Talk*, 1916, quoted in Greenfield, *English Rustics in Black Skin*, p. 172.

all Caribbean governments, suffrage (except in the French colonies) was severely restricted, and black and coloured men held few prestigious positions. Today non-whites predominate in all the governments and occupy most places of public eminence.

Although this transformation leaves Caribbean social structures essentially intact, it has induced great changes in public attitudes. Anti-colonial, anti-white, and anti-establishment views were earlier articulated by pan-Africanists like Marcus Garvey in the 1910s and 1920s, by British West Indian labour leaders who fought discrimination in the 1920s and 1930s, by Haitian and French Antillean forerunners of Aimé Césaire's *négritude*. Returning migrants forced out of Central America and the United States in the 1930s, embittered by racial and social disparities, organized protests against West Indian living conditions, and during the depression decade this landless and impatient proletariat leavened the conservatism of the labouring population.[1] But only since the Second World War have radical views gained substantial West Indian support.

Both world wars triggered change. Many West Indians experienced the outside world as soldiers in Europe and chafed at the old ways when they returned home. Islands with American bases acquired new perspectives; Trinidad especially was Americanized in its tempo of life, in its demands for modern consumer goods, and in its impatience with Old World forms. Trinidad oilfield workers mounted the first effective West Indian strike against discriminatory hiring.[2]

As the political franchise broadened, the common man gained new significance in the eyes of local politicians and cultural leaders. No longer a figure to ignore or despise, he now exemplified the local spirit essential to the mystique of autonomy. Ethnographers in Haiti, poets in the French Antilles, and novelists in the British Caribbean concentrated creative talent on folk life, extolling the black proletariat's struggle against oppressors at home and abroad. Even in territories now independent, literary figures continue to assail the powers that were.[3] The habit of protest—like that of accommodation—dies hard. And the social structures and relationships born of West Indian history go far to account for West Indian attitudes today.

[1] Jesse Harris Proctor, Jr., 'British West Indian Society and Government in Transition 1920–1960', *SES*, Vol. 11, 1962, pp. 273–304, ref. p. 283; O. W. Phelps, 'Rise of the Labour Movement in Jamaica', *SES*, Vol. 9, 1960, pp. 417–68; G. E. Cumper, 'Labour Demand and Supply in the Jamaican Sugar Industry, 1830–1950', *SES*, Vol. 2, No. 4, March 1954, pp. 37–86, ref. pp. 80–1.

[2] W. F. Elkins, 'Black Power in the British West Indies: The Trinidad Longshoreman's Strike of 1919', *Science and Society*, Vol. XXXIII, No. 1, 1969, pp. 71–5.

[3] A. J. Seymour, 'The Novel in the British Caribbean—III', *Bim*, Vol. 11, No. 44, January–June 1967, pp. 238–42, ref. p. 239.

CHAPTER III

Social Structure

A common thread runs through most Caribbean societies, reflecting their similar and interconnected histories. Yet the West Indies are not one but many, and though the resemblances are evident, ways of life are far from identical. Geographical size, number of people, racial patterns, ethnic awareness, and resource use are only some of the obvious distinguishing criteria. Each society displays features unique to itself. But to simplify discussion, they may be grouped into categories, ranging from least to most complex: (1) homogeneous societies without distinctions of colour or class; (2) societies differentiated by colour but not stratified by class; (3) societies stratified by both colour and class; (4) societies stratified by colour and class but lacking white Creole elites; and (5) societies stratified by colour and class, and also containing sizeable ethnic groups in large measure outside the colour–class hierarchy, with distinctive culture, institutions, and values. Only the last three types are numerically populous, as the table on pp. 78–9 shows.

Homogeneous societies. Several small Caribbean islands are peopled by folk of a single colour, class, and way of life, in all cases but one by descendants of Africans. The 6,000 folk of Carriacou (save for an isolated village of light-skinned fishermen), the 1,000 Barbudans, the 3,000 Caicos Islanders include no whites and few coloured people as distinct from blacks; occupation and wealth hardly differ among them. Each island is a relic of slavery: Carriacou was a feudal sugar and cotton domain until the post-emancipation decline of sugar, when the planter class withdrew; Barbuda was a hunting and slave-breeding preserve maintained by the Codrington family of Barbados; South Caicos was settled by Southern royalist refugees from the American Revolution; North Caicos was a salt mine. In all of them work is now scarce and emigration for jobs a normal way of life. Yet these islands display remarkable social stability, most inhabitants belonging to families native there for centuries.[1]

[1] M. G. Smith, *Kinship and Community in Carriacou*, 1962; Richard J. Russell and William G. McIntire, *Barbuda Reconnaissance*, 1966; Edwin Doran, Jr., 'The Caicos

French St. Barthélemy likewise exhibits extreme homogeneity of class and race: except for a few English-speaking non-whites in Gustavia, the capital (and only) town, the 2,000 islanders are the unmixed descendants of seventeenth-century Breton settlers. Their mode of life is strongly patriarchal and family-centred, and they are strictly endogamous not only by race but by locality. But like the predominantly black peasants of other islands, the rural St. Barthois are mostly poor and unlettered, living together on equal terms as farmers, traders, and smugglers.[1]

Societies differentiated by colour but not by class. Hierarchy is of little moment in several small islands where white and black, or coloured and black, co-exist without much commingling. On Saba, Bequia, Anguilla, the Saintes, and Désirade, groups differentiated by colour tend to dwell apart, though their occupations, fortunes, and aspirations hardly differ. Colour divisions vary: thus in Bequia and Anguilla coloured are distinct from black, in Saba and Désirade white from non-white; but endogamy is nowhere so strict as in St. Barthélemy.

Désirade exemplifies several types of racial convergence. Almost half the 1,400 Désiradeans are formally 'white', but only 250 of these are genetically unmixed. As with Carriacou, planters abandoned Désirade after emancipation. But unlike Carriacou, Désirade contained white smallholders, descendants of prisoners deported from France or inmates and provisioners of the leper asylum maintained there from 1728 until 1954. These whites remained in Désirade as peasant farmers, substituting family for slave labour, while non-whites engrossed abandoned estate lands. Family structures likewise converged. Better off non-whites emulated the nuclear and patriarchal European ideal, whereas in white families women took on a greater share of authority along with field labour. Désiradean family organization today correlates with economic status, not with race. Endogamy is minimal, but in establishing mixed unions coloured men normally marry, white men take concubines. White and coloured (there are few unmixed blacks) both make a meagre living from farming and fishing and

Conch Trade', *GR*, Vol. 48, 1958, pp. 388–401; Doreen Collins, 'The Turks and Caicos Islands—Some Impressions of an English Visitor', *CQ*, Vol. 7, No. 3, December 1961, pp. 163–7.

[1] Jean Benoist, 'Du social au biologique: étude de quelques interactions', *L'Homme*, Vol. VI, No. 1, 1966, pp. 5–26, ref. pp. 10–18; Charles Robequain, 'Saint-Barthélemy: terre français', *CO-M*, Vol. II, 1949, pp. 14–37; Guy Lasserre, *La Guadeloupe: étude géographique*, 1961, Vol. II, pp. 806–9, 845–83; Jean Benoist, 'Saint-Barthélemy: Physical Anthropology of an Isolate', *American Journal of Physical Anthropology*, Vol. 22, 1964, pp. 473–87. Early visitors characterize the St. Barthois as mostly poor and unlettered, but a recent visitor reports quite a high level of culture and prosperity, stemming from the re-export of French merchandise to the Caribbean and South America (Arno Castel, 'St. Barts: Pure French, Even Sans Gendarmes', *New York Times* Travel Section, 12 April 1970, p. 29).

The West Indies: A Tabular Summary

Territory	Social Type[a]	Area (km²)[b]	Population[b,c] (000)	Administrative Affiliation		Folk Speech
				Caribbean	Metropolitan	
Anguilla	2	91	6	(St. Kitts)[d]	United Kingdom	English
Antigua	3m	280	62		United Kingdom	English
Aruba	3m	190	59	Curaçao	Netherlands	Papiamento
Bahamas	3, 1m	11,400	169[e,f]		United Kingdom	English
Barbuda	1	155	1	Antigua	United Kingdom	English
Barbados	3mp	433	238[e]		(United Kingdom)[d]	English
Bay Islands[h]	3	373	10[g]		Honduras	English
Bequia[h]	2m	18	3	St. Vincent	United Kingdom	English
Bonaire		281	8	Curaçao	Netherlands	Papiamento
British Honduras	5	23,000	120[e]		United Kingdom	English, Spanish
Carriacou[h]	1[i]	29	6[e]	Grenada	United Kingdom	English
Cayman Islands	2p	260	11[e,f]	(Jamaica)[d]	United Kingdom	English
Corn Islands	1	16	2		Nicaragua[k]	English
Curaçao	3m	472	141		Netherlands	Papiamento
Désirade	2p	21	2	Guadeloupe	France	French
Dominica	4	751	70[e]		United Kingdom	French[i]
French Guiana	4	91,000	44		France	French
Gonâve, Île de la	1	658	27	Haiti	(France)[d]	French
Grenada	4	308	89[e]		United Kingdom	French, English
Grenadines[m]	1	78	13	St. Vincent	United Kingdom	English
Guadeloupe	3mp	1,432	273		France	French
Guyana	5	210,000	714[e]		(United Kingdom)[d]	English
Haiti	4	27,750	4,674		(France)[d]	French
Jamaica	3m	11,425	1,861[e]		(United Kingdom)[d]	English
Marie Galante	1	158	20	Guadeloupe	France	French
Martinique	3m	1,080	324		France	French
Montserrat	4m	101	12[e]		United Kingdom	English

Nevis	4	93	11[e]	St. Kitts	United Kingdom	English
Providencia	2, 3P	31	2		Colombia	English
Saba	2	13	1	Curaçao	Netherlands	English
Les Saintes	2p	13	3	Guadeloupe	France	French
St. Barthélemy	1p	21	2	Guadeloupe	France	French
St. Kitts	3	168	34[e]		United Kingdom	English
St. Lucia	4	616	100[e]		United Kingdom	French
St. Martin/Sint Maarten[n]	4p	86	15	Guadeloupe/Curaçao	France/Netherlands	English
St. Vincent	3	344	90[e]		United Kingdom	English
San Andrés	4m	23	15[o]		Colombia	English
Sint Eustatius	1, 2	21	1	Curaçao	Netherlands	English
Surinam	5	181,455	400		Netherlands	Sranan
Tobago	3, 4m	300	35	Trinidad	(United Kingdom)[d]	English
Tortue, Île de la	1	181	12	Haiti	(France)[d]	French
Trinidad	5	4,828	955		(United Kingdom)[d]	English
Turks and Caicos	1	430	6[e,p]	Grand Turk	United Kingdom	English
Virgin Islands (Br.)	1, 2	174	10[e,q]		United Kingdom	English
Virgin Islands (U.S.)	4mp	344	59[e,r]		United States	English

a 1 Homogeneous societies without distinctions of colour or class.
2 Societies differentiated by colour but not stratified by class.
3 Societies stratified by both colour and class.
4 Societies stratified by colour and class but with white Creole elites absent or insignificant.
5 Societies stratified by colour and class and containing sizeable ethnic groups in large measure outside the colour-class hierarchy.
p=poor whites significant; m=metropolitan whites significant.
b Exclusive of offshore dependencies.
c 1969 estimate unless otherwise noted.
d Former colonial ties.
e 1970 census, provisional figures.
f New Providence, 101; Grand Bahama, 26; Andros, 9; Eleuthera, 6; Great Abaco, 6.5; Exuma, 4; Harbour and Spanish Wells, 3; seven other islands, together more than 4.
g Roatán, 4; Guanaja, 2; Utila 1 (based on 1950 census).
h One of the Grenadines.

i Mainly black except for two isolated coloured communities.
j Grand Cayman, 9.3; other islands, 1.3.
k Leased to the United States.
l English in the north-east.
m Union, Cannouan, and Mayreau islands.
n St. Martin (French) 52 square kilometres and 10,000 population; Sint Maarten (Netherlands) 34 square kilometres and 5,000 population.
o Natives, 8; Spanish mainlanders, 7.
p Grand Turk, 2; North Caicos, 1; South Caicos, 1; Middle Caicos, Providenciales, and Salt Cay each 0.5. All are black except for a few white and coloured on Grand Turk.
q Tortola, 9; Virgin Gorda, 1; other islands together about 0.5. Anegada (0.3) is all coloured; Tortola has a few coloured and white; the other islands are entirely black.
r St. Croix, 31; St. Thomas, 26; St. John, 2. These figures exclude about 16–20,000 British West Indian aliens.

are reputed similarly fond of alcohol, cock-fighting, and gambling.[1]

On tiny, mountainous Saba white and non-white are more differenti-ated than in Désirade. Families of European origin among the 1,000 inhabitants long held aloof from the rest, the men traditionally sea-farers, the women busy with drawn-thread work. Each Saban com-munity was racially exclusive or segregated by colour, though white and black levels of income and education differed little. But since the Second World War many whites have departed or died, and non-whites have moved into formerly white localities. Whites tend to emigrate permanently, whereas black and coloured Sabans who take temporary work in nearby St. Maarten and the Virgin Islands often bring back wives from these islands. Saba is now half non-white, and even in Windwardside, the principal white settlement, more blacks are born than whites. The Saban Administrator is coloured, and mixed couples are served in bars, which 'could not have occurred, a decade ago, without scandalous and condemnatory comment'; but at Wind-wardside's 'Lido' black men still do not dance with white women.[2]

Less segregated than Saba but more stratified than Désirade are the Cayman Islands, whose 1960 population was given as 1,500 European, 5,500 mixed, and 1,500 African. Like the St. Barthois, Cayman whites do not marry non-whites; inbreeding accounts for much deaf-mutism, tooth decay, and other genetic defects. Occupational differences also distinguish the races: coloured Caymanians are mostly peasant farmers and fishermen; whites are seamen, who emigrate for years at a time and then return with their savings. This seafaring tradition and fiscal links with the United States have made many white Caymanians prosperous. But despite the economic disparity between white and non-white, the Caymans lack the hierarchical ideology of the larger West Indian territories; by no means an aristocracy eschewing manual work, white Caymanians remain close to the sea, if not to the soil.[3]

The Bay Islands of Honduras, another seafaring and remittance society, have a social structure similar to the Caymans, from where, along with Jamaica, much of their population derives. Some 6,500

[1] Claude Bariteau, 'Organisation économique et organisation familiale dans une île antillaise: la Désirade', 1968. See also Lasserre, La Guadeloupe, Vol. II, pp. 883–917; Jean Raspail, Secouons le cocotier, 1966, pp. 26–7.

[2] John Y. Keur and Dorothy L. Keur, Windward Children: A Study in Human Ecology of the Three Dutch Windward Islands in the Caribbean, 1960; Dorothy Keur, 'The Nature of Recent Change in the Dutch Windward Islands', International Journal of Comparative Sociology, Vol. V, No. 1, March 1964, pp. 40–7; Julia G. Crane, 'Concomitants of Selected Emigration on a Caribbean Island: Saba', 1966; Era Bell Thompson, 'Saba's Youngest Ruler', Ebony, October 1969, pp. 116–22.

[3] Edwin Doran, Jr., 'Inbreeding in an Isolated Island Community', Journal of Heredity, Vol. XLIII, 1952, pp. 263–6; 'Saving and Development', WIE, Vol. 5, No. 2, August/September 1962, pp. 10–21, ref. pp. 13–16.

blacks and 3,000 whites, together with small remnants of Black Caribs, inhabit Roatán, Guanaja, and Utila. A substantial contingent of white Americans, dating from the Civil War, segregates whites from blacks more than in Caymans, but all Bay Islanders unite against Spanish Honduran mainlanders.[1]

Societies stratified by both class and colour. Most West Indian territories contain a hierarchy of classes, corresponding to colour gradations from white through brown to black. The conjunction was until recently taken for granted. 'When as children we sang hymns like: The rich man in his castle, The poor man at his gate; God made them one and all, And ordered their estate. We know from our experiences that the man in the castle was always white and the one at the gate always black like us.'[2] The old order has supposedly vanished. At least in public affairs colour stratification no longer prevails. 'Black people can rise to the highest rank', observes a visitor in Jamaica; 'the Governor-General is a black man. . . . The members of the government are coloured. . . . The civil service and the teaching staff at the university are almost all coloured'.[3] Overt job discrimination is a thing of the past; shops no longer openly advertise for light-coloured girls, and government brings pressure on private enterprise to give better jobs to blacks. But 'economic power still resides to a great extent with the white and fair groups', a local scholar notes, 'and individuals within these groups still do not generally accept black people as equals.'[4]

The endurance of racial hierarchy is traditionally ascribed locally to economics. 'In any expensive hotel or restaurant all the guests are white, the manager is brown, the waiters and the dish-washer are black. Nothing to do with colour, you are told, it is simply an economic fact that black people cannot afford expensive restaurants'.[5] The real reasons, of course, go beyond this, but the extent of economic inequality emerges sharply in various statistics of landholding, income, and education. Of Barbadian estates over 100 acres, whites owned 186, coloured 25, blacks 8, figures *inversely* proportional to population size. The Jamaican median wage for 'Europeans' was almost twice that for 'Afro-Europeans' (coloured), thirteen times that for 'Africans' (blacks). In Trinidad the median income for 'European' males was $500 a

---

[1] I am indebted to William V. Davidson, Department of Geography, University of Wisconsin, Milwaukee, for information from his study of the Bay Islands. See also David R. W. Jones, 'The Caribbean Coast of Central America: A Case of Multiple Fragmentation', *Professional Geographer*, Vol. XXII, 1970, pp. 260–6.

[2] Warren D. Armstrong, 'Why They Carried Their Protest within the Church's Walls', *Trinidad Express*, 1 March 1970, p. 5.

[3] George Mikes, *Not by Sun Alone*, 1967, p. 48.

[4] Errol L. Miller, 'Body Image, Physical Beauty, and Colour among Jamaican Adolescents', *SES*, Vol. 18, 1969, pp. 72–89, ref. pp. 72–3.

[5] Mikes, *Not by Sun Alone*, pp. 48–9.

month, for 'mixed' (coloured) \$113, for 'Africans' (blacks) \$104, and for (East) 'Indians' \$77. Educational differentials are still greater: in 1943, 48 per cent of the white Jamaicans had attended secondary school, but only 10 per cent of the coloured and 1 per cent of the black population had done so. Trinidad's 1960 school-certificate holders included 53 per cent of the Europeans, 10 per cent of the mixed, and less than 4 per cent of the Africans and East Indians.[1]

With status, as with wealth and education, blacks have the least, whites the most. Among sixty Jamaicans locally identified in 1961 as men of greatest influence, one-third were white, though only one Jamaican in a hundred is white; white Barbadians are 56 per cent of the 'influential' though only 4 per cent of the total population; white Dominicans are 14 per cent of the 'influential' but 0·5 per cent of the whole population. Ethnic minorities are also disproportionately influential; less than three out of ten 'influential' people in any of these islands come from the overwhelming majority that is black and coloured.[2]

But just as some blacks are elite, not all whites are upper class. Remnants of a European proletariat survive, especially in Martinique and Barbados, where small family farms with white indentured labourers antedated the great sugar estates. Like Sabans and Désiradeans, these 'poor whites'—'Redlegs' in Barbados, 'Cha-Chas' in St. Thomas, *békés Goyaves* and *blancs Matignons* in the French Antilles—hardly differ from the black peasantry in occupation or culture but keep residentially and socially apart. Other poor whites—a few hundred Barbadians in St. Vincent and Grenada, farmers of nineteenth-century German origin in Jamaica, European ex-convicts exiled in French Guiana, St. Barthois domiciled in St. Thomas—only minimally affect the local society.[3]

The role of elite whites also varies. Barbados contains most whites, both absolutely and proportionately—10,000, or 4 per cent of the Barbadian population. Although displaced from political power, whites still own most Barbadian sugar estates, rum distilleries, major business firms, and export and import agencies. Coastal tourist resorts divide

[1] Barbados estates from *West Indian Census 1946, Part B, Census of Agriculture*, 1950, Table 6, p. 4; Jamaican wages extrapolated from Colin G. Clarke, *Social Structure and Social Change in Kingston, Jamaica*, MS. Table 45; Trinidad wages (1960) from 'The Problems', *Tapia*, No. 1, 28 September 1969, p. 1. Dollars are in local currency.

[2] Extrapolated from data furnished by Charles C. Moskos, Jr., based on a series of interviews between November 1961 and January 1962. See also idem, *The Sociology of Political Independence: A Study of Nationalist Attitudes among West Indian Leaders*, 1967.

[3] A. Grenfell Price, *White Settlers in the Tropics*, 1939, pp. 20–32, 77–102; Edward T. Price, 'The Redlegs of Barbados', *Yearbook Association of Pacific Coast Geographers*, Vol. 19, 1957, pp. 35–9; Warren T. Morrill and Bennet Dyke, 'A French Community on St. Thomas', *CS*, Vol. 5, No. 4, January 1966, pp. 39–47; Francine Chartrand, 'Au sujet des "blancs-Matignon"', *Bulletin de la Société d'Histoire de la Guadeloupe*, No. 2, 1964, pp. 8–11.

Barbados physically between white elite (and visitors) and black folk. Internal group homogeneity now tends to harden colour lines. In the past, two white cricket clubs, one for resident planters and high officials, the other for estate employees, shopkeepers, bank clerks, and petty civil servants, mirrored status distinctions among Barbadian whites; but white population decline and general class erosion have all but erased this line today. Even back-country Redlegs, favoured by white employers over the black peasantry, can reach managerial positions, and two generations of wealth and astute marriages suffice to make them elite.

Neither does colour conspicuously differentiate middle- from working-class Barbadians. Because resident whites were many and powerful, the free coloured, though numerous, made relatively little headway in Barbados during slavery. After emancipation many former free-coloured Barbadians had the capital to acquire freeholds that validated their middle-class status, whereas most ex-slaves were at best able to rent pieces of estate land. Numerous blacks who subsequently left for jobs in Panama and Cuba later returned with money enough to become smallholders as well, so that the Barbadian middle class came to include a substantial number of the dark-skinned as well as the light. Thus non-white shade distinctions are trivial next to the gulf dividing white from non-white. Barbados is a three-class, but virtually a two-colour, society.[1]

Not so Martinique, where an exclusive middle class developed out of a strongly entrenched free-coloured group. 'What is remarkable in Martinique', notes an anthropologist, 'is the distance which separates the middle class from the mass of the population.' A Martinican of working-class background, who had become Professor of Law at the University of Dakar, could not come back to live in Martinique because the coloured bourgeoisie refused to accept him.[2] Martinicans further distinguish light-skinned *grands mulâtres*—estate owners and professionals linked by fortune and style of life with elite whites—and a darker *petit-bourgeoisie* of school teachers, shopkeepers, and minor civil servants. Aloof from each other, both groups shun the masses but are in turn shut out by the whites. Economic, even fraternal, connections across the colour line generate only the most restricted social contacts.

The 2,300 *békés*, or resident whites—less than 1 per cent of Martinique's population—maintain a far more elaborate internal hierarchy

[1] Otis P. Starkey, *The Economic Geography of Barbados: A Study of the Relationships between Environmental Variations and Economic Development*, 1939; Sidney M. Greenfield, *English Rustics in Black Skins: A Study of Modern Family Forms in a Pre-Industrialized Society*, 1966; David Callender, 'The Relationship between the Social Structure and Public Reaction to the Sugar Depression of 1884–1914 in Barbados and Trinidad'.

[2] Edith Kovats-Beaudoux, 'Une minorité dominante: les blancs créoles de la Martinique' [1969], pp. 56, 211.

than their Barbadian counterparts. Some of the 500 *petit blanc* peasantry work for elite whites, but they lack the mobility Barbadian Redlegs enjoy. *Grands blancs* shun them less for their poverty than for being culturally non-white: *petit blanc* patois speech, dress, and, above all, deportment brand them akin to blacks and put them socially beyond the pale. In Barbados, speech and manner vary little with class or locality, and the variance is not crucial for status; in the French Antilles, elite whites place a feudal emphasis on these differences, formalized in 'titles of nobility' locally acquired by their *béké* ancestors.

Distinctions further divide Martinique's upper- and middle-class whites. Select branches of a dozen families constitute the true elite, controlling most of the estates and intermarrying among themselves. In second rank are families of less distinguished or more recent Caribbean vintage, together with impoverished, but genteel, elite branches. Still lower come folk denoted 'pas tout-à-fait blanc', who though considered tainted by remote coloured ancestry are none the less treated formally as white. All three groups avoid marriage not only with coloured Antilleans, but also with poor whites, and even with mainland French, lest marriage to any outsider erode *béké* family control over the sugar industry.[1]

Societies lacking white Creole elites. The structures outlined for Barbados and Martinique are reproduced with less rigour in West Indian societies that have smaller white elites—Jamaica, Trinidad, St. Kitts, Antigua, St. Vincent, Guadeloupe. But even the absence of white Creoles scarcely attenuates stratification. 'A white minority need not be resident to produce this pattern'; in many territories, as in Grenada, 'the brown middle class maintain their links with the metropolitan power as well as with their own Creole society. However, the black mass find it difficult, if not impossible, to cross the class–color barrier, particularly . . . where the class and color lines have remained virtually frozen.'[2]

Elite, middle class, and folk are as severely differentiated in Haiti as anywhere else. The mulatto aristocracy, much reduced by Duvalier, shares power and wealth with a small black elite. The black middle class is remote from, and disdainful of, the black peasantry. 'The real masters are not the decorated blacks,' wrote a refugee in 1955, 'but the white settlers, who control the finance, the economy, public health, public works, diplomacy, and agriculture.'[3] Although blacks have since come to dominate some of these realms, foreign whites are still the envied avatars.

[1] Ibid., pp. 68–92.

[2] A. W. Singham, *The Hero and the Crowd in a Colonial Polity*, 1968, p. 94.

[3] Alfred Viau, *Noirs, mulâtres, blancs ou rien que du sang*, 1955, p. 44. See also Roland Wingfield and Vernon J. Parenton, 'Class Structure and Class Conflict in Haitian Society', *Social Forces*, Vol. 43, 1965, pp. 338–48.

Virtually no Creole whites remain in the British Windward Islands of Grenada, St. Lucia, and Dominica. A handful of foreign whites staff governments, banks, schools, churches, and hotels. More intimately involved in the local scene than Europeans in Haiti, they play no determinative role. Their origin, colour, and wealth notwithstanding, they are a frosting on the social cake rather than its bakers. Coloured Creoles, not whites, today comprise the Windward elite, such as it is; the saying that 'the only reason the coloreds got St. Lucia is that the whites didn't want it'[1] expresses a typically rueful self-mockery. The closely interrelated, light-skinned upper class sharply distinguish themselves from all others of whatever shade. Much of the peasantry is in fact mixed, owing largely to early French settlement, but family connection as well as colour determines status. Of an aspiring rural youngster, back home with a university degree, one of the Dominica elite recently remarked to me, 'How can he suppose that *we*'—the ruling class, the first families, the 'town'—'would take his pretensions seriously? After all, he is nothing but a black boy from the country.' These islands are like Martinique minus the *békés*; their social structure collapses three classes into two.

The British Leeward island of Montserrat exemplifies another type of social attenuation. It too has lost its resident white elite, but unlike the Windwards has little tradition of intermixture between free and slave, white and non-white; Montserrat's 12,000 population is overwhelmingly black, the coloured group there comprising only 2 per cent by contrast with 40 to 60 per cent in the Windwards. Lacking a sizeable free-coloured group, Montserrat failed to develop a middle class of its own and instead has regularly imported coloured shopkeepers and professionals from nearby Antigua and St. Kitts.

The dynamics of class rivalry depend on the divergent island histories. In the Windwards the strongly entrenched coloured elite usually co-opt and absorb popular leaders and dominate the expatriate element; in Montserrat popular leaders neutralize the weak coloured middle class, who are linked neither with the former white elite nor with the black peasantry and who perforce become clients of expatriate entrepreneurs.

Resident expatriate whites are much more influential in other territories, sharing power with Creole whites in Curaçao and Aruba, with a coloured elite in the United States Virgin Islands, and with both in the Bahamas. In Curaçao conflicts of interest among Dutch representatives of petroleum and tourist establishments, Venezuelan traders, Sephardic Jewish merchants, British West Indian migrant labourers,

[1] Daniel J. Crowley, 'Conservatism and Change in Saint Lucia', *Actas del XXXIII Congreso Internacional de Americanistas, San José, 20–27 Julio 1958*, 1959, Vol. II, pp. 704–15, ref. p. 710.

and the majority black and coloured community have eroded the former sense of fraternity beyond the point of violence.[1]

American Virgin Islands society contains at least six distinct groups. The coloured elite maintain political power through government hand-outs for the native black majority. Both classes despise the St. Barthois in St. Thomas as poor whites and fear the Puerto Ricans in St. Croix as competitors. Some 16,000 black West Indian immigrants from nearby British islands, who comprise more than half the working force, are excluded from local political participation and denied social and economic benefits; a labour spokesman detects 'a racist mentality among the native blacks toward the alien blacks'.[2] Toward mainland Americans, 'native' islanders maintain a guarded reserve. 'Every new white resident is rapidly made to feel that it is the white minority that lives on sufferance . . . in a society in which an aristocracy of mixed blood of high social status . . . calls the tune.'[3] But it is mainland money that hires the band; Americans own most of the land, the banks, and the local industries.

To keep power the Virgin Islands coloured elite treads a tight-rope between the demands and complaints of its rival clients—black elector-ate and white capital—meanwhile remaining in the good graces of Congress and the federal agencies, the greatest sugar-daddies of them all. Amid the claims and countercharges of racial harmony and conflict, 'there is little social mixing between the old aristocracy of upper-class Negro birth and the new aristocracy of American wealth'. Unlike most West Indian societies, here 'both the upper-class and the lower-class . . . constitute hermetic cultures sealed off, with the occasional exception, from even the most friendly of Americans.'[4]

Stratified societies containing additional ethnic groups. A sub-stantial East Indian and Javanese population adds another dimension to the colour-class hierarchy in Trinidad and the Guianas. In Guyana endemic conflict between East Indians and Creoles overshadows, with-out eliminating, friction between black proletariat and white or light elite. In Surinam, where East Indians and Javanese dominate most rural districts, black villagers and country folk increasingly migrate to the city, but economic development and the multiplicity of ethnic groups attenuate social stress. In Trinidad, East Indians and Creoles coexist in uneasy peace, Indians emphasizing their separateness,

[1] Harmannus Hoetink, 'Curazao como sociedad segmentada', *Revista de Ciencias Sociales*, Vol. IV, 1960, pp. 179–92; Jacques Dupuis, 'Les paradoxes de Curaçao: à travers les provinces de l'empire Shell', *CO-M*, Vol. 22, 1969, pp. 63–74.

[2] Franklin S. Anderson, quoted in Jack Star, 'Virgin Islands: Shame in the U.S. Tropics', *Look*, 10 March 1970, p. 18.

[3] Gordon K. Lewis, 'An Introductory Note to the Study of the Virgin Islands', *CS*, Vol. 8, No. 2, July 1968, pp. 5–21, ref. p. 16.

[4] Ibid., p. 16.

Creoles ignoring Indian subculture or reprobating it as divisive.

American Indians, mestizos, and Black Caribs—African in ancestry, Indian in language, Creole in culture—complicate a basic Creole social structure in British Honduras. Indians and mestizos, earlier excluded from the local power system, have combined with other non-Creole elements that lean more toward Central America than the West Indies. These groups are generally Roman Catholic, Spanish-speaking, and anti-British, unlike the West Indian Creoles. All value whiteness, but colour lines are less significant in British Honduras than are divisions based on religion, language, and cultural tradition.[1]

PLURALISM

Social differentiation thus varies markedly from one Caribbean territory to another. Certain small islands display no systems of stratification and little difference in wealth, status, or power. But in most Caribbean societies such distinctions are commonplace and persistent, correlating with, and reinforced by, colour and ethnicity.

Class stratification is most apt to be disruptive when it is externally imposed. By contrast, any indigenous social hierarchy presupposes a community of culture and some durable ties between people and the land that may validate the structure even for the least advantaged. But stratification imposed by conquest, enslavement, or forced migration polarizes and exacerbates differences of race and culture, which in turn further aggravate other animosities. Lacking genuine popular support, the elite—often a racial or ethnic minority—maintain supremacy through economic control and police power. The use of force perpetuates antecedent divisions; segregation and discrimination create new ones.

No clear line distinguishes these two types of stratified society. Some indigenous hierarchies are turbulent; some imposed orders are relatively placid. In time, even conquerors and slaves may coalesce in a domestic state, and integration may overcome antecedent differences of race and culture. The distinction is useful, though, in comparing traditional societies, primitive or advanced, with those complicated by European conquest and colonization. Western European and North American countries are relatively unified in language and culture; whereas in much of Africa, South-East Asia, Latin America, and the Caribbean, deep differences and structural inequalities reflect European imperialism and its aftermath. A general consensus of values, attained over

[1] C. H. Grant, 'The Civil Service Strike in British Honduras: A Case Study of Politics and the Civil Service', *CQ*, Vol. 12, No. 3, September 1966, pp. 37–49. See also S. R. R. Allsopp, 'British Honduras—The Linguistic Dilemma', *CQ*, Vol. 11, Nos. 3 and 4, September–December 1965, pp. 54–61; Gordon K. Lewis, *The Growth of the Modern West Indies*, 1968, pp. 289–307.

centuries of coexistence and based on widespread compatibility of interests and culture, holds the typical Western society together. But in post-colonial states the interests and modes of life of ruling minorities are typically in conflict with those of subordinate classes; consensus and emulation are inadequate to unify the society, and force is required to prevent social dissolution.

All West Indian slave societies were based on force, openly avowed by slave-owners and governments and more or less resisted by slaves. After emancipation a few whites, many of the coloured middle class, and some of the former slaves worked to build a society based on consensus and social integration. But such a society has not yet come into being. The elite minority kept its predominance and with imperial support preserved the old distinctions—distinctions based now on colour rather than on servitude. In several territories later immigrants of alien heritage made class differences still more complex; for their status was based anew on servitude and on ethnic identity. Certain values today permeate the entire social order, but in everyday life Caribbean classes remain sharply divided, and divergent social institutions and modes of culture underscore class divisions.

This kind of society is often termed 'plural', following Furnivall's analysis of the Netherlands East Indies in 1939 and subsequent studies of other colonial and ex-colonial societies in Africa and Asia. The theory of pluralism has been further articulated, with specific Caribbean reference, by M. G. Smith.[1] I shall use the plural hypothesis as a convenient framework for discussing West Indian social differences and the tensions they generate. But it is necessary first to outline the attitudes and contradictions the plural hypothesis itself arouses.

The meaning of 'plural' to begin with needs clarification. As defined by most social anthropologists, pluralism is quite different from its ordinary use in, for example, American political and social discussions. In the United States the term 'pluralism' commonly refers to the melting pot, in which European groups of diverse ethnic and cultural backgrounds, though retaining some Old World values, are believed to have pooled their differences in a consensual stew. American democracy and libertarian individualism are often ascribed to the capacity to make such differences culturally enriching rather than socially divisive. A multiplicity of fraternal, religious, economic, and occupational organizations, with memberships that overlap and cut across ethnic groups, is said to prevent social polarization and cleavage. American pluralism encourages ceremonial diversity but renders

---

[1] J. S. Furnivall, *Netherlands India: A Study of Plural Economy*, 1939; idem, *Colonial Policy and Practice: A Comparative Study of Burma and Netherlands India*, 1948, especially pp. 303–12; M. G. Smith, *The Plural Society in the British West Indies*, 1965; Leo Kuper and M. G. Smith, eds., *Pluralism in Africa*, 1969.

cultural differences trivial and harmless; it thus promotes consensus and compromise rather than communalism and conflict. For political scientists and moralists, American pluralism validates the existing system and dignifies its virtues.[1]

For many European social anthropologists, on the other hand, pluralism marks societies in which class cleavages are deep and persistent, cultural differences are institutionalized, and force is the main regulative mechanism. This school of thought sees Euro-American society, with its superficial cultural differences and pervasive national institutions, as a 'heterogeneous' rather than a 'plural' society.

Contrasting views of social structure and evolution parallel these two types of pluralism. According to the traditional model of society developed by Talcott Parsons and other functionalists, consensual interests and values hold societies together and enable them to operate in equilibrium. Pluralists in the European sense argue that the consensus model disregards conflict, ignores the use of force and coercion, and fails to account for social change. Functionalists in turn criticize pluralist theory as self-contradictory, since integration by coercion negates their definition of society, and as catastrophist, since without a community of interest, only revolution or disintegration can resolve social conflict.

In the West Indies, related suppositions reinforce opposing judgements about the nature and prospects of society. Pluralists focus on institutional differences, class rivalries, coercion from above, and hostility throughout the system; functionalists—notably R. T. Smith and Lloyd Braithwaite—point out that West Indian society survives despite these elements of stress, and they draw attention to aims and values shared by all classes and ethnic groups.[2]

This characterization oversimplifies both approaches, to be sure. The

[1] Talcott Parsons, *The Social System*, 1951; Talcott Parsons and Edward A. Shils, eds., *Toward a General Theory of Action*, 1951; William Kornhauser, *The Politics of Mass Society*, 1959; Edward A. Shils, 'The Theories of Mass Society', *Diogenes*, No. 39, 1962, pp. 45–66; Henry S. Kariel, 'Pluralism', in *International Encyclopedia of the Social Sciences*, 1968, Vol. 12, pp. 164–9. Advocates of this concept of pluralism tend to emphasize the cultural interpenetration and resemblances of white and black social orders and to ignore or understate the structural effects of racialism in the United States. See Charles A. Valentine, 'Blackston: Progress Report on a Community Study in Urban Afro-America', 1970, especially p. 65; Robert Blauner, 'Black Culture: Myth or Reality?' in Norman E. Whitten Jr., and John F. Szwed, eds., *Afro-American Anthropology: Contemporary Perspectives*, 1970, pp. 347–66.

[2] Lloyd Braithwaite, 'Social Stratification and Cultural Pluralism', *Annals New York Academy of Sciences*, Vol. 83, 1960, pp. 816–36; R. T. Smith, 'Social Stratification, Cultural Pluralism and Integration in West Indian Societies', in S. Lewis and T. G. Mathews, *Caribbean Integration: Papers on Social, Political, and Economic Integration*, 1967, pp. 226–58; idem, 'Social Stratification in the Caribbean', in Leonard Plotnicov and Arthur Tuden, eds., *Essays in Comparative Social Stratification*, 1970, pp. 43–76.

'consensus' school is not blind to conflict. Neither do the pluralists neglect integration; they merely conceive it differently. Values are not co-terminous with norms, nor norms with behaviour; West Indian social groups often maintain separate institutions and exhibit divergent behaviour while they share underlying values. In the Caribbean, as has been said in a different context, even divisive 'cultural differences . . . usually do not extend to an obvious and uncompromising contradiction of basic norms or values.'[1] And though pluralism predicts conflict, it does not assume inevitable collapse: in a Guyanese case study, Despres shows how 'broker' institutions integrate plural segments at the national level. Throughout the West Indies, endemic hostility occasionally surfaces in violence against the rule of law or scapegoat minorities, but elite coercion, economic necessity, and widespread emulation of elitist values may keep a plural society in indefinite, albeit uneasy, equilibrium.[2]

Java and Burma, the first plural models, were highly complex colonial systems, comprising European rulers and traders, Chinese merchants, and a wide range of indigenous ethnic elements and classes. In the Caribbean, Trinidad, Guyana, Surinam, and British Honduras —where East Indians and other ethnic groups co-exist and compete with Creoles—most closely resemble the Asian models. But the plural hypothesis is also applied to other Caribbean societies, where such ethnic blocs are absent or insignificant, and where Creole classes divide approximately along lines of colour. Some of these societies exhibit more, or different, evidences of pluralism than others. Aspects of pluralism vary in intensity, in interrelatedness, in degree of formalism, in historical stability, in functional import, and in the extent to which they are locally perceived. One or more determinants of social stratification—colour, descent, wealth, occupation, age, sex—may more or less inhibit freedom of choice or expression in various realms of activity.

Difficulties of segregating and classifying social institutions compound the problem of applying plural theory over so wide a range of actual circumstances. There is a real distinction between heterogeneous and plural, but apparent similarities often conceal fundamental diversities and vice versa. It is not easy to determine at what point different ways of life become socially incompatible. How much social mobility, actual

[1] Gerald D. Suttles, *The Social Order of the Slum: Ethnicity and Territory in the Inner City*, 1968, p. 62. For attempts to reconcile pluralist and functionalist positions, see Malcolm Cross, 'Cultural Pluralism and Sociological Theory: A Critique and Reevaluation', *SES*, Vol. 17, 1968, pp. 381–97.

[2] Leo A. Despres, *Cultural Pluralism and Nationalist Politics in British Guiana*, 1967. As early as 1950, British colonial policy was consciously designed to contain communal conflict aroused by plural tensions (J. M. Lee, *Colonial Development and Good Government: A Study of the Ideas Expressed by the British Official Classes in Planning Decolonization 1939–1964*, 1967, pp. 189–90).

or perceived, makes a plural society merely heterogeneous? How large must an institutionally distinctive minority be to qualify the whole society as plural? Does the size of the group effectively measure its significance? In these and other ways, plural and non-plural societies grade imperceptibly into one another. But notwithstanding the difficulties of generalization, the plural concept is relevant to many aspects of West Indian social structure. And differences between ethnically segmented societies, such as Trinidad and the Guianas, and those that divide principally by class and colour can be explored with the help of a distinction, articulated by van den Berghe, between social and cultural pluralism.[1]

The shape and structure of West Indian societies depend on three basic elements: class hierarchy, social pluralism, and cultural pluralism. The rigidity of stratification varies from place to place, but the social pyramid is almost everywhere identical: a small upper class controls access to power and rewards; successively larger middle and lower classes have less and less status, wealth, and self-esteem.

Formal similarity to outmoded European social systems validates this structure in West Indian eyes. More than most ex-colonies, the Caribbean territories preserve imperial values and standards of behaviour that were current when hereditary distinctions were taken for granted. These distinctions are more firmly embedded because the Caribbean is a place of retirement for vice-regal relicts who do not enjoy 'life without a subject race.'[2] West Indians themselves are still dominated by a 'habit of mind which thinks it . . . natural and desirable, that different sections of a community should be distinguished from each other by sharp differences of economic status, of environment, of education, and culture and habit of life . . . [and] regards with approval the social institutions and economic arrangements by which such differences are emphasized and enhanced'.[3]

The range and rigidity of West Indian stratification do not stem from class distinctions alone, however, but also from racial and ethnic differences. Racial and ethnic categories overlap in reality and are

---

[1] Pierre L. van den Berghe, *Race and Racism: A Comparative Perspective*, 1967; David Lowenthal, 'The Range and Variation of Caribbean Societies', *Annals New York Academy of Sciences*, Vol. 83, 1960, pp. 786–95; Burton Benedict, 'Stratification in Plural Societies', *AA*, Vol. 64, 1962, pp. 1235–46; idem, 'Pluralism and Stratification', in Plotnicov and Tuden, eds., *Essays in Comparative Social Stratification*, pp. 29–42. R. L. Bryce-Laporte, 'Crisis, Contraculture, and Religion among West Indians in the Panama Canal Zone', in Whitten and Szwed, eds., *Afro-American Anthropology*, pp. 103–18, analyses a plural situation involving a white American majority and a lower-class minority of West Indian origin.

[2] Lady Reynolds, cited in *News Chronicle*, quoted in 'This England', *New Statesman*, 23 January 1960, p. 95.

[3] R. H. Tawney, *Equality* [1931], p. 49.

locally confused with one another, but different social and cultural consequences tend to flow from each. A *racial* category is different by virtue of *perceived physical* characteristics, presumed to be innate and immutable, from which particular moral, intellectual, and other attributes and abilities are believed to derive. An *ethnic group*, which may or may not appear physically unique, displays unique *cultural* characteristics such as language or religion and, unlike most racial aggregates, has a clear sense of identity and cohesion based on this shared cultural tradition, including presumed descent; 'an ethnic group consists of people who conceive of themselves as being alike by virtue of common ancestry, real or fictitious, and are so regarded by others.'[1]

Ethnicity thus involves many orders of distinctiveness, whereas race requires only one, an awareness of differences in physical appearance, which is not an essential aspect of ethnicity. The line between race and ethnicity is not fixed, however. Appearance may be altered by cosmetics or surgery or dress; cultural images of race affect perceptions of physical differences; and those who consider cultural traits to be genetically inherited view ethnic groups as racially distinct. But racial differences usually involve stratification, with a social hierarchy graded according to colour or some other physical attribute. By contrast, ethnic groups often coexist side by side, either unranked or without general agreement about their rank.

In the Caribbean, these definitions of race and ethnicity set off distinctions within the white-coloured-black Creole hierarchy from relationships between Creoles and other groups—East Indians, Chinese, Javanese, Amerindians, and, to some extent, Syrians, Portuguese, and even Bush Negroes. To distinguish these two types of difference is not to insist on a rigid dichotomy but rather to emphasize the essential qualities of each.

Creole relationships with other Caribbean groups will be described here in terms of ethnicity, because these feature behaviour based on *antecedent* socio-cultural tradition and a keen sense of corporate identity. The resultant stress and conflict are frequently expressed in racial terms and have indeed a racial component, since the ethnic groups are partly stereotyped and ranked by physical appearance; but perceived physical distinction is only one aspect of the difference rather than a prime determinant, as it is within the Creole colour hierarchy.

Race and colour have always supplied critical distinctions among Creoles. Segregated by law or by custom since the seventeenth century, white and non-white have played distinct social roles. Codified differences forced each class to institutionalize separate modes of organiza-

[1] Tamotsu Shibutani and Kian M. Kwan, *Ethnic Stratification: A Comparative Approach*, 1965, p. 572; van den Berghe, *Race and Racism*, pp. 21–30.

tion and ways of living. Of course, whites and blacks in the West Indies were at first ethnically and culturally, as well as socially, distinct, but the African slaves were stripped of their ethnic identities, were left with only scattered remnants of their cultural heritage, and were forced to undergo creolization. Slave culture became in large measure a creolized form of European culture, and African ethnic identity among the Creole-born, slave and free, a matter for despair rather than for pride.

The culture and behaviour of ordinary West Indians do differ from those of the elite and middle class. Distinctive folk customs are often ascribed locally to fixed racial traits and are taken by some scholars to be African tribal remnants; working-class culture, institutions, and values, still denigrated as 'African' by white Creoles, now commend themselves to black-power leaders for the same supposed antecedents. But few of these cultural differences are residual *ethnic* survivals; they are the consequences of *racial* segregation and of inequalities of power, status, and rewards, which stem from slavery and social pluralism.

The rest of this chapter describes West Indian social structure in terms of colour–class stratification and assesses the consequences of social pluralism for institutions and cultural values. Later chapters examine the ethnic dimensions of cultural pluralism and the nature and role of West Indian minorities.

COLOUR

Race and colour are not the sole determinants of status in the West Indies. But class distinctions are mainly seen, and grievances expressed, in racial terms.

Colour in the sense of physical appearance carries extraordinary weight. A comparison is revealing: in Britain aspects of build, hair, and facial structure may connote a Welsh or Scottish, elite or working class, identity, but such features neither denote group qualities nor divide allegiances. West Indians, on the other hand, habitually conceive differences of appearance in terms of social segmentation. Describing various national cricket teams, a Barbadian emphasizes West Indian particularity: 'When the Indian team takes the field at Lords, it is a team of Indians. Some are short and some are tall; but they *look* alike.' And so with the Australian team or any other. 'But when a West Indian team takes the field . . . what do we see? Short and tall, yes; but Indian, Negro, Chinese, White, Portuguese mixed with Syrian.' Physical differences take on an extra dimension. 'To the English eye,' he adds, 'the mixtures are as weird and promising as the rainbow.'[1] To his own West Indian eye the mixture is by implication less *outré* but also less encouraging. It can seem dismaying. A Guyanese novelist returning home describes his 'feeling almost of shock when confronted with the

[1] George Lamming, *The Pleasures of Exile*, 1960, p. 37.

West Indian mass in the dining saloon. Shock, yes, and confusion and alarm and even, paradoxically, repulsion. This polyglot mass, this composite, this hybrid, this mongrel—who were these people? I suspect that the answer to this question keeps many a reflective West Indian abroad.'[1]

Before examining further what West Indian Creoles make of their physical differences, let us see what their genetic inheritance and racial distribution actually are. African ancestry predominates throughout the Caribbean, but degrees of European admixture vary greatly. Where all three elements are present blacks may comprise as much as nine-tenths or as little as a third, coloured or mixed from a substantial majority to an insignificant minority, whites from 5 per cent to less than 1 per cent. Less than one-third of all non-white Creoles are mixed or coloured—a far smaller proportion than that among 'black' Americans. Some isolated groups show no evidence of mixing: the inhabitants of Barbuda and of the Île de la Tortue off Haiti, are genetically so West African as to preclude European admixture.[2] Parts of rural Haiti and Jamaica appear similarly close to Africa, but unmixed descent cannot be assumed. Martinique, Trinidad, and Dominica everywhere evince European as well as African genetic antecedents.

Local perception of racial identity varies from time to time as well as from place to place; census shifts underscore the ambiguity of West Indian colour classification. Whites are too few and individually too well known to allow for much latitude in counting them, though St. Lucia's census officer noted that the 950 whites reported in 1891 included 'many who are not white, even by courtesy.'[3] But the line between coloured and black fluctuates widely with the bias of the census-taker or the mood of the populace. Dominica reported a 'coloured' proportion of 30 per cent in 1921, 75 per cent in 1946, and 33 per cent in 1960—variations explicable only as shifts of evaluation, not of population. Jamaica exhibits similar anomalies: between 1943 and 1960 the 'coloured' proportion of Kingston declined from 33 to 14 per cent. The explanation lies in nomenclature as well as in-migration; dark-skinned Kingstonians were less content to be labelled 'black' in 1943 than 'African' in 1960.[4]

[1] Denis Williams, 'The 1969 Edgar Mittelholzer Memorial Lectures', National History and Arts Council, Guyana, 1st lecture, quoted in Patrick Guckian, 'The Balance of Colour: A Re-assessment of the Work of Edgar Mittelholzer', *JJ*, Vol. 4, No. 1, March 1970, pp. 38–45, ref. p. 45.

[2] Jean Benoist, 'Anthropologie physique de la population de l'île de la Tortue (Haïti): contribution à l'étude de l'origine des noirs des Antilles', *Bulletins et Mémoires de la Société d'Anthropologie de Paris*, Ser. XI, Vol. 3, 1962, pp. 315–35.

[3] Alex. Clavier, comp., *Report on the Census of the Island of Saint Lucia 1891*, p. 4.

[4] O. C. Francis, *The Population of Modern Jamaica*, 1963, pp. 4-4, 4-5; *W.I. Population Census 1960, Bulletin No. 20 (Jamaica)*, 1962.

Distinctions made in everyday life are both finer and more flexible than the broad census categories. Rural villagers in Montserrat ranging phenotypically from medium to dark brown refer to some as 'clearer' than others. One scholar reports 'a fairly prevalent Jamaican assumption that a man is called coloured if he has any white ancestry at all.'[1] Yet Jamaican 'samboes' (one-fourth white) are said usually to classify themselves as black, 'the term coloured having by custom come to be applied to persons of a distinctly brown or clear complexion.'[2] In Guadeloupe, the strict genetic meaning of *mulâtre* (half white, half black) has similarly shifted to denote fair-skinned quadroons and octoroons (three-fourths and seven-eighths white). Darker folk there are *câpres*, the genetic equivalent of samboes. But in Martinique and Trinidad the size of the mixed element tends to be exaggerated.[3]

West Indian racial distinctions are unlikely to merge in the foreseeable future. The early growth of the mixed population at the expense of both whites and blacks owed less to coloured fecundity than to accretions of mixed offspring from white–non-white unions. Since emancipation, a smaller white population with less access to non-white women has produced fewer mixed offspring. Relatively few coloured West Indians today can point to a white father or grandfather; their white progenitors are generally of earlier vintage.

The light-coloured elite in most territories, moreover, socialize and marry among themselves. Darker illegitimate offspring tend to merge with the bulk of the black population. Access to foreign opportunity further depletes light-coloured ranks. Generally better off and better educated than darker West Indians, they more readily gain professional and other positions abroad, and a larger proportion of them emigrate.

Few Creoles will not in time share white ancestry. But for most of them this share will be so small that even in West Indian terms they will count as black. Yet the continuing presence of influential white and coloured minorities will make colour differences hard to ignore. Real change would require that West Indians cease to value colour according to the standards of past centuries.

Pragmatic integrationists, West Indians are theoretical racists. Despite their ambiguous colour designations, manifold shade distinctions, and tolerance of mixing, West Indians' genetic beliefs are closer to Lord Monboddo than to UNESCO. They view types of behaviour,

---

[1] Madeline Kerr, *Personality and Conflict in Jamaica*, 1952, p. 101.

[2] H. G. de Lisser, *Twentieth Century Jamaica*, 1913, p. 44.

[3] Lasserre, *La Guadeloupe*, Vol. I, p. 324; Jean Benoist, 'Les Martiniquais: anthropologie d'une population métissée', *Bulletins et Mémoires de la Société d'Anthropologie de Paris*, Ser. XI, Vol. 4, No. 2, 1963, p. 265; Lloyd Braithwaite, 'Social Stratification in Trinidad', *SES*, Vol. 2, Nos. 2 and 3, October 1953, pp. 5–175, ref. p. 160.

attitudes toward life, and personality traits as no less 'racial' than skin colour and hair texture. Racial inheritance is specifically linked with blood, as exemplified in the Guyanese novelist Mittelholzer's constant references to his characters' 'good blood' and 'bad blood', 'weak blood' and 'strong blood', supposedly derived from one or another ancestor.[1]

West Indians do not confine genetic determinism to whites and blacks, East Indians and Chinese; they extend it to mixed and inter-graded races. Although brown-skinned Creoles are now the official ideal type in song and slogan, Bennett limns a characteristic West Indian contempt and envy toward 'mixed' inheritance:

> Dem don't know wey dem stan'
> One granpa w'ite, an t'oder granpa
> Big, black, African.[2]

Resembling neither, the mulatto endures rejection by both:

> Because we are not black . . .
> the black man questions what we say . . .
> Because we are not white, . . .
> the white man questions what we say.[3]

'These red people are all cross-bred and worthless', a black Barbadian comments. 'They ain't got personality.'[4] The mulatto is usually 'a spectator, always on the fringe,' notes a fictional protagonist. 'In the country they called him *"ti béché"* and in the town . . . "white nigger".'[5] Albinos, too, encounter revulsion and harsh jocularity as 'white Negroes'.[6]

That the 'mixed blood' ideal conflicts with popular views about race mixture is clear from complaints that beauty contests 'automatically eliminate Jamaican girls of pure races in favour of the girls of mixed races'. Critics demanded—and got—official reassurance that the multi-racial national motto, 'Out of Many One People', did not mean the Government would compel miscegenation.[7]

---

[1] Joyce L. Sparer, 'Edgar Mittelholzer—Obsession with "Blood": Attitudes towards Race in Guyanese Literature, [Parts] 2 and 3', *Georgetown Sunday Chronicle*, 16 and 23 April 1967 (republished in her 'Attitudes towards "Race" in Guyanese Literature', *CS*, Vol. 8, No. 2, July 1968, pp. 23–63), referring to Edgar Mittelholzer's *Children of Kaywana*, 1952, *The Harrowing of Hubertus*, 1954 (reissued as *Kaywana Stock*, 1959), and *Kaywana Blood*, 1958.

[2] Louise Bennett, *Jamaica Labrish*, 1966, p. 211.

[3] A. L. Hendriks, 'What Colour Is a Kiss?', *Bim*, Vol. 13, No. 49, July–December 1969, p. 57.

[4] Paule Marshall, *The Chosen Place, the Timeless People*, 1969, p. 31.

[5] Garth St. Omer, *Shades of Grey*, 1968, p. 116.

[6] Frederic G. Cassidy and David DeCamp, 'Names for an Albino among Jamaican Negroes', *Names*, Vol. 14, 1966, pp. 129–33.

[7] F. A. Glasspole, 'Motto Had Nothing to Do with Miscegenation', and Alva Ramsay, 'Sportsman Calls for Multi-racial Queens', *West Indian Sportsman*, November–December 1969, pp. 22–3, and 39, respectively.

Colour appearance in the West Indies is not a matter of pigmentation alone; it involves a constellation of physical traits. Along with shade, the most important are hair type and facial structure ('looks'). Light skin, straight hair, thin lips, and narrow nose are considered 'good'; dark skin, kinky hair, thick lips, and flat nose are 'bad'. Complex formulae connect all these traits: middle-class Vincentians are said to be 'preoccupied with marrying lighter-skinned persons' in order to 'have nice straight-hair children.'[1] 'Good' hair may compensate for a dark skin; a light-coloured Guyanese father found his son's straight locks some consolation for the boy's swarthy complexion.[2] In Jamaica 'a dark person with "good" hair and features ranks above a fair person with "bad" hair and features.' But other traits do not erase the stigma of darkness; Henriques recalls that his upper middle-class family were derided as 'coolies' (East Indians) for their dark skins. European 'looks' generally count for more than straight hair, but colour classification requires a combined assessment:

A person might exhibit European-like features, but his hair might be more negroid than European. In such a case, his colour status in the society would be determined by the texture of his skin. This individual would rank above a person of similar complexion with 'good' hair, but whose features were more African.[3]

Physical features matter at all levels. Among Guyanese Negro villagers an anthropologist found 'the tendency to see beauty in a straight nose, a skin a shade lighter, or hair which is less "kinky" or "hard". Mothers even pull their children's noses to make them longer.'[4]

Among West Indian Creoles, however, pigmentation is the diagnostic trait, if not the sole determinant, of perceived colour. Hair and facial features seem to matter relatively less than in Latin America, where the presence of Indians and larger numbers of Europeans affect status judgements. It is the colour spectrum that West Indian racial names always denote, and gradations refer only to skin shade. A Jamaican beauty contest a decade ago selected a dozen winners of different hues, named for trees, fruit, and flowers of analogous colour.[5] Hair and features were not mentioned; earlier they might not even have been noticed. African faces in old West Indian engravings resemble dark-skinned Europeans. West Indians indeed often assume pigmentation to be the sole determinant of 'colour'; some pregnant women

---

[1] K. R. V. John, 'Footnotes on Slavery', *Flambeau*, No. 3, January 1966, pp. 10–14, ref. p. 14.

[2] Edgar Mittelholzer, *A Swarthy Boy*, 1963, pp. 117–18.

[3] Fernando Henriques, *Family and Colour in Jamaica*, 1953, p. 47.

[4] Raymond T. Smith, *The Negro Family in British Guiana*, 1956, p. 212.

[5] Ebony, Mahogany, Satinwood, Allspice, Sandalwood, Golden Apple, Jasmine, Pomegranate, Lotus, Appleblossom.

abstain from coffee and chocolate lest their babies be born darker.[1]

Details that differentiate the light from the white receive special attention. 'She had that flawless alabaster skin that white-skinned people with a small weak strain of Negro often showed', a novelist describes a near-elite Jamaican.[2] A Guyanese girl 'didn't look coloured,' writes another, but 'her skin took tan too easily, and the flesh on the inside of her thighs or under her arms—where the sun did not reach—was dead white', instead of tinged with pink.[3]

Yet for many pigmentation has been the least of the barriers. Blackness was the badge of slavery, but Europeans regarded it without the abhorrence they professed for other presumably African features. Today even those who exalt black as beautiful single out black skins for praise, seldom lauding African hair or 'looks'.

Preference for European appearance persists despite public avowals of multi-racial ideals. A secondary-school survey reveals that Jamaicans of all shades favour long, blond, straight or wavy hair and straight noses; those who lack them are dissatisfied with their own looks. In the last twenty years only the ideal skin colour has changed. 'Fair' or 'clear' complexions a shade or two removed from white are now most admired; a Jamaican ought not be too 'porky'. The author suggests that 'racial integration and equality . . . have brought about a compromise in the colour of the ideal', but the shift more probably mirrors changes in Caucasian aesthetic taste, notably sun-tanning. The preferred complexion is in any case far lighter than the typical West Indian dark brown, as far from the norm as are the desired straight hair and noses from the usual Jamaican. 'These early adolescents have been growing up at a time when racial equality is extolled,' the survey concludes, 'yet their concept of beauty is to a great extent congruent with the ideas of beauty reported . . . during the 1940s when colour discrimination was commonly evidenced.'[4] Their own personal experiences, reinforced by

[1] Eric Williams, *The Negro in the Caribbean*, 1942, p. 66. African beauty was, of course, judged by European standards (Edward Brathwaite, 'Creative Literature of the British West Indies during the Period of Slavery', *Savacou*, Vol. 1, No. 1, June 1970, pp. 46–73, ref. p. 51). In Brazil and Puerto Rico, by contrast, hair type is often a better social gauge than pigmentation. See Harmannus Hoetink, *The Two Variants in Caribbean Race Relations*, 1967, pp. 161–89; Donald Pierson, *Negroes in Brazil: A Study of Race Contact at Bahia*, 1967; Gilberto Freyre, *The Racial Factor in Contemporary Politics*, 1966, p. 25; Charles Wagley, *Amazon Town: A Study of Man in the Tropics*, 1953, pp. 130–1; Sidney W. Mintz, 'Cañamelar: The Subculture of a Rural Sugar Plantation Proletariat', in Julian H. Steward et al., *The People of Puerto Rico: A Study in Social Anthropology*, 1956, pp. 314–417, ref. p. 410; Charles C. Rogler, 'The Role of Semantics in the Study of Race Distance in Puerto Rico', *Social Forces*, Vol. 22, 1943–4, pp. 448–53.   [2] Peter Abrahams, *This Island Now*, 1966, p. 16.

[3] Christopher Nicole, *White Boy*, 1966, p. 66.

[4] Miller, 'Body Image, Physical Beauty and Colour among Jamaican Adolescents', p. 88.

mass media, continue to overshadow national mottoes and models of racial egalitarianism.

Physiognomy in all its aspects, however, is only one of many ways West Indians perceive and order colour. Ancestry, wealth, education, way of life, and associates all play important parts in colour ascription, as they do in social classification.

Where ancestry is a matter of common knowledge, it may outweigh appearance: in Grenada, for example, genealogy indicates class more precisely than physiognomy.[1] Birth counts for relatively less in larger or less traditionalist societies. But the interplay of ancestry and appearance takes place in even the most rigidly stratified orders. Endogamy is the general rule among Barbadian whites, but as an elite Creole remarked, 'No sensible person whose family has been here for over two hundred years would claim he's all white—for sure.' Episodes of miscegenation are openly recognized. 'Graham's not Negro', comments a Barbadian friend; 'his mother was, but he'd pass as white'—not mistaken for white, that is, but socially accepted as virtually white.[2]

Colour is very much a matter of culture. The saying that 'every rich Negro is a mulatto, every poor mulatto is a Negro' remains as true today as ever. Whatever their actual appearance, middle-class folk tend to be seen as 'coloured', lower-class folk as 'black'. Thus a black Jamaican maid identifies as 'white' a 'pitch-black' but elegantly dressed visitor with long, white gloves and a long, golden cigarette holder. Her dress made her white; 'the white gloves reaching up to her elbows, made her even whiter. The long holder, of course, made her snow-white.' Similarly, a black Jamaican professor one night awaits a friend in vain because the black college porter refuses to admit a black man. 'That's a peculiar rule', the professor comments, 'but then why do you let *me* in?' The porter could see the joke. 'You are not a black man, sir,' he smiled; 'you are a professor.' When a lady is elegant and a man a professor, in Jamaican eyes they are not black.[3]

Colour may ultimately depend on one's associates. 'I don't like too many dark people around me,' says a working-class Trinidadian; he wants to be with somebody 'to lighten up my complexion'.[4] 'The surest sign of a man's having arrived', a West Indian concludes, 'is the fact that he keeps company with people lighter in complexion than himself.'[5]

Variations in background and ways of life make distinctions between

[1] M. G. Smith, *Stratification in Grenada*, 1965.

[2] Raymond W. Mack, 'Race, Class and Power in Barbados', in Wendell Bell, ed., *The Democratic Revolution in the West Indies: Studies in Nationalism, Leadership, and the Belief in Progress*, 1967, pp. 140–64, ref. pp. 140, 160–1.

[3] Mikes, *Not by Sun Alone*, pp. 44–5.

[4] Lloyd Braithwaite, 'Social Stratification in Trinidad', p. 132.

[5] C. L. R. James, *The Case for West-Indian Self Government*, 1933, p. 9.

coloured and white almost as flexible as those between black and coloured. Some Trinidadians 'bear fairly marked Negroid characteristics but are by definition white', comments a local scholar. 'The term "Trinidad white" . . . indicat[es] that the person is not really white but passes for white in Trinidad society.' A Vincentian student relates that 'even plainly negro folk by virtue of the mixing with the Whites in clubs and organisations are counted as pass-for-Whites, or Vincentian Whites'.[1]

Nationalist and black-power pressures in one sense reverse colour ambitions. Today West Indians may opt for darker identities; lack of evidence has not prevented politically prominent Jamaicans from claiming African ancestry. A Barbadian, three-fourths white, runs for public office as a 'Negro', while his sister is a member of an 'exclusively white' club. With the same ancestry and appearance 'one has chosen to be white; the other prefers to be colored for the political advantages this offers in a predominantly colored society.'[2]

Culture and association thus strongly affect West Indian colour attribution. But appearance and descent remain intimately linked with status. An analysis of the Grenadian elite and middle class reveals a statistical association of 0·73 between status and genotype, of 0·68 between status and phenotype.

There are high positive correlations between light pigment and high status, medium pigment and medium status, dark pigment and low status. 'Poor whites' . . . are excluded from the elite on cultural and social grounds. The high-ranking dark families, in turn, owe their status to cultural and social identification with the elite.

Other circumstances do modify inherited colour criteria, 'but the limits within which these biological differences are overridden . . . are rather narrow; and as a rule, differences of pigment and status correspond'.[3]

SOCIAL INSTITUTIONS

West Indian classes are separated not merely by differences of colour and status, power and wealth; they also exhibit diverse cultural patterns and social frameworks. The legal, religious, educational, and

[1] Lloyd Braithwaite, 'Social Stratification in Trinidad', p. 88; John, 'Footnotes on Slavery', p. 14.

[2] Mack, 'Race, Class and Power in Barbados', p. 160.

[3] M. G. Smith, *Stratification in Grenada*, pp. 160, 166. A study in rural Jamaica likewise shows a high coefficient of correlation between colour and status (Robert A. Ellis, 'Color and Class in a Jamaican Market Town', *Sociology and Social Research*, Vol. 41, 1957, pp. 354–60, ref. p. 356). But colour emerges as 'less important than culture in depicting the critical boundaries in the social structure of Kingston' (Colin G. Clarke, 'Aspects of the Urban Geography of Kingston, Jamaica', 1967, Vol. I, p. 377).

family institutions of the elite connect only tangentially with most West Indian lives. The rural peasantry and urban proletariat are aware of elite mores and are encouraged to emulate them, but working-class life is mainly guided by institutions unlike those of the elite in structure, style, leadership, purpose, and ideology. The folk institutions give rise to new cultural distinctions, which social disjunctions intensify. All these differences are reflected in, and help to validate, class stereotypes.

The tensions aroused by these divergent institutions lie at the heart of social pluralism. It is not the differences alone, but also the common ground, the mutual hopes and fears, that shape West Indian social classes and personality. Elite, middle class, and folk have various stakes now in minimizing, now in maximizing, the gulfs that separate them.

Class distinctions in many societies tend to reinforce old differences and to create new ones. Where ascriptive stratification is negligible (as in the United States, except between blacks and whites) or where cultural integration is far reaching (as generally in Britain), these differences may be of minor consequence. But in the West Indies, notwithstanding the legal abolition of racial discrimination a century ago or more, the legacies of conquest and forced labour still set classes apart. Although European tradition is paramount among all classes, the culture and behaviour of the Caribbean elite and middle class and those of the rural peasantry and urban proletariat are highly disparate. The differences reflect great inequalities in circumstances, status, and access to power; to this day the West Indian working class are more bystanders than participants in the decisions, goals, and publicly expressed values of their own societies.

These disparities do not, however, totally isolate or seal off classes from one another. Ideals and structural bonds connect West Indians throughout the social hierarchy. But class links and resemblances, like their differences, may generate stress as well as solidarity. Let us examine these patterns in the context of specific West Indian institutions.

Legal institutions illustrate how the gulf between ideal and reality divides West Indian classes. If law in the British Caribbean is 'English law in all its stages of development', a West Indian judge finds it 'hopelessly inadequate to fulfil the requirements of our society [because it is] unrelated to the verities of our life, economy, and customs'.[1]

Though suffrage and jury service are in theory open to all, lawmaking and law-enforcing agencies remain in elite hands and reflect elite social views. One of these views is that the masses are innately criminal. The belief is self-validating; local legal codes interdict such

[1] K. W. Patchett, 'English Law in the West Indies', and Hugh Wooding, 'Foreword', in *Law in the West Indies: Some Recent Trends*, 1966, pp. 1–53 and vii–viii, respectively, ref. pp. 52 and vii.

customary folk 'practices' as bastardy, praedial larceny, obscenity, obeah, marijuana, and, indeed, poverty itself: the Speaker of the Jamaica House of Representatives argued that the West Kingston slums 'constitute perfect hide-outs for criminals and wrong-doers . . . due to the absence of streets and lights, the great number of labyrinthine tracks, and the numerous little shacks housing the dense population'.[1]

The masses see formal law as an elite weapon and the police as their natural enemies; the elite expect and get preferential treatment. 'When the apparent offender against the law is black the police approach is rude'; if he is white 'the police approach if they do at all with trepidation and respect and, at times, even with apology.' Lower-class blacks charged with an offence are assumed to be lying; 'only white people don't lie'.[2]

> In Laventille and John John [two Trinidad slum areas]
> They treat a man like a Viet-Cong
> Police hounding you everyday
> Magistrate want to jail you right away
> All because you come from behind the bridge.[3]

In court, unfamiliarity with the forms, if not outright illiteracy, gravely disadvantages the folk litigant. He finds legal aid costly and often futile; for the whole system seems to conspire against him. A colloquy in a Walcott play conveys the sense of being foredoomed by ignorance: 'My noble judges,' intones the prosecutor, 'when this crime has been categorically examined by due process of law, and when the motive of the hereby accused by whereas and adhoc shall be established without dychotomy, and long after we have perambulated through the labyrinthine bewilderment of the defendant's ignorance'. The judges applaud, and the prosecutor concludes: 'Ignorance is no excuse. Ignorance of the law is no excuse. Ignorance of one's own ignorance is no excuse. This is the prisoner. I will ask the prisoner to lift up his face. *Levez la tête ous!*'[4]—the minatory patois command accentuating the gulf between high and low.

---

[1] E. C. L. Parkinson, letter of 11 November, quoted in *Jamaica Daily Gleaner*, 20 November 1968, p. 16.

[2] Earl Lewis, 'Discrimination at Home', *Moko*, No. 12, 11 April 1969, p. 4; Augustus Ramrekersingh, 'Black Boy', *Moko*, No. 18, 4 July 1969, p. 3. See also Colin McGlashan, 'The Two Jamaicas', *Sunday Observer Review*, 23 November 1969, p. 25.

[3] A calypso by 'Young Creole', quoted in 'The Carnival Is Over', *Embryo*, 'After the Carnival' Supplement, n.d., p. S2.

[4] Derek Walcott, 'The Dream on Monkey Mountain', *CQ*, Vol. 14, Nos. 1 and 2, March–June 1968, pp. 110–26, ref. p. 116. A century ago a judge from Jamaica reported similar bias, noting 'gross neglect of duty by Attorneys towards their Clients when these are poor and practically powerless to do anything about it'. He had never heard 'of a labouring man having ever so just a complaint [against] his

The mass of West Indians regard law as 'an alien thing, not felt as applying to their daily life because there are so many basic points at which it runs counter to their habits of thought.'[1] Identifying law with elite oppression, they maintain a solid front against it. Embroiled country folk seldom invoke legal processes; law officers seeking presumed criminals meet unco-operative silence if not deliberate evasion—to be hunted by the police, whatever the cause, is reason enough for protection. 'Any West Indian criminal of working-class origins', remarks an observer, 'can count . . . on that fund of sympathy'.[2] Official encouragement to shoot suspects on sight, such as the Jamaican Prime Minister reputedly gave the police in 1970, may win middle-class support but hardly allays folk mistrust of police motives. 'An over-worked, underpaid and basically illiterate police force', a critic suggests, 'shares the same anarchic vision of life as the criminals it hunts down.'[3] Proficiency in undermining, disobeying, or circumventing the law gains young men status among their peers. Rural Haitians accept crime and delinquency as necessary forms of survival and value criminal skills like those of any artisan.[4]

Similar circumstances exist elsewhere, to be sure, even when folk and elite are ethnically alike, as for instance in the Appalachian Mountains of the United States. Wealth and class in most countries affect the likelihood of apprehension, access to legal aid, availability of bail, probability of conviction, and severity of punishment. What distinguishes Caribbean legal systems is that those discriminated against constitute the great majority of West Indians. Their own habitual mode of life, officially vilified for its illegal or extra-legal transgressions, is validated for them by a separate institutional system.

Some aspects of this alternate legal structure are rooted in the custom of slave courts; others developed after emancipation, outside the nexus of estates and towns. Systems of peasant land tenure, for example, are seamed with unwritten but binding rules allocating family rights to house sites, to produce, to pasturage, and to the division of acreage and tree crops among descendants—rules at variance with the European real estate and inheritance codes in local statute books.

Widespread adherence to uncodified family rights makes many legal

Lawyer for gross neglect of duty taking any steps. . . . He has no practical remedy' (Noelle Chutkan, 'The Administration of Justice in Jamaica as a Contributing Factor to the Morant Bay Riot of 1865', 1969, pp. 19–20).

[1] 'The Conditions Affecting Demand', *WIE*, Vol. 2, No. 10, April 1960, p. 7.

[2] Derek Bickerton, *The Murders of Boysie Singh*, 1962, p. 155.

[3] 'Sans humanité: Violence in Jamaica—Part II', *Moko*, No. 14, 9 April 1969, pp. 3–4.

[4] Emerson Douyon, 'La délinquence juvenile en Haïti', *Transcultural Psychiatric Research Review and Newsletter*, Vol. V, April 1968, pp. 75–7. See also Peter J. Wilson, 'The Possibilities of Caribbean Social Organization' [1968].

sanctions hazardous, if not impossible, to enforce. Local authorities condemn 'family land' tenure as uneconomic, wasteful, a prime cause of soil exhaustion and erosion, an obstacle to agricultural modernization; but to outlaw it would disrupt kinship ties, multiply litigation beyond court capacities, and jeopardize untold smallholdings.[1]

Folk institutions override formal law in still other ways. Even under colonial rule, peasant and working-class solidarity hampered law enforcement. Official action against illicit distillers, tax defaulters, rent-delinquent tenants, and contraband smugglers often met community resistance. The police did not always win the resulting frays. Local juries have refused to convict folk arrested for fomenting disorder; folk solidarity or fear of local reprisal sometimes won acquittals even when the venue was moved to another territory. Prosecution failures taught a few attorneys-general and police chiefs to move slowly and cautiously against 'transgressions' validated by local custom.

The connection with colonial rule made police service traditionally unpopular in West Indian territories. Compulsory free-coloured enlistment soured Trinidadians on police careers from the start (1797), and as late as 1922, the majority of the Trinidad police force were from other islands.[2] Universal suffrage and self-government have further intimidated Caribbean police forces. Mass leaders incite their followers, activate armed bands, and alarm law enforcers with threats of uprisings among the poor and the disaffected. In Jamaica the two major political parties accuse each other of suborning the police. No cause more readily enlists the sympathy and aid of politicians than complaints of police victimization; and popular leaders themselves enjoy, and are condoned for, flouting the law. During recent disturbances in Montego Bay, which reflected folk hostility toward the tourist industry, the Jamaican constabulary was 'unable to find enough "natives" willing to protect the property of foreigners. . . . Looting still takes place', reported a local Jamaican journal, because 'the firemen and police are

---

[1] A. de K. Frampton, 'Land Tenure in Relation to the British West Indies', *Caribbean Economic Review*, Vol. IV, Nos. 1 and 2, December 1952, pp. 113–39; Edith Clarke, 'Land Tenure and the Family in Four Selected Communities in Jamaica', *SES*, Vol. 1, No. 4, August 1953, pp. 81–118; idem, *My Mother Who Fathered Me: A Study of the Family in Three Selected Communities in Jamaica*, 1957, pp. 33–72; Arthur Thelwell, *Report on Squatter Problem and Land Use, Island of Dominica*, 1950; Herman J. Finkel, 'Patterns of Land Tenure in the Leeward and Windward Islands and Their Relevance to Problems of Agricultural Development in the West Indies', *Economic Geography*, Vol. 40, 1964, pp. 163–72; M. G. Smith, 'The Transformation of Land Rights by Transmission in Carriacou', *SES*, Vol. 5, 1956, pp. 103–38; Guy Lasserre, 'Petite propriété et réforme foncière aux Antilles françaises', *Colloque Internationale Centre de la Recherche Scientifique*, 1965, pp. 109–24.

[2] Carlton Robert Ottley, *A Historical Account of the Trinidad and Tobago Police Force*, 1964, pp. 17, 126. 'To be a policeman was for the Trinidadian a great disgrace' (ibid., p. 106).

more sympathetic to the sufferers than to the propertied and privileged.'[1]

But racial bitterness poses less of a problem in Caribbean law enforcement than in the United States, where an essentially white police force often clashes with a black populace. In the West Indies such collisions are limited to expatriate troop actions. Up to a generation ago, most police chiefs and high-ranking officers were white expatriates, but the bulk of the police have long been black. Comparing his native Virgin Islands with Harlem, the black leader Roy Innis proudly recalls that on the island his 'father was a cop, and the symbol of authority.'[2]

Family forms exemplify the divergence of West Indian social structure and attitudes. Monogamy is the ideal type for all classes, but each approaches it by a different route and to a different degree. Formal marriage among rural folk is commonly deferred until the man can afford to build or buy a house, put on an elaborate wedding, and support a wife who need not go out to work. Because young men rarely command such resources, a legal ceremony often marks a culmination rather than the commencement of a relationship. Although two out of three West Indian children are born illegitimate, most parents eventually wed; four out of five British West Indians over 65 are, or have been, married.[3]

In this respect, as in many others, West Indian folk practice diverges from that of the elite and middle class. But the differences can only be assessed in the context of behaviour patterns they share—patterns in many ways unlike contemporary American or European norms. The Creole family characteristically includes widely ramified kindred. It is not an extended family in the communal sense, but rather a loose network that recognizes and links even fourth and fifth cousins. Geographical distance never wholly severs these bonds; a relative who returns after any length of time may claim family attention, respect, or support.

Such linkages animate the entire social hierarchy. Elite, middle class, and folk keep up to date on their relations' marriages, offspring, and collateral connections. Among Martinican *békés*, 'the name of a family immediately identifies an individual, to the detriment of any individuality', states an anthropologist. 'This great family spirit involves all

---

[1] 'Foreign Whites Patrol Mobay', *Abeng*, 15 February 1969, p. 4.

[2] Alex Poinsett, 'Roy Innis: Nation Builder', *Ebony*, October 1969, p. 170.

[3] William Goode, 'Illegitimacy in the Caribbean Social Structure', *American Sociological Review*, Vol. 25, 1960, pp. 21–30, ref. p. 25, based on the 1943–6 West Indian censuses. Edith Clarke's *My Mother Who Fathered Me* is the pioneer study in this realm; the voluminous literature is summarized in M. G. Smith's 'Introduction' to the second edition of her book (1966), pp. i–xliv. See also R. T. Smith, *The Negro Family in British Guiana*; and Sidney W. Mintz and William Davenport, eds., 'Caribbean Social Organization', *SES*, Vol. 10, No. 4, 1961.

the generations including the allied branches. Many parties and gatherings are held for members of the extended family only, and holidays as well as vacations are passed together.'[1]

Elite Creoles who must demonstrate unequivocal white ancestry are most conspicuously familial, but descent connotes status in the coloured middle class as well. A Dominican spells out some consequences of small-island relationships:

Dedication to the family tree makes some people . . . happy in the knowledge that they belong to a family with a great tradition. . . . Searching out for those people in that large family circle (which is so closely knit) in positions of influence and great wealth, [people] finding themselves in difficulties will often summon one of the species in a high office to intercede on their behalf in order to preserve the good name of the family. . . . Quite a number . . . would like to make their way through life merely by recalling what their father may (or may not) have done . . . hundreds of years ago.[2]

Even the peasantry are assiduous genealogists, well informed about connections the elite and middle class might prefer to forget. Because most West Indian societies are small, insular, and highly stratified, distant relatives are apt to be literally unavoidable.

Relations between man and wife, parent and child, also bear a distinctive West Indian stamp. Married or not, West Indian men and women spend little leisure time together. Clubs, gatherings, outings, games, are separated by sex at all social levels. Among the folk, men typically congregate at bars and rum shops, in front-room stores, under cotton or palm trees, and on street corners; women meet at home, at market, and in the churches. Although the sexes are not stringently segregated, in the Latin American and Mediterranean fashion, regular companionship between men and women is rare.

The tie between parents and children—especially mothers and sons— is closer and more durable than that between most marital partners. Young men often continue to depend on maternal care well into their twenties and thirties, and in some communities 'a man rarely thinks of marrying so long as he has [his mother] to look after his meals, mend his clothes, and care for his living quarters.'[3] West Indians of all classes

---

[1] Kovats-Beaudoux, 'Une minorité dominante', pp. 101–2. See also H. Orlando Patterson, 'The Ritual of Cricket', *JJ*, Vol. 3, No. 1, March 1969, pp. 22–5.

[2] C. A. Maynard, 'A Carricature of a Small Society', *Dawnlit*, Vol. I, No. 2, March 1962, pp. 16–17, 31, ref. p. 16.

[3] Peter J. Wilson, 'Reputation and Respectability: A Suggestion for Caribbean Ethnology', *Man*, N.S., Vol. 4, No. 1, March 1969, pp. 70–84, ref. pp. 79–81. On the separation of the sexes, see Yehudi Cohen, 'Adolescent Conflict in a Jamaican Community' [1955], in his *Social Structure and Personality: A Casebook*, 1961, pp. 167–81; idem, 'Character Formation and Social Structure in a Jamaican Community', *Psychiatry*, Vol. 18, 1955, pp. 275–96. The symbiosis between mother and child in

regard children as blessings. Proud to give birth, happy to cherish babies, ready to make sacrifices for a child's future, parents look forward to support and companionship in old age. 'If you have enough children,' a Barbadian woman surmises, 'one is bound to turn out good and keep you when you're old'.[1] Where 'lonely old people in England take in dogs or cats', remarks a West Indian, 'lonely old people in Jamaica take in children.'[2]

Upbringing is felt to require physical chastisement; parents regularly resort to the rod. Outsiders may interpret frequent beatings as symptoms of parental insecurity, but West Indians consider them normal and appropriate. Flogging is considered essential not only for effective punishment but for education; teachers vie with parents as disciplinarians. Beatings are no evidence of cruelty, opines a local authority: 'people of nearly all classes in Jamaica . . . who are very violent with children at any other given moment are often at other times very loving and warmhearted.'[3] West Indians also approve a show of authority from man to wife: 'They don't love you 'less they beat you', as the saying goes.[4] In New York, West Indian husbands a generation ago gained a reputation for savage cruelty; Harlemites wondered why their women put up with it. Black Americans continue to view West Indian families as 'slaves to the man of the house'; West Indians say that 'American Negroes do not discipline their children.'[5]

Martinique is said to militate against the acquisition of theoretical and intellectual knowledge. And 'under the influence of maternal care so prominent in Martinique, the young man does not really feel the need to find work. His mother takes care of him just as in his early childhood, trying to make his daily life as easy as possible in this prolonged infancy' (Jean-Luc Morel, 'Jeunesse et emploi: de l'insertion des jeunes martiniquais dans le milieu social', *CERAG*, No. 13, 1968, pp. 86, 57). Eva E. Abraham–van der Mark, 'Yu'i mama: enkele facetten van gezinsstructuur op Curaçao (1969) discusses the importance of the maternal link in Curaçao.

[1] Brian Spear, 'Family Planning in Barbados', *New Society*, Vol. 14, 4 September 1969, p. 357.

[2] Noel White, 'To Study about African Culture', *Abeng*, 27 September 1969, p. 2.

[3] John Figueroa, 'Education for Jamaica's Needs', *CQ*, Vol. 15, No. 1, March 1969, pp. 5–33, ref. p. 30.

[4] Roger D. Abrahams, 'The Shaping of Folklore Traditions in the British West Indies', *Journal of Inter-American Studies*, Vol. IX, 1967, pp. 456–80, ref. p. 475. 'The amount of beating, whipping and flogging in the life of the West Indian is really startling to the outsider' (ibid.). See also Edward Seaga, 'Parent-Teacher Relationships in a Jamaican Village', *SES*, Vol. 4, 1955, pp. 289–302, ref. pp. 292–3; Cohen, 'Character Formation and Social Structure in a Jamaican Community', pp. 278–81.

[5] Garrie Ward Moore, 'A Study of a Group of West Indian Negroes in New York City', 1923, p. 5, cited in Gilbert Osofsky, *Harlem: The Making of a Ghetto: Negro New York, 1890–1930*, 1968, p. 134. Osofsky notes that West Indian families are patriarchal and that men don't help with domestic chores (ibid.). See also John Jasper Spurling, *Social Relationships between American Negroes and West Indian Negroes in a Long Island Community*, 1969, pp. 60–1.

These traits—social distance between the sexes, demonstrative love mingled with continual chastisement—are residual forms of behaviour once characteristic of both slavery and earlier western society. Victorian or pre-Victorian patterns can be seen in these as in many other aspects of West Indian life. But the degree and nature of the residue differ from class to class.

Certain elite habits clearly antedate Victorianism. During slavery white men customarily took 'housekeepers'—brown girls for planters and colonial officials, black for overseers and underlings. When slavery ended and nineteenth-century moral standards filtered into the Caribbean, concubinage became less general and open, but it remains common. European officials and professionals today are apt to arrive married or to wed a West Indian rather than merely to take a mistress. But among white Creoles the double standard still prevails: girls must be chaste and boys adventurous, wives strictly monogamous and husbands free to roam.

Such arrangements are simple for the non-elite St. Barthois: white women stay shut up at home; white men consort with non-white women in other islands. Martinican *békés* maintain seventeenth-century mores: family heads arrange marriages, paternal control is strict and absolute, women remain cloistered, divorce is unheard of. The men keep coloured or black mistresses. Their liaisons were once frankly recognized, and coloured offspring were brought into family enterprises, linking *béké* and middle-class interests. This open avowal of closeness is now taboo, 'but a large number of *békés*, married or not, have coloured mistresses, and this fact is known and admitted. It is only necessary to avoid scandals.'[1]

European Christianity likewise once accepted the coexistence of legitimate with informal, temporary, and sometimes plural sexual unions. Spanish common law distinguished, for inheritance, between the offspring of common-law and of casual unions, and recognition was extended even to the natural heirs of priests and married men; dual marital arrangements were also common in France and Britain. But in the West Indies such alternative forms, and the double standard underlying them, have lasted much longer than in Europe. Their universality and durability stem in large measure from sexual exploitation by whites and, when marriage was forbidden, from consensual slave mating systems.[2]

---

[1] Kovats-Beaudoux, 'Une minorité dominante', p. 114.

[2] See M. G. Smith, *West Indian Family Structure*, 1962, pp. 259–60; and idem, 'Introduction', in Edith Clarke, *My Mother Who Fathered Me*, 2nd ed., pp. i–xliv. For some European antecedents, see Woodrow Borah and Sherburne F. Cook, 'Marriage and Legitimacy in Mexican Culture: Mexico and California', *California Law Review*, Vol. LIV, 1966, pp. 946–1008, ref. pp. 950–1, 980.

Few aspects of Caribbean life, however, are more variously explained or keenly debated than the origins of Creole folk family structure. Local elites habitually accounted for them in terms of 'inherent Negro promiscuity' or reversions to African 'customs', racialist views still current. Some scholars, with Herskovits, see the mother-centred West Indian family, however much creolized, as a West African tribal heritage, though much of West Africa was in fact traditionally patriarchial and patrifocal. Others contend that African family structure did not survive enslavement and have remarked on West Indian folk similarities to early European family systems. Lower-class Barbadians may practise some of the same marriage customs as the medieval English. But in the absence of historical connection this fact would not demonstrate European origin any more than an Ashanti similarity would prove West African origin.[1]

Questions of origin have taken on a latter-day significance with the search for 'heritage'. But they tend to obscure rather than to illuminate comprehension of the dynamics of West Indian family life. To understand current patterns, one must turn to the slave past and to the pressures of the present. The example set by white elite males, and widespread impoverishment among the masses, go far to account for the reluctance to marry and the high rates of illegitimacy prevalent throughout West Indian society. The occasional sponsors of monogamy met little success in the face of prevailing mores. Slaves looked to masters as models to emulate, as one official was told when he advised a slave to marry: 'Massa, you telly me to marry one wife, which is no good! You no tinky I see you buckra no content wid one, two, tree, or four wifes'.[2]

Whites also set standards of paternal irresponsibility. 'Every attempt to get a Bastardy Bill through the House of Assembly has failed, simply because honourable members were unwilling to cut a stick which they knew would be used for their own backs.'[3] A Jamaican girl in 1870 thought it pointless to seek a court order to claim support for her child; for 'bukras had so many bastards themselves, they would never make

---

[1] Donald W. Hogg, review of Greenfield, *English Rustics in Black Skins*, in *CS*, Vol. 9, No. 1, April 1969, pp. 84–5. For the African heritage debate, see Melville J. Herskovits, *The Myth of the Negro Past* [1941], idem, 'Problem, Method, and Theory in Afroamerican Studies' [1945], and 'The Ahistorical Approach to Afroamerican Studies: A Critique' [1960], both in his *The New World Negro: Selected Papers in Afroamerican Studies*, 1966, pp. 43–61 and 122–34, respectively; M. G. Smith, 'A Framework for Caribbean Studies' [1955], in his *The Plural Society in the British West Indies*, especially pp. 24–37.

[2] Slave of Henry Shirley, quoted in Maria Nugent, *Lady Nugent's Journal* (Philip Wright, ed.), 1966, p. 87.

[3] Henry Clarke, letter to *The Times*, quoted in Sydney Olivier, *The Myth of Governor Eyre*, 1933, p. 343.

negroes maintain their bastards'.[1] The failure of the Jamaican mass marriage campaign of the late 1940s underscored the futility of moral exhortation by an elite itself notorious for dual family arrangements. Slavery taught West Indians to admire formal marriage and paternal responsibility in theory and to eschew them in practice.

Middle-class mating and family patterns emulate those of the elite. The French Antillean coloured bourgeoisie, like the *békes*, maintain both wives and mistresses. Small-island men of affairs, after the fashion of slave-owning planters, abjure marriage, take whatever women they desire, and father as many children as possible. Half the children in Dominica are reputedly fathered by Shillingfords, with several men of the name accounting for over a hundred offspring each. Beneath a veneer of shocked respectability, many fellow islanders vicariously enjoy the fabulous sexual reputations, the arrogant disregard for genteel convention, and the progenitive feats of these patriarchs. The habit of *droit de seigneur* pervades business and other establishments. Throughout the West Indies, hopes of promotion or fears of disfavour constrain shop girls, clerks, and teachers to sleep with their employers or superiors. 'For a girl to work in a certain business place her answer must never be NO', writes a small-island correspondent; 'I am speaking from experience'.[2]

The double standard rules the middle class still more strictly. No breath of scandal may tarnish a married woman's reputation. Whether respectable or profligate, the husband and father has complete authority in the home. Antiquated moral and religious exhortations bolster middle-class family standards, and the prevalence of spinsters extends the Victorian parallel. The West Indies are infested with maiden ladies, socially precluded from concubinage or casual affairs, who devote themselves to spoiling their nieces and nephews, promoting good works, and arbitering class mores.

Mating patterns among the peasantry and urban working class typically follow a sequential pattern. A young man begins by visiting a girl at home; the girl's family, reluctantly or not, often rears the offspring of this more or less casual union, while the mother takes domestic or other work in town. After one or more such 'visiting' relationships, a couple enters without ceremony into what is variously

[1] Quoted in the Rev. Henry Clarke to the Hon. Edward Rushworth, 10 February 1870, Letterbook 9, No. 5, Edith Clarke Papers. See also Molly Green Huggins, *Too Much to Tell*, 1967, pp. 106, 116.

[2] 'Our Young Women', letter signed 'A Married One', *Dominica Star*, 7 September 1968, p. 13. See also Edgar Mittelholzer, *With a Carib Eye*, 1958, pp. 125–7. For similar elite behaviour, see Hugh Carlton Greene, 'On the Track of Great Uncle Charles', *History Today*, Vol. XX, No. 1, January 1970, pp. 61–3; André Breton with André Masson, *Martinique charmeuse de serpents*, 1948, p. 74. Comparable male attitudes in rural Trinidad are detailed by Morris Freilich, 'Sex, Secrets, and Systems', in Stanford N. Gerber, ed., *The Family in the Caribbean*, 1968, pp. 47–62.

called a 'keeper union', 'faithful concubinage', or 'common-law marriage'. In such a consensual union the woman frequently owns or rents the house, and the household includes her children by former partners. Formal marriage may follow, but often not until late in life; marriage is felt to require an established position in the community and maintenance of the wife 'in style'.

These patterns of course vary with locale. Formal marriage is more usual and comes earlier for folk in small homogeneous islands and in formally Catholic territories. However, when Dominica, nine-tenths Catholic, recorded 82 per cent illegitimate births in 1969 one local commentator mockingly suspected that 'the 18% legitimate "drop outs" . . . were probably Protestant spoil-sports.'[1] Community norms also differ within any one island. In Jamaica casual unions are the rule among part-time, migrant labourers in a sugar-estate area, whereas among peasant farmers legal and 'keeper' unions prevail in proportions that vary with land ownership and productivity.

Manifold results flow from these circumstances. Throughout the West Indies the need to supplement livelihoods with temporary migrant labour leaves women in charge of households much of the time. Many children are raised solely by women—a condition made memorable in the phrase 'my mother who fathered me'. There are mothers who care for children but lack regular male support, grandmothers who bring up daughters' offspring, legal or common-law wives whose husbands are away seasonally or permanently. Men frequently lack authority even when they are physically present; common-law unions are in general more egalitarian than marriages. The women in such relationships are independent agents, not subservient chattels. They are apt to make the important decisions about children, jobs, and so on, abetted by their own relatives; those on the man's side play less of a part.

Formal marriage may have definite drawbacks for both partners. For women it entails a loss of equality, less freedom to move about, fewer contacts, more loneliness. For men it means an economic burden, a less carefree or venturesome style of life, a more demanding and perhaps less satisfying relationship. Martinican peasants complain that women who are docile and agreeable before marriage, afterwards become arrogant and demanding.[2] Married women in Jamaica are said to insist on material evidence of their change in status, 'for example, shoes,

[1] Polygraph's Fun Column, *Dominica Star*, 10 January 1970, p. 7. In Haiti, by contrast, 'marriage is still dominated by the parents who choose their children's mates from among their own friends. . . . The traditional family is still the patriarchal type', but now that authority is being transferred to the mother the father is becoming 'increasingly aggressive' (Hubert de Ronceray, 'Le changement social dans les familles haïtiennes: première partie: familles urbaines', *Cahiers du CHISS*, Vol. 3, No. 4, May 1969, pp. 1–34, ref. pp. 6, 24).

[2] Michael M. Horowitz, *Morne-Paysan: Peasant Village in Martinique*, 1967, pp. 54–5.

maid service, and so on.'[1] The wife who quits her job and becomes a drone is immortalized in the tale of the Trinidadian girl who at long last married her lover and thenceforth went about singing 'Now My Daily Task is O'er'.[2]

Yet the advantages of marriage often outweigh these perils. Status induces many young women to wed; young men are more apt to avoid tying themselves down. A man who waits too long, however, may be permanently left out. The West Indian mother can usually count on her children's support; a father can command it only by regularizing the relationship.

Obligation to the father varies with how much he has been around. . . . As time goes on, the non-participating father finds it increasingly difficult to get a foothold in any family group. Each time he fails in a duty, the woman learns better how to do without him. . . . In the end the tables are completely turned and when he wants to start participating, he is no longer wanted. . . . The old bachelor is a pathetic creature, at best tolerated by an old girl-friend or a relative in the status of near-beggar.[3]

The practical advantages of legitimacy also favour marriage. At the baptism of illegitimate children in Martinique it is customary to propose a toast 'que le prochain soit légitime'. Legitimate birth confers social but not moral status; the working class attaches no shame or condemnation to illegitimacy. Yet many West Indians acquire legitimacy retroactively. Life-long partners may marry in old age as much to please their children as themselves; many weddings mark the birth of a first grandchild, others are celebrated as a religious duty when death nears. *Ex post facto* or otherwise, legitimacy may be essential to secure an inheritance. Under the *Code Napoléon* of 1802, illegitimate French Antilleans inherit only half as much from parents as do legitimate offspring. In Barbados, if no legitimate heirs appear, intestate property reverts to the deceased's siblings; common-law wives and illegitimate children receive nothing. Acknowledgement of paternity helps assure maintenance but is no aid to inheritance; only a written will can leave property to an illegitimate child, since 'where family inheritance rules exist, those children will have no claim.'[4]

---

[1] 'Report of Study Group VI', in George Cumper, ed., *Report of the Conference on Social Development Held at the University College of the West Indies*, 1961, p. 170.

[2] Hyman Rodman, 'Marital Relationships in a Trinidad Village', *Marriage and Family Living*, Vol. 23, 1961, pp. 166–70, ref. p. 169.

[3] Katrin FitzHerbert, *West Indian Children in London*, 1967, p. 26.

[4] Patchett, 'English Law in the West Indies', p. 31. Of two hundred Negro women interviewed in Trinidad, only one-fifth reported any family stigma against illegitimacy, but 95 per cent thought it very important to marry for the purpose of conferring legitimacy on children (Robert R. Bell, 'Marriage and Family Differences among Lower-class Negro and East Indian Women in Trinidad', *Race*, Vol. XII, 1970–1, pp. 59–73, ref. pp. 68–9).

Whereas illegitimacy carries little social stigma among the folk, the middle class profess to regard it as shameful. They blame the lower class for the supposed European image of West Indians as promiscuous and immoral. Dissociation enhances their own status; only the elite male, whose social position is assured, can afford a less rigid morality.

Divergent class behaviour and attitudes about family life are not, of course, unique to the Caribbean. Black ghetto dwellers in the United States, like West Indian folk, have been stigmatized for illegitimacy, broken homes, mother-centred families, absent fathers, and inadequate father images. Structurally similar, the heritage of slavery and discrimination is evaluated quite differently in the two areas. Unlike West Indians, both black and white Americans have, until recently, viewed departures from white norms as aberrant or pathological. Critics of the Moynihan Report, for example, concentrated on finding or imputing moral condemnation to disclosures about mother-centred Negro families, though the fact that white families at similar economic levels are similarly 'broken' invalidates 'any social-psychological pattern of matriarchy peculiarly characteristic of the Negro family'.[1]

In the West Indies the middle class scores illegitimacy as immoral and irresponsible, but most Creoles take for granted the difference between elite and folk family patterns, and few regard the latter as aberrant or pathological. All West Indians 'appear to subscribe in theory to a Christian, God fearing ideal of monogamy and family unity', as one anthropologist puts it, 'yet only a very small proportion of all households act out this ideal, or even make much of an effort to do so'.[2] The folk are, after all, the overwhelming majority; what they do is at least statistically normative. Illegitimacy and the mother-centred home are not symptoms of social disorganization; they are accepted features of folk life. The 'absent father' may affect West Indian personality, but

[1] Herbert H. Hyman and John Shelton Reed, '"Black Matriarchy" Reconsidered: Evidence from Secondary Analysis of Sample Surveys', *Public Opinion Quarterly*, Vol. 33, 1969, pp. 346–54, ref. pp. 346, 352. The loose use of the terms 'matrifocal', 'matrilocal', and 'matriarchal' adds to the confusion of the whole issue. The extent to which black American families express mainstream patrifocal values is often unrecognized or underestimated by white interviewers and social scientists unfamiliar with ghetto subcultures (Valentine, 'Blackston', pp. 48–9). Moreover, matrifocality and consensual unions 'turn out to be traits . . . in many parts of the world and among peoples who have had no history of slavery' (Oscar Lewis, *A Study of Slum Culture: Backgrounds for La Vida*, 1968, p. 19). For a general discussion, see Nancie L. González, 'Toward a Definition of Matrifocality', in Whitten and Szwed, eds., *Afro-American Anthropology*, pp. 231–44.

[2] Peter J. Wilson, 'Caribbean Crews: Some Unconsidered Aspects of Social Structure', 1967, pp. 8–9. For an opposing view, that the lower class regard non-legal marriage as deviant, see Goode, 'Illegitimacy in the Caribbean Social Structure', pp. 21–30; and Judith Blake with J. Mayone Stycos and Kingsley Davis, *Family Structure in Jamaica: The Social Context of Reproduction*, 1961.

this is not locally seen to be psychologically crippling, as in the United States, much less a self-perpetuating 'tangle of pathology', in Moynihan's notorious phrase.[1] To have a father present in the home may be useful, but in the Caribbean context a fatherless household is no predictor of social deviance or, necessarily, of mental ill-health. Whether or not the father is present, the child's closest ties are with the mother and her kin. 'Whenever the child is exposed to a model of adult male behaviour,' suggests one observer, 'it is normally self-reliant and achievement oriented.'[2] In sum, when family structure in the United States departs from the middle-class ideals, personality disorganization and community dislocation are assumed to follow. Caribbean family structure, though more remote from middle-class ideals, permits adjustments to a wider range of normative options.

Religious faith and practice likewise differ sharply from class to class throughout the Caribbean. Nominally Christian and temperamentally agnostic, West Indian elites attend church less as a religious duty than to affirm their role as social, if no longer as national, exemplars. Middle-class Protestants take religion more seriously; theirs is a literal, not a perfunctory, creed and, whatever their behaviour, a symbol of private as well as public morality. Denominational adherence reflects Anglican elitism, or Methodist, Baptist, and Presbyterian missionary efforts. In whatever sect, doctrine is more fundamentalist, church attendance more regular, and religion more relevant to everyday life among the middle class than the elite, except where both are strictly Roman Catholic.

Most working-class Creoles are no less formally Christian than the elite and middle class, but the institutional structures, systems of belief, and emotional significance of religious faith differ profoundly. Carib-

[1] West Indian folk view as illegitimate only the offspring of promiscuous sexual relationships. Children of other extra-residential unions are maintained by their fathers for as long as the law requires. Children of consensual unions are subject to full paternal rights and responsibilities (M. G. Smith, *West Indian Family Structure*, pp. 221–2; Yehudi A. Cohen, 'Structure and Function: Family Organization and Socialization in a Jamaican Community', *AA*, Vol. 58, 1956, pp. 664–86, ref. pp. 668–70). See also Hazel Du Bois, 'Working Mothers and Absent Fathers: Family Organization in the Caribbean', 1964. On Moynihan's characterizations of black culture and institutions, see Charles A. Valentine, *Culture and Poverty: Critique and Counter-Proposals*, 1968; Ira Katznelson, 'White Social Science and the Black Man's World', *Race Today*, Vol. 2, 1970, pp. 47–8; Seymour Parker and Robert J. Kleiner, 'The Culture of Poverty: An Adjustive Dimension', *AA*, Vol. 72, 1970, pp. 5:6–27. Virginia Heyer Young, 'Family and Childhood in a Southern Negro Community', *AA*, Vol. 72, 1970, pp. 269–88, documents a lack of concern about illegitimacy in the rural South resembling Caribbean attitudes (p. 274); the fondness for young children and the degree of aggression also duplicate West Indian patterns (pp. 283–7).

[2] Carole Yawney, 'Drinking Patterns and Alcoholism in Trinidad', in Frances Henry, ed., *McGill Studies in Caribbean Anthropology*, 1969, pp. 34–48, ref. pp. 41–2.

bean peasantries and proletariats combine traditional, evangelical, and fundamentalist forms of Christianity with revivalism and spiritualism. Their deity is accessible to direct persuasion. They believe both in salvation by faith and in a spirit world, where the dead possess supernatural powers and mediate among the living. Folk sects—Pentecostal, Seventh Day Adventist, Shouter, Pocomania, Vodun—demand active congregational participation. Their rites frequently generate intense emotions, often culminating in group-induced spirit possession and public conversion.

Generally transitional between African religions and formal Christianity, folk sects have various historical antecedents. Revival, Revival Zion, Pocomania, Convince, and other Jamaican Afro-Christian cults stem from a revivalist movement sparked by 'Native Baptist' slaves of Loyalist refugees from the American Revolution. By contrast, Trinidad's Shouters, or Spiritual Baptists, remained in established denominations and shunned revivalism, resembling American Negro Baptist and Methodist sects in their more orthodox behaviour.[1]

Denominational choices also reflect church colonialism. Native Baptists and other cults flourished in Protestant territories partly because formal Christian creeds rebuffed non-white ministers even for non-white congregations. The Catholic Church still treats the French Antilles and the French-speaking British Windwards as mission stations to be staffed with clergy from Irish, Flemish, and Canadian orders. Trinidad, too, was supplied by Dominican Fathers 'who were first of all French and then Irish and hence almost inevitably white, [and] it is only quite recently that the Church has reached the point where there are sufficient local Secular priests to consider a new arrangement.'[2] Black-power demonstrations in the Port-of-Spain cathedral reflected long-standing resentment against the structure of white religious domination.

African and other non-Christian features persist in West Indian folk religion but are greatly modified by liturgical syncretism. Shango in Grenada and Trinidad blends African deities and Christian saints. In Haiti the Christian deity *Bondieu* heads the Vodun hierarchy; the powers invoked, the *loa*, can be identified as specific saints; Catholic services may begin with the Vodun prayer for the dead. The Church

[1] George Eaton Simpson, 'Baptismal, "Mourning", and "Building" Ceremonies of the Shouters in Trinidad', *Journal of American Folklore*, Vol. 79, 1966, pp. 537–50, ref. pp. 538, 541, 548. The Trinidad Shouters did, in fact, practise spirit possession, though this was proscribed by law from 1917 until 1951, so that the sect's regular services had to be conventionally Baptist (Melville J. Herskovits and Frances S. Herskovits, *Trinidad Village*, 1947, pp. 190–223; George Eaton Simpson, 'The Shango Cult in Trinidad', 1965, especially p. 79).

[2] Gilbert Boyd Reid, 'Answer Me That! and Fr. Boyd-Reid Talks about Church in Trinidad', *Trinidad Sunday Guardian*, 8 March 1970, p. 10.

long encouraged some of these amalgamations. But Christianity in Haiti, unlike the rest of the Caribbean, is superficial; Vodun, now the official state creed, is a comprehensive system influencing most aspects of life. The essentially foreign character of the Catholic Church in Haiti, where the local coloured elite preferred French priests to locals, helps to account for its weakness against Vodun.

Rather than rival religious systems, the West Indies exhibits a continuum fusing African and other elements with Christian faith. In using the 'ticket-and-leader' system Baptist circuit-riders in nineteenth-century Jamaica themselves moved unwittingly toward Afro-Christian synthesis; the peasantry were said to regard the tickets, designed to control church dues and attendance, as fetishes equivalent to passports to heaven. Missionaries were also confused about the roles played by Obeah and Myalism. Obeah manipulates evil spirits through black magic, and the Jamaican folk fought Obeah with Myalism, the folk religion of the Ashanti. But Baptist and Methodist missionaries, assuming Obeah to be 'African religion', mistook Myalist opposition to it for conversion to Christianity.[1]

Tracing origins thus complicates rather than clarifies efforts to categorize folk faiths. 'Is pocomania an African cult influenced by Christian worship,' asks a local scholar, 'or Christian religious practise reinterpreted and restructured in the mould of an African cult?'[2] Vodun incorporates not merely New World syncretism but African religion previously modified by Portuguese missionaries in fifteenth-century Dahomey. Then, after enslavement by French and Spanish planters, 'the chief West African practitioners of Voodoo were once again brought into contact with Catholicism,' and the renewed contact reinforced Vodun-Christian resemblances.[3]

Whereas the African affinities of Vodun in Haiti and Shango in Trinidad are evident, African elements in other West Indian folk

---

[1] Mary Jo Willeford, 'Negro New World Religions and Witchcraft', *Bim*, Vol. 12, No. 48, January–June 1969, pp. 216–22, ref. p. 220. See Philip D. Curtin, *Two Jamaicas: The Role of Ideas in a Tropical Colony, 1830–1865*, 1955, pp. 29–30, 37, 169–71. The Church of England in Barbados also used the 'ticket-and-leader' system (ibid., pp. 37–8).

[2] Mervin C. Alleyne, 'The Cultural Matrix of Caribbean Dialects', in Dell Hymes, ed., *Pidginization and Creolization of Language*, 1971 (forthcoming). The name itself reflects uncertainties about origin. The customary spelling suggests a pattern of behaviour derived from the Spanish, 'little madness', but there is no evidence of Spanish derivation, and a more likely semantic link is with Kumina, an African religious cult introduced by Africans into Jamaica about 1850; Cassidy links poco-mania with the Twi root *kom*, a frenzied dance (F. G. Cassidy and R. B. Le Page, *Dictionary of Jamaican English*, 1967, p. 356; Edward Seaga, 'Revival Cults in Jamaica', *JJ*, Vol. 3, No. 2, June 1969, pp. 3–13, ref. p. 4). See also Vittorio Lanternari, *The Religions of the Oppressed: A Study of Modern Messianic Cults* [1960], pp. 133–41.

[3] Willeford, 'Negro New World Religions and Witchcraft', p. 217.

religions are much more tenuous. Visitors often mistake as 'African' relics of European folk belief that commingle pagan and Christian forms. The 'omens of death believed in by Jamaican Negroes', a folklorist concluded, 'differ in no way from European patterns and are most likely taken directly from the whites'.[1] Sources of recipes for potions and formulae used to invoke supernatural powers range from pre-Columbian Carib to contemporary Chicago; the De Laurence Company of Chicago is the main Caribbean supplier of talismanic instructions and magic texts, notably the best-selling *Great Book of Magical Art, Hindu Magic, and Indian Occultism*.[2]

Respectable West Indians emphasize their remoteness from what they reprobate as heathen superstitions, even when they in fact share them. 'The middle and the rising middle classes will deny hotly that magic plays any part in their lives', notes a psychologist, 'yet in cases of breakdown many people will revert to magical practices and healing'.[3]

Folk and elite faith in the Southern United States diverged for reasons similar to those discussed for the West Indies. But white and Afro-American differences in liturgy, creed, and organization are less consequential than those in the Caribbean. Black Americans tended to duplicate white church systems rather than develop alternative forms of worship. Only in their emphasis on participation and catharsis, and in occasional convergence with para-political groups such as the Black Muslims, do black churches significantly depart from white American norms.

In the Caribbean, by contrast, folk and elite faiths seem worlds apart. Nothing could be more remote from the orthodox churches than the faith of West Kingston slum dwellers Colin Clarke describes:

Afro-Christian cults stressed continuous revelation, prophecy in tongues, interpretation of omens and dreams, and the manipulation of the dead. . . . While water was abstracted from the Hope River to provide for the city's needs, the cultists regarded the river as the Jordan, and . . . baptised their converts in its depleted stream. . . . Towering prayer flags . . . fluttered over the balm yards. These were frequented by the sick who attributed their illness to obeah. . . . In this way 'religion' in West Kingston competed with orthodox Christianity, agnosticism and with the government's medical services.[4]

[1] Martha Warren Beckwith, *Black Roadways: A Study of Jamaican Folk Life*, 1929, p. 84.
[2] Seaga, 'Revival Cults in Jamaica', p. 11, who refers to L. W. De Laurence, *Great Book of Magical Art, Hindu Magic and East Indian Occultism, now Combined with the Book of Secret Hindu, Ceremonial and Talismanic Magic*, rev. ed., Chicago, De Laurence, 1915. See also Erika Bourguignon, 'Ritual Dissociation and Possession Belief in Caribbean Negro Religion', in Whitten and Szwed, eds., *Afro-American Anthropology*, pp. 87–101.
[3] Kerr, *Personality and Conflict in Jamaica*, p. 173.
[4] Colin G. Clarke, 'Aspects of the Urban Geography of Kingston, Jamaica', p. 350.

Educational patterns throughout the Caribbean reflect, validate, and reinforce these class differences. Initially the elite were taught in Europe, the slaves not at all. Dissimilar systems of education later developed, for the elite and rising middle class and for the masses.

The elitist secondary-school system catered for whites unable to afford education abroad and for non-whites on their way up the social ladder. Entrance was essentially limited by status. The curriculum, classical and Europe-oriented, was designed less to train than to confer prestige on future leaders of colonial societies.

Mass primary schooling involved the rudiments of book learning and desultory 'practical' studies, but it was chiefly an exercise in humility. Too much literacy, as the elite saw it, would teach folk to disdain manual labour and would dissatisfy them with their station in life. 'Give them some . . . reading and writing, but no more', a sugar planter recommended for East Indian labourers in Trinidad as late as 1926. 'Even then I would say educate only the bright ones. . . . If you do educate the whole mass of the agricultural population, you will be deliberately ruining the country.'[1] The primary schools were intended mainly to inculcate respect for, and submission to, superiors, while keeping children out of mischief.

Today most Caribbean territories are striving toward universal education and equal opportunity. But the persistence of colonial patterns of reward and prestige, together with shortages of funds and personnel, keeps school systems elitist and unsuited to local needs. Trinidad has progressed fastest, yet only one Trinidadian child in three goes to secondary school, most who attend stay less than two years, and only one in twenty graduates. Even in Barbados, which takes pride in its traditional role of schoolmaster to the rest of the Caribbean, only 4·5 per cent of those over 15 had secondary-school certificates in 1960. Elsewhere, far fewer are schooled; of the 12 to 18 age group, just one in six Windward Island children were in secondary school in 1964, one in seven Jamaicans, one in ten in the Leewards.[2] Recent educational statistics in Dominica make a more graphic point: of about 1,500 children of primary school-leaving age in 1970, 707 sat entrance exams for secondary school; 248 passed, of whom 73 will get Government financial aid.[3]

Advanced education is also for the few in the French Antilles and,

[1] Testimony of E. A. Robinson at a Select Committee of the Legislative Council, 1926, quoted in Eric Williams, *History of the People of Trinidad and Tobago*, 1962, p. 214.
[2] G. W. Roberts, 'A Note on School Enrolment in Trinidad and Tobago, 1960', *SES*, Vol. 16, 1967, pp. 113–26; *Report of the Tripartite Economic Survey of the Eastern Caribbean, January–April 1966*, 1967, Table I, p. 84; M. G. Smith, 'A Study of West Indian Development Trends and Their Relation to the Future Development of the U.W.I.', 1965, Table 6.
[3] *Dominica Star*, 4 July 1970, p. 11.

above all, in Haiti, where primary students outnumber advanced by
13 to 1. Haiti in 1960–2 had 1,600 university students, 0·03 per cent of
the population.[1] Of Martinicans aged 20–24, only 3·5 per cent were
attending college at home or abroad in 1967–8, as compared with 16
per cent of the same age group in France.[2] The English-speaking Caribbean has about 10,000 university-trained people, or about 0·3 per
cent of the population, as compared with 13 per cent for the United
States and 5 per cent for Puerto Rico.[3]

Secondary scholars are predominantly elite and middle class, and
the smaller the proportion of students to the population the more elite
they are. Managerial and professional families—mainly white, light-
coloured, Portuguese, and Chinese—constitute half the secondary
enrolment in Guyana and Surinam.[4] Agricultural and manual
labourers make up more than half the population of Martinique but
account for only one-fifth the enrolment of the girls' *lycée* and one-
seventh of the local university students.[5] The system is self-perpetuating:
elite children attend private primary schools and are encouraged to
study at home; folk children have few facilities for study and many
competing demands on their time.

They will sit for the scholarship examinations and fail. . . . They will fail
them because there is always water to be fetched, chickens to be fed, rice to
be dried, and a host of other chores which children are expected to perform
once they are home. They will fail them because most parents, though willing,
are unable to help their children understand the lessons taught at school.
They will fail them because by 6:30 in the evening it is too dark to read a
book or do what little homework has been assigned. With no electricity, night
effectively envelops and suffocates school work. In the end the children will
fail the examinations because they have had the misfortune to have been born
in Canelot [a rural village].[6]

Costs also constrain rural folk; secondary schools are concentrated in
the capital towns, public transport from country districts is inadequate
or non-existent, and the expense of boarding a child in school or in
town is prohibitive. Thus almost two-thirds of Martinique's secondary-
school students are from Fort-de-France, which has only one-fourth of

[1] Klébert Viélot, 'L'enseignement primaire en Haïti', in Richard P. Schaedel,
ed., *Papers of the Conference on Research and Resources of Haiti*, 1969, pp. 281–346, ref.
p. 336.
[2] José Nosel, 'Les étudiants à la Martinique', in 'Problèmes universitaires des
Antilles-Guyane françaises', *CERAG*, No. 18, 1969, pp. 36–71, ref. pp. 37–8.
[3] Thomas G. Mathews, 'Caribbean Cooperation in the Field of Higher Education',
in Roy Preiswerk, ed., *Regionalism and the Commonwealth Caribbean*, 1969, pp. 151–6,
ref. p. 154.
[4] Louis W. Bone, *Secondary Education in the Guianas*, 1962, pp. 46–7.
[5] Nosel, 'Les étudiants à la Martinique', p. 58; Miguel Chamoiseau, 'Les élèves des
classes terminales de lycée', *CERAG*, No. 18, 1969, pp. 98–112, ref. p. 109.
[6] Allen S. Ehrlich, 'East Indian Cane Workers in Jamaica', 1969, p. 82.

the school-age population.[1] In Haiti, nine-tenths rural, urban students outnumber rural even at the primary level.[2] Differences between rural and urban school opportunities—notably in the larger islands where many children live a full day's travel from school—may exceed colour differentials.

The secondary-school curriculum too remains elite—academic rather than practical, focused on Europe rather than on the Caribbean, affording prestige rather than social utility. The most successful graduates elect careers in medicine, law, and government; to opt for a technical vocation is to be thought a failure. Patterns of reward thus perpetuate West Indian disdain for manual labour. Even the new Trinidad Draft Education Plan 'unwittingly perpetuate[s] social distinctions' by banishing craft education from the normal secondary curriculum. Geared to the Cambridge General Certificate of Education examinations, secondary education strikes more than one observer as 'essentially fashioned to ape English Grammar schools.'[3] In Martinique the post-primary teachers 'are the inheritors of a culture and the keepers of a classical and humanistic tradition. Thus . . . they resist change, they believe they have a mission to safeguard . . . the present social structure'. They do not make students face local responsibilities but 'keep them at a distance from the realities of the country.'[4] In Haiti alienation begins earlier. 'The rural school is not really a part of the local milieu. . . . Instead of including the child in his environment, the school seeks to help him escape it.'[5]

Not even Trinidad's spectacular enrolment spurt has integrated its secondary students into the society. There are many new schools, especially in rural areas; between 1956 and 1966 secondary enrolment almost trebled; government scholarship awards increased from 230 in 1950 to 6,370 in 1966; today 'the majority of parents look upon secondary education for their children as a social norm'. But the norm is more social than educational; as enrolment increases, the proportion of graduates declines. Between 1962 and 1967, those who passed the O-level examination in mathematics dropped from 83 to 35 per cent, in English from 74 to 43 per cent. Fewer students gained certificates in biology, French, English, and geography though many more sat the examinations. A-levels, the terminal secondary examinations, declined

---

[1] Ch. Beringuier, 'L'espace regional martiniquais', *CERAG*, No. 3 [1966], 2nd ed., 1969, pp. 11–12.

[2] Viélot, 'L'enseignement primaire en Haïti', p. 336.

[3] Leo Pujadas, 'A Note on Education Development in Trinidad and Tobago 1956–1966', *Trinidad and Tobago C.S.O. Research Papers*, No. 6, 1969, pp. 1–46, ref. pp. 29, 32.

[4] François Gresle, 'Les enseignants et l'école': une analyse socio-demographique des instituteurs et des professeurs de la Martinique', *CERAG*, No. 19, 1969, pp. 120, 123, 136.

[5] Viélot, 'L'enseignement primaire en Haïti', p. 343.

still more severely between 1956 and 1966: the proportion of government-school successes fell from 72 to 26 per cent, private schools from 41 to 8 per cent. Of the failures, 20 per cent were estimated jobless in 1969.[1] 'The nearer a student gets to the certificate without actually getting it,' a local critic noted, 'the worse his chances of finding employment.'[2] In Martinique, too, 'everyone who goes to secondary school does so in the hope of getting a degree . . . and people spend years training for this, an ambition which 70 per cent of the time is brutally destroyed in the examinations, leaving them at 18 without either diploma or trade.'[3]

For the West Indian majority, formal education is brief and perfunctory. Primary schooling is mostly free and in theory compulsory, but there are too few schools and teachers to enforce attendance. Many in the poorer islands have never been to school at all—one out of four St. Lucians, one Dominican in seven, one Montserratian in nine. Farm and other chores cut down school attendance. In Jamaica fewer than two-thirds of those on the rolls ordinarily turn up.[4]

Class-room conditions do not spur intellectual advance. Furnished with decrepit equipment and ancient tattered texts, West Indian primary schools are principally staffed by untrained older pupils, supervised by head teachers more concerned to keep order than to instil knowledge. Rote recitation is the rule among classes of sixty to a hundred, separated from one another by thin or no partitions. St. Vincent spent only 53 cents per primary-school child for all requisites in 1968. At a Jamaican rural primary school in 1969 text books sent by the Ministry of Education were kept in the principal's office solely for the use of the teachers; in the class-rooms only Bibles were in evidence. Publication dates had been deleted from some texts used in Barbados to conceal their embarrassing age, in one case dating from the 1870s.[5]

Although formal illiteracy is now rare, many West Indians can barely read and write. A 1963–4 survey found only one Jamaican in three

[1] Pujadas, 'A Note on Education Development in Trinidad and Tobago 1956–1966', pp. 7, 29, 30.

[2] 'The Problems', *Tapia*, No. 1, 28 September 1969, p. 4.

[3] Morel, 'Jeunesse et emploi', p. 34.

[4] G. W. Roberts and N. Abdulah, 'Some Observations on the Educational Position of the British Caribbean', *SES*, Vol. 14, 1965, pp. 144–54, ref. p. 145; *Spotlight*, Vol. 27, Nos. 9 and 10, September–October 1966, p. 15. See also Seaga, 'Parent-Teacher Relationships in a Jamaican Village', p. 229. Primary schools in the Montego Bay area, Jamaica, turned back hundreds of would-be entrants for the 1970–1 school year owing to lack of space; the local girls' school, built for 725 students, now houses 1379 (*Jamaica Weekly Gleaner*, 16 September 1970, p. 17).

[5] *The Development Problem in St. Vincent: A Report by a University of the West Indies Development Mission* [1969], p. 118; UWI, Institute of Education, 'Textbook Survey Draft', 1969, pp. 18–19.

unable to read, but three out of five could not read well.[1] Much of what they read in school has little value in any local context. Sparrow's calypso, 'Dan Is the Man', satirizes the irrelevance of formal colonial folk education:

> . . . in my days in school they teach me like a fool . . .
> Pussy has finished his work long ago and now he resting . . .
> Solomon Agrundy was born on a Monday.
> The ass in the lion's skin.
> Winken, Blinken and Nod sail off in a wooden sloop . . .
> De alligator fighting to make monkey into soup.
> And Dan is de man in de van.
> De poems and de lessons dey write an' send from England
> Impress me they were trying to cultivate comedians.
> Comic books make more sense, you know it is fictitious without pretense . . .
> How I happen to get some education my friends me en' know,
> All dey teach me is about brer rabbit and rumpelstilskin-o
> They wanted to keep me down indeed, they try they best
>   but didn't succeed,
> You see, me head was duncy enough to know ah cyan' read.

Many Caribbean states, though less stinting than heretofore, still lag behind national goals in their support of schooling. The Jamaican 'government is still thinking in terms of "primary" education for the vast majority of the 12 through 14 age-group', a UNESCO team concluded, 'in circumstances which can tend only to perpetuate the present social distinctions and class barriers.'[2] Even in more progressive Trinidad, 'those who drew up the [1968] Draft Education plan not only are living in the past but are not learning anything from it', a critic charges. 'We shall produce clerks with the ability to tinker [and] end up [in] the same place—with great numbers of frustrated 16-year olds on our hands'.[3]

Class differences as striking as those described for law, the family, religion, and education exist in most other aspects of Caribbean life, from patterns of marketing to preferences in sports. But such distinctions, though profound, are not absolute; elite patterns and tastes figure in folk life, while the upper-class evince, and even enjoy, aspects of folk culture. 'Between the Jamaican peasant and the Jamaican middle class sophisticate' there is a gap, but it is being crossed all the time.

As a peasant boy of six or seven living in what was then regarded as one of the 'darkest' and most folksy parts of Jamaica, I remember singing big chunks of Handel's 'Messiah', Haydn's 'Creation' and of course that old favourite 'The Lost Chord'. Grandmother and . . . country aunties . . . were exposed to some of the best liturgical music out of a European culture. These same people would

[1] *Spotlight*, Vol. 26, Nos. 7 and 8, July–August, 1965.

[2] *Jamaica Educational Planning Mission, September–November 1964*, 1965, p. 15.

[3] 'How Can This Education Plan Help the Poor Society?' *Trinidad Express*, 6 July 1968, p. 10.

participate in pocomania, and I have had my dose of 'groaning and shouting' as well as healing in the balmyard and the obeahman.[1]

And it would be hard to find a Jamaican at the top of the social ladder who did not eat rice and peas or ackee, drink coconut water, or dance to local music. The personality of West Indians in each class depends on the entire complex of traits, attitudes, and behaviour in all realms of life, overlapping as well as unique, interacting as well as isolating.

SOCIAL DISTANCE

In most aspects of life, class sharply differentiates West Indian patterns of thought and behaviour. Isolation reinforces these differences. Elite and middle-class West Indians, in daily contact with domestic servants and other employees, remain extraordinarily ignorant of working-class circumstances. Interclass contacts are attenuated by physical and cultural barriers and constrained by custom. Social distance is one reason agricultural-extension and social-welfare work are so often ineffectual: reforms advocated by light-skinned, urban visitors without local understanding or insight seldom commend themselves to peasant families and rural cultivators.[2]

How little one class knows of another was poignantly brought out in the Jamaica Family Life Project of the late 1950s. 'The advent of the middle-class Jamaican "lady"' engaged to elicit peasant views about family size and birth control 'was about as unusual as the arrival of an anthropologist to a pre-literate community; and in all areas her arrival . . . cause[d] some suspicion.' Interviewers nearly lost their lives in one locality, whose inhabitants interpreted their promises of secrecy as threats of witchcraft.

Misunderstandings were mutual. Many interviewers were so

[1] Rex Nettleford, 'The Dance as an Art Form—Its Place in the West Indies', *CQ*, Vol. 14, Nos. 1 and 2, 1968, pp. 127–35, ref. pp. 130–1. Similarly in Freetown, 'Creole society could appreciate the rhythm and pathos of the Kru Dance of Death as much as the new-found pleasure in a formal ball. . . . They could respect the power of the *oje* as well as the intricate secrets of the Masonic Lodge. They enjoyed palm wine and West Indian rum as much as Bass's Imported Ale on tap at Porter's Royal Hotel' (John Peterson, 'Sierra Leone Creole: A Reappraisal', in Christopher Fyfe and Eldred Jones, eds., *Freetown: A Symposium*, 1968, pp. 100–17, ref. pp. 114–15).

[2] Hyman Rodman, 'On Understanding Lower-Class Behaviour' (*SES*, Vol. 8, 1959, pp. 441–50) describes the problems involved; M. G. Smith and G. J. Kruijer, *A Sociological Manual for Extension Workers in the Caribbean* (1957) issue an extended warning against neglecting to tackle them; James M. Blaut et al., 'A Study of Cultural Determinants of Soil Erosion and Conservation in the Blue Mountains of Jamaica: A Progress Report' (*SES*, Vol. 8, 1959, pp. 403–20) and David T. Edwards, *Report on an Economic Study of Small Farming in Jamaica* (1961) illustrate the effects of failures of communication in agriculture. Lloyd Braithwaite, 'Social and Political Aspects of Rural Development in the West Indies', *SES*, Vol. 17, 1968, pp. 264–75, adds that peasants see extension workers as motivated by individual goals rather than by good-will and understanding.

unfamiliar with the country that they sallied forth in stockings and high heels to communities accessible only by mule track. Rejecting mules as undignified, they ended by crawling on hands and knees to places they could scarcely believe human beings lived in. 'I was very upset', one woman later wrote, 'as the house was filthy. . . . The mattress was stuffed with banana trash which almost suffocated me with the smell of urine. The bed was covered with flies.' Crowding, dirt, and abject poverty were disturbing novelties; the city women confronted people and conditions whose existence they had not hitherto imagined.[1]

Geographical remoteness is both a condition and a cause of social distance. Although segregation is formally outlawed, circumstances of West Indian work and life physically separate the folk from the elite, whose country plantation houses and town villas, characteristically set deep in their own grounds, fenced off and guarded by dogs, are virtually inaccessible on foot. Immobility further isolates the lower class; bus or truck rides to field, factory, and market are for many the only journeys away from home. Easy access to a wider realm is limited to car owners, who are seldom tempted to explore shabby rural—or urban—areas barely reachable by road. Thus elite–folk contacts are normally confined to superior–subordinate relationships in environments that emphasize social distance.

Physical isolation, like class difference, varies considerably from territory to territory. 'The absence of urban ghettoes', suggests an observer of Trinidad, makes 'the proximity of conflicting or disparate ways of life . . . even more acute'.[2] By contrast, 'abysmal and total ignorance . . . of the people of the country' is charged to the Jamaican middle class[3] and adduced to explain 'how the plight of such a high percentage of people is not more conspicuous'.[4]

Interclass isolation, like many cultural differences, originated in slavery. Creole life enforced some community of interests and habits between master and slave, to be sure, and a few planters could be found 'mixing with, and actually working familiarly with their own negroes.'[5] But such contact was rare, a Jamaican noted:

The great bulk of the slaves . . . are beyond the ken of their master's immediate observation: indeed there are many of the attorneys [managers] who do not

[1] Kurt W. Back and J. Mayone Stycos, *The Survey under Unusual Conditions: Methodological Facets of the Jamaica Human Fertility Investigation*, 1959, pp. 9, 5. Results of the study appear in J. Mayone Stycos and Kurt W. Back, *The Control of Human Fertility in Jamaica*, 1964.

[2] Ivar Oxaal, *Black Intellectuals Come to Power*, 1968, p. 24.

[3] Ken Hill, 'It Is Difficult to Fathom the Mood of Jamaica These Days', *Trinidad Express*, 21 March 1970, p. 9.

[4] *The Church and Unemployment*, n.d., p. 3.

[5] Governor Valentine Morris of St. Vincent, quoted in Ivor Waters, *The Unfortunate Valentine Morris*, 1964, p. 56.

personally know a tenth part of the numerous slaves belonging to their constituents. They see them once a year, collected to receive their annual allowance of clothing, and this is the only opportunity they have of knowing anything about them, except by report.[1]

The infrequent contact with whites permitted slaves not only to develop the alternative institutions discussed, but to erect an elaborate framework of ceremonies, court trials, and secret societies, which functioned partly as jest and partly as an apparatus for rebellion. 'The planter, looking at his Negroes and seeing only Negroes, never knew. He might know that certain Negroes dressed in cast-off clothes, . . . a mimicry in the Negro-yards of white entertaining. But he didn't know that the Negro carter . . . was a king at night, with 12 courtiers and a uniform of his own', in charge of a slave regiment. One such Trinidadian potentate 'belonged in real life to the Attorney-General, who was not really an attorney-general; one make-believe mingling with another.'[2]

Classes self-cloistered in isolation and fantasy still characterize the Caribbean from Haiti to Surinam. In suburban Jamaica the absentee nostalgia of the elite mirrors the alienation of the slum dispossessed:

The West Kingston Rastafarians refuse to work for Babylon, think of themselves as the chosen people, regard their repatriation to Africa as a matter of right, and hold the King of Ethiopia to be a god. The St. Andrew Rastafarians [that is, the elite] refuse to work for anyone but their own kind, think of themselves as being of a different calibre, as well as of a different and superior race, regard England as their spiritual home, and hold the throne of England in that reverence befitting the Divine Right of Kings. . . . Yet the horror with which they regard the Rastafarians of the slums is equalled only by the horror with which the Rastafarians of the slums regard them. . . . The two groups are the only people who can be said really to share a common culture. . . . It is only the use of soap that stands between them.[3]

Linguistic differences also inhibit interclass contacts. The language of the elite—formal English, French, or Dutch—is not the mother tongue of most West Indians, who customarily speak a creolized variant of one of the European languages. But each territory exhibits not a single dichotomy but a speech continuum, ranging from a more or less fossilized version of a European tongue, through mixtures grammatically European but flavoured with West Indian expressions and pronunciation, to the most heavily creolized speech. Along this continuum West Indian ways of speaking alter with occasion, context, and associates, often shifting in mid-sentence. No elite, however sequestered,

---

[1] J. Stewart, *A View of the Past and Present State of the Island of Jamaica*, 1823, pp. 252–3.

[2] V. S. Naipaul, *The Loss of El Dorado*, 1969, pp. 251–5.

[3] *Jamaica Daily Gleaner*, 20 July 1966, quoted in Leonard E. Barrett, 'The Rastafarians: A Study in Messianic Cultism in Jamaica', 1968, p. 164.

is wholly ignorant of Creolese; no peasantry, however isolated, lacks a smattering of standard French or English. As popular media spread and education expands, both linguistic extremes give way to mixtures. European words and sounds increasingly influence Creolese, and metropolitan French and English yield to West Indian standard variants with local pronunciation and colloquialisms.[1]

But though speech patterns overlap, they do not merge; the peasantry is ill at ease with standard European, and the elite never entirely comprehends folk dialect. Connectivity varies: in Barbados the elite speak a strongly creolized 'official' language, the folk are generally conversant with formal English, and the linguistic community transcends class divisions; all is more or less 'Bajan'.[2] In Jamaica everyone is partly bilingual, but educated people find some folk speech incomprehensible, while rural folk have trouble both with standard English and with Creole variants in localities other than their own. In Haiti patois is familiar to all, but the rural majority speak a version remote from the urban, and, in turn, are virtually ignorant of French. The linguistic gulf there is great because the revolutionary wars, in dispersing the rural elite, virtually isolated the two speech systems. Haitian formal French and rural patois are mutually unintelligible, though there is some convergence today. But even Haiti exhibits a range of forms from standard French to *français cetolisé* to *créole urbain* to *le gros créole*, the speech of the countryside.[3] Elsewhere in the Caribbean, standard and Creole speech have continuously interacted.

Elite and folk are especially isolated where 'official' and majority speech have different European roots. In St. Lucia and Dominica the formal language is English, but French patois is the mother tongue of 90 per cent of the population. The ruling class in the Netherlands Caribbean speak Dutch, but the folk in the Netherlands Windwards speak English, in the Leewards a Spanish-based Papiamento, in Surinam an English-based Sranan; indeed, Sranan and Papiamento are less Creolese variants than separate, though low-status, languages. Papiamento was, in fact, long Curaçao's elite as well as folk *lingua*

[1] F. G. Cassidy and R. B. Le Page, 'Lexicographical Problems of the Dictionary of Jamaican English', in *Proceedings of the Conference on Creole Language Studies*, 1961, pp. 17–36, ref. pp. 22–3; Albert Valdman, 'The Language Situation in Haiti', in Schaedel, ed., *Papers of the Conference on Research and Resources of Haiti*, pp. 155–203, ref. pp. 180–1; Kenneth Ramchand, 'The Negro and the English Language in the West Indies', *Savacou*, Vol. 1, No. 1, June 1970, pp. 33–44.

[2] See Frank A. Collymore *Notes for a Glossary of Words and Phrases of Barbadian Dialect*, 1955.

[3] Mervin C. Alleyne, 'Communication between the Elite and the Masses', in F. M. Andic and T. G. Mathews, eds., *The Caribbean in Transition, Papers on Social, Political, and Economic Development*, 1965, pp. 12–19; idem, review of R. B. Le Page, *The National Language Question*, in *CS*, Vol. 5, No. 1, April 1965, pp. 53–4, ref. p. 54; Valdman, 'The Language Situation in Haiti', pp. 167–76.

franca; Portuguese-speaking Jews and Dutch-speaking Protestants used Papiamento to communicate not only with subordinates, but with each other.[1] In the other truly bilingual territories, judges, civil servants, and doctors often need interpreters to communicate with country folk.

Reliance on interpreters obviously limits contact. But even given the same European language base, prejudices about standard and Creolese speech attenuate communication between folk and elite. However sensitive, the elite speaker uses Creolese differently from the masses and is seen as talking down. 'Education an' class just twist that girl mouth right out o' shape', complains a character in a Lamming novel.

She learn fast how to talk two ways. . . . Tonight she go talk great with the stranger man, grammar an' clause, where do turn into does, plural an' singular in correct formation, an' all that. But inside, like between you an' me, she tongue make the same rat-trap noise. Then she talk real, an' sentences come tumblin' down.[2]

The peasant or labourer dealing with an official or an employer in standard European has to contend not only with its unfamiliarity but with its prestige; to use English or French 'correctly' is a mark of status. The girl who admires her boy friend because he 'could talk English so good, that when he finish, you ain't understand a word he said', exemplifies the West Indian folk dilemma.[3] Fear of error or loss of face often reduces the folk speaker to silence. In St. Lucian legal and business transactions, the Creole-speaker often refuses 'the services of an English–Creole interpreter' because he 'is afraid of revealing his ignorance of English.'[4] West Indian folk resemble Chicago slum dwellers unfamiliar with English, who find that

all the subtleties that are usually incorporated into speech are suddenly lost.... Left adrift without the ordinary innuendos, graces, overtones, and insinuations, . . . their own self-presentation becomes equally coarse, abrupt, and impolite . . . [and they] either avoid those encounters requiring communication in English or at best submit to them with considerable uneasiness.[5]

That Creolese is rarely written accentuates distinctions between literate and unlettered. Folk in an oral culture behave and respond differently from people accustomed to writing. Most West Indians are

[1] Sidney W. Mintz, 'The Socio-Historical Background to Pidginization and Creolization', in Hymes, *Pidginization and Creolization of Language*, pp. 154–68.

[2] George Lamming, *Season of Adventure*, 1960, p. 21. See also Kenneth Ramchand, 'The Artist in the Balm-Yard: "Season of Adventure"', *NWQ*, Vol. 5, Nos. 1 and 2, Dead Season and Croptime 1969, pp. 13–21.

[3] Clifford Sealy, 'The Professor', in Errol Hill, ed., *Caribbean Plays*, Vol. II, 1965, pp. 119–48, ref. p. 143.

[4] Mervin C. Alleyne, 'Language and Society in St. Lucia', *CS*, Vol. 1, No. 1, April 1961, pp. 1–10, ref. p. 7.

[5] Suttles, *The Social Order of the Slum*, pp. 63–4.

partially literate, and all are influenced by written language, but the Creolese subculture is none the less 'pre-literate' in its traditionalism and conservatism, in its taste for the concrete and the personal, in its addiction to polemics and the repetition of formulae, and in some concomitants of personality.[1] West Indian elites condemn these manifestations just as they repudiate Creolese itself.

Local writers have only begun to assimilate the rich oral traditions of calypso, mento, and folk speech. Educated West Indians learn to appreciate spoken Creolese but still object to its being written. 'Nobody ever recognized me as a writer', recalls Louise Bennett, the leading expositor of Jamaican Creolese. People would say, '"Well, she is 'doing' dialect"; it wasn't even writing you know. Up to now a lot of people don't even think I write. They say "Oh, you just stand up and say these things!"'[2]

Most elite attitudes toward Creolese are much less kind. The upper classes abominate Creole speech for its supposed links with Africa and blackness. Haiti long prohibited patois for 'official' communications; the 90 per cent who know only patois are still 'totally excluded from participation in . . . administrative and legal procedures.'[3] Status was not the only motive; insistence on French enabled the ruling elite to maintain tight control over an uninformed populace, for they feared 'its eventual recalcitrance if it should become better educated.'[4]

Throughout the Caribbean the respectable reprobate the use of patois. Interclass contacts are limited not only by real ignorance, but by the refusal of educated people to employ Creolese except in jest or mockery. Some who habitually speak it at home still publicly deny that they can understand it. The West Indian returning from abroad typically insists 'to all who will listen that he has forgotten how to speak Creole'.[5] Educated West Indians often wrongly assume that habitual Creole speakers know no standard tongue. 'I wasn't ever asked to a Jamaican Poetry League meeting', Louise Bennett remembers; 'most people thought that . . . they couldn't discourse with me at all because I was going to talk to them in Jamaican dialect which they couldn't understand.'[6] Language use is a major component, then, of West Indian

---

[1] Walter J. Ong, 'World as View and World as Event', *AA*, Vol. 71, 1969, pp. 634–47.

[2] Dennis Scott, 'Bennett on Bennett', *CQ*, Vol. 14, Nos. 1 and 2, March–June 1968, pp. 97–101, ref. p. 98. The mento is a Jamaican folk song.

[3] Valdman, 'The Language Situation in Haiti', p. 165.

[4] Edmund Wilson, *Red, Black, Blonde and Olive: Studies in Four Civilizations: Zuñi, Haiti, Soviet Russia, Israel*, 1956, p. 99.

[5] Edith Efron, 'French and Creole Patois in Haiti', *CQ*, Vol. 3, No. 4, August 1954, pp. 199–213, ref. p. 203.

[6] Scott, 'Bennett on Bennett', p. 98. See also Pierre van den Berghe, 'European Languages and Black Mandarins', *Transition*, Vol. 7, No. 34, 1968, pp. 19–23.

class distance. And attitudes about what constitutes proper speech tend to increase that distance.

Relationships across class lines are circumscribed by hierarchical habits derived from medieval Europe and from master–slave contacts. An observer in Guadeloupe is 'struck by the exaggerated, fearful respect' many Negroes show to whites; Barbadians report similar 'rites of deference'.[1] Social distance separates middle class from rural folk as well. Jamaican teachers and administrators, characterized as 'the opposite sect', are set apart residentially and morally. 'Our father was the head teacher, and we were "teacher daughter"', recalls a Jamaican, 'to be picked for the side in games because of our social place, not our prowess; to be asked favours, not to be bosom friends.'[2] If rural folk are less obsequious and elites less presumptuous than before, a sizeable residue of formal deference persists.

To transgress class lines or to presume equality is to risk discomfiture. Carew's *Black Midas*, who strikes it rich in Guyanese gold diggings and takes a white man's house in Georgetown, deludes himself that money can buy equality: 'I felt very proud entering that house, for there was I, a black man from a village, stepping into the shoes of the great ones.' But he never felt at home there. 'We were all conscious of the white man's presence.' His woman could not 'sleep well until she had an obeahman come in to drive out the white man's spirit'.[3] Without education, money brings only limited benefits. In a small community any man of property has middle-class rank. But at higher social levels and in wider arenas wealth will not secure membership if appearance, accent, and manner betray folk origins.

Neither does political power bring parity of status. The West Indian who fancies folk leadership as a spring-board to the elite is often disappointed. Elected officials can command elite material perquisites— big houses, chauffeured limousines, elegant clothes, a servant entourage —but may still be denied elite social intercourse. Robert Bradshaw, who has ruled St. Kitts for twenty years, remains a parvenu to middle-class Kitticians. In Grenada Premier Eric Gairy brought the local planters to terms through his control of the labour union, but he could not persuade them to accept him socially. 'Although he became a good tennis player at the Tanteen Club and developed a cultivated "English" accent, . . . he was made pointedly aware that neither the government

[1] Jacques Zylberberg, 'Outline of the Sociology of La Guadeloupe', *Civilisations*, Vol. 16, 1966, pp. 478–99, ref. p. 493; Paule Marshall, *Soul Clap Hands and Sing*, 1961, pp. 8–9.

[2] Joyce Gladwell, *Brown Face, Big Master*, 1969, p. 10. See also Seaga, 'Parent-Teacher Relationships in a Jamaican Village'.

[3] Jan Carew, *Black Midas*, 1958, pp. 184–94. See also Joyce L. Sparer, 'Carew—An Unfinished Search for Identity: Attitudes towards Race in Guyanese Literature, Part 4', *Georgetown Sunday Chronicle*, 30 April 1967.

officials nor the white and brown elites would take tea with him or play tennis with him'.[1]

Ceremonial efforts to bridge gaps of race and class can be mortifying experiences, like the Government House luncheon for Trinidad's newly elected legislators described in *The Mystic Masseur*:

Ganesh came in dhoti and *koortah* and turban; the member for one of the Port of Spain wards wore a khaki suit and a sun helmet; a third came in jodhpurs; a fourth, adhering for the moment to his pre-election principles, came in short trousers and an open shirt; the blackest M.L.C. wore a three-piece blue suit, yellow woollen gloves and a monocle. . . . He [Ganesh] saw with alarm that the people from whom he had hoped to learn the eating drill were too far away. The members looked at the waiters who looked away quickly. Then the members looked at each other. The man in jodhpurs muttered, 'Is why black people can't get on. You see how these waiters behaving? And they black like hell too, you know.' . . . Soup came. 'Meat?' Ganesh asked. The waiter nodded. 'Take it away,' Ganesh said with quick disgust. The man in jodhpurs said, 'You was wrong there. You shoulda toy with the soup.' 'Toy with it?' 'Is what the book say.' . . .

Unoriginal disaster befell Mr. Primrose. His monocle fell into his soup. The Governor's lady looked quickly away. But Mr. Primrose drew her attention to the monocle. 'Eh, eh,' he chuckled, 'but see how it fall down!' The M.L.C.'s looked on with sympathy. Mr. Primrose turned on them. 'What you all staring at? All you ain't see nigger before?' The man in jodhpurs whispered to Ganesh, 'But we wasn't saying anything.' 'Eh,' Mr. Primrose snapped. 'Black people don't wear monocle?' He fished out the monocle, wiped it, and put it in his coat pocket. . . .

The meal was torture to Ganesh. He felt alien and uncomfortable. He grew sulkier and sulkier and refused all the courses. He felt as if he were a boy again, going to the Queen's Royal College for the first time.[2]

Back home, he called out for food. 'But, man,' said his wife, 'I thought you was *dining* with the Governor.' 'Don't make joke, girl. Done dine. Want to eat now. Going to show them,' he mumbled, as his fingers ploughed through the rice and *dal* and curry, 'going to show them.'

What Europeans find incongruous—the monocle, woollen gloves in the tropics, imperial show in a colonial backwater, the medley of outworn traditions—is not locally thought out of place. Such features neither amuse nor perturb most West Indians, who are at home in this assemblage. But the juxtaposition of elite and folk behaviour is felt to be not merely egregious but painfully demeaning.

Patterns of West Indian social life reflect and reinforce class distance. Homogeneity of colour and class remains the general rule. In Trinidad even dramatic societies developed along lines of colour; 'the appearance of a mixed racial group', especially in European plays, 'would probably

---

[1] Singham, *The Hero and the Crowd in a Colonial Polity*, p. 188.
[2] V. S. Naipaul, *The Mystic Masseur*, 1957, pp. 201–4.

have appeared incongruous to the audience'.[1] In elite social clubs the occasional light-skinned Creole or the *pro forma* membership of a black Governor hardly constitute colour mixing. Three-fifths of the members in the most prestigious social clubs of Kingston in 1960 were white expatriates and Creoles, Jews, and 'Jamaican whites'.[2]

Trinidad too maintains a 'very efficient colour "sieve"':

There is a club for the black middle class, [one for the] black lower class, one for the 'high-brown' with European features, one for the brown with less pronounced European features, and of course, there are exclusively white clubs. These never refuse membership because of colour, but always on some other ground. In any case people nearly always go to a club where they are easily accepted.

In 1965 a Trinidadian noted that though this description was ten years old, 'today very little of it has changed'.[3] A 1969 inquiry into complaints of discrimination at the Trinidad Country Club revealed an unaltered situation; two black American couples were refused ready access to the Club's tennis courts and bar; the Club in theory forbade non-members these privileges but in practice regularly extended them to foreign visitors, generally white. A black Trinidadian depicted the Club's racial ambience:

The white people seemed to be disporting themselves in various ways—some playing tennis, some sipping cool drinks, others frolicking in the swimming pool. . . . The black people, on the other hand, consisted of ball boys . . . retrieving balls, uniformed servants in the children's playground, chauffeurs . . . , uniformed black waiters, also a black security guard who later accosted me and took objection to my presence.

He felt 'like Alice in a South African wonderland.' A member of the Club's management committee, asked about colour policy, could not 'recall any instance of any black person being refused membership *on any ground whatever*.'[4] But since only about 50 of the 6,000 members were

---

[1] Lloyd Braithwaite, 'The Problem of Cultural Integration in Trinidad', *SES*, Vol. 3, 1954, pp. 82–96, ref. p. 89.

[2] I am indebted to Valerie Bloomfield for Jamaican club lists and colour assessments. See also Colin G. Clarke, 'Aspects of the Urban Geography of Kingston, Jamaica', pp. 380, 383. For similar circumstances in Puerto Rico see Robert A. Manners, 'Tabara: Subcultures of a Tobacco and Mixed Crops Municipality', in Steward et al., *The People of Puerto Rico*, pp. 93–170, ref. pp. 132–3.

[3] A condensation of C. L. R. James (*Beyond a Boundary*, 1963, pp. 55–7), with comments, by Elliott Bastien, 'The Weary Road to Whiteness and the Hasty Retreat into Nationalism', in Henri Tajfel and John L. Dawson, eds., *Disappointed Guests: Essays by African, Asian, and West Indian Students*, 1965, pp. 38–54, ref. p. 43.

[4] *Report of the Commission Appointed by His Excellency the Governor-General to Investigate Allegations of Discriminatory Practices by the Management of the Trinidad Country Club*, 1969, pp. 5, 25, 29, 30–1.

black, 'it would seem', as the Inquiry's Commissioner wryly concluded, 'that there are not many black applicants'.[1]

Even in Dominica, with no white Creole families, the 'white' club endures as the haunt of British and Canadian bank staff, American businessmen, the better-educated Syrians, a few coloured professionals with British and American wives, and a handful of the light-skinned Creole elite. In the early 1960s dark-skinned young people—especially girls—were invited to occasional 'open' dances, an exception that underscored the distinction. This exclusiveness was a frequent topic of conversation at the other leading club, frequented by the coloured elite and middle class, though some found it pleasant or expedient to belong to both clubs. Double membership would be impossible among French Antilleans, who maintain stricter colour barriers.

Such barriers are the more significant because public social arenas are virtually absent in the West Indies. Cafés, restaurants, hotels, and other places to sit and chat tend to cater exclusively for folk or elite trade but not for both. Some islands lack any convenient place for informal meetings among people of diverse backgrounds. Two former schoolmates, one from the coloured near-elite, the other the daughter of a self-made contractor of peasant origin, seldom cross paths in the small-island capital where both now live. 'The only place we ever meet', the latter, now a schoolteacher, commented to me, 'are the airport and the supermarket'.

Durable formal associations—chambers of commerce, agricultural societies, and welfare, co-operative, and trade-union groups—are usually homogeneous in class. Literary, theatrical, and cultural clubs, sporadically fostered by university representatives or optimistic expatriates, soon perish from lack of intimacy among members. Those that endure, usually under church or school aegis, tend toward uniformity of class, colour, and occupation. Community improvement and charity groups that in small-town Britain include everyone from local squire to greengrocer are rare in the Caribbean.

West Indian cocktail parties deceive visitors into supposing that class and colour distinctions are dead. Large gatherings commonly include the entire colour spectrum, but guests are all elite or near-elite. At a typical spread for two hundred Dominicans of all shades, for example, will appear most of the expatriate whites, perhaps a fifth of the coloured elite and urban middle class, and a small proportion of the black population—politicians, professional men, civil servants. All of these, black, coloured, and white, are in the best-educated, best-off 2 or 3 per cent of the population.

Moreover, those who mingle at large functions seldom meet on more intimate social occasions. At home, in their clubs, and on holiday jaunts

[1] Clement Phillips, quoted in *Trinidad Guardian*, 16 August 1969, p. 2.

West Indians habitually consort with those closest in colour and social background. Even on the university campus, according to a Trinidadian student, 'the high-browns "lime" by themselves. The Indians stick together. The Whites stick together and the few Chinese that we have on campus come into one small group, or associate with the richer Indians.'[1]

Parades, political rallies, and legislative and court sessions are almost the only public events that bring people of different classes together. Cricket excepted, elite sports have small interest for the peasantry, and vice versa. Once or twice a year a Christmas or Carnival spirit animates the whole community; people of all classes make merry, dance in the street, and express pleasure in being together. But even then class and colour play a part: followers of each carnival band come from a single social stratum.

Of all instrumentalities that separate classes, the most deliberate and durable is endogamy. Nowhere in the Caribbean is miscegenation legally banned or publicly censured. None the less white Creole inter-marriage remains customary if not mandatory; whites who marry non-white West Indians are, in the main, expatriates unconstrained by Creole family ties.

In the French Antilles endogamy is vital to *béké* economic as well as social dominance and demands social exclusion against the risk of forbidden attachments. Male friendships across colour lines, however warm and enduring, never extend into family lives. *Grands mulâtres* on friendly terms with *békés* may be invited to funerals, but, one of them confides, 'never to baptisms nor weddings.'[2]

Severe penalties underscore these sanctions. If a white Martinican 'marries a coloured person he is rejected by his family and by the other whites. Socially he is completely ostracized. . . . A white man who marries a coloured person becomes for the group a "béké sauté barrière"; he is no longer in the group.' His descendants are also excluded, even though the element of colour originated several genera-tions back. Some fourteen Martinique families are 'somatically com-pletely similar to whites, and only one thoroughly familiar with their genealogy would call them anything else. . . . But the distinction remains; they are not whites, and [though] some of them are very rich indeed, socially they are beyond the pale.'[3]

British Caribbean whites who marry non-whites suffer less extreme ostracism. To wed a renowned coloured barrister, subsequently the

---

[1] In *Trinidad Express*, 24 November 1968, p. 23, quoted in Anthony P. Maingot, 'From Ethnocentric to National History Writing in the Plural Society', *CS*, Vol. 9, No. 3, October 1969, pp. 68–86, ref. p. 68.

[2] Kovats-Beaudoux, 'Une minorité dominante', p. 72.

[3] Ibid., pp. 121–2, 129, 89.

island's Premier and later Prime Minister of the West Indies Federation, the daughter of a white Barbadian planter fled from her parents' home.[1] This marriage has not established a precedent nor broken down Barbadian social barriers.

Despite egalitarian credos, despite the eradication of overt discrimination, despite the fluidity of colour lines, West Indian racial stratification is not likely to dissolve soon. West Indians are well aware of this. 'In Brazil and the Dominican Republic', comments a sociologist, one often hears the remark that 'We are becoming one people'.[2] But in the non-Iberian Caribbean such a remark is made only facetiously or for export.

Because social distance pervades all aspects of life, public as well as intimate, West Indians stereotype one another by class and colour. Even intimates at school or on a job are referred to by race or ethnic stock. French Antillean *békés* 'speak with one voice', and all classes speak of them generically. A short story depicts similar clustering among light-skinned Trinidadians:

In Trinidad I was not a Negro, I was a Creole. The Negroes were the poor people who lived in the slums or worked as unskilled labour in the oil fields and on the sugar plantations. We Creoles believed that we were the elite of Trinidad and there was a tacit agreement among the little groups of which our society consisted that everyone else should be kept out. We were particularly afraid that some Negro might enter into our cliques and 'get at' one of our daughters or sisters. . . . As our groups were formed by people who for the most part were close relatives, . . . the only love affairs there were, were incestuous.[3]

Race and colour are shorthand designations of class, but they often overwhelm all other connotations; colour visibility may transcend other elements of class. Racial awareness is instilled in West Indians from early childhood. And the habit of racial stereotyping encourages isolation. In Park's phrase, 'it is the essence of race relations that they are the relations of strangers'.[4] Even in small West Indian societies, some people of different colours scarcely know one another as individuals. Back home after a few years' absence from the most easy-going of islands, a white spinster told me: 'It was sad to walk out in the street and not to recognize anyone. We never met the coloured people when

[1] F. A. Hoyos, *The Rise of West Indian Democracy: The Life and Times of Sir Grantley Adams*, 1963, p. 38.

[2] Hoetink, *The Two Variants in Caribbean Race Relations*, p. 189.

[3] Colin Hope, 'Gabrielle', *CQ*, Vol. 15, Nos. 2 and 3, June–September 1969, pp. 109–18, ref. pp. 109–11.

[4] Robert E. Park, 'The Nature of Race Relations', in Edgar T. Thompson, ed., *Race Relations and the Race Problem: A Definition and an Analysis* [1939], pp. 3–45, ref. p. 43.

we were children, and I never did learn to distinguish among them.'
All she had learned was their colour. This is what many West Indians
still know best about one another.

The West Indian class hierarchy is steeply stratified; differences
between classes are profound; contacts across class lines are restricted.
The association of colour with class intensifies awareness of, and adherence to, the differences. Generally the most intransigent class characteristic, colour offers least opportunity for mobility. Yet Caribbean
class systems lack the rigidity common to many other racial hierarchies.
Neither ancestry nor appearance is wholly determinative in the West
Indies; one changes 'colour' by acquiring education, manners, wealth,
associates. Personal status and class affiliation can be altered; indeed,
the prospect of such changes obsesses many West Indians.

Perpetual attrition at the top also makes West Indian society
relatively fluid. The emigration or natural decrease of Caribbean elites
encourages upward mobility: as members of the old elite depart or die
off, darker Creoles move up to take their places. Autonomy and universal suffrage have hastened the process; political power has created
competing sub-elites, and the near-elite and middle class are in constant
flux.

Status may be lost as well as gained. The downward paths of many
careers are routes familiar to West Indians. Decline is in one sense
inescapable; since Caribbean elites are by tradition absentee, merely to
live there is to forfeit status. Further loss accrues to whites who go 'bush'
—take to heavy drinking, become overly intimate with lower-class
folk, or do manual labour for hire. The white peasantry of the French
Antilles are *déclassé* not because they are poor but because they lack
'European' manners and live like 'Africans'. One Martinican *béké*
socially inferior to his wife is called *negre blanc* on account of his passion
for football and cock-fighting.[1]

Risks are graver for the light-coloured sub-elite and middle class.
Idiosyncratic lapses forgivable in a white are not tolerated in a socially
striving coloured man. Above all, he should not marry beneath him. 'A
fair man who marries a dark or black woman ruins his social career',
Henriques wrote of Jamaica twenty years ago.[2] The penalty today
would be less severe, but many educated and talented black women
still are left husbandless.

The ideal of upward mobility is more pervasive than the occurrence.
Opportunities to rise are scarce, because the elite and middle class
comprise but a small proportion of any West Indian population. Only a
few in any generation escape the confines of folk life. But the popular

[1] Kovats-Beaudoux, 'Une minorité dominante', p. 126.
[2] Henriques, *Family and Colour in Jamaica*, p. 55. I am indebted to H. Orlando
Patterson for his unpublished typescript, 'A Jamaican Dilemma'.

view exaggerates and multiplies the occasional success stories. It is an article of faith that luck and pluck alone, regardless of colour, parentage, intelligence, or aptitude, can push anyone up the narrow ladder to elite status. The flavour of Samuel Smiles exhortations or rags-to-riches Frank Merriwell tales suffuses the West Indian air, making colour as malleable a barrier to ultimate triumph as lower-class origins seemed to nineteenth-century British or American social utopians. Although social structures have changed little since slavery, a dynamic sense of individual mobility animates West Indian life. Myth outruns fact, but in the process makes its own reality.

West Indians who achieve high status slough off plebeian associates. Neither those who make good nor those left behind consider such aloofness reprehensible, though it may be resented: 'they get so civilise that they looking at you as if you is nothing and your hopes and dreams and your life is nothing too.'[1] Everyone knows there is room at the top only for the lucky few; indeed, it is because they are few that the goal is worth striving for. Fortune widely shared loses its value.

Many young West Indians are socially ambitious; getting ahead is the main stimulus to effort. But success comes to individuals, not groups. 'The head of the family [traditionally] . . . selected one out of six children whom he wanted to be a doctor, and "rat bite the others."'[2] The sacrifice is often considerable: 'Who here does not remember how mothers used to wash the shirts at night and iron them in the morning, to put the sons through school? Who has forgotten the mad scramble every January to buy shoes and ties and uniform? Who does not know the scrimping and the saving, the drudgery and the slaving?'[3] The child who wins a coveted scholarship enhances the family's prestige and ensures them a measure of practical support, but a Trinidad secondary school survey showed that 'the recognition of economic obligation to their parents on the part of lower-class students . . . [entails no] psychological closeness to them.'[4]

Parental sacrifice indeed required that the successful scholar neglect the group, as St. Omer's school-leaving protagonist makes poignantly plain: 'For him and for others like him, nothing but this driving force towards personal satisfaction and achievement could matter now, nor

[1] Earl Lovelace, 'The Wine of Astonishment', *Voices*, Vol. 2, No. 1, September–December 1969, pp. 3–7, ref. p. 6.

[2] Karl Hudson-Phillips, quoted in *Trinidad Express*, 27 March 1970, p. 12.

[3] Lloyd Best, 'Black Power and National Reconstruction: Proposals Following the February Revolution', *Tapia Pamphlet* [1970], p. 3.

[4] Marisa Zavalloni, *Adolescents' Values in a Changing Society: A Study of Trinidad Youth*, 1968, p. 23. See also Andrew C. Pearse, 'Education in the British Caribbean: Social and Economic Background', *Vox Guyanae*, Vol. II, No. 1, February 1956, pp. 9–24, ref. pp. 21–2.

would matter for a very long time to come.' He agrees it is selfish to study law instead of staying home to teach. 'My children might consider educating their people. I cannot.' His mother had not toiled for him to submerge himself in the mass, but to escape out of black anonymity and become a *person*.[1]

Education is the most potent mechanism for achieving status. The goal of schooling is not to acquire knowledge but to win prizes and to come out on top with an appropriate set of manners—speech, dress, deportment, classical allusions. A West Indian who is black and poor needs both prizes and manners to get far, but the panache of professional training in London or Paris may in time open any door. A career in medicine or law is not only prestigeful but also provides access to wealth through contacts with men of power.

A 'good' marriage consolidates and perpetuates status, however gained. In most colour-graded societies, 'raising the colour' is a familiar process. But in the West Indies it has been habitual. At least until recently, aspiring West Indians sought light-skinned wives as a matter of course. A brown Jamaican recalls that her 'mother considered it a feather in her cap that she had married a "good brown man"'; her father 'remained aloof from considerations of colour, though we suspected his vanity was touched by my mother's reverent regard for the colour of his skin.' The children were expected to do as their mother had done; 'to raise the colour of the family was to raise its social status.'[2] A prestigious union is still felt to outweigh accompanying drawbacks. 'A sallow skin is believed to make up for lack of intelligence', a Dominican observes, 'and middle-class males often marry sallow-skinned girls who are glaringly incompatible with them in intelligence.'[3] Such a marriage is 'a necessary embarrassment', explains a fellow islander, which 'helps some to climb and intrude into other circles . . . for maintenance of an imaginary "high society" status.'[4] The consequences also help to explain the absence of marital companionship.

In West Indian–metropolitan marriages colour and class are apt to be dissonant. 'Most of the [coloured] men who marry "white"', asserts a Jamaican, 'marry below their social and economic class. Lower-class Caucasian women are always glad to marry distinguished coloured men because it ensures them of a social status and standard of living

[1] St. Omer, *Shades of Grey*, pp. 220–1.

[2] Gladwell, *Brown Face, Big Master*, pp. 23–4. See also Henriques, *Family and Colour in Jamaica*, p. 55. Other observers in Jamaica query, however, the extent to which such marriages occur (Ellis, 'Color and Class in a Jamaican Market Town', p. 357).

[3] Bernard M. Christopher, 'Middle-Class and Their European Values', *Dawnlit*, Vol. V, 1965, pp. 22–6, ref. pp. 22–5.

[4] 'Is It True?' *Dominica Herald*, 5 August 1967, p. 2.

far above what they would enjoy if they married into their own race and class.'[1] Motives for such marriages are, to be sure, more complex than this suggests. But the plebeian ways of some English wives embarrass their coloured husbands in the West Indies, where white skins are felt to be incongruous with common conduct.

West Indian colour preferences are male-oriented; women seldom achieve or transmit status through personal merit. Thus marrying light is a man's perquisite, whereas marriage to a darker man may give a woman a 'greater economic security because only the more successful men can obtain a fairer mate.'[2]

But marrying light may be a surrogate for upward mobility rather than its cap-stone. Few West Indians can ascend the narrow educational ladder, whereas many can find wives lighter than themselves. A young black Barbadian whose mother urges him to 'always look for something higher than you, son,' is depicted dreaming of marriage to a light-skinned girl as perhaps his only step up the social scale;[3] his children may rise from there. Status striving prevails throughout West Indian society.

Compared with South Africa or the United States, the one ideologically and the other institutionally racialist, the West Indies are in most ways open. South African Bantu and American blacks, living in larger, more industrialized, and less ascriptive societies, may reach goals unavailable to non-white West Indians. But race sets obvious limits for the Bantu: he cannot gain national status in white-dominated South Africa. Within black America mobility is considerable, but colour restricts wider roles. In white America blacks can gain prestige but little power; and the greater their success the more they tend to be lost to the black community, which remains a world apart. In America as in the West Indies the upwardly mobile leave families and humble origins behind, but the black man who makes good in the United States is more *déraciné* than the West Indian. And he is ultimately less successful because America remains white; the black West Indian increasingly inherits his own society.

Racial demography mirrors these three social structures and partly explains differences in mobility. Whites professing egalitarianism among themselves but addicted to racial endogamy comprise the overwhelming American majority and the all-powerful South African minority. In both countries the social elite is symbolically inconsequential; status striving is not a major aspect of life. The small West Indian white minority, by contrast, is elitist in habit but less racially

---

[1] Ambrose Mason, letter in *Newday*, Vol. 5, No. 5, May 1961, p. 38.
[2] Fernando Henriques, *Family and Colour in Jamaica*, 2nd ed., 1968, p. 58.
[3] Frank A. Collymore, 'To Meet Her Mother', *Bim*, Vol. 11, No. 44, January–June 1967, pp. 290–5, ref. p. 292.

exclusive in policy and practice. Status obsesses many West Indians but colour groupings are blurred and fragmented rather than dichotomized, and the attrition of white and light elites facilitates black mobility. The numerical weakness of the elite forces cognizance of pressures from below, and the entire class hierarchy is knit together by intermixing, acculturation, and assimilation.

Each territory displays its own style of consensus. In Barbados colour consciousness and class barriers inhibit social contact, but common cultural features and modes of behaviour, including a keen parochial pride, pervade the entire community. In Trinidad a live-and-let-live tolerance and a leavening sense of the absurd take the edge off intermittent divisive crises. 'What will keep this society together, is not the army and the police,' mocks a local critic, 'but the general indifference of the people to any action which reduces comfort, and the easy acceptance of dishonesty.'[1] In most of the Windwards, despite profound cultural differences between peasantry and elite, colour tolerance makes contact easy in a wide range of milieus.

Post-emancipation plantation decline or dissolution in many small territories brought people together by eliminating the worst inequities. 'Sugar had ceased to be king and consequently . . . there were no barons at all, . . . no glaring inequalities and no hardened stratifications', explains a Dominican, appreciative of 'a harmony induced by the relative poverty of all sections, plus the social mobility of a racially mixed society of land-owning farmers.' Social flexibility is enhanced, he adds, by the ambiguous status of many elite offspring; 'widespread illegitimacy makes it difficult to maintain hardened race and class structures.'[2]

The social structure is more rigid and mobility more limited in Montserrat, but there, too, differences are lessened because no one has been even moderately affluent for a long time. Some of the early planters knew great luxury, but emancipation, free trade, and hurricanes ended sumptuous living. In 1888 the President could find no well-to-do class on the island. The absence of glaring contrasts between rich and poor enables Montserratians to feel, at times, that they are all one community. The few Montserratian elite, though socially exclusive, are none the less in everyday contact with some of the folk. The Government itself, on which most Montserratians directly depend,

[1] Y. Lord, 'No Dam Dog Bark', *Moko*, No. 15, 23 May 1969, pp. 2–3, ref. p. 3. 'We are all Trinidadians, but our citizenship has not been gained by an act of parliament or by statistics on a passport. We are Trinidadians because we have an instinct to live and to let live' (Benedict Wight, 'A Soliloquy: I Am a Trinidadian', *Trinidad Express*, 9 March 1970, p. 9). See also Eugène Revert, *La Martinique: étude géographique*, 1949, pp. 501–2.

[2] L. A. Roberts, 'Freedom Party Speech . . . June 1st', *Dominica Star*, 13–14 June 1969, p. 2.

is small enough to promote intimacy.[1] Likewise in the British Virgin Islands 'common experiences under difficult economic circumstances . . . contributed towards the creation of an indissoluble bond between all sectors of the population which is still a characteristic of society'.[2]

Environmental and structural conditions thus induce interclass solidarity and damp down conflict. West Indians unite against outside dangers, real or imaginary. Natural catastrophes—droughts, floods, earthquakes, above all hurricanes—cut across class lines to promote community co-operation. Normally little concerned about back-country poverty, the urban elite rally around with food, clothing, shelter, and transport when a hurricane hits. Island-wide sympathy and gifts go to other territories at times of disaster. Smallness of scale facilitates contacts in every West Indian society. 'An island . . . is a small self-contained unit which knows its own boundaries, its own nature, its own idiosyncrasies. People who live on islands know each other, and are in touch with what is going on over in [the next] parish'.[3]

Constant propinquity can be a drawback as well as a virtue, to be sure. 'One can feel very quickly at home on an island, . . . but on the other hand one may feel hemmed in, even claustrophobic; the very familiarity of everything becomes a burden and a limitation; then one longs for the anonymity of a great city'.[4] Small-islanders at the University of the West Indies in Jamaica are a thousand miles from home but even so they find home ties constraining; 'no family or friend is ever out of reach: no one gets lost in the way that an American midwesterner can anonymously attempt to reshape himself'.[5] In this sense no West Indian can ever entirely escape his background.

Expressions of both solidarity and conflict in Caribbean societies are seldom abstract; they reflect face-to-face intimacies among a wide range of the population. Interclass contacts may be rare for the rural peasantry, but elite and folk leaders are in daily proximity. It would be logistically difficult for employers' and workers' representatives not to

---

[1] John Spencer Churchill to Chamberlain, in Register of Letters from the President of Montserrat (1884–9), No. 180, 13 December 1888. See also David Lowenthal, 'Montserrat: Autonomy in Microcosm', 1961, p. 74. The lack of resources and of a landed or an absentee planter class promoted a similar egalitarianism, along with general miscegenation, in Anguilla (Della M. Walker, 'Family and Social Structure in Anguilla', in Gerber, ed., *The Family in the Caribbean*, pp. 111–16).

[2] I. Dookhan, 'A History of the British Virgin Islands: Some Notes on Its Writing and Bibliography', 1967, p. 6.

[3] Barbara Howes, ed., 'Introduction', in idem, *From the Green Antilles: Writings of the Caribbean*, 1966, p. xi.

[4] Ibid.

[5] Lucille Mathurin-Mair, 'The Student and the University's Civilising Role', *CQ*, Vol. 15, Nos. 2 and 3, 1969, pp. 8–19, ref. p. 18.

run across each other in any small West Indian capital. In these circumstances factionalism and gossip abound, quarrels based on collective interests merge with private hostilities, and group disputes became personalized.

But the frequency of encounters may make social divisions seem more intense than they actually are. Circumscribed arenas ensure that champions of rival causes will often also meet as allies. The limitations of local enterprise, the risks of entrepreneurship, the need to insure against catastrophe, encourage West Indians to engage in several pursuits at once; and occupational multiplicity increases up the socio-economic scale. Representatives of class interests are therefore seldom uncompromising ideologues. The planter and the labour leader who lock horns in the legislature or in a strike will also be co-operating on welcoming committees, tourist boards, chambers of commerce, school boards, and church vestries. Both will visit hospitals, organize outdoor relief, officiate at cricket matches and beauty contests, and attend gas-station or Coca-Cola plant openings. Neither could forgo this all-inclusive round and remain potent in the local society.

Joint participation at so many levels tempers partisan passions and curtails the emotional force of class conflict. Rival leaders often acquire a high mutual regard, especially where other able men have emigrated. Long publicly embattled, the white Creole estate representative and the black labour leader of Montserrat expressed admiration for one another as men of energy and ability.

Among the mass of the people as well, the small size of West Indian societies promotes a familiarity that makes it hard to sustain uncompromising hostility. West Indians who have to live in the same small island all their lives learn early how to get along with those from whom they differ. And personal intimacies transcend expectations based on abstract morality or causes. 'Outspoken categorical judgements of other groups are continually vitiated by individual exceptions known to the speaker.' Knowledge of one another's private shortcomings leads people to discredit any claims or pretensions to an unrelenting moral uprightness. A sociologist characterizes Trinidad as 'a heterogeneous society, in which many members recognize . . . that ultimate values may be relative and arbitrary'.[1] In the West Indies generally, personalism usually overrides divisive moral imperatives.

[1] Ivar Oxaal, 'Race, Pluralism and Nationalism in the British Caribbean', *Journal of Biosocial Science*, Supp. No. 1, July 1969, pp. 153–62, ref. p. 161. As in a small Chicago community, 'gossip and scandal are so rife . . . that they destroy the illusion that public norms either provide a dependable picture of reality or a reliable view of each other' (Suttles, *The Social Order of the Slum*, p. 79). For a discussion of these social circumstances see David Lowenthal and Lambros Comitas, 'Emigration and Depopulation: Some Neglected Aspects of Population Geography', *GR*, Vol. 52, 1962, pp. 195–210; Lambros Comitas, 'Occupational Multiplicity in Rural Jamaica',

Values that transcend class lend a sense of community to most West Indian societies. To be sure, goals are variously defined, ordered, and reached by each class, and the gulf between folk and elite circumstances is a source of envy and distress as well as a spur to ambition and emulation. But all classes tend to *believe* that their ideals are universally held; except for Ras Tafari, and more lately some black-power spokesmen, no Creole group expresses a creed that is not integrative and majoritarian. Marriage and freehold property, for example, are seen as desirable alike by those who normally enjoy them and by those who rarely do. That this ideal is a commonplace for some and a remote or unrealizable prospect for others gives rise to much misunderstanding and tension but does not preclude all unity.

Unity is possible partly because the social structure itself is a shared value. Differential rewards occasion much grief, but West Indians still tend to accept stratification as natural, even inevitable. Status aspirations blunt the impetus of reform but also stitch together the social fabric. Mass heroes are often from upper-class backgrounds. Thus Trinidad's urban proletariat revered Captain A. A. Cipriani; no 'objection was ever raised', avers a local historian, 'to having a white French creole planter lead a predominantly black lower class social protest movement'.[1] Indeed, his followers felt that Cipriani's whiteness made the local elite and the Colonial Office more apt to heed him. Jamaica's trade-union movement has likewise 'consistently drawn its leadership from outside its own ranks' because, it is suggested, the rank and file feel they themselves lack the linguistic skills to deal with local employers and government.[2] Ambassadors should similarly be light-skinned; the 'fair and brown are more capable of representing Jamaica either at home or abroad'; for it is believed that in 'a white world it is easier for the fair Jamaican to elicit support'.[3]

Intellectual prestige is a major factor in leadership appeal. Many West Indian popular figures have had brilliant scholastic records—Adams of Barbados, Burnham of Guyana, Manley of Jamaica, Césaire of Martinique, Williams of Trinidad. Neither social nor cultural distance inhibits academics from vigorous political participation. The West Indian 'doctor', whether real or self-styled, derives authority

in Viola Garfield and Ernestine Friedl, eds., *Proceedings of the American Ethnological Society, 1963*, 1964, pp. 41–56; Burton Benedict, 'Sociological Aspects of Smallness', in Benedict, ed., *Problems of Smaller Territories*, 1967, pp. 45–55; Urias Forbes, 'The West Indies Associated States: Some Aspects of the Constitutional Arrangements', *SES*, Vol. 19, 1970, pp. 57–88; and, in another context, William A. Christian, Jr., *Divided Island: Faction and Unity on Saint Pierre*, 1969.

[1] Selwyn D. Ryan, 'Rise and Fall of the Barefooted Man', *Trinidad and Tobago Index*, No. 3, Winter 1966, pp. 4–15, ref. p. 8.

[2] Alleyne, 'Communication between the Elite and the Masses', p. 15.

[3] Henriques, *Family and Colour in Jamaica*, 2nd ed., p. 174.

from both science and witchcraft. Professional panache, scholarly self-assurance, productivity as pamphleteer and historian are prime features of Eric Williams's charisma. Indeed, for an acceptable opposition candidate East Indians sought a 'doctor' possibly even more erudite. Scholarly achievement has been a vital asset in West Indian political success.

West Indian willingness to be led from above was patent at a recent Caribbean consumers' seminar. The middle-class origins of the various consumer movements were openly acknowledged, and 'instead of behaving as if this were something to be rather ashamed of, it was regarded as inescapable', the British Consumer Council's director reported. Because 'the middle class set the standard for a country', according to an ancillary report, 'we should make wise consumption a prestige symbol.'[1] Ironic advice, in view of the middle-class habits of conspicuous consumption inherited from the elite, and of the grinding poverty that puts most middle-class consumer goods, however economically selected, beyond the reach of peasantry and proletariat.

The very features that make West Indian societies intensely hierarchical and West Indian classes so remote from one another thus also help to bridge these differences. An acceptance of hierarchy, a traditionalistic regard for manners and background, a dominance of family over personal and national interests, a multiplicity of individual pursuits, the personalization of politics, the effects, both confining and gregarious, of small size and insularity—these give West Indian classes common interests, shared values, and mutual familiarity.

West Indian stratification systems and ideas of status have antecedents in European as well as Caribbean history. But two particular points of strain differentiate Caribbean from most other societies in the New World and the Old. One is the hierarchy of race and colour, deeply affecting the lives of white, coloured, and black, which has been the subject of this chapter. The other is ethnicity, involving relations between East Indians and Creoles. To this we now turn.

[1] Elizabeth Ackroyd, 'Caribbean Jaunt', *New Statesman*, 18 April 1969.

CHAPTER IV

East Indians and Creoles

The colour–class hierarchy embraces most differences among West Indians of European and African descent. Several circumstances alleviate the resulting strains and tensions. One is acquiescence in the idea of stratification, even by many relegated to the bottom; another is the widespread expectation of upward mobility, partly validated by Creole replacement of European elites. Finally, the colour hierarchy is graded rather than polarized. The elaboration and significance of colour differences varies with locale and with context, but West Indian Creoles seldom dichotomize white and black. Instead, the whole colour spectrum intergrades and overlaps.

These features of Creole society—hierarchical gradation, individual and group mobility, general acceptance of the structure—are conspicuously missing in relationships between Creoles and other West Indians. The term 'Creole' often differentiates West Indians of North European, African, and mixed descent both from aboriginal American Indians and from more recent immigrants—Portuguese, Chinese, East Indians, Javanese, and Syrian. These five groups vary in their differences from, and resemblances to, Creoles. But each group, an entity identified by itself and others as culturally distinctive, enjoys cohesion based on a shared ethnic tradition. Between ethnic and racial distinctions there is no fixed line, and ethnic identities and conflicts are often perceived and expressed in racial terms. Indeed, most West Indians do not use the word 'ethnic' and automatically transfer its meanings to 'race'. But in their sense of identity and in their relationships with others, these groups are predominantly *ethnic* rather than *racial*.

Most of them came to the Caribbean on a temporary basis, intending soon to return home. Some, notably the Javanese in Surinam, retain their ancestral citizenship. But the majority have lost ties with their original homelands, many consider themselves truly West Indian, and some have gained high local status. Whether sojourners or settlers, however, they stand in some measure outside the Creole hierarchy, and Creole exclusion reinforces their own aloofness.

Ethnic seclusion has several consequences. First, it encourages Creole and non-Creole to view each other as organic entities rather than as congeries of individuals or intergraded groups. Creole social classes similarly stereotype one another, but individual mobility and status changes blunt the force of these attributions. Between Creoles and non-Creoles, group identification is more homogeneous, intense, and rigidly ascriptive. East Indians differentiate between whites and blacks, to be sure, just as Creoles do. But the East Indian social universe often divides into two realms, their own and that of all Creoles; and most Creoles likewise set East Indians apart.

Second, exclusion from the Creole hierarchy impedes non-Creole access to status, wealth, and power. Adherence to separate traditions and ideals makes mobility less rewarding and at the same time more difficult. Non-Creoles may disdain Creole values, but they none the less want a fair share of local rewards; ethnic inequities constitute a major East Indian grievance against Creoles. Third, non-Creole groups accept West Indian institutions only with considerable reservation and at times reject them entirely. Political parties are ethnically polarized, patriotism may refer to the country of origin, and in time of stress, in Guyana, both sides threatened territorial partitioning.

Grievances within the Creole hierarchy generate considerable resentment and verbal antagonism. But Creole–non-Creole disagreements, reinforced by group stereotypes, are apt to explode in communal violence. East Indian–'African' conflict in Guyana alone, during the pre-independence decade, took more lives than did all the West Indian labour clashes of the 1930s. Ethnic violence is not confined to lands where Creoles and East Indians compete as powerful rivals. Anti-Syrian outbursts in Martinique and the episodic destruction of Chinese shops in Jamaica exemplify Creole resentment toward traders who seem aloof from Creole society. Small ethnic minorities are perennial scapegoats for frustrations rooted in economic causes. But these minorities interact with Creoles in ways unlike the larger East Indian populations, as will be shown in Chapter V.

East Indians are by far the largest non-Creole group and have had the most profound impact on Caribbean society. Nine-tenths of the indentured Indian immigrants were from the Ganges River basin and embarked at Calcutta; the South Indian remainder came from Madras. One in six were Muslims, the rest Hindus. The aegis and dates of migration varied, but the purpose was always to supply plantation labour. And since estate conditions were roughly similar everywhere in the Caribbean, East Indian disparities of caste, religion, and occupation tended to fade into insignificance. East Indians throughout the West Indies are more alike than are Indians within India itself.

The nature of the East Indian group in each Caribbean territory is, however, a function of its size. In Trinidad, Guyana, and Surinam, where they comprise one-third to one-half of the population, Indians manifest a distinctive, flourishing culture and community and compete with Creoles for national power and status. Because their birth rate outdistances that of Creoles, East Indian political dominance is an early prospect in all three territories.

The East Indians of Jamaica, Martinique, Guadeloupe, and the Windward Islands, by contrast, are only small minorities—2 to 4 per cent of the population. Far from challenging Creole hegemony, they hardly constitute viable separate entities and are in large measure subsets of the rural lower class. Although they are, with few exceptions, culturally similar to Creoles and physically dispersed among them, they are by no means integrated within Creole society. Indeed, they display many of the separatist features that mark the larger East Indian communities in Trinidad and the Guianas—group endogamy, a stereotyped (and reciprocated) hostility toward Negroes, and pride in what they view as 'Indianness'. But they lack the distinctive religious tradition, family structure, and material culture that Indians in Trinidad and the Guianas maintain.

Cultural differentiation, in short, is not a prerequisite for East Indian solidarity, nor is the survival of East Indian culture the sole determinant of Caribbean inter-ethnic relations. Much of what passes for Indianness in Trinidad and the Guianas is, indeed, a result as well as a cause of East Indian–Creole stress.

REMOTENESS FROM INDIA

However 'Indian' East Indians in the West Indies may be, they are not much like Indians in India. Less that is ancestral survives in the Caribbean than in most other overseas Indian communities. The extent to which those long cut off from intimate contact with the homeland retain Indian ways depends on how cultural persistence is understood. 'The customs and organizational principles of peasant communities of Oudh before the Mutiny persist in, say, Trinidad, whereas in all likelihood they have changed in India', one scholar points out. 'If the Kenyan grandsons of a Patidar farmer from Gujarat lead the life of the Bombay urban upper class, learned from the *Indian Illustrated Weekly*, does this represent persistence or change?'[1] The Trinidadian Naipaul, otherwise no traditionalist, records his sense of 'outrage when I heard that in Bombay they used candles and electric bulbs for the Diwali festival, and not the rustic clay lamps, of immemorial design, which in Trinidad we still used'.[2]

---

[1] Chandra Jayawardena, 'Migration and Social Change: A Survey of Indian Communities Overseas', *GR*, Vol. 58, 1968, pp. 426–49, ref. p. 439.

[2] V. S. Naipaul, *An Area of Darkness*, 1964, p. 38.

Outsiders and insiders are apt to disagree about what Caribbean Indians have inherited. The features that foreign visitors find strikingly Indian are not those East Indians themselves emphasize, which are in any case radically altered and indeed creolized. Indians themselves are often unaware that they have adopted Creole forms. Even when they are conscious that their culture is changing, they seldom recognize change as an adaptation to the wider West Indian world. 'We were steadily adopting the food styles of others: the Portuguese stew, . . . the Negro way with yams, plaintains, breadfruit and bananas', but, adds Naipaul, 'everything we adopted became our own; the outside was still to be dreaded'.[1]

Of all Indian folkways, the institution of caste has suffered the greatest attrition. Caste adherents among Caribbean immigrants included a fair sampling of those in Hindu India. Agents first recruited hill-country peasants and agricultural castes but finally enlisted anyone from Brahmans to Untouchables. As many as fifty different caste affiliations were likely to appear on the manifest of a shipload bound for the Caribbean.

Indian sub-castes and castes (*jati*)[2] are customarily ranked within the four traditional *varna*—Brahmana (priests), Kshatriya or Rajanya (warriors and princes), Vaishya (merchants, artisans, agriculturalists), and Sudra (servants and labourers); beneath are the outcaste Untouchables. Only those in the first three *varna* are 'twice-born', entitled to perform Vedic ritual and to undergo spiritual rebirth. Caste proportions among Caribbean migrants are hard to estimate; widely separated areas and eras were involved, and many Indians altered their affiliation *en route*. The Creole stereotype that all East Indian migrants were low-caste was baseless; there were Brahmans on almost every ship. But those of high caste were a smaller minority than in India. Brahmans in the Caribbean comprised only 2 per cent (British Guiana) to 5 per cent (Surinam), compared with 11 per cent in the United Provinces of India; and Brahmana and Kshatriya together were only 15 to 20 per cent of the Caribbean Hindus.

The proportion of Hindu immigrants belonging to twice-born castes is in doubt, because many agricultural castes were Vaishya by adherence but Sudra by occupation. But both landowners and labourers were numerous among incomers. So were the more menial Sudra, for whom emigration offered escape from a depressed situation. Low-caste

---

[1] Ibid., p. 35.

[2] The nomenclature of caste is complex, and there is no general agreement about the various levels of the caste hierarchy. For this book I have adopted the classification systems of M. N. Srinivas, *Religion and Society among the Coorgs of South India*, 1952, pp. 24–31; Adrian C. Mayer, 'The Indian Caste System', and H. S. Morris, 'Ethnic Groups', in David Sills, ed., *International Encyclopedia of the Social Sciences*, 1968, Vol. 2, pp. 339–44, and Vol. 5, pp. 167–72, respectively.

Hindus ranged from an estimated 23 per cent of the Hindu total in British Guiana and 33 per cent in Surinam to 40 or 50 per cent in Trinidad. Most numerous and degraded among these were the *Chamars*, traditionally leather workers. Untouchables were rare among the Calcutta emigrants but, with Sudra castes, were a substantial proportion among those who shipped from Madras.[1]

West Indian estate conditions made caste structure difficult to maintain, however. Even those able to withstand the polluting effects traditionally attached to an ocean voyage found caste habits inconsistent with plantation life. Many recruited as agriculturalists were in fact small proprietors unaccustomed to manual labour; others were skilled gardeners physically unable to cope with estate work. Brahmans, however impoverished, felt it demeaning to become common labourers. Caste distinctions soon blurred among those who stayed on the plantations. Field and factory work and enforced barrack residence were incompatible with rituals of caste distance in food preparation and ablutions; estate labour requirements vitiated caste occupational roles. Creole planters largely ignored caste hierarchy in allocating authority and sometimes even reversed ascribed rank; managers and overseers tended to regard low-caste Hindus as better workers than the more assertive Brahmans.

Hindus were unable to maintain a functional distribution of caste skills on any one estate. 'Our community, though seemingly self-contained, was imperfect. Sweepers we had quickly learned to do without. Others supplied the skills of carpenters, masons and cobblers. But we were also without weavers and dyers, workers in brass and makers of string-beds.'[2] And the scarcity of women—only one migrant in three or four was female—made caste endogamy impossible from the start.

Traditional India's major unit of caste organization, the *jati*, has

[1] For caste percentages and other demographic data see C. J. M. de Klerk, *De Immigratie der Hindostanen in Suriname*, 1953, pp. 103–8; Judith Ann Weller, 'The East Indian Indenture in Trinidad', 1968, p. 135; Donald Wood, *Trinidad in Transition: The Years after Slavery*, 1968, pp. 144–5; Raymond T. Smith and Chandra Jayawardena, 'Caste and Social Status among the Indians of Guyana', in Barton M. Schwartz, ed., *Caste in Overseas Indian Communities*, 1967, pp. 43–92, ref. p. 48; Raymond T. Smith, 'Some Social Characteristics of Indian Immigrants to British Guiana', *Population Studies*, Vol. XIII, 1959, pp. 34–9, ref. Table III, pp. 35, 38; Dwarka Nath, *A History of Indians in British Guiana*, 1950, Table 19, pp. 208–10. The Creole belief that most East Indians were low caste stemmed from their assumption that no others would have accepted emigration to the 'slavery' they themselves despised; 'the coolies belonged to the worst elements in British India, and only thieves, murderers and prostitutes would participate in such a scheme' (Johan D. Speckmann, 'The Indian Group in the Segmented Society of Surinam', *CS*, Vol. 3, No. 1, April 1963, pp. 3–17, ref. p. 8).

[2] Naipaul, *An Area of Darkness*, pp. 31–2.

almost entirely disintegrated in the West Indies. In India the *jati* defines status, determines marriage, and organizes religious ritual; in the West Indies it serves none of these functions. Occupational specialization has disappeared save for the priesthood, which is still reserved to Brahmans. 'There is no caste organization, no caste council, and no set of rules to regulate intercaste relationships and obligations at either a personal or group level. Children are not initiated into caste, and castes do not discipline their members for breaking caste rules; indeed, there are no rules.'[1] Unable to name their own *jati* were 13 per cent of those queried in Trinidad, 25 per cent in Guyana, and most Hindus in rural Jamaica. Intra-caste (*jati*) marriages account for less than half of all Hindu unions in Trinidad, one-fourth of those in Guyana.[2]

Although the caste as a functioning endogamous unit is gone, *varna* to some degree substitutes for *jati* corporate identity. Indeed, many East Indians scarcely differentiate the two. 'Varna is rarely mentioned explicitly when caste is discussed by Hindus' in San Fernando, Trinidad, 'but they think in terms of high, medium, and low castes, and varna adequately expresses this rank order.'[3] The dissolution of *jati* and the persistence of *varna* somewhat resembles earlier Vedic forms; such caste features as *jajmani* (patron–client relationships) and hierarchies of purity and pollution are dispensed with, others, such as endogamy and the private avoidance of caste commensality (eating together), are kept. Extreme incongruities of caste are avoided by habitual *varna* endogamy. In the Caribbean, then, *varna* roughly correspond with class but lack *jati* prescriptive and proscriptive power; they do not organize ritual and are only broadly indicative of occupation.

Concepts of pollution and purity have also been standardized in the Caribbean. Good Hindus consider it sufficient to undertake periodic ritual cleansing, to shun beef and pork, and to eschew such occupations as butchering, shoemaking, and laundering. Residential segregation, customary in India, in Trinidad affects only 'impure' Sudras and outcastes, who raise pigs, eat pork, or catch crabs. Dwelling apart at the margins of towns and rural villages, these folk move into other neighbourhoods when they cease practices other Hindus consider polluting.[4]

Caste attribution endures as a mark of status, but it has acquired a

[1] Colin G. Clarke, 'Caste among Hindus in a Town in Trinidad: San Fernando', in Schwartz, ed., *Caste in Overseas Indian Communities*, pp. 165–99, ref. p. 168.

[2] Clarke, 'Caste among Hindus in a Town in Trinidad', p. 172; Raymond T. Smith and Jayawardena, 'Caste and Social Status among the Indians of Guyana', p. 71; Allen S. Ehrlich, 'East Indian Cane Workers in Jamaica', 1969, p. 123 and footnote 11, p. 246.

[3] Clarke, 'Caste among Hindus in a Town in Trinidad', p. 174.

[4] Arthur Niehoff and Juanita Niehoff, *East Indians in the West Indies*, 1960, p. 93. See also Morton Klass, *East Indians in Trinidad: A Study of Cultural Persistence*, 1961, pp. 59, 62, 64.

Creole-like flexibility. 'Brahman' is a term of general respect, and there are Indians who like to 'clothe their leaders in traditional dignity, and refer to the late Dr. J. B. Singh [a British Guiana leader of the 1920s and 1930s] as an "Indian prince" because of his Kshatriya origin,' but these are understood to be 'symbolic statements', not literal descriptions.[1] In like manner, low-caste names are common terms of insult and abuse—thus in Trinidad, 'Man, you're a jackass and from the lowest "nation" on earth, the Chamars', or in Guyana, '"You dirty Chamar bitch"'. But this has no reference to the caste of the person abused, who may be . . . of any caste', or, indeed, a Creole.[2]

Caste has, in short, dissolved as a functional form but survived as an aspect of prejudice, a matter of style, an ingredient of personality. 'In Trinidad caste had no meaning in our day-to-day life; the caste we occasionally played at was no more than an acknowledgement of latent qualities; the assurance it offered was such as might have been offered by a palmist or a reader of handwriting.' Yet when it was rumoured that Naipaul's distant relative had married a *Chamar*, rich, travelled, successful, but a *Chamar* none the less, the notion appalled him, and 'the thought still occurs whenever we meet and that initial sniffing for difference is now involuntary.'[3] A Surinamese Brahman similarly remarked of a young Hindu that though 'he may have studied in the Netherlands and he may hold an important position here, he nevertheless remains a Chamar; you can always notice it by his way of life and his manners.'[4] Caste codes continue to flavour Caribbean life long after they have ceased to be dominant.

If caste has lost most of its relevance in the Caribbean, this is by no means true of Indian religion. Where the Indians are a small minority they are generally Christianized—Catholic in the French Antilles, Protestant in Jamaica—but in the Guianas and Trinidad the great majority remain Hindu and Muslim. Doctrines of *dharma* (righteous conduct) and *karma* (moral causation), of reincarnation and the wheel of life, intimately connect Hinduism and caste. But the erosion of caste leaves formal religion as the major focus of communal activities and beliefs.

Hindu–Muslim dissension, carried over from India, still endures in the Caribbean. More than caste distinctions, religious differences long preoccupied East Indians there. 'To our condition as Indians in a multi-racial society we gave no thought', Naipaul recalls of his schooldays, but 'Muslims were somewhat more different than others. They

[1] Raymond T. Smith and Jayawardena, 'Caste and Social Status among the Indians of Guyana', p. 89.

[2] Niehoff and Niehoff, *East Indians in the West Indies*, p. 91; Raymond T. Smith and Jayawardena, 'Caste and Social Status among the Indians of Guyana', p. 62.

[3] Naipaul, *An Area of Darkness*, p. 36.

[4] Quoted in Johan D. Speckmann, 'The Caste System and the Hindustani Group in Surinam', in Schwartz, ed., *Caste in Overseas Indian Communities*, pp. 201–12, ref. p. 209.

were not to be trusted; they would always do you down', and hostile suspicions were made vivid by the continuous presence of a Muslim 'in whose cap and grey beard, avowals of his special difference, lay every sort of threat.'[1] Hindu mistrust of Muslims endures, but Creole dominance has diminished Hindu-Muslim tensions. In Trinidad 'it is not uncommon to find Muslims attending Hindu prayer meetings held at the home of friends, or vice versa.'[2] And in Surinam Hindus and Muslims together present a closed front to all outsiders, Creoles and Javanese alike.

Among Caribbean East Indians Islam has lost its proselytizing force, and despite their relatively small numbers, Muslims there are divided by factionalism (mainly traditional versus reformist). Islam remains most potent in Surinam, where Javanese share that creed with East Indians. Despite formal equality with Hinduism, Muslims lack community strength, and some of them treat religious affiliation as purely nominal: thus a Trinidad Muslim who had never heard of the Koran testified that his religion was 'Indian'.[3] Perhaps as a consequence, Muslims have often become more creolized than Hindus, but they generally follow Hindu social patterns and attitudes, live in the same villages, and are considered one people with them, both in their own eyes and those of others.

Hinduism is the principal focus for expressing ethnic solidarity and disseminating Indian culture. Even among Christian Indians (Presbyterians, Anglicans, and Catholics), Hinduism has come to stand for 'Indian'; in Surinam Christian couples sometimes marry in Hindu style to reaffirm their membership in the Indian group. In Trinidad and Guyana likewise, a Christian Indian is assumed to be 'Hindu' in culture, and in this sense a member of the Indian community. But these new roles have forced traditional Hinduism into new forms, notably through the establishment of local Sanatan Dharma, similar to orthodox Hindu organizations in India.

Trends have led from village and caste beliefs and practices to wider, more universalistic, definitions of Hinduism that cut across local and caste differences. . . . Development of the Sanatan Dharm and the decline of all smaller sects . . . [stem from] a consciousness of being all Indians in a multiethnic society, where . . . finer distinctions of caste, ritual, and belief were unappreciated and ignored.[4]

[1] Naipaul, *An Area of Darkness*, p. 33.
[2] Carole D. Yawney, 'Drinking Patterns and Alcoholism among East Indians and Negroes in Trinidad', 1968, p. 33, also p. 72. See also Selwyn D. Ryan, 'The Struggle for Afro-Indian Solidarity in Trinidad and Tobago', *Trinidad and Tobago Index*, No. 4, September 1966, pp. 3–28, ref. p. 24, footnote 12; V. S. Naipaul, *The Suffrage of Elvira*, 1958, pp. 74, 129–30, 161; Johan D. Speckmann, *Marriage and Kinship among the Indians in Surinam*, 1965, pp. 110–11, 131.
[3] Derek Bickerton, *The Murders of Boysie Singh*, 1962, p. 128.
[4] Jayawardena, 'Migration and Social Change', p. 444.

Hinduism in the Caribbean is a simpler and more homogeneous creed than in India. And in aspects of structure and function it strikingly resembles Christianity. Competition is the root cause: to counter Christian proselytization, Hinduism has achieved a comparable conceptual scope and organizational range. Brahman priests today dispense standard ritual at all community temples; they hold services at weekends, respond to calls for private domestic ceremonies, visit hospitals, and advise their parishioners much as Christian ministers do. Hindu priests like Christian frown on magical healing and spirit possession as 'pagan'.

Yet West Indian Hindus are more self-consciously 'Hindu' than are others overseas or even, perhaps, in India. Discriminatory social controls exerted through Church-run schools and Christian marriage legislation impelled Caribbean Hindus to reaffirm their philosophic creed and to elaborate its ceremonies. Competition thus led Hindus to emphasize uniqueness in belief and ritual while emulating Christian structure and function.

Quite different are the cult-followers of South Indian descent—the Madrasi of the French Antilles and a few localities in Trinidad and Guyana. Dark-skinned, of Dravidian rather than Aryan origin, most Madrasi are treated as low caste or outcaste in the Caribbean. 'Madrassi and Nigger is de same ting', was one Trinidadian's scornful reaction to her new son-in-law, although both were not only East Indian but Christian.[1] Many Madrasi retain no trace of formal Hinduism; those in the French Antilles are Roman Catholic. But since their origins were mainly Sudra or Untouchable, Sanskritic gods were of less consequence in their pattern of worship than the propitiation of local deities by shamanistic possession and animal sacrifice. The latter practices are still current both on the Courantyne Coast of Guyana and —Catholicism notwithstanding—in the French Antilles. Hindu leaders condemn Madrasi pantheism, spirit possession, healing rituals, and autonomous temples, but Creoles accept them as genuine folk faith; in Guyana the majority of Obeah practitioners today are reputed to be East Indians. French Antillean Creoles often seek advice from East Indian priests, who share curative and other powers with Creole magicians, and who celebrate rituals honouring a pantheon headed by the deity Maldevidan, variously identified with Christ, Vishnu, and St. Michael.[2] In Guyana an annual Kali Mai Puja ceremony, conducted

[1] Clarke, 'Caste among Hindus in a Town in Trinidad', p. 175.

[2] Michael M. Horowitz and Morton Klass, 'The Martiniquan East Indian Cult of Maldevidan', *SES*, Vol. 10, 1961, pp. 93–100. See also Jayawardena, 'Migration and Social Change', pp. 425–6, 446; idem, *Conflict and Solidarity in a Guianese Plantation*, 1963, pp. 22–5; Raymond T. Smith, *British Guiana*, 1962, pp. 124–7; André Nègre, 'Les "Indiens" de la Guadeloupe et leurs rites religieux', *Bulletin de la Société d'Histoire de la Guadeloupe*, No. 1, 1964, pp. 33–43.

not by Brahmans but by South Indian priests and generally regarded as 'Madrasi', attracts many Creole devotees. Trinidad Creoles term the comparable, secularized, North Indian ceremony of Ramlila 'Coolie Carnival'.

Indian religions in the Caribbean thus exhibit a two-fold departure from ancestral forms and convergence with Creole culture. At the national level, especially in Trinidad and Guyana, Hinduism emphasizes symbolic distinctiveness while adopting Christian institutional forms; at the folk level, remnants of local cults, pantheism, magical practices, and spirit possession coalesce with pre-Christian and pagan aspects of Creole faith.

Most East Indians consider the patrilineal extended family the ideal form. But Caribbean estate life made this ideal economically and socially impracticable. Indians who left the plantations to become peasant farmers secured limited control over their children's families through land ownership, but this dominion was of brief duration, except in Surinam and in parts of rural Trinidad. And where East Indians remain tenants and wage earners, the nuclear household has generally supplanted the extended family. A son may continue to live with his parents after he marries, but a separate home usually follows the birth of his first child, even though that home may be close by.

Dying out along with the extended family is much of the traditional Indian dominance of husband over wife, father over son. As scarce and hence valuable commodities, Indian women drove hard bargains from the start; today many of them go out to work, keep their own money, and, except in the realm of sexual behaviour, resemble Creoles in their lack of subservience to men. Traditional marriage to a chosen groom may be terminated by separation and followed by a second union, formal or consensual, giving the woman more independence and power. Urban migration requires many East Indian men to work far from home or renders them jobless, leaving women to shoulder responsibility for children and old people. Even in rural homes where fathers still rule, reverence for paternal authority is but a shadow of what it used to be.[1]

The most pervasive links with the Indian past are in the realm of material culture. 'India lay about us in things', Naipaul has put it;

in a string bed or two, grimy, tattered, no longer serving any function, never repaired because there was no one with this caste skill in Trinidad; . . . in wooden printing blocks, never used because printed cotton was abundant and cheap and because the secret of the dyes had been forgotten, no dyer being at

[1] Leo Davids, 'The East Indian Family Overseas', SES, Vol. 13, 1964, pp. 383–96; Lauchmonen, Old Thom's Harvest, 1965; Johanna M. Lessinger, 'Produce Vendors in the Princes Town Market, 1968, pp. 41, 52; Speckmann, Marriage and Kinship among the Indians in Surinam, p. 198.

hand; . . . in brightly coloured pictures of deities on pink lotus or radiant against Himalayan snow; and in all the paraphernalia of the prayer-room.[1]

Clothing, food, and language display a common sequence of retention, gradual disappearance, then self-conscious revival in ethnic separatism. The elaborate *pagadi* headdresses, the ubiquitous long skirts and *orhnis*, *dhotis* and *shalwars*, gave way by the time of the Second World War to dress differentiated from Creole mainly by the vestigial head veils of East Indian women and the ceremonial *dhotis* of some men. But imminent independence in India and rising ethnic tensions in the Caribbean impelled many East Indians to adopt imported saris and other items of 'national' dress.

The decline and rejuvenation of Hindi follow the same pattern. Within a generation of their Caribbean arrival, indentured East Indians, save those in Surinam, spoke English and had begun to forget their native Hindi, Tamil, or Telegu. Although many rural Indians in Trinidad and Surinam continue to speak Hindi at home, almost all are bilingual in Creolese. National sentiment reanimated by Indian independence spurred prominent East Indians to advocate Hindi instruction in schools, and Hindi has become an anti-Creole focus for urban Indians, even those whose ancestral tongue it was not.

Cuisine is the most ubiquitous and in some ways the most consequential Indian cultural survival. Indians throughout the Caribbean cling to traditional dietary habits. The use of rice and edible oils, the preponderance of curry, and the indispensability of *masala* distinguish East Indian meals. Foods such as *dahl*, *roti*, and *powah* are virtually all that remain of Indian material culture in Jamaica. Women still grind spices and colour them with turmeric grown in their own gardens.

Rice is the principal Indian food transplanted to the Caribbean. Upland rice had long been grown by Creoles, but Indians were used to and preferred irrigated varieties. Indentured immigrants brought over wet rice, which became the staple crop among East Indian peasant farmers. Wet-rice cultivation today is distinctively Indian in Surinam and Guyana and is exclusively Indian in Trinidad, Jamaica, and the French Antilles, but as a food rice now belongs as much to the Creole as the Indian diet, even in territories devoid of East Indians.

East Indians in the Caribbean thus remain more 'Indian' in some ways than in others. But trait-by-trait generalizations grossly over-simplify; degrees and types of 'Indianness' vary from place to place, from city to countryside, from old to young. Surinam's rural East Indians remain most traditional, urban Trinidad's least. In Trinidad the Oropouche Lagoon, an area affected both by Presbyterian missions and by industrialization, is more creolized than conservative Caroni,

[1] Naipaul, *An Area of Darkness*, p. 31.

where outside influences hardly affect peasant farmers. The Mahasabha resists urban creolization with indianization; the countryside is unselfconsciously Indian. In localities remote from city life, 'any traditional manifestations of East Indian life-styles . . . are *real*, not artificial.'[1]

How Indian the East Indians remain, and how Creole they have become, are two quite different, though related, questions. Some Indians express the wish to be 'just like a Creole'; others derogate Creole-like behaviour. These opposing values lead some to overlook, others to exaggerate, the extent to which they have forgotten Indian and have adopted Creole ways.

Attitudes may range widely in a single household; an East Indian in Chaguanas, Trinidad, assured an interlocutor, 'I'm completely Creolized, man,' while his wife and daughters were in the kitchen singing Indian songs and dancing steps learned from Indian movies.[2] Market vendors make 'no attempt to disclaim knowledge of Hindi, or familiarity with food, customs, or music which are identified as "Indian" in Trinidad', but 'their children would often deny knowing about such "old fashion" things.'[3]

Some '"creolized" Indian women', charges an opponent of assimilation, 'not only disclaim . . . any knowledge of Indian [ways] of life, but actually scoff at it!'[4] Like Indians in South Africa who expressed 'anxiety at a book which discussed their way of life as being in any way different from that of white South Africans',[5] they are less confident about being Creole than desirous to show they are creolized. Thus in a Selvon story, a Negro overhears Indians and says to a friend, 'Listen to them two Indian how they arguing about we creole calypso.' An Indian retorts, 'Man, I is a creolise Trinidadian, oui.'[6] The points of mutual reference, the use of the patois phrase, the ease of banter reflect the common wish to seem creolized.

To emphasize the Indian and ignore Creole aspects, to deny that the wider West Indian world has made any substantial inroads, is more characteristic.

Country Indians have a distinct manner of speaking, family structure, code of behaviour, amusement, even a different diet from the Creoles. . . . They may not care for rented houses, fêtes, carnival, English movies. . . . Contact with the Creole world is minimal, limited to a vague togetherness at Christmas or

---

[1] Yawney, Drinking Patterns and Alcoholism among East Indians and Negroes in Trinidad', p. 33. See also Ivar Oxaal, *Black Intellectuals Come to Power*, 1968, pp. 26–7.

[2] F. T. Cloak, Jr., *A Natural Order of Cultural Adoption and Loss in Trinidad*, 1966, pp. 110–11.

[3] Lessinger, 'Produce Vendors in the Princes Town Market', p. 40.

[4] H. P. Singh, *The Indian Enigma*, 1965, p. 7.

[5] Hilda Kuper, *Indian People in Natal*, 1960, p. xx.

[6] Samuel Selvon, 'Calypsonian', in G. R. Coulthard, ed., *Caribbean Literature: An Anthology*, 1966, pp. 72–83, ref. p. 79.

Carnival. Such Indians . . . simply ignore the Creole life as much as they can. They do not read newspapers, they use their radios for Indian music, and they seldom visit towns.[1]

But purely ancestral culture and social institutions survive as ideals rather than as realities or endure in name but are creolized in character and function. Many insistent aspects of Indianness are either syncretized adaptations to Creole life or deliberate resuscitations of all but forgotten folkways.

East Indians who have gone home are most keenly aware of being, if not fully West Indian, at least no longer Indian in any traditional sense. An East Indian who visited Calcutta a century ago came back to Trinidad warning that 'there was no use in those who were accustomed to the ways of this country returning to India', because 'the manners of the East were different and utterly opposed to the freedom of life that they were accustomed to here'.[2] Low-caste Hindus especially found it hard 'to reassume their traditionally subordinate positions in a village in India after life and work in an island where the chance to better themselves was more easily attainable.'[3] Even as a temporary visitor, the Caribbean East Indian is now an alien in India.

INDIAN–CREOLE DIFFERENCES

Yet East Indian ways of life and thought differ substantially from Creole patterns. Although little traditional remains and creolization is pervasive, East Indian culture and social organization, personality traits and values, are markedly unlike those of other West Indians. 'The average Indian knows little of his past, would be unable to argue well for his way of life or his religion, but he believes in it nonetheless.' Indians, one of them contends, 'remain separate because they have little in common with the urban Negro people.'[4] Heightened by isolation, ignorance, and fear, these differences have engendered negative, persistent, and inclusive group stereotypes.

One early, widely held view denied the very possibility of creolization. Few Creoles expected East Indians to give up 'an alien high culture, satisfied with its own values'. English preconceptions of Indians as intractable Orientals spread rapidly among Creoles. The Africans had been considered 'clay which could easily be moulded into a Christian and Western shape, the Hindus (and Muslims) of India were more like a stone that could only be worked painfully and with much toil.'[5]

[1] Ramdath Jagessar, 'East Indians and Integration', *Moko*, No. 6, 17 January 1969, p. 2.

[2] Trinidad Immigration Report, 1871–2, C.O. 295/266, quoted in Wood, *Trinidad in Transition*, p. 276.

[3] Weller, 'The East Indian Indenture in Trinidad', p. 112.

[4] Ramdath Jagessar, 'Indian Iceberg', *Tapia*, No. 3, 16 November 1969, p. 7.

[5] Wood, *Trinidad in Transition*, p. 110.

Little was done, in truth, to bring East Indians and Creoles together. Indians were imported specifically to work on plantations, which were long the only places that they were legally permitted to be. And where East Indians settled, Creoles generally departed. Not all East Indians are rural nor are all Creoles urban, but that is substantially the pattern. The resident plantation labour force in Trinidad and the Guianas is almost wholly East Indian, and Indians off the estates are mainly agriculturalists. Indian indentures hastened the Negro plantation exodus, and over the next century more and more Creoles abandoned agriculture for the mines of Guiana, the oilfields of Trinidad, and government and other white-collar jobs in Port-of-Spain, Georgetown, and Paramaribo.

Occupational specialization further divides rural East Indians and Creoles. Although nine-tenths of their labour force is Indian, sugar estates generally reserve certain critical and well-paid tasks for Creoles. Because Indians were initially seen as temporary migrants, planters saw no point in teaching them highly skilled factory operations, which thus became exclusively Creole. Creole physique and reputed stamina led planters to favour them for cane cutting, which Creoles find attractive as a well paid seasonal task. Guyanese planters and estate managers, marooned amidst a large East Indian population, feel less insecure with Creole guards and watchmen. And they prefer Creole domestics, as more acculturated than East Indians to European food habits, customs, and traditions.[1]

The remaining Creole peasantry, numerous in Guyana and sporadic elsewhere, practise farming unlike the East Indian. Alternating subsistence agriculture with estate wage-labour, they raise provisions, fruit, and livestock for local markets. But Creole productivity suffers from land fragmentation, family claims to property and produce, a lack of capital and equipment, and a continuous townward exodus of the more enterprising. By contrast, East Indians concentrate on rice. Rice growing and milling require explicit control of large acreage and capital accumulation. The successful Indian turns miller and buys more land for his sons; the Creole who makes good leaves for the city.

Ethnic patterns of community organization, family ties, religious life, and education reinforce these economic differences. However attenuated the extended family may be, East Indian household arrangements and kinship bonds are not like those of Creoles. Indians still marry young, seek to control wives and daughters, and rely on community kinship groups. As in Northern India, daughters marry outside the village, often outside the district; married sons remain close to the

[1] Ibid., pp. 136–9; Leo A. Despres, 'Differential Adaptations and Micro-Cultural Evolution in Guyana', *Southwestern Journal of Anthropology*, Vol. 25, 1969, pp. 14–44, ref. pp. 31–2.

parental home. Thus while Creoles tend to act as individuals, East Indians operate as nuclear family units, with clusters of families often forming village factions.

Everyday pursuits also differentiate the two ethnic groups. In rural Guyana 'Africans and Indians engage in similar kinds of recreational activities, but these activities are structured differently, they occur in terms of a different time schedule, and they involve the expression of different kinds of values.' Guyana Day independence celebrations mirrored these distinctions. 'Each group exhibited its own cultural wares in terms of its own pageants. . . . The Africans hoisted the flag of Ghana . . . the Indians elevated the flag of India.' Afterwards, Africans went to a steel-band concert and dance, and Indians listened to traditional Indian music; only 'a few African and Indian village politicians mingled with one another and discussed the future of Guiana as the "land of six peoples." '[1]

Inter-ethnic participation is more common in Trinidad. Obeah exerts an influence over the lives of Creole and Indian villagers alike. And 'an orthodox Brahman who has never eaten meat', an anthropologist notes, 'may still be the organizer of a Creole carnival band representing Vikings or Scottish clansmen, or play the guitar at a Spanish-Venezuelan "cross-wake"'.[2] But to remark on such events shows their uniqueness, as with the Trinidad Prime Minister's pleasure in seeing 'a Negro singer singing and dancing the East Indian music, and all the East Indian children dancing African folklore [sic]'[3] at a community-centre opening. The occasion evoked comment chiefly because it was unusual.

Achievement takes different forms and entails different consequences among East Indians (especially Hindus) and Creoles. Ritual obligations require a wealthy Hindu to spend money in good works, whereas the Creole image of wordly attainment is the planter, a lavish spender little noted for piety. Creoles gain status through schooling in European —that is, Christian—language, culture, and manners; East Indians both desire education as the highway to success and fear its anti-Indian bias. Indians long avoided sending children to school lest they be converted to Christianity and thereby lost to the family and community. The Canadian Presbyterian mission schools and Teachers' College in Trinidad did stress Hindi, to be sure. But the typical Indian felt, as a future Chief Justice of Guyana wrote in 1919, that 'to send his

[1] Leo A. Despres, *Cultural Pluralism and Nationalist Politics in British Guiana*, 1967, pp. 111–12.
[2] Daniel J. Crowley, 'Plural and Differential Acculturation in Trinidad', *AA*, Vol. 59, 1957, pp. 817–24, ref. p. 823.
[3] Eric Williams, cited in *Trinidad Guardian*, 20 September 1965, p. 1, quoted in Krishna Bahadoorsingh, *Trinidad Electoral Politics: The Persistence of the Race Factor*, 1968, p. 78.

boy to a denominational school to be taught English is to denationalize him and jeopardize his religious faith'.[1]

Different values, goals, and personality structures reflect these disparities. Thus the East Indian family traditionally encourages dependency and discourages initiative, engendering great conflict between parents and children, especially in rural Caribbean areas. Boys resent leaving school to help their fathers as field hands; girls prefer education and careers to remaining at home or becoming docile daughters-in-law. The sex composition of Trinidad school rolls shows that more girls than boys manage to escape the traditional responsibilities.[2]

Young East Indians who reach secondary school are even more competitive than Creoles. 'One sets one's sights on long-range goals; achievement brings power and prestige; lack of achievement brings disgrace, and failure is due to some external force', summarizes the Indian stance.[3] By comparison with Creoles, Trinidadian East Indian students interviewed in 1957 expressed more concern about attaining prestige, displayed greater willingness to eschew present gratifications for future rewards, seemed more dependent on external approval, and felt more apprehensive about being let down or defrauded. Ambition none the less does submerge some ethnic differences in aspiration; lower-class Creole as well as Indian secondary scholars are motivated 'to defer present gratifications and to undergo deprivation for the attainment of future goals'.[4]

Their responses substantiate other disparities of attitude, however. Rural East Indians especially find the social environment threatening and discriminatory, but with this perception of a hostile world goes an exceptional confidence that they can realize their ambitions. Educational aspirations, notably among Indian girls, surpass those of Creoles,

---

[1] J. A. Luckhoo, 'The East Indian in British Guiana', *Timehri*, Vol. 6, 1919, p. 61, quoted in Despres, *Cultural Pluralism and Nationalist Politics in British Guiana*, p. 102. 'An Indian will not send his child to a Creole school; he is afraid of injustice being done to his children by the Creole teachers, and of ill usage from Creole pupils' (Robert Moor of Anglican Mission Indian Schools to Governor of Trinidad, 12 March 1890, in Shirley C. Gordon, *A Century of West Indian Education: A Source Book*, 1963, p. 122).

[2] Malcolm Cross and Allen M. Schwartzbaum, 'Social Mobility and Secondary School Selection in Trinidad and Tobago', *SES*, Vol. 18, 1969, pp. 189–207, ref. p. 205.

[3] Vera Rubin, 'Approaches to the Study of National Characteristics in a Multicultural Society', *International Journal of Social Psychiatry*, Vol. V, No. 1, Summer 1969, pp. 20–6, ref. pp. 24–5. See also Walter Mischel, 'Delay of Gratification, Need for Achievement and Acquiescence in Another Culture', *Journal of Abnormal and Social Psychology*, Vol. 62, 1961, pp. 543–52.

[4] Vera Rubin and Marisa Zavalloni, *We Wish to Be Looked Upon: A Study of the Aspirations of Youth in a Developing Society*, 1969, pp. 56, 198–9.

black or white. Without apparent self-doubt, East Indian students yearn for omnipotence. 'I am always thinking that one day I will be one great man in the world', a boy writes; 'that thought is constantly reverberating in my mind'. Fame in their eyes also has a large post-humous component. Their faith in limitless self-perfection may derive partly from Hindu values stressing the power of will, the achievement of salvation through individual self-improvement, but it also reflects East Indian experiences and social seclusion in the Caribbean.[1]

People of other classes manifest similar ethnic differences. Creoles exhibit greater concern with the present, Indians both with the past, in terms of family and religious heritage, and with the future. The psychological evidence is slim and unreliable, but as a rough generalization conformity, internalization, and self-control seem to characterize Indian personality structure; independence and expressiveness that of Creoles. Criminal as well as everyday behaviour reflects these distinctive traits. East Indians in Trinidad are often charged with acts of premeditated revenge against personal or family enemies, stemming from insults or from property disputes; among Creoles, larceny and impulsive violence are more common.[2]

Derogatory stereotypes express and buttress these differences. Many Creole attitudes stem from the nineteenth century, when some planters found Indians 'industrious, cheerful, contented, docile, [and] obedient', but most took a more jaundiced view of the indentured immigrants as a necessary evil at best. Lurid stories of Indian 'customs' such as infanticide, *suttee*, and *thuggee* caused West Indian planters to shudder for their own safety. And after the Indian Mutiny of 1857, Cawnpore joined Haiti as an ominous precedent of white massacre. Creole estate owners and officials generally characterized East Indians as stubborn, untrustworthy, and deceitful, with perjury a universal failing.[3]

This is the common coin of prejudice against depressed newcomers, but some complaints were more specific. Indian behaviour with money and property, a striking contrast to that of Creole West Indians, excited much invidious comment. The thrift Creoles so sadly lacked was condemned as avarice in Indians. Whites scorned the vulgar ostentation of 'Negroes or coloured men dressed in finery . . . and supposedly with all their wealth on their backs', but joined with other Creoles in deriding East Indians as naked heathens, too mean to dress

[1] Marisa Zavalloni, *Adolescents' Values in a Changing Society: A Study of Trinidad Youth*, 1968, pp. 30, 50–53; Rubin and Zavalloni, *We Wish to Be Looked Upon*, pp. 103–9, 185.

[2] Helen Bagenstose Green, 'Values of Negro and East Indian School Children in Trinidad', *SES*, Vol. 14, 1965, pp. 204–16, ref. pp. 208–9; idem, *Socialization Values in the Negro and East Indian Sub-Cultures of Trinidad*, 1963; Bickerton, *The Murders of Boysie Singh*, p. 214.

[3] Wood, *Trinidad in Transition*, pp. 110–12, 114, 153–5.

in a civilized fashion. Indian women wearing gold chains and jewellery were, on the other hand, walking repositories of their husbands' wealth. The melting down of coins for gold bangles severely depleted currency supplies in Trinidad, and Indians were accused of depressing internal trade because they refused to spend their money.[1]

Creoles still tend to regard East Indians as avaricious, stingy, and secretive. Negro farmers in Guyana attribute Indian success to 'Coolie deviousness' and fear being deprived of the little they have. An anthropologist records a villager's suspicion that

de coolieman taking over de whole country. Dey band themselves together to get all we own. . . . Dey rent we land and take it away. Dey loan black people money and take all dey own. Dey smart people, you know. Cunning. Dey work cheap, eat cheap, and save and save. Black people can't punish themselves so. If we punish ourselves like coolieman, we slaves again.[2]

East Indians respond that Creoles are feckless, childish, vain, pompous, promiscuous: they feel 'contempt for the Negro . . . who allows his womenfolk complete sexual freedom, and does not even exhibit shame when his sister becomes an unmarried mother. . . . The Negro is too interested in "fêting": dancing, carnival, and expensive clothes . . . [to] know how to save money.'[3] Indian attachment to property fuelled their mistrust of black-power demonstrations in Trinidad in 1970. 'We want no part of your struggle because you talk nothing but destruction', one Indian explained. 'We have toiled too long and too hard to give up what we have (and we have a hell of a lot).'[4]

Improvidence is one Indian stereotype that Creoles readily confess to, bemoaning their own inability to save, to plan, to sacrifice present pleasures.

With us it is a good time and a fete for everything imaginable—christenings, confirmation, first communion, birthdays, farewells and even death. Our school boys and girls must be in a soul fete on Friday, Saturday and Sunday nights whilst the other races are at home with a book. . . . There are many Indians who are poor or poorer than us and yet they find the time to study with the result that they are more qualified than us.[5]

[1] Ibid., pp. 155–9.

[2] Despres, *Cultural Pluralism and Nationalist Politics in British Guiana*, p. 93. 'It was precisely because they were not readily accepted in the dominant sector of the society that the East Indians substituted the goal of wealth accumulation for status goals within the overall society' (M. K. Bacchus, *Education and Socio-Cultural Integration in a 'Plural' Society*, 1970, p. 21).

[3] Klass, *East Indians in Trinidad*, p. 244. See also Peter Simms, *Trouble in Guyana*, 1966, pp. 57–8.

[4] Grace Maharaj, 'To the Black People in T'dad', *Embryo*, Vol. 2, No. 19, 24 March 1970, p. 9.

[5] Clyde Belgrave, 'Why Black Power in Our Society Is a Farce', letter in *Trinidad Express*, 6 March 1970, p. 4.

The actual existence of the differences such stereotypes imply is not essential to their expression. Throughout the Caribbean, Indians and Creoles similarly disparage one another, whether the disparity between them is great or small. Stereotypes common in Surinam and Guyana, Trinidad and Martinique, are reiterated almost word for word by culturally undifferentiated Indians and Negroes living side by side in rural Jamaica. Negro villagers there, who view acquisitiveness as a genetic trait, are convinced their Indian neighbours camouflage their wealth: 'Indians have plenty of money, but they don't show it.' Even well-educated Jamaicans believe that all Indians have lots of money hidden away. Creoles complain that Indians are stingy and keep to themselves, but those who resent Indian clannishness and frugality also envy them their ability to save.[1]

More uncompromising is the Jamaican Indian view of Negroes as lazy, and wanting only to sport and drink rum. The Indian minority, who suffer as scapegoats when things go wrong, believe that Creoles behave 'Negrish'—each man for himself, covetous, irresponsible, aggressive, never planning for the morrow but vexed and argumentative when thwarted. Indians believe no Negro would scruple to steal. 'The Niggers sleep during the day and at night they walk around and steal. Stealing and killing—that's their work.' This behaviour is ascribed to racial history: 'They're the last people God made. They're an evil race.'[2]

INDIAN–CREOLE SEGREGATION

The antipathies these images express depend only partly on the differences they emphasize. Physical and social distance, as much as cultural distinctiveness, sustains the negative stereotypes, which in turn validate segregation. The main components of ethnic isolation are endogamy and residential separation.

East Indians generally disapprove of ethnic intermarriage. For Guyanese Hindus a prospective spouse may be Muslim or Christian but should be Indian in any case. In Paramaribo one household in twenty-five is interracial, in San Fernando one household in nineteen, but in rural areas intermarriage is extremely rare. A study of Guyana in 1965 found 'little evidence of any coalescing process between the Indian and African components of the population.'[3]

[1] Ehrlich, 'East Indian Cane Workers in Jamaica', pp. 129, 130, and footnote 8, p. 242.   [2] Ibid., pp. 129, 133, 134.

[3] R. T. Smith and Chandra Jayawardena, 'Marriage and the Family amongst East Indians in British Guiana', *SES*, Vol. 8, 1959, pp. 321–76, ref. p. 356; Speckmann, 'The Indian Group in the Segmented Society of Surinam', pp. 3–17; Colin G. Clarke, 'Residential Segregation and Intermarriage in San Fernando, Trinidad', *GR*, Vol. 61, 1971, pp. 198–218, ref. Table 3, p. 212; *Racial Problems in the Public Service: Report of the British Guiana Commission of Inquiry*, 1965, p. 27.

Indian attachment to endogamy stems from residual caste exclusions, from their desire to preserve a separate community, and from their stereotype of Negroes as lascivious, ugly, and evil. Blacks who advocate creolization, Indians charge, are 'interested more in sexual union between Indians and Negroes than in unity of minds between the two races.'[1] Negro animality in quest of Indian beauty is a frequent theme of tales in which pure Indian girls are ravished by blacks. Liaisons with Negroes are considered polluting; parental disinheritance is a common, though perhaps often an empty, threat. 'If me dawta take up with black man,' Indian villagers in Guyana ask, 'who will take she fo wife?'[2] But Creoles often fancy Indian girls as thrifty and tractable wives, and some Indian men keep Negro mistresses. In San Fernando, despite the stereotype, there are more Creole women living with, or married to, East Indian men than there are Creole men with East Indian women.[3]

Indian–Creole offspring, commonly called 'douglas', are said to suffer no special disability in Guyana and in urban Surinam, but mixed families seldom belong to Indian communities in rural Surinam and are more acceptable among Creoles than among Indians in Trinidad. The name is more widely applied, however, to the mixed offspring of dark Creoles than of light, let alone of white. As in one Creole colloquy, 'What else you could call her if she's Indian-Creole? It ain't no insult.' 'You don't mean Indian-*Creole* you mean Indian-Negro.'[4]

Similar attitudes toward ethnic mixing entail quite different consequences where East Indians are a small minority. In the French Antilles and in rural Jamaica formal intermarriage is rare, but casual unions are common, despite parental antipathy. 'Older people,' reports a young Jamaican Indian, 'are prejudiced against the Negroes. . . . With us things are different. We don't know about the old Indian ways. We're all mixed up.'[5] Indian–Creole mixtures, 'rials' in Jamaica, *chappé-coolies* in Martinique and Guadeloupe, are in fact almost as numerous as pure Indians. In Jamaica, unlike Trinidad and the Guianas, they usually adhere to the Indian community, especially if the father is Indian; but in Guadeloupe they seek to merge with Creoles.

Residential segregation, though less intense than endogamy, also

---

[1] Singh, *The Indian Enigma*, p. 14.

[2] Despres, *Cultural Pluralism and Nationalist Politics in British Guiana*, p. 93.

[3] Clarke, 'Residential Segregation and Intermarriage in San Fernando', p. 216.

[4] Michael Anthony, *Green Days by the River*, 1967, p. 10. See also R. T. Smith and Jayawardena, 'Marriage and the Family amongst East Indians in British Guiana', p. 356; Speckmann, *Marriage and Kinship among the Indians in Surinam*, p. 118; Niehoff and Niehoff, *East Indians in the West Indies*, p. 67.

[5] Ehrlich, 'East Indian Cane Workers in Jamaica', p. 138. For Guadeloupe see Guy Lasserre, 'Les "Indiens" de Guadeloupe', *CO-M*, Vol. VI, 1953, pp. 128–58. In Jamaica the ratio of Afro–East Indians to East Indians increased from 1:5 in 1943 to 9:10 in 1960.

limits face-to-face contacts between Caribbean Indians and Creoles. Separation is most conspicuous in rural Surinam, where topography emphasizes the isolation of government-sponsored ethnic settlements; river transport alone connects many rural communities. Moreover, each ethnic element clusters in certain regions. Thus the 1950 census showed Creoles to be 90 per cent of rural Coronie, Hindustanis 85 per cent of western Nickerie, Indonesians 80 per cent of north-western Commewijne.

Ethnic separation is somewhat less intense in Guyana. More than three-fifths of the rural population is East Indian, but even on the Courantyne Coast, where Creoles are least in evidence, they are one-sixth of the population. Road and railway offer easy means of contact among Creole and Indian villages interdigitated along the coast. Few communities are entirely homogenous; not many Creoles live in 'Indian' villages, but almost all the so-called 'Negro' villages contain at least a few East Indian families.[1] Mixture generates stress, however; 'when large numbers of both groups live together in the same village, the community is usually riven by hostile factionalism.'[2] In most cases one major ethnic group heavily preponderates and endeavours to maintain its dominance. Creole village leaders try to keep land to themselves; Indians resolutely do likewise. Mixed villages today are less common than before; during the riots of the early 1960s, Indian and Creole minorities fled from their villages to ethnic refugee settlements.

Trinidad is ethnically divided in a different manner. East Indians initially came to the sugar estates of the western plains and coastal strip, and many subsequently settled nearby as small farmers. Here most of them remain. Only recently have East Indians thronged into urban areas, and in 1960 they were only 9 per cent of Port-of-Spain, 26 per cent of San Fernando. By contrast, Indians were two-thirds the population of rural Siparia, Savana Grande, Naparima, and Caroni— nine-tenths in many localities. Many rural East Indians are quite remote from Creoles and the Creole life of the towns, but urban Creoles and East Indians are better described as polarized than segregated. In San Fernando, no street is devoid of Creoles even where East Indians are most numerous. Whites live more apart from both than Negroes and East Indians from one another. But a recent building boom has increased segregation, with Negroes concentrated in government housing, East Indians in private suburban developments.[3]

East Indian residential concentration in the French Antilles is also

[1] David Lowenthal, 'Population Contrasts in the Guianas', *GR*, Vol. 50, 1960, pp. 41–58.

[2] Despres, *Cultural Pluralism and Nationalist Politics in British Guiana*, pp. 70, 86.

[3] Clarke, 'Residential Segregation and Intermarriage in San Fernando', pp. 201–8.

striking. Two circumscribed districts contain half Guadeloupe's 15,000 Indians, most of them in seven wholly East Indian rural communities. Martinique's Indians are similarly concentrated. In Jamaica, two-thirds of the 28,000 East Indians live in small sectors of four parishes, but few villages are preponderantly Indian; Indians and Creoles instead reside in loosely demarcated areas within each village. Wide dispersal of the relatively few East Indians throughout Jamaica's sugar plantations from the start handicapped Indian retention of their culture and helps to account for their high degree of creolization.[1]

Residential mixing is no guarantee of ethnic amity, however. Creole and East Indian neighbours in Chaguanas, Trinidad, are on good speaking terms, yet ethnic neighbourliness is usually confined to casual encounters in street and yard. East Indians only occasionally attend Creole fêtes: Creoles are onlookers rather than invited guests at Indian weddings and Hindu festivals. Indoor visits are limited to a brief paying of respects; one does not stay to eat, drink, sing, or play cards.[2]

Conflict may be acute when disparate ethnic groups are in proximity. Both Indians and Creoles in Jamaica cite near neighbours of the other ethnic stock as frequent sources of stress. Political strife so exacerbated Guyanese ethnic factionalism that the appearance of amity noted in 1951 among 'people of all races liv[ing] side by side in the villages' gave way by 1965 to widespread suspicion and distrust.[3]

Thus endogamy greatly, and residential segregation moderately, constrain the number, frequency, and intensity of East Indian–Creole contacts. But the chief cause of ethnic conflict today is not the paucity of contact but its increasing frequency. In its origins, ethnic stress arises from group isolation and differences. In its dynamics, it reflects a growing realization that the two groups must coexist, sharing power, rewards, and status.

FOCI OF STRESS

Ethnic stress is complex, and perceptions of its intensity vary widely with observer and locale. It is more pervasive in Guyana than Trinidad, in national politics than local affairs, among taxi drivers than small farmers. Indenture history accounts for certain national differences: Guyanese planters reduced Negro pay to defray Indian import costs and used indentured Indians to keep Creole wages low. In Trinidad, by contrast, estate work went begging; Creole livelihood in skilled and other labour was assured, and the ex-slaves regarded Indians less as

[1] Guy Lasserre, *La Guadeloupe: étude géographique*, 1961, Vol. I, pp. 315–19; Ehrlich, 'East Indian Cane Workers in Jamaica', pp. 148–63.

[2] Cloak, *A Natural Order of Cultural Adoption and Loss in Trinidad*, pp. 108–9.

[3] *British Guiana Constitution Report of 1951* (the Waddington Report), quoted in *Racial Problems in the Public Service*, p. 27.

competitors than as drudges for submitting to plantation routines reminiscent of slavery. Conflicts on Guyanese plantations tend to be ethnically divisive, whereas in Trinidad ethnic criteria figure in day-to-day affairs but, remarks an observer at a land development project, play little part in crises.[1]

Ethnic rivals seldom distinguish specific or remediable complaints from inherent socio-cultural issues. Thus Trinidadian Indians tend to blame their political powerlessness on Creole discrimination, when in fact their own culture and institutions impede their ambitions in the national arena. Some Indian grievances, however, are matters of fact: that Creoles are preferred in certain civil-service jobs, for example, or that Trinidad's Expo '67 pavilion in Montreal presented a predominantly Creole image of Trinidad. On these verifiable aspects of stress I shall focus first, later discussing Creole–East Indian disagreements about West Indian culture and society in general.

Most ethnic complaints concern supposed inequities in employment, education, and welfare, recognition of specifically 'Indian' cultural features, and Creole fears of Indian dominance. Independence has exacerbated stress; having lost their mutual imperial adversary, Creoles and Indians now compete for the power and status formerly held by expatriates and local whites.

East Indians in the Caribbean long remained unassertive, as a consequence, in part, of planter aims to keep them 'backward, agricultural and uneducated so as to ensure a supply of agricultural labour for the sugar and rice industries.'[2] Many Indians subordinated desire for local success to hopes of returning to India. Rice millers and merchants who amassed wealth kept aloof, even in Port-of-Spain, Georgetown, and Paramaribo, from the Creole mainstream.

Only after the turn of the century did East Indians begin to take an active part in Caribbean affairs. Indian small farmers bought and sold in Creole markets, and other transactions grew out of this traffic. The termination of indentured immigration during the First World War ended the most invidious distinction between Indian and Creole, and the whole corpus of ethnic law gradually passed away. The 1930s and early 1940s saw the repeal of all discriminatory legislation, legitimizing Hindu and Muslim marriages and enabling Indian children to be schooled without risking enforced conversion.

New employment opportunities during the Second World War and adult suffrage soon afterward further stimulated Indian participation in West Indian life. Nehru's 1950 declaration that overseas Indians should no longer look to India as their homeland also spurred Carib-

---

[1] Jayawardena, *Conflict and Solidarity in a Guianese Plantation*, pp. 54–5; Michael G. Benson, 'Social Interaction on a Trinidad Land Development Project' [Waller Field], 1968, p. 35.   [2] *Racial Problems in the Public Service*, p. 26.

bean Indian creolization. The end of empire forced East Indians to compete out of fear of Creole rule, if not out of desire to share that rule.

Close links between ethnicity and occupation were formerly taken for granted. But Indians today aspire to civil-service and white-collar jobs once exclusively held by Creoles, and some Creoles venture into occupations, like taxi-driving, once customarily Indian. A survey in Guyana shows that Indians and Creoles rank occupations in the same order of prestige.[1] And in all territories tension accompanies increased East Indian participation in many walks of life. Creoles resent Indian incursions; Indians claim Creoles still hold them back.

East Indian complaints focus particularly on the civil service, the police force, and the schools. Each involves unique problems that contribute to ethnic stress. The civil service in the Caribbean, as in many small countries, has supreme local importance. Governments employ a high proportion of the total labour force, and civil servants may comprise a majority of the small educated class. Social prestige, security of tenure, and pensions enhance the value of official jobs. The civil service offers men of talent and ambition better opportunities, with less distinction of colour and family background, than equivalent careers in commerce. Civil servants are powers in the land: if they do not make policy they implement it, and they have inherited the prerogatives and the powers of the former overlords. In demanding equality in civil-service employment, East Indians are laying claim not just to jobs but to status and power.

Starting from nothing their progress may seem impressive. Five times as many Indians held British Guianese professional and public posts in 1946 as in 1897, but this was an increase only from 0·2 to 1 per cent of the total Indian population. Significant rises in recent government employment have not yet brought equality. The Indian component of the civil service rose from one-eleventh in 1931 to one-third in 1964; but Indians are more than half the Guyanese population. The Trinidad situation is even less equitable: in 1962 Indians comprised 40 per cent of the population but only 11 per cent of the civil service.[2]

[1] Sara Graham and David Beckles, 'The Prestige Ranking of Occupations: Problems of Method and Interpretation Suggested by a Study in Guyana', *SES*, Vol. 17, 1968, pp. 367–80, ref. p. 370.

[2] Despres, *Cultural Pluralism and Nationalist Politics in British Guiana*, p. 130; *Racial Problems in the Public Service*, Tables 2 and 3, pp. 32, 33, and G. W. Roberts, with J. A. Byrne, 'Memorandum on the Racial Composition of British Guiana's Public Service', pp. 139–61; Raymond T. Smith, *British Guiana*, p. 112; representative of Hindu Youth Association, quoted in *Verbatim Notes on Proceedings of Meeting on Draft Constitution*, 1962, p. 77, cited in Selwyn Douglas Ryan, 'Decolonization in a Multi-Racial Society: A Case Study of Trinidad and Tobago' [1967], p. 398. Creole leaders frequently sought to refute East Indian allegations of inequalities by means of selected statistics, of which those in Eric Williams, *Inward Hunger: The Education of a Prime Minister* (1969, pp. 282–3), are good examples.

In senior positions the Indians lag still further behind. Of the pensionable staff in 1960, Afro-Guyanese accounted for 58 per cent, East Indians only 16 per cent. Top posts vacated by Europeans have gone mostly to Creoles. The professional advisory staff, more East Indian than other senior branches, lost power and prestige after independence, when administrative chiefs (most of them light-coloured Creoles) took charge of departments.[1]

These imbalances imperilled Guyana's future. Creoles resisted Indian demands for civil-service entry on a proportional basis. And some 'Indian politicians told Indian workers that only they could get the workers the Government jobs which were now being denied to them in favour of the Africans', Chief Minister Cheddi Jagan, himself an Indian, recounted.[2] Tension diminished after 1965 when a Commission of Inquiry reported that the imbalance was transitory; Indians were progressing rapidly, and specific charges of ethnic discrimination were few. The Creole-dominated Government has since placed more Indians in Cabinet and committee posts. But Indians view these appointments as mere palliatives; their grievances, if no longer incendiary, remain unallayed.

In Trinidad, as in Guyana, independence activated East Indian resentment against government job discrimination. Employment disparities confirm their suspicions that the Creole-dominated People's National Movement, the party in power, favours its own supporters and that 'Negroes are getting into positions at the expense of East Indians because they supported the PNM.'[3] By 1970 the situation was no better. 'It is not enough to have persons of Indian origin appointed to ministries, to the Senate, to statutory boards and Commissions', wrote an Indian analyst. 'The reaction is that these have been bought out. . . . Every move made by the Government is suspected of having pro-Negro, anti-Indian (or anti-white) motives; there is no field of activity whatsoever which is exempt from this sort of suspicion.'[4]

Negro dominance of the police is another major cause of grievance among Indians, who as recently as 1964 accounted for only one-fifth of the Guyanese force and one-fortieth of Trinidad's. But old habits as much as deliberate favouritism hampered Indian recruitment, a Guyanese inquiry showed. Minimum height and girth requirements automatically excluded many East Indians; a stipulation of bachelor status also militated against Indians, who marry younger than Creoles.

[1] M. K. Bacchus, 'The Ministerial System at Work: A Case Study of Guyana', *SES*, Vol. 16, 1967, pp. 34–56, ref. p. 50.

[2] Cheddi Jagan, *Forbidden Freedom: The Story of British Guiana*, 1954, p. 43. Jagan referred, of course, to politicians of the East Indian Association, not to those of his own party.   [3] Quoted in Bahadoorsingh, *Trinidad Electoral Politics*, p. 68.

[4] Martin Sampath, 'Joint Racial Leadership—the Logical Way Out', *Trinidad Express*, 10 March 1970, p. 8.

The disruption of Hindu dietary custom in police barracks discouraged potential recruits. And the senior officers who screened and interviewed applicants were almost all Creoles.[1]

In the 1963–4 riots Creole police were both aggressors and targets in Indian villages and on sugar estates, and any remaining confidence was dissolved. 'Discrimination and injustices practiced by the Police with increasing frequency and absolute immunity' frustrated Janet Jagan's Ministry of Home Affairs; the Government planned to reconstitute the force entirely 'to reflect a broad cross section of our multi-racial community'.[2] Despite the Jaganites' 1964 election defeat, the incoming Creole-led regime instituted a crash programme to recruit Indian police. But many of the new recruits soon dropped out, and the 1965 Commission of Inquiry concluded that there were still 'not sufficient Indians in the Police Force for it to command the general support of the population as a whole.'[3]

Guianese and Trinidadian schools, like the civil service and police force, have long been dominated by Creoles, white or coloured. Fears of proselytization formerly prevented many East Indians from seeking an education; non-Christians everywhere suffered neglect. Before 1933 most Guyanese Indians never attended school; as recently as 1960 two-fifths of those over fifteen in a solidly Indian section of Chaguanas, Trinidad, had had no education.[4] In 1946 almost half the Guyanese Indians over ten could not read or write English, and in Trinidad, despite numerous Presbyterian converts, Indian illiteracy was at least 60 per cent. Indians still get less schooling than Creoles, an average of three and half years as compared with six, for example, in rural Guyana.[5] And since most Indians live in rural areas they are even more disadvantaged at higher levels of education.

Indians complain of educational discrimination on three specific counts: denominational school systems suffused with European and Creole elite values, a preponderance of Negro teachers, and inadequate rewards to Indian students. 'A terrific number of university scholarships

[1] *Racial Problems in the Public Service*, pp. 41–2; B. A. N. Collins, 'Racial Imbalance in Public Services and Security Forces', *Race*, Vol. VII, 1965–6, pp. 235–53, ref. p. 244; representative of Hindu Youth Association, cited in Ryan, 'Decolonization in a Multi-Racial Society', pp. 398, 483.

[2] People's Progressive Party *Manifesto*, 7 December 1964, p. 24. See also Felix Cummings, speech, 7 September 1966, 'Guyana before the United Nations', People's Progressive Party, p. 10.

[3] *Racial Problems in the Public Service*, p. 42; Collins, 'Racial Imbalance in Public Services and Security Forces'.

[4] Calculated from Chaguanas enumeration districts 12 through 20 in *Trinidad and Tobago Population Census 1960*, Vol. II, Part A, Tables 5 and 8B.

[5] Despres, *Cultural Pluralism and Nationalist Politics in British Guiana*, p. 129; Murli J. Kirpalani et al., *Indian Centenary Review, One Hundred Years of Progress*, 1945, p. 55, cited in Niehoff and Niehoff, *East Indians in the West Indies*, p. 77.

have been awarded to Negroes by the Government', averred one prominent Trinidadian, 'when it is known that applications by better qualified Indians have been rejected.'[1] Some Creoles admit that Indians have had to turn Christian to secure teaching positions or win promotions in rural Guyana. And the under-representation of East Indians among secondary students shows that Trinidad government schools either prefer Negro applicants or are still avoided by Indians.[2]

The supposed Creole domination of teaching, however, is much exaggerated. Among Guyanese teachers in 1965, Negroes outnumbered Indians only four to three, and as many Indians as Negroes staff Guyanese secondary schools. But suspicions of inequity die hard.

The denial of legitimacy to Indian culture is a long-standing source of East Indian discontent with West Indian educational systems. Not until the 1940s did Caribbean governments sanction 'Indian' schools. Yet by 1950 there were fifty such schools in Trinidad alone, including thirty-three Mahasabha, specifically designed to promote Indian self-awareness. Indian nationalists today seek the same 'mother tongue' status for Hindi and Urdu as for French and Spanish, languages required in Trinidad's schools. But Hindi and Urdu teaching is little related to folk remnants of these tongues, which most older Indians cannot read or write. Instruction is all the more difficult because Indians disparage their own speech as inferior to the 'real' Indian they hear in Indian movies.[3]

Indian complaints led the Guyanese Government under Jagan to take over the educational system from the churches in 1961. But reform of Creole 'apartheid' and Christian 'fascism' was transformed into a drive for Indian control. New schools in Indian areas were staffed exclusively by Indian teachers. Segregated schooling gained further impetus after the 1964 riots, when thousands of Indians and Creoles forced out of mixed areas improvised schools on a strictly ethnic basis.[4]

In education, as in employment, Indians look for a fairer apportionment of national benefits and rewards. But certain demands foster the Indian subculture at the expense of broader social participation; other goals combine national equity with cultural autonomy. East Indian

---

[1] Quoted in Bahadoorsingh, *Trinidad Electoral Politics*, p. 68.

[2] Despres, *Cultural Pluralism and Nationalist Politics in British Guiana*, pp. 101–2; Cross and Schwartzbaum, 'Social Mobility and Secondary School Selection in Trinidad and Tobago', p. 201 and Tables 8 and 9, p. 204.

[3] Ryan, 'The Struggle for Afro-Indian Solidarity in Trinidad and Tobago', pp. 14–15; Niehoff and Niehoff, *East Indians in the West Indies*, pp. 83–7; Ryan, 'Decolonization in a Multi-Racial Society', p. 172.

[4] Collins, 'Racial Imbalance in Public Services and Security Forces', p. 244 fn.; Despres, *Cultural Pluralism and Nationalist Politics in British Guiana*, pp. 237–8. These schools have subsequently become 'non-denominational' under government auspices (Bacchus, *Education and Socio-Cultural Integration in a 'Plural' Society*, p. 35).

complaints that public holidays were exclusively Christian led to the addition of Hindu and Muslim festivals to the calendar in the late 1960s. As national holidays, Christian, Hindu, and Muslim holy days increasingly lose their sectarian character. Non-Hindus now play Phagwa, non-Muslims celebrate Hosein, and at Easter everyone in Guyana flies kites, symbolizing Christ's resurrection on the third day.

But such adjustments only partly mitigate Indian feelings of neglect and discrimination. Although Caribbean governments now lend vocal support to a wide range of Indian cultural activities—even islands that are devoid of East Indians celebrate Gandhi's birthday—most Indians remain convinced that more is done for the Negro subculture than for their own.

Radio stations give only two hours Indian music a day. Neither newspaper pays more than token attention to them, and a casual reading would never show a stranger that Indians form one third of the population. . . . The Ministry of Culture has conveniently forgotten to encourage Indian cultural activites, but it has pushed the Creole version. And the Indians are angry about . . . the unequal expenditure, the unequal radio time, and the obvious ignoring of their interests as a group.

Trinidad's development expenditures in housing, manufacturing, and the Civil Service do little for Indians, they charge; for 'these are all Creole areas.' Even the vaunted Agricultural Year (1969) programme to help the small farmer left Indians 'singularly unimpressed. . . . They feel that this is really Negro Agricultural year'.[1]

Creoles view the East Indian drive for equal opportunity more sympathetically than their quest for cultural autonomy. Opportunity seems a natural consequence of participation in West Indian life; autonomy strikes them as retrograde and divisive. High East Indian birth rates arouse Creole fears of exclusive Indian control. By means of proportional representation in Guyana, gerrymandering in Trinidad, and spoils sharing in Surinam, Creoles still (or again) dominate governments in all three territories. But Indian populations are increasing at about 5 per cent a year, almost double the Creole rate. Thus the balance of power is soon bound to shift.

Staving off demographic subjugation, Creole leaders attempt to divide the East Indians, to woo aggrieved minorities, and to recruit outside support. In Trinidad the ruling P.N.M. for many years included no Hindu but several Muslim Cabinet members, one of whom suggested 'an affinity between Islam and the African population based on the theory that many of the slaves had originally been Muslims';[2] Muslim leaders describe Prime Minister Williams as

[1] Ramdath Jagessar, 'East Indians and Agriculture', *Moko*, No. 6, 17 January 1969, p. 2. See also Ryan, 'Decolonization in a Multi-Racial Society', p. 633.

[2] Oxaal, *Black Intellectuals Come to Power*, p. 22.

'Defender of the Faith'. Hindus characterize Muslim and other Indian appointees as the scum of the Indian community, selected not to represent but to discredit Indian ability and culture. 'In every field of activity where the government is concerned, the best or ablest Indian is not given a chance. . . . Only the third raters of the Indian community are placed. . . . Just look at the award of scholarship, [at] the Indians appointed by Government to the Senate'.[1]

Creoles have also sought links with predominantly Negro islands to the north, which explains why many East Indians opposed the now defunct West Indies Federation. In the 1960s, Guyanese Creoles unsuccessfully bid for island immigrants to offset East Indian demographic gains, and then bolstered their narrow electoral majority by 'registering' overseas Guyanese, most of them Creoles. Trinidad Indians accuse the P.N.M. of seeking 'to make sure that the "creole" or "indigenous" population is not outnumbered by East Indians';[2] this accusation is consonant with some Creole fears, but Trinidad's subsequent rejection of union with Grenada suggests that rising local unemployment worried the Creole Government more than the prospect of Indian dominance. In Surinam Creoles sought electoral strength through an anti-Indian alliance with Bush Negroes.

Parties in all three territories are ethnically constituted, and pressures of self-rule have polarized politics. An independent Guyana under Jagan, Creoles feared, 'would be a country with Africans as slaves to East Indians,' whereas an Indian political leader charges that 'the Negroes have drunk the goblet of power and now see no necessity to share anything with the East Indians.'[3] In Trinidad, where a prominent Muslim maintains that up to 1950 he had 'never heard or found the problem of racialism', Indians in the mid-1960s claimed that 'Negroes would rather have a dishonest Negro than an honest East Indian as Prime Minister', and an Indian leader in 1970 interpreted black revolt against the Creole-led Government as 'the first step towards multi-racialism'.[4] By contrast, the prospect of governmental responsibility and concern for Creole economic stability so unnerved Surinam's

[1] Singh, *The Indian Enigma*, pp. 18–20.

[2] 'The Three R's', *Trinidad Nation*, 23 June 1961, p. 8. See also Jesse Harris Proctor, Jr., 'East Indians and the Federation of the British West Indies', *India Quarterly*, Vol. XVII, 1961, pp. 370–95; Ryan, 'The Struggle for Afro-Indian Solidarity in Trinidad and Tobago', pp. 15–18.

[3] Society for Racial Equality, quoted in Despres, *Cultural Pluralism and Nationalist Politics in British Guiana*, p. 264; Fenton Ramsahoye, speech of November 1968, Georgetown, Guyana, as reported by Frank J. McDonald, to whom I am indebted for the quotation.

[4] Kamaluddin Mohammed, *Unifying Our Cosmopolitan Community* [1960], p. 2; Indians quoted in Krishna Bahadoorsingh, 'What Trinidad's Leaders Believe about Race and Politics', *Trinidad and Tobago Index*, No. 4, September 1966, pp. 38–45, ref. p. 40; Dennis Mahabir, quoted in *Trinidad Express*, 16 March 1970, p. 3.

United Hindustani party that after winning the 1969 elections they sought a Creole to head the new Government.

Creole reactions to the Indian 'threat' stem in part from divergent interpretations of cultural assimilation. The closer Indians approach power, the more Creoles worry about Indian unwillingness to be truly West Indian. The extent to which East Indians are already creolized— that is, like other West Indians—is a question that Creoles argue with vehemence and passion. Yet 'one of the prime obstacles in the way of better relationships', according to a Trinidadian Creole, 'is the stubborn belief on the part of the [Creole] majority . . . that those Indians that protest are a handful of mischievous and misguided professional racists.'[1] The mystique of assimilation is precious but fragile; when an anthropologist concluded that a Caroni village was 'in basic structure . . . an "Indian" community and not a "West Indian" community,' the Prime Minister himself denied the findings and denounced the author's motives.[2] As a subsequent analyst remarks, the trouble was not that no such place existed, but that this was a place 'which some leading P.N.M. politicians felt *ought not* to exist.'[3]

Assertions that differences are negligible and should be forgotten, and statements of faith in national integration, are the common coin of public discourse. 'Everybody in public life pretends' that ethnic differences do not exist, writes an eminent Trinidadian; 'they talk about them only to one another and in whispers.'[4] Even in Guyana, where East Indian and Creole political leaders have been stoned on the hustings, both major parties continuously preach integration and publicly abjure ethnic factionalism.

Caribbean reform groups have really transcended ethnic loyalties only in opposition, however. Indians and Creoles combined in Trinidadian trade-union action against expatriate oil and sugar interests in the 1940s, but the coalition collapsed soon after its leaders won legislative seats. In Guyana the People's Progressive Party in the early 1950s united rural Indians and working-class Creoles in opposition to British colonialism and the local elite. After gaining office and being ejected by colonial fiat, the party split along ethnic lines, and an Indian–Creole

[1] Ryan, 'Decolonization in a Multi-Racial Society', p. 484.

[2] Klass, *East Indians in Trinidad*, p. 239; Eric Williams, *History of the People of Trinidad and Tobago*, 1962, p. 280. A friendly critic of Williams's book charges that social scientists who doubted Trinidadian unity were projecting their own minority malaise: 'American academic imperialists . . . of Jewish background . . . being themselves the product of the well-known revolt . . . against the ghetto-culture of their parents, are thereby temperamentally incapable of sympathising with the effort of the emancipated colonial peoples to rediscover their national cultural heritage against the specious argumentation of a spurious cosmopolitanism' (Gordon K. Lewis, review in *CS*, Vol. 3, No. 1, April 1963, pp. 100–5, ref. p. 104).

[3] Oxaal, *Black Intellectuals Come to Power*, p. 26.

[4] C. L. R. James, *West Indians of East Indian Descent* [1965], p. 2.

power struggle has gone on ever since. None the less, some Guyanese Creoles still assert comradeship with East Indian workers in opposition to whites and foreigners. 'In most of the criticisms of Dr. Jagan which I heard from Africans', an observer reports, 'I was hastily assured that "our Cheddi" was not really to blame; he had been led astray or persuaded in his actions by his White American wife.'[1]

The solidarity such statements profess is superficial, however. There is an Indian–Creole *modus vivendi*, but one scholar suggests that 'the usual response of the majority of Trinidad Negroes toward East Indian folkways and mores, and of East Indians toward Negro traits,' is based less on intermingling than on *'negative indifference*, frequently accompanied by ridicule or sarcastic expressions of anti-pathy, mistrust and hostility.'[2] Overt ethnic conflict is rare in Trinidad owing not to acculturation but rather to dissociation, a live-and-let-live propensity to mind one's own affairs.

Behind Creole tolerance lies wishful thinking and ignorance of Indian mores. Not only do Indians keep apart, but Creoles misread separatism as jealousy and regard Indian ways as useless relics of the dead past or as the mischievous contrivances of a 'recalcitrant minority', in the Trinidad Prime Minister's famous phrase. Creoles too readily assume that Indian culture is of trivial importance to Indians, whereas, to themselves,

Indians are another people with a defined traditional way of life, of religion, of behaviour, of thought. . . . They do not have to argue, to shout aloud that Indians are beautiful. They do not have to justify their existence and claim equality. To them Indians are a superior people, and no question about it. . . . The lotus blooms in the west, but it is still a lotus.[3]

Creoles who believe themselves the only true West Indians also fail to recognize Indian traits in Creole culture. That carnival drumming has roots in Muslim Hosein and in Hindu drummers' skills, Creoles have forgotten. That rice in its present form is an East Indian contribution to the basic Creole diet, they seldom acknowledge. Curried goat is such a universal favourite that most Jamaicans are unaware of its Indian provenance. Creoles characteristically see even *roti* as simply Trini-dadian, not Indian.

Despite all the evidence of syncretism, Creoles are essentially unaware that they have borrowed Indian traits. They take for granted that East Indians should become West Indian by adopting Creole ways, never the reverse. The mere 'existence of Javanese and Indian culture in Surinam', suggested a Creole nationalist, 'was a barrier to the develop-

---

[1] Judith Roback, 'Bases of Social Differentiation in a Guyana Mining Town', 1968, p. 136, note 7. See also Jayawardena, *Conflict and Solidarity in a Guianese Plantation.*

[2] Oxaal, *Black Intellectuals Come to Power*, p. 23.

[3] Ramdath Jagessar, 'Indian Iceberg', *Tapia*, No. 3, 16 November 1969, p. 7.

ment of a national culture'.[1] A black Trinidadian confirms that 'creole elements on the whole still do not consider the Indian subculture to be legitimate and worthy of promotion.' Indeed, the Trinidad Government tends to regard Creole as *the* culture, and Indian separatism as refractory if not treasonable. The Prime Minister is said to refuse to 'concede minority communities the right to elect their own kind, or to articulate their own version of national community.'[2]

Middle-class Creoles laud the national scene as 'cosmopolitan' but demand cultural homogeneity and social integration on their own terms. They view 'the existing alienation of a large percentage of the East Indian population . . . as an aberration' from their own standards. Thus they think of 'Carnival as a "national" festival when in fact it is almost exclusively a Creole event, and . . . equate the predominantly Creole P.N.M. with the nation.'[3] At the same time they regard Indians as an inferior subspecies and continue to term even Indian business and professional men 'Coolies'.

Indians bitterly resent the Creole 'habit of looking at Trinidadians of Indian descent as Indians and not as Trinidadians. . . . When a Negro does or says something, he is a Trinidadian, or a West Indian. When an Indian does or says something, he is an Indian.' Integration, Indians feel, should be recognized as a two-way street: 'Bread is no more West Indian than Roti is. Cricket is no more West Indian than hockey is. And [C. L. R.] James is no more West Indian than Bhadase Maraj is.'[4] Caribbean integration, Indians insist, must involve Indian as well as Eur-African culture and values; creolization by itself is unacceptable because it requires Indians, but not Creoles, to forgo their identity.

One Indian problem is that they alone treasure a sense of separate identity. East Indians want integration but resist assimilation. Those who creolize can participate in West Indian society, but Creoles cannot correspondingly indianize. Although one Indian suggests that 'Indian culture should become a part of the way of life of all Trinidadians', another warns Creoles to 'give up the feeling that Indians are similar to Negroes except for minor differences of ideas and physical appearance.

[1] Quoted in V. S. Naipaul, *The Middle Passage*, 1962, p. 170.

[2] Ryan, 'Decolonization in a Multi-Racial Society', pp. 485, 480.

[3] Oxaal, *Black Intellectuals Come to Power*, p. 23. In rural Trinidad Indian children play 'country carnival', which, like Hindi calypsoes, is dissociated from the Creole version. Creole assumptions of universalism may be quite unconscious. Thus one Creole scholar criticizes an East Indian author's 'hatred of the steel band and all it indicates' not only as a 'rejection of West Indian culture, but a rejection of the single common ground where Trinidadians of all races meet on a basis of equality' (Gordon Rohlehr, 'The Ironic Approach: The Novels of V. S. Naipaul', in Louis James, ed., *The Islands in Between: Essays on West Indian Literature*, 1968, pp. 121–39, ref. p. 131; see also Edward Brathwaite, 'Caribbean Critics', *NWQ*, Vol. 5, Nos. 1 and 2, Dead Season and Croptime 1969, pp. 5–12).

[4] Singh, *The Indian Enigma*, pp. 11–12, 14.

Indians . . . are not a subculture, but a rival culture—and a strong resistant one. . . . They are not, and do not care to be, part of Trinidad's cultural callalloo.'[1]

East Indian seclusion arouses Creole animosity because it is based not merely on cultural pride but on racial aversion. Caribbean experience and Creole values have reinforced the traditional *varna* hierarchy, ranking lighter castes above darker, which follows earlier racial distinctions in India. Indians regard as outcastes only the *black* Creoles, not the light-skinned, still less the white. 'East Indians do not refuse all association with Creoles of European origin, who can justifiably claim a respectable identity. But they do refuse much contact with Negroes'.[2] A survey of secondary-school children in Trinidad disclosed an explicit white bias; 'more East Indian boys than those in any other group . . . spontaneously express the desire to marry a white girl.'[3] A sociologist explains that Indians 'realized what few Negroes would be willing to concede—that as a group East Indians far more closely resembled the Europeans in racial characteristics than did the Negroes.'[4] Since Indians found the comparison advantageous, the realization is hardly surprising; it reflects their initiation into, and imitation of, the Creole system of colour ranking.

Many Caribbean East Indians are as dark as Africans but otherwise Caucasian in appearance. They value all aspects of physiognomy that set them apart from blacks. Thin lips and narrow noses are 'desirable' East Indian features, but most important, in their view, is long, straight hair. Facial hair is another diagnostic trait; an East Indian physician in predominantly black St. Vincent flaunted tufts of hair in his ears as a mark of Caucasian ancestry.

The impoverished East Indians of rural Jamaica likewise presume that white is good and black is bad and arrogate to themselves the status of European culture heroes they feel they resemble. Of a litho-graph of Christ with shoulder-length golden hair, an Indian exclaimed: 'He's just like us!' He pointed to his own head of straight grey hair: 'Look at it! Touch it! It's not like Nigger hair! You ever see Niggers who have hair like Jesus? No, man. They don't have nice hair like us.'[5] Indian antipathy to being thought black was one factor in their reluctance to join the 1970 black-power demonstrations in Trinidad.

---

[1] Cecil Seetahal, in 'Indian Iceberg', *Tapia* No. 6, 8 March 1970, p. 7; Ramdath Jagessar, 'Indian Iceberg', *Tapia*, No. 13, 16 November 1969, p. 7. See de Klerk, *De Immigratie der Hindostanen in Suriname*, p. 211.

[2] Ramdath Jagessar, 'East Indians and Integration', *Moko*, No. 6, 17 January 1969, p. 2.

[3] Rubin and Zavalloni, *We Wish To Be Looked Upon*, p. 130.

[4] Oxaal, *Black Intellectuals Come to Power*, p. 179; see also Wood, *Trinidad in Transition*, pp. 137–9.

[5] Quoted in Ehrlich, 'East Indian Cane Workers in Jamaica', p. 128.

'Indians are insulted at being considered black in the Negro sense of the word. . . . Physically they are not black, emotionally they do not feel the Negro stigma of blackness'.[1]

Indian identification with things white and European transcends physiognomy. Despite their disdain for Creole schooling, East Indians compete energetically for professional status and European manners. 'Each claiming to be whiter than the other, Indians and Negroes appeal to the unacknowledged white audience to see how much they despise one another . . . by reference to the whites.'[2]

If East Indians use Creole colour values to bolster their ethnic status, Creoles correspondingly emphasize or re-invent an antecedent ethnicity. It is precisely in Trinidad and Guyana, where Indianness requires the reiteration of Indian ancestral glories, that black and coloured Creoles find African roots most important. A taste for African dress, African nationalism, even African language, today creates a black pride as self-conscious as Indian uniqueness. This new-found ethnicity scarcely replaces the general yearning for things European, but the cloak of ethnic equality validates acerbities of colour. East Indians confronting black power found it even less to their taste than Creole culture:

We fear the black man is trying to use us for some sinister purpose. . . . Every Indian is united today. . . . We are closer together now than we have been for centuries. . . . Approaching us in *your* tightly knit band, will drive us into *our* tightly knit band. . . . We distrust strangers, especially you, who have behave[d] like strangers all these years.[3]

Interaction further complicates distinctions between the Creole order and East Indian ethnic awareness. Indians stress physical racial characteristics as components of ethnic distinctiveness and as evidence of its innate, immutable, genetic quality. Racial emphasis validates both subcultural separatism and endogamy; it also establishes a high rank for East Indians when measured against Creole colour values. Creoles similarly racialize their stereotypes of East Indian traits because they do not like to concede them broader cultural validity, and also because Creoles, too, conceive them to be genetically inherited.

[1] Brinley Samaroo, in 'African-Indian Solidarity: Two Views', *Vanguard*, 21 March 1970; Ramdath Jagessar, 'Indian Iceberg', *Tapia*, No. 3, 16 November 1969, p. 7.
[2] Naipaul, *The Middle Passage*, p. 80; see also Kuper, *Indian People in Natal*, pp. 69–70.
[3] Maharaj, 'To the Black People in T'dad'.

CHAPTER V

Ethnic Minorities

A half dozen smaller minorities stand, like the East Indians, partly outside the Creole class hierarchy, maintain distinctive ethnic or socio-cultural identities, and play unique roles in West Indian societies. These minorities are of two structurally distinct types: virtual outcasts relegated to positions beneath the whole Creole hierarchy, and adaptive groups accorded relatively high status. The former comprise American Indians, Bush Negroes, and Javanese; the latter Jews, Portuguese, Chinese, and Syrians.

ETHNIC OUTCASTS

Caribbean outcast minorities have little in common, except that Creoles generally neglect all of them as curiosities or condemn them as nuisances. Amerindians were the earliest inhabitants and are still widely dispersed; Javanese are among the most recent arrivals and are practically exclusive to Surinam; Bush Negroes descend from escaped plantation slaves. Great diversity of culture and social organization parallel these differences of date and location. Yet the three occupy roughly analogous social positions; they are at once the most impoverished and the least assimilated of West Indians. Non-participants in the larger society, they are not merely excluded but choose to remain aloof.

Amerindians. Amerindians scarcely survive as an ethnic entity in the West Indian islands. The 1960 censuses of Trinidad and the Windwards enumerated 2,000 'Caribs', but in few of them does Amerindian ancestry preponderate; perhaps none are pure Indian. A visitor in 1878 reported twenty 'uncontaminated' Carib families in Dominica and half a dozen in St. Vincent.[1] By 1940 only a hundred inhabitants of Dominica's Carib Reserve—one-fifth of the total—'appeared and believed themselves to be "full-blooded" Indians'.[2] Today perhaps

---

[1] Frederick A. Ober, *Camps in the Caribbees*, 1886, p. 100.

[2] Douglas MacRae Taylor, *The Black Carib of British Honduras*, 1951, pp. 26–27n. See also idem, 'The Caribs of Dominica', in *Smithsonian Institution Bulletin 119: Anthropological Papers*, 1938, pp. 103–60.

fifteen to twenty appear unmixed. The so-called Carib communities of St. Vincent and St. Lucia are wholly intermixed with Creoles. In the French Antilles no Amerindians remain; 'the few Martinican families who claim Indian descent based on their physical appearance', concludes a physical anthropologist, 'are in reality much more likely to have a Chinese ancestor.'[1]

In the mainland Caribbean the Amerindian presence is more palpable. With an estimated 28,000 in Guyana, 4,500 in Surinam, and 1,000 in French Guiana, about 3 per cent of each country's population, the Guianas together contain some 34,000 Amerindians, slightly more than half along the coastal littoral, the remainder in the interior forests and savannas.[2] The 1960 British Honduran census enumerates 11,000 Indians of Mayan stock, 10 per cent of the population, plus 7,000 Black Caribs, Indian in speech and presumed cultural identity though phenotypically African. However defined, only about 50,000 Amerindians inhabit the West Indian culture realm, a small fraction of the one or two million living there at the time of Columbus.

The history of Amerindian decline was sketched in Chapter 2. The surviving remnants are dwindling, socially demoralized, progressively less Indian in character. Ironically, those who display the greatest pride in 'Indian' identity are the Black Caribs of Central America. Nothing could be more anomalous than the circumstances of these descendants of fugitive slaves from Barbados and other islands who took refuge in St. Vincent, where they adopted the language and culture of the Caribs whose mountain retreats they shared. African and Amerindian intermittently fought, enslaved, and intermixed with one another throughout the seventeenth and eighteenth centuries. In the process Black Caribs gradually supplanted the aboriginal Indians. In 1795 English troops thwarted a Black Carib attempt to capture the whole island, rounded them up, and two years later deported them, 4,000-strong, to Roatán, one of the Bay Islands off Honduras. Their descendants filtered westward from Honduras into Guatemala and northward to Toledo and Stann Creek in southern British Honduras, maintaining fairly homogeneous settlements but also intermingling with Creoles, mestizos, and Indians along the coast.[3]

---

[1] Jean Benoist, 'Les Martiniquais: anthropologie d'une population métissée, *Bulletins et Mémoires de la Société d'Anthropologie de Paris*, Séries XI, Vol. 4, No. 2, 1963, p. 257.
[2] Audrey J. Butt, 'The Guianas', *Bulletin of the International Committee on Urgent Anthropological and Ethnological Research*, No. 7, 1965, pp. 69–70; Jean Hurault, 'La population des Indiens de Guyana française', *Population*, Vol. 20, 1965, pp. 603–32, 801–28. According to a more recent estimate, however, the Amerindian population of Guyana alone is 40,000 (*Report by the Amerindian Lands Commission*, 1969, p. 17).
[3] Taylor, *The Black Carib of British Honduras*; Nancie L. Solien González, *Black Carib Household Structure: A Study of Migration and Modernization*, 1969.

Contemporary Black Carib lore makes their wanderings still more fabulous:

When Christopher Columbus discovered the West Indies about the year 1493. he found there a race of white people (half-breeds) with wooly hair whom he called Caribs . . . a highly cultured people who had absorbed the Civilization of the Spaniards under whose rule they had lived unmolested for about two centuries. They were sea-faring hunters and tillers of the soil, peaceful and united. They hated aggression. Their religion was Mohammedanism, and their language presumably Arabic.[1]

Other than language, few elements of Black Carib culture are truly 'Carib' or, indeed, markedly unlike those of neighbouring Creoles. The coastal location of closely knit, densely settled Carib villages reflects their traditional dependence on the sea. Labour is divided by custom: after the men cut and clear the tropical forest, the women plant, till, and harvest, while the men return to fishing, supplemented by occasional wage labour on near-by plantations or in town. Today Black Carib men engage more in agriculture, focusing on cacao, rice, beans, coconuts, and bananas for sale; women continue to raise the traditional garden crops—manioc, plaintains, yams, pineapples.

Certain craft skills, family patterns, and aspects of folklore also set them apart from neighbouring Creoles. Black Caribs are nominally Catholic, but some customary religious beliefs serve as symbols of Carib identity. Polygyny is likewise traditional, but Black Carib households today are markedly consanguineal, since male dependence on migrant labour leaves women in charge at home.

In this as in most other respects Black Caribs resemble the Creole and mestizo folk with whom they have long mingled. Even their linguistic uniqueness is declining; 80 per cent of the Carib-speaking British Hondurans are now bilingual in English, though their accent marks them off from local Creoles. Some differences from Creoles, locally ascribed to Carib heritage, are in fact the opposite. A recent study notes that 'Caribs have preserved many West Indian culture traits which have long since disappeared among the Jamaicans and other West Indians who also inhabit this coast'[2]—for example, the costumes and movements of the 'John Canoe' masked dances typical of early Jamaica. In short, Black Caribs are in some respects more 'West Indian', in the sense of being less Latin American, than their black British Honduran neighbours.

Physical appearance differentiates them from West Indian Creoles

[1] P. V. Ramos, 'History of the Caribs', *Belize Daily Clarion*, 5 November 1946, quoted in Taylor, *The Black Carib of British Honduras*, p. 37.

[2] González, *Black Carib Household Structure*, p. 27; see also idem, 'West Indian Characteristics of the Black Carib', *Southwestern Journal of Anthropology*, Vol. 15, 1959, pp. 300–7.

hardly more than culture does. Short, stocky stature and high cheek-bones are said to reflect Amerindian ancestry, and some Caribs think themselves slightly lighter-skinned than Creoles; but Creoles claim Caribs are darker, having less European blood. Creole intermixture increases the African and reduces the Amerindian component among Black Caribs; for 'children resulting from mixed unions nearly always are raised as Caribs, being abandoned by their Negro parent.'[1]

Physical and cultural creolization notwithstanding, Black Carib cohesiveness and pride in non-African ancestry remain potent. 'I could go and kill every Negro in Africa for having spoiled our race', a young Black Carib school teacher told an anthropologist in 1949.[2] They cling to a belief that 'pure'—that is, light-skinned—Caribs survive in the islands. In 1968 a British Honduran Black Carib leader arranged a visit from the St. Vincent Carib community as an expression of cultural and ethnic solidarity.[3] To the dismay of their British Honduran hosts, the Vincentians were not the blue-eyed blonds they had expected and could neither speak nor understand the Carib tongue.

Black Caribs, despite their pride, occupy an inferior status in British Honduras. Creoles deride them for being superstitious, lazy, clannish, slovenly, and for having 'big heads' and 'big feet'—the former allegedly due to Indian ancestry, the latter to walking barefoot. Black Caribs are better regarded by Mayan Indians and mestizos, who are rural and Catholic like themselves.[4] They excel as linguists and staff many rural schools but only recently began to compete for civil-service jobs and to engage in politics, aligned with other Catholics against Creoles. Once in Belize, however, they quickly tend to become acculturated, look down on village Caribs, give up Carib speech, and 'pass' as Creoles.

More so than Black Caribs, most 'true' Indians are dispirited and disappearing. The Mayans of British Honduras are no long-settled tribe, but descendants of nineteenth-century refugees from Mexico and Guatemala. The mestizoized Mopañero Mayans of the north generally repudiate their Indian ancestry and emphasize Spanish background. In the west the Yucatañeco Mayans at Soccótz rely wholly on a nearby Spanish-Ladino community to supply their needs.[5] In the south the Kekchi Mayans at Punta Gorda and Toledo are much 'anglicized' by manifold connections with Black Carib neighbours.

The remaining Lesser Antillean Caribs are almost completely

[1] González, *Black Carib Household Structure*, p. 29.

[2] In Taylor, *The Black Carib of British Honduras*, p. 39.

[3] David L. McKoy, *A Memorable Visit . . . by the Vincentian Delegation to (Belize) British Honduras*, 1967.

[4] Sheila Cosminsky, 'Interethnic Relations in Punta Gorda, British Honduras: A Preliminary Report', 1966, pp. 28, 8, 11.

[5] Marcella Mazzarelli, 'Intercommunity Relations in British Honduras', *Human Organization*, Vol. 26, 1967, pp. 222-9, ref. pp. 223-6.

creolized. Basket-making (promoted by Social Welfare officers) and inheritance through the male line are the only 'Indian' traits of the Dominica Caribs. The Dominica Carib Reserve, along with the Carib Chief and Council, are early twentieth-century creations. The Governor who formalized the Carib Reserve tried 'to make them realize that they are the last remnant of a fine race and that they should try to keep their breed pure',[1] but a generation later a Commission reported that 'they have no folklore, no songs or music, no dances or customs, no costume or ornament to distinguish them from the other inhabitants of Dominica.'[2] The Caribs, like their Creole neighbours, are Roman Catholic, French-patois-speaking subsistence farmers.

In the Guianas the 10,000 coastal Arawaks, Warraus, and Galibis, long under mission influence, have intermixed with Creoles and lost much of their own culture and language, particularly in north-western Guyana. The Amerindians of the interior follow more traditional ways of life, but European agricultural technology augments their tropical forest economy. In Guyana an airstrip network, anti-malarial campaigns, and mechanical wells and wind-pumps have dramatically increased tribal populations: the Wapishana of the Rupununi savanna, who numbered 1,700 in 1945, were estimated at 4,000 in 1963. But modernization also subjects them to mission and plantation exploitation. Medical and technical progress involves working on livestock ranches, wearing shirts, brushing teeth, singing English folk songs, and giving up *cassiri* (fermented cassava). The hinterland Amerindians of Surinam and French Guiana, on the other hand, seem doomed to extinction. Despite repeated epidemics they have acquired little immunity to respiratory diseases; medical and other intervention has meanwhile eroded their traditional social organization.[3]

Guyana today promotes Amerindian integration, reversing the reservation policy of the colonial era. 'Recognizing their weak and exploitable condition,' the new Guyanese constitution 'envisages and permits . . . [what] amounts to racial discrimination in their favour', according to an international commission that pronounced government policy 'humane and enlightened'.[4] The Prime Minister warned that

[1] Henry Hesketh Bell, *Glimpses of a Governor's Life*, 1946, p. 21.

[2] J. Stanley Rae and Sidney A. Armitage-Smith, *Conditions in the Carib Reserve and the Disturbance of 18th September, 1930, Dominica*, Cmd. 3990, p. 22. See also E. P. Banks 'A Carib Village in Dominica', *SES*, Vol. 5, 1956, pp. 74–86; Taylor, 'The Caribs of Dominica'.

[3] Richard F. Salisbury, 'Ethnographic Notes on Wapishana Agriculture', in R. F. Salisbury et al., *Ethnographic Notes on Amerindian Agriculture*, 1968, pp. 7–20, ref. p. 7. Butt ('The Guianas', p. 85) gives the number of the Wapishana as 2,200 in 1946. See also Raymond T. Smith, *British Guiana*, 1962, pp. 112–13; Michael Swan, *The Marches of El Dorado: British Guiana, Brazil, Venezuela*, 1958, pp. 195–9.

[4] *Racial Problems in the Public Service: Report of the British Guiana Commission of Inquiry*, 1965, p. 23.

'our hinterland is not a mere showcase for the passing admiration of curious anthropologists, archaeologists and tourists but a vast place to be peopled and developed', and explained to the Indians themselves that they could no longer be treated 'as children of the forest or inferior beings' but must become an integral part of Guyana.[1] Rival political parties now bid for Amerindian support. But many Indians mistrust integration as a cloak for land expropriation. Dissatisfaction with government adjudication of Indian territorial rights flared up in 1969 in a Rupununi rebellion led by American-born ranchers. Several Amerindians were killed by government forces quelling the revolt, some were later tried for, and acquitted of, murder, and others fled across the Brazilian and Venezuelan borders.[2]

In Surinam and French Guiana, Indians are far fewer and tribal areas remain under semi-colonial or metropolitan control. Surinam rules with benevolent passivity: some tribes have been commercialized for tourist display; others make contact only through Bush Negro intermediaries; still others, such as the Trio, are subject to 'civilizing' mission influence.[3]

By contrast, French Guiana rigorously guards Amerindians against assimilation, save for the already creolized coastal tribes. Until a few years ago, indiscriminate contacts with Creoles and tourists were decimating some interior tribes and corrupting the remainder. Five years with Creole gold panners, for example, had destroyed the Emerillon Indians through malaria, tuberculosis, prostitution, and alcoholism. The neighbouring Wayana and Oyampi, looking for tourist handouts, had moved their villages close to administrative centres. To protect the Indians against these vices of civilization, the French Government in 1962 restricted visits to tribal areas. Thanks to the absence of epidemic disease since then, Indian births have exceeded deaths for the first time in a generation.[4]

Creole behaviour toward Amerindians reveals ambivalent feelings.

---

[1] Linden Forbes Sampson Burnham, 'We Must Integrate or Perish' (1967), in *A Destiny to Mould: Discourses by the Prime Minister of Guyana*, 1970, pp. 246–50, ref. p. 250; *News from Guyana*, Ministry of Information release no. 20, 2 July 1970.

[2] Burnham, 'Radio Broadcast to the Nation on Disturbances in the Rupununi Savannahs', 4 January 1969, in *A Destiny to Mould*, pp. 171–6; *Report by the Amerindian Lands Commission*, pp. 65–6.

[3] P. G. Rivière, 'A Policy for the Trio Indians of Surinam', *Nieuwe West-Indische Gids*, Vol. 45, 1966, pp. 95–120. See also idem, *Marriage among the Trio: A Principle of Social Organisation*, 1969.

[4] Jean Hurault and P. Frenay, 'Les Indiens Emerillon de la Guyane française, *Journal de la Société des Américanistes*, Vol. 52, 1963, pp. 132–56; Etienne P. Bois, *Les Amerindiens de la Haute-Guyane française*, 1967; Jean Hurault, *Les Indiens Wayana de la Guyane française: structure sociale et coutume familiale*, 1968; idem, 'La population des Indiens de Guyane française'; Dominique Darbois, *Yanamale: Village of the Amazon*, 1956.

On the one hand they are despised as backward and ignorant savages: Guyanese and Dominican Creoles regularly revile Amerindians as filthy, lecherous, traitorous, unteachable. These pejoratives serve to enhance Creole self-esteem; the Amerindian stands for all that the Creole rejects in the European stereotype of himself. That most Amerindians are also subsistence farmers confirms the Creole image of agriculture as degrading. As a lower social order, Amerindians inflate Creole status. The Dominican coloured elite frequently adopt Carib children, treating them partly as pets, partly as servants. Black Carib boys in British Honduras and in Honduras are often sent to live with upper-class townfolk, who educate and acculturate them in exchange for household help. At the same time, the Mayans of Punta Gorda find *compadres* and *comadres* among Black Caribs, who take pride in adopting Indian children and sending them to school.[1]

Creole hostility toward Amerindians has additional roots. Large-scale African slavery was instituted in part to 'save' the Indians, after Las Casas's long crusade finally persuaded the Spanish crown to outlaw Indian slavery. Thereafter Europeans ruthlessly enslaved Africans and romanticized Indians as noble savages. The stereotype that Indians preferred death to loss of liberty reinforced the distinction. The white planter felt closer to the Indians in spirit than to the Negroes 'who had made his fortune by their toil and then had the bad taste to survive to remind him of it.'[2] Indians were regularly employed to apprehend escaped Negroes. 'Everyone knows that Amerindians hunted down runaway slaves; it was something I heard again and again,' affirmed a Trinidadian visiting British Guiana, 'and wherever one sees Amerindians, it is a chilling memory.'[3] This helps to explain why black and coloured West Indians resent outside concern for Amerindians. In French Guiana the Indian reservation policy is unpopular with Creoles,

---

[1] González, *Black Carib Household Structure*, pp. 53–4; Cosminsky, 'Interethnic Relations in Punta Gorda, British Honduras', p. 35.

[2] Jack Corzani, *Splendeur et misère: l'exotisme littéraire aux Antilles*, 1969, p. 57. For the conflict over Indian slavery, see Lewis Hanke, *Aristotle and the American Indian: A Study of Race Prejudice in the Modern World*, 1959, and John Paddock, 'The War of the Myths: Spanish and English Treatment of the Native Americans', *America Indigena*, Vol. 18, 1958, pp. 281–92. For European views of Indians and Africans, see Henri Baudet, *Paradise on Earth: Some Thoughts on European Images of Non-European Man*, 1965, pp. 30–1.

[3] V. S. Naipaul, *The Middle Passage*, 1962, p. 99. 'Our Caribs', noted a Dutch Governor in Guiana, 'have loyally done their best. . . . These occurrences cause a great bitterness between the blacks and them, which, if well and reasonably stimulated, cannot fail to be of much use and service in the future to the Colonies' (Laurens Storm van 's Gravesande, Governor of Essequibo, 1738–1772, Despatch, 9 April 1764, P.R.O. 472/32, in Storm van 's Gravesande, *The Rise of British Guiana*, The Hakluyt Society, 2nd Series, No. 26, 1911, Vol. II, p. 446). For North American parallels, see William S. Willis, 'Divide and Rule: Red, White, and Black in the Southeast', *Journal of Negro History*, Vol. XLVIII, 1963, pp. 157–76.

who want free access to the interior and complain that Indian protection perpetuates French colonialism. In Dominica even the trifling autonomy of the Carib Reserve draws perennial criticism.

Yet Creoles also find much to admire in Amerindians. In St. Lucia and Dominica light skin and straight hair make Caribs enviable. 'Dey're maad people,' a black Dominican told a traveller, 'but dey got lovely, lovely hair.'[1] Supposed Indian ancestry was advantageous to elite French Antilleans who claimed Carib descent for themselves or for their coloured wives; for a sufficient reward even a black man migh be proclaimed Indian. Dominican Creoles exaggerate Carib antecedents to emphasize that they are lighter than other islanders. Even in Trinidad and Jamaica, light-skinned Creoles are given to calling themselves part Indian. Haitian literature satirizes mulattoes who 'insist that they are quite free of Negro blood and ascribe their ineffaceable tan to the aboriginal San Domingan Indians'.[2]

Yet this hardly reflects unmixed delight in Amerindian origins. Carib racial vanity in St. Lucia and Dominica is apt to be inversely related to Carib ancestry: the purest Amerindians are regarded as backward and primitive, whereas Creoles without apparent Indian admixture are fond of referring to their Carib origins.[3] At Mackenzie, in Guyana, a woman of mixed Indian descent spoke 'disparagingly of the "pure Amerindian girl" to whom her brother is married and [of] the "little savages" who are her nieces and nephews, though she later claimed pride in being part Amerindian and quoted her brother as saying "If you don't have Amerindian blood in you, you aren't a member of the master race."'[4]

Creoles in Dominica alternate veneration and execration of the island's aborigines. The Government took credit in 1969 for 'voluntarily' increasing its allowance to the Carib Chief and Council to $14 and $9 (Eastern Caribbean currency) a month, respectively; yet government ministers at the same time vilified the Caribs as 'drunken', 'lazy', and 'dishonest'.[5] Opposition party accusations of duplicity reveal

[1] Patrick Leigh Fermor, *The Traveller's Tree: A Journey through the Caribbean Islands*, 1950, p. 122.

[2] Poem by Émile Roumer, in Edmund Wilson, *Red, Black, Blond and Olive: Studies in Four Civilizations: Zuñi, Haiti, Soviet Russia, Israel*, 1956, p. 142.

[3] Pierre Vérin, 'Sainte-Lucie et ses derniers Caraïbes', *CO-M*, Vol. XII, 1959, pp. 349–61, ref. p. 361; idem, 'Notes sur la vie sociale du village de la Pointe Caraïbe (Sainte-Lucie, Antilles)', *Annales de l'Université de Madagascar*, Série Lettres et Sciences Humaines, No. 6, 1967, pp. 139–64, ref. p. 158.

[4] Judith Roback, 'Bases of Social Differentiation in a Guyana Mining Town', 1968, p. 79.

[5] Dominica Government Information Service, release no. 371/69, 13 September 1969; Androcles, 'Those Whom the Gods . . .', *Dominica Star*, 4 January 1969, pp. 2 and 4. See also 'Carib Council or Salybia Village Council?' *Dominica Herald*, 23 November 1968, p. 2.

an equivalent ambivalence about Amerindians: 'Everyone knows that the Premier has Carib blood in him', charges a local paper, 'yet he is seeking to portion out their land to others.'[1]

As indigenous inhabitants, Amerindians play an important symbolic role in the West Indian search for identity. The very absence of Indians is a source of regret to Creoles, who find it hard to feel at home in lands lacking visible remains of an ancient past. Cultural nationalism throughout the Caribbean today promotes the search for Arawak and Carib remains. Finding them will not meet the need for roots, however; for living West Indians have little real connection with Amerindian culture or descent. 'The meaningful legacies in Jamaica's history', concludes one critic, 'are the slave chains and the mantraps preserved in the Folk Museum. Arawak remains . . . are presumably of some interest to the archaeologist but they are hardly sufficient for an original cultural reorientation and definition.'[2]

Bush Negroes. As exemplars of West Indian identity, flourishing groups of unmixed African descent might seem more appropriate than the remote and dwindling Amerindians. The Bush Negroes of Surinam and French Guiana and some of the Maroons of Jamaica maintain folkways little changed since their slave forebears escaped from plantations, holding out against local forces and European militia until governments and planters finally conceded their freedom and autonomy.

Although they still dwell apart, these groups are by no means racially distinctive. They share African ancestry with most West Indian Creoles, many of whom are equally unmixed. Unlike most Creoles, however, Bush Negroes take pride in their African ancestry and believe that most elements of their culture stem from Africa, including some that clearly do not. In this they separate themselves from the Creole mainstream more deliberately than even the Amerindians. But Bush Negro self-esteem requires no ties of fellowship with the wider black world; still determined to keep to themselves, they rely on traditional bonds of community to resist creolization, nationalization, and modernization.

In this endeavour the Bush Negroes surpass the Jamaican Maroons, thanks to greater numbers, tribal cohesion, territorial remoteness, ethnic segregation, and economic viability. The Bush Negroes number some 38,000 (36,000 in Surinam, 2,000 in French Guiana) divided among six tribes (Saramacca, Auka or Djuka, Boni, Matuari, Koffiemacca or Coeroenti, Paramacca) inhabiting the middle reaches of the major river systems. Up-river to the south dwell Amerindian tribal

---

[1] 'Is It True?' *Dominica Herald*, 30 September 1967, p. 2.

[2] W. I. Carr, 'The West Indian Novelist: Prelude and Context', *CQ*, Vol. 11, Nos. 1 and 2, March–June 1965, pp. 71–84, ref. p. 84. This theme is discussed in Wilson Harris, 'History, Fable and Myth in the Caribbean and Guianas', *CQ*, Vol. 16, No. 2, June 1970, pp. 1–32.

remnants; down-river on the northern coastal plain are plantations and agricultural settlements, tenanted mainly by East Indians and Javanese.

Bush Negroes won a monopoly of river transport in eighteenth-century Surinam. Their descendants remain canoe-builders and river mariners, dominating trade between the interior and the coast. As woodsmen and loggers, Bush Negroes also supply half of Surinam's timber needs, though the proportion is diminishing with the advent of mechanized logging. Others, including Bush Negroes from French Guiana, supplement subsistence agriculture with temporary mining and construction jobs in Surinam. In this manner they continue to thrive, despite primitive technology, soil exhaustion, and economically restricting ritual observances. Unlike their Amerindian neighbours, Bush Negroes suffer little from tuberculosis, and their rate of natural increase is the highest in Surinam.[1]

The two or three thousand Jamaican Maroons enjoy few such advantages. They inhabit a desolate and rugged limestone region in north-central Jamaica, unrewarding for agriculture and difficult for transport. Lacking resources adequate to maintain group cohesion, the Maroons are gradually coalescing with surrounding peasantry, whom they resemble in appearance and mode of life. Maroon autonomy originally required isolation, but with Jamaican independence they no longer feel the same need to keep apart. And those who go out to market their produce are said to find 'a broader freedom down in the plains now than in their mountain strongholds.'[2]

As the most isolated and least creolized Africans in the New World, Bush Negroes and Maroons have long allured travellers fascinated by 'jungle voodoo' rites, missionaries eager to save 'primitive' souls, and anthropologists interested in African 'survivals'. Blood-type studies have demonstrated the genetic likeness between Bush Negroes and West Africans. And fieldwork among the Saramacca a generation ago persuaded Herskovits of their African socio-cultural heritage. Religion, folklore, tribal organization, family patterns, modes of agriculture, art

[1] Peter Neumann, *Wirtschaft und materielle Kultur der Bushneger Surinames: Ein Beitrag zur Erforschung afroamerikanischer Probleme*, 1967, pp. 25–7; Jean Hurault, 'Histoire des noirs réfugiés Boni de la Guyane française', *Revue Française d'Histoire d'Outre-Mer*, Vol. 47, No. 166, 1960, pp. 76–137; André Sausse, 'Pathologie comparée des populations primitives noirs et indiennes de la Guyane française', *Bulletin de la Société de Pathologie Exotique*, Vol. 44, 1951, pp. 455–60; idem, *Populations primitives du Maroni (Guyane française)*, 1951; J. D. G. Schaad, 'Epidemiological Observations in Bush Negroes and Amerindians in Surinam', *Tropical and Geographical Medicine*, Vol. 12, 1960, pp. 38–46.

[2] Peter Abrahams, *Jamaica: An Island Mosaic*, 1957, p. 61. See also R. C. Dallas, *The History of the Maroons* [1803]; A. E. Furness, 'The Maroon War of 1795', *JHR*, Vol. V, No. 2, November 1965, pp. 30–49. For the favourable connotations of the word 'Maroon', see Frederic G. Cassidy, *Jamaica Talk: Three Hundred Years of the English Language in Jamaica*, 1961, pp. 160–1.

forms, and linguistic structure seemed to combine elements from Ashanti, Dahomey, Benin, and the Congo.[1]

Yet there are departures, as Herskovits recognized. Cut off from Africa for two and a half centuries, Bush Negroes could hardly have followed the same road as their Old World congeners. Indeed, their villages remained static by comparison with much of Africa; Bush Negro culture is less that of Africa today than that of seventeenth-century Africa. Like Creoles and East Indians, the Bush Negroes keep many Old World ways that the Old World has forgotten.

But Bush Negroes are in no sense purely African. New World life and culture contacts have profoundly altered them. Even their rebel slave forebears were partly creolized. By the time their tribal organization was firmly fixed, almost all Bush Negroes were Creole-born. Tribal anomalies reflect Guianese geography and military exigencies, along with African institutional modes, and in ways that they are all alike Bush Negro tribes often diverge markedly from Africans. Thus the matrilineal and matrilocal character of Bush Negro society, both more rigorous and more uniform than the wide range of ancestral African forms, may reflect local reactions against coercion, 'pushing to its logical conclusion', in one scholar's view, 'an attitude prevalent among the Negroes of the New World in general.'[2] In the authority of headmen, in the divisions of labour between men and women, Bush Negro tribal systems are not Old World retentions but responses to New World conditions. Indeed, the market-place activity of Paramaribo is more reminiscent of West Africa than are the trade patterns of Bush Negro settlements.

Bush Negro material culture is likewise a *mélange* of African, European, and Amerindian traits in a New World context. Agricultural crops and techniques derive in large measure from the eighteenth-century plantation economy. Bush Negro hunting and fishing methods owe more to Amerindian than to African techniques. Moreover, their livelihood has always depended on European colonial co-operation and on commerce with Amerindians and Creoles. Wood cutting and river trading are not just supplements to subsistence but basic and durable features of Bush Negro economy.[3] Mid-nineteenth-century government efforts to stop the Djukas from smuggling and trading with slaves and to persuade them to return to their tribal grounds up-river succeeded

[1] Melville J. Herskovits and Frances S. Herskovits, *Rebel Destiny: Among the Bush Negroes of Dutch Guiana*, 1934.

[2] Jean Hurault, 'Comment on Review of "Les noirs réfugiés Boni de la Guyane française"', *CS*, Vol. 7, No. 4, January 1968, pp. 65–7, ref. p. 66. See André J. F. Köbben, 'Law at the Village Level: The Cottica Djuka of Surinam', in Laura Nader, ed., *Law in Culture and Society*, 1969, pp. 117–40.

[3] Neumann, *Wirtschaft und materielle Kultur der Buschneger Surinames*, pp. 41, 89–90, 194.

no better than have subsequent integration attempts.[1] Tribal migration has been opportunistic: gold and diamond mines drew Bonis and Saramaccas from Surinam to French Guiana in the late nineteenth century. Bush Negroes today are increasingly numerous as bauxite workers and as day labourers in Paramaribo.

Money is not the only attraction; the bright lights, shops, movies, and reputed sexual license of the city entice young men from the Bush Negro villages. Many are also pushed out for some breach of law or custom, often for contravening rigid tribal sexual codes. Yet economic development has induced some creolization even in the hinterland. The Afobaka Dam on the Suriname River compelled many Bush Negroes to relocate nearer the inhabited coastal belt. Their new villages boast electricity and tap water, and tar-papered wooden shacks replace their former palm-covered, dirt-floored huts, 'benefits' secured only at the cost of increased dependence on the central government.[2]

Although Creole pressures are altering Bush Negro ways, their social solidarity remains secure. Even in Paramaribo they live by themselves, returning to their villages within a few years. Moreover, contact with the world outside is confined to men; women remain at home, where they control inheritance, dominate ritual, and maintain tribal integrity. 'I will send my son to your country', a Bush Negro mother told Herskovits. 'The men who go . . . say it is good to know how to count the white man's way. My woman-child I will never send.'[3]

Pride as blacks and mistrust of whites figure prominently in the Bush Negro sense of identity. Recalling ancestral struggles against slave-owners, they treat whites as potential enemies and condemn Creoles for their white bias. Trustworthy information about Bush Negroes is meagre partly because they fear that to divulge it may lead to re-enslavement or death. A Djuka group that had totally misled Creole census takers proudly told an anthropologist, 'They can count everyone, the Creoles, the Hindustani, the Javanese, but not us'.[4]

[1] Silvia W. de Groot, 'Migration Movements of the Djuka Tribe in Surinam from 1845 to 1863', *Nieuwe West-Indische Gids*, Vol. 44, 1965, pp. 133–50; idem, *Djuka Society and Social Change: History of an Attempt to Develop a Bush Negro Community in Surinam, 1917–1926*, 1969.

[2] H. E. Lamur, 'De levensomstandigheden van de in Paramaribo werkende Aukaner arbeiders', *Nieuwe West-Indische Gids*, Vol. 44, 1965, pp. 119–32; Thomas G. Mathews, 'The Three Guianas', *Current History*, Vol. 51, 1966, pp. 333–7, and 365–6, ref. pp. 336–7.

[3] Herskovits and Herskovits, *Rebel Destiny*, p. 154.

[4] André J. F. Köbben, 'Participation and Quantification: Field Work among the Djuka (Bush Negroes of Surinam)', in D. G. Jongmans and P. C. W. Gutkind, eds., *Anthropologists in the Field*, 1967, pp. 35–55, ref. p. 50. For similar Boni secretiveness, see Thomas J. Price, 'Ethnohistory and Self-Image in Three New World Negro Societies', in Norman E. Whitten, Jr., and John F. Szwed, eds., *Afro-American Anthropology: Contemporary Perspectives*, 1970, pp. 63–73.

Many Creoles vaunt a 'European' superiority toward Bush Negroes, whom they chide for being deliberately 'primitive' and 'African'. Bush Negroes in Paramaribo, underpaid and overcharged, are shunned and derided as 'stupid', 'heathen', and 'naked'.[1] But Jamaicans have always admired the Maroons as early freedom fighters, and in Surinam some Creole politicians now pay court to Bush Negroes as 'Bush Creoles', urging 'black solidarity' against Asians.

Javanese. Neither indigenes nor rebels, 46,000 Javanese inhabit Surinam because both their former and their present homelands were parts of the Dutch Empire. They are the most recent Caribbean immigrants and also the least assimilated. Although the Javanese dwell with Creoles and Hindustanis on the cultivated coastal lands, they are hardly more creolized than the Bush Negroes of the interior. Resigned to residence in Surinam, not even third-generation Javanese are truly at home there. Only fraud and sorcery, they (like some East Indians) feel, could have induced their forefathers to quit Java. As an immigrant explained:

I met a stranger on the road. . . . He asked me if I would not like to earn a lot of money [and] told me that he could arrange for me to work in another country for a couple of years where I would be well-paid, so that I could return to my *desa* [village] as a wealthy man. I told him that I could not leave my family. Then the stranger stepped on my foot, mumbling a spell in a strange language, and suddenly I no longer remembered having a family. So then I said 'All right, I will go to that country.' . . . When the ship was only a few yards from the shore I remembered everything. [The magic only worked on Java.] I wept, and everyone else wept, but it was too late.[2]

Such legends absolve the individual from blame for leaving his family and village and also reinforce Javanese solidarity in Surinam.

The actual circumstances of Javanese migration were similar to that from India. Population pressure and poverty in Netherlands India and need for plantation labour in Surinam persuaded Dutch authorities to begin Javanese recruitment in 1890. Five thousand immigrants entered Surinam by 1901, 6,000 more by 1914, an additional 20,000 between 1917 and 1929, and a final 1,000 in 1939. Javanese indentures resembled East Indian, including provision for home passages. One out of four did return, but many who wished to go back home were ashamed to because they had failed to gain wealth. Most re-indentured themselves on Surinam coffee estates or took up land in coastal villages or

---

[1] Lamur, 'De levensomstandigheden van de in Paramaribo werkende Aukaner arbeiders'.

[2] Annemarie de Waal Malefijt, *The Javanese of Surinam: Segment of a Plural Society*, 1963, p. 29. For similar migration myths, see Morton Klass, *East Indians in Trinidad: A Study in Cultural Persistence*, 1961, p. 10; Allen S. Ehrlich, 'East Indian Cane Workers in Jamaica', 1969, p. 37.

abandoned plantations, supplementing rice farming with coconut cultivation and fishing. Those still on plantations endure the obloquy of the others.[1]

The Javanese were thoroughly isolated from the rest of Surinam society. Remote from Creoles and Hindustanis (East Indians), they had little contact with Dutch estate owners and government officials. Unless a Javanese went to Paramaribo he might not see any non-Javanese for years on end. Walled off in their own world, they retained many ancestral features of culture and social organization. But the disorienting effects of the voyage itself, the immigration of single persons rather than families, the shortage of women, and submission to plantation control all took a toll of cherished folkways and values. Traditional *desa* modes of authority, for example, have been lost or altered. The sacred Javanese relationship to land is absent, community solidarity has crumbled, and residential patterns have changed. Parents still arrange marriages for offspring, but concubinage is common, and Muslim family sanctions are much weakened.[2]

One serious schism stemmed from divergent judgements concerning the location of Surinam *vis-à-vis* the Holy Land. Newcomers from Java at first prayed as at home, facing west towards Mecca. Subsequently an educated Surinam Javanese asserted that the shortest route to Mecca was eastward. Some favoured his view, others rejected it, and the ensuing quarrel so divided the community that east-facing and west-facing Javanese would not intermarry, attend the same ceremonies, or even speak to one another. Community need has partly reconciled the opposing factions, but the Mecca question remains unresolved; to this day both cardinal directions compete for adherence.[3]

Divided among themselves, Javanese seldom make common cause with other ethnic groups. All-Muslim solidarity, a political venture of the late 1940s, soon dissolved into Javanese and East Indian factions. Javanese involvement in Surinam affairs was in any case minimal; it was Indonesian nationalism that claimed their allegiance. After Indonesia became independent in 1949, half the Javanese in Surinam gave up Dutch for Indonesian citizenship, and many of them returned home. The remainder, committed to a Surinamese destiny, have elected their own local legislative representatives since 1955, but,

---

[1] Joseph Ismael, *De Immigratie van Indonesiërs* in Surinam, 1949, pp. 26, 95; Malefijt, *The Javanese of Surinam*, p. 35. See also R. M. N. Panday, *Agriculture in Surinam 1650–1950: An Inquiry into the Causes of Its Decline*, 1959, pp. 151, 154–5, 210–11.

[2] J. Prins, 'Twintig jaar praktijk van de aziatische huwelijkswetgeving in Suriname', *Nieuwe West-Indische Gids*, Vol. 44, 1965, pp. 78–108; Malefijt, *The Javanese of Surinam*, pp. 36, 188–92.

[3] Justus M. van der Kroef, 'The Indonesian Minority in Surinam', *American Sociological Review*, Vol. 16, 1951, pp. 672–9; Malefijt, *The Javanese of Surinam*, pp. 164–5.

unaffiliated with any major party, their influence is small.[1] The Javanese birthrate—unlike the East Indian—is relatively low, and the Javanese proportion of the population is unlikely to rise above its present 16 per cent.

Javanese seldom take part in other Surinamese institutions. Apparently lacking ambition or reluctant to learn Dutch, few of them enter the civil service or the professions. Creoles reprobate the Javanese for their self-imposed seclusion and 'backwardness'. But Hindustanis, because they too resist creolization, view the Dutch and Creoles as competitors, the Javanese as allies. Since the Javanese are fellow Asians with a strong tradition of their own, their presence in Surinam lends support to East Indian insistence on cultural autonomy.[2]

As West Indian minorities, Amerindians, Bush Negroes, and Javanese play analogous social roles. Greatly outnumbered everywhere, controlling little of consequence, they are seldom powers to reckon with. In any event they have small desire to exercise power; their ambitions *vis-à-vis* Creole society are few. They wish mainly to be left to themselves. Secluded by endogamy and residence, they place a high value on ethnic custom and tradition. Group awareness helps them to maintain autonomy and distinguishes them from Creoles in personality as in social organization.

Derogatory stereotypes reflect their apartness. The minorities scorn Creoles as ambitious, corrupt, and individualistic, despising some for being black, others for striving to be white. Creoles disparage the minorities as feckless, clannish, immoral, and lascivious—stereotypical derogations given extra force by the deliberate 'rejection' of 'civilization'. Creoles who seek status by emulating European ideals are outraged when despised minorities simply disdain those ideals. That is why these minorities are considered not merely lower-class but outcast.

Outcast–Creole relationships resemble those between East Indians and Creoles, but with significant structural differences. Near-majority status in Trinidad and Guyana, cultural demands at the national level, and competitiveness within the wider society make East Indians rivals of Creoles rather than outcasts. And the smaller, feebler East Indian minorities in Jamaica and the French Antilles tend to merge into the Creole lower class, again unlike the Javanese, Amerindians, and Bush Negroes.

[1] Albert L. Gastmann, 'The Politics of Surinam and the Netherlands Antilles', 1968, pp. 51–2, 73–4.

[2] Annemarie de Waal Malefijt, 'Het sociaal-economisch vermogen van de Javanen in Suriname', *Tijdschrift van het Koninklijk Nederlandsch Aardrijksundig Genootschap*, Vol. LXXX, 1963, pp. 467–73; Prins, 'Twintig jaar praktijk van de aziatische huwelijkswetgeving in Suriname'.

Of the outcast groups, the Javanese most closely approach the East Indian situation. In Surinam they are almost as numerous as the Hindustanis, and the two populations share common circumstances of migration, estate labour, ancestral retention and loss, and loyalty to an Asian homeland. But the tenacity of Javanese communalism and their enduring aloofness toward the larger Surinam society cause Creoles to relegate them to a deeper limbo. Javanese uniqueness is deplored but is also used to justify their continued exclusion, as with Bush Negroes.

Between social outcast and ethnic competitor no firm line can be drawn; a larger or more ambitious Javanese community would clearly enjoy a different status in Surinam. The East Indians too were at first an outcast minority in Caribbean societies. As for the Amerindians and Bush Negroes, technology and nationalism threaten their isolation and autonomy and make extinction or assimilation their probable fate.

Four other ethnic minorities—Jews, Portuguese, Chinese, and Syrians —occupy positions in Caribbean society not in the least like those of the groups described. Far from being outcasts, they fill gaps within West Indian economic and social structure left vacant by, or taken over from, Creoles. Whether present for three centuries or for three decades, these minorities dominate many aspects of Caribbean commerce, and as successful entrepreneurs they have gained social status on par with the Creole elite or middle class. Status-gap minorities, like outcasts, retain an ethnic identity and a degree of communal autonomy. But their economic role precludes social and physical isolation and, though clannish, they are far less endogamous than the outcast groups.

Status-gap people nevertheless also become Creole scapegoats. Creoles both envy and reprobate their 'inherent' shrewdness, acquisitiveness, frugality, familism. Ethnic minorities are felt to gain only at the expense of others. Not rooted in the West Indian community, they amassed wealth without sharing it, whereas well-off Creoles often had to distribute largesse throughout a ramified circle of relatives and associates. Social self-sufficiency gave minorities a further economic advantage; unlike Creoles, they could not be seduced or shamed into charity, debt remission, or conspicuous consumption. Creole entrepreneurs might be ostracized for accumulating without spending, but there was little to impede those already socially marginal from the single-minded pursuit of profits.[1]

Elitist Creole values denigrate entrepreneurial activity; small-

[1] Simon Rottenberg, 'Entrepreneurship and Economic Progress in Jamaica', *Inter-American Economic Affairs*, Vol. 7, No. 2, Autumn 1953, pp. 74–9, ref. p. 78.

society networks of obligation render it inefficient. Thus Creoles readily yielded almost every economic arena. Chinese, Portuguese, Jews, and Syrians dominate many aspects of commerce not only by having bested Creole competitors, but because Creoles often chose not to compete. The minorities had little difficulty engrossing occupations shunned by other West Indians.

The West Indian plantation system had stifled local shopkeeping just as it truncated local elites. European merchants and their Caribbean agents controlled imports and exports and distributed goods in bulk to the estates. Retailing was difficult to carry on and poorly regarded. Free coloured people, even where they were not barred from shop-keeping by law, had great trouble acquiring sufficient capital or credit. White prestige models based on a landed proprietary moreover dero-gated commerce and shopkeeping. The rising coloured middle class aped these elitist values, eschewing trade for the learned professions. Lack of opportunity, lack of familiarity, and lack of interest put com-merce beyond their ken. And when minorities took up retailing, most Creoles retreated with little regret into more prestigious, if less lucrative, occupations.

Slavery and colonial subjection also habituated many Creoles to shrink from managerial responsibility. 'It never cross my mind', remarks a small-islander in a Naipaul novel, 'that I could open a shop of my own. Is how it is with black people. They get so used to working for other people that they get to believe that because they black they can't do nothing else but work for other people.'[1] By contrast with Creole entrepreneurial diffidence, status-gap minorities seem all the more aggressive.

Conspicuous as these minorities still are, they are unlikely to survive as structurally separate groups. Political independence and Creole majority rule increasingly force them to integrate through inter-marriage and creolization. As their Creole connections ramify and the rising generation acquires Creole distaste for trade, minority groups become less familist, thrifty, and parsimonious. Unless newcomers from abroad swell their numbers, most of them will eventually merge into the Creole elite and middle class, leaving only exotic family names and out-worn Creole stereotypes as evidence that such differences once mattered.

Jews. Sephardic Jews, the earliest and most enduring local minority, spread throughout the Caribbean during the seventeenth century, first with the Dutch from Brazil, later directly from western Europe. The cemeteries of Surinam and St. Kitts, of Barbados and Nevis, of Martin-ique and St. Eustatius, attest the early prominence of Jews, but emigra-tion and Creole amalgamation in the eighteenth century then reduced

[1] V. S. Naipaul, *A Flag on the Island*, 1967, p. 140.

their numbers. Today only Jamaica and Curaçao have significant Jewish elements.[1]

In common with European Jews, those in the Caribbean at first endured severe disabilities. Martinique forbade them to engage in commerce; Barbados did not let them indenture Christian servants; Jamaica refused them the franchise and required a special group tax from them. But discrimination against Jews was less often enforced and sooner repealed than in Europe, because in West Indian eyes it mattered greatly that Jews were white. And because many of them lacked a European homeland of their own, Jews in the West Indies manifested less of the absentee spirit than other whites. After 1773 when an Amsterdam stock market crisis forced Dutch owners to yield their Surinam estates into corporate hands, Jews were, in fact, almost the only resident white Creoles left, and they dominated Surinam's economic and political life up to the twentieth century.[2]

Owning considerable capital, Jews were all the more valuable to dwindling white communities. Martinique lifted its interdiction against Jewish trade in 1659, Denmark appointed a Jewish Governor in St. Thomas in 1684, Jews dominated commerce in Curaçao, and in Jamaica, relieved of all economic and social impediments, Jews comprised one-third of the white population in the mid-nineteenth century. In deference to its eight Jewish members (out of forty-seven) the Jamaican House of Assembly adjourned for Yom Kippur in 1849. In 'no country under the sun', exclaimed a local Jewish journal, 'are the blessings of toleration and of unbounded civil liberty more diffused and enjoyed . . . than in this island.'[3]

Jews in Jamaica today number only 600, 5 per cent of the local

[1] Gordon Merrill, 'The Role of Sephardic Jews in the British Caribbean Area during the Seventeenth Century', *CS*, Vol. 4, No. 3, October 1964, pp. 32–49.

[2] L. L. E. Rens, 'Analysis of Annals Relating to Early Jewish Settlement in Surinam', *Vox Guyanae*, Vol. I, No. 1, May 1954, pp. 19–38; P. A. Hilfman, 'Notes on the History of the Jews in Surinam', *Publications of the American Jewish Historical Society*, No. 18, 1909, pp. 179–207; Harmannus Hoetink, 'Diferencias en relaciones raciales entre Curazao y Surinam', *Revista de Ciencias Sociales*, Vol. V, 1961, pp. 499–514.

[3] *First Fruits*, Vol. I, Nos. 7–8, 1844, quoted in Samuel J. Hurwitz and Edith Hurwitz, 'A Beacon for Judaism: First Fruits of the West', *American Jewish Historical Quarterly*, Vol. 56, 1966, pp. 3–76, ref. pp. 11–12. For Martinique, see Jacques Petitjean-Roget, 'Les juifs à la Martinique sous l'ancien régime', *Revue d'Histoire des Colonies*, 1956, pp. 138–58 (Jews were expelled thence by the Jesuits in 1683); for St. Thomas, see Alexander Alland, 'The Jews of the Virgin Islands', *American Hebrew*, Vol. 146, Nos. 20–4, Vol. 147, No. 1, March–May 1940; and Gordon K. Lewis, 'An Introductory Note to the Study of the Virgin Islands', *CS*, Vol. 8, No. 2, July 1968, pp. 5–21, ref. p. 9; for Jamaica, see 'History of the United Congregation of Israelites, Duke Street', p. 1; Jacob A. P. M. Andrade, *A Record of the Jews in Jamaica from the English Conquest to the Present Time*, 1941; Samuel J. Hurwitz and Edith Hurwitz, 'The New World Sets an Example for the Old: The Jews of Jamaica and Political Rights 1661–1831', *American Jewish Historical Quarterly*, Vol. 55, 1965, pp. 37–56.

whites, but they play a role disproportionate to their numbers. They occupy high places in the island's business and social affairs, especially in Kingston. Jewish families control many import and export firms, the cement works, the only daily newspaper, the radio station, and the telephone company. Many of them hold strategic civil-service and appointive posts. Of the dozen most 'influential' white Jamaicans named in a 1962 survey, half were Jewish.[1]

Considered middle class, like free coloured people, until the early nineteenth century, Jamaican Jews have since risen to near-elite or elite status. Concomitantly, they moved out of commercial Kingston to the St. Andrew suburbs. Living near other upper-class whites, they also live like them and subscribe wholeheartedly to Jamaican elite institutions and values. Jamaican Jews are ardent sportsmen and lavish entertainers, known for amateur theatricals, dancing, gambling, and 'highlife'.

Both affinity and self-interest link Jamaican Jews to Creole high society. But they still tend toward endogamy in both religion and colour. The synagogue remains a social focus even though their present reform congregation places little emphasis on creed or observance. And they generally marry among themselves or Jews of American and English extraction. Within their own circle, family leadership dominates individual lives, as epitomized by the Isaacs clan in Abrahams's *This Island Now*. One powerful set of Jamaican Jewish brothers is habitually referred to as a unit—'The Matalons'.[2]

Attitudes towards Jamaican Jews reflect both their assimilation and their familism. During times of crisis in the eighteenth century, other whites charged Jews with receiving stolen goods, aiding free coloured people, selling ammunition to Maroons, and the like. Later the coloured middle class, envying Jewish whiteness and commercial success, reprobated their aloofness. As a visibly clannish enclave within the white elite, Jamaican Jews still arouse some suspicion and antipathy. But thanks to integration and good public relations they have avoided special religious odium, and as scapegoats they hardly suffer more than other Jamaican whites.

The Jewish community in Curaçao prospered early through shipping and slave-trading. Initially Dutch and Brazilian in origin, its ranks were swelled by other Sephardim from the French Antilles, from

---

[1] Extrapolated from data furnished by Charles C. Moskos, Jr., based on a series of interviews between November 1961 and January 1962. See also Benjamin Schlesinger, 'The Jews of Jamaica: A Historical Review', *CQ*, Vol. 13, No. 1, March 1967, pp. 46–53.

[2] Peter Abrahams, *This Island Now*, 1966. See also Colin G. Clarke, 'Aspects of the Urban Geography of Kingston, Jamaica', 1967, pp. 36, 70, 79–90, 99, 157, 366–7, 386–7; Leonard Broom, 'The Social Differentiation of Jamaica', *American Sociological Review*, Vol. 19, 1954, pp. 115–25.

St. Thomas, and from Portugal. The Sephardic community in Curaçao consolidated its position through strict parental control, cross-cousin marriage, and social exclusion of outsiders; the entire religious congregation formed one great *famiya*, which worshipped, worked, played, and was educated together. As among the *békés* of Martinique, 'persons who did not conform to the "rules" . . . were usually no longer considered part of the family'. But coloured concubines were condoned, and Sephardic fathers recognized their illegitimate offspring, who became family business adjuncts. By the mid-eighteenth century the Sephardic community numbered close to 2,000.[1]

There was little contact between Curaçaoan Jews and the Dutch Protestants, from whom they were separated not only by religion but by language and residential location on the island. Social isolation continued even after 1825 when the Jews were accorded civil rights and began to enter the local civil service and, ultimately, politics. Whereas business acumen and community brought the Sephardim increasing prosperity, factions weakened and divided the Dutch elite and petty bourgeoisie, so that by the early twentieth century the Jews had become socially as well as economically pre-eminent.

The establishment of the Royal Dutch Shell refinery in Curaçao after 1910 brought the Sephardim, as owners of most of the real estate around Willemstad, still greater wealth, but at the same time initiated the decline of group control and identity. Marriage to the Europeans who thronged into Curaçao became increasingly common. Meanwhile, more Jews who went abroad to study failed to return, and local religious and social patterns became less restrictive. Sephardic family concerns, no longer favoured with large numbers of sons and requiring additional technical expertise, have opened their doors to collateral relatives and well-qualified outsiders, American, Dutch, Curaçao coloured, and even Ashkenazim. The last are East European Jewish refugees attracted to Curaçao by local Jewish status and Dutch liberality during the 1930s and 1940s. The Ashkenazim proved formidable business competitors and have begun to cross Sephardic social barriers as well. By 1968 only half of the 800 Jews in Curaçao belonged to the old Sephardic community.[2]

---

[1] Frances P. Karner, *The Sephardics of Curaçao: A Study of Socio-cultural Patterns in Flux*, 1969, pp. 12, 15, 24, 29.

[2] Hoetink, 'Diferencias en relaciones raciales entre Curazao y Surinam'; Karner, *The Sephardics of Curaçao*, pp. 33, 36, 44–5, 52, 68; I. S. Emmanuel, 'Joodse gemeenten in de Nederlandse Antillen: Curaçao', *Encyclopedie van de Nederlandse Antillen*, 1969, pp. 313–16. Jewish financiers and traders from St. Thomas and Curaçao have played significant roles in the Dominican Republic since the 1840s (see E. Ucko, *La fusión de los Sefardíes con los Dominicanos*, 1944, cited in Harmannus Hoetink, 'The Dominican Republic in the Nineteenth Century: Some Notes on Stratification, Immigration, and Race', in Magnus Mörner, ed., *Race and Class in Latin America*, 1970, pp. 96–121, ref. pp. 104–5).

Local autonomy and universal suffrage have forced Curaçao's Jewish community to take a political back seat to the rising coloured middle class, but like the Jamaican Jews they remain economically entrenched. Jewish shops in Willemstad were singled out for arson during the labour disturbances of May 1969. But though the European Jewish community was reported to be 'convinced that the riots were the work of anti-Semitic black-power groups financed by mysterious Arab money',[1] Sephardic business leaders continue to operate on the assumption that nothing more specific was involved than general resentment against local and Dutch whites.

More than any other Caribbean group the Curaçao Sephardim exemplify the circum-Caribbean linkages that make the West Indian realm culturally homogeneous. Not only are their origins Caribbean-wide, but when the local community became too numerous to be able to provide places for all offspring, young men emigrated to other Caribbean lands. From the eighteenth century on, Curaçaoan Jewish enclaves were established in Aruba, Venezuela, Colombia, Panama, Cuba, St. Thomas, the Dominican Republic, and elsewhere. Migrants remained in close touch with family and congregation, and retained their Curaçaoan identity, even when they married local women and their children became Catholics. These satellite communities kept the Curaçaoan Sephardim conversant with local conditions and personalities throughout the Caribbean and immeasurably expanded their commercial scope. From time to time individuals and occasionally whole groups returned to marry and to reintegrate themselves in Curaçao, a process that still continues.[2]

Portuguese. Like the Jamaican Jews, the Portuguese in Guyana have achieved elite positions by overcoming early prejudice and outlasting other resident whites. But these similar endings disguise disparate histories. The Portuguese, most of them from the island of Madeira, initially came not as entrepreneurs but as nineteenth-century indentured labourers, and in fact set the stage for subsequent indentures from China, India, and Java. The least satisfactory estate workers, they soon became the most successful merchants.

Madeiran plantation history in some ways paralleled Caribbean. Portugal had colonized Madeira in the fifteenth century and raised sugar-cane with Moorish and African slave labour. Before slavery was abolished there, cane had given way to grapes, and British interests

[1] H. J. Maidenberg, 'Radical Ex-Teacher in Curaçao Considered Big Threat by Some', *New York Times*, 1 March 1970, p. 22. See E. A. de Jongh, *E dia di mas historiko*, 1970; and *30 Mai 1969, Rapport van de Commissie tot onderzoek van de achtergronden en oorzaken van de onlusten welke op 30 Mai 1969 op Curaçao hebben plaatsgehad*, 1970.

[2] Karner, *The Sephardics of Curaçao*, pp. 14, 30, 70–1. See Ucko, in Hoetink, 'The Dominican Republic in the Nineteenth Century', pp. 104–5.

became substantially involved in the wine trade. But erosion, soil exhaustion, population pressure, and a swing of taste away from fortified Madeira wines posed problems there just at the time emancipation threatened Caribbean sugar production.[1] Through contacts with local British agencies, planters in Surinam, British Guiana, Trinidad, Martinique, and Guadeloupe indentured Madeiran labourers in the 1830s, but large-scale immigration was confined to British Guiana, where labour was most scarce. Guianese planters also hoped that Madeirans might form the nucleus of a European middle class and serve as an inducement to attract other Europeans as skilled estate labourers.

Appalling mortality among the early arrivals deterred neither Guianese planters nor Madeirans faced by the prospect of starvation at home, after the *oideum* disease wiped out their vines in 1852. By 1861 almost 28,000 Madeirans had reached British Guiana, but only 10,000 were enumerated in the census: a few had gone home, but more than half had died. Yellow fever decimated the first-comers; crowded barracks and bad sanitation on the estates took a continuous toll of the rest. Planters had imagined Madeira to be much like Guiana, but the humid climate and the stiff clay soils made Guianese estate labour too arduous for the newcomers. The survivors soon quit the plantations for petty commerce, first travelling along the coast with packs on their backs and then opening shops in Georgetown and the Negro villages. The freed slaves could afford, and find room to store, only small quantities of such staples as salt fish, rice, spices, clothing, and household utensils; the Madeirans catered to their needs. By 1842 they had opened more than fifty shops in Georgetown, and two years later the Governor reported that the Portuguese, as they came to be known, dominated internal commerce; 'there is scarcely a mile of road without a retail shop kept by them'. In 1851 they owned two-thirds of the rural shops and more than half of those in Georgetown, where they also outfitted and grubstaked gold, diamond, and timber prospectors.[2]

Portuguese success stemmed from several circumstances. Generally better educated than their ex-slave competitors, and already familiar with imported goods, they were more confident and aggressive entrepreneurs. Predisposed to saving rather than to spending, the Portuguese regularly re-invested their profits. And as newcomers, they did not feel obligated to share with the community. Endogamy reinforced Portuguese

[1] Orlando Ribeiro, *L'île de Madère: étude géographique*, 1949, pp. 52, 55–6, 87, 144–5; Donald Wood, *Trinidad in Transition: The Years after Slavery*, 1968, pp. 25, 101–6.

[2] K. O. Laurence, 'The Establishment of the Portuguese Community in British Guiana', *JHR*, Vol. V, No. 2, November 1965, pp. 50–74, ref. pp. 50–1. See also R. R. Kuczynski, *Demographic Survey of the British Colonial Empire*, 1953, Vol. III, pp. 16–17; Henry G. Dalton, *The History of British Guiana*, 1855, Vol. I, pp. 454–67; *Official Gazette*, 16 October 1852, in Raymond T. Smith, *British Guiana*, pp. 44–5.

social isolation. Intending to stay, they had migrated as families; 'the high proportion of women and children always present among them was unique in the annals of nineteenth century West Indian emigration.'[1] And it made for a settled community that mixed little with Creoles.

Thrift, business acumen, and social self-sufficiency were not the only reasons for Portuguese prosperity. Their colour gained them preferential treatment and access to credit from influential Europeans and white Creoles. By the 1850s, when East Indians and Chinese were filling estate needs, Madeirans were encouraged to migrate as shopkeepers, and neither indentures nor agricultural contracts were required of them. All this enabled them to prosper sooner and faster than the East Indians, Chinese, or Negroes.

White favouritism did not extend to other realms of Portuguese life, however. 'The Portuguese have had access to the plantocracy,' a scholar concludes, 'but they have never belonged to it.'[2] In the eyes of the colonial elite, the Portuguese were scarcely even 'white' in appearance; peasant origins, commercial careers, and Roman Catholicism all kept them out of the inner circle. In the late nineteenth century they joined coloured Creoles in seeking a measure of local self-government, and as merchants their interests sometimes ran counter to those of white planters. Portuguese often took leadership in predominantly black villages; at the turn of the century, when they were 4 per cent of the Guianese population, they held 10 per cent of all village council seats.[3] Only later, as British whites departed, did well-to-do Portuguese turn from shopkeeping to the professions and the civil service. The 6,000 Portuguese in Guyana in 1966 were less than 1 per cent of the population, yet they still accounted for 4 per cent of the secondary school-teachers and a disproportionate share of senior civil-service posts.[4]

Successive ethnic ascriptions reflect Portuguese status changes. Indentured Madeirans were not identified as whites, both because they were dark-skinned Mediterraneans who did servile field labour and because they were regarded, like Jews and Syrians, as ethnically

[1] Laurence, 'The Establishment of the Portuguese Community in British Guiana', p. 72.
[2] Leo A. Despres, *Cultural Pluralism and Nationalist Politics in British Guiana*, 1967, p. 63.
[3] Raymond T. Smith, *British Guiana*, p. 103; Allan Young, *The Approaches to Local Self-Government in British Guiana*, 1958, p. 149. In Guyana 'white' specifically excludes the Portuguese (Clive Y. Thomas, 'British Guiana', *NWQ*, Vol. 1, No. 1, March 1963, pp. 87–96, ref. pp. 91–2).
[4] Despres, *Cultural Pluralism and Nationalist Politics in British Guiana*, p. 163; *Racial Problems in the Public Service*, p. 93; 'Guyana', *Caribbean Monthly Bulletin*, Vol. 4, No. 11, September 1967, pp. 2–3.

distinct. Official Guianese documents always differentiated 'Portuguese' from 'European' until the 1946 census, which called them 'other
Europeans'. The 1960 census made no distinctions among 'whites'. At
first remote from both white and black, the Portuguese in Guyana were
later seen as closer to white and are now virtually assimilated with them.

Guianese Negroes taunted the plantation 'Portugee' as 'white
niggers' for undertaking work they themselves shunned as demeaning.
Portuguese behaviour as shopkeepers initially reinforced this image;
they addressed Negro customers as 'Sir' and 'Ma'am' and spoke of
black ladies and gentlemen, implying that these were their betters. But
as Portuguese gained wealth, education, and white approval, Negro
hostility towards them grew, erupting in arson and looting in 1848 and
again in 1856, following the trial of a fanatic anti-Catholic Creole. The
riots were ostensibly of religious origin, but the Portuguese were not
ardent Catholics, and the Negroes not bigots; religious differences
merely sanctioned aggression against an envied but exposed and powerless minority.[1]

Portuguese business methods continued to incense both Creoles and
Indians. Mittelholzer's novels reflect enduring Guianese stereotypes of
the Portuguese as 'a mean, contemptible sort of Jew class out to grasp
everything for themselves'. To the elite and near-elite they remained
descendants of 'greasy pedlars and greasier salt-goods-shop-keepers.'[2]

Long denied a social status in keeping with their business success, the
Guianese Portuguese became embittered partners of the British and
expatriates whose power and prestige they did not share. They looked
down on both Negroes and Indians, who in turn derided the Portuguese
for their elite pretensions. These acerbities are significant in the context
of contemporary Guyanese politics. Portuguese businessmen were torn
between economic mistrust of the more radical East Indian-led
People's Progressive Party and racial prejudice against Negroes who
dominated the People's National Congress. Portuguese unwillingness to
be guided by those they viewed as 'inferiors' caused them to break with
Burnham.[3] Following an abortive collaboration with the P.N.C., the
predominantly Portuguese United Front now functions as a catch-all
for propertied and other minority groups.

In Trinidad, Jamaica, Curaçao, and Grenada, where the Portuguese
from Madeira and elsewhere formed smaller bodies of immigrants, they
filtered into sub-elite and elite circles more rapidly. But the route was

[1] V. O. Chan, 'The Riots of 1856 in British Guiana', *CQ*, Vol. 16, No. 1, March
1970, pp. 39–50; Young, *The Approaches to Local Self-Government in British Guiana*, pp.
51–2; Laurence, 'The Establishment of the Portuguese Community in British Guiana',
pp. 67–71.

[2] Edgar Mittelholzer, *With a Carib Eye*, 1958, p. 19; idem, *A Morning at the Office*,
1950, p. 217.

[3] Despres, *Cultural Pluralism and Nationalist Politics in British Guiana*, pp. 256–60.

generally similar: off the estates and into retailing, then with money acquired, emulation of the social and educational standards of the British-based elite. In Trinidad and Jamaica their control of the dry-goods business gave way to Chinese competition during the 1860s, but they remained essentially an urban group, increasingly prominent in the professions and the civil service. None the less the old stigma of alien ethnicity and of 'trade' still attaches to them as a stereotype, and the survival of exclusively Portuguese social clubs in Trinidad attests not only to bonds within that community, numbering 3,400 in 1960, but also to their incomplete integration in Creole society.[1]

Chinese. The Chinese, much more dispersed through the Caribbean than the Portuguese, also began as indentured estate labourers and soon moved into shopkeeping. Chinese commercial success and clannishness likewise aroused envy and hostility, the more virulent because they were non-white and initially non-Christian.

Chinese indentured immigration to the Caribbean dates (discounting an abortive venture of 1806–7 in Trinidad) from the 1850s and early 1860s, when 9,000 workers were recruited from Fukien and Kwang-tung, by way of Amoy, Canton, and Hong Kong, for Jamaica, Trinidad, the French Antilles, British Guiana, and Surinam. The Chinese were no better suited to estate work than the Portuguese; large numbers died, many were deemed intractable, and most soon found their way to the villages and towns. The fact that only men customarily migrated was also felt to be a drawback; 'as they have no females amongst them', explained a Governor of Jamaica, 'in a short time they must die out, and so become expensive immigrants'.[2] Even before the Kung Convention of 1866 put an end to organized migration, most West Indian territories had become disenchanted with Chinese estate labourers. Only Trinidad and, especially, British Guiana, chronically short of labour, persevered through 'family recruitment' of an additional 9,000 Chinese, though individual migrants continued to enter all the territories as petty traders and craftsmen.

Family recruitment, more than the earlier indentures, brought in

[1] Elliott Bastien, 'The Weary Road to Whiteness and the Hasty Retreat into Nationalism', in Henri Tajfel and John L. Dawson, eds., *Disappointed Guests: Essays by African, Asian and West Indian Students*, 1965, pp. 38–54, ref. pp. 42–3; Jacques Dupuis, 'Les paradoxes de Curaçao: à travers les provinces de l'empire Shell', *CO-M*, Vol. 22, 1969, pp. 63–74, ref. p. 66; M. G. Smith, *Stratification in Grenada*, 1965, pp. 10, 208–9, 212–13, 239; Wood, *Trinidad in Transition*, pp. 101–6; Lloyd Braithwaite, 'Social Stratification in Trinidad: A Preliminary Analysis', *SES*, Vol. 2, Nos. 2 and 3, October 1953, pp. 5–175, ref. pp. 66, 69, 78.

[2] Henry Barkly to Lord John Russell, 30 April 1855, in *Papers Relating to the West Indies Colonies and Mauritius*, p. 266, quoted in Andrew W. Lind, 'Adjustment Patterns among the Jamaican Chinese', *SES*, Vol. 7, 1958, pp. 144–64, ref. p. 148. For the Caribbean Chinese generally, see Morton H. Fried, 'The Chinese in the British Caribbean', in idem, ed., *Colloquium on Overseas Chinese*, 1958, pp. 49–58.

bona fide farmers, who remained on the land after serving their indentures. In Trinidad many Chinese succeeded as market gardeners, the
cultivation of sweet potatoes being one of several specialties. The
British Guiana Government offered Christian Chinese free land in
Hopetown, fifteen miles up the Demerara River. Hopetown reached a
peak population of 567 in 1871, thenceforth declining owing to drainage
problems, soil exhaustion, and a shortage of women; the proportion
of non-Chinese increased as the Chinese died off or filtered back
to Georgetown, and before 1900 the settlement was abandoned
altogether.[1]

The whole Chinese community in British Guiana similarly declined.
From 5,000 in 1881 their numbers dropped to 2,600 in 1911, owing to
mortality, repatriation, and substantial emigration to Jamaica, Trinidad, and Surinam. Caribbean Chinese whose ancestors were indentured
labourers differ from those who came later as merchants. And distinctions also endure between original Cantonese, or Punti, and Hakka, or
'Guest People'; from British Guiana the Hakka mainly emigrated to
Surinam, the Cantonese to Trinidad, but they are everywhere residentially and socially exclusive.[2]

The Chinese soon came to dominate retail trade in all these territories save Guyana, where they share it with the Portuguese. In Jamaica
not all shopkeepers are Chinese nor are all Chinese shopkeepers; yet in
1960 almost half of the Chinese wage earners were in trade. But unlike
the Portuguese in Guiana, who became wholesalers and merchants on a
larger scale, the Chinese tended to remain small retailers. The Chinese
shopkeeper is a stereotype as ubiquitous in the Caribbean as the Chinese
laundryman or restaurateur in the United States; any grocery is a
'China shop'. The wide divergence between the facts and the local myth
of Chinese monopoly stems from their high visibility and from their
comparative success, not in owning the most shops but in doing more
business than anyone else.[3]

In shopkeeping the Chinese succeeded for the same reasons as the
Portuguese: familism, frugality, social aloofness, a willingness to
sacrifice present comfort for future security. And like the Portuguese,
the Chinese have lately moved into the civil service and the professions.
In 1960 Chinese clerical workers were five times their proportion of
the Jamaican population. In British Guiana the Chinese accounted for
10 per cent of the pensionable civil servants, though they form only

[1] Young, *The Approaches to Local Self-Government in British Guiana*, pp. 149–52; Morton
H. Fried, 'Some Observations on the Chinese in British Guiana', *SES*, Vol. 5, 1956,
pp. 54–73; Cecil Clementi, *The Chinese in British Guiana*, 1915, pp. 284–318.

[2] Wood, *Trinidad in Transition*, pp. 160–7.

[3] Jacqueline Levy, 'The Economic Role of the Chinese in Jamaica: The Grocery
Retail Trade', 1967, p. 18; F. G. Cassidy and R. B. Le Page, eds., *Dictionary of Jamaican
English*, 1967, p. 102.

half of 1 per cent of the population.[1] Chinese men are conspicuous in Caribbean commerce and real estate; Chinese women serve in banks and as typists and airline stewardesses. In both Trinidad and Jamaica a higher proportion of Chinese than of any other ethnic or racial category attend secondary school.[2] The Chinese are reputed to be among the most reliable and effective business leaders in Jamaica and Trinidad,[3] and the appointments of Chinese as Trinidad's first native-born Governor-General and as Guyana's first President underscore their local reputation.

Entrepreneurial success puts the Chinese among the richest as well as the best educated of West Indian ethnic groups. The average Chinese income was almost five times that of blacks and thrice that of coloured Jamaicans in 1960,[4] and the Chinese of Trinidad and Surinam prosper similarly. Well-to-do younger Chinese have moved into upper-class white neighbourhoods in the suburbs of Port-of-Spain, Georgetown, Kingston, and Paramaribo.

Many West Indian Chinese, like the Jews in Jamaica and the Portuguese in Guyana, are advancing from middle- toward upper-class status. Complete absorption into the elite is hampered, however, by the large size of the Chinese community, by their oriental appearance, and by their close relationships with non-elite Creoles. Partly because almost all the early Chinese immigrants were male, they—more than any other ethnic minority—mingled with dark Creole women, whom they were reputed to treat well. Chinese-coloured West Indians are everywhere nearly as numerous today as pure Chinese, and mixed children are readily accepted by their Chinese parent.

Residential segregation, like endogamy, is rare among Caribbean Chinese. They are today the most urbanized of West Indians, but because they usually live in their retail shops, there is no exclusive Chinese quarter in any city; even Kingston's 'Chinatown' is only 40 per cent Chinese. Chinese West Indians are extremely dispersed; one finds a Chinese shopkeeper in even the most remote village.

Most West Indian Chinese are largely creolized in culture, though

---

[1] Colin G. Clarke, *Social Structure and Social Change in Kingston, Jamaica* (in press), ms. Table 44, pp. 588, 591; Despres, *Cultural Pluralism and Nationalist Politics in British Guiana*, p. 163; 'Guyana', *Caribbean Monthly Bulletin*, Vol. 4, No. 11, September 1967, pp. 2–3.

[2] Malcolm Cross and Allan M. Schwartzbaum, 'Social Mobility and Secondary School Selection in Trinidad and Tobago', *SES*, Vol. 18, 1969, pp. 189–207, ref. p. 203; *Newday*, Vol. 5, No. 5, May 1961, p. 33.

[3] Tony H. Bonaparte, 'The Influence of Culture on Business in a Pluralistic Society: A Study of Trinidad, West Indies', *American Journal of Economics and Sociology*, Vol. 28, 1969, pp. 285–301, ref. pp. 296, 299.

[4] Calculated from Clarke, *Social Structure and Social Change in Kingston, Jamaica*, ms. Table 45, p. 595.

Chinese script, marriage celebrations, the sale of gunpowder, certain festivals, and the stereotypical Chinese preoccupation with gambling still persist. Some still speak Chinese, but few have ever been to China, and almost all are now Christians. The Chinese revolution has severed the older generation's links with the homeland, though a few well-to-do Chinese still send offspring back for a year or two of schooling. One observer in Guyana remarked on a son and daughter, home from Hong Kong, 'speaking to each other in Chinese as they work in their shop while their father and mother still know only English.'[1] Today, North American universities are more often selected by West Indian Chinese.

The Chinese differ sharply among themselves about creolization and West Indian integration. Older Chinese in Trinidad and Jamaica prefer endogamy and threaten to disown children who marry Creoles; the young, impatient of parental control, favour Creole ways. The two generations have separate social organizations, as distinct in activity as in attitude. The politically conservative older Chinese devote themselves to trade associations, the Chinese benevolent society, the Masonic lodge, and a predominately Chinese public school; they attend Chinese-language films, and a few are still Confucian or Buddhist. They look back on colonial days with nostalgia and suspect the young of Maoist sympathies.

The younger Chinese regard themselves as West Indians, mix with their middle-class Creole peers, and have 'outside' children by black or coloured women; the Chinese-coloured population has increased faster than the Chinese, and Afro-Chinese girls are locally extolled as beauties. Nevertheless, even the younger group are somewhat isolated from the Creole middle-class mainstream.[2]

The Chinese have, however, internalized Creole colour values. Chinese physical preferences and aesthetic standards, like those of most Creoles, are based on ideal 'European' types. Chinese adolescents in Jamaica are happy about having straight hair and light skins but express dissatisfaction with themselves both for features that are uniquely Chinese (slant eyes) and for those that are negroid (flat noses).[3] Those Chinese who marry outside their own group prefer white

[1] Peter Simms, *Trouble in Guyana*, 1966, p. 61; Fried, 'Some Observations on the Chinese in British Guiana', p. 64.

[2] Clarke, 'Aspects of the Urban Geography of Kingston, Jamaica', pp. 388–9; Gerald Bentley and Frances Henry, 'Some Preliminary Observations on the Chinese in Trinidad', in *McGill Studies in Caribbean Anthropology*, 1969, pp. 19–33, ref. pp. 23, 29. The number of Chinese painters and their full-time dedication to art distinguishes them in Trinidad; painting is valued by most, but for a younger Chinese to become a painter is also a form of creolization (Hans Guggenheim, *Social and Political Change in the Art World of Trinidad during the Period of Transition from Colony to New Nation*, 1968, pp. 24–6).

[3] Errol L. Miller, 'Body Image, Physical Beauty and Colour among Jamaican Adolescents', *SES*, Vol. 18, 1969, pp. 72–89. Creole colour values only partly explain

or European mates. Non-negroid features and Chinese emulation of white standards, along with their educational and commercial prowess, excite coloured Creole envy and antipathy.

In Jamaica Chinese engrossment of retail trade especially provoked Creole complaints of duplicity and miserliness. 'Every native shop-keeper finds it necessary to circulate his earnings', wrote a rural observer in 1913, 'whilst the Chinaman simply hoards up his cash'.[1] They were regarded as a race, even a species, apart; newspapers alleged a 'Yellow Peril' in gambling, cheating with weights and measures, falsifying of records, fraudulent bankruptcies, smuggling, and arson for insurance—though in fact fires were less often set by Chinese owners than by jealous Creoles. Anti-Chinese feeling reached a peak during an unemployment crisis in 1938, when legislators sought to restrict their business permits.

Most Jamaicans are less hostile toward the Chinese than ambivalent, alternating praise with excoriation. Thus in 1949 a local journal extolled the Chinese as 'more Jamaican than the children born in Jamaica of European parents. . . . They think Jamaican, Jamaica is their home, and they never miss an opportunity to show their love for and patriotism for the country of their birth and upbringing.'[2] Yet three years later the same paper assailed Chinese exclusion as racist:

They hate Negroes more than all . . . though they have bred more half-Negro children than any other group. . . . Only Chinese are employed in Chinese businesses; only Chinese are accepted in the Chinese public school; only Chinese are admitted to membership in the Chinese Athletic Club. Few Chinese even bother to vote.

Instead of removing the barrier between themselves and the rest of Jamaica, 'the Chinese keep piling up wealth and hate behind that wall, giving back nothing to the community'.[3] On balance, public comment is perhaps less amiable than acerbic.

Chinese status became more precarious as Jamaican sovereignty approached. They seemed likely inheritors less of expatriate rewards than of their role as scapegoats. Cautioned to 'learn to be Jamaican first,' the Chinese Benevolent Association in 1961 opened the Chinese

---

this bias, however; the Chinese in Hong Kong manifest a similar, though less marked, tendency to prefer and identify with Caucasian appearance (J. Kenneth Morland, 'Race Awareness among American and Hong Kong Chinese Children', *American Journal of Sociology*, Vol. 75, 1969, pp. 360–74).

[1] *Jamaica Daily Gleaner*, 18 June 1913, quoted in Lind, 'Adjustment Patterns among the Jamaican Chinese', p. 157; see also pp. 156–60.

[2] *Spotlight*, May 1949 and October 1952, quoted in Lind, 'Adjustment Patterns among the Jamaican Chinese', pp. 162–3.

[3] 'Occidental Chinese Wall', *Spotlight*, October 1952, quoted in ibid., p. 162.

public school to non-Chinese Jamaicans,[1] and other hitherto exclusive Chinese organizations likewise began admitting Creoles.

Chinese expressions of loyalty to Jamaica have not dissipated anti-Chinese feeling; the stereotype of the selfish Chinese merchant is too firmly implanted to be exorcised by public disavowals. 'Though they draw their seeming success from the whole community around them, the Chinese manage to carry nobody aboard the success vehicle except their own relatives', noted a prominent journalist. 'In this land of job-less non-Chinese, the[ir] supermarkets . . . manage to get along without employing anyone but Chinese.'[2] Alleged Chinese mistreatment of a Negro employee sparked a 1965 Kingston riot in which many Chinese stores were looted and burned. A recent accusation that the Jamaican Chinese 'were extracting all they could . . . and were pushing this "black" society around' drew a retort rare from a Chinese that his immigrant father 'had to get up at 5 a.m. week-day[s] to be ready to serve "the blacks"! . . . He ate while he served the "blacks"! . . . He had one pair of pants, two shirts and never had holidays like the "blacks".' The writer himself recalled 'being abused, insulted, rude to, robbed', yet 'my best friends are all Negroes.'[3]

Elsewhere in the Caribbean the Chinese excite less animosity. The 3,000 Chinese in Surinam engross retailing, but Surinamese society is too fragmented to unite against any particular ethnic element. And in Trinidad and Guyana, Creole–East Indian rivalry casts the Chinese in the role of conciliators more than of scapegoats. 'They blended into the colour scheme. They could accommodate themselves to any winning side. They have their own clubs and national newspapers. But nobody troubles them. Because they trouble nobody. It is no discredit to them if disunity among Negroes and Indians exists.'[4] But that role itself carries risks. Decisions by Chinese West Indian umpires in England–West Indies cricket test matches sparked off mass riots in Trinidad (1959–60), Guyana (1953–4), and Jamaica (1968). The ordinary Jamaican saw the game as a replica of the society, symbolized 'in the person of the [Chinese] umpire . . . a racial type inevitably associated with the dominant capitalist class in the West Indies.'[5]

As titular national leaders, Chinese can scarcely avoid identification with colonial models. Guyana's selection of a Chinese President aroused a Trinidadian reaction that 'to have a member of the Chinese or any

[1] *Newday*, Vol. 5, No. 5, May 1961, p. 33.

[2] Evon Blake, 'Chinese and Jobs' [1963–4], in *The Best of Evon Blake*, pp. 36–7.

[3] Ronald Wong, 'Chinese and Blacks', letter in *Jamaica Daily Gleaner*, 13 March 1970, p. 14.

[4] Dennis Mahabir, 'The Next Time, Let Us Select a Negro or an Indian GG, Okay?' *Trinidad Express*, 26 March 1970, p. 9.

[5] H. Orlando Patterson, 'The Ritual of Cricket', *JJ*, Vol. 3, No. 1, March 1969, pp. 23–5, ref. p. 25.

other small community appointed head of state is a slap in the face for all Negroes and Indians—here and in Guyana.'[1] President Arthur Chung and Governor-General Solomon Hochoy, in this view, celebrate the success of multi-racialism less than they point up its failure.

Syrians. A small group of relative newcomers from the Middle East is more widely dispersed throughout the Caribbean than any other minority. Palestinians, Lebanese, and others, all usually termed 'Syrians' in the Caribbean, have migrated there since the 1890s as itinerant pedlars and merchants. Most of the early migrants were Greek Orthodox; later arrivals have been Roman Catholic, and these have absorbed the earlier group. From Haiti to Surinam, from Jamaica to St. Kitts, Syrians now dominate the import trade and the dry-goods business, rivalled only by the Portuguese in Guyana and the Jews in Jamaica. 'They would buy a few dress lengths or suit lengths or what have you,' notes a descendant, 'and in the country parts travel around with their wares on a mule, from house to house, selling their stock mostly on credit. . . . They intended to make money and go back home, so they didn't care how they lived, they didn't care what others thought about them, because there was no feeling of permanence.'[2]

Many Syrians did stay, however, going up the economic ladder faster than the Portuguese and higher than the Chinese.

Poor as Job, going on foot along the roads carrying his suitcase full of notions, the day soon comes when he has a small store. Here, in the midst of an indescribable jumble, the Guadeloupean woman can at one and the same time find flowered prints for dresses, a tire for her bicycle, and casseroles for her kitchen. Within a few months, the Syrian imitates patois well enough to make himself understood; at the end of a few years, the former pedlar has become a well-to-do tradesman with a house of his own on Rue Frébault in Pointe-à-Pitre and a Dodge or a Studebaker. Marrying generally among themselves, the Lebanese and Syrians together with their fellow countrymen from the neighbouring British islands tend to form a closed group, encysted on the country, draining out of it the wealth that the often nonchalant and unorganized Creoles fail to exploit.[3]

Their success is proverbial. Almost every territory numbers Syrians among its principal merchants, and few of them fail to achieve at least a modest competence. They own the largest department store in Jamaica, the only ones in St. Kitts and Dominica. Syrians operate a high proportion of Caribbean hotels and cafés, movie houses and soft-drink plants; they figure prominently on local tourist boards and chambers of commerce.

[1] Mahabir, 'The Next Time'.
[2] Nellie Ammar, 'They Came from the Middle East', *JJ*, Vol. 4, No. 1, March 1970, pp. 2–6, ref. p. 4.
[3] Guy Lasserre, *La Guadeloupe: étude géographique*, 1961. Vol. I, p. 322.

More than most minorities, however, the Syrians remain sojourners rather than settlers in the Caribbean. Many retain Levantine or acquire Canadian or American citizenship; they often return to the Middle East; relatives visit back and forth. Syrian properties are as divided as their loyalties; they engage in international trade along with West Indian and have sizeable holdings and bank accounts outside the Caribbean. Within it they are pan-West Indian, moving constantly from territory to territory. With kinfolk so widely dispersed, Syrian gatherings and family councils often involve participants from South and Central America as well as several of the islands.

Some successful Syrians retire to the Middle East, but more today enter the mainstream of West Indian life. They buy rural properties, spend week-ends in the country, and play at being planters; they socialize with whites and light-coloured Creoles, whom their children increasingly marry. Syrians in Jamaica leave the Club Alaif to frequent non-Syrian social groups; in Trinidad, as one of them expresses it, 'regardless of what many may like to think, the Syrians . . . belong to Trinidad and Tobago.'[1] Their ambiguous background—white but not European, rich but not 'cultured', Roman Catholic but Semitic, English- or French-speaking but 'Arab'—makes their social status analogous to that of nineteenth-century Jamaican Jews. Indeed, Syrian-Jewish partnerships formalize their mutual Jamaican interests, and in the popular mind Syrians and Jews are linked as acquisitive and clannish, and, at times, extortionate; a Trinidadian complains that 'black girls . . . have been and are consistently abused by the Syrians and Jews in the smaller stores'.[2]

Syrian prosperity, like that of other minorities, excites envy and hostility. Newspapers in Guadeloupe periodically denounce the 'foreign' (that is, Syrian) monopoly of business and threaten Creole takeovers; Creole businessmen in Martinique resist Syrian commercial incursions; black-power spokesmen in Dominica call for Syrian abdication of property. In Trinidad, however, a prominent Syrian asserts that he has 'never been insulted by any black man' and predicts that he would succeed 'in any election because of the good I have done for the people of Trinidad and Tobago.'[3] And in Jamaica the presence of Chinese scapegoats enables Syrians to gain high status while arousing little animosity.

The extent to which Syrians become scapegoats depends on various factors. Their small numbers leave them vulnerable to local pressures

---

[1] Nagib Elias, 'How I Made My Millions', *Trinidad Express*, reprinted in *Torch*, 13 February 1970, p. 3.
[2] B. G., 'It Would Be a Waste of Time Just Talking', in 'Letters from Our Readers', *Trinidad Express*, 15 March 1970, p. 8.
[3] Elias, 'How I Made My Millions'.

but likewise diminish causes of conflict. Despite their familism Syrian employment practices are not exclusive; unlike the family-staffed Chinese stores, for example, Syrian establishments hire Creole employees. But Syrians, like the Jews and Portuguese, increasingly incur black hostility as whites. West Indian nationalisms render their 'foreign' status perilous; for political independence is apt to trigger resentment against prosperous alien minorities.

In this precarious marginal situation, Syrians take pains to avoid any appearance of colour bias. In many territories they belong both to predominately white and to coloured clubs and marry into coloured as well as white Creole families. Such unions not only demonstrate Syrian good faith but cement alliances with powerful Creole interests. West-Indian-born Syrians now outnumber those from abroad. The careers of Abe Issa, prominent Jamaican hotelier and ardent West Indian federalist, and of Edward Seaga, Jamaican Finance Minister and ardent separatist, exemplify the range of Syrian involvement in matters local and West Indian.

Caribbean social structure discloses three distinct types of group relationships. Most extensive are stratified hierarchies ranked roughly by colour, broadly defined. Access to power, wealth, and other rewards depends on one's place in this hierarchy, and most Creoles at all status levels accept the system as a whole. Ways of life within this hierarchy differ profoundly, but distinctive folk features are not so much ancestral ethnic residues as by-products of slavery, racial discrimination, unequal access to benefits, and cultural lag. Modification of 'colour' through achievement, confidence in individual mobility, creation of new elites by white emigration and colonial devolution, and diffusion of elite-oriented goods and values constantly attenuate cultural and social differences. Goods and services are still inequitably distributed, perhaps more than before, and expectations have risen faster than rewards; yet the gulf separating classes no longer seems quite so unbridgeable as West Indians once habitually thought.

In addition to the class–colour hierarchy, Trinidad, Guyana, and Surinam also exhibit ethnically segmented structures. People of East Indian origin, numerically almost equal to the Creoles, interact with the Creole hierarchy in a wholly different manner. Long kept from power and prestige, the East Indians resent exclusion but at the same time reject many Creole values, especially those of non-whites. Caribbean experience has deprived them of much of their heritage, but they retain far more of it than the African slaves did. Attending a Creole literary discussion, an East Indian realizes that

> I was the only one whose fathers
> were not chained in the long

journey out
whose fathers came and kept
if not the kernel, then the shell
of an ancient culture;
who had felt the lash but not the
hopelessness, the forced descent
into oblivion
nor that basement worse than death.[1]

However much altered or syncretized Indian culture may be, both East Indians and Creoles still style it 'Indian'. Most Creole–East Indian differences have ethnic roots, by contrast with the by-products of slavery, colonialism, and racism that mainly differentiate Creole classes. And compared to distinctions of colour, those of ethnicity remain rigid; miscegenation seldom blurs ethnic boundaries.

Tensions between East Indian and Creole social segments are today aggravated by competition for preferment and power. Colonial devolution and expatriate emigration increase each group's fear of tyranny by the other. East Indian economic gains, social progress, and population growth have reduced discrimination and promoted acculturation but also generated new conflicts by enlarging the arena of confrontation.

A third pattern marks relationships between Creoles and smaller minorities, including East Indians where their numbers are few. Origins have little bearing on a minority's place or function in Caribbean society. Indigenous or newcomer, plebeian or patrician, all occupy ambiguous positions partly within, partly outside, the traditional Creole hierarchy. In many respects they are interstitial between the racially stratified Creoles and the ethnically segmented East Indian–Creole relationship. Minorities close to the elite are culturally assimilated and participate in most Creole institutions, and they dominate some aspects of them; those at the bottom remain physically and socially isolated, retain unique folkways, and live by their own social institutions. Both types of minority play distinctive economic roles and both serve as majority scapegoats. But status-gap groups tend to fade away through acculturation and intermarriage; outcast groups are reduced by economic deprivation, heavy mortality, and social anomie.

These three systems are not formally exclusive, however, nor are their distinctive qualities always apparent. Racial, ethnic, and minority circumstances range from cultural pluralism to assimilation, apartheid to integration, heterogeneous to homogeneous values, seclusion to amalgamation, endogamy to miscegenation, and placidity to violence. Each Caribbean social system occupies many points along these continua. Thus ethnic pluralism increases from Guyana to Trinidad to

[1] Ramdath Jagessar, 'On Attending a Literary Discussion', *Moko*, No. 5, 27 December 1968, p. 3.

Surinam, but political and social stress correspondingly decrease. The Creole hierarchies of Jamaica, Barbados, Trinidad, and Martinique all differ from one another, as do those in territories that lack Creole whites. Social stress may well be graver among Creole classes in the French Antilles, for example, than among ethnic segments in Surinam.

All these aspects of social structure change through time. Since slavery ended, the class–colour hierarchy has become less ascriptive and more egalitarian, while demographic change has altered the status of other ethnic groups *vis-à-vis* Creoles. Indeed, minority–majority relations are by their very nature demographically defined. Immigration or natural increase may transform a minority into a full-fledged ethnic community; population loss may reduce a segmented ethnic community to minority status; assimilation may eliminate its reason for separate existence and may bring it within that Creole sphere engaged in the search for its own West Indian identity.

CHAPTER VI

Emigration and Neo-Colonialism

Insularity notwithstanding, West Indian connections with the world outside profoundly influence Caribbean societies. Two particular agencies exert pressure on traditional relationships. One is emigration: thousands of West Indians go abroad; their departure and return vitally affect their homelands. The other is movement into the Caribbean: in-migration has dwindled to short-term visits by expatriate experts, businessmen, and tourists, but overseas goods and values continue to impinge on Caribbean ways of life. Both processes leave West Indians as dependent as ever on the outside world. This chapter reviews the causes and consequences of dependency, first in terms of migration, then of neo-colonialism.

EMIGRATION

The West Indies have been emigrant societies ever since European settlement. Emigration was a corollary of the absentee spirit. The yearning for Europe pervaded Creole life; for even those who lacked personal connections there regarded it as home. Not only whites went 'home'; thousands of their coloured descendants were assimilated into eighteenth- and nineteenth-century European society, never to return to the Caribbean.

Europe continues to attract those who are ambitious, energetic, and impatient with, or fearful of, local conditions. Elite and middle-class West Indians regularly travel abroad for business or pleasure. To many, a first-class education still means a European education. The University of the West Indies, too elite to cater for most local needs, is not elite enough to suit some; more than half of all Commonwealth Caribbean college students attend British and North American institutions. For French West Indians, university and professional training still more frequently entails Paris.

But many emigrants are less pulled toward 'home' than pushed out of the Caribbean by economic need. Since the seventeenth century hundreds of thousands, perhaps millions, of West Indians have been forced out by agricultural unemployment. And emigration will remain all but inevitable as long as population growth outstrips economic development. Most Caribbean birthrates hover between 3 and 4 per cent a year—twice those of developed nations; public-health programmes have reduced infant and adult mortality to low levels. Government sponsorship of birth control in Barbados, Trinidad, Jamaica, and the French Antilles cannot soon overcome West Indian pride in procreation, suspicions of racist motives, and local apathy and ignorance—not to forget the real advantages of large families in parental eyes. Without any further increase the West Indies would still be over-populated; there are too many people now for the jobs available.

Moreover, job opportunities are contracting. Both industrial and agricultural development require more skilled and fewer unskilled labourers. Sugar mechanization is the prime example: using less than half the man-hours of work today, the Caribbean produces five times as much sugar as fifty years ago. Large-scale agriculture is increasingly labour intensive, and since agriculture employs four-fifths of the labour force, technological advance throws many out of work. One West Indian worker in four is now unemployed; seasonal imbalances in estate labour needs, fragmentation of peasant holdings, and fluctuations of demand and supply leave many more chronically underemployed than jobless. Technology not only displaces labour; it increases its seasonality. A century ago it required 250 days in the year to cope with the sugar crop; today no more than 150 days are needed. The toll of agricultural under-employment is probably most severe in Martinique, where out of 39,000 farm employees only 800 have permanent jobs; in other words 97 per cent work only seasonally.[1]

Scale further constrains West Indian opportunities. Production, processing, and marketing are more costly for small territories than for large, and the disadvantage widens with technological progress. Montserrat grows quality bananas but cannot sell them profitably because it produces too few to pay for good harbour facilities or to attract shippers geared to regular interisland schedules. The smaller the island, the greater the relative cost of marketing any product.

Small-island goods and public services are likewise costly. West Indian societies of 10,000 cannot afford a hospital, nor islands of 100,000 a university, because they cannot use so wide a range of services continuously or economically. Students and patients instead

---

[1] Andrew Peter Phillips, *The Development of a Modern Labor Force in Antigua*, 1969, p. 62; Jean-Luc Morel, 'Jeunesse et emploi: de l'insertion des jeunes Martiniquais dans le milieu social', *CERAG*, No. 13, 1968, p. 12. Impending mechanization of cane cutting and loading, however, may cause relatively little further labour displacement (B. Persaud, 'Problems of the Commonwealth Caribbean Sugar Industry', *Cane Farmer*, Vol. 11, No. 2, February 1970, p. 30).

must leave home, which is expensive and socially disruptive. Smallness puts many ordinary amenities out of question. Paved roads, electricity, telephones, and movies may all require equipment, capital outlay, and levels of consumption beyond small-island capacities.

Small size handicaps public services too. In larger lands, bigger schools replace one-room schoolhouses, suppliers of books and furniture are geared to bulk distribution and consumption, and everything is concentrated in ever larger centres. But physical smallness prevents this process of consolidation. In an island of 50,000 what seemed adequate a generation ago is today outmoded by advances that are not locally realizeable. Yet Caribbean islanders want the things they learn about from radio, television, magazines, and returned migrants. Thus even if the population remains stable, each passing year leaves a small territory less viable.[1]

Stable populations are a rarity. Small islanders regularly leave home for larger places to find better pay and a wider range of goods and services. At the same time, social and cultural impoverishment magnifies the difficulties of rejuvenating their homelands. It is the rare school teacher or mechanic who elects to live in a place too small to afford the rudiments of modern comfort. Life in Grenada or Guadeloupe holds out no great lure, but trained West Indians from these islands understandably regard assignment to the isolated Grenadines or Désirade as a worse hardship. In response to a visitor's surprise at finding that all the teachers on Désirade were mainland French, a local gendarme exclaimed: 'Qu-est-ce que vous croyez? Qu'un Antillais accepterait un poste merdeux comme celui-là?'[2] Those required to teach in such rural outposts typically seek to escape the tedium by living in town, far away.

West Indians abroad resist appeals to come back home not only because salaries are low but because aside from work there is so little to do. A Guyanese reports that

a lot of bright young people are afraid that if they return home they won't be able to bear the boredom of their leisure hours. . . . The old social round, in

---

[1] These problems are exemplified in H. A. Moisley, 'The Deserted Hebrides', *Scottish Studies*, Vol. 10, Part 1, 1966, pp. 44–68; R. G. Ward, 'The Consequences of Smallness in Polynesia', and A. D. Knox, 'Some Economic Problems of Small Countries', in Burton Benedict, ed., *Problems of Smaller Territories*, 1967, pp. 81–96 and 35–44 respectively; and David Lowenthal and Lambros Comitas, 'Emigration and Depopulation: Some Neglected Aspects of Population Geography', *GR*, Vol. 52, 1962, pp. 195–210.

[2] Jean Raspail, *Secouons le cocotier*, 1966, p. 33. See also François Gresle, 'Les enseignants et l'école: une analyse socio-démographique des instituteurs et des professeurs de la Martinique', *CERAG*, No. 19, 1969, pp. 94–5; David Lowenthal, 'Levels of West Indian Government', *SES*, Vol. 11, 1962, pp. 363–91; Burton Benedict, 'Sociological Aspects of Smallness', in Benedict, ed., *Problems of Smaller Territories*, pp. 45–55.

which you meet the same characters over the same cups and exchange the same gaff and gossip, becomes a bore. . . . You have to be highly liquored to feel alive.[1]

All Caribbean territories suffer a steady attrition of young people who find local rewards meagre and local society stultifying. The bonding of scholarship students only briefly detains West Indian teachers, doctors, and other professionals; between 1955 and 1959, eighty-five Trinidad government scholarship winners defaulted on their five-year service obligations. With these *émigrés* go others, politically beyond the local pale or unwilling to tolerate coercion; a majority of Haiti's professional men, for example, are political exiles today.[2]

The local prospects of West Indian writers are no less discouraging. No Caribbean market is large enough to support much cultural creativity; authors who stay or return home must combine writing with teaching, journalism, broadcasting, or public relations. Lionized by small local followings, they often cease to be artistically productive and become merely local celebrities who write.

To escape creative paralysis or impoverishment West Indian authors generally go to New York, London, or Paris, in search of a publisher and a public. Even as *émigrés*, they find a psychological and spiritual refuge in the metropolitan milieu of words and ideas, philosophy and world affairs. The liveliest minds of West Indian society and many of its potential chroniclers thus absent themselves; what they might contribute to West Indian life is never born or is soon lost to local view.[3]

West Indians learn early that success, psychological as well as economic and social, requires emigration. 'This place, I tell you, is nowhere', exclaims a West Indian in a novel. 'It doesn't exist. People are just born here. They all want to go away'.[4] Willingness to sell anything to buy passage led one observer to conclude that 'tens of thousands of West Indians would prefer to live anywhere rather than in the West Indies.'[5]

Built-in pressures keep pushing West Indians, especially the

---

[1] Robert Moore, 'Defeating the "Come Back Home" Call', *Action Radio Times*, Vol. 1, No. 1, October 1969, p. 23.

[2] Eric Williams, broadcast, 23 March 1970, in *Trinidad Express*, 24 March 1970, p. 15; François Latortue, 'Considerations sur la main-d'oeuvre haïtienne', in Richard P. Schaedel, ed., *Papers of the Conference on Research and Resources of Haiti*, 1969, pp. 486–523, ref. pp. 513–14.

[3] See George Lamming, 'Caribbean Literature: The Black Rock of Africa', *African Forum*, Vol. 1, No. 4, Spring 1966, pp. 32–53; Derek Walcott, in 'The 7 Year Itch . . . and 7 Members of the Theatre Workshop Give Reasons Why', *Art and Man*, Act II, Scene II, June 1969, pp. 34–8, 61, 64; Mervyn Morris, 'Some West Indian Problems of Audience', *English*, Vol. XVI, Spring 1967, pp. 127–31; Wilson Harris, 'Impressions after Seven Years', *New World Fortnightly*, No. 44, 25 July 1966, pp. 17–20.

[4] V. S. Naipaul, *A Flag on the Island*, 1967, p. 187.

[5] 'Nationalism in the Sixties', *WIE*, Vol. 3, No. 7, January 1961, pp. 3–7, ref. p. 7.

educated, out of the Caribbean. Were all economic and social problems resolved the process would still continue. No West Indian university could cater for all needs, let alone every new specialty. Breadth of experience and intimacy with science and scholarship moreover require study, travel, and contacts in a larger society. From such sojourns many never return, many more but briefly.

Scope and destination. Emigrant numbers, destinations, and purposes vary with time and place of departure. From some islands the outward stream is small but steady, from others substantial or episodic. Jamaican emigrants probably outnumber any other. Owing to a net outflow of 200,000 during the 1950s and 1960s, one Jamaican in ten now lives abroad. But emigrant proportions are higher in the eastern Caribbean. The years 1959–61 saw almost 6,000 people depart from St. Kitts–Nevis, 10 per cent of the inhabitants; Montserrat lost 5 to 10 per cent of its people *each year* over the same period.[1] On small islands where migration is endemic, still larger proportions may be away. One Carriacouan in four is normally off the island, and Anguilla, with only 6,000 residents, keeps close ties with nearly 8,000 Anguillans living elsewhere.

Many West Indian migrants, perhaps most, stay within the Caribbean. More seventeenth-century Barbadian and Kittician 'poor whites' went to Jamaica than to North America. Many refugees from the Haitian Revolution fled to Trinidad, which remains a favoured destination of Windward and Leeward islanders. Both white royalists and free coloured revolutionaries from Guadeloupe took refuge in Dominica. Thousands of St. Lucians and Dominicans have sought fortunes in the French Guiana gold fields since the 1880s. The 50,000 Barbadians and Windward and Leeward islanders who manned the Curaçao and Aruba oil refineries after 1928 have mostly died or returned home, but 15 per cent of Curaçao's population in 1968 was still foreign-born. Sizeable and durable Jamaican communities in the Dominican Republic, Haiti, the Bahamas, and British Honduras send their children back to Jamaica for schooling. Tens of thousands of Haitians live in the Bahamas, Cuba, and the Dominican Republic. British West Indians continuously filter in to the United States by way of St. Thomas. And countless West Indians throughout the archipelago are always moving back and forth between neighbouring islands.[2]

But the greatest employment opportunities lie farther afield. At

[1] See Lowenthal and Comitas, 'Emigration and Depopulation'; Ceri Peach, *West Indian Migration to Britain: A Social Geography*, 1968, p. 15.

[2] Raphaël Bogat, 'Dominique, terre de refuge', *Bulletin de la Société d'Histoire de la Guadeloupe*, No. 8, 1967, pp. 79–94; *Nederlandse Antillen Statistisch Jaarboek 1969*, 1970, p. 27; Malcolm J. Proudfoot, *Population Movements in the Caribbean*, 1950; Aaron Segal with Kent C. Earnhardt, *Politics and Population in the Caribbean*, 1969.

least 100,000 West Indians helped to build the Panama Canal during the early 1900s, and many subsequently found work on United Fruit Company plantations in Central America; two generations later scores of West Indian communities along the coast remain in touch with their island homelands. Between the First World War and the Depression another 100,000 settled in the United States, notably New York and Boston, where their families retain a definite West Indian identity. In the 1950s the tide of emigration turned toward Europe, and by 1968, 320,000 West Indians were in Britain, 150,000 in France, and 20,000 in the Netherlands. The late 1960s witnessed a renewed flow into the United States and Canada.

Many migrants intend to return when they make good. Some do come home as successes, others as failures; but most remain abroad, except for brief visits. Another type of migrant leaves home for specified periods. Jamaican labourers spend summers as farm workers in Florida or New Jersey; Windward and Leeward islanders cut cane in Puerto Rico and Barbados; Carriacou and Cayman Island seamen serve hitches on ocean liners and freighters. No sharp line separates permanent from temporary migrants, however. An intended absence of a few months may stretch to a lifetime, whereas someone who means to pull out for good may shortly come back disillusioned. But each type of migrant plays a distinctive role, from which different consequences ensue.

One consequence is foreign hostility, often racially expressed. The West Indian student, tourist, or pensioner seldom meets closed doors abroad. But wherever working-class migrants are numerous they face difficulties. Panamanians and Americans discriminated against Barbadian and Jamaican workers in the Canal Zone. Central American governments still keep West Indians at arm's length, censuring English-speaking Negroes as unassimilable. West Indians in New York and Boston faced hostility from both black and white, and the United States Emigration Act of 1924 specifically limited non-white entry.

Europe in recent decades has become increasingly unfriendly. Large-scale Antillean and Surinamese immigration has aroused racial prejudices in both France and the Netherlands. Commonwealth citizens from the West Indies, India, and Pakistan have excited much overt racism in Britain, leading in 1962 to Parliamentary restrictions on 'coloured' immigration. With major outlets in Western Europe closed, West Indians have turned again to Canada, which has absorbed thousands of islanders, and to the United States, where the 1965 immigration law eased entry. American residence visas for Jamaicans alone rose from 5,000 in 1966 to 17,000 in 1968, and 3,000 Jamaicans a year emigrate to Canada.

Effects of migration: the home community. Migrant departure and return have profound impacts on West Indian societies. The typical emigrant is a young man or woman who can find no work at home. From some territories men traditionally leave for several years, returning to buy or build a house and settle down. The smaller islands are habitually depleted of young adults, especially males. Off-island agricultural work or sponge fishing at times claims one-third the married men of South Andros in the Bahamas; British Virgin Islanders habitually take work in St. Thomas. In 1960 Cayman Island females outnumbered resident males by four to three; in Anguilla the ratio was five to four, and the 15–44 age group had three women to every two men. Such imbalances are enduring features of small-island life: in Carriacou, where women outnumber men by almost three to one, the ratio has been at least two to one throughout the past century.[1]

The paucity of men is not limited to minuscule islands where emigration is a constant way of life. The entire British Caribbean in 1946 had only 932 males per 1,000 females, and in Barbados and in Grenada the ratio was only four to five. Among those of working age the discrepancy was still greater: fewer than two men to three women in Grenada, three to four in St. Vincent.[2]

The social consequences depend on how institutionalized the sexual imbalance is. Where out-migration is habitual and socially obligatory, family and household organization adjust to the skewed sex ratio. Extra-residential mating involving single women is sanctioned in Carriacou, the Cayman Islands, and South Andros. Barbadian family structure adjusts to sexual imbalance by idealizing the nuclear household and reasserting emigrants' obligations to dependants.

Large-scale, permanent migration has altogether different effects. Young men leave first, typically followed by young women and later by some of their children. The early stages, when wage earners alone are away, can be most burdensome. One inhabitant in three of St. George parish, Montserrat, went to Britain between 1948 and 1962, and three-fifths of these emigrants were aged 15 to 25; estate agriculture was abandoned in 1962 because only 191 folk of working age remained in the parish.[3] Of Jamaica's 162,000 net emigrants to the

[1] Keith F. Otterbein, *The Andros Islanders: A Study of Family Organization in the Bahamas*, 1966, pp. 12–13; Della M. Walker, 'Family and Social Structure in Anguilla', in Stanford N. Gerber, ed., *The Family in the Caribbean*, 1968, pp. 111–16; M. G. Smith, *Kinship and Community in Carriacou*, 1962, pp. 20–1. For comparable effects see Ward, 'The Consequences of Smallness in Polynesia', pp. 81–96.

[2] David Lowenthal, 'The Population of Barbados', *SES*, Vol. 6, 1957, pp. 445–501, ref. p. 468; Anthony Marino, 'Family, Fertility, and Sex Ratios in the British Caribbean', *Population Studies*, Vol. XXIV, 1970, pp. 159–72, ref. pp. 163–4.

[3] Beverly J. Holcomb, 'Colonialism, Cooperation and Cash in a West Indian Society', 1964, p. 55.

United Kingdom during 1953–62, 52 per cent were men, 40 per cent women, and only 8 per cent children. Adults who left the island between 1955 and 1960 took 6,500 of their offspring with them but left 90,000 behind.[1]

From the whole British Caribbean during the 1950s only one emigrant in twenty was a child; and by 1960, 250,000 children had one or both parents in Britain. At home the proportion of able-bodied to dependents declined steeply. In Jamaica the working-age segment dropped from 47 per cent in 1943 to 40 per cent in 1960; in Martinique in 1968 it was 41 per cent. In many West Indian rural districts less than one-third of the remaining population is able-bodied. The burden of dependency is great: in Martinique for every 100 working age adults there are 125 children and 18 persons over 60, compared with 64 and 35 respectively in mainland France.[2]

Acute distress often ensues. Some emigrating parents make little or no provision for their offspring. One 12-year-old Jamaican girl was 'left entirely alone in a house with a few pounds when the rest of the family, *en bloc*, went to England. . . . In another case a woman left her child with a complete stranger as she was about to board a plane for England.' Complaints that emigrant fathers neglected their families were heard from every territory. Difficulties arise even when parents remit regular sums. Foster agencies frequently neglect or ill-treat their charges. At one Jamaican 'baby-farm' an eye-witness observed 'about twenty little children queuing up for food' in Dickensian fashion.[3]

Conditions were not usually this bad, to be sure. Most children were—and are—left in the care of grandparents or other relatives, often in remote districts. Grandparental upbringing is a common feature of West Indian family life, but mass emigration magnifies its incidence and effects. Growing up in these confining circumstances deprives many children of adequate schooling, supervision, and contact with the modern world.

For elderly adults left at home, child care is not the only problem. The scarcity of the able-bodied makes it hard, if not impossible, to cultivate family farms, to cope with marketing and transport, and to keep up community organization. Moreover, migrants often sell their land, livestock, or standing crops to buy passage, leaving those behind propertyless. With little income except what is remitted, some are so bereft that they try to prevent children from joining their parents

[1] Gene Tidrick, 'Some Aspects of Jamaican Emigration to the United Kingdom, 1953–1962', *SES*, Vol. 15, 1966, pp. 22–39, ref. p. 26; R. B. Davison, 'W. I. Migration to Britain, 1955–61', *WIE*, Vol. 4, No. 4, October 1961, pp. 6–16, ref. p. 8.

[2] G. E. Cumper, 'Preliminary Analysis of Population Growth and Social Characteristics in Jamaica, 1943–60', *SES*, Vol. 12, 1963, pp. 393–431, ref. pp. 398, 424; Morel, 'Jeunesse et emploi', p. 10.

[3] R. B. Davison, 'W. I. Migration to Britain', p. 7.

abroad. Accounts from Montserrat describe children forcibly being taken from grandparents loath to lose their best claim for support.[1]

Once emigrants establish themselves abroad, they regularly bring over their children. The British immigration act of 1962, limiting entry except for dependents, accelerated this trend. Thus in 1966 only 1,400 adults but more than 8,000 children left the West Indies for Britain, and 25,000 more children were expected to migrate by 1970. Jamaica alone experienced a net exodus of 10,500 children during 1967–8 whereas 4,500 more adults returned from Britain than went there.[2]

Money sent home helps to offset the absence of the able-bodied. Indeed, remittances are a *raison d'être* of emigration, and the sums involved are substantial. Postal and money orders from Jamaican emigrants during 1953–62 totalled £28,566,000 over the cost of passage to Britain. In 1963 alone, net Jamaican remittances totalled £8·1 million, 3·2 per cent of Jamaica's gross domestic product and half her visible trade deficit. In 1968 Jamaica netted £6·5 million from migrants; in 1966–7 postal and money orders from Britain to the West Indies were £8·6 million.[3]

Small-island remittances may play a still greater role. Montserratians abroad sent back nearly one-fourth of the island's 1960 income. Remittances are the principal resources of Barbuda and Anguilla. Goods flow in along with money; parcels of clothing are frequent gifts, especially at Christmas. Although few depend entirely on emigrant aid, remittances enable many to eschew ill-paid or distasteful labour, making do with occasional jobs such as road mending. Governments frankly schedule public works to help people anxious to 'meet the food bill until they receive the next remittance from overseas.'[4]

Large-scale emigration may simultaneously raise living standards while undermining the local economy. As the labour force dwindles, field crops give way to cattle and coconuts, pasture succeeds tillage,

[1] Stuart B. Philpott, 'Remittance Obligations, Social Networks and Choice among Monserratian Migrants in Britain', *Man*, N.S. Vol. 3, 1968, pp. 465–76, ref. p. 469.
[2] E. J. B. Rose et al., *Colour and Citizenship: A Report on British Race Relations*, 1969, Appendix Table VIII.i, p. 796; *Economic Survey Jamaica, 1968*, p. 48.
[3] Tidrick, 'Some Aspects of Jamaican Emigration to the United Kingdom', pp. 23, 30; R. B. Davison, *Black British: Immigrants to England*, 1966, p. 119; *Economic Survey Jamaica, 1968*, pp. 15, 23; Sheila Patterson, *Immigration and Race Relations in Britain, 1960–1967*, 1969, p. 5.
[4] Kenneth John, 'Political Crisis in St. Vincent', *NWQ*, Vol. 3, No. 3, High Season, 1967, pp. 51–6, ref. p. 55. For Montserrat, see Philpott, 'Remittance Obligations, Social Networks and Choice among Monserratian Migrants to Britain', p. 466. See also Richard J. Russell and William G. McIntire, *Barbuda Reconnaissance*, 1966, pp. 4–5.

and wilderness encroaches on pasture; in Montserrat well over half the arable acreage now lies idle, and production steadily diminishes. But remittances have noticeably improved health, nutrition, housing, and education.[1]

The net economic impact of emigration is far from certain. Some maintain that the debits—the price of passage, the expense of raising children to become wage earners abroad, the cost of training and then replacing skilled workers—outweigh remittance benefits. Trinidad and Tobago, for example, trained 696 nurses between 1965 and 1969, but in the same period 586 nurses resigned and emigrated. But others cite population relief and income gains; emigration was a prime factor in Jamaica's phenomenal 6·8 per cent annual rise in per capita gross domestic product over the decade 1953–62.[2]

The social consequences of large-scale emigration are more obviously negative. Emigration, even of the unskilled, deprives communities of the most progressive and ambitious inhabitants. In the absence of vigorous adults, community guidance, like child rearing, rests with the elderly or the weak. Mass emigration aggravates the normal attrition of the educated; almost nine-tenths of Montserrat's secondary-school graduates since 1950 have gone away. Everywhere, the coloured middle class leave in disproportionate numbers, because they are better educated and more knowledgeable about opportunities, can more easily raise passage money, and are more apt to gain acceptance abroad than the rest. Thus the coloured population of Montserrat declined from 2,503 in 1921 to 287 in 1960; that of Nevis from 2,288 in 1881 to 616 in 1960. Their departure opens up opportunities for the working class, but education and talent remain in short supply. High turnover in government, education, and commerce causes administrative chaos; with skilled persons unavailable, the untrained get 'temporary' appointments, and the unqualified are seconded to senior positions.

Large-scale emigration also undermines village and rural community relationships. Communal work groups and reciprocal labour services fade away, remittance receipts magnify real or imagined differences in wealth and arouse jealousy, people do not get along together as well as they did before emigration. Loneliness is pervasive; people complain that all their best friends have gone away, leaving behind only idlers and vagabonds. When too many people leave, the

[1] Lowenthal and Comitas, 'Emigration and Depopulation'; Carleen O'Loughlin, *Economic and Political Change in the Leeward and Windward Islands*, 1968, pp. 32–4; idem, 'The Economy of Montserrat: A National Accounts Study', *SES*, Vol. 8, 1959, pp. 147–78.

[2] Eric Williams, broadcast, 23 March, in *Trinidad Express*, 24 March 1970, p. 15; Tidrick, 'Some Aspects of Jamaican Emigration to the United Kingdom', pp. 33, 36, 39.

remainder lose both social nexus and self-respect, and life becomes altogether less rewarding.[1]

Effects of migration: the emigrant. Some West Indian societies adjust to migration as the norm, others endure it as a trauma. The effects on emigrants themselves are also manifold: often atypical from the start, experience abroad makes them yet more unlike those at home. But insights acquired overseas ultimately affect the homeland too. Many migrants return only briefly or late in life, if ever. But others come home to play significant roles in Caribbean society. Their energy and self-awareness equip them at least to articulate if not to solve problems that defy traditional West Indian approaches. Virtually every major Caribbean leader, in fact, has spent several years abroad.

New perceptions of colour are basic to West Indian emigrant experience. To leave a land where blacks are the great majority for one where they are a small minority can be a profound shock. Non-whites from the French Antilles, unaccustomed to large numbers of whites, express alarm at seeing them everywhere in Paris and dread at being caught in a white crowd.[2]

The awareness of being alien also conflicts with images of a familiar and welcoming 'mother country' inculcated by generations of laudatory schoolbooks. Before going to Europe, many West Indians tend to think of themselves as European and, by extension, white. In Europe they learn that they are 'African'—that is, black. When the Antillean in France 'hears Negroes mentioned he will recognize that the word includes himself as well as the Senegalese'. A Jamaican migrant recalls that his 'first lesson on arriving in Britain [was that] I was not one of the "mother country's" children. I was one of her black children.'[3]

When migrants are few and generally well educated, class makes colour less consequential. 'Everybody disapproves of the coloured stowaway but . . . all sorts of people are only too flattered to be introduced to the Indian Maharajah or the African chief whose title and genealogy ensure him an upper-class status.'[4] To show they were not working-class immigrants, coloured scholars at one time wore college scarves or other distinctive garb. But the practice proved too imitable:

[1] Lowenthal and Comitas, 'Emigration and Depopulation', pp. 207–9; Roger Abrahams, 'Patterns of Performance in the British West Indies', in Norman E. Whitten, Jr., and John F. Szwed, eds., *Afro-American Anthropology: Contemporary Perspectives*, 1970, pp. 163–78, ref. p. 176.

[2] François H. M. Raveau, 'Caste and Race in the Psychodynamics of Acculturation', in Anthony de Reuck and Julie Knight, eds., *Caste and Race: Comparative Approaches*, 1967, pp. 266–75, ref. p. 271.

[3] Frantz Fanon, *Black Skin, White Masks*, 1967, pp. 147–8, 153; Donald Hinds, *Journey to an Illusion: The West Indian in Britain*, 1966, p. 51.

[4] Michael Banton, *White and Coloured: The Behaviour of British People towards Coloured Immigrants*, 1959, pp. 46–7.

'former seamen in Manchester who wished to be taken for students might sport such scarves, and even illiterates could be seen with folded copies of *The Times* or *Manchester Guardian* under their arms.'[1]

Mass immigration dooms such distinctions to insignificance; by the late 1950s colour was the decisive factor affecting migrants into Britain. West Indians are more familiar with, and better disposed toward, English patterns of language and culture than most immigrant Indians and Pakistanis are, but this advantage is offset by social and personality differences that perturb both migrant and host. West Indian family patterns, time sense, and habitual spontaneity upset many Britons, who tend variously to stereotype them as musicians and athletes, to reprobate them as irresponsible and self-indulgent, or to condemn them as dirty and lazy.[2]

Similar stereotypes are applied to 'blacks' from any land. But even those who differentiate Caribbean from African migrants are prone to lump all West Indians as black. A former West Indian political leader who settled in Britain recalls that 'I was accepted as a white person in Trinidad. For all practical purposes, I am "coloured" in England.'[3] English inability or unwillingness to distinguish colour gradations violates West Indian sensitivity. Differences of culture and background, along with shade, are swallowed up in the pervasive prejudice against all non-whites. 'Home, you belong to a Church and a family and a circle', says one London migrant to another. 'Yes. But here you black. Anything goes. We is all the same tarbrush and everybody walk 'pon we.'[4]

The gulf between precept and behaviour exacerbates the West Indian's dilemma. Britain 'offers inducements for a particular kind of behaviour,' one analyst remarks, 'while at the same time punishing or at least discouraging the logical outcome of such inducements.' The migrant 'must strive, but he may not succeed', and in seeking jobs and

[1] Michael Banton, *Race Relations*, 1967, p. 377.
[2] Rose, *Colour and Citizenship*, pp. 551–604; Ruth Landes, 'Race and Recognition', *Listener*, Vol. 48, 6 November 1952, pp. 751, 763. 'Do you play in the band?' a Britisher asks a Trinidadian at a party in Edinburgh. 'No.' 'Do you play Cricket, then?' 'No.' Long silence. 'Cheerio' (Kenneth Ramchand, 'The Colour Problem at the University: A West Indian's Changing Attitudes', in Henri Tajfel and John L. Dawson, eds., *Disappointed Guests: Essays by African, Asian, and West Indian Students*, 1965, pp. 27–37, ref. p. 36). For similar American stereotypes of Negroes, see Marvin Karlins, Thomas L. Coffman, and Gary Walters, 'On the Fading of Social Stereotypes: Studies in Three Generations of College Students', *Journal of Personality and Social Psychology*, Vol. 13, No. 1, 1969, pp. 1–16.
[3] Albert Maria Gomes, 'I Am an Immigrant', *Listener*, Vol. 80, 3 October 1968, quoted in Rose, *Colour and Citizenship*, p. 437.
[4] O. R. Dathorne, *Dumplings in the Soup*, 1963, p. 74. See also Kenneth Little, 'Some Aspects of Color, Class, and Culture in Britain', in 'Color and Race', *Daedalus*, Vol. 96, No. 2, 1967, pp. 512–26, ref. p. 516; Rose, *Colour and Citizenship*, pp. 420–40.

housing 'he is constantly aware . . . that he is being discriminated against.'[1] Racial animosity increasingly alienates migrants, who are becoming 'less and less West Indians in English society, more and more black men in a white society.'[2] Most agree that race relations in Britain are deteriorating. 'The situation is getting closer and closer, more hostile now to coloured people,' remarked a Jamaican, returning home after thirteen years in England.[3] In France, Martinicans and Guadeloupeans are said to be treated 'no worse' than other 'foreigners', which is small comfort to Antilleans, formally and spiritually French. As the Caribbean migrant community grows, racism appears to increase in both France and the Netherlands.[4]

In the United States, West Indian adjustments reflect the greater severity of the American racial order. Gradations of family background, culture, and shade matter far less in black American than in West Indian society, and American whites, like the British, ignore such differences; a West Indian 'pass-for-white' would simply be a 'black' or 'Negro' in the United States. American whites relegate light and dark, educated and illiterate, alike to the black ghetto. Middle-class West Indians of the 1930s and 1940s were outraged to see light-coloured Americans accepting without overt protest the same treatment accorded poor blacks.

Caribbean immigrants themselves have traditionally offered a striking contrast to reputed American Negro subservience. Well-educated and well-to-do descendants of West Indian *gens de couleur* in ante-bellum New Orleans were noted for their self-respect. 'In their contact with white men,' one observer wrote, 'they did not assume that creeping posture of debasement—nor did the whites expect it'.[5] Both before and after emancipation, West Indians in the United States

[1] Christopher Bagley, 'The Social Aetiology of Schizophrenia in Immigrant Groups', *Race Today*, Vol. 1, 1969, pp. 170–4, ref. p. 174.

[2] Gordon K. Lewis, 'Race Relations in Britain: A View from the Caribbean', *Race Today*, Vol. 1, 1969, pp. 78–80, ref. p. 79.

[3] Betty Davison, 'No Place Back Home: A Study of Jamaicans Returning to Kingston, Jamaica', *Race*, Vol. IX, 1967–8, pp. 499–509, ref. p. 504.

[4] For France see 'Discussion: Symbolic Expression of Racial Tension', in De Reuck and Knight, eds., *Caste and Race*, pp. 276–91, ref. p. 276; Godula Castles, 'Racial Prejudice in France', *Race Today*, Vol. 2, 1970, pp. 10–13. For the Netherlands, see J. Tholenaar-Van Raalte, 'De integratie van Westindische immigraten in Groot-Brittannië en in Nederland', *Nieuwe West-Indische Gids*, Vol. 46, 1968, pp. 150–63; A. E. Bayer, *Surinaamse arbeiders in Nederland*, 1965; G. A. de Bruijne, 'Surinamers naar Nederland—een nieuwe vorm van urbanisatie', E. E. Sluisdom, 'Het aantal Surinamers in Nederland', and 'Statistisch compendium', all in *Enig zicht op Suriname*, 1969, pp. VII-1–5, VII-6–7, and VIII-1–16 respectively.

[5] Charles Gayarré, quoted in Grace King, *New Orleans, The Place and The People*, 1896, p. 345. The discussion that follows is abridged and updated from my 'Race and Color in the West Indies', in 'Color and Race', *Daedalus*, Vol. 96, No. 2, 1967, pp. 580–626.

played a major role in American Negro efforts, whether toward assimilation and integration with whites or toward defiance and departure.

Later Caribbean immigrants often felt superior to American Negroes because they 'had never experienced the open racial "jimcrow" discrimination of the United States', one of them suggests.[1] 'The West Indian comes to New York with a supreme advantage', writes a Trinidadian, namely, ignorance of American patterns of segregation. 'Unaccustomed to the local mores, . . . he goes out . . . and swings through every door.' Asked to comment on his own success, C. L. R. James avers that 'if I was ahead it was because I came from the Caribbean, . . . [where] we blacks form a majority. So that our attitude is that things can happen if we will only do it. That's why we are able to go abroad and take part; we have the feeling that we are not defeated in any way.'[2]

Migrants to the United States enjoy tangible as well as psychological advantages. Most black Americans get inferior schooling in circumstances that hamper learning; ambitious West Indians have either had reasonably good schooling at home or are pushed to do well in America by traditions that accord status to academic success, in a Trinidadian's frank phrase, 'as a path to another niche in the elite of skinocracy.'[3]

West Indians in the United States are also ambitious to acquire property, associated in the Caribbean with freedom, economic security, and high status. Marshall's description of Barbadians in Brooklyn, scrimping and saving to buy brownstone houses, conveys something of the West Indian passion for home ownership.[4] Their own stereotype of spendthrift, Cadillac-buying, American blacks—'they could do *more*. They could own their own houses. . . . They spend too much money in bars. Education is free in New York: they could get some'[5]— mirrors certain foreign images of the West Indian at home.

West Indian ambitions have paid off in America. Although less than

[1] Cheddi Jagan, *The West on Trial: My Fight for Guyana's Freedom*, 1966, p. 51.

[2] Lennox Raphael, 'West Indians and Afro-Americans', *Freedomways*, Vol. 4, 1964, pp. 438–45, ref. p. 445; 'The *Black Scholar* Interviews: C. L. R. James', *Black Scholar*, Vol. 2, No. 1, September 1970, pp. 35–43, ref. pp. 36, 38.

[3] Raphael, 'West Indians and Afro-Americans', p. 442. West Indian success is noted in Carter G. Woodson, *The Negro Professional Man and the Community*, 1934, p. 83. For a more recent and contrary view, see John Jasper Spurling, *Social Relationships between American Negroes and West Indian Negroes in a Long Island Community*, 1969, pp. 66–8.

[4] Paule Marshall, *Brown Girl, Brownstones*, 1959; Gene Grove, 'American Scene: The West Indians', *Tuesday Magazine*, Vol. 2, No. 3, November 1966, pp. 12–15. See also C. Gerald Fraser, 'Neighborhoods: West Indians Flavor Bedford-Stuyvesant', *New York Times*, 28 October 1970, pp. 49, 57.

[5] Orde Coombs, 'West Indians in New York: Moving beyond the Limbo Pole', *New York Magazine*, 13 July 1970, pp. 28–32, ref. p. 30; Spurling, *Social Relationships between American Negroes and West Indian Negroes*, p. 61.

1 per cent of the American Negro population in 1930, West Indians were 7·8 per cent of *Who's Who in Colored America* and one-third of all Negro professionals in New York City. A generation later they were still 'powerful in Harlem's business, financial, labor, and political worlds.... They are a hustling, vital people, and the influence they have on colored affairs is far out of proportion to their numbers.'[1] Not all West Indians adjusted so successfully to American conditions. But enough West Indians prospered to engender an American Negro stereotype of them as 'Black Jews'—aggressive, efficient, acquisitive, calculating, and clannish—an image extraordinarily similar to the Creole stereotype of Portuguese, Chinese, and Syrian minorities in the Caribbean. Black American opprobrium against West Indians is now less open, but the same underlying attitudes remain, reinforced by a renewed flood of migrants since 1965. In Harlem and Brooklyn, in Queens and the Bronx, West Indians are considered pushy, boastful, tight with money, given to social snobbery, and vain-glorious about their island backgrounds. American black resentment stems, in part, from West Indian dealings with *white* Americans, emphasizing their differences from black Americans and the European character of their background.[2]

British West Indians in the United States seldom break their home ties, as the scores of West Indian benevolent and social organizations testify. The islands are remembered, through a nostalgic haze that screens out the actual lot of the black majority, as places 'where every human being, regardless, was a man'.[3] French West Indians and Haitians likewise place a high value on personal liberty regardless of colour, resent American segregation, and are critical of black Americans for having submitted to it.

Many West Indians in the United States still adhere to formal 'European' nationality. Foreign passports not only emphasize their difference from Americans but help them in dealing with the white world. The 'West Indian population has checked out of the islands,' one writer commented a generation ago, but 'it has retained the pawn tickets.'[4] The ties remain as strong today. 'It doesn't matter how long you have been in America . . . [or] that you have no intention of

---

[1] J. M. Flagler, 'Well Caught, Mr. Holder!' *New Yorker*, Vol. 30, 25 September 1954, pp. 65–85, ref. p. 65. See also Ira de Augustine Reid, *The Negro Immigrant: His Background, Characteristics and Social Adjustment, 1899–1937*, 1939, p. 221; Woodson, *The Negro Professional Man and the Community*, p. 83.

[2] Coombs, 'West Indians in New York', pp. 30–1; Spurling, *Social Relationships between American Negroes and West Indian Negroes*, pp. 58–60; Charles A. Valentine, 'Blackston: Progress Report on a Community Study in Urban Afro-America', 1970, p. 94.

[3] Hugh Panton Morrison, 'Home Is the Hunter', in Edna Manley, ed., *Focus: An Anthology of Contemporary Jamaican Writing*, 1956, pp. 13–25, ref. p. 18.

[4] Quoted in Reid, *The Negro Immigrant*, p. 219.

returning to the islands during your working life. *America is not your home.*' This applies to second- and third-generation West Indians as well. 'Very often "one of us" has never seen the West Indies, and has no accent. What he or she does have is a West Indian grandmother, and that is sufficient.'[1]

West Indians abroad gain new perspectives of whites. Caribbean whites are overwhelmingly elite and middle class: 'a white person represents the Governor, Parson, Director of Education and so on'.[2] The West Indian model is the white middle class. In Europe, however, most whites are working class, and West Indians who have seen 'the conditions under which poor whites lived in metropolitan countries' cease to view whites as a homogeneous, superior race.[3] Nor do European and American whites consider manual labour demeaning. In the West Indies 'they make Englishmen like a god', but in England a Jamaican 'found they worked like everyone else, they even swept roads, everyone worked so hard'.[4]

White behaviour toward non-whites abroad likewise differs from West Indian patterns, though it varies from country to country. Britons pretend to be colour-blind, the French emphasize cultural equality, Americans often seem blatantly hostile. Despite recent changes, West Indian migrants in the United States still experience harsher discrimination than at home, and customary segregation makes America unutterably bleak to many Caribbean visitors. Foreign criteria of social distance also differ from the West Indian norm. Thus Britons might readily accept West Indians as fellow workers but seldom invite them home—a general British pattern mistaken for, if not compounded by, colour prejudice.

Sex is a realm of particular ambiguity for West Indians in Europe. What is permissible at home may be taboo abroad and vice versa. The frequency of interracial marriage in Britain strikes some observers as evidence of 'interracial Utopia', but West Indians retort that 'inferior' women are their only British friends: 'You can have what the Englishmen don't want. You can get the room he won't live in, the job he won't take and the woman he throws out.'[5]

[1] Coombs, 'West Indians in New York', pp. 28, 30.

[2] Neville Maxwell, *The Power of Negro Action*, 1965, p. 21.

[3] B. L. St. John Hamilton, *Problems of Administration in an Emergent Nation*, 1964, p. 53.

[4] Quoted in Betty Davison, 'No Place Back Home: A Study of Jamaicans Returning to Kingston', p. 508. See also Selwyn Douglas Ryan, 'Decolonization in a Multi-Racial Society: A Case Study of Trinidad and Tobago' [1967], p. 70.

[5] Quoted in Ruth Landes, 'A Preliminary Statement of a Survey of Negro-White Relationships in Britain', *Man*, O.S., Vol. LII, September 1952, p. 133; idem, 'Biracialism in American Society: A Comparative View', *AA*, Vol. 57, 1955, pp. 1253–63. J. A. G. Griffith et al., *Coloured Immigrants in Britain* (1960), R. B. Davison, *Black British* (pp. 125–6), and Dilip Hiro, 'The Coloured Man's View of the British' (*New Society*, Vol. 11, 22 February 1968, pp. 263–6) discuss the sexual stereotypes.

Residence abroad alters ideas of nationality along with those of race. Notwithstanding a plethora of local emigrant societies, a wider West Indian nationalism also emerges. Most Europeans and Americans can scarcely identify the individual islands, let alone appreciate their unique qualities. And West Indians abroad seek mutual support in an alien world; homesickness fosters the discovery of common backgrounds, problems, and aspirations. Shared experiences impel a sense of West Indian unity. 'Outside the world of cricket the West Indies is not a nation and does not act as one. Yet the migrant in Britain speaks of himself as a West Indian.' The whole migration experience is 'slowly but steadily making breaches in the walls of insularity thrown up by each island and territory.'[1] Where ethnicity was significant it too becomes less divisive. Surinamers at home think of themselves primarily as Creoles, Hindustanis, and so on; 'in the Netherlands the different ethnic groups come together as Surinamers.'[2]

Emigration affects ideas about class structure too. Many of the values Caribbean society idealizes in theory are living realities only abroad, where mobility is widespread, reward is based on achievement, work is a virtue, and entrepreneurial effort is less encumbered by patronage. The West Indian who is poor and black crosses the ocean not only to make his fortune but to break out of a system that keeps him at the bottom. Some find foreign colour bars less galling than the class system at home. 'In the West Indies there are more barriers between jobs than there are in Britain. . . . I would never have worked as a bus conductor back home', relates a Jamaican migrant, 'partly because . . . in the West Indies for a bus conductor to be dating a State Registered Nurse might be the talk of the town'. But in Britain 'very few people seem to look down on you because of the job you are doing.' Many a suitor successful in Britain 'would not have got anywhere near his lady if they had been back in the West Indies. . . . Migration to Britain has contributed largely to the smashing of West Indian class consciousness',[3] at least in England.

The aspiring migrant may, however, use overseas opportunity as a path to status in the old system. In America if he takes a menial job it is only until he 'gets straightened out'; as quickly as possible he acquires the respectability his poverty denied him at home, for 'he is on this earth to reaffirm the validity of middle-class values'.[4]

---

[1] Hinds, *Journey to an Illusion*, pp. 208, 128. See also George Lamming, *The Pleasures of Exile*, 1960, p. 214; Hugh W. Springer, 'Barbados as a Sovereign State', *Journal of the Royal Society of Arts*, Vol. CXV, 1967, pp. 627–41. Unifying effects are by no means universal, however; racial disturbances in Britain for some time exacerbated animosities between Jamaican and Eastern Caribbean migrants.

[2] Bruijne, 'Surinamers naar Nederland', p. VII-5.

[3] Hinds, *Journey to an Illusion*, pp. 74, 128.

[4] Coombs, 'West Indians in New York', p. 28.

The migrant's return. All these perspectives affect Caribbean society through the migrant who comes home. The impact varies with his background, the duration of his stay abroad, and the circumstances of his return. But much is expected of him. 'He cannot return home as penniless as he left', says a Vincentian. 'He must progress, because his island peers know that he came to America to work or to study and they are waiting for word about him.'[1] A Jamaican in England warns that 'you should only go back when you can do so with good clothes on your back, a spare suit or so, and money in your pockets to treat the home folk'.[2] Material success reflects their transformation in the eyes of home folk. In the French Antilles 'the Negro who knows the mother country is a demigod. . . . Many of them . . . go home to be deified.'[3] Trinidadians likewise hold an 'almost magical belief in the possibilities of a visit abroad which somehow transformed the individual into a new person. He was likely not only to assume a new status but to have this new status thrust upon him.'[4] Homecoming at all social levels is a triumphal occasion. The Montserrat youngster who goes away 'to make himself a man' is feasted on his return to signalize his adult status.[5]

Adulation entails obligation. Not only must the returned migrant bring gifts, buy drinks, and generally spread money around the community; he is also supposed to maintain a higher standard of living. 'Because he has been to England', writes one migrant, 'everybody will expect him when he gets back home to build the biggest house that anybody has ever seen in that area.' This expectation is a major spur to emigrant effort. 'As long as he is convinced he is going to go back home, he will walk until his ankles are swollen to find a job' to make enough money to build that house.[6]

Prosperity often proves elusive, however. 'It takes a hell of a lot of money to make a fresh start in Jamaica,' remarked one emigrant:

I know a man who returned to Jamaica with just over £2,000. He made a big splash. First of all he bought a car. . . . Then he started doing the town. At last somebody got through to him that he ought to invest his money. . . . He was busted clean in less than a year. That man was so ashamed . . . that he killed himself.[7]

Few returned migrants can get regular jobs. Unemployment and high living costs persuade many to return to Britain, despite its racial ten-

---

[1] Coombs, 'West Indians in New York', p. 30.

[2] Peter J. Wilson, 'Reputation and Respectability: A Suggestion for Caribbean Ethnology', *Man*, N.S., Vol. 4, 1969, pp. 70–84, ref. p. 76.

[3] Fanon, *Black Skin, White Masks*, p. 19.

[4] Lloyd Braithwaite, 'The Problem of Cultural Integration in Trinidad', *SES*, Vol. 3, 1954–5, pp. 82–96, ref. p. 84.

[5] Philpott, 'Remittance Obligations, Social Networks and Choice among Montserratian Migrants in Britain', p. 467.

[6] Hinds, *Journey to an Illusion*, p. 189.   [7] Ibid., p. 189.

sions. 'I was homesick', confessed one man in Kingston; 'Now I am homesick to go back.'[1]

West Indians who return home with university degrees often automatically become cultural, community, and political leaders. Many are tapped for leadership while they are still students abroad; others are swept into prominence the moment they return. Some consequently view the Caribbean as 'missionaries looked toward Africa'; as one migrant put it, 'they talk about going to the West Indies and making a contribution'.[2]

Many graduates do not live up to their advance billing. Early promise and high visibility erode their zeal; those famous before accomplishing anything often remain men of whom wonders are anticipated, the expectation being a career in itself. Some become professional Europeans, basking for the rest of their lives on highly embroidered familiarity with the great world. Others shuttle back and forth across the Atlantic and around the Caribbean, perennial promoters of visionary ventures. As exiles responsible to some larger loyalty they avoid serious commitment to West Indian society. The majority settle back comfortably into preferred positions in the local hierarchy and gradually lose sight of unsettling insights acquired abroad.

More than a few, however, react strongly against local conditions. Many returning West Indians are appalled by local insularity, poverty, and apathy. One Jamaican's sojourn in England 'made me see my own country better', another's 'opened my eyes to a lot of things';[3] Surinamese back from the Netherlands find the pace of social and economic reform unbearably slow; Guyanese home again find shoddy what they previously viewed as merely shabby. By contrast with the tempo of the world outside, the West Indies seem static, bound by old memories, early habits, and past failures.

Those bent on change are pushed into the forefront of reform movements by their dynamism, zeal, and broad experience. Some falter for lack of means, of associates, or of endurance; some react to frustration by expressing an iconoclastic contempt for existing institutions; some re-emigrate; some make peace with things as they are while avoiding complete conformity. Whether a success or a failure, the returned migrant leaves his mark on West Indian society.

Colour stratification is one traditional value many migrants shed abroad and return home to struggle against, though often in vain. To the light-skinned scholar, radicalized in Britain, 'shade differences no longer mean anything'. But the local society still defers to the old

[1] Betty Davison, 'No Place Back Home', p. 508.

[2] Hinds, *Journey to an Illusion*, p. 183.

[3] Quoted in H. Orlando Patterson, 'West Indian Migrants Returning Home: Some Observations', *Race*, Vol. X, 1968–9, pp. 69–77, ref. p. 77.

gradations, and 'for the rest of his life he will be thought "odd" by his family and former friends, though the prestige accruing to him as a graduate will in part make up for this oddity.'[1] The black graduate's readjustment may be more difficult; he is apt to be resented by less trained but lighter-skinned seniors and by the old middle class.

Emancipation from concern with shade distinctions by no means blinds returned migrants to colour; on the contrary, it fosters local awareness of world-wide racism. Under ex-migrant urging, non-white West Indians become more self-consciously black. 'You're a black man; a Negro', one Jamaican tells another. 'And you live in a white world. Perhaps not in Jamaica, but . . . Uncle Sam's breathing down our backside every moment.' Neither is America their only bugbear. 'The colonial past is still here in this country. . . . We are black men in a white civilization'.[2]

Migrants and students home from abroad have helped to lead the West Indies toward democracy and independence. Yet they also bring with them a keen consciousness of continuing West Indian bondage to the world outside. They goad change, but their impact is blunted not only by the force of local tradition but also by the persistence of dependency.

NEO-COLONIALISM

Movement in as well as out reflects West Indian dependence on the external world. People, goods, ideas, and values continually flow in from abroad. Some importations impel change, but most buttress the West Indian *status quo*, no matter what domestic or foreign sponsors may intend.

External agencies dominate the Caribbean enough to warrant the term 'neo-colonial'. West Indians have achieved sovereignty only to find, like the slaves emancipated a century ago, that they gained the appearance without the substance of freedom. Today they are more dependent than ever on the great powers. 'Nominal political independence [may] sever the formal ties of colonialism with the "mother" country,' writes Guyana's former Prime Minister; but despite all 'the trappings of national sovereignty [we] still remain a colony.' Similarly, a Jamaican commented to him that 'we have our own Governor-General, Prime Minister, flag, National Anthem, and Coat of Arms, but everything has remained the same'[3]—foreign bases, trade agreements, fiscal controls, import preferences, favours to overseas investors and to tourists:

---

[1] Patricia Madoo, 'The Transition from "Light Skinned" to "Coloured"', in Tajfel and Dawson, eds., *Disappointed Guests*, pp. 55–62, ref. p. 61.

[2] H. Orlando Patterson, *An Absence of Ruins*, 1967, p. 50.

[3] Jagan, *The West on Trial*, p. 402.

Independence for each island is really nothing more than a flag, an anthem, a diplomatic corps that gets rich and ever more pretentious, poverty, exploitation of the land by British and American interests, and governments so fatuous that they believe that true independence is the ability to bar the occasional white reporter who says something the ruling class does not like.[1]

New forms of dependency reinforce old colonial habits. Political, economic, and cultural constraints are intimately interlinked—commercial ties lead to strategic accommodations, cultural dependency stems from overseas economic dominance. But such connections imply no grand conspiracy to control West Indian affairs. On the contrary, many European, North American, and Caribbean statesmen strive consciously to make West Indians masters in their own houses. But great-power strategic aims, global economic patterns, the diffusion of technology and of expectations, and the endurance of colonial attitudes all subvert true independence.

Independence is largely a mirage in the modern world, above all for small, over-populated islands. Yet ex-colonial lands avidly seek a greater measure of autonomy, both for its own sake and as a presumed prerequisite of power and prosperity. The frustration of that aspiration engenders stress and animus throughout the Caribbean.

Political sovereignty. 'The crux of the West Indian problem', asserted Trinidad's Prime Minister in 1965, 'is that America does not want the West Indies, Canada wants them less, and Britain wants them least of all.'[2] The great powers all shun formal possession, in truth. During the Second World War the United States exchanged some over-age destroyers for 99-year leases of half a dozen strategic sites in the British Caribbean but rejected complete takeover as a racial liability; as President Roosevelt put it, 'if we can get our naval bases, why . . . buy with them two million headaches?'[3] France and the Netherlands achieved formal Antillean decolonization some years ago, and during the 1950s and 1960s, Britain steadily sloughed off West Indian sovereignty.

But though Europe no longer wants territorial ownership, it is reluctant to relinquish West Indian control. Threats to local order invite a heavy ex-imperial hand. The British military presence ensured British Guiana's peaceable transition to sovereignty despite ethnic tensions. Metropolitan French troops put down riots in Martinique and Guadeloupe, and Paris treats as 'seditious' Antillean complaints

[1] Coombs, 'West Indians in New York', p. 32.

[2] Eric Williams, *Reflections on the Caribbean Economic Community*, 1965, p. 39. Williams was alluding to the futile small-island overtures, after the break-up of the Federation, for association with Canada or the United States.

[3] Franklin D. Roosevelt to Cordell Hull, 11 January 1941, in *Foreign Relations of the United States, 1941*, 1959, Vol. III, p. 3.

that the *départements* are colonies in disguise. Dutch militia in 1969 quelled striker protests against the Curaçao Government. A British frigate long hovered about Kingstown, St. Vincent, lest political acerbities flare into violence. And tiny Anguilla, which for years had vainly beseeched Britain for protection, had only to declare itself a republic in 1969 to incur a paratroop invasion from London. Small-island sovereignty, a West Indian editor concludes, is 'a sour joke':

Britain with the big stick will always stand poised ready to crack the skulls of the weak, defenseless Associated States when they or their satellites step out of line. These States . . . are not independent and cannot be accepted as member countries of the U.N. And they are not colonies so they do not come within the sphere of influence of the U.N.'s committee on Colonialism. In truth, they are out on a limb, without protection, and at the mercy of the big powers.[1]

Various motives animate intervention. Defence and foreign relations are metropolitan responsibilities in the British Associated States and in the French and Netherlands Caribbean. Britain occupied Anguilla ostensibly to protect local citizens from 'Mafia-type' American adventurers. The Dutch largely direct Netherlands Caribbean development programmes. French civilization in the Antilles is a sacred trust never to be relinquished by Paris. Behind such aims lie purposes less openly avowed: a shield for metropolitan economic interests, a paternalistic concern, a nostalgia for past glories. Smaller Caribbean remnants are no longer profitable as colonies but cost little enough to keep as imperial retirement communities.

Some West Indians find such intrusions demeaning; others see no practicable alternative, like the Anguillan opponent of autonomy who pointed out that 'a man does not leave his father and mother to be independent, but to link up with a girl. Who is Anguilla going to link up with?'[2] West Indian dependence on great-power favour is seldom so explicitly acknowledged, but in time of crisis few West Indian leaders care to rely solely on local police and defence forces. And they are not averse to having expatriates bear the onus for keeping law and order. Several Commonwealth Caribbean states joined in urging Britain to resolve the Anguilla crisis, in part to avoid having to intervene themselves. West Indian rulers also value metropolitan ties as safeguards against revolution, especially through contamination by way of Haiti or Cuba. 'For too many people, the very mention of the name "Cuba" conjures up visions of subversion, Communism, repressive rule, ruthless regimentation and abbreviation of several of the

[1] 'A Sledgehammer to Swat a Fly', *Dominica Herald*, 22 March 1969, p. 2. For the Anguilla story, see Colin G. Clarke, 'Political Fragmentation in the Caribbean: The Case of Anguilla', *Canadian Geographer*, Vol. XV, 1971, pp. 13–29.

[2] *Anguilla Beacon*, 28 December 1968, p. 3.

fundamental freedoms'.[1] Anything untoward, unexplained, and even faintly menacing in the Caribbean is almost instantly rumoured to stem from Castro—or from the C.I.A.

The American presence is a far more formidable deterrent to effective West Indian autonomy than Cuba is. The 1915–34 American occupation of Haiti, for example, was a regime as brutal and racist as any in the Caribbean. Americans generally considered Haitians, like other blacks, inferior and incapable of self-government. Although abjuring annexation, the United States sought 'an unquestioned predominance and an unshakable control,' a contemporary editorialist declared, simply in order to free all the West Indies from misery, starvation, corruption, disease, and violence. But the National City Bank of New York, having bought up the outstanding French loan to Haiti, revised the constitution and ran Haiti in its own interests. Land was opened up to foreign ownership, freedom of speech curtailed, martial law imposed, and virtual slave-labour reintroduced under the United States Marines, who killed thousands of Haitians in order to 'pacify' the country, build a few roads, and collect customs receipts.[2]

The Caribbean today, no longer of strategic concern to Europe, matters in some ways more than ever to the United States. Formal freedom from Britain or France has only symbolic significance when one is a small fish in an American sea. Trinidad's effort to terminate the United States naval-base lease at Chaguaramas underscored local pride in nationhood, but the ensuing *modus vivendi* kept Trinidad firmly attached to American strategic interests.[3] Naval rocket-launching and orbital tracking stations up and down the archipelago manifest America's military strength—and bolster local revenues. Fearful of another Cuba, America intervened in British Guiana during the 1960s to alter both the constitution and the political succession.[4]

[1] Norman Girwar, 'Should We Open Our Doors to Cuba?' *Trinidad Express*, 8 March 1970, p. 14.

[2] John W. Blassingame, 'The Press and American Intervention in Haiti and the Dominican Republic, 1904–1920', *CS*, Vol. 9, No. 2, July 1969, pp. 27–43, ref. pp. 29–32, 40–1. See also Arthur C. Millspaugh, *Haiti under American Control, 1915–30*, 1931; Ludwell Lee Montague, *Haiti and the United States, 1714–1938*, 1940.

[3] Eric Williams, *Slavery to Chaguaramas*, 1959; Lloyd Best, 'Chaguaramas to Slavery?' *NWQ*, Vol. 2, No. 1, Dead Season 1965, p. 43–70, especially p. 67; *The Annexation of Chaguaramas*, 1963, especially p. 3. Much of the Chaguaramas site was in fact relinquished by the United States in 1967 (Eric Williams, *Inward Hunger: The Education of a Prime Minister*, 1969, p. 244); Williams regards the settlement as a major nationalist accomplishment (*From Columbus to Castro: The History of the Caribbean, 1492–1969*, 1970, pp. 475–6).

[4] 'An independent British Guiana under Burnham . . . would cause us many fewer problems than an independent British Guiana under Jagan. And the way was open to bring it about, because Jagan's parliamentary strength was larger than his popular strength' (Arthur Schlesinger, Jr., *A Thousand Days: John F. Kennedy in the White*

The prospect of a black-power takeover in Trinidad in 1970 sped thousands of marines from Guantanamo to Port-of-Spain. 'Neutrality within the Caribbean is apparently not a position allowed by the masterminds of our State and Military Departments', a recent study concludes.[1] Washington considers the new West Indian nations only marginally viable. United States naval officers in the Caribbean claim they have 'enough power to cope with any foreseeable trouble . . . and [that] "we expect trouble anywhere"'.[2] Strategically 'the Caribbean is *mare nostrum*. . . . The United States is not under any circumstances going to permit these states to align themselves with elements openly hostile to this country in the cold war, it is not going to allow situations . . . in which there is a realistic possibility of Communist domination. It simply is not.'[3]

America's overwhelming might, threats of intervention, and reactions to Caribbean problems make many West Indians suspicious of any American activity, including social service. Thus in 1969 a radical newspaper warned Jamaicans that the 'so-called peace-corps' had 'white foreigners throughout the Jamaican countryside spying on black people, inciting and harassing them'; volunteers were said to be 'carrying out subversive work . . . in a sort of double-agent fashion' to protect 'America's interest in the Caribbean'.[4]

West Indians in authority tend to identify American interests closely with their own. They regard American goodwill as crucial and take it for granted that America's presence is permanent. 'Much of the thinking in the Caribbean assumes', a West Indian observes, 'that the marines will always be in Guantanamo.'[5] Guyana seeks American protection against Venezuelan territorial claims, Jamaican leaders take comfort that the United States will prevent Castro-type crusades, and Trinidad relies on arms from Uncle Sam. The West Indies can ill afford the public display of anti-American feelings. It is no accident

House, 1965, p. 779). See also Jagan, *The West on Trial*, pp. 274, 298–300; Leo A. Despres, *Cultural Pluralism and Nationalist Politics in British Guiana*, 1967, pp. 182–3, 198–9, 282; Philip Reno, 'The Ordeal of British Guiana', *Monthly Review*, Vol. 16, Nos. 3 and 4, July-August 1964; Ernst Halperin, 'Racism and Communism in British Guiana', *Journal of Inter-American Studies*, Vol. VII, No. 1, January 1965, pp. 95–134.

[1] Thomas Mathews, 'Problems and Leaders in the Caribbean', in A. Curtis Wilgus, ed., *The Caribbean: Its Hemispheric Role*, 1967, pp. 28–40, ref. p. 38.

[2] Comdr. Robert M. Casey, cited in Anthony Maingot, 'National Sovereignty, Collective Security and the Realities of Power in the Caribbean Area', in Roy Presiwerk, ed., *Regionalism and the Commonwealth*, 1969, pp. 220–45, ref. p. 241.

[3] John N. Plank, 'Neighborly Relations in the Caribbean', in Wilgus, ed., *The Caribbean: Its Hemispheric Role*, pp. 161–70, ref. pp. 168–9.

[4] *Abeng*, 26 April 1969, p. 2, and 3 May 1969, p. 4.

[5] Lloyd Best, 'Independent Thought and Caribbean Freedom', *NWQ*, Vol. 3 No. 4, Cropover 1967, pp. 13–34, ref. p. 20.

that Haiti and the Commonwealth Caribbean were the only places that greeted Nelson Rockefeller's 1969 good-will tour without open hostility.

Economic dominance. The West Indians depend on the great powers not only for defence in time of emergency but for their livelihood. 'If you want independence, you must have economic independence', a former British Colonial Secretary used to tell West Indians. Trinidad's Prime Minister finally retorted, 'Fine! We don't want a penny from you. Give us the independence now.'[1] Brave words, but vain. Underneath their 'loud and . . . exuberant . . . nationalism', Caribbean leaders 'knew that the sovereign nation state was an atavism in the age of giant international corporations and capital markets and big power politics.'[2]

The West Indies are least sovereign in the economic realm. 'The smaller the country', states a Barbadian, 'the more it depends on its external environment. There is no cure for this dependence.'[3] Moreover, Caribbean physical resources and economic institutions were developed for, and remain dominated by, outsiders. Classic instances of mercantilism, the West Indies supplied Europe with tropical foodstuffs and bought metropolitan manufactures in return. To this role they still adhere, today exporting oil and bauxite along with sugar, bananas, and other crops. The major Caribbean territories all have export economies, selling a few primary products and purchasing many consumer goods. 'Political independence', notes a West Indian, 'has not changed the fact that . . . the external markets depend on the policies and practices of foreign governments.'[4]

Foreigners control more than this. Substantial local resources—land, plants, machinery, even railroads and port facilities—belong to Europeans and Americans. West Indians 'are still to own and manage oil, asphalt and bauxite, or even sugar which they have produced for hundreds of years.' International firms, like colonial planters, standardize Caribbean economies by controlling the key export commodities.

Tate and Lyle integrate sections of Trinidad and Tobago with sections of Jamaica and sections of British Honduras. Demba, Alcan, Kaiser, Alcoa and Reynolds integrate the West Indian bauxite industry through their operations in Jamaica, Guyana, Haiti, Surinam and the Dominican Republic. The oil companies integrate the marketing and refining of oil in the Caribbean.[5]

Foreigners own most major West Indian enterprises, and almost

[1] Williams, *Slavery to Chaguaramas*, pp. 24–5.
[2] Selwyn Ryan, 'Restructuring the Trinidad Economy', *NWQ*, Vol. 4, No. 4, Cropover 1968, pp. 7–23, ref. p. 19.
[3] Springer, 'Barbados as a Sovereign State', pp. 636–7.
[4] Philip Sherlock, *West Indies*, 1966, p. 99.
[5] James Millette, 'The Caribbean Free Trade Association: The West Indies at the Crossroads', *NWQ*, Vol. 4, No. 4, Cropover 1968, pp. 30–48, ref. pp. 33–4.

totally dominate export commodities. In Trinidad, for example, three foreign firms control 90 per cent of the economy, foreign branch plants generate 83 per cent of taxable company revenues, and thus 'the economy of Trinidad and Tobago is essentially an appendage of the overseas economy of the American and European corporations.'[1] External control partly explains why West Indians neglect local markets in favour of exports. Because outsiders own better arable lands, command more capital, and offer surer returns, agricultural research and technology (also dependent on overseas capital and skills) focus on export rather than on subsistence crops. Planter and peasant alike prefer regular payments for sugar or bananas to the risks of praedial larceny, price fluctuations, marketing chaos, storage inadequacies, and problems of scale that beset most local foodstuffs. 'The authorities have repeatedly suggested that the farmer with a small acreage of land should concentrate on food production for the local market. For over 130 years the small scale farmer has resisted this interpretation of his role and continued to produce crops for export.'[2]

Caribbean export crops depend, however, on commodity prices pegged well above world market levels; 'if the West Indies sugar industry did not have the price support of the Commonwealth Sugar Agreement,' one expert bluntly states, 'the industry will go bust within a year or two.'[3] The French and Netherlands Caribbean enjoy duty-free access to the European Economic Community; the Commonwealth territories have preferential agreements with Britain and the United States. The sugar, bananas, citrus fruits, and other crops thus sold comprise more than 90 per cent of Caribbean agricultural exports. Originally designed to protect West Indian interests against foreign competition, these arrangements today keep export agriculture alive at the cost of profound economic dependence, and a continuing bias against domestic agriculture.[4]

[1] Lloyd Best, 'The Puzzled Afro-American', *Trinidad Guardian*, 16 March 1969, p. 9. See also Ryan, 'Restructuring the Trinidad Economy', p. 16.

[2] Janet D. Momsen, 'Small Scale Farming in Barbados, St. Lucia and Martinique', 1970, pp. 15–16. See also Dayanand Maharaj, 'The Small Farmer in the Trinidad Sugar Industry', 1970, p. 12; Alan Eyre, *Land and Population in the Sugar Belt of Jamaica* [1965], p. 8; William G. Demas, *The Economics of Development in Small Countries with Special Reference to the Caribbean*, 1965, pp. 104–18; David T. Edwards, 'An Economic View of Agricultural Research in Jamaica', *SES*, Vol. 10, 1961, pp. 306–39; G. L. Beckford, 'Toward Rationalization of West Indian Agriculture', in *Papers Presented at the Regional Conference on Devaluation*, 1968, pp. 147–54, ref. p. 152.

[3] S. Norman Girwar, 'Economic Diversification in the Context of the Future of Sugar Protection in Some of the Caribbean Commonwealth Territories', 1969, p. 6.

[4] Aaron Segal, *The Politics of Caribbean Economic Integration*, 1968; Demas, *The Economics of Development in Small Countries*, pp. 103–9; Clive Y. Thomas, 'Diversification and the Burden of Sugar to Jamaica', *NWQ*, Vol. 5, Nos. 1 and 2, Dead Season and Croptime 1969, pp. 41–7, ref. p. 43.

Benefits accrue to growers and their agents at the expense of outside domination, depressed incomes, inefficient production, and other drawbacks. Producers have small incentive to grow more than set quotas; for they must sell any surplus at the lower world-market prices. Therefore they seek mainly to minimize current production costs. Trade unions, often backed by local governments, resist labour-saving innovations and delay technological modernization; nevertheless, employment in export agriculture steadily diminishes. Heavy capital requirements moreover necessitate borrowing abroad. Public debt charges grew from less than 7 per cent of Jamaica's government revenues in 1957 to more than 9 per cent in 1967.[1] Earnings drain away not only as interest on loans but also as profit for metropolitan shareholders, salaries to metropolitan employees, and fees to metropolitan marketing and shipping firms.

Local demands for what is *not* locally grown also offset export receipts. Because the West Indies ship out four-fifths of what they produce, they must buy foreign goods to feed, to clothe, and to house the local populace. Barbados's sugar crop—practically its sole export—brings the island $35 to $40 million (Eastern Caribbean) a year, but the island's annual food import bill is $30 million; locally grown food provides only 40 per cent of the calories, 32 per cent of the monetary value of what is consumed.[2] Potentially, at least, 'we possess everything we need', writes a French West Indian, 'and presently we import it all'.[3] The vast foreign trade benefits metropolitan agencies but steadily impoverishes the Caribbean, partly because of adverse trade balances. The food import bill for the British West Indies increased from $38 million (Trinidad and Tobago) before the Second World War to $245 million in 1964. Exports tend to remain static, while population growth and increased import costs saddle West Indian countries with heavy foreign-payments deficits. In Surinam between 1954 and 1964 exports doubled but imports tripled.[4] Exports cover only about 40 per cent of Martinique's import costs; Government grants make up the balance. Jamaica sustained a 1968 trade deficit of £66·4 million, with imports 70 per cent above exports. Jamaican agricultural output

---

[1] Ransford W. Palmer, *The Jamaican Economy*, 1968, p. 129.

[2] E. G. B. Gooding, 'Diversification of Agriculture in Barbados', in John I. McKigney and Robert Cook, eds., *Protein Foods for the Caribbean* [1968], pp. 48–9. See also E. G. B. Gooding, 'Crop Diversification in Barbados', *World Crops*, Vol. 20, March 1968, pp. 34–9.

[3] Remy Nainsouta, quoted in Daniel Guérin, *The West Indies and Their Future*, 1961, p. 45.

[4] G. M. Sammy, 'W. I. Technical Officers are Frustrated: Politicians Blamed', *Trinidad Sunday Guardian*, 8 March 1970, p. 12; Fuat M. Andic and Suphan Andic, 'Government Finance and Planned Development: Fiscal Surveys of Surinam and the Netherlands Antilles', 1968, p. 64.

increases 2 per cent annually, while food demands rise 5 per cent; in 1950 Jamaica imported 17 per cent of its food, in 1965, 27 per cent. Projected protein needs will indefinitely outstrip domestic production of fish, meat, and dairy products.[1] Trinidad by 1968 was nearly self-sufficient in fresh meat and poultry, but the $9·8 million saved in meat and milk imports was all but dissipated in the expenditure of $8 million for animal feeds and concentrates.[2]

Agricultural preferences perpetuate other aspects of dependence. Most trade arrangements require Caribbean producers to buy where they sell, crippling local initiative and bargaining power. Nine-tenths of Martinique's exports go to metropolitan France, which in turn supplies four-fifths of local imports. Britain, the United States, and Canada together engross three-fourths of Commonwealth Caribbean commerce. Dependent on metropolitan processors and markets and exporting only a small fraction of world production in any commodity, Caribbean economies are exceedingly vulnerable to trade fluctuations they cannot control. Decisions that vitally affect Caribbean welfare are made by European and North American buyers, seldom by West Indian suppliers.

Economic development programmes increase Caribbean dependence, because foreign investors also dominate the new industries. Local entrepreneurs remain diffident; West Indians 'are still to develop an indigenous banking system so that the money which they save will be applied to purposes which they determine'. Instead they 'continue to borrow their money via the foreign banks and use more of that money to pay interest on the loans thus obtained.'[3] Private overseas investment accounts for more than half the domestic capital formation in the Commonwealth Caribbean.

Tax-free incentives encourage reliance on foreign capital. Trinidad's pioneer industries policy strengthens Anglo-American economic dominance. The overwhelming majority of the new concerns set up under Jamaican industrial incentive laws are American-owned or controlled; the ostensible Jamaican heads are locally dismissed as 'para-

[1] Owen Jefferson, 'Some Aspects of the Post-War Economic Development of Jamaica', *NWQ*, Vol. 3, No. 3, High Season 1967, pp. 1–11; P. Mahadevan, 'Animal Protein Supplies for the Caribbean', in McKigney and Cook, eds., *Protein Foods for the Caribbean*, pp. 20–2; G. L. Beckford and E. A. Brown, 'Economic Aspects of Food Availability in Jamaica', *CQ*, Vol. 14, No. 4, December 1968, pp. 61–5; *Jamaica, Trinidad and Tobago, Leeward Islands, Windward Islands, Barbados, and British Guiana: Projected Levels of Demand, Supply, and Imports of Agricultural Products to 1975* [1954], pp. 12–14.

[2] Trinidad and Tobago, *Third Five-Year Plan, 1969–1973*, 1970, p. 215.

[3] Millette, 'The Caribbean Free Trade Association', p. 33. For the scope and impact of overseas investment, see A. McIntyre and B. Watson, *Studies in Foreign Investment in the Commonwealth Caribbean: No. 1 Trinidad and Tobago*, 1970.

sites who rise and fall with American fortunes.'[1] Small factories modelled on Puerto Rico's Operation Bootstrap proliferate in Jamaica and Trinidad, but their local impact is negligible. Profits go mainly to overseas investors; employment is minuscule. New plants in Trinidad hired only 11,000 during 1960–8, whereas the labour force increased by 200,000.[2] Because they utilize labour-intensive technology with high ratios of capital input, pioneer concerns sometimes force competing local firms to lay off more workers than the new plants themselves employ.

Local skills like local labour are in low demand. Research on product design is conducted abroad; local needs and resources are scarcely noticed. An artist in Martinique,

after many months of exploration, and great financial outlay, found an appropriate type of clay *in Martinique* to make tile; and then developed the required mixing and baking formula. . . . He presented his results to the Director [of the government art school], and prepared to conduct classes in art-tile making. Apparently he was too successful! He was told that now that he was ready to teach tile work the School would import clay for that purpose from France![3]

Expatriate manufacturers commonly eschew local materials as well. 'Industrialization . . . seems to be a process of filling imported tubes and tins with various imported substances. Whenever we went beyond this we were likely to get in trouble.'[4] Few opportunities to go further are available. The foreign entrepreneur prefers to do most of the work abroad. 'A final finishing and assembly operation—which is often very suited to a quickly trained and not expensive local labour force—is all that is required to give him a large measure of local protection and attractive tax concessions', a British manufacturer's representative explains.[5] Many a Caribbean enterprise is 'not a manufacturing process within the wildest stretch of imagination', but merely a 'screwdriver industry' putting together knocked-down merchandise.[6] Another kind of tax advantage explains why the United States Virgin Islands watch industry accounted for half the local exports to the

[1] Blackman, 'Time Now . . . to Work Out the New Imperialism', *Abeng*, 13 September 1969, p. 4.

[2] Edwin Carrington, 'Industrialization in Trinidad and Tobago since 1950', *NWQ*, Vol. 4, No. 2, Croptime 1968, pp. 37–43; 'Role of Trade Unions in Unemployment', *Trinidad Guardian*, 24 March 1970, p. 8.

[3] H. Merrill Jackson, 'Caribbean–West African Field Study: First Report', 1969, p. 11.

[4] V. S. Naipaul, *The Mimic Men*, 1967, p. 258.

[5] J. R. M. Rocke, 'Market Where Britain Must Do More', *The Times*, 8 October 1968.

[6] Thomas Wright, 'Candidly Yours', *Jamaica Daily Gleaner*, 18 February 1970, p. 12.

mainland in the mid-1960s, whereas wages for the 800 West Indian employees who put together watch parts and sub-assemblies imported from Japan, Germany, and France came to less than one-tenth the mainland wholesale price of the watches.[1] The Trinidad blank-sock industry exemplifies the West Indian consequences of sub-assembly:

The 'blank' sock is about 99·9% foreign made. It is in fact a completely made-up sock which has the toe-hole open; and one of our newest and most prestigious foreign manufacturing firms has been given a concession to import 100,000 dozen of these items in order to 'manufacture' socks. . . . A local firm with the capacity to produce socks from the basic raw material was virtually ruined to facilitate the introduction of the foreign establishment under pioneer aid.[2]

The tourist industry, like other pioneer developments, is largely foreign-owned and controlled. Tourism is the fastest-growing sector of half a dozen Caribbean economies. Barbadian tourist revenue approaches that from sugar; Jamaica's 352,000 tourists in 1968 spent £36·6 million. But more than half of the income is dissipated in profits to foreign investors, expatriate staff salaries, and payments for imported goods, especially food. 'We are loath to sell foreigners a local bill of fare', one West Indian avers, because 'we have no confidence in it and therefore have not developed it.'[3] At Coco Point resort, Barbuda, everything is flown in from Florida, food, equipment, and service personnel, along with tourists, whose money never leaves the United States. Tobago has imported landscape as well. 'There is now a part of Tobago which is forever and irrevocably American. The Mt. Irvine golf course . . . reposes on a carpet of green grass imported from Kentucky, U.S.A. We know that tourists thrive on imported food; now they will play on imported grass.'[4]

External 'charity' augments outside influence. Grant-aided British Caribbean colonies and French Antillean social-welfare programmes are under direct metropolitan surveillance. American aid, tied to the importation of American goods or services, helps to 'maintain the openness of our economy', a West Indian economist asserts, 'and with it our dependence and our vulnerability to the slightest foreign whim or fancy.'[5]

The greed or naïveté of some local leaders attracts foreign exploitation. Independence has not taught the small islands to husband

[1] F. E. Oxtoby, 'The Role of Political Factors in the Virgin Islands Watch Industry', GR, Vol. 60, 1970, pp. 463–74.

[2] Millette, 'The Caribbean Free Trade Association', p. 46.

[3] 'Devaluation', New World Occasional Bulletin No. 3, January 1968, p. 11. See also Trinidad Third Five-Year Plan, p. 258; Jamaica Economic Survey, 1968, p. 5.

[4] 'Call That George', Moko, No. 10, 14 March 1969, p. 3. For Coco Point see Jean Raspail, Punch Caraïbe, 1970, pp. 111–12.

[5] 'Devaluation', p. 12.

resources or to define, let alone protect, long-range local interests. A recent St. Vincent regime is said to have leased two Grenadine islands to American developers for fifty cents a year, and a Dominican government put pressure on local landowners to sell out to an international consortium that collapsed shortly afterward.

Subservience to metropolitan interests arouses some local criticism. University economists charge that the Jamaican sugar industry uses 'the best lands in the country, is supported by unusually high price and quota supports, has rationalized its labor force by 25% over the past ten years *and yet*' its production costs are 'uncomfortably high, its profit rather low, and the wage which it pays the mass of its wretched workers barely sufficient to cover the expenses of subsistence.'[1] And in Trinidad a radical group declared that 'owners are taking too large a share of the wealth produced and the [expatriate] staff too large a share of the wages' and concluded that 'the bankrupt sugar cane plantation system must go'.[2] As descendants of slaves, West Indians are said to

remember with horror what the sugar estate has meant. Do we ask the Jew to live and work in the concentration camps of Germany? . . . The sociological case against the sugar plantation is unanswerable. . . . It is psychologically demoralizing and as such is an obstacle to progress. And last but not least, it is morally repugnant.[3]

Emotional considerations affect the economic views of producers no less than those of reformers, where sugar is concerned. When the rationale of dependence is questioned, West Indian governments and businesses raise the spectre of starvation and misery. 'The first and only concern is: How can we save the sugar industry. . . . The question is not: what best can we do for Jamaica with our capital. Sugar is deemed to be Jamaica! And that's the end of the matter.'[4] The criticism cited above provoked Jamaican newspaper alarums of 'revolution' based on 'falsehoods and economic ruin,' a sugar manufacturer's retort that 'people who want to see real poverty should go to India, or Haiti,'[5] and government warnings that abolition of the sugar industry would plunge Jamaica into chaos. Trinidad officials joined

[1] Havelock Brewster, 'Jamaica's Life or Death: The Sugar Industry', in 'The Sugar Industry: Our Life or Death?' *New World Pamphlet No. 4*, December 1967, p. 7.

[2] Trinidad Workers and Farmers Party spokesmen, quoted in Ryan, 'Restructuring the Trinidad Economy', pp. 14, 12.

[3] H. Orlando Patterson, 'Social Aspects of the Sugar Industry', *NWQ*, Vol. 5, Nos. 1 and 2, Dead Season and Croptime 1969, pp. 47–9, ref. p. 49. See also G. Arthur Brown, 'Sugar without Emotion', ibid., pp. 40–1.

[4] Havelock Brewster, 'Sugar—Mechanizing Our Life or Death', ibid., pp. 55–7.

[5] James Kirkwood, 'New World Revolution Based on Falsehoods and Economic Ruin', *Jamaica Daily Gleaner*, 13 January 1968, quoted in 'King Sugar and the New World: The Story of the Great Sugar Debate', *New World Pamphlet No. 5*, June 1968, pp. 7–8.

producers in asserting that sugar abandonment would kill the economy. The Government admits that 'continued reliance of the economy on sugar and citrus production requiring preferential shelter in metropolitan markets is a sign of structural weakness' but considers it 'utopian to advocate an instantaneous discarding of such links.' And the Prime Minister warns that 'the reduction or elimination of preferences in the sugar industry will present insoluble social and economic problems as no satisfactory substitute for sugar can be foreseen that would accommodate the increasing population and maintain even existing standards of living.'[1]

Reformers consider government defence of sugar and other foreign interests demeaning if not self-serving. 'The PNM and the "Black Massa"', Trinidad radicals feel, have sold out to the 'world-wide net of capitalist exploitation'; Caribbean governments 'deliberately assume the role of house-slave . . . to metropolitan business.'[2]

In Trinidad, at least, government leaders appear no happier than their critics about external influence. 'Dependence on foreign sources of finance, apart from being psychologically prejudicial, is practically dangerous', notes the Prime Minister. 'Many foreign interests behave as if they have a God-given right to be exempt from paying taxes to a national government, as if private enterprise from overseas is entitled to any privileges which it demands.'[3] To achieve a measure of self-sufficiency, Trinidad has shifted development support from the plantation to the subsistence sector of the economy, the latest Five Year Plan aims at 'a greater role for the public sector in running industries traditionally reserved for foreign enterprise such as oil and sugar', and the People's National Movement urges 'speedy and positive action' towards government control of these sectors of the economy.[4] But the harsh fact remains that the 'human, physical and financial resources of Trinidad are inadequate to a programme of nationalization. Some measure of dependence is inevitable'.[5]

At issue is the nature and extent of that dependence. Williams is 'strongly aware of the need to create . . . a more autonomous Caribbean economy. We are . . . taking steps . . . to shift the locus of economic decision-making from the metropolis to the home country' by means of national sugar and oil companies, banks and mass media. Moreover, 'we are watching American economic penetration of the Caribbean closely—there is a danger of domination here, as there may be too

[1] *Trinidad Third Five-Year Plan*, p. 49; Williams, *Inward Hunger*, p. 115.
[2] Ryan, 'Restructuring the Trinidad Economy', p. 17; Best, 'Independent Thought and Caribbean Freedom', p. 14.
[3] Eric Williams, quoted in Ryan, 'Restructuring the Trinidad Economy', p. 22.
[4] *Trinidad Third Five-Year Plan*, p. 37; 'Gov't Told to Get More Control', *Trinidad Guardian*, 22 March 1970, p. 1.
[5] Ryan, 'Restructuring the Trinidad Economy', p. 10.

from other infant imperialisms in our area.'[1] But many feel it is late to speak of 'the danger' of American domination. And the avowal of local decision-making seems to critics merely a smoke-screen for new foreign commitments. In C. L. R. James's cogent phrase, 'there is no neo-colonialism in . . . Trinidad and Tobago: it is the same old colonialism which has existed since the beginning and continues, independence or no independence.'[2]

Cultural dependence. Submission to external cultural criteria is an inevitable concomitant of West Indian political and economic dependence. 'It is accepted as natural and even desirable that the rhythm and style of life in the territory should be dominated by events in the metropolis.'[3] Trinidad government planners themselves depict an environment in which 'the local Government and local producers abdicate to foreign firms and individuals the making of crucial [financial] decisions . . . , the images and messages of the communications media, tastes in goods, and even ideas of proper national economic and social goals and instruments'.[4]

The role of the West Indian middle class is crucial in this process. With ready access to foreign goods and easy credit arrangements, an expanding bourgeoisie emulates the buying habits of the local elite and of more affluent societies. Martinique in 1968 had 36,000 cars, or one for every eight inhabitants. The Jamaican appetite for foreign luxuries weighs heavily in the adverse trade balance, yet the Government hesitates to restrict imports, fearing that a public 'accustomed to these tastes . . . will not be willing to give them up.' Trinidadian consumer expectations 'influenced by foreign communications media' threaten to put even more strain on that country's resources.[5] Exposure to metropolitan standards affects all levels of West Indian society; governments feel compelled to promise welfare benefits they cannot afford—and often do not deliver; the 1970 poor relief allowance in Dominica is as little as a dollar per week, and a St. Vincent advisory report recommends increasing the $5 (E.C.) a month paid to destitute families.[6]

[1] Eric Williams, *Britain and the West Indies: Historical and Contemporary Aspects of the Relationship between Britain and the West Indies*, 1969, pp. 22–3; and idem, quoted in 'The Times Diary', *The Times*, 19 March 1969.

[2] C. L. R. James, 'Expatriate Island', *New Society*, Vol. 13, 17 April 1969, p. 607. See also idem, 'The Caribbean Confrontation Begins', *Race Today*, Vol. 2, 1970, pp. 311–14.   [3] Best, 'Chaguaramas to Slavery?' p. 54.

[4] *Trinidad Third Five-Year Plan*, p. 36.

[5] George Huggins, 'The French West Indies Today', *Moko*, No. 11, 28 March 1969, p. 2; 'Foreign Trade', *Jamaica Daily Gleaner*, 6 July 1968; 'Trinidad Gets Whiff of Gas', *New York Times*, 20 January 1969, p. 67.

[6] Androcles, 'Well Played, Sir!' *Dominica Star*, 14 March 1970, p. 2; *The Development Problem in St. Vincent: A Report by a University of the West Indies Development Mission* [1969], p. 144.

In order to attract foreign capital West Indians not only import metropolitan goods but cater for expatriate tastes. Foreign entrepreneurs receive elite living conditions, public deference, and assurances of social harmony along with their tax exemptions. Attentiveness to the confidence of metropolitan investors restricts West Indian public policy, discouraging economic reform and muting consideration of social needs. 'A country that has got used to depending on external factors', Trinidad's planners explain, 'always finds it difficult to make . . . decisive structural changes'.[1] Foreign investments affect the very structure of government, for overseas confidence is felt to require adherence to overseas constitutional forms: thus Bahamian whites, accusing black leaders of undermining investor confidence with demands for independence, campaigned in 1968 on the slogan, 'Don't turn your back on the Union Jack.' But the new black Prime Minister, a self-styled 'conservative with a social conscience', has sweetened foreign investment with reassuring talk of 'democratic Parliamentary Government' and with concessions exempting manufacturers from property 'and any other foreseeable tax' until 1990.[2]

Subservience to metropolitan norms and values affects all aspects of West Indian life.

Patterns are set by adaptations to the business ethos of a transient class of metropolitan entrepreneurs and managers reinforced by tourists. . . . This metropolitan class . . . determines the changes in the rules of cuisine, dress, working hours etc. And as the reward for conformity to these rules is not just personal advancement . . . but also economic growth for the territory as a whole, the deviant is open to the charge of being anti-national.[3]

Tourism plays a multiple role in this process. The Bahamian reformers who swept the 'Bay Street Boys' (white merchants) out of office in 1967 have not tampered with the old colonial aura so attractive to visitors. In Antigua where government forces confronted rebellious labour unions in 1968, the spectre of frightened tourists brought an early compromise. In Jamaica the Tourist Board purveys images of a land of servile mammies and nannies while denying Jamaicans access to hotels and beaches. 'Tourism is whorism', a British Honduran asserts. 'What is good for the tourist industry may be bad for Martinicans' because the very things that tourists enjoy are detrimental to local progress.[4] Because West Indians provide mainly

[1] *Trinidad Third Five-Year Plan*, pp. 35–6.

[2] Henry Giniger, 'More Autonomy Is Seen in Wake of Bahamas Vote', *New York Times*, 12 April 1968, p. 15; 'Bahamas Tax Plan Gains', ibid., 1 March 1970, p. 46; Bahamas advertisement, ibid., 10 August 1970, p. 60.

[3] Best, 'Chaguaramas to Slavery?' p. 57. See also Martin Sampath, 'We Can't Forgive the Violent Minority', *Trinidad Express*, 20 March 1970, p. 9.

[4] Evan Hyde, quoted in *Time*, 3 August 1970, p. 22; 'Prostitution to Tourism', *Abeng*, 22 February 1969, p. 1; 'Tourisme et développement en Martinique', *CERAG*,

the menial services and foreigners the capital and management, tourism emphasizes both the fact and the feeling of helpless dependence.

The resort areas, once small enclaves, have become major power centres. 'Kingston is run from Montego Bay as Port of Spain soon will be run by Scarborough and Chaguaramas, and Barbados is already run by its coral reef of hotels. The tourist ethnic [*sic*] flourishes and the native, trapped by the smallness of his environment, becomes more and more a tourist in his own society.'[1] Prisoner is perhaps a more accurate term. The Mill Reef Club on the eastern end of Antigua, which shuts out the rest of the island behind a high barbed-wire fence, is only less egregious than Barbuda's Coco Point, one of the Caribbean's most expensive resorts. The thousand villagers of Codrington, Barbuda's sole inhabitants, are said to be kept apart behind their cactus barricade, under the surveillance of Antiguan policemen. A local newspaper recently counselled Barbadians to learn a second language—that is, standard English—'for encountering tourists'.[2]

Some West Indians emulate tourist tastes; others conform to tourist stereotypes, imploring visitors to buy their 'native beads' and 'native earrings'. 'Because of our poverty and because of our basic lack of self-respect and self-confidence, we treat the tourist as a rich man to be robbed or a god to be propitiated', a Jamaican observes. 'We beg for alms, we demand tips, we tell him how much we need him, and we try our best to show him what happy dancing souls the "natives" are. Some of these features are common to tourism everywhere; but we are marked by a lack of confidence in our own house, and an absence of real pride in our possessions'.[3] Lack of self-confidence extends to most West Indian enterprises.

Accustomed to advancing by denying our own worth, we have found it easier to rely on outside help in our quest for change. . . . We hoped for economic transformation by borrowing capital, by borrowing management, by borrowing technology, by borrowing this and borrowing that, and by cowtowing before every manner of alien expert we could find.[4]

The external standards West Indians emulate include not only European but American modes of thought, behaviour, and material goods, not to overlook Indian and African. Films and broadcasts, books and magazines, ensure that anything truly local will be swamped by sights and sounds of exotic origin, from classical music to jazz and rock, from

No. 16, 1969; Jean-Luc Morel and François Gresle, 'Les touristes en Martinique', *CERAG*, No. 14, 1968, pp. 46–7, 56.

[1] Millette, 'The Caribbean Free Trade Association', p. 33.

[2] *Barbados Advocate-News*, reported in *Dominica Star*, 5 July 1969, p. 3.

[3] Douglas G. Hall, 'The Colonial Legacy in Jamaica', *NWQ*, Vol. 4, No. 3, High Season 1968, pp. 7–22, ref. p. 19.

[4] Lloyd Best, 'Black Power and National Reconstruction: Proposals Following the February Revolution', *Tapia Pamphlet* [1970], p. 4.

lithographs of the Royal Family to Impressionist reproductions.
In culture as in livelihood, Caribbean dependence has increased
since most West Indians gained national sovereignty. In the new
nations, which seek a self-reliant identity, cultural dependence is even
more galling than economic or strategic subordination. The disparity
between the freedom West Indians are told they have and the neo-
colonial realities with which they live engenders widespread confusion, disappointment, and stress. For the ordinary West Indian,

life goes on in much the same way as when 'de man at King's House' was
English, white and alien. . . . He still walks on streets and lanes with alien
names. When he goes to the big open space . . . it is George 'de Six' Memorial
Park. If his wife is to have a baby she still goes to Victoria Jubilee Hospital. . . .
And so on. So he wonders what kind of independent Jamaica this is in which
every public thing and place is named after some foreigner.[1]

A few West Indians resent the neo-colonial pattern, expose its
demerits, and often proclaim its imminent demise. 'People are simply
not prepared like the Mandarins of Branch-Plant Society,' one
reformer predicts, 'to spend their time fudging bright undergraduate
essays for university and international conferences . . . while the real
decisions . . . are prepared in the Head Offices of the financial intermediaries and the bauxite, petroleum and sugar corporations.'[2] But
indignation by itself is unlikely to alter that harsh reality.

Emigration and external dependence are cardinal facts of West Indian
life. Residence abroad and the inflow of metropolitan goods and ideas
widen local horizons. But these processes not only enhance West
Indian life, they also diminish it; for they lend credence to the local
prejudice that things West Indian are second-rate, impotent, not
worth having. Extreme episodes may subvert society altogether: a
mass exodus of young adults or a sudden takeover by a foreign power
can be catastrophic. But emigration and dependency are so endemic
in the Caribbean that West Indian society now largely accommodates
them. They are not spasmodic events but part of the enduring institutional structure.
The two processes are causally linked. Colonial and neo-colonial ties
are a price West Indians pay for the chance to escape to the mother
country. 'Potential and actual ability to emigrate *en masse*', notes a
scholar, 'is one of the most politically, economically, and psychologically valuable aspects of the [colonial] relationship'.[3] French and

---

[1] Evon Blake, 'The Psychology of Independence' [1963–4], in *The Best of Evon
Blake*, pp. 37–8.
[2] Lloyd Best, 'Guest Editor's Statement: The Next Round', *NWQ*, Vol. 4, No. 2,
Croptime 1968, pp. 1–7, ref. p. 5.
[3] Segal with Earnhardt, *Politics and Population in the Caribbean*, p. 7.

Dutch West Indians enjoy 'free' access in return for a binding association. Even British West Indians, whose entry Britain has severely curtailed, still tend to expect Commonwealth ties to pave the way for
some welcoming warmth.

The emigration habit has convinced West Indians that the way to
get ahead is to get out, and they see that those who stay behind stag-
nate. The acceptance of dependency adds a corollary: West Indians,
powerless to control their collective fate, must bend to the great
powers. Both conditions militate against a sense of community.
'Obsession with emigration as a solution', as Singham says of Grenada,
'has further reinforced the attitude bred by colonialism of finding
solutions to problems outside the society.'[1]

Frequent migration also enhances local tolerance of colonial ties.
Emigration continually drains away potential rebels, leaving behind
those more prone to endure neo-colonialism. 'One of the reasons that
the British West Indies have remained statically conservative, impoverished and without a revolutionary movement', remarks Cruse, 'is
that all such radicals leave home, like other ambitious locals, and go
off to make revolutions somewhere else.'[2] Yet most emigrants are not
radical, let alone revolutionary; their goals are strongly middle class.
'We come here to work, man, not to fight the white man',[3] typifies the
West Indian migrant's response to black power. By contrast with the
few black militants, the average West Indian overseas is apt to resent
being reminded that 'the song is we shall overcome, not we shall come
over.'[4]

The less ambitious stay-at-home is still more passive; black West
Indians are said to be 'the most conformist and accommodative people
in the Caribbean.'[5] But the local temper is too complex to be summed
up in such generalizations. It is equally true that West Indians at
home share the absentee spirit of those away, and 'because we are all
expatriates', a Trinidadian declares, 'West Indians are extremists';[6]
they readily take ideas to logical extremes because they envisage no
prospect of local application.

We now turn to the consequences of emigration and external
dependence, together with other aspects of West Indian institutions
and values, for the West Indian sense of racial and national identity.

---

[1] A. W. Singham, *The Hero and the Crowd in a Colonial Polity*, 1968, p. 71.
[2] Harold Cruse, *The Crisis of the Negro Intellectual*, 1967, p. 435.
[3] Clyde K. Picon, letter, 19 July, in *Trinidad Guardian*, 31 July 1967.
[4] Lewis, 'Race Relations in Britain', p. 79.
[5] Cruse, *The Crisis of the Negro Intellectual*, p. 135.
[6] C. L. R. James, 'Introduction', in Errol Hill, ed., *Caribbean Plays*, Vol. II, 1965,
pp. v–viii, ref. p. vi. See also Lamming, 'Caribbean Literature'; Morris, 'Some West
Indian Problems of Audience'; Harris, 'Impressions after Seven Years', p. 18.

CHAPTER VII

Racial and National Identity

A striking feature of West Indian identity is the low esteem in which it is locally held. West Indians at home often wish they were not West Indian. This desire permeates Caribbean life not only because life is for many inflexibly hard, but also because West Indians genuinely believe their identity can be altered. The wish is often realized in imagination; they easily persuade themselves they are something else. This delusion is most prevalent in the elite and middle class, but the desire extends throughout the social order; both Kingston suburbanites and West Kingston Ras Tafari believe themselves to be citizens of some remote land. Even for non-Rastas conventional allegiance entails private dissent. Instead of rejecting the system, West Indians deny their own identity. Indeed, the greatest conformists have the strongest yearning not to be West Indian.

West Indian self-negation has two principal components, colour and nationality. As a consequence of slavery and colonialism, black and coloured Creoles strive to be both white and European. These two goals are intimately interrelated in origin but differ in their rationale and effect. The structural significance of colour and colonialism were explored in earlier chapters; their internalization and psychological consequences will now be surveyed.

RACIAL IDENTITY

When blackness meant slavery and whiteness meant mastery, it was little wonder that blacks wished to be white. Many Caribbean slaves, like colonized people anywhere, sought to improve their lot by copying their masters. 'The first ambition of the colonized', in Memmi's phrase, 'is to become equal to that splendid model and to resemble him to the point of disappearing in him.'[1] The West Indian slave could not achieve such convergence but often found emulation essential for survival, if not for self-advantage. To imitate whites was the only path to success in a white-dominated society. 'The white man was superior in every way; . . . to ameliorate ourselves . . . we had to ape him as closely as

[1] Albert Memmi, *The Colonizer and the Colonized* [1957], p. 120.

possible—do what he did, like what he liked, wear what he wore'. The process is now less deliberate, but it still goes on. 'We think white alright, but unconsciously. . . . Our minds are all enslaved and emasculated by the values of our colonial fathers.'[1] A small-islander asserts that 'if the Creator offered the black Dominican the opportunity, . . . eight out of every ten black persons in Dominica would want to become white.'[2]

Some dark West Indians seem deeply convinced that they *are* white. Until recently, according to Fanon, 'no Antillean found it possible to think of himself as a Negro':

I am a white man. For unconsciously I distrust what is black in me, that is, the whole of my being. I am a Negro—but of course I do not know it, simply because I am one. . . . My mother sings me French love songs in which there is never a word about Negroes. When I disobey, when I make too much noise, I am told 'stop acting like a nigger'.[3]

Expatriation sometimes reinforces delusions of whiteness. Coloured children of West Indian descent in England tend to regard themselves as white and to be aggressive toward non-whites. 'I really did not know that I was coloured until I was twelve years old', relates an Anglo–West Indian; 'if I saw that I was not as pale as some girls it did not mean anything to me.'[4] The delusion can endure past childhood. 'We white men', a dark-skinned Surinamese minister reprimanded his congregation in Holland; 'what are *we* doing for our black people?'[5]

Race and colour play a major role in West Indian mental illness. Martinicans dream of being turned white by magic. Hallucinations of French Antilleans in Paris concern racial segregation, exclusion, and pursuit, with whites the victorious enemy. Africans and Haitians, more willing to accept their own blackness, are prone to blame persecution on nationality rather than race.[6]

[1] Swinburne Lestrade, 'Carnival Princess, Slavery, Decolonialised Minds', letter in *Dominica Herald*, 15 March 1969, p. 8.

[2] 'Black Power Say!!!' *Dominica Star*, 10 May 1969, pp. 6–7. In Haiti too, 'there is probably not a single member of the élite who does not feel as if half life's problems would disappear if only one were white' (James G. Leyburn, *The Haitian People*, 1966, p. 286).

[3] Frantz Fanon, *Black Skin, White Masks*, 1967, pp. 153, 191.

[4] Quoted in Donald Hinds, *Journey to an Illusion: The West Indian in Britain*, 1966, p. 55. See also Christopher Bagley, 'Migration, Race and Mental Health: A Review of Some Recent Research', *Race*, Vol. IX, 1967–8, pp. 343–56, ref. p. 348.

[5] Quoted in Era Bell Thompson, 'Surinam: Multiracial Paradise at the Crossroads', *Ebony* (New York), February 1967, p. 120.

[6] François H. M. Raveau, 'Caste and Race in the Psychodynamics of Acculturation', in Anthony de Reuck and Julie Knight, eds., *Caste and Race: Comparative Approaches*, 1967, pp. 266–75, ref. p. 268; Raveau, 'An Outline of the Role of Color in Adaptation Phenomena', in 'Color and Race', *Daedalus*, Vol. 96, No. 2, 1967, pp. 376–89, ref. pp. 380–1.

Because West Indian society is largely black-skinned but white-oriented, it is not only the mentally ill who are confused about colour. A dark five-year-old Martinican school-girl empties her inkwell over a white boy's head to turn him black, but she soon learns it is better to be white. Unable to blacken the world, she tries 'in her own body and in her own mind, to bleach it. To start, she would become a laundress. . . . Whiten the race, save the race . . . make sure it will be white.'[1]

In white eyes, however, blacks cannot become white. Racial immutability bars folk from elite as it did slave from master, colonized from colonizer. The black, like the 'native', is urged to assimilate, but his efforts meet 'with disdain from the colonial masters. . . . He can never succeed in becoming identified with the colonizer, nor even in copying his role correctly.'[2]

Black West Indian efforts to become white are doomed to perpetual failure, but unlike Memmi's colonial archetype, the West Indian seldom gives up the struggle to integrate. Yet to emulate is to invite rejection. In the French Antilles, 'school inspectors and government functionaries . . . poured every effort into the programs that would make the Negro a white man. In the end, they dropped him and told him, "You have an indisputable complex of dependence on the white man."'[3]

The non-white status-seeker suffers constant anxiety about his acceptability. Insecurity leads him to exaggerate 'white' tastes and to conceal even from himself preferences that do not conform. Social climbers are adjudged to lose their true selves; to get into the charmed circle 'they give up warm relationships for those that bring status, give up identity for image, turn from cooperation to a crab-barrel rivalry'.[4] The achievement is scored as incompatible with lasting happiness. 'Ah know you would mek a good doctor, me boy', a mother tells her eight-year-old. 'But dat not for you. . . . Your skin black and you poor.' Even professional success would never get him into the country club 'no matter how big a shot he became. The very most he could hope for socially was an invitation to Government House. . . . He would be smiled at and flattered, but he would know that . . . behind his back they would sigh and say what an awful nuisance

[1] Fanon, *Black Skin, White Masks*, pp. 45–7 (referring to Mayotte Capécia, *Je suis martiniquaise*, 1948).

[2] Memmi, *The Colonizer and the Colonized*, p. 124.

[3] Fanon, *Black Skin, White Masks*, p. 216.

[4] Joyce L. Sparer, 'A Composite Picture . . .: Attitudes towards Race in Guyanese Literature, Final Instalment', *Georgetown Sunday Chronicle*, 18 June 1967. See also Fernando Henriques, *Family and Colour in Jamaica*, 1953, p. 45; Christopher Nicole, *White Boy*, 1966; Aristide R. Zolberg, 'Frantz Fanon: A Gospel for the Damned', *Encounter*, No. 27, November 1966, pp. 56–63.

it was having to make oneself pleasant to these parvenu niggers.'[1]

To outsiders West Indians often give the impression of taking colour distinctions for granted, but most in fact give them painstaking consideration. Touring the Caribbean, a Trinidadian remarked 'how deep in nearly every West Indian, high and low, were the prejudices of race; how often these prejudices were rooted in self-contempt; and how much important action they prompted.'[2] Prejudice against darkness prevails throughout Caribbean society. 'West Indian leaders are carbon copies of the European slave master', complains an emigrant. 'But what they have retained are his worst vices, . . . the kind of values which causes a West Indian mother to tell her fair-skinned daughter: "Don't marry a dark man"'.[3] These attitudes have hardly changed since slavery, a Vincentian points out. 'Then as now people were obsessed with skin colour and shade. People would go to ridiculous lengths in retracing a family tree to see whether . . . a tear-drop of white blood flowed in their veins. Today it is the same; people are no longer Black, they are coffee-brown, they are not Negro, they are mixed'.[4] West Indians in New York, too, 'have . . . spent their lives trying not to be black. They proclaim their Chinese, Indian, English, or Portuguese blood, but they never give equal time to the glaring African strain.'[5]

Awareness of colour varies with class. The elite take for granted their own identity as whites; colour becomes an overt issue among them only in gross transgressions of the social code. Nor is colour *per se* a constant concern in peasant communities. But for the Caribbean middle class colour is the crucial determinant of status and suffuses most relationships. A Jamaican shows what colour prejudice could mean in family life:

Colour- and shade-consciousness was a family affliction. . . . The black forbears of my mother's family were spoken of regretfully and as if they belonged to a dim distant past. . . . In my mother's family the black ancestor could not be disowned because his marks were obvious among them. But in my father's family . . . he was never mentioned; we turned our backs resolutely against him.

Her great-grandparents were part Scottish, part Jewish, she was told.

[1] Edgar Mittelholzer, *A Morning at the Office*, 1950, pp. 7, 156.
[2] V. S. Naipaul, *The Middle Passage*, 1962, p. 230.
[3] 'Wanted—A Leader', *Flamingo*, No. 6, February 1962, p. 1.
[4] K. R. V. John, 'Footnotes on Slavery', *Flambeau*, No. 3, January 1966, pp. 10–14, ref. p. 13. Post-bellum American mulattoes were similarly renowned for 'their aptness is tracing their ancestry . . . to the times of William the Silent and bring you up to 18 so and so to show you how illustrious is his lineage and pedigree' (John E. Bruce, quoted in E. Franklin Frazier, *Black Bourgeoisie*, 1965, p. 197).
[5] Orde Coombs, 'West Indians in New York: Moving beyond the Limbo Pole', *New York Magazine*, 13 July 1970, pp. 28–32, ref. p. 32.

What the other part of their racial inheritance was, was never mentioned. It was without doubt African, slave, black—unspeakable. . . . 'Pass over the black faces. Greet the brown face! Ah, a white face! Gaze upon it with pleasure and admiration!' . . . So I disintegrated myself. . . . I could not change my brown face, but I was pleased only with a white face and wanted to forget the black faces altogether.[1]

Middle-class obsession with colour is exemplified in the legendary remark that at Government House one used to be sure of meeting no one darker than oneself. Now that blacks are not only guests but governors, some of the lighter skinned stay at home instead. In the presence of the lower orders, they walk 'round and round with their heads . . . in the air as if they were staring at a distant mountain and sniffing its strange air.'[2] Whiteness preoccupies even territories lacking white Creoles. Mulattoes in Dominica are said to 'impersonate white, hate their [own] colour, . . . and criticise their Black Brothers.'[3] And in Haiti 'nothing has changed' since the 1791 Revolution, a recent exile declares. 'The Haitian mulatto considers himself equal to the white who in turn looks upon him as a larva.'[4]

Hyperbole aside, colour consciousness varies in degree and import from place to place. As a Trinidadian recounts,

one of the futile skills unconsciously acquired by anyone who has grown up in the West Indies is the ability to distinguish persons of Negro ancestry. I thought I possessed this skill to a reasonable degree until I went to Martinique. Time and again I was told that a white-skinned, light-eyed, straight-haired person I had just met was really 'coloured'. . . . Trinidad is more humane and allows people who look reasonably white to pass as white. [But] . . . this generosity can occasionally impose on the Trinidadian a burden of deception which the Martiniquan, who openly calls himself 'coloured' because the whole island knows he is only fifteen-sixteenths white, never has to bear. . . . Nevertheless there is in Trinidad an intention of tolerance and a general laxity which would appal the Martiniquan. . . . No social prejudice, no social sanction really matters in Trinidad: standards are too diverse and society is split into too many cliques. . . . The division of Martinique society into white (of certifiable purity), mulatto and black is accepted as valid and unalterable by all sections. . . . Negro blood is like an ineradicable commonness.[5]

[1] Joyce Gladwell, *Brown Face, Big Master*, 1969, pp. 23–5.
[2] Trevor Yearwood, 'Maureen', *Bim*, Vol. 13, No. 50, January–June 1970, pp. 96–109, ref. p. 98.
[3] 'Selfish Black Brother', letter signed 'Proud to Be Black', *Dominica Herald*, 17 May 1969, p. 4.
[4] Alfred Viau, *Noirs, mulâtres, blancs ou rien que du sang*, 1955, pp. 44, 62.
[5] Naipaul, *The Middle Passage*, pp. 196–8. A perceptive observer, familiar with West Indian culture and with Aimé Césaire, nevertheless discerned in Martinique 'fewer evidences of a colour bar or of racial discrimination' than in any other stratified Caribbean society (Patrick Leigh Fermor, *The Traveller's Tree: A Journey through the Caribbean Islands*, 1950, pp. 51–2).

An hierarchy of accepted worth accompanies this colour division. In the text of a Martinican song,

> The white man does call his woman *chérie*;
> The mulatto does call his woman *dou-dou*;
> The nigger does call his woman a stinking bitch.
> Nigger ain't have manners, for truth.

> White man eating out of porcelain plate;
> Mulatto eating out of earthenware;
> Nigger eating out of calabash.
> Nigger ain't have manners, for truth.

Prejudice of shade continues to afflict West Indians who move to less racially stratified Latin-American societies. Speaking for second-generation Turks Islands immigrants in the Dominican Republic, an 'elderly retired Episcopalian minister, himself a lighter-skinned West Indian . . . expressed official opposition to the appointment of a Negro West Indian descendant to a parish . . . because of his dark skin color. The parishioners themselves, he reported, "resented a black Simon."'[1]

Photographs, physical grooming, and beauty contests reflect the West Indian white bias. Black Jamaicans of a generation ago considered a picture of the Negro face itself 'a reminder of a shameful past, an inferior, primitive culture,' a local novelist concluded.[2] Country and city people alike still express disappointment with their photographs: a young Jamaican woman destroys a picture of herself 'because it is printed too black';[3] a Government Minister explodes in fury when he sees his official photograph—'God, man, why you make me so black?'[4] Local newspapers learn to flatter by lightening likenesses of important black men.

Despising blackness, West Indians seek to expunge it from their features. A generation ago cosmetic whitening was rare in the Caribbean simply because West Indians lacked the technical resources. But now hair straightening is practically universal even in rural areas. Almost every West Indian woman 'fixes' her hair with a hot comb; in the most remote islands her first luxury is a more elaborate treatment. Girls appearing at a 1970 carnival celebration in 'wave after wave of straightened, cold creamed, hot combed, stringy hair' were immortalized

---

[1] Glenn Hendricks, *The British West Indian Immigrant Group of Puerto Plata*, 1967, p. 30.

[2] John Hearne, 'European Heritage and Asian Influence in Jamaica', in John Hearne and Rex Nettleford, *Our Heritage*, pp. 7–34, ref. p. 25. See also Madeline Kerr, *Personality and Conflict in Jamaica*, 1963, p. 99.

[3] Rex Nettleford, 'National Identity and Attitudes to Race in Jamaica', *Race*, Vol. VII, 1965–6, pp. 59–72, ref. p. 70.

[4] Colin McGlashan, 'The Two Jamaicas', *Sunday Observer Review*, 23 November 1969, p. 25.

as 'The Glory That Was Grease'.[1] The 'Afro' style popular in black America is much less known in the Caribbean and is viewed askance by West Indians embarrassed by the exposure of 'bad' hair.

Skin-bleaching creams and lotions, introduced from America during the Second World War, are widely used, as are peroxide and face powder. The West Indian who in the nineteenth century was seen as 'burning to be a white man' now bleaches instead.[2] Rural women visiting town are often so heavily powdered they appear ghost-like. West Indians are less ambivalent than Americans about whitening agents. In the United States black is now beautiful, but bleaching and hairdressing remain multimillion dollar industries. By contrast, few West Indians profess to admire the 'natural' look; their ideal types are avowedly white-oriented.

White aesthetic standards put black West Indians at a disadvantage in most realms of life. Grenada's dark-skinned Governor, recalling her local convent school days, remarks that 'Grenada then knew nothing of colour prejudice—but discrimination was there nevertheless, of a social kind, and the ranks were pretty well closed. In plays the nuns put on, black girls were usually pixies, mulatto girls had the envied roles of fairies.' Twenty years ago, a Dominican retorts, 'black girls like myself could not even get parts as pixies unless their parents were well-to-do.'[3]

In the West Indies black is not yet thought beautiful. Colour ambivalence surfaces periodically in beauty contests, where internalized white values and new 'mixed blood' maxims are both cruelly at odds with the preponderantly dark-skinned population. Business sponsors who clothe and chaperone contestants aim to satisfy traditional colour tastes; donors at a Trinidad beauty contest in the late 1950s asserted that the island was 'not "ready" to have a coloured girl serve as its ambassador abroad . . . [and] threatened to withdraw their prizes if blacks were chosen.'[4] Contests were subsequently desegregated by government fiat, but this resulted in little more than 'putting each year a lonely Miss Ebony into the creamy flocks of the Carnival Queens.'[5] In Dominica the selection of a white carnival princess in

[1] 'This University Carnival', *Tussle*, Vol. 2, No. 2, February 1970, pp. 8–9. See also Bunny Cunningham, 'Women, How about Natural Hair?' *Scope*, Vol. 3, No. 1 [November 1968], p. 10.

[2] John, 'Footnotes on Slavery', p. 14. 'Burning to be a white man' is a paraphrase of Anthony Trollope, *The West Indies and the Spanish Main*, 1860, p. 56.

[3] Hilda Bynoe, quoted in 'Dame Hilda: Government Is a Family Affair', *Dominica Star*, 26 April 1969, p. 15; 'Discrimination', letter signed 'Congolese', *Dominica Star*, 3 May 1969, pp. 12, 16.

[4] Selwyn Douglas Ryan, 'Decolonization in a Multi-Racial Society: A Case Study of Trinidad and Tobago' [1967], p. 217.

[5] Adrian Espinet and Jacques Farmer, 'Pussonal Nonarchy: The Paradox of Power in Trinidad', *Tapia*, No. 3, 16 November 1969, p. 6.

1969 aroused great resentment and complaints that the significance of Carnival was destroyed. 'Dominica is a black country beyond any doubt. Our representatives (be they Carnival Queen, Princess, Premier, Governor, etc.) have to be black—not just "any colour". . . . I curdle in understanding pity at the fact that my Carnival Princess 1969 is a white girl'.[1]

In Jamaican beauty contests black girls have seldom appeared among the finalists. The judges' rejection of a dark favourite with an 'Afro' hairdo in the 1967 Miss Jamaica contest evoked public demands that a dark girl be given a chance; that the only 'representative' Jamaican type failed to place among the winners seemed a sad reflection on national identity. 'The rejection of the huge masses of blacks here in the annual Beauty Contest and through the writings and comments of some politicians, intellectuals, and reporters has been deeply damaging', it was said, to 'the morale of the country.'[2]

One surrogate for whiteness is sexual conquest. 'Marrying light' goes beyond taste and status, even beyond aesthetics; it is a mode of self-approval. Fanon details the wish-fulfilling fantasy of a black West Indian about his white inamorata: 'By loving me she proves that I am worthy of white love. I am loved like a white man. I am a white man. . . . I marry white culture, white beauty, white whiteness. When my restless hands caress those white breasts, they grasp white civilization and dignity and make them mine.'[3] West Indians abroad often 'marry persons of a class or a culture inferior to their own whom they would not have chosen as spouses in their own race and whose chief asset seems to be the assurance that the partner will achieve denaturalization and . . . "deracialization".'[4]

Colour constrains feeling among the folk too. 'I could never love a black man', asserts a dark Jamaican. 'Black and black breed picknies like monkeys. I always want my picknies to be as light as possible.'[5] No level of relationship is immune from consideration of colour. 'Every woman in the Antilles, whether in a casual flirtation or a serious

[1] Lestrade, 'Carnival Princess, Slavery, Decolonialised Minds', p. 8. See also 'Carnival Princess Must Be West Indian, Say Students' (letter), and 'Carbon Copy Carnival Again', *Dominica Herald*, 15 February 1969, pp. 5, 8, and 2, 10, respectively.

[2] Alva Ramsay, '"Jamaica Will Become Fundamentally a Black Society" Says Sir Philip Sherlock', *West Indian Sportsman*, November–December 1969, p. 28; H. S. Burns, 'Revamp Festival', letter in *Spotlight*, Vol. 28, Nos. 10 and 11, October–November 1967, p. 3. See also *Jamaican Weekly Gleaner*, 16–23 August 1967, especially p. 27.

[3] Fanon, *Black Skin, White Masks*, p. 63.

[4] Louis-T. Achille, *Rythmes du monde*, 1949, p. 113, quoted in Fanon, *Black Skin, White Masks*, p. 71. See also Mervyn Morris, 'Feeling, Affection, Respect', in Henri Tajfel and John L. Dawson, eds., *Disappointed Guests: Essays by African, Asian, and West Indian Students*, 1965, pp. 5–26.

[5] Kerr, *Personality and Conflict in Jamaica*, p. 96.

affair, is determined to select the least black of the men. . . . A great number of girls from Martinique . . . admitted to me with complete candor—completely white candor—that they would find it impossible to marry black men.'[1]

Coloured and black West Indians not only admire whiteness, they follow whites in linking blackness with poverty, laziness, stupidity, and vice. 'The black man was always pictured as a villain', a Jamaican journalist recalls his school-days. 'The only black picture I ever saw was in Standard III Royal Reader. . . . The artist made that face so doggoned ugly that we boys . . . taunted each other with it. The next most notable black picture I saw . . . was of Satan.'[2] Most Dominicans 'still conform to the thought pattern where "naygur" means "bad" and "white" means "good".'[3] Everyday circumstances are minutely compartmentalized in 'black' and 'white' traits. Colour frustration is endemic: the more a non-white West Indian accepts European evaluations, the more he rejects his own blackness.

Self-contempt is the most damaging consequence of West Indian internalization of white values. 'It is normal for the Antillean to be anti-Negro', according to Fanon, because 'in the collective unconscious, . . . one is a Negro to the degree that one is wicked, sloppy, malicious, instinctual. . . . If I order my life like that of a moral man, I simply am not a Negro.'[4] The typical Creole poet is 'crammed full of white morality, white culture, white education, and white prejudices,' another Martinican notes. 'He takes a special pride in the fact that a white man can read his book without ever guessing the color of his skin.' Shorn of sensuous images that might seem African, his writing reflects a bygone Europe; 'the bourgeois of the Antilles refuses to adopt any poetic model that a hundred years of white experimentation have not sanctioned.'[5]

Self-contempt characterizes the black Jamaican who is glad to see her child 'marry brown, and forget the roots'; folk who praise the college graduate because he 'use the white people dem word good good'; the maid who would never work for black people; the black watchman who claims authorities told him not to let any black people pass; the industrial worker who resents his black supervisor yet insists 'there is no hope for the black man'; the black woman who supports a white candidate, 'for no black man can help me in this yah country

[1] Fanon, *Black Skin, White Masks*, pp. 47–8.
[2] Evon Blake, 'The Black Man Must Find Himself' [1963–4], in *The Best of Evon Blake*, pp. 34–5.
[3] 'Black Power Say!!!', pp. 6–7.
[4] Fanon, *Black Skin, White Masks*, pp. 191–2.
[5] Étienne Léro, *Légitime défense*, 1932, quoted in Norman R. Shapiro, 'Negro Poets of the French Caribbean: A Sampler', *Antioch Review*, Vol. XXVII, 1967, pp. 211–28, ref. pp. 212–13.

these days.'[1] To disclaim one's own blackness requires a more emphatic rejection of other blacks. Rural West Indians still reflect the old imperial view of black incapacity. 'A Government is seen as a complex organization needing the white man's "big brain" to run it efficiently', whereas the Negro is said to assert authority 'so that no one will be confused about his status because of the color of his skin.'[2] The prevalence of such stereotypes justifies the Trinidad black-power leader's response to a suggestion that 'black men with white minds' be expelled from the movement: 'If we got rid of all the black men like that here, we wouldn't have anybody'.[3]

Colour schizophrenia leads West Indians into remarkable self-contradictions. Thus the negroid appearance of the statue of the nineteenth-century coloured martyr, George William Gordon, elicited a black Jamaican's criticism: 'if he wasn't a black man, they wouldn't have made him so black.'[4] Ambivalence is habitual; West Indians continually alternate between receiving racial hostility and expressing it, being victim and being offender. 'One day a person will be bitter and anti-white' and another day 'concerned with fears and dislike only of people darker than himself. In some constellations he is the almost white man with white ideals, in others he is the dark man resenting white domination.'[5] Perplexed and insecure, West Indians 'identify with the aggressor but . . . at the same time . . . [are] consumed with rage against their oppressors'.[6]

To face one's own blackness, the dark Hyde to the white Jekyll, can be the fearsome experience the poet Damas describes.

> So many times I'm frightened by my consciousness of race
> and like a dog at night
> baying at some
> impending death
> I always feel ready to foam with rage
> against the things around me
> against the things that keep me
> forever from being
> a man.[7]

Imprisoned in self-hatred, the West Indian may be compulsively phobic. 'Find me rage and I will raze the colony', a poet puts

[1] Nettleford, 'National Identity and Attitudes to Race in Jamaica', pp. 69–70.
[2] Allen S. Ehrlich, 'East Indian Cane Workers in Jamaica', 1969, pp. 182–3.
[3] Geddes Grainger, quoted in *Trinidad Guardian*, 27 February 1970, p. 15.
[4] George Mikes, *Not by Sun Alone*, 1967, p. 57.
[5] Kerr, *Personality and Conflict in Jamaica*, p. 96. See also Gladwell, *Brown Face, Big Master*, p. 111.
[6] A. W. Singham, *The Hero and the Crowd in a Colonial Polity*, 1968, p. 90.
[7] Léon Damas, 'So Many Times', quoted in Shapiro, 'Negro Poets of the French Caribbean', p. 223.

it.[1] But rage is sometimes exaggerated for effect, and the professionally angry black makes an easy target of satire in small West Indian societies.

'I don't know whether any of us really knew Mr. Blackwhite,' I said. 'He was a man who moved with the times.' . . . [His] book . . . was called *I Hate You*, with the sub-title *One Man's Search for Identity*. . . . 'I am a man without identity. Hate has consumed my identity. My personality has been distorted by hate. My hymns have not been hymns of praise, but of hate. How terrible to be Caliban, you say. But I say, how tremendous.'[2]

West Indians who vainly seek a white identity avoid other racial attributions. Following emancipation former slaves sought to obliterate public references to colour. Census-takers classifying race were sometimes repulsed with violence. Folk felt that to be listed as 'black' perpetuated racial inequities and even invited re-enslavement. The instructions warning Jamaica's 1960 census enumerators that 'at all costs, you should not argue with a man about his racial origin',[3] reflect a similar anxiety. 'What can be the possible point of asking this question' abour 'race', asked a Trinidadian apropos the 1970 census, 'unless it is to supply the politicians, semi-intellectuals and other agitators with some phoney figures which will be misused to draw erroneous conclusions[?] . . . The whole country should simply answer "not stated". . . . Thereby we should prove to the world that race and colour is "IRRELEVANT" in Trinidad and Tobago.'[4] Racial euphemism succeeds euphemism, each outworn by an accumulation of evil connotations. 'African', 'Negro', 'black', 'coloured', and 'Creole' are in turn adopted as polite to be later abandoned as derogatory.

West Indians resist being pinpointed at all. No possible designation would be flattering to them; better the chaotic medley of

> Black brown yellow pink and cream
>
> *　　　*　　　*
>
> Our English hymns creole proverbs
> Steel band calypso rock-n-roll
> Anancy-stories obeah and Christ

than to be fixed in 'one quick-drying definition.'[5]

A Guyanese novelist maintains that 'only the utterly vulgar would

---

[1] Edward Brathwaite, 'Negus', *CQ*, Vol. 15, Nos. 2 and 3, June–September 1969, pp. 130–2, ref. p. 132. See also Dennis Solomon, 'Derek Walcott's *Dream on Monkey Mountain*', *Tapia*, No. 7, 19 April 1970, p. 6.

[2] V. S. Naipaul, *A Flag on the Island*, 1967, p. 154.

[3] *1960 Population Census—Jamaica: Enumerators Manual and Visitation Record*, West Indies Census 3, n.d., mimeo., p. 26.

[4] 'Race and Colour Totally Irrelevant', letter signed 'Gulliver', *Trinidad Guardian*, 25 March 1970, p. 12.

[5] Mervyn Morris, 'To a West Indian Definer', in G. R. Coulthard, ed., *Caribbean Literature: An Anthology*, 1966, pp. 86–7.

raise his voice to discuss the racial origins of his neighbor.'[1] In the French Antilles, no statistics deal with colour, no one of tact even mentions it.

One says nothing at all, neither Negro, nor black, nor coloured, nor dark, *ni Martin ni son chien.* . . . The circumlocutions are comic. Taking care that the maid and coloured employees are not within hearing. . . , one leans toward one's questioner, and whispers: 'Him? He is like that . . .'. One designates at the same time an object of appropriate colour, a black watch-band, a telephone, a wooden table. . . . And everyone understands. . . . One also avoids saying that someone is white, because this would be to mark the essential difference.[2]

Jamaicans use a different style, combining colour designations to soften their impact; Radio Jamaica on several occasions has described missing persons as being of 'lightdark' complexion.[3]

West Indians are as sensitive about their attitudes as about their identities. Explicit questions elicit misleading answers; indirect queries are met—or evaded—with cautious circumspection. 'We like to say that colour does not matter to us', a friend told me in 1960. 'We know very well that this is not true. But we do not want to admit it to an outsider or to have anyone else suggest it to us.' On the occasion of Jamaican independence, when a foreign reporter asked 'whether the fact that in a predominantly black country the Cabinet was not predominantly black indicated any control by a special group', a Minister replied acidly that the Government was 'less worried about the colour problem than the correspondent seemed to be.'[4] The Trinidad Government likewise strove to explain the 1970 black-power riots in terms of economic rather than racial disaffection.[5] At the 1969 inquiry into alleged discrimination at the Trinidad Country Club, criticism of the club's social set-up was dismissed as stemming from a (racial) chip on the shoulder. The fact that only fifty of the 6,000 club members were black did not, the inquiry concluded, warrant the 'facile assumption that there is a colour bar'.[6]

In the West Indies to 'talk about "the colour question" or "race relations" is to pick a way through thorns while walking on eggshells,

---

[1] Edgar Mittelholzer, 'Color, Class and Letters', *Nation* (New York), 17 January 1959, p. 55.

[2] Jean Raspail, *Secouons le cocotier*, 1966, pp. 45–6. For comparable reticence among the American black bourgeoisie, see Nathan Hare, *The Black Anglo-Saxons*, 1970, p. 68.

[3] O. G. Harding, letter in *Jamaica Daily Gleaner*, 9 March 1970, p. 12.

[4] Robert Lightbourne, quoted in *Jamaica Weekly Gleaner*, 10 August 1962, p. 12.

[5] This is not to imply that they were mistaken, but merely to note that they felt it in their best interests to emphasize economic rather than racial causes.

[6] Trinidad Government, *Report of the Commission Appointed by His Excellency the Governor-General to Investigate Allegations of Discriminatory Practices by the Management of the Trinidad Country Club*, 1969, pp. 24, 30.

as even the commonest adjectives of description appear to bear allusive barbs.' But to ignore it is no better; for 'too great a circumspection . . . may also arouse hostility'.[1] The dilemma recurs throughout the Caribbean. 'The mere mention of colour on the part of the stranger is liable to put the average Guianese on the defensive', a visitor found, but 'the effort of avoiding pitfalls can result in a stiltedness that may in itself be considered indirectly insulting.'[2]

Even from insiders, questions about colour may meet open hostility. A Haitian describes colour prejudice as 'a shameful disease of which nobody dares to speak but which is the cause of a sure death.'[3] And a Jamaican's campus survey elicited vehement reactions; many undergraduates refused to discuss colour at all. 'Why don't they leave it alone?' asked one. 'That way people would be less conscious of it and the problem would solve itself.'[4]

Colour awareness is a corrosive and enervating preoccupation that hampers West Indian efforts to cope with most other problems. 'The individual himself never offends, it is always someone else who does something to him or "puts something on him." Disaster is never self-caused but always emanates from some external agency'.[5] Since those in control are white or light, discrimination is assumed to play a major role in misfortune. 'The black man in Jamaica is lucky', averred a local columnist. 'If the white man fails, he can only blame himself. If the black man fails, he can always blame colour prejudice. Now that the whites are so few . . . some of our more shiftless types are blaming the brown man.'[6] Blacks echo this accusation. 'Jamaica's main psychological problem is . . . the attitude of the black population towards themselves'; the Jamaican needs 'to develop a sense and feeling of equality as against aggressive unfounded superiority. . . . He has spent too much time being BLACK instead of being a MAN.'[7]

Preoccupation with race leads many West Indians today, as in the past, to attribute every action to it. 'Anything that is done pro or con, either by white or coloured people, [is] . . . nearly never attributed to this or that good or bad feeling, idea, intention, or cause, but to racial hatred or the question of colour.'[8] Haitian colour complexes are said

[1] A. P. Thornton, 'Aspects of West Indian Society', *International Journal*, Vol. XV, 1960, pp. 113–21, ref. p. 113.

[2] Zahra Freeth, *Run Softly Demerara*, 1960, p. 62.

[3] Viau, *Noirs, mulâtres, blancs ou rien que du sang*, p. 62.

[4] H. Orlando Patterson, 'The Social Structure of a University Hall of Residence', *Pelican*, Vol. IX, No. 3, March 1962, pp. 22–39, ref. p. 30.

[5] Kerr, *Personality and Conflict in Jamaica*, p. 167.

[6] Thomas Wright, 'Candidly Yours', *Jamaica Daily Gleaner*, 25 April 1961, p. 12.

[7] Evon Blake, 'Blackman Time Now', and 'The Black Man Must Find Himself' [1963–4], both in *The Best of Evon Blake*, pp. 33–4.

[8] *The Dominican*, 15 April 1897.

to have 'caused every crime from Toussaint L'Ouverture' to the present.[1] Just as all issues may be judged as racial, so any criticism may be imputed to prejudice. To avoid saying anything that might be felt as a racial slur, West Indians often refrain from any comment whatever. Inadequacies, even affronts, are passed over in silence, lest the response be misconstrued. Colour consciousness thus makes plain speaking impossible and stultifies constructive criticism. 'You know that the person to whom you are talking is quite convinced that if you snub him, it is because of his colour, and not because he is merely tedious'. So you 'smile as sweetly as you can and let it pass. Which is bad for you, for you are in a false position, and bad for him, because... it's such a convenient way of avoiding self-knowledge.'[2]

The public airing of colour complaints strikes a few West Indians as a sign of progress. Formerly, one 'seldom if ever heard talk and protest about this colour thing', a Jamaican asserted;

for when something is accepted—accepted so deeply that to drag it up to the surface would be unbearably painful—nobody talks about it. . . . It's only when the pain gets less, when you see an end to it just around the corner, that you dare to drag it into the open and face it. That's why we talk about it endlessly in Jamaica today. For we are, today, nearer to beating it than anywhere else in the world.[3]

By contrast, a prominent Trinidadian considered it odd that 'awareness of disparity in pigmentation is greatest at a time when everyone is most eager to disavow this kind of discrimination.'[4] But straightforward views on race are not only hard to elicit, they are seldom consistent. 'To discuss racism in a West Indian context is to become hopelessly confused', avers another Trinidadian. 'One gets lost in a mass of contradictions, and vacillation seems to be the rule of the day.'[5]

Many multi-racial societies exhibit colour ambivalence not unlike the West Indian. Langston Hughes's 'high-class' Negro who had married 'the lightest woman he could find' and sought 'Nordic manners, Nordic faces, Nordic hair, Nordic art (if any), and an Episcopal heaven'[6] still is part of the American scene, both North and South.

---

[1] Viau, *Noirs, mulâtres, blancs ou rien que du sang*, p. 62.
[2] Thomas Wright, 'Candidly Yours', *Jamaica Daily Gleaner*, 4 May 1962, p. 4.
[3] Ibid., 25 April 1961, p. 12.
[4] Albert Gomes, 'West Indies Facing Moment of Truth?' *Trinidad Guardian*, 1 October 1961, p. 8.
[5] Elliott Bastien, 'The Weary Road to Whiteness and the Hasty Retreat into Nationalism', in Tajfel and Dawson, eds., *Disappointed Guests*, pp. 38–54, ref. pp. 38–9.
[6] Langston Hughes, 'The Negro Artist and the Racial Mountain', *Nation*, 23 June 1926, pp. 692–4, in Francis L. Broderick and August Meier, eds., *Negro Protest Thought in the Twentieth Century*, 1965, pp. 92–7, ref. p. 93.

Notwithstanding the recent upsurge of black pride, white ideals remain ingrained long after they are consciously proscribed. But even before black separatism became a significant force, rigid polarization made 'whiteness' too remote for black Americans to aim for. 'Most dark Negroes', concluded a pioneering study of the Chicago ghetto, 'do not sit around wishing they were light.'[1] By contrast with the fraternal colour-blindness of black Americans, awareness of shade prolongs colour striving in West Indian society.

They continue to insist, proudly, that they are a 'mixture'. When they are confronted with the physicality of blackness, a fact so lasting, so incontrovertible, they take hope in the possible deliverance of their children from this stigma. 'Put a little cream in your coffee,' the black Barbadian mother tells her educated, unmarried son, and he knows that she is not talking about beverages. . . . Although jet-black men politically rule the islands and administer justice, their adulation of the white mystique remains formidable.[2]

NATIONAL IDENTITY

West Indians are as uneasy about their national as their racial identity. 'They have no country of their own,' wrote Trollope a century ago, but were only 'a servile people in a foreign land.'[3] They remain rootless still; as an island novelist says, it 'was the only home they know, an' it was no home.'[4] They find little to identify with in the Caribbean past, 'except the haunting recollection of each passing moment', a sense of coming 'from nowhere worth mentioning. . . . I cannot say whether I am civilized or savage, standing as I do outside of race, outside of culture, outside of history, outside of any value'.[5] Those who recognize no local roots resent the term 'native' all the more as signifying not indigenous but poor, primitive, black, 'African'. Despising his own origins, the West Indian came to feel he existed only as an outsider—'outside the master's big house on the plantation; . . . outside the pleasure, pomp and plenty in the city, outside power and rights in the society.'[6]

This sense of inferiority, involving both colour and nationality, is part of the colonial heritage.

We saw ourselves through other eyes. The newspapers, the books, the comics, the cinema, all showed us ourselves as second-class people. All the evidence

---

[1] St. Clair Drake and Horace R. Cayton, *Black Metropolis: A Study of Negro Life in a Northern City* [1945], Vol. II, p. 502.

[2] Coombs, 'West Indians in New York', p. 32.

[3] Trollope, *The West Indies and the Spanish Main*, p. 55.

[4] George Lamming, *Of Age and Innocence*, 1958, p. 69.

[5] H. Orlando Patterson, *An Absence of Ruins*, 1967, p. 160.

[6] Joyce L. Sparer, 'Attitudes towards "Race" in Guyanese Literature', *CS*, Vol. 8, No. 2, July 1968, pp. 23–63, ref. p. 59.

said we were nothing. . . . We became a sick people, torn by conflict about ourselves. . . . We dressed up in other people's clothes. We tried to look like them. We tried in every way to save ourselves by denying ourselves. We denied our music while we loved it. We suppressed our art. We became Afro-Saxons; black skins, white masks.

Until independence 'all groups save some Europeans were second class citizens', but afterwards matters were worse: 'the whole range of groups regarded themselves as second-class citizens. Responsibility . . . was accepted by no one.'[1] A sense of insignificance doomed West Indians to apathy. 'We knew something was wrong with our society, [but] we made no attempt to assess it. Trinidad was too unimportant and we could never be convinced of the value of reading the history of a place which was, as everyone said, only a dot on the map'.[2]

The measure of importance is European nationality. Long tutelage makes West Indians yearn for Europe. Metropolitan exemplars pervade West Indian home and school life from the earliest years; subsequent disappointments do not dim the lustre. The more contact the more disillusionment, Jahoda observes of a comparable African situation; 'Europeans ceased to inspire profound awe, as their weaknesses and limits became . . . apparent'.[3] West Indians are both more familiar with, and more tolerant of, European limitations. They assume that excellence, like eliteness, is an absentee virtue, and seldom expect it of expatriates. Their idealized European is not the Caribbean sojourner but a fictitious composite drawn from school books, magazines, films, and folklore. West Indians of all colours view themselves as more truly European than many of the Europeans they see in the Caribbean.

Identification with Europe is strongest in the French-colonized Caribbean. The black Haitian revolutionary Toussaint L'Ouverture is said to have adored France and disdained Africa. Even after six generations of independence French education and manners remain precious to the Haitian elite: 'French our institutions, French our public and civil legislation, French our literature, French our university, French the curriculum of our schools,' intoned the Haitian ambassador to Paris in 1938.[4] French remains the language of authority

---

[1] 'The Problems', *Tapia*, No. 1, 28 September 1969, p. 7.

[2] Naipaul, *The Middle Passage*, p. 42.

[3] Gustav Jahoda, *White Man: A Study of the Attitudes of Africans to Europeans in Ghana before Independence*, 1961, p. 125. See also Guy Hunter, *The New Societies of Tropical Africa*, 1962, p. 318.

[4] Quoted in C. L. R. James, *The Black Jacobins: Toussaint L'Ouverture and the San Domingo Revolution* [1938], p. 393. See also Leyburn, *The Haitian People*, pp. 109–10; Mervin C. Alleyne, review of Pradel Pompilus, *La langue française en Haïti*, in *CS*, Vol. 3, No. 4, January 1964, pp. 51–4; Sidney W. Mintz, 'Caribbean Nationhood in Anthropological Perspective', in S. Lewis and T. G. Mathews, eds., *Caribbean Integration: Papers on Social, Political and Economic Integration*, 1967, pp. 141–54, ref. p.

and of polite society; though it is now politic to extol folk speech, most educated Haitians pay patois only lip service.

Francophile and white values converge in Martinique and Guadeloupe, where the Negro is said to 'be proportionately whiter in direct ratio of his mastery of the French language.'[1] But French feeling goes beyond language and literature. 'The Antilles cannot and do not want to be anything other than French', declares a Martinican. 'They are French in spirit, in heart, in blood.'[2] Disgust with *départementalisation* has not weakened this bond even for the fiercest *autonomistes*. The mayor of Fort-de-France, Aimé Césaire, the best-known critic of colonialism, is now immensely disillusioned with *départementalisation*. Yet documentation of Martinican objections to the situation is not to be found in Fort-de-France; a recent inquirer at the municipal archives was referred to Césaire's private library *in Paris*. Antillean Frenchness and servility were both noted by De Gaulle on a visit there in 1964: 'Comme vous êtes foncés [coloured]!' he exclaimed in a speech, the pun mimicking the Creole dropping of the 'r'; 'that the audience broke into loud applause is a sign of the depth of the French Antillean malady.'[3]

Frenchness is no less strong in French Guiana. 'What a solid bulwark this South American *département* represents for France!' a recent *préfet* exclaimed. Ten thousand kilometres from the mother country, here was 'an intensely French territory, where everyone speaks, reads, and writes French, and above all thinks French with never a discordant note to trouble their sincere patriotism.'[4] Paris is the goal of ambitious youngsters in Cayenne, as in any provincial capital. A number of Guianese have won fame in the metropolis; the poet Léon Damas, the colonial administrator Felix Eboué, French Senate President Gaston Monnerville. But the homeland is not really remote; in Guiana, uninterruptedly French since the seventeenth century, one is in France, though perhaps France of 1900 rather than of 1970. The marks

153. The popularity of Jean Price-Mars's *Ainsi parla l'oncle* (1928), the departure of the United States Marines, and other developments began to change the Haitian self-image a generation ago, notes James (*The Black Jacobins* [1963 ed.], pp. 393–6).

[1] Fanon, *Black Skin, White Masks*, p. 18.

[2] Victor Sablé, *La transformation des isles d'Amérique en départements français*, 1955, p. 176. See also Ève Dessarre, *Cauchemar Antillais*, 1965, p. 77.

[3] H. Merrill Jackson, 'Caribbean–West African Field Study: First Report', 1969, p. 10. For French West Indian discontent with *départementalisation*, see Gérard R. Latortue, 'Political Status of the French Caribbean', in T. G. Mathews et al., *Politics and Economics in the Caribbean*, 1966, pp. 148–83; Gérard R. Latortue, 'French West Indian Autonomy', *Caribbean Review*, Vol. 2, No. 2, Summer 1970, pp. 8–9; idem, 'The European Lands', in Tad Szulc, ed., *The United States and the Caribbean*, 1971, pp. 173–92.

[4] R. Vignon, 'French Guiana—Looking Ahead', *Caribbean Commission Monthly Bulletin*, Vol. 7, 1954, p. 254.

are evident everywhere: café life, school curricula, books and journals, French bread baked in even the most remote settlement. Wine, champagne, and liqueurs are not merely articles of commerce, they are sacrosanct emblems of Gallic culture.[1]

Devotion to France transcends Antillean awareness of imperfections. 'To be sure, race prejudice would break out from time to time; to be sure, the West Indian settler class oppressed and condemned the agricultural workers to endemic famine, but the title of French citizen was surely worth these few unpleasantnesses.' And exemplary individual successes in the metropolis likewise atone for general exploitation. 'Three hundred tons of gold left the Guianan territory every year to fill the cellars of the Banque de France, but was not Mr. Monnerville, as the second or third in the rank of French citizens, both a symbol and the payment of a debt?'[2]

British West Indians are stereotypically less 'anglicized' than French West Indians are 'gallicized'. 'The representatives of revolutionary France deliberately sided with coloured men against their white masters', one Frenchman seeks to explain the difference, and 'the French colonist has never displayed the Britisher's icy racism, and, checked by no Puritan scruples, he has been father to countless half-caste children.'[3] Gallic chauvinism and sexual behaviour are less likely causes, however, than British insularity: 'The British have never attempted to turn their colonials into Englishmen.' The West Indian 'in the French territories aimed at Frenchness, in the Dutch territories at Dutchness; in the English territories he aimed at simple whiteness and modernity, Englishness being impossible.'[4]

Today four former British colonies are independent, yet fealty more than physiography still makes Barbados 'Little England'. Jamaicans, Trinidadians, and small-islanders all emulate English manners, take pride in Commonwealth status, and pursue British honours—'a socially and psychologically corrupting [system] for taming the colonial natives', that 'causes middle-aged "social workers" with big bosoms and M.B.E.'s to say "sixpence" instead of "twelve cents".' This implies full acceptance of the ascribed role of '"good" West Indians—yes, Sir Uncle Tom.'[5] A Naipaul novel describes an encounter at Oxford with a Trinidad East Indian thus elevated: 'I looked . . . for

---

[1] David Lowenthal, 'French Guiana: Myths and Realities', *Transactions New York Academy of Sciences*, Series II, Vol. 22, 1960, pp. 528–40, ref. pp. 536–8.

[2] Frantz Fanon, 'Blood Flows in the Antilles under French Domination' [1960], in his *Toward the African Revolution*, 1967, pp. 167–9, ref. p. 167.

[3] Daniel Guérin, *The West Indies and Their Future*, 1961, p. 145.

[4] Naipaul, *The Middle Passage*, pp. 169, 68. See also J. J. Thomas, *Froudacity* [1889], p. 115.

[5] Adrian Espinet, 'Honours and *Paquotille*', *NWQ*, Vol. 2, No. 1, Dead Season 1965, pp. 19–22, ref. p. 21.

someone with a nigrescent face. It was easy to spot him, impeccably dressed, coming out of a first-class carriage. I gave a shout of joy. "Pundit Ganesh!" I cried, running towards him. "Pundit Ganesh Ramsumair!" "G. Ramsay Muir," he said coldly.'[1]

West Indians unsure of their Englishness convert their anxiety into absurdity; humour becomes a weapon and a shield. A Jamaican novelist delineates a black physicist who is completely English in manner, speech, and dress: 'Being acutely conscious of it, and of its absurdity in the eyes of everyone he confronted, he constantly sought to parody himself' and overdid his Oxford accent so that it would be seen he was consciously overdoing it. 'Not only was his desire to be English somewhat tenuously satisfied, but the insecurities and self-contempt which it implied were allayed, indeed smothered, . . . by caricaturing and laughing at it.' He employed patois in the same exaggerated self-mocking fashion, talking 'not so much in an affected dialect but more in the manner of someone affecting an Englishman affecting the dialect.' As the protagonist concludes, 'everything here seems to mock itself either by laughing at itself, or cursing itself: . . . two black workers cursing each other about their blackness; . . . a group of brown-skinned upstarts sweating themselves to death drinking tea on a hot afternoon'; and beyond this, a culture hard to identify as a whole because 'in essence it is an absence.'[2]

But Anglomania fills this vacuum in fact, not just in fantasy. A black Guyanese recalls, without regret, having 'grown up British in every way. Myself, my parents, and my parents' parents, none of us knew or could know any other way of living, of thinking, of being; we knew no other cultural pattern . . . and it was absolutely natural for me to identify myself with the British heroes of the adventure stories'.[3] A Vincentian remembers

Sunday school and church picnics, cricket and soccer, and afternoon teas that brought us black popinjays into the realm of English grace. Our British affectations, 4,000 miles removed from their source, seem, on reflection, absurd. But there was no absurdity when, as children, we prayed for Sir Francis Drake and Sir Walter Raleigh; . . . and we wore, uncomplainingly, green woolen blazers and gray flannel trousers to school, not because they were comfortable (the wool itched and stank in the tropical heat) but because on some decaying street in Liverpool as well as at a posh public school a British teenager wore the same get-up.[4]

---

[1] V. S. Naipaul, *The Mystic Masseur*, 1957, p. 215.
[2] Patterson, *An Absence of Ruins*, pp. 61–3, 84. See also Gordon Rohlehr, 'Character and Rebellion in "A House for Mr. Biswas" by V. S. Naipaul', *NWQ*, Vol. 4, No. 4, Cropover 1968, pp. 66–72, ref. p. 72.
[3] E. R. Braithwaite, *To Sir, with Love*, 1959, pp. 41–2.
[4] Coombs, 'West Indians in New York', pp. 31–2.

Distance does not diminish Britain's repute; second-generation British West Indians in the Dominican Republic are said to retain 'an exaggerated idea of the superiority of a United Kingdom they have never seen'.[1] West Indians brought up in the British imperial tradition consider themselves part of that branch of western civilization with all the accrued values of the Christian-Hellenic tradition.

Everything European is admired in the West Indies—people, ideas, culture, clothing. Public life in the islands still requires formal business suits, and even in Guyana, where informality is a Prime Ministerial fetish, a juror's request to serve without coat and tie was refused; 'we have not yet . . . disposed of all wigs and gowns', noted the judge, 'therefore, it is imperative that gentlemen who wish to sit as members of the panel must be properly clad.'[2] Barbadian football teams in 1969 selected English names and colours—Arsenal, Tottenham Hotspurs, Liverpool, Coventry City.[3]

Caribbean educational theory and equipment often reflect antiquated metropolitan standards. The arithmetic recently taught in St. Kitts featured systems of weights, measures, and coinage outdated in England and probably never used in the West Indies. Some European models are not obsolete; Cayenne's secondary school teaches dressmaking on precision machines of the most modern Paris design, but no other such machines are to be found in French Guiana.[4] Such circumstances clarify the wonderment implicit in a Dominican's statement that 'we are living in Modern, even in neo-Modern, days.'[5]

Overseas visitors are made much of not only because new faces are a welcome change, but also because foreigners are presumed superior. 'We adore outsiders and make them feel that we are lunatics or paupers out here, who need someone like them from the world beyond to make us "see the light".'[6] Dominicans 'make a big fuss of strangers', a local editor observes, 'and view their own kind as substandard'.[7] Titled visitors receive special deference; a local newspaper notes that 'a commendatory letter from the Marquis of Bristol, Hereditary High Steward of the Liberty of St. Edmund, will be read' at a Best Village competition.[8] Ignorance about the Liberty of St. Edmund presumably would not detract from Dominican pleasure in the aristocratic connection.

[1] J. Halcro Ferguson, *Latin America: The Balance of Race Redressed*, 1961, p. 81.
[2] Horace Mitchell, quoted in 'Juror Barred', *Jamaica Daily Gleaner*, 2 December 1968.
[3] John Wickham, 'West Indian Writing', *Bim*, Vol. 13, No. 50, January–June 1970, pp. 68–80, ref. pp. 71–2.
[4] Louis W. Bone, *Secondary Education in the Guianas*, 1962, pp. 32–3.
[5] O. M. Morris, quoted in *Dominica Star*, 14 March 1970, p. 11.
[6] 'Marjorie Talking', *Dominica Herald*, 3 December 1966, p. 7.
[7] 'Carbon Copy Carnival Again', *Dominica Herald*, 15 February 1969, p. 2.
[8] *Dominica Chronicle*, 16 December 1967, p. 1.

Local West Indian leaders, even self-styled 'socialists' heading labour parties, were no less pro-European than their expatriate predecessors. They and their followers adhered to the precepts a Jamaican union head spelled out in 1938: 'Leaders are what the labourers want. Good leaders, Temperate Speeches, work within the bounds of British Principles and Policies'.[1] In newly independent Jamaica, both politicians and bureaucrats fell back on traditional attitudes, acting on the time-honoured principle that troubles could be resolved if only 'the British way of life would be more fully understood and more closely followed.'[2] Trinidad too is still dominated by imperial guidelines. 'Our education, civil service, trade unions and business are in general indistinguishable from their British models. . . . The most powerful trade union in the country apes British trade unionism of the thirties or even earlier, complete with outdated slogans'.[3]

West Indians remain European even in their manner of breaking away from the mother country. To show his fitness for independence a Trinidadian was supposed to 'have the special additional qualification of being able to behave like an Englishman.'[4] Good manners are required, churlishness deplored. Although 'we want to remove the [imperial] "trappings"', chides a small-island editor, 'prominent members of the ruling Party should [not] have been so discourteous as to ignore the playing of God Save the Queen while imbibing whiskey with some English invitees at Saturday's "At Home" at Government House.'[5] Parliamentary procedures are available for any grievances, as black-power marchers who stormed the Trinidad cathedral were lectured: 'If the demonstrators wanted a black God and black saints, they should have gone about it in the right way. The Prime Minister could have been approached and asked to form a committee under the chairmanship of [the] Archbishop'.[6]

New nations West-Indianize their civil services only to have local

---

[1] A. G. S. Coombs, quoted in K. W. J. Post, 'The Politics of Protest in Jamaica, 1938: Some Problems of Analysis and Conceptualization', *SES*, Vol. 18, 1969, pp. 374–90, ref. p. 382. In Trinidad, Cipriani similarly beat the British with their own stick; what was good enough for the British Labour movement, he used to say, was good enough for him (Lloyd Braithwaite, 'The Problem of Cultural Integration in Trinidad', *SES*, Vol. 3, 1954, pp. 82–96, ref. p. 85).

[2] B. L. St. John Hamilton, *Problems of Administration in an Emergent Nation: A Case Study of Jamaica*, 1964, p. 139. See also T. S. Simey, *Welfare and Planning in the West Indies*, 1946, p. 238.

[3] 'Neo-Colonialism', 29 April 1967, in *The State of the Nation: Trinidad and Tobago in the Later 1960's*, pp. 80–1.

[4] Lloyd Taylor, 'The Seven Years' War: Queen's Hall, 1962, to Whitehall, 1969', *Tapia*, No. 6, 8 March 1970, pp. 5–6.

[5] 'Listen', *Dominica Herald*, 17 June 1967, p. 8.

[6] 'Power Is Already in the Hands of the Blacks', letter signed 'Blasted Vex', *Trinidad Express*, 11 March 1970, p. 4.

officials demand the same 'home leave' privileges their expatriate predecessors enjoyed. Portraits of Queen Elizabeth remain in West Indian legislative halls, pictures of Queen Victoria adorn peasant cottages, and one small-island labour leader expresses disdain for the Establishment by substituting a photograph of Edward VIII!

In the late 1960s a dozen young West Indians met informally in New York to further West Indian causes. Talk grew animated, people were interrupted; at length someone exclaimed: 'Mr. Speaker, Sir! Point of order!' 'I was dismayed', one of them told me. 'There we were, radicals far from home talking about *West Indian* identity, and we still respond "Mr. Speaker, Sir! Point of order!" How British can you get?'

A corollary of West Indian attachment to 'European' criteria is that everything local seems inadequate or second-rate. Scotch and gin rather than rum, roast beef and Yorkshire pudding instead of pepper-pot, tinned food above fresh, European furniture, utilities, and clothing regardless of comfort or cost—these are what West Indians prefer. In Grenada anything local is termed *foo-foo*, a dish considered inferior because it was originally associated with slaves. 'Irish potatoes constitute a higher symbol of status than locally-grown sweet potatoes and, the products of developing local industries, equal in quality and lower in price, still experience severe competition from the imported article.'[1] Middle-class West Indians generally choose imported staples over local roots or ground provisions.

These prejudices are traditional. A century ago travellers noted that 'Jamaicans are fond of English dishes, and that they despise, or affect to despise, their own productions. They will give you ox-tail soup when turtle would be much cheaper'.[2] When an enterprising Trinidadian planter made chocolate locally, 'the fair Creoles would not buy it. It could not be good; it could not be the real article, unless it had crossed the Atlantic twice to and from that centre of fashion, Paris.'[3] It is still standard practice to dismiss local produce in favour of foreign. 'The excellent coffee which is grown in Trinidad is used only by the very poor and a few middle-class English expatriates. Everyone else drinks Nescafé or Maxwell House or Chase and Sanborn, which is more expensive but is advertised in the magazines and therefore acceptable.'[4]

Local forms of speech are also despised; like what goes in West

[1] Alister Hughes, 'Non-Standard English of Grenada', *CQ*, Vol. 12, No. 4, December 1966, pp. 47–54, ref. p. 52.

[2] Trollope, *The West Indies and the Spanish Main*, p. 21.

[3] Charles Kingsley, *At Last: A Christmas in the West Indies*, 1900, p. 127.

[4] Naipaul, *The Middle Passage*, p. 46. See also Alfred P. Thorne, 'An Economic Phenomenon (Study of an Apparent Psychological Trait and Its Probable Effect on Regional Economic Development)', *CQ*, Vol. 6, No. 4, 1960, pp. 270–8.

Indian mouths, what comes out should be 'European'. The prejudice is strongest in the French Antilles. Martinican teachers scorn patois as *le français déformé* and forbid its use in school; at home a black child who speaks patois is scolded—'tu parles comme un nègre'. 'The middle class in the Antilles never speak Creole except to their servants. . . . Some families completely forbid the use of Creole,'[1] and mothers berate their children:

> shut up I told you you must speak French
> the French of France
> the Frenchman's French
> French French.[2]

Creole speech is likewise abhorrent to the respectable in the British Caribbean. 'The Grenadian child has but to utter the word *jook* or some other non-standard word or expression, and his parent or teacher will take such a *lag* at him that he will be for ever convinced of the "undesirability" of his non-standard-English.'[3]

A patois unrelated to the official tongue is utterly anathematized. Although almost all St. Lucians speak French dialect, the educated view it as suitable only for proverbs and curses. Local teachers discourage its use by reiterating that 'Patois cannot be written, Patois has no grammar, it is only "broken French"'. One head teacher, on his evening walks through the village, would flog any child he heard speaking patois. To a UNESCO plea to preserve local languages, St. Lucia's Education Officer responded that 'these instructions do not in any way concern us, since Creole is not a language.'[4] A few radicals champion patois as intrinsically St. Lucian, but folk speakers themselves prefer English as the language of status and opportunity. 'This class not only has repugnance to speaking in Creole but considers itself gravely insulted and dishonoured if a person who normally expresses himself in English condescends to address them in Creole.'[5]

West Indian country folk everywhere deprecate their own speech. Trinidad villagers whose *lingua franca* is French patois claim they cannot speak it and refer to it as an ugly 'Negro' language. Any

[1] Fanon, *Black Skin, White Masks*, p. 20. See also Michael M. Horowitz, *Morne-Paysan: Peasant Village in Martinique*, 1967, p. 63.

[2] Léon-G. Damas, 'Hoquet', in Léopold S.-Senghor, ed., *Anthologie de la nouvelle poésie nègre et malgache de langue française*, 1948, pp. 15–17.

[3] Hughes, 'Non-Standard English of Grenada', p. 52 (my italics). *Jook*, to prick or pierce; *lag* (or 'take a lag at'), to attack (pp. 50–1).

[4] Pierre Vérin, 'The Rivalry of Creole and English in the West Indies', *West-Indische Gids*, Vol. 38, 1958, pp. 163–7, ref. pp. 164, 166. See also Lawrence D. Carrington, 'St. Lucian Creole—A Descriptive Analysis of its Phonology and Morpho-Syntax', 1967, pp. 20–2.

[5] Mervin C. Alleyne, 'Language and Society in St. Lucia', *CS*, Vol. I, No. 1, April 1961, pp. 1–10, ref. p. 7.

language as spoken elsewhere is 'purer' than the Trinidadian variant; local Spanish is 'broken' by contrast with 'real' Venezuelan Spanish, local patois is 'broken' French by contrast even with French Antillean patois.[1] Trinidad Hindus similarly belittle their Hindi as a debased corruption of 'real' Hindi in India.

Although stigmatized as inferior, Creolese none the less embodies certain virtues. In Antigua, for example, 'Creole is intrinsically felt to be the code of the genuine'; it symbolizes what is 'natural' and deeply felt, whereas standard English carries an aura of falseness. Haitian folk similarly mistrust French as the tongue of deception and duplicity—the patois phrase for speaking French also means 'glossing over... dishonest thoughts and actions' and 'offer[ing] a bribe'—but they have no false illusions about the practical virtues of patois. A programme of literacy in Creolese, however attractive on nationalistic grounds, 'may be hard to sell—or even to give away—to much of the population. . . . There are neither motives of status or personal advantage to learn to read in Creole'.[2]

Creoles educated abroad epitomize West Indian obeisance to metropolitan linguistic standards. The Haitian home from France emphasizes his French pronunciation and garnishes his remarks with the latest Paris argot. The Antillean author of *Guadeloupe's Contribution to French Thought* wrote home to get 'corrections' of Creole text, 'adding ingenuously that he had lost the use of his native tongue.'[3] The Martinican newly returned from Paris pretends not to understand patois and makes it clear that he is now a real Frenchman temporarily exiled to the Antilles: 'I am so happy to be back with you. Good lord it is hot in this country, I shall certainly not be able to endure it very long'.[4] British West Indians stress 'better' English both as a preparation for, and as a major benefit of, residence abroad. 'I set to work to suppress the familiar phrases and pronunciation', a Jamaican recalls her local boarding-school days.

I accepted [standard English] as the language that ought to be used at all times everywhere, and if I modified it at any time . . . I would feel guilty. . . . But in spite of the pain of isolation and conflict. . . , I cannot entirely regret this

[1] Carroll McClure Pastner, 'A Sociolinguistic Study of a Rural Trinidad Community', 1967.

[2] Karl Reisman, 'Cultural and Linguistic Ambiguity in a West Indian Village', in Norman E. Whitten, Jr., and John F. Szwed, eds., *Afro-American Anthropology: Contemporary Perspectives*, 1970, pp. 128–44, ref. p. 140; Robert A. Hall, Jr., *Pidgin and Creole Languages*, 1966, p. 133; Paul Berry, 'Literacy and the Question of Creole', in Richard P. Schaedel, ed., *Papers of the Conference on Research and Resources of Haiti*, 1969, pp. 204–80, ref. pp. 230–1, 215.

[3] Léon Hennique, referred to in Jack Corzani, *Splendeur et misère: l'exotisme littéraire aux Antilles*, 1969, p. 35.

[4] Fanon, *Black Skin, White Masks*, p. 37.

legacy of speech and manners from St. Hilary's, for when I came to England I found acceptance and ease in social contacts.[1]

Islanders may poke fun at the returned migrant for talking 'with a hot potato in his mouth', but they are critical if he shows no change. 'Noh Lickle Twang' upbraids the young Jamaican who comes back from America without a new 'accent':

> Byoy yuh couldn' improve yuhself!
> An yuh get soh much pay?
> Yuh spen six mont' a foreign, an
> Come back ugly same way?[2]

Nationalism and academic approbation today lend Creolese new respectability, but it remains a target of middle-class snobbery and still carries a lower-class stigma. Creolese expressions are exaggerated when 'the speaker wants you to know that they are part of his dialect and not his educated vocabulary.' Thus *nyam* (eat), a Creolese word of West African origin natural to most Jamaican folk, is avoided by educated Jamaicans except pejoratively or 'in a spirit of tolerant reminiscent humor'. *Nyam* is all right in folk tales and Anancy stories, but elsewhere it is a sign of ignorance and backwardness.[3]

West Indian folk tales were, until recently, also scorned, and middle-class repugnance was reflected in folk devaluations. Martinicans were ashamed of their traditional stories because they were 'ugly'. A local collector of Guyanese East Indian lore recalls how hard it was 'to explain to them that their folk songs were of any worth—to them, these songs were the symbol of their backwardness', and they implored him, 'don' ask we nothin' to laugh at we.'[4] Local folk tales discomfit the educated West Indian by reminding him of things he deliberately avoids. The Trinidadian 'who spurned the calypso for the English folk song [and] listened to Grimm's fairy tales but withdrew with horror at acquaintance with "Anansi"'[5] linked the European legends with civilization, the local tales with savagery. A Trinidadian is depicted trying 'to debunk the old West Indian nancy-story':

[1] Gladwell, *Brown Face, Big Master*, p. 34.

[2] Louise Bennett, *Jamaica Labrish*, 1966, pp. 209–10.

[3] F. G. Cassidy and R. B. Le Page, 'Lexicographical Problems of *The Dictionary of Jamaican English*', in *Proceedings of the Conference on Creole Language Studies*, 1961, pp. 17–36, ref. pp. 24, 29.

[4] Ved Prakash Vatuk, *British Guiana*, 1963, p. 7, quoted in Raymond T. Smith, 'Social Stratification, Cultural Pluralism and Integration in West Indian Societies', in Lewis and Mathews, eds., *Caribbean Integration*, p. 253. For Martinique, see Anca Bertrand, cited in Jackson, 'Caribbean–West African Field Study: First Report', p. 13.

[5] Lloyd Braithwaite, 'The Development of Higher Education in the British West Indies', *SES*, Vol. 7, 1958, pp. 1–64, ref. p. 55.

Faddists were trying to dig up everything they could pertaining to negro folk-lore in the West Indies: the *cumfa* dance, *shango*, the nancy-story. They were glorifying the calypso and encouraging primitive institutions like the steel band. . . . It was a mistaken idea . . . that West Indian literature and art should be based on these primitive tales. West Indians were not primitives. Only a handful of backwoods peasants were familiar with the nancy-stories.[1]

A tourist official in another novel analogously explains to a carnival visitor that 'you see before you the vestiges of the dead past . . . the darkness and the fumblings of prehistoric man to find himself. Culture and breeding take time, my friend . . . time. But it shan't be long now before we rid ourselves of all this nonsense and make ourselves a credit to the Empire.'[2]

Jamaica's Christmas pantomime—a largely English event—exemplifies West Indian ambivalence toward local folkways. In one critic's view, the 1969 pantomime

was clearly conceived in the self-contempt that subscribes to the myth of the happy negro, and in the blindness which regards folk forms and idioms as amenable solely to humour. Jamaican folksongs were used only when a broadly 'folksy' atmosphere was required, while songs from an American show like 'The West Side Story' were used whenever there was need to express love and tenderness. . . . Underlying the entire Pantomime was the well-educated hypocrisy which enables the middle class simultaneously to ape and scorn the illiterate masses.[3]

Efforts to instil a positive sense of 'West Indian' or 'Creole' identity are recent and largely opportunistic. Creole speech has come to denote folk solidarity; under adult suffrage mass support often requires a display of patois. But once popular leaders get elevated to the legislature they often abandon Creolese and revert to French, English, or Dutch.

Caribbean leaders today promise release from the European incubus that hinders the realization of West Indian identity. Employment, resources, language, architecture, the arts are all in principle to be nationalized. Xenophobia supports every cause; petitioners against relocating an old market in a new building entreated Trinidad's Prime Minister not to 'imitate european and american standards'.[4] Black and coloured West Indians are canonized; Paul Bogle and Marcus Garvey, leaders of black disaffection in 1865 and in the 1920s respectively, have been elevated to the official Jamaican pantheon. Guyana made a national hero of Cuffy, chose the anniversary of the slave revolt he led to become a republic, and removed paintings of the

[1] Mittelholzer, *A Morning at the Office*, pp. 238, 242.

[2] Ismith Khan, *The Obeah Man*, 1964, p. 139.

[3] Gordon Rohlehr, 'Cultural Dilemma', *Moko*, No. 3, 29 November 1968, p. 1.

[4] Placard carried by Port-of-Spain market vendors, cited in John Barr, 'Carnival, Cricket and The Mighty Sparrow', *New Society*, 8 February 1968, p. 201.

Royal Family out of Parliament into the Guyana museum to remind Guyanese, said the Prime Minister, 'of the past to which we must not and cannot return.'[1]

Yet even the most aggressive West Indianizers continue to interpret local custom in accordance with European criteria. Thus steel-pan expertise—a popular symbol of Creole culture because visibly 'folk' but clearly indigenous rather than African—is habitually judged by performances of European 'classics' rather than of West Indian compositions, their true innovative idiom. 'All the bands played pieces by European composers—Handel, Mozart, Bizet, Suppé—and even the locally composed test pieces sounded like something from a Viennese operetta.' The most defiant local pride submits in the end to the metropolitan bias of local culture. The captain of the Guinness Cavaliers, a steel band, 'after insisting that studying music would destroy his inspiration as a Trinidadian, announced later that his band was no longer interested in local competitions. The most recent festival, with another foreign adjudicator and a test piece by Benjamin Britten, found nearly all the top bands abroad.'[2] The 1969 carnival calypso competition run by the Dominica Junior Chamber of Commerce rejected one folk song 'as having too many patois words';[3] the calypso is imported, the patois local.

As a conscious movement, creolization in the broad sense of the term has made little headway outside of Haiti. European preferences and modes of thought are deeply embedded, and West Indians on the whole are not eager to uproot them. The West Indianization of intellectual life hardly goes beyond school texts with a Caribbean focus and *New World*, a radical quarterly that substituted sugar plantation periods—'dead season', 'crop time', 'high season', and 'crop over'—for the traditional European seasons of the year. The journal reproached a former university vice-chancellor, a devoted West Indian nationalist, for referring 'to "spring, summer, autumn and winter" when talking about and to a West Indian audience'.[4]

The triviality of the complaint underscores the endurance of European bias among the reformers themselves. Their efforts to substitute the study of the hibiscus for that of the daffodil, West Indian or African history for English, have simply replaced one instrumental

[1] Linden Forbes Sampson Burnham, speech in the National Assembly, August 1969, and 'The Cooperative Republic' (1969), in *A Destiny to Mould: Selected Discourses by the Prime Minister of Guyana*, 1970, pp. 68–9 and 156.

[2] Landeg E. White, 'Steelbands: A Personal Record', *CQ*, Vol. 15, No. 4, December 1969, pp. 32–9, ref. pp. 32–4. For the role of steel bands, see Gordon K. Lewis, *The Growth of the Modern West Indies*, 1968, pp. 30–4.

[3] 'Carbon Copy Carnival Again', *Dominica Herald*, 15 February 1969, p. 2.

[4] 'The Intellectual Tradition and Social Change in the Caribbean', *New World Pamphlet* [1966], p. 12.

goal with another. To be sure, the hibiscus is more meaningful in the local environment and easier to study in its living form, but few West Indianizers have asked the more basic questions, 'why is Biology taught in the first place and are the aims and purpose of teaching the subject the same whether one is dealing with children in industrialized urban societies as in rural agricultural societies?' Implicit in most Caribbean educational development plans 'is a universal concept of "best education" for all societies',[1] an ideal model that West Indian societies should strive for.

New World also criticizes West Indian writers for 'pre-occupation with being published abroad.' But 'it is a melancholy fact', a local reviewer asserts, 'that our society is still too timid to acknowledge excellence before it has had the stamp of foreign approbation. It still too often has to be by success abroad that one establishes one's right to this society's serious attention.'[2] And nationalism has increased cultural schizophrenia. 'There are still "educated" people among us who believe that literature, like history ("real" literature, or "real" history), must be British; and even the most enlightened of us find it hard to reject beliefs fed into us from birth.'[3]

Public professions of West Indianization are often belied by private deeds. With much fanfare the Jamaican legislature in 1968 abolished British honours awards; yet a few weeks later the Jamaican Prime Minister became a member of the Queen's Privy Council. Critics of Trinidad's Prime Minister mock that 'the highest sounding honours must be given to those who have sold out most completely'; where 'lesser men covet colonial knighthoods, Williams' excellence claims nothing beneath the rare dignities of C.H. and Her Majesty's Privy Council—surely the final proofs of stature in this white man's world.'[4] Titular etiquette in the new Caribbean nations met a formidable challenge in the person of Lionel Luckhoo, a knighted Guyanese who up to early 1970 was jointly responsible for the affairs of Guyana and Barbados in the United Kingdom. Guyana had officially abolished British titles, but Barbados had not, so West Indians carefully referred to him 'as Mr. Luckhoo when representing Guyana, and as Sir Lionel a moment later in the role of Bajan Lord High Everything Else.'[5]

Local radicals who profess grave concern about the persistence of

---

[1] Kassim Bacchus, 'Education and Change', *NWQ*, Vol. 5, Nos. 1 and 2, Dead Season and Croptime 1969, pp. 63–73, ref. pp. 68–9.

[2] Mervyn Morris, 'Walcott and the Audience for Poetry', *CQ*, Vol. 14, Nos. 1 and 2, March–June 1968, pp. 7–24, ref. p. 12.

[3] Edward Baugh, 'Towards a West Indian Criticism', *CQ*, Vol. 14, Nos. 1 and 2, March–June 1968, pp. 140–4, ref. p. 141.

[4] 'Call That George!' *Moko*, No. 18, 4 July 1969, p. 3; Espinet and Farmer, 'Pussonal Nonarchy'.

[5] 'Sundry Topics, by the Hawk', *Guyana Sun*, 28 March 1970, p. 8.

colonial attitudes charge that 'independence has meant no more than . . . substitution of imitative "Afro-Saxon" Caribbeans for metropolitan carpetbaggers.'[1] But their own protests against the old order are often quixotic or perfunctory. The local intelligentsia who regularly assail Britain or France none the less end up on leave in London and Paris. And students who refused to bear the train of Princess Alice, the Chancellor, at the 1970 university graduation exercises continue on protest marches to wear their own red gowns, 'as much a feudal status hang-up as the Chancellor's train.'[2]

The leisurely pace of West Indianization contrasts with the nationalist fervour of other new states. Most ex-colonies are now rid of ethnically alien tyranny; 'Afro-Asian intellectuals . . . are no longer being exploited, maltreated, or insulted by white men in their own countries.'[3] But they still feel excluded from centres of action and power, and independence multiplies their educational needs and their intellectual dependence on Europe. Hence 'the typical ex-colonial will forego the use of the colonizer's language, even if all the locks of the country turn with that key. . . . He will prefer a long period of educational mistakes to the continuation of the colonizer's school organization. He will . . . destroy the institutions built by the colonizer as soon as possible'.[4] But this violent rejection of things European would strike most West Indians as ludicrous and self-defeating.

Unlike Afro-Asians, most West Indians tacitly take dependence for granted. They view local society as an extension of that centred in London or Paris. They find European hegemony natural and appropriate; politics apart, the West Indies must remain tributaries to the mainstream. In education, many West Indian administrators refuse to countenance independent local examinations or professional certification not tied to metropolitan standards. In the arts, many West Indians dismiss local forms as trivial or synthetic. It is hard to find much creativity that is uniquely West Indian, harder to persuade people that specifically West Indian aspects of culture matter. Middle-class antipathy to the steel band, the mento, the folk tale, the calypso, and local dance styles may be dying out, but few West Indians dream of these becoming major local commodities.

The promotion of 'national culture' excites much local derision. Most West Indians concur with the judgement that 'much of what is

---

[1] Ryan, 'Decolonization in a Multi-Racial Society', p. 427. See also George Lamming, 'The West Indian People', *NWQ*, Vol. 2, No. 2, Croptime 1966, pp. 63–74, ref. p. 68.

[2] Sylvia Wynter, 'New Standards or High Standards—A Matter of Emphasis', *Jamaica Sunday Gleaner*, 15 March 1970, p. 10.

[3] Edward Shils, 'Color, the Universal Intellectual Community and the Afro-Asian Intellectual,, in 'Color and Race', *Daedalus*, Vol. 96, No. 2, 1967, p. 281.

[4] Memmi, *The Colonizer and the Colonized*, pp. 137–8.

good is . . . only slightly West Indian, and much of what is thoroughly West Indian is inferior.'[1]

Everybody gone local and nobody singing anything by them foreign people with name like Beethoven and Chopin and so forth. All that foolishness done with. Today is 'Ride de Donkey', 'Tina', 'Cocoa Tea' and 'Doo Doo'. In fack I hear that one night the Music Festival performance was so poor and it had so few people in the audience they had to refund the money people pay.[2]

Celebrations of local culture tend to be cursory genuflections toward an otherwise neglected past. 'Those whose duty it is to be familiar with our folk ways are totally in the dark as to the customs and culture of our forefathers', a Dominican charges. Commentators at the National Day fête 'did not know anything historical, cultural or technical about either the Quadrille or the Belair.' Nor is there much effort to build on these folkways. Instead 'we keep repeating the past every year for two days with nothing new added from our own background'.[3]

Caribbean products have yet to gain general respect, let alone popular esteem. Businessmen do not stock local goods of equal or better quality than the foreign-made for fear of losing customers. European-oriented culture at school persuades West Indians that it is best to ignore most aspects of local life. 'Anything that touched on everyday life excited laughter when it was mentioned in a classroom', a Naipaul protagonist recalls. 'We denied the landscape and the people we could see out of open doors and windows, we who took apples to the teacher and wrote essays about visits to temperate farms.'[4]

To enhance local pride, West Indian governments now promote steel-band and calypso contests and subsidize local authors. But foreign visitors are the most affluent bidders for Caribbean 'culture', and all local art forms risk being regarded as assets for tourism. West Indians striving for self-determination, no less than those still essentially European, deplore alike the self-conscious search for roots and the pandering to the tourist stereotype of the sensuous, carefree, primitive, 'African' West Indian.

One need not be sensitive to such nuances to question the viability of West Indian national identity. Pride in nationhood does exist, though anyone hearing the Barbadian national song, 'God Bless Bim',

---

[1] D. A. G. Waddell, *The West Indies and the Guianas*, 1967, p. 13. See also Keith Hunte, review of Waddell, *CS*, Vol. 8, No. 4, January 1969, pp. 99–100. The transition from intensely felt ambivalence to pallid respectability is traced in Barbara E. Powrie, 'The Changing Attitude of the Coloured Middle Class Towards Carnival', *CQ*, Vol. 4, Nos. 3 and 4, March–June 1956, pp. 224–32.

[2] 'Dear Boysie', *Trinidad Guardian*, 22 March 1970, p. 5.

[3] 'Where Do We Go from Contes?' *Dominica Herald*, 9 November 1968, p. 2.

[4] V. S. Naipaul, *The Mimic Men*, 1967, pp. 114–15. See also Marjorie Thorpe, '"The Mimic Men": A Study of Isolation', *NWQ*, Vol. 4, No. 4, Cropover 1968, pp. 55–9, ref. p. 56.

might easily imagine it celebrated a regimental reunion rather than the birth of a nation. Of those Jamaicans who had heard of their new national hero, Paul Bogle, not a few shared the dismay of the middle-class lady who was said to have exclaimed, 'What, that wicked black devil?' But the taxi driver displeased with his country's new flag expresses the quintessential West Indian tone: 'To tell the truth I prefer the old Union Jack. . . . They send us this thing and they try to sweeten us up with some old talk . . . but I prefer the old Union Jack. It look like a real flag. This look like something they make up. You know, like foreign money?'[1]

NÉGRITUDE AND BLACK POWER

Africa is one place most West Indians shun even more than the Caribbean. Save for the Ras Tafari, few West Indians wish to return to Africa, identify themselves with things African, or like being linked with Africans. Little is known and much is misunderstood about what is African in West Indian life, but whatever is locally perceived as African is widely disapproved. Working-class Jamaicans reject apparent Africanisms in speech, dress, and food; elite Haitians deny there is anything African in local folk culture, characterizing patois as 'Spanish' and Vodun as seventeenth-century Breton. 'African' is a general term of reproach; British colonial officials recruited out of the Africa service were abhorrent to West Indians for their 'African mannerisms and want of manners'—that is, for treating West Indians like 'natives'.[2]

West Indians abroad resent being mistaken for Africans, whom they consider less 'civilized' than themselves. In France, before 1939, the African was a Negro, the West Indian a European; 'when a boss made too great demands on a Martiniquan in a work situation, he would . . . be told, "If it's a nigger you want, go and look for him in Africa"'.[3] Some Africans themselves acquiesced in this pecking order; Fanon knew 'people born in Dahomey or the Congo who pretend to be natives of the Antilles'.[4]

West Indians in Britain expressed equivalent distress at being identified as African. Caribbean students there habitually adopted 'some acuteness, some witticism, some easy friendliness, some inter-

---

[1] Naipaul, *A Flag on the Island*, pp. 156–7.
[2] George Eaton Simpson, 'Jamaican Revivalist Cults', *SES*, Vol. 5, 1956, p. 433; R. A. Hall, *Pidgin and Creole Languages*, pp. 47, 143; L. D. 'Lully' Punch, *A Journey to Remember (39 Years in the Civil Service)* [1967], pp. 49–50. At least until recently, 'African' was a term reserved specifically for post-emancipation immigrants from Africa and their descendants (M. G. Smith, *Dark Puritan*, 1963, p. 10).
[3] Fanon, 'West Indians and Africans', *Esprit* (1955), in his *Toward the African Revolution*, pp. 17–27, ref. p. 21.
[4] Fanon, *Black Skin, White Masks*, p. 25.

national sophistication'[1] to emphasize that they were more 'English' than the Africans were. In a fictional retaliation against African ascription, a Trinidadian on a bus utters 'a variety of rich gibberish, which . . . anybody hearing him would of course conclude' was African; a friend responds in the same jargon, ending with 'an English phrase like the "town of Manchester" or . . . "ate his arm and kept the thighs for the Sunday joint",' and finally, in an Oxford accent 'bubbling with culture, . . . "I say old chaps, I do think we should get off here, what!"'[2]

For the West Indian, Africa remains a sad and sinister continent. Reluctant to acknowledge the legacy, he slanders his African ancestry, but the rejection hints at an underlying ambivalence. Young West Indians laugh scornfully at movies depicting African tribesmen, yet 'it is precisely because Africa has not been forgotten', a local critic observes, 'that the West Indian embarrassment takes the form of derisive laughter.'[3] In one Jamaican novel, a folk figure, who represents both Africa and the folk, intones: 'We is in you mind when you sleeping and when you wake up. We is you past and present, any day at all, argue or not. We is part of you, 'cestors, and you children to come after you. You can't lose we at all. . . . You can't escape you own blood!'[4] A pull toward Africa is also variously manifest in the philosophy of *négritude*, in West Indian political sympathies, and in racial and ethnic tensions stemming from continuing social inequities.

Caribbean *négritude* is both a literary movement and a political faith, but the two are largely unrelated; West Indian *littérateurs* are little known to mass leaders of black protest. As a concept, *négritude* recognizes a unique black (or Negro, or African, depending on the context) culture and personality and deliberately rejects white values in their favour. White or European culture is viewed as excessively cerebral, arid, and compartmentalized. Traits deemed specifically black or African include a poetic and mythic sense of life, a rapport with nature, a subordination of individual to group, and a merging of artistic expression with everyday experience:

I am black; I am the incarnation of a complete fusion with the world, an intuitive understanding of the earth, an abandonment of my ego in the heart

---

[1] Morris, 'Feeling, Affection, Respect', p. 15.

[2] O. R. Dathorne, *Dumplings in the Soup*, 1963, pp. 142–3.

[3] George Lamming, *The Pleasures of Exile*, 1960, p. 224, referring to a Naipaul review in *New Statesman*, 6 December 1958, pp. 826–7. See also Lamming, 'Caribbean Literature: The Black Rock of Africa', *African Forum*, Vol. 1, No. 4, Spring 1966, pp. 32–52, ref. pp. 33–4; G. R. Coulthard, *Race and Colour in Caribbean Literature*, 1962, p. 70; O. R. Dathorne, 'Africa in West Indian Literature', *Black Orpheus*, No. 16, October 1964, pp. 42–54; Lilyan Kesteloot, *Aimé Césaire*, 1962, p. 195.

[4] Andrew Salkey, *A Quality of Violence*, 1959, p. 202. See also Edward Brathwaite, 'Caribbean Critics', *NWQ*, Vol. 5, Nos. 1 and 2, Dead Season and Croptime 1969, pp. 5–12, ref. pp. 7–11.

of the cosmos, and no white man ... can ever understand Louis Armstrong and the music of the Congo. If I am black, it is not the result of a curse but it is because, having offered my skin, I have been able to absorb all the cosmic effluvia.[1]

The term *négritude* was coined during the 1930s by its greatest exponent, the Martinican poet Aimé Césaire. Its literary antecedents are partly Cuban, its philosophic tenets derive from Haitian folklorists. In Haiti, Price-Mars and his school of ethnology in the 1920s taught that the elite, 'trying to be what they were not, European instead of African,' had rejected the country's intrinsic personality. The folklore movement of the 1930s embraced the entire Haitian peasant tradition, including patois, primitive art and music, and Vodun.[2] *Négritude* gave rise to a Caribbean-wide literature praising blackness and ennobling the African heritage. West Indian intellectuals made common cause with black Africa; collaboration between Césaire and Léopold Senghor of Senegal fructified *négritude* in both hemispheres.

It is significant, however, that *négritude* originated not in Africa but in the Caribbean (or, more precisely, in Paris, where student emigrés gathered).[3] *Négritude* is by definition less an affirmation than a protest against white dominance: 'Césaire makes so much display about accepting his race,' a Martinican suggests, only 'because he really feels it as a curse. Do the whites boast like that about theirs?'[4] Not only is *négritude* negative in essence, it is equivocal in practice. 'When the Negro declares in French that he rejects French culture, he takes in one hand that which he has pushed aside with the other'. *Négritude* 'is dedicated to its own destruction, it is passage and not objective, means and not the ultimate goal.'[5]

[1] Fanon, *Black Skin, White Masks*, p. 45. For definitions of négritude, see Coulthard, *Race and Colour in Caribbean Literature*, especially pp. 58–70; idem, 'Négritude—Reality and Mystification', *CS*, Vol. 10, No. 1, April 1970, pp. 42–51; Albert H. Berrian and Richard A. Long, eds., *Négritude: Essays and Studies*, 1967; René Piquion, *Manuel de négritude* [1965].

[2] Harold Courlander, 'Vodoun in Haitian Culture', and Rémy Bastien, 'Vodoun and Politics in Haiti', in Courlander and Bastien, *Religion and Politics in Haiti*, 1966, pp. 1–26, ref. p. 24; and pp. 39–68, ref. pp. 54–5, respectively. See also Richard P. Schaedel, 'Introduction', in *Papers of the Conference on Research and Resources of Haiti*, pp. 5–15, ref. pp. 8–9.

[3] Lilyan Kesteloot, 'Naissance de la négritude: "l'étudiant noir"', in idem, *Les écrivains noirs de langue française: naissance d'une littérature*, 1965, pp. 91–210; Jacques Louis Hymans, 'French Influences on Leopold Senghor's Theory of Négritude, 1928–48', *Race*, Vol. VII, 1965–6, pp. 365–70. 'The headquarters was in Paris. But which of them would have dreamed of travelling around the Soudan or the Congo to come into close contact with the soul of our ancient ancestors, the Mandingos or the Bantus? ... They prefer the Boulevard des Italiens to the swamps of Bahr-el Gazal or the mountains of Kilimanjaro' (Sténio Vincent, *En posant les jalons*, 1939, pp. 153–4, quoted in Coulthard, 'Négritude—Reality and Mystification', p. 44).

[4] Quoted in Fanon, *Black Skins, White Masks*, p. 48.

[5] Jean-Paul Sartre, *Black Orpheus* [1963], pp. 23, 60.

Literary *négritude* tends to be all-embracing but passive. 'La Beauté est nègre / et nègre la sagesse', / 'l'endurance est nègre / et nègre le courage'.[1] But this is hardly an inducement to action. As an African critic puts it, 'a tiger does not go about proclaiming its tigritude. It just pounces.'[2]

Passivity and negation help explain why *négritude* has touched West Indian life and thought only lightly. Its devotees do not recall an African heritage; they manufacture one anew. African nationhood kindled West Indian pride, but Africa and *négritude* are not vivid memories, they are metaphors meaningful mainly to poets and visionaries. Identification with Africa is inversely proportional to its relevance in everyday West Indian life. It is the light-skinned cosmopolite who is most conscious of Africa, not the folk in rural backwaters where speech, folklore, religion, and social organization most bespeak that past.

Awareness remains superficial even in Haiti, whose peasantry provide obvious African parallels. But the French-educated intellectuals who rediscovered this peasant heritage showed more concern for mystique than for misery; 'the Haitian *clercs* mistook their passionate interest in folklore for the active care they should have taken of their illiterate brothers.'[3] Literary followers of *négritude*, however radical in theory, have been concerned more with symbolic truth than with practical reform.

West Indian *négritude* assumes political significance by emphasizing a return to Africa, actual or symbolic. The back-to-Africa movement began with slaves repatriated to Sierra Leone as free men in the late eighteenth century. For Jamaican Maroons and Guianese Bush Negroes Africa is sufficiently present in the Caribbean. But more recently disaffected Creoles, who eke out a precarious existence on the margins of Caribbean society, have sought to alter it radically or to leave it entirely.

Many black West Indians have held prophetic or apocalyptic visions of imminent return to Africa, sometimes by way of paradise. A Jamaican, Alexander Bedward, prophesied in 1920 that he would ascend to heaven with the elect of African ancestry, returning later to colonize a new earth. In the 1910s and 1920s Marcus Garvey crystallized mass Jamaican—and later American Negro—discontent in his mission to recolonize Africa with the New World black diaspora, culminating with his Black Star Line but foundering with its misfortunes. In the 1940s and 1950s the Ras Tafari 'built themselves a bizarre myth of an

[1] Léon-G. Damas, *Black-Label*, 1956, p. 52.
[2] Attributed to Wole Soyinka, in Slade Hopkinson, 'Two Poems', *Bim*, Vol. 11, No. 44, p. 274.
[3] Bastien, 'Vodoun and Politics in Haiti', p. 62.

Africa that does not exist and that never was',[1] yet they fashioned a repatriation movement so militant that fear for domestic safety impelled the Jamaican Government to sponsor missions to assess colonization prospects in Africa. Although the return to Africa now seems more remote than ever, the prospect is occasionally rekindled by the arrival of some African cargo vessel. And the 70,000 Ras Tafari remain socially aloof in Jamaica, demanding a territorially separate state as an interim homeland. Meanwhile the fearful Jamaican elite and middle class generally urge that 'every means of sending the Rastas somewhere else should be carefully explored.'[2] Satirizing the concept of repatriation as a panacea, a Jamaican asks:

> Why not send us all back home?
> Ship all Catholics to Rome
> Ship our Scots back to their heather,
> English back to rainy weather.
>
>   *   *   *
>
> Send every single person back
> To Syria, China, Cayman Brac;
> And should we population lack
> Go out and find an Arawak.[3]

West Indian political and religious *négritude* parallel the American Black Muslim and black-power movements in impetus but diverge in impact. The facts of American demography make black 'control' there a remote prospect, but in some Caribbean territories it is a reality, and in all it is a potential; severe economic decline, heavy unemployment, or an oppressive 'brown' government may anywhere spark widespread revolt.

In Haiti black power is already state power. Duvalier subdued the mulatto elite and the Christian churches; Vodun, Haitian patois, and the black peasant now symbolize national cohesion. Open defiance of the white world was a key factor in Duvalier's success with the folk. When he proclaimed that 'Haiti is black and must be ruled by blacks', Haitians interpreted this to mean true freedom from white control.[4]

West Indian black nationalism thus cannot be assessed in literal

---

[1] Louis James, 'Introduction', in idem, ed., *The Islands in Between: Essays on West Indian Literature*, 1968, pp. 1–49, ref. p. 11.

[2] Leonard E. Barrett, 'The Rastafarians: A Study in Messianic Cultism in Jamaica', 1968, pp. 164, 191–6. See also George E. Simpson, 'Political Cultism in West Kingston, Jamaica', *SES*, Vol. 4, 1955, pp. 133–49; M. G. Smith, Roy Augier, and Rex Nettleford, *The Ras Tafari Movement in Kingston, Jamaica*, 1960; Sheila Kitzinger, 'The Rastafarian Brethren of Jamaica', *Comparative Studies in Society and History*, Vol. IX, 1966, pp. 33–9.

[3] Thomas Wright, 'Candidly Yours', *Jamaica Daily Gleaner*, 4 August 1960.

[4] Bastien, 'Vodoun and Politics in Haiti', pp. 59, 61. See also Bernard Diederich and Al Burt, *Papa Doc: The Truth about Haiti Today*, 1969.

terms alone. Its underlying aim is not so much African repatriation or even political revolution as the articulation of a separate and prideful black personality—an identity not yet possible in multi-racial West Indian societies. Black power fuses with *négritude*, as expressed by Edward Brathwaite:[1]

Down, down	back back
white	to the black
man, con	man lan'
man, brown	back back
man, . . .	to Af-
kill	rica.
dem an' go	

Africanist efforts to liberate West Indian folk consciousness arouse conflicting responses. 'A Trinidadian described his deep feeling when he first became aware of his African past; a Jamaican denied any interest in or awareness of Africa—yet . . . she was most evidently moved'[2] by Brathwaite's reading. Some, converted from disdain for a savage 'dark' continent to admiration for Africa's ancient civilization, proclaim their freedom from 'inevitable and ever-lasting tutelage to European culture';[3] others feel threatened by the prospect of such a shift in allegiance.

Négritude today extols African culture in order to transform West Indian tastes. 'Black consciousness has opened the minds of many young people', says a Trinidadian. 'Europe's astringent rhythms will find themselves supplanted in the popular mind by the native rhythm of drum, steelband and parang. . . . New styles of dress and personal adornment are a signal that a black renaissance is at hand.' The *agbada* is an advocated point of departure for exploring black history; the *dashiki* 'goes deeper than mere consideration of style . . . [to] clothes designed for a tropical climate.' In short, 'black men and women are . . . finding meaning in their own culture and their own environment',[4] even if the environment referred to is 'their own' only by ethnic extension.

Black rebirth implies white eclipse. 'No longer must our race look for whites for guidance and leadership', insists a Dominican; stores should 'stop carrying skin bleaching and hair straightening advertisements [that] . . . make our people feel they must try to look like white

[1] Edward Brathwaite, 'Wings of a Dove', in his *Rights of Passage*, 1967, pp. 41-4, ref. p. 42.

[2] Anne Walmsley, 'Second C.A.M. Conference', *Bim*, Vol. 12, No. 48, January–June 1969, pp. 233-6, ref. p. 235.

[3] G. Coulthard, review of Berrian and Long, eds., *Négritude: Essays and Studies*, in *CS*, Vol. 9, No. 1, April 1969, pp. 81-3, ref. p. 81.

[4] David Murray, 'Afro-Carib Consciousness', *Tapia*, No. 1, 28 September 1969, p. 5.

people to "be somebody".' West Indians are exhorted to 'take down the pictures of white women from your walls. Elevate your own women to that place of honour.'[1] Black-power movements have activated nascent anti-white feeling in many territories, paralleling or mirroring black self-assertion in the United States, and numerous racial incidents reflect the local sense that it is 'black man time now'.

But black power in the West Indies is not only anti-white, it is also anti-*coloured*. Black hostility toward the Caribbean light-skinned elite and middle class accords with the 'white' status they have always sought and partially achieved. West Indian pan-Africanists have historically rejected mulattoes as allies of whites and Europeans. Blyden, the island-born nineteenth-century advocate of Negro repatriation to Africa, openly and unremittingly detested mulattoes and urged the extension of Southern American anti-miscegenation laws to forbid marriage or fornication between 'genuine Negroes' and 'half-castes'.[2]

Garvey, Blyden's spiritual successor, spoke for a black peasantry that was left leaderless because, he explained, 'the educated class of my own people...are the bitterest enemies of their own race.'[3] Black unity was the crux of Garvey's appeal. He affirmed pride in being Negro, denounced coloured men who sought assimilation with whites, and taught his followers to venerate their Africanness. In Jamaica Garvey made little headway against black apathy and self-abasement. But in the United States after 1916, Garvey's Universal Negro Improvement Association aroused a tremendous response among the darker, less-educated Negroes who seemed forgotten by the light-skinned leaders of 'the Talented Tenth'.[4]

West Indian status distinctions between black and mulatto had only limited relevance, however, to Negroes in the United States. To be sure, Negro society in most American cities was dominated by descendants of old free-coloured families, and 'successful' Negroes still are usually lighter than the rest. But these distinctions, unimportant to whites,

[1] 'Black Power Say!!!' *Dominica Star*, 10 May 1969, p. 6.
[2] Hollis R. Lynch, *Edward Wilmot Blyden: Pan-Negro Patriot, 1832–1912*, 1967, pp. vii, 118, 139.
[3] Marcus Garvey to Robert Russa Moton, 29 February 1916, Moton Collection, Tuskegee Institute Archives (courtesy of Carl S. Matthews).
[4] August Meier, *Negro Thought in America, 1880–1915: Racial Ideologies in the Age of Booker T. Washington*, 1964, especially chapters 12–14; Harold R. Isaacs, *The New World of Negro Americans*, 1963, pp. 133–46; Edmund David Cronon, *Black Moses: The Story of Marcus Garvey and the Universal Negro Improvement Association*, 1964. On colour distinctions among Negro Americans see E. Franklin Frazier, *The Negro Family in the United States*, 1951, chapters 19 and 20; Edward Byron Reuter, *The Mulatto in the United States* [1918], pp. 177–80; Andrew Billingsley, *Black Families in White America*, 1968, pp. 122–46.

were seldom formalized by blacks. The very idea of colour stratification was at odds with what Negro Americans sought, and those who
did not deny its existence tended to minimize its significance. Garvey's
appeals to black men victimized by the West-Indian colour–class
system alienated Americans of mixed blood as well as black Americans
unwilling to regard mulattoes as their oppressors. The impassable white
barrier, the strong prejudice against all non-whites alike, then as now
gave American Negroes a sense of community regardless of shade, which
is still absent in the West Indies.

Both independence and the black-power movement have reactivated
conflict between black and brown. 'We have identified the mulatto with
the betrayal of the Revolution', writes a Guyanese celebrant of slave
insurrection; when brown men do the right thing they are said to have
'repudiated the mulatto heritage'.[1] A Trinidadian notes that 'today
there are fewer and fewer "red niggers" and more and more Black
men of light complexion, who have healed the psychological and moral
gaps in their consciousness, and understood that their salvation and
identity lie in their self-identification with the Black masses'.[2] A more
realistic appraisal, perhaps, is that 'for years people like me playing
white and the day of reckoning come. . . . People whose colour red . . .
[are] getting curse up all over the place.'[3] West Indians of many shades
have begun to wear Afro wigs, some to affirm their pride in blackness,
others to forestall black harassment. Some political leaders in the
self-governing West Indies seek solidarity with the electorate by
exaggerating their own 'blackness'; thus Bradshaw of St. Kitts has
claimed to be a full-blooded Ashanti, and the lighter-skinned Premier
of Dominica, when not asserting Carib ancestry, emphasizes African
antecedents.

West Indian black power is unlikely to remain viable in this racially
emphatic form, however; for many of its principal advocates are themselves light-skinned, and local views of colour are too fine-grained, local
societies too personalized, to tolerate American-style polarization.
When a Barbadian terms himself the 'black' leader of the 'suffering
black masses', a local columnist retorts that if 'this half white, half
black gentleman . . . is black, the rest of us are Amerindians.'[4] A
Dominican 'Mongrel' castigates a local black-power spokesman—
'may I still call him "Little" Rosie'—for ignoring racial facts:

So, we are Africans now! God bless us all! What utter nonsense! I'll bet there
isn't a single negro in this island who doesn't have some white blood in him.

[1] P. H. Daly, *Revolution to Republic*, 1970, pp. 67, 69.
[2] 'After the Carnival', *Embryo*, Supplement, n.d., p. S1.
[3] 'Dear Boysie', *Trinidad Sunday Guardian*, 8 March 1970, p. 8.
[4] 'Madness on Tuesday Night', letter signed 'Archie', *Barbados Beacon*, reprinted in
Dominica Star, 7 December 1968, p. 1.

Rosie himself . . . has got quite a bit! For heaven's sake, man, Rosie, I mean, we all know that all of this is political. . . . But go at it in a different manner, man.[1]

When students protested Jamaica's 1968 exclusion of a Guyanese lecturer with the slogan 'This, above all, to thine own colour be true', a small-island editor asked 'What colour? There are so many shades!'[2]

Black power is 'a forceful weapon for the American Negro', concedes a small-island journal, but 'may be a suicidal one for the West Indian, falsifying both his inter-racial origins and his quickly deepening culture.'[3] American Negro origins are, to be sure, no less 'inter-racial' than are West Indian; it is the perception of colour that differs. It is all very well to insist that 'blackness' has little to do with skin colour and to claim with Stokely Carmichael that Castro is really the 'blackest' man in the Caribbean; but it is not easy to convince most West Indians that by analogy some of the 'whitest' figures are black leaders like Bradshaw of St. Kitts, Bird of Antigua, or Gairy of Grenada.[4] And when Carmichael refers to his early life in Trinidad with pride because the school-teachers and the police were black, local realities conform still less with black power, 'since these figures of authority, in full complaisance to colonial policy, often used their powers not to liberate our people, but to maintain us in a condition of servility.' Carmichael's naïveté 'makes nonsense of black power in the West Indies where we are revolting against a black-skinned Afro-Saxon administration.'[5] And so the West Indian returns to what he has always known; whether or not 'Massa Day Done', in Williams's optimistic phrase, 'not all whites were Massa, . . . not all Massas were white.'[6]

In Trinidad and the Guianas, where East Indians are a major element in the population, black power poses additional problems of definition and, still more, of safety; for as one Indian put it during the Trinidad disturbances of 1970, 'If Afro-Indian racism is used against whites, there can be no guarantee that in future years, . . . one of the two major ethnic groups will not use the same destructive battle cry of race in a new contest for power.'[7] Black American prescriptions for

[1] 'Be Yourself?' letter signed 'Mongrel', *Dominica Chronicle*, 6 June 1970, p. 2.

[2] 'Black Pride or Black Power', *Dominica Star*, 16 November 1968, p. 1.

[3] Ibid.

[4] 'Tapia Special on the Current National Crisis', p. 2, in *Tapia*, No. 6, 8 March 1970.

[5] 'Rt. Hon. Dead Horse, C.H.: Filling the Political Vacuum', *Tapia*, No. 7, 19 April 1970, p. 2.

[6] Eric Williams, *Massa Day Done: A Masterpiece of Political and Sociological Analysis*, 1961, p. 7.

[7] R. K. Richardson, '"Majority Power" Would Be Better', *Trinidad Guardian*, 26 March 1970, p. 10.

ending white domination, adds a Guyanese, 'are hopelessly and dangerously wrong.'[1]

Whatever its utility or consistency pan-Africanism engenders no
enduring appeal, partly because West Indian links to Africa are too
tenuous to be sustained by sheer rhetoric. Apart from diplomats and
dashikis, African–West Indian culture contact is minimal. Unlike
Brazil, where constant commerce has kept West Africa vivid and
meaningful, the Caribbean has had only sporadic communication
since the slave trade ended, and even the migration of free Africans to
the West Indies during the post-emancipation decades had little impact
on most local cultures and institutions. 'Black Power leaders . . . say
that we must throw off the White Imperialist Culture and adopt
Black African ways', notes a small-island 'Africus'. 'It seems bad that
our young men ape their white masters by playing cricket—a truly
white man's game. . . . Isn't there a good African game our young men
could play in the Botanical Gardens on Sundays?'[2]

Serious or sardonic, this query reflects the common conviction that
European culture is for West Indians inevitable, if not superior. 'The
more educated West Indians agree almost to the man that the white
race everywhere is more advanced, generally, than the blacks in
Africa', a Dominican avers. 'How then can it ever make sense to discard
the civilization of the whites for that of the blacks which they themselves classify as "developing"?'[3] The old colonial bugbear of Haiti
still terrifies West Indians who fear black anarchy:

No country has ever profited by getting rid of white people. One of the first to
try it was Haiti, and after 300 years the black people there are still mainly in
poverty, misery and oppression. . . . Jamaica as a nation of mainly black people
cannot succeed . . . unless it maintains excellent relations and friendships
with white people abroad, [which requires] good relations with white people
in Jamaica.[4]

Sparrow's calypso 'Congo Man', a gloss on the reported rape of
European nuns in the Belgian Congo in 1964, exemplifies West Indian
racial and national ambivalence. 'Congo Man' enjoying his first taste
of white meat is 'an obvious sexual metaphor for the black who has at

[1] Kit Nascimento, 'Imported Black Power Is Hopelessly Dangerously Wrong',
Action Radio Times, Vol. 1, No. 2, November 1969, p. 6. A black American scholar
expresses similar concern lest 'Pan-Negroism encourage . . . disquieting "Ethiopianist"
escapism among the Jamaican masses', and finds 'emphasis upon Negro solidarity . . .
actually dysfunctional in such countries as Trinidad and Guyana' (St. Clair Drake,
'Reflections on the Black Diaspora', *NWQ*, Vol. 4, No. 4, Cropover 1968, pp. 73–8,
ref. p. 77).

[2] 'Away with Cricket', letter in *Dominica Star*, 17 May 1969, p. 13.

[3] Peter Simple, 'For Dominica—Brown Power', *Dominica Chronicle*, reprinted in
Dominica Star, 3 May 1969, p. 1.

[4] 'The Sentry', *Jamaica Daily Gleaner*, 14 January 1970.

last fulfilled his dream of being equal to the white master, by sleeping with the white man's woman.' But the song makes 'the sort of joke about cannibalism of which only the white world ought to be capable, [and thus] mercilessly and unconsciously reveals the cultural limbo in which the West Indian moves'. According to a local critic,

Sparrow has used the white man's stereotype of the African—which reveals his divorce from the African—to make a deep and serious joke against the white—which reveals his alienation from the whites. But in so doing, he reveals a deep psychic need within the West Indian to prove his manhood through a fulfilled phallic vengeance for ancestral rape—which reveals his alienation from himself.[1]

Africans themselves are understandably skeptical about black Antillean rediscovery of ancestral virtues. The West Indian who once implored Europeans not to 'pay attention to my black skin, it's the sun that has burned me, my soul is as white as yours', now asks Africans not to 'pay attention to my white skin, my soul is as black as yours'; but the transition is too sudden and superficial to be convincing. In Fanon's trenchant phrase, 'the West Indian, after the great white error, is now living in the great black mirage.'[2]

At the United Nations Jamaica is regarded as 'a reactionary black English outpost in the lap of America', and West Indians, submissive still to European models, are reprobated as 'Afro-Saxons'.[3] West Indians impatient for reform find this a just assessment. 'Despite all the official ballyhoo,' writes a Trinidadian, 'we have met the times by resorting to blackface ads for Ovaltine and Guinness, by erecting selected black mannequins in the shopwindows, and by a destructive sponsorship of steelbands. . . . But we have never rejected the assumption of blackness as illegitimacy.'[4]

African elements, like folk culture, are generally more stifled than stimulated by official recognition that is both partial and paternalistic. 'The Church *now* tries to use folk masses, jazz masses, African masses and the like. . . . They haven't, however, stopped referring to African religion as primitive fetish-worship, or stigmatising states of possession as diabolical.'[5] But middle-class opprobrium is only one obstacle to

---

[1] Gordon Rohlehr, 'Bizarre Satire: Social Context of Sparrow's Calypsoes—Part 5', *Trinidad Sunday Guardian*, 25 February 1968, p. 10.

[2] Fanon, 'West Indians and Africans', pp. 25, 27.

[3] Rex Nettleford, 'The African Connexion—The Significance for Jamaica', in Hearne and Nettleford, *Our Heritage*, p. 52; Nettleford, 'National Identity and Attitudes to Race in Jamaica', p. 62.

[4] Espinet and Farmer, 'Pussonal Nonarchy', p. 6. The symbols of black pride are often insufficient, even as symbols. 'A Negro is used on T.V. as the painter for a certain brand of well-known paint, while only white babies drink Lactogen milk', a Trinidadian avers (Frank Lee, 'National Lottery', *Moko*, No. 14, p. 4).

[5] 'After the Carnival', p. S6.

Africanist ambitions in the West Indies. A graver impediment is the inadequacy of things African to symbolize anything more than freedom from European trappings. 'Foreign influence' is exorcised in strictly limited fashion.

Nobody wears blue serge suits; only the Jamaican upper class plus St. Kitts' Mr. Bradshaw wear waistcoats; and the day is near when we shall all throw away ties. Scotch will be thrown away and all patriots will drink rum, post my mortem. These are the conventional radicalisms. And every year some more will be added. Afro shirts, bushy hair, sandals. But the absence of an intellectual tradition cannot be so swiftly and engagingly corrected.[1]

In black power as in so much else, the West Indian intellectual tradition is to emulate and imitate. 'The present rash of African sentiment contains a fair proportion of the West Indian tendency to look everywhere but at the West Indies.'[2] The minutest details of Caribbean black power reflect Africa, if at all, by way of the United States. Malcolm X begets Michael X, Black Panthers generate Black Eagles. 'Leaders of the protest movement are apparently so deficient in innovation', charges a Trinidadian, 'that they find it necessary to copy their nomenclature, syllable by syllable, and their ornamentation (beards, black jerseys, clenched fist salute, etc.) from the American "black power" movement'.[3]

The radicals respond that those who imitate Europe have no right to complain about other borrowings. The middle class wants them to 'stop importing foreign habits, like mini-skirts, Afro-hair-dos, Black Power (in its American version)', but they do not see 'anything wrong with importing foreign habits like the Governor-General's Imperial Crest, like beating prisoners to death in police stations (in its American version), like having Carnival Queens.'[4] West Indians view the conscious use of exotic elements as a necessary stage in the identity search. 'I look upon it only as a start', explains a Trinidadian promoter of African garb. After 'we have worn them for a while and the novelty wears off we will have to find something of our own. Out of this we will arrive at our own culture.'[5]

West Indians seem unwilling to begin any journey, however, unless outsiders lead the way. At Guyana's Republic Day fête, the Prime Minister ate food from a calabash.

[1] Randolph Rawlins, 'Black Power', *Art and Man*, Act II, Scene II, June 1969, pp. 47–51, ref. p. 48. See also V. S. Naipaul, 'Power to the Caribbean People', *New York Review of Books*, 3 September 1970, pp. 32–4.

[2] Wickham, 'West Indian Writing', p. 71.

[3] David Renwick, 'How Jamadar Views the Unrest', *Trinidad Sunday Guardian*, 29 March 1970, p. 13.

[4] Adrian Espinet, 'Plenty Parties, Plenty Balls', *Tapia*, No. 5, 1 February 1970, p. 1.

[5] Irma Simonette, quoted in Rosemary Stone, 'Eye', *Trinidad Express*, 26 March 1970, p. 8.

But don't think that because Mr. Burnham was eating in calabash it means that we going take it up too. Noh! Not yet. The people in America have to start using it first, then we bound to follow suit. . . . They chewing gum, we chewing it faster. For years we drinking rum with water, they say it good with Coca-Cola, we agree. Remember how we used to turn up noses at roti? The Yankees came and say it too nice. So now roti in every social fete. Is that kind of people we are yes.[1]

West Indians readily accept foreign idioms to explain and to resolve problems of cultural definition. But since these solutions are external they perennially dissatisfy and become new sets of problems. Each resolution entails new obligations to outside sources. As one critic says, 'the West Indian, in searching for an identity, is expressing one.'[2] The quest is a lifetime preoccupation.

[1] 'Dear Boysie', *Trinidad Sunday Guardian*, 1 March 1970, p. 8.
[2] C. L. R. James, cited in Winston Hackett, 'Identity in the Poetry of Walcott', *Moko*, No. 8, 14 February 1969, p. 2.

CHAPTER VIII

Conclusion

West Indian societies have proved remarkably resistant to fundamental alteration. The high promise and repeated disappointment of hopes engendered by historic events, from emancipation to independence, are themselves constants that have shaped Caribbean temperament. The West Indies always seem on the verge of developments that fail to occur or that leave things much as before. But in recent years external forces and internal pressures have visibly affected traditional ways. The old class system still dominates many aspects of life, but the composition of the hierarchy is changing, stratification counts for less in personal relations, and colour distinctions are more flexible than before.

Most striking is the penetration of barriers between white and non-white. Except in the French Antilles, social elites are no longer exclusively white, nor does apparent whiteness determine membership in elite circles. Overt racial exclusion ended in the 1940s; since then self-government and expatriate withdrawal have further liberalized elite criteria. Middle-class status, too, is now less linked to colour. Many black West Indians move directly from folk backgrounds into emerging political and professional elites. And among the peasantry and urban proletariat colour is seldom a feature of status distinctions.

Non-whites have gained increasing prominence in almost every Caribbean territory. Thirty years ago only two of Jamaica's top twenty-five officials were coloured, and five-sixths of the Governor-General's guest list was white;[1] today brown and black men occupy most top posts, and whites are a small minority at any official function. In 1906 a Martinican *béké* caused a furor by shaking hands in public with a mulatto leader;[2] to omit such a civility today would be unthinkable. In the Netherlands Windwards, interracial mixing, common at dances in the 1960s, 'could not have occurred, a decade [earlier], without

---

[1] Paul Blanshard, *Democracy and Empire in the Caribbean: A Contemporary Review*, 1947, p. 101.

[2] Shelby T. McCloy, *The Negro in the French West Indies*, 1966, pp. 270–1.

scandalous and condemnatory comment.'[1] Although expatriate sugar interests still dominate St. Kitts, 'nowadays we see cross sections at social gatherings where once only marked exclusiveness prevailed.'[2] In Barbados, stigmatized as a segregated society in 1950, institutional segregation has since disappeared, and no gathering of the powerful could fail to include coloured and black men.[3]

As class–colour composition changes, new political, educational, and entrepreneurial elites also erode class lines.

The steady expansion of the cash-nexus in the West Indies brought time-sanctioned values and behaviour under assault. . . . The attainment of the political kingdom by the coloured colonial has had salutory ramifications extending far beyond the political arena itself. The African descendant has not only attained power . . . he has now attained a level of status and dignity.[4]

But those who gain high status now find the very principle of hierarchy undermined. Twenty years ago, ordinary Antiguans tipped their hats and curtsied to the white and light elite who went to Government House functions. Status dispersal makes deference both anachronistic and less rewarding; now that anyone can go to Government House, many no longer bother. Traditional status no longer dominates the marriage market; working-class youngsters of high promise may be preferred to more humdrum scions of the old elite. In Guyana a 'general egalitarian climate of opinion' is said to have replaced the previous 'social discrimination accepted in both public and private life.'[5] A Kittician contends that 'the old stiff and rigid social system is completely shattered and people have become more flexible and approachable.'[6] As more persons of working-class origin take up professional careers, social background counts for less. Class is neither so sharply defined nor so potent, colour is less crucial for status, and high social rank no longer elicits automatic deference.

Yet ascription still largely determines place and reward throughout the Caribbean. A hierarchical proclivity characterizes Creole rulers no less than their expatriate predecessors. Despite lip-service to equal

[1] Dorothy L. Keur, 'The Nature of Recent Change in the Dutch Windward Islands', *International Journal of Comparative Sociology*, Vol. V, No. 1, March 1964, pp. 40–8, ref. p. 46.

[2] *St. Kitts Union Messenger*, 3 December 1960, p. 2.

[3] Patrick Leigh Fermor, *The Traveller's Tree: A Journey through the Caribbean Islands*, 1950, p. 153; Raymond W. Mack, 'Race, Class, and Power in Barbados', in Wendell Bell, ed., *The Democratic Revolution in the West Indies: Studies in Nationalism, Leadership, and the Belief in Progress*, 1967, pp. 140–64, ref. pp. 157, 160–1.

[4] Ivar Oxaal, 'Race, Pluralism and Nationalism in the British Caribbean', *Journal of Biosocial Science*, Supplement No. 1, July 1969, pp. 153–62, ref. pp. 155–6.

[5] B. A. N. Collins, 'The Public Service of Guyana: The Report of the Commission of Inquiry', 1969, p. 7, para. 17.

[6] *St. Kitts Union Messenger*, 3 December 1960, p. 2.

opportunity, few leaders actively promote social or economic equality.[1] Under self-government, Jamaican senior officials began 'to treat their subordinates in the civil service as they did their domestic employees at home. . . . The relationship of subordinate to superior followed the line of almost military discipline and the colonial pattern of "keeping the native at a respectable distance".'[2] In Guyana self-rule initially magnified class bias in the public service; black and East Indian professionals who wielded power under expatriate chiefs were displaced by light-coloured career civil servants of elite background.[3]

Personnel shifts attendant on the transfer of sovereignty are apt to be mistaken as evidence of social mobility. Senators in newly independent Trinidad saw their own positions as proof that 'Trinidad's is an open society with equality of opportunity.' But they themselves were anything but self-made men; their middle-class professional backgrounds virtually assured them high office when metropolitan rule ended.[4]

Darker aspirants are more conscious of the gulf between reform credos and local realities.

Because they are black and have not gone to the right schools, and do not have the right social connections . . . people with the training and ability to become part of the *élite* have remained just on the fringe of the *élite*; highly placed and highly paid, but knowing that were it not for their colour they would be higher than those above them because their abilities are greater.[5]

Black Trinidadians entering the public service are 'disgruntled' by the knowledge 'that others, in no ways superior to themselves, are getting better breaks.'[6]

Those who get breaks tend to forget social reform and accept the system. Overseas-trained black Guyanese at the bauxite mines find that 'the company would prefer them not to mix too freely with their fellow Guyanese in the village' and adjust accordingly—'he is well established . . . , he is company-oriented, when he says "we" he means management.'[7] Behaviour toward superiors and subordinates reflects the endurance of West Indian hierarchical habits. In commerce as in the civil service, 'chances of prompt service increase if the individual is

[1] Wendell Bell, *Jamaican Leaders: Political Attitudes in a New Nation*, 1964, pp. 35, 106.
[2] B. L. St. John Hamilton, *Problems of Administration in an Emergent Nation: A Case Study of Jamaica*, 1964, pp. 123, 159.
[3] M. K. Bacchus, 'The Ministerial System at Work: A Case Study of Guyana', *SES*, Vol. 16, 1967, pp. 34–56, ref. p. 50.
[4] Ann Spackman, 'The Senate of Trinidad and Tobago', *SES*, Vol. 16, 1967, pp. 77–100, ref. p. 85.
[5] Peter Abrahams, *This Island Now*, 1966, p. 134.
[6] 'Millette: Too Little, Too Late', *Trinidad Guardian*, 1 April 1970, p. 6.
[7] Maurice St. Pierre, 'Industrial Unrest in Mackenzie, Guyana', in Frances Henry, ed., *McGill Studies in Caribbean Anthropology*, 1969, pp. 65–92, ref. p. 79.

white, wears a coat and tie, or bears himself with starchy dignity'.[1] The police treat elite offenders with lenient deference, while they haul up black suspects as criminals for lesser offences or none at all.[2]

Status schooling remains a major function of West Indian education. Secondary-school curricula continue to produce a ruling elite remote from the folk. And many nationalist politicians go on intoning old colonial values. Effort and obedience are especially extolled. 'If we work hard', a Jamaican senator asserts, 'there will be no poverty in Jamaica.'[3] At Grenada's 1970 prize-day ceremonies Premier Eric Gairy 'urged pupils to . . . be obedient, polite and respectful'.[4]

West Indians are right to believe that who they know matters more than what they know. 'In spite of their lack of skills, [Jamaicans] who want to work with the bauxite companies . . . assiduously compile "letters" from clergymen and politicians . . . on the naive assumption that at such levels politics, religion, and capital converge.'[5] This apparent naïveté reflects reality in most spheres of activity. Academic honours and influence peddling determine the recruitment of civil servants more than administrative or technical competence. Promotion in Martinique, for example, 'depends much less on how well one works than on the favour of the powerful. . . . To gain access to the managerial elite, politics are often more useful than proved competence or great intellectual capacity.'[6]

Family connections buttress privilege. Scholarships, appointments, and promotions are generally assumed to be at the disposal of highly placed relatives. Nepotism flourishes in many small societies, but West Indians carry the practice to extremes. For example, the Public Works Department in Dominica's second town reportedly 'consists of one family—clerks A, B, C, D, E, [and] F. A is the brother of B and the husband of C. A and B are first cousins of D. B is the brother-in-law of E. C is the sister-in-law of B. F, I do not know how to place her. But I guess she is some kind of relative to E.'[7]

Any position once gained outweighs job performance. Thus the directorship of a local radio station made a Guyanese barrister a success

[1] Selwyn Douglas Ryan, 'Decolonization in a Multi-Racial Society: A Case Study of Trinidad and Tobago' [1967], p. 434.
[2] 'The Case for Law Reform: Return to the Rule of Law', *WIE*, Vol. 2, No. 9, March 1960, pp. 7–8; Earl Lewis, 'Discrimination at Home', *Moko*, No. 12, 11 April 1969, pp. 2 and 4; Augustus Ramrekersingh, 'Black Boy', *Moko*, No. 18, 2 July 1969, p. 3.
[3] Ivan Moore, in *Jamaica Daily Gleaner*, 2 December 1968, p. 10.
[4] 'Youth Told: Be Obedient', *Trinidad Guardian*, 17 March 1970, p. 7.
[5] *The Church and Unemployment*, p. 7.
[6] Jean-Luc Morel, 'Jeunesse et emploi: de l'insertion des jeunes martiniquais dans le milieu social', *CERAG*, No. 13, April 1968, p. 67.
[7] 'Is It True?' *Dominica Herald*, 9 December 1967, p. 2.

in the eyes of his peers: 'It did not matter that he had done nothing outstanding at B.G. Broadcasting. What was important was that he had been the first colored man in the West Indies to hold such a position.'[1]

Gulfs in living standards reflect and reinforce class distance. The more static societies exhibit old divisions between the only moderately well-off elites and the impoverished masses. In Haiti a few families are said to 'enjoy life as kings' in view of the fact that 'they eat every day— three or four times a day', whereas four out of five are illiterate and hungry, and 'fatal starvation is commonplace in rural areas'.[2] In St. Vincent a few live in comfort, while for most life is little more than 'a study in poverty.'[3]

Disparities between rich and poor are still greater where mineral extraction, tourism, and industrialization have spurred development. During 1952–63 Jamaica achieved the world's highest per capita productivity increase, and income in the Commonwealth Caribbean generally ranks well above most Third World countries. But this benefits few West Indians.[4] The bauxite and oil operations that employ little labour account for the bulk of the increase. Their permanent working force, together with that in export agriculture, is far better off than the mass of peasant proprietors, estate tenants, sharecroppers, and casual labourers, not to mention the totally unemployed.[5]

Poverty and rural desuetude propel thousands townward, but most migrants' hopes prove delusory. In Martinique 'young people leave the countryside in droves, attracted by the mirage of city life, but end up simply wandering around the city streets.'[6] Urban unemployment far exceeds rural and the city jobless are worse off: no family land, no provision crops, no community share-pot stands between them and starvation. Slum and shanty-town dwellers scuffle for scraps in garbage dumps while they wait for work, for emigration, or for some miracle. The absence of jobs deters few rural emigrants; 'people

[1] Paule Marshall, *Soul Clap Hands and Sing*, 1961, p. 97.

[2] Gérard R. Latortue, 'Political Crisis in Haiti', *NWQ*, Vol. 3, No. 2, High Season, 1967, pp. 45–50, ref. p. 46; Kendall W. King, 'Nutrition Research in Haiti', in Richard P. Schaedel, ed., *Papers of the Conference on Research and Resources of Haiti*, 1969, pp. 347–70, ref. p. 354. See also I. D. Beghin, W. Fougère, and Kendall W. King, *Food and Nutrition in Haiti*, 1968.

[3] K. R. V. John, 'Political Crisis in St. Vincent', *NWQ*, Vol. 3, No. 3, High Season 1967, pp. 51–6, ref. p. 51.

[4] William G. Demas, *The Economics of Development in Small Countries with Special Reference to the Caribbean*, 1965, pp. 101–2; E. Ahiram, 'Income Distribution in Jamaica, 1958', *SES*, Vol. 13, 1964, pp. 333–69, ref. p. 343.

[5] Owen Jefferson, 'Some Aspects of the Post-War Economic Development of Jamaica', *NWQ*, Vol. 3, No. 3, High Season 1967, pp. 1–11, ref. pp. 2–4.

[6] Morel, 'Jeunesse et emploi', p. 19.

are attracted . . . [to the city] in the vague hope of being able to get a job, even if in practice the probability of succeeding is not very great.'[1]

Living standards among the elite and the rising middle class contrast sharply with those of the masses. Jamaica's income distribution is most unequal, with the best-off 5 per cent of the population getting 30 per cent of the national income, and the poorest 20 per cent getting only 2 per cent; the well-off make sixty times what the poor do. In the mid-1960s it was Jamaica's dubious distinction to have the world's highest rate of income inequality. Other West Indian territories display analogous, if less extreme, inequalities.[2]

These flagrant disparities are acutely felt to contradict professed ideals. The West Indian poor have seen promise after government promise degenerate to palliatives. Jamaican leaders in the 1950s 'thought they could solve the unemployment problem by industrialization; but they failed. In the 1960s both Parties seem to feel that the problem cannot be solved. Political patronage, "Christmas work" and "Independence Work" have replaced whatever genuine intention there ever was to eradicate unemployment.'[3] At the height of Trinidad's 1970 black-power demonstrations, the Christian Council of Churches responded to the crisis by agreeing to observe 'Unemployment Week' with Hindu and Muslim co-operation.[4] Proffered such solutions as this, it is little wonder that the black majority, in a local reformer's view, is depressed and unhappy.[5]

Government passivity in the face of gross disparities breeds apathy and hostility. Slum dwellers and jobless come to regard the new leaders as stooges of the old, 'charlatans who run the plantation for whites'.[6] The elite and middle class in return construe folk behaviour as a threat to their homes and their lives. During recurring crises 'nervous people sipping Scotch by the poinsettias on their patios . . . asked one

[1] Nassau A. Adams, 'Internal Migration in Jamaica: An Economic Analysis', SES, Vol. 18, 1969, pp. 137–51, ref. p. 151.

[2] Ahiram, 'Income Distribution in Jamaica, 1958', pp. 335–44; E. Ahiram, 'Distribution of Income in Trinidad-Tobago and Comparison with Distribution of Income in Jamaica', SES, Vol. 15, 1966, pp. 103–20, ref. p. 108. One-sixth of Trinidad's workers earn more than $300 a month, while one-fourth take home less than $50 (Ryan, 'Decolonization in a Multi-Racial Society', p. 511). In Guyana, levels of income have become more disparate between skilled and unskilled labour (Havelock Brewster, 'The Pattern of Change in Wages, Prices and Productivity in British Guyana, 1948 to 1962', SES, Vol. 18, 1969, pp. 107–36, ref. p. 132).

[3] 'Unemployment', New World Pamphlet, September 1967, p. 2.

[4] 'This Challenge Must Be Faced', Trinidad Sunday Guardian, 22 March 1970, p. 10.

[5] James Millette, 'Leading Politically', Moko, No. 24, 20 March 1970, p. 3.

[6] James Millette, quoted in Thomas A. Johnson, 'What Caribbean Black Power Means', New York Times, 25 April 1970.

another how long they will be safe in their beds'.[1] Most Jamaican leaders queried in 1962 judged the folk majority 'hostile'.[2] Criminal violence, however defined, has since become a graver problem throughout the Caribbean. 'Serious crimes' in Trinidad more than doubled between 1960 and 1967.[3] In the United States Virgin Islands, where 'serious crime was almost unheard of' in 1960, 'the white community is [now] racked with fear', and the Commissioner of Public Safety asserts that the sharp rise 'caught the police with their pants down.'[4] The Jamaican murder rate increased by 70 per cent between 1962–3 and 1966–7.

The gulf between rich and poor is a widely recognized threat to social and national stability.

The privileged can only survive by suspecting everyone who is black and badly dressed, by sleeping with one ear open and a gun beneath the pillow, and by keeping savage dogs. The Government can only survive by arming and increasing the police and encouraging them to drop the traditional colonial niceties, and by expanding the army and using it in frequent shows of naked force. The quality of human life and human relationships is soured and bloodied.[5]

Ultimately the most repressive measures cannot assure the maintenance of law and order, or protect the property of the rich. 'The police are a frightened and demoralized body of men whose sole trust is in their guns and batons, and the owners of those splendid houses on the hill are beginning to realize that bigger and more savage watch-dogs and stronger burglar bars are insufficient deterrent to men prepared to shoot their way into homes', observed a Jamaican in 1969. 'Some of the crimes of violence have been part of a bitter protest at the entrenched supremacy of the upper classes.'[6]

The stress is often expressed in terms of race. If colour no longer determines class boundaries, it increasingly symbolizes the differences that lie beyond them. Precisely because status and rewards are in flux, racial inequalities are no longer accepted as inevitable concomitants of a hierarchical system but are construed as deliberate, malign, and hence corrigible. 'If there was justice and equality for us black people',

---

[1] Marjorie Hughes, *The Fairest Island*, 1962, p. 12, quoted in James A. Mau, *Social Change and Images of the Future: A Study of the Pursuit of Progress in Jamaica*, 1968, p. 99.

[2] Mau, *Social Change and Images of the Future*, p. 102.

[3] Dudley Seers, 'A Step Towards a Political Economy of Development (Illustrated by the Case of Trinidad/Tobago)', *SES*, Vol. 18, 1969, pp. 218–53, ref. p. 239.

[4] Glynn Mapes, 'Uneasy Islands: Rise of Black Power Brings Racial Strife To Caribbean Region', *Wall Street Journal*, 22 December 1970, p. 15.

[5] 'Sans Humanité: Violence in Jamaica', *Moko*, No. 13, 25 April 1969, p. 4, and No. 14, 9 May 1969, p. 4.

[6] 'Unemployment', p. 13.

a Jamaican argues, 'there wouldn't be so many of us starving while white people . . . are feeding their dogs with beefsteak. . . . The white people's dogs live better than the black man in this country'.[1] As the majority see it, 'the black man eats the least, wears the least, owns the least, prays the most, works the most, suffers the most and dies the most.'[2]

West Indian leaders, unable to resolve these disparities, are tempted to deny their existence. 'To talk about bad conditions in Jamaica at the present time', according to one senator, is 'a fairy tale'.[3] For most Jamaicans, the facts of life make such a statement incredible. Deep-seated structural inequalities cannot now be concealed behind the façades of black governors and prime ministers. In the eyes of many who are poor and dark, national leaders are puppets manipulated by foreign imperial and local white or light-coloured interests. Economic and social awareness thus heighten consciousness of colour and generate racial acerbity.

Mass antagonism toward foreign whites is keen and outspoken. Nationalism calls for replacing foreigners with natives, whatever their qualifications. West Indianization is deliberate policy in most Common-wealth Caribbean countries, and metropolitans are 'looked upon with general disfavour' in the Netherlands and French territories.[4] Few senior personnel from abroad remain in West Indian public services, except in the French Antilles, where *départementalisation* ironically increased the metropolitan presence. As colonies the French Antilles had been administered largely by West Indians under mainland French governors. Departmental status subordinated them to the central government in Paris and opened the Antillean civil service and the *gendarmerie* to thousands of European and Algerian French, whose presence West Indians bitterly resent.[5]

West Indianization at the University of the West Indies has special significance as symbolic of trans-Caribbean leadership. Complaints about expatriates' 'colonial' habits sped their replacement in the early 1960s, and the proportion of West Indian staff continues to rise. Euro-pean and American academics nowadays are treated with reserve, kept on the periphery, and remain for brief periods only; not even local marriage insures against local animus. One university board member has expressed the hope that 'it will not be long before U.W.I. is purged

[1] 'Black Shadow Over "Paradise Isle"', *Newday*, Vol. 5, No. 6, June 1961, p. 20.

[2] Millard Johnson, cited in S. George Minott, 'The P.P.P. and Charges of Race Hatred', *Jamaica Times*, 29 June 1961, p. 9.

[3] Ivan Moore, quoted in *Jamaica Daily Gleaner*, 2 December 1968, p. 10.

[4] See Keur, 'The Nature of Recent Change in the Dutch Windward Islands', p. 45.

[5] See Gilbert Gratiant, *Île fédérée française de la Martinique*, 1961, pp. 31–6.

of any foreign influences so that it can be a truly West Indian university in faculty, student body, and subject matter.'[1]

The shift from the early collaborative spirit to conscious exclusion based on race and nationality is well expressed in a West Indian's poem 'To an Expatriate Friend':

> Colour meant nothing. Anyone
> who wanted help, had humour or was kind
> was brother to you; categories of skin
> were foreign; you were colour-blind.
>
> And then the revolution. Black
> and loud the horns of anger blew
> against the long oppression; sufferers
> cast off the precious values of the few.
>
> New powers re-enslaved us all;
> each person manacled in skin, in race.
> You could not wear your paid-up dues;
> the keen discriminators typed your face.
>
> The future darkening, you thought it time
> to say good-bye. It may be you were right.
> It hurt to see you go; but, more,
> it hurt to see you slowly going white.[2]

Among young West Indian radicals it is almost mandatory to reject foreign whites and to condemn expatriate help. Their hostility is sharpened by the enduring self-abasement of some folk, who still express the view that black leaders are doomed to fail because only whites know how to run things. An anti-Jaganite Guyanese, poor, old, and black, exempts Jagan's American wife from criticism, because 'that big, nice, great white lady come all the way from America to help we, comrade.' This remark sums up, the narrator adds, 'the story of her way of life and mine too—the ugly history of the movement from slavery to parasitism.'[3]

West Indianization is less pervasive in private than in public employment. Official pressure requires foreign-owned mining companies, factories, and banks, which have a quasi-public visibility, to train local replacements for expatriate staff. Nor can foreign firms afford the appearance of exclusion, as Antiguan hoteliers who hired English

---

[1] Cited by Thomas G. Mathews, 'Caribbean Cooperation in the Field of Higher Education', in Roy Preiswerk, ed., *Regionalism and the Commonwealth Caribbean*, 1969, pp. 151–6, ref. p. 152.

[2] Mervyn Morris, 'To An Expatriate Friend', *JJ*, Vol. 3, No. 4, December 1969, p. 38.

[3] Martin Carter, 'A Question of Self-Contempt', *NWQ*, Guyana Independence Issue, Vol. 2, No. 3, High Season 1966, pp. 10–12, ref. p. 11.

hostesses and cashiers for want of trained locals discovered at the cost of a severe strike in 1968. But despite business claims to the contrary, the proportion of West Indians at managerial levels is still small. In government as well, leaders who lay great public emphasis on local decision-making often welcome expatriate advisers through the back door. Alien employment restrictions are regularly disregarded on the ground that without 'a steady supply of competent experts . . . investors will be reluctant to gamble their savings.'[1] And in facilitating foreign aid, expatriate expertise and contacts are often essential.

As outsiders, expatriates may also be more malleable than local lieutenants. The foreigner who displeases is a ready scapegoat: he can easily be dismissed and sent home. But when a local aide falls out with his chief there is a risk of retaliation; he may even form a rival political party. After representing the English expatriate 'presence as an indignity and an intolerable strain on our Treasury . . . we were beginning to discover in ourselves a deep reluctance to render the civil service more local. . . . Some people preferred to be served by men who were no threats to them, who at the end of their service would return to their own country.'[2]

West Indianization may be the symbolic order of the day, but independence also increases the local need for doctors, technicians, teachers, and a host of other expatriate experts, reinforcing metropolitan institutions and culture. The psychological impact of their presence is likewise profound. To be sure, the new foreigners are often quite unlike the old colonial officials. They have come to do special jobs, are unconcerned with status and social nuance, and are apt to be racially and socially egalitarian. Tourism and real-estate development are notable exceptions, however. Fears are widely expressed that tourists will foment racial segregation in the Caribbean. A 'self-defence' patrol reportedly organized by American Rotarian vacationers aroused Jamaican trepidation that 'we will soon have white foreigners patrolling the streets of Montego Bay with the authority to arrest, shoot or kill black Jamaicans'.[3]

Between the Rotary tourist and the foreign economic planner or volunteer service worker many West Indians consider it fruitless or frivolous to distinguish. However well-intentioned white expatriates may be, colour and wealth at once give them an advantage over most West Indians. Concerned about 'the arrogant behaviour of certain expatriate whites', one small-island editor would 'prefer to do without white investors than have the cancer of race prejudice and colour bar

[1] Ryan, 'Decolonization in a Multi-Racial Society', p. 631.
[2] V. S. Naipaul, *The Mimic Men*, 1967, pp. 250–1.
[3] 'Foreign Whites Patrol Mobay', *Abeng*, 15 February 1969, p. 4.

eating into the lives of our happy, friendly people.'[1] But few West Indians seriously consider rejecting foreign investment.

White Creole roles and reactions arouse more ambivalence. Family alliances sustain *béké* entrepreneurs in Martinique, and resident whites remain the principal estate owners in Barbados. But elsewhere, apart from tourist and retirement enclaves, the white elite and middle class are largely confined to urban areas and occupations. In the smaller territories the white-Creole presence may be limited to elderly or reclusive relicts, living out their days in crumbling plantation houses or shabby rooms in small capital towns, the last remnants of 'planters/. . . colonels hard as the commonwealth's greenheart/middlemen . . . bully-boy roarers of the Empire club,/Gray apparitions at veranda ends'.[2]

Three decades ago, white Creoles shared governmental control with metropolitan officials in every colony; today adult suffrage puts most such positions beyond their reach. An occasional white wins an election in Barbados, a rural Trinidad constituency has selected a white businessman, and some of the Jamaican proletariat lionize a local Syrian. But these are exceptions contingent on party favour or the support of some special minority. Few white Creoles today seek elective office.

They have withdrawn from administration as well. Many whites are said to have quit the Trinidad civil service after 1956 rather than work under, or be victimized by, a 'black' government. 'West Indianizing the [Civil] Service was taken by many to mean "Negrofying" it', and rumour had it that 'the promotion of native whites was suspended for some time'; senior posts were demanded for non-whites 'excluded from them in the past', and only those whites were kept who were extremely competent or could not have been dismissed without 'doing violence to the multiracial ideology.'[3] White youngsters who would formerly have entered the civil service instead go into business, often in family concerns; for in other firms they may now find jobs or advancement difficult.

Whites no longer dominate public affairs even in plantation strongholds. In Jamaica the honorific position of county Custos, once a white-Creole social perquisite, has passed to brown and black Creoles. In Trinidad, where metropolitan and white-Creole district wardens used to be 'a virtual power elite', authority has devolved on to elected county

[1] 'Is It True?' and 'Our Government and Rhodesia', *Dominica Herald*, 23 March 1968, pp. 2 and 4. See also Roger Brown Mandeville, 'Conversation with a Jamaica White Man', *Abeng*, 3 May 1969, p. 3, and Neville Linton, 'The Role of the Expatriate in Developing Countries', *International Development Review*, Vol. XII, No. 2, 1970, pp. 24–7.

[2] Derek Walcott, 'Veranda', in idem, *The Castaway and Other Poems*, 1965, pp. 38–9.

[3] Ryan, 'Decolonization in a Multi-Racial Society', pp. 432–3, 211–12. See also 'Strong Words From Grenada', by Crab Back, *Dominica Star*, 15 August 1970 p. 11; Spartan, 'The Elusive Cause', *Trinidad Express*, 13 March 1970, p. 9.

councils and the national Finance Ministry, while the wardenship itself has passed to darker men.[1]

The search for heroes to signalize sovereign status further excludes white Creoles; for West Indians tacitly assume that these exemplars should be non-whites, and by extension 'that a black or coloured citizen is somehow more of a Jamaican than a white one'.[2] Memories of the past along with their inherited privileges make whites ready targets of hostility. A black nationalist in a Jamaican novel reflects 'a world of latent prejudice among dark-skinned people against those whose skins were fair. . . . We're not going to be as rough as they were; we're not going to put them in chains and make slaves of them; we're not even going to have colour bars to keep them out. . . . But . . . we're not going to serve them any more. . . . It is our turn now and we've taken over.'[3]

Apprehensive that majority rule, middle-class envy, and mass misery may jeopardize their economic and social interests, many West Indian whites have left for Europe or North America. Others hedge against local disaster with bank accounts outside the Caribbean and standing orders for plane reservations; during periods of stress, flight bookings are rumoured to be filled for weeks ahead. But the white Creole with outside alternatives can afford to keep somewhat aloof and avoid accommodating to local interests. The white establishment 'won't take my hand', a Curaçao radical commented. 'Why should they? They have a sweet deal going taking money out of the island and living here like lords.'[4]

Yet most whites are quick to disavow colour prejudice and condemn colonialism. French Antillean *békés* took the lead in denouncing the racism of metropolitan and Algerian functionaries in Martinique and Guadeloupe. No one deplores tourist misbehaviour in Jamaica, Barbados, and Antigua more than local whites do. A Trinidadian finds 'whites scourging themselves for the prejudices of their group before black audiences, . . . by reporting outrageous statements made by members of their group, and dissociating themselves from the senti- ments.'[5] In Barbados whites are said to refrain from publicly criticizing the Government for fear of victimization.

Racial privilege and absentee attitude have left white West Indians—

---

[1] Ryan, 'Decolonization in a Multi-Racial Society', p. 620; L. D. 'Lully' Punch, *A Journey to Remember* (*39 Years in the Civil Service*) [1967], pp. 102–3.

[2] Gloria Cumper, 'In Search of a New Identity', in 'Jamaica: A Special Report', *The Times*, 26 September 1968, p. 1.

[3] Abrahams, *This Island Now*, pp. 199 and 197.

[4] Stanley C. Brown, quoted in H. J. Maidenberg, 'Radical Ex-Teacher in Curaçao Considered Big Threat by Some', *New York Times*, 1 March 1970, p. 22.

[5] V. S. Naipaul, *The Middle Passage*, 1962, p. 78. See also Gratiant, *Île fédérée française de la Martinique*, p. 36.

Anglo-Saxon, Celtic, French, or whatever—with what has been described as much 'the same face: unlined, satisfied, with that incongruous,
youthful plumpness of the cheeks'.[1] Their assured places in local
societies typically leave them without further ambition. Statements by
white Trinidadian schoolboys reflect extraordinarily prosaic aspirations, seldom going beyond the time-honoured routines. 'A recurrent
theme in the essays of white students is that "Comfort . . . breeds
indifference to the future." . . . "As I become older I become lazier and
slack off. I am almost on the brink of doing nothing."'[2] As non-white
critics view them, Europeans were 'the most backward ruling class
imaginable. For all the leisure of their wealth, they have created nothing, invented nothing. . . . There is not among them a novelist or a poet
of any rank; not an innovator of any standing, not an historian, not a
painter. They stand on the sidelines revealing no human insight'.[3] West
Indians in the process of redressing old racial wrongs find it hard to
remember that 'the white West Indian is one of us, even although he is
white.'[4] Instead, 'white people' are now defined as those who choose 'to
adopt or to continue in a European rather than a local way of life and
thinking.'[5]

The coloured middle classes, though scarcely less 'European', have
succeeded to white positions of status and prestige. They dominate civil
services, control affairs through a cadre of quasi-governmental agencies, and get the lion's share of new jobs and rewards. Except in the
French Antilles, the middle class are the principal beneficiaries of
government education and housing programmes. Yet they do not
control the mainsprings of either economic or political affairs. 'They
had never belonged to a property owning or a business operating class
and rarely understood what was happening', avers a Trinidadian.
'Between them, probably half a dozen Cabinet Ministers in the West
Indies have even ever seen a share certificate.'[6] A cachet attaches to the
planter way of life but not to planting as a business; successful shopkeepers buy estates for status, and their offspring shun commerce for the
professions. Middle-class West Indians are entrepreneurial only as
fund-raisers. Leaders in other new nations talk of steel mills, dams, and
power plants, but 'a West Indian politician talks about how much

[1] John Morris, *Fever Grass*, 1969, p. 97.

[2] Vera Rubin and Marisa Zavalloni, *We Wish To Be Looked Upon: A Study of the
Aspirations of Youth in a Developing Society*, 1969, p. 57.

[3] Lloyd Best, 'Black Power & National Reconstruction: Proposals Following the
February Revolution', *Tapia Pamphlet* [1970], p. 4.

[4] Mervyn Morris, review of *New Beacon Reviews: Collection One* (ed. John La Rose)
in *Bim*, Vol. 13, No. 50, January–June 1970, p. 132.

[5] Douglas G. Hall, 'The Colonial Legacy in Jamaica', *NWQ*, Vol. 4, No. 3, High
Season 1968, pp. 7–22, ref. p. 20.

[6] Randolph Rawlins, 'Black Power', *Art and Man*, Act II, Scene II, June 1969,
pp. 47–51, ref. p. 50.

money he will get from the British government or from the United States. It is because the class from which he comes had and has had no experience whatever in matters of production. . . . They have never had anything to do with the big sugar estates. Banking is out of their hands and always has been.'[1]

Mistrusting their own skills, the middle class echo the old planter class in considering the folk capable of nothing.

One hundred and fifty years ago, when the Non-conformists told the slave-owners, 'You cannot continue to keep human beings in this condition,' all the slave-owners could reply was 'You will ruin the economy, and further what can you expect from people like these?' When you try to tell the middle classes of today, 'Why not place responsibility for the economy on the people?' their reply is the same as that of the old slave-owners: 'You will ruin the economy, and further what can you expect from people like these?'[2]

Within the middle class, self-interest is expected to outweigh broader social concerns. School-leavers a generation ago, a Trinidadian complained, showed 'no interest in public movements'.[3] Federation and self-government fleetingly aroused nationalist ardour, but three years after independence Trinidad's Prime Minister characterized his junior civil servants as 'frankly not adequate. It's not just lack of ability. It's also often lack of sympathy—a kind of indifference bred by the colonial system.'[4] Aiming only to reap colonial benefits previously dispensed to whites, they multiplied their paperwork and ignored the public welfare. They sought not to reform the colonial bureaucratic apparatus but to inherit it; 'nationalism and independence means that you with a black face must now have' what whites formerly had.[5]

The middle class, critics contend,

has cars, good jobs, 'respectable' manners, and an awful lot of 'white' habits. . . . It dominates all the powerful Institutions in the society. . . . It is materialistic, complacent and (despite all its formal education) illiterate. It is multi-racial and cosmopolitan in composition, and believes that this society is the happiest and most peaceful society on God's earth, that all our little differences are drowned and resolved eventually by Carnival, rum, women and parliamentary democracy. It titters at the mention of words like 'revolution'.[6]

Yet the middle class fears that revolution may cost them these perqui-

[1] C. L. R. James, *Party Politics in the West Indies*, 1962, pp. 131 and 136.

[2] Ibid., p. 139. See also Maurice Zeitlin, 'Economic Insecurity and Political Attitudes of Cuban Workers', *American Sociological Review*, Vol. 31, No. 1, February 1966, pp. 35–51.

[3] Tito Achong, in *The People*, 22 January 1938, quoted in Ryan, 'Decolonization in a Multi-Racial Society', pp. 540–1.

[4] Eric Williams, quoted in Bernard Taper, 'Letter From Port of Spain', *New Yorker*, 23 October 1965, pp. 203–26, ref. pp. 219, 223.

[5] Selwyn Douglas Ryan, and Eric Williams, 5 September 1962, in Ryan, 'Decolonization in a Multi-Racial Society', pp. 459, 627. See also p. 440.

[6] 'The Middle Class', *Vanguard*, 21 March 1970, p. 2.

sites. Local autonomy brings anxieties along with benefits. 'No class is louder in proclaiming Jamaica as an example to the world of successful effort to abolish distinctions based on race and colour. Yet no class is more terrified of upheaval' that might destroy its inherited privileges.[1] The least threat to status may seem intolerable. One of Trinidad's first black wardens recalls that a subordinate 'of a half white caste . . . could not stand a junior position he held with me at the top. . . . To have a negro at the head of the administration was too much for him.'[2] The West Indian governing class sometimes seems to exemplify libertarian ideals, but Singham's interviews of the Grenadian economic elite in 1962 probably convey a more accurate picture of their views. A substantial majority 'thought the introduction of adult suffrage had been a mistake, . . . advocated the return to a limited franchise based on literacy or educational qualifications', and castigated the masses as 'lacking in intelligence, gullible, easily led (i.e. misled), and, worst of all, "they are in the majority"!'[3]

Middle-class wealth is increasingly assailed by black-power advocates and apparent riches may endanger a brown man's political career. The ruling party in Dominica charged that mulattoes of the opposition sought 'to "protect their interests" and to hell with the "ordinary labourer"'; this 'story that not even a fly would believe'[4] evoked popular sympathy and helped the Government to poor-mouth its way to re-election in 1970.

Ordinary West Indians envy and emulate the middle class but profoundly mistrust their professions of concern. A folk leader in a Lamming novel fears ultimate betrayal by a light-skinned sympathizer because it is impossible 'for people of her type to break with their traditional attitudes to the black masses. . . . "I learn how any playing 'bout with your lot bound to end. You know the rules too good"'.[5]

Middle-class privilege is insecurely based. Active political engagement, especially in the smaller societies, is open to few of them, partly because such activity would be *déclassé*, partly because it would conflict with their traditional occupational interests. 'The power elites' in Grenada, for example, conceive politics 'as a game indulged in either by the playboy members of their own class, members of the lower middle classes trying to climb the social ladder, or . . . rural rabble-rousers.'[6] Partisan roles are proscribed for teachers and civil servants;

[1] 'Independence for Jamaica', *WIE*, Vol. 5, No. 1, 1962, pp. 4–17, ref. p. 17.
[2] Punch, *A Journey to Remember*, p. 129.
[3] A. W. Singham, *The Hero and the Crowd in a Colonial Polity*, 1968, pp. 195–6.
[4] 'Is it True?' *Dominica Herald*, 19 October 1968, p. 9.
[5] Kenneth Ramchand, 'The Artist in the Balm-Yard: "Season of Adventure"', *NWQ*, Vol. 5, Nos. 1 and 2, Dead Season and Croptime 1969, pp. 13–21, ref. p. 15, and George Lamming, *Season of Adventure*, 1960, p. 328.
[6] Singham, *The Hero and the Crowd in a Colonial Polity*, p. 198.

merchants and traders find neutrality risky but cannot afford openly to take sides. Yet place and property are at the mercy of elected leaders. 'Many appointments in the civil service and in statutory boards . . . are based solely on political patronage,' the head of the Trinidad Civil-Service Association asserts, and some officials 'are openly victimized for being manly enough to express independent opinions and to voice their honest dissent'.[1] In Dominica, 'if civil servants want to talk to certain friends . . . they prefer to drive them out of town in their cars and have a tête-à-tête behind . . . a cluster of banana trees in the interest of their jobs.'[2] Officials learn 'to play the courtier in the interest of survival and advancement'.[3]

The coloured middle class must yield to pressure because they usually lack the white option of departure. However European they may feel, exile is apt to involve racial discrimination and material loss. This helps to explain their caution and conservatism in local affairs. The white can afford to 'give the poor coolie boy and his nigger friends a taste of power,' as a Guyanese novelist put it, because he's not risking anything; he can leave without losing much. The coloured man cannot and so must temporize, compromise, accommodate. And the lighter he is, the more difficulty he has in avoiding being made a scapegoat. 'Unless you happen to be pure white . . . the more white blood you have the more vulnerable you become'.[4]

The middle-class West Indian has achieved a remarkable range of satisfactions. His distance from the black majority is institutionalized and still largely accepted on both sides. He has succeeded to elite positions and privileges and today has greater prestige and power than ever before. He can retain them, however, only by coercion and the maintenance of hierarchical values based on preferences for things European and white. Since structural reform would tend to equalize opportunity and redistribute access to benefits, the coloured elite and middle class are almost bound to favour the *status quo*.

The West Indian majority under self-government has gained little beyond greater expectations. Only in elected politics is every door now open; with adult suffrage, blacks are said to 'feel that they . . . have a divine right to rule.'[5] Yet folk leaders are often as aloof as their white and coloured predecessors were. For many of them, 'politics has meant getting ahead . . . from being a rural primary school headmaster for

---

[1] President of the Civil Service Association, in *Civil Service Review*, July 1965, quoted in Ryan, 'Decolonization in a Multi-Racial Society', p. 443.

[2] 'Uncle Toms, Yes-Men, Line-Toe-ers', *Dominica Herald*, 29 July 1967, p. 4.

[3] Ryan, 'Decolonization in a Multi-Racial Society', p. 443.

[4] Christopher Nicole, *White Boy*, 1966, pp. 253-4.

[5] Henry Forde, 'Barbadians Are Hypocritical about Colour', *Barbados Advocate*, 21 February 1962.

example, to an Honourable Minister of Government'.[1] Office and status won, the people are forgotten. The 'eddicated sons-o'-bitches' elected to the Assembly, in a Barbadian's view, were 'so damn important that they ain't farting on their own people.'[2] And a Jamaican peasant surmises that 'black men in the Legislative Council today . . . would massacre all the black people in this island, if the Governor invited them to dinner and gave them a "Sir".'[3] Most rural Jamaicans, a 1962 survey revealed, thought there were only two or three black Assemblymen when there were in fact sixteen. The 'error' reflected the distance between legislators' origins and reputed behaviour; many were perhaps 'black, but they've got white minds.'[4]

In private enterprise, as in public affairs, black success arouses suspicion among the folk. 'A rich black man is anomalous on two counts. Either society will prevent him from accumulating wealth, or he will accumulate it at the expense of his race . . . by assimilating [the] values . . . of the white world . . . adopting its religion, serving its politics and joining in the general exploitation of the black man.'[5]

Yet the resentment is mixed with admiration. A self-made Barbadian evokes 'a queer blend of pride and prejudice' by keeping the rural people at a distance; yet the people also found it 'gratifying to see an ordinary black man owning land and property and really prospering.'[6]

Even under self-rule most West Indians regard their rulers as alien. 'There is a feeling that the government is one thing; the people are another. Government is something remote. . . . It is conceived of . . . as all-powerful, as responsible for everything and as an object apart from ourselves to be praised or blamed'.[7] The new leaders inherit the obloquy of the old along with their privilege.

Folk champions willy-nilly appear in the guise of magicians, even as demi-gods, promising miracles beyond the capacity of ordinary mortals. To satisfy popular demands for heroic leadership, 'messiahs had to come along and do something big that nobody could understand'.[8]

[1] Trevor Munroe, 'Nationalism and Democracy in Jamaica', *NWQ*, Vol. 4, No. 4, Cropover 1968, pp. 24–9, ref. p. 26.

[2] Austin C. Clarke, *The Survivors of the Crossing*, 1964, p. 169.

[3] Sylvia Wynter, *The Hills of Hebron: A Jamaican Novel*, 1962, p. 268.

[4] Public-opinion survey undertaken in 1961 by Cyril Rogers, to whom I am obliged for these data. For the actual composition of the Assembly see Bell, *Jamaican Leaders*, p. 83.

[5] *The Church and Unemployment*, p. 7.

[6] Millicent Payne, 'The Chink in His Armour', *Bim*, Vol. 10, No. 41, June–December 1965, pp. 17–23, ref. p. 17.

[7] David Coore, 'Government and the Community', in George Cumper, ed., *Report of the Conference on Social Development Held at the University College of the West Indies, 1961*, pp. 108–10, ref. p. 109.

[8] Androcles, 'General Election Post Mortem, No. 3', *Dominica Star*, 14 November 1970, p. 2.

Political leaders do not always object to being deified, their detractors charge:

A very definite attempt was made in the Election campaign to make people believe that LeBlanc, the leader of the successful Party, partook of the nature of a god. This is not an exaggeration. . . . The attempt to divinize LeBlanc began with the posting of large pictures of him at strategic points all over Dominica. . . . Satellites took over from there and in a variety of ways hinted that LeBlanc was no ordinary mortal and that he was something of a god. Consequently it would be impious not to vote for him.[1]

The new demigod is bound to disappoint his following; his transition from hero to villain, 'mismanaging the affairs of the nation, robbing the rich to enrich himself . . . ruthlessly suppressing opposition and dissent', is almost as certain and swift in the West Indies as in any former colony.[2] 'Who are our friends?' asks a Trinidadian. 'Who are our enemies? . . . These political vagabonds have to play ball with the economic interests while at the same time stage a BIG SHOW to fool the population'.[3]

West Indians who decry graft and corruption at the same time view them as facts of life. 'The exercise of influence by politicians in all sorts of spheres' seems entirely natural; 'if one has power one should use it'. People by and large 'accept as fair the proposition that the adherents of the party in power should get whatever is going.'[4] While a handful of radicals denounce local leaders as colonial overseers, most West Indians simply complain that they are more extortionate than former rulers. 'The old colonial days were much better than now. At least bones used to shake the branches and some leaves used to fall in our pockets, although he took all the fruits. Since . . . [self-government], fruits, leaves, branches, tree-trunks, everything go in the big boys pockets. Nothing comes to us, the poor people.'[5]

Cynicism, tolerance of chicanery, and above all poverty vitiate any programme requiring co-operative effort or private sacrifice. Most West Indians are too impoverished to secure or support responsible leadership. 'When people dwell like most Vincentians on the threshold of ever-threatening starvation they cannot readily appreciate an intellectual approach to politics that . . . emphasizes . . . co-ordinated long-

[1] 'The Problems', *Tapia*, No. 1, 28 September 1969, p. 7.
[2] Bernth Lindfors, 'The African Politician's Changing Image in African Literature in English', *Journal of Developing Areas*, Vol. 4, 1969–70, pp. 13–28, ref. p. 13.
[3] J. L. Hichaels, 'Who Are Our Friends? Who Are Our Enemies?' *Trinidad Vanguard*, 7 March 1970, p. 5.
[4] Gloria Cumper, 'Middle Class Is Growing', in 'Jamaica: A Special Report', *The Times*, 14 September 1970, p. III.
[5] 'Call That George', *Moko*, No. 13, 25 April 1969, p. 3; Vernon Arnett, 'Jamaica—Dictatorship or Democracy?' *Moko*, No. 4, 13 December 1968, p. 2.

term development. . . . Bread-and-butter politics is the only type they understand.'[1]

Beyond survival, the West Indian labourers' aim is not class welfare but to become middle class. They do not view themselves as a group; mass awareness is limited to an egalitarianism of underprivilege, a common front in the face of catastrophe. 'Indeed,' predicts a student, 'a revolutionary change tomorrow, or in the future, will result in the masses claiming that the revolution owes them a living.'[2] In the meantime, however much they mistrust their leaders' motives, they are only too ready to lean on them for initiative in all matters: 'Deprived of responsibility, we degraded our own capacity. We looked for "Doctors" whether they were benevolent planters, or cunning labour leaders or our bright sons.'[3] In the Trinidad 'Independence' calypso,

> Annabella stocking want patching
> She want de doctah help she wid dat
> Johnson trousers falling
> He want de doctah help he wid dat
> Dorothy loss she man
> She want to complain to Doctah Williams.[4]

In freedom as in bondage, West Indians have 'found it easier to rely on a Doctor than to take up our own beds and walk.'[5]

Local leaders bolstered by sovereignty and by mass adulation now fancy themselves masters of their own destiny. After generations of being told that non-whites could never rule themselves, they are sometimes surprised to find that they can. 'Our enemies said . . . we would never be fit for freedom', Trinidad's Prime Minister writes. 'They said we could never govern ourselves. They said that we were a lazy, servile race, desirous only of sitting in the sun and eating yams and pumpkins. . . . They said we could never operate democratic institutions, we could never be governed along European lines.'[6]

Current West Indian governmental forms do, in fact, reflect colonial tutelage. 'Not only did each minister dress like the last colonial governor', in one critic's view of the new order, 'but he thought [the] powers of a minister were exactly those of the powers of a man whom he

---

[1] John, 'Political Crisis in St. Vincent', p. 55.

[2] Paul Thomas, 'Let Me Look Out For Me', *Scope*, Vol. 3, No. 1 [November 1968], p. 7. For egalitarianism of underprivilege see Gordon Rohlehr, 'Character and Rebellion in "A House for Mr. Biswas" by V. S. Naipaul', *NWQ*, Vol. 4, No. 4, Cropover 1968, pp. 66–72, ref. p. 71, and Chandra Jayawardena, 'Ideology and Conflict in Lower Class Communities', *Comparative Studies in Society and History*, Vol. X, 1968, pp. 416–66, ref. p. 422.

[3] 'The Problems', p. 7.

[4] The Mighty Striker, 'Annabella'.

[5] Best, 'Black Power & National Reconstruction', p. 4.

[6] Eric Williams, *Inward Hunger: The Education of a Prime Minister*, 1969, p. 232.

would have called a "foreign imperialist overlord."[1] It is said of one island ruler that 'no decision is too large for his single capacities, or too small to be beneath his notice.'[2]

West Indian premiers are typically seen, 'proper in dress and formal in mien, . . . sitting in the back of large cars, preceded by outriders. . . . This style is derived from the bad old colonial days and is meant both to emphasize and hallow the power they wield.'[3] With one another leaders are apt to deal, as the West Indian Federal Prime Minister bitterly remarked when his Jamaican and Trinidadian rivals met, 'like the Pope and the Emperor dividing the world between them.'[4]

The roots of authoritarian behaviour lie deep in the colonial past. Today, political office enables new masters, with 'a peculiar quality of arrogance,' to realize an 'overweening desire to lord it over the rest of the parish like a feudal baron . . . to ride rough shod over other human beings.'[5] But 'this is as much the fault of the ordinary citizen as of the politician', a Jamaican states. 'The desire to please those in authority often results in increasing substantially the opportunities for the use of political influence, and who is going to resist such opportunities?'[6]

The self-importance of newly elected rulers has eroded established liberties. Heads of government demand public recognition of their high status, consider themselves above the law, and exult in their power over the people:

> Watch dem bow and scrape
> When dem see dat is Me
> I is rulin powah, gal!
> I is Authority!
> I mek dis country jump wid joy,
> Or rock wid misary![7]

Viewing their own positions as proof of progress, rulers in many territories tend to treat any opposition as ill-motivated if not seditious. 'Newness to eminence has bred an acute nervousness,' a Trinidadian points out, 'and this nervousness defines dissent with treachery.'[8] According to the Prime Minister of Jamaica, it is not enough to be loyal; 'there should be "a passionate belief and confidence" in the

---

[1] John J. Figueroa, 'Education for Jamaica's Needs', *CQ*, Vol. 15, No. 1, March 1969, pp. 5–33, ref. pp. 23–4.

[2] Adrian Espinet and Jacques Farmer, 'Pussonal Nonarchy: The Paradox of Power in Trinidad', *Tapia*, No. 3, 16 November 1969, p. 6.

[3] Rawlins, 'Black Power', p. 47.

[4] Grantley Adams, quoted in John Mordecai, *The West Indies: The Federal Negotiations*, 1968, p. 253.

[5] Picong, 'What Power Does to the West Indian', *Dominica Star*, 19 April 1969, p. 1.

[6] Cumper, 'In Search of a New Identity'.

[7] Louise Bennett, 'Is Me', in her *Jamaica Labrish*, 1966, p. 140.

[8] Rawlins, 'Black Power', pp. 50–1.

stability of the country.'[1] In response to protests against a Seditious and Undesirable Publications Act that threatened to throttle the local press, a Government release urged 'all sections of the community to recognise that the present Government is the lawfully elected Government of Dominica . . . and not for ever try to purvey . . . to the world that the people of Dominica have been so foolish as to have elected a totally bad government.'[2] Petitioned to repeal the Act, the Premier replied that he had been elected and would rule as he saw fit as long as he held office.[3]

Long years in impotent opposition have made many leaders unused to tact or compromise, or to the belief that any opponent could be sincere, let alone sensible. When Eric Williams's reinstatement of an erring Minister met with some public protest, he angrily added that anyone who didn't like his decision could 'Get to Hell Out a Here' in the words of Sparrow's calypso: 'Who gave you the privilege to object?/ Pay your taxes, shut up and have respect.'[4] Many West Indian leaders consider the people incapable of independent judgement, lambs to be led, children to be chastised.

The loss of civil liberties in the name of nationalism is exacerbated by West Indian insularity and small size, by economic and cultural dependence, by social and ethnic stratification, and by the lack of any widely shared national purpose. From free Jamaica to free Guyana, political opposition is silenced, criticism suppressed, freedom of assembly abridged, and scapegoats coerced by governments that have just won autonomy. As an opposition leader on Grand Flamingo, Christopher Nicole's fictitious island, cogently remarks: 'You think we achieved our independence three years ago? That was a preliminary skirmish. The real task awaiting our people . . . is to achieve their independence from the people who achieved their independence for them.'[5]

Jamaica reveres the memory of Marcus Garvey, who is safely dead, but bans the writings of Malcolm X, Stokely Carmichael, and Frantz Fanon. 'Seditious intention' in Dominica embraces any criticism of government, and any publication the Minister of Home Affairs considers 'prejudicial to the public interest' may be silenced.[6] Nor is the

[1] Hugh Shearer, quoted in 'Greater Commitment to Society Urged by PM', *Jamaica Daily Gleaner*, 25 November 1968, p. 1.

[2] Dominica Government release, 'The Seditious and Undesirable Publications Bill', 4 July 1968.

[3] Androcles, 'Resignation, Dismissal or Retirement', *Dominica Star*, 4 October 1968, pp. 2 and 4; 'Scribe . . .', *Dominica Herald*, 12 October 1968, pp. 4, 9.

[4] Gordon Rohlehr, 'The Social Context of Sparrow's Calypsoes—Part 6: Death of a Federation', *Trinidad Guardian*, 26 February 1968. See also Ryan, 'Decolonization in a Multi-Racial Society', p. 470.

[5] Christopher Nicole, *The Self Lovers*, 1968, p. 207.

[6] *Seditious and Undesirable Publications*, Dominica Act No. 16, 1968, sections 3(1) and 6(1). See also 'Dominica Madness', *Jamaica Daily Gleaner*, 3 August 1968.

tendency to tyranny confined to former British territories; in Curaçao and Guadeloupe separatist sentiments are curbed and branded as seditious.

Stringent precautions against subversion have characterized many new nations; America's Alien and Subversion Acts of the 1790s reflect similar anxieties about a hostile and dangerous world. But West Indian authorities exhibit a still more insular xenophobia directed against close West Indian neighbours. Inter-island freedom of movement is more and more curtailed, work permits are required of resident aliens, and 'security risks' from other islands are summarily deported —Montserratians brought to St. Kitts as infants fifty years ago, Dominicans who have spent seven years away, small-islanders suspected of irregular entry in Trinidad, may all be sent 'home'. The exclusion of the Guyanese Walter Rodney from Jamaica in 1968, and later government charges that Jamaican students at the University of the West Indies were subverted by Eastern Caribbean radicals,[1] are typical instances of the new insularity. At the same time the Bahamas deported hundreds of 'illegal' Jamaicans accused of trading in drugs and harlots: the plane from Jamaica is known in Nassau as the 'Ganja Special'. When the *Jamaican Daily Gleaner* complains that 'old-guard Bahamians are only using the dopesters and visa-beaters as an excuse for their dislike of the radicalism [that] Jamaican example and Jamaican migrants have contributed',[2] one wonders if those 'Jamaican radicals' perhaps came from the 'subversive' Eastern Caribbean.

Explanations for curtailing liberty differ, but the root causes are the same throughout the West Indies. Leaders revel in self-rule, yet habit or need tempt them to invoke imperial authority. When Anguilla broke away from St. Kitts, Chief Minister Bradshaw's first thought was to summon a British frigate from nearby Antigua. But the frigate's commander refused to come; now that St. Kitts–Nevis–Anguilla was internally self-governing, the use of British force would be inappropriate.[3] Lacking frigates, leaders of the new West Indian states feel compelled to mount their own defences. Self-protection takes precedence over sympathy with oppressed brethren; West Indians commiserate with black Americans, but 'we have our own skins to protect as an up and coming nation struggling for survival', notes a Trinidadian. 'We are determined to keep our policy of inter-racial solidarity intact, there-

---

[1] 'On Campus Jamaica is still a colony ruled by the mistique [*sic*] of a region with which it is still not at ease; and constantly being indoctrinated under hypnosis by the Eastern Caribbean. A Jamaican youngster going to Mona is going to a foreign land, as strange as any campus overseas. We shall need to take over the University . . .' (*Jamaica Daily Gleaner*, 19 September 1968).

[2] 'The Bahamas', *Jamaica Daily Gleaner*, 24 June 1968, p. 14.

[3] *Anguilla Beacon*, 2 December 1967, p. 1.

fore we intend to keep Stokely and his black power policy as far as possible from these shores.'[1]

Security is maintained at the expense of social reform; indeed, fundamental change is seen as the ultimate threat to stability. But governments can prevent change only by keeping their people in ignorance. In Trinidad, the works of the Trinidadian Carmichael are banned; soon it may be necessary to ban the early writings of the Prime Minister himself.[2] A Jamaican wonders if some day we'll 'begin to feel that it would be better not to teach the masses how to read as once they do so they'll be exposed to thoughts which may be subversive'.[3]

Contempt for the people is not confined to those in power; it is equally characteristic of those who oppose tyranny. Dominica's 'Freedom fighters' blamed the Seditious Publications Act on stupidity; 'this is happening', an opposition leader charged, 'because Dominica people [are] so ignorant they don't even know their rights are endangered and won't listen to warnings.'[4] A Grenadian assumes that most people are unable to 'distinguish between the liberator and those who . . . [seek] the return of the days of the whip.'[5] 'The people here are ignorant', a Curaçao radical characterizes his fellow countrymen, 'and behave like animals. We must use Madison Avenue techniques and brainwash them into being human.'[6]

Contemptuous of the masses they must court, politicians are insecure in their relations with the educated who serve them. An elected leader who refuses to listen to technical advice from his own professional staff may be trying to conceal graft, or he may simply be seeking to avoid confessing ignorance or error.

The politician is sensitive about his newly acquired status and views with considerable skepticism the advice tendered to him by the civil servants; the latter are equally skeptical about the capacity of the politician to direct the government. If the situation deteriorates sufficiently, the politician terrorizes the civil servant by attacking him personally in the market place. The civil servant retaliates by hiding files and trying to sabotage the politician.[7]

The Kittician premier Bradshaw's famous dictum, 'Studyation is

[1] Mr. Subero, Secretary of the Arima Constituency, at P.N.M. Tenth Annual Convention, quoted in 'Tide Runs Against Revolution', *Trinidad Nation*, 6 October 1967, pp. 1 and 10.

[2] Gordon K. Lewis, 'The Politics of the Caribbean', in Tad Szulc, ed., *The United States and the Caribbean*, 1971, pp. 5–35.

[3] Colin Gregory, 'Of This and That', *Jamaica Daily Gleaner*, 29 November 1968, p. 16.

[4] Elkin Henry, in Dominica Legislative Council, 5 July 1968.

[5] *Grenada Star*, 13 January 1962, quoted in Singham, *The Hero and the Crowd in a Colonial Polity*, pp. 226–7.

[6] Stanley C. Brown, quoted by Maidenberg, in *New York Times*, 1 March 1970, p. 22.

[7] Singham, *The Hero and the Crowd in a Colonial Polity*, pp. 205–6.

better than education,'[1] epitomizes the folk leader's response to learning and to the learned.

Anti-intellectual feelings are by no means confined to politicians, however. Senior civil servants themselves, while they envy the freedom of university staff and students, are deeply suspicious of academic abstractions and reformist doctrines. One radical activist, himself a campus figure, observes: 'Governments do not trust the intellectual community in general and the College or University men in particular.'[2]

The attribution of magical powers to doctors and scientists reinforces fears of academic malevolence. Middle-class criticism of the University of the West Indies in 1968 conveyed the impression that physics students were busy manufacturing minibombs, 'Biologists [were] breeding new diseases to inflict on our children, Chemists planning to poison the Cabinet at one of its cocktail parties, and History–Economics students ready with replacements.'[3]

The middle class links the university with atheism and the destruction of private property. 'The hearts of West Indian intellectuals are as black as Black Art and Mau Mau and the hearts of the fetishistic worshippers of Africa,' in one Jamaican's view.[4] Another accused intellectuals of 'indoctrinating as many students as possible in the historical inevitability of Communism'.[5] To journey at all in the realm of ideas may arouse suspicion. Graduates who return to the smaller islands find that intellectual discussion there 'is not merely taboo: it is actively, sometimes violently suppressed.'[6]

The West Indian masses often find their intellectual 'saviours' no less remote and authoritarian than the present government leaders. Neither of Trinidad's rival campus radicals 'has been able to speak to the common man for any length of time in a language he can fully understand', a critic complains.[7] 'They continue to fill their paper with intellectualism', in effect saying that 'if other people want to know anything worthwhile they have to pick up a dictionary and follow us'. Such radicals 'are so far away from the masses that they do not see that it will take more than a dictionary to bridge the gap'.[8] Trinidad's Black

[1] V. S. Naipaul, 'St. Kitts: Papa and the Power Set', *New York Review of Books*, 8 May 1969, p. 23.

[2] Lloyd Best, 'University... Boiling Pot', *Tapia*, No. 2, 19 October 1969, p. 1.

[3] John J. Searchwell, letter, 'Government, Rodney and the University', *Public Opinion*, 15 November 1968, p. 5.

[4] Keith Chance, letter in *Jamaica Daily Gleaner*, 12 November 1968, p. 16.

[5] Political Reporter, 'Communist Subversion, the University and Jamaica', *Jamaica Sunday Gleaner*, 3 November 1968, p. 8.

[6] 'Grenada', *Moko*, No. 11, 28 March 1969, p. 3.

[7] Warren D. Armstrong, 'Patterns of Politics Splitting the Country', *Trinidad Express*, March 1970.

[8] 'A Reply to Benedict Wight, Dr. Julien and Lloyd Best, from the Black Liberation Organisation . . .', *Trinidad Express*, 23 March 1970, p. 9.

Panther party, in resentment against high-handed academics, pledged to 'ruthlessly destroy any attempt to force campus politicians on the people.'[1]

Adult suffrage is a two-edged sword; it gives elected leaders a mandate enjoyed by no colonial forerunners but requires them continuously to court deprived and evanescent followers, who view political action as a chance to vent anger against the established order. The West Indian normally responds not to planners 'but rather to leaders who can articulate his hostility. . . . Electoral politicians . . . exploit this hostility and provide temporary relief for the mass through crowd catharsis. . . . Since they are denied responsibility, there is a strong tendency to irresponsible action and behavior.'[2]

Beleaguered by their own supporters, West Indian leaders confront economic and social problems that they are powerless to cope with. Their dawning awareness of this, coupled with a fear that the populace may reach the same conclusion, impels them to seek stability at all costs. Only a police state, however, can secure a stability that benefits so few. 'A society that permits such a large percentage of its citizens to be without the responsibility of ownership can have no real protection for the goods possessed by the rest of the citizens', a Jamaican editor points out.[3] 'When middle-class and upper-class people, and their spokesmen, panic before social unrest,' adds a clergyman, 'their very fear often pressures their government into agreeing to more and more repressive measures, and dictatorship is then not very far away.'[4]

Factors of scale exacerbate political problems just as they do economic and social difficulties. Lacking adherence to any larger constituency, 'a small island falls easily under the domination of a boss, who crudely or subtly intimidates the police, the newspapers, the magistrates and private employers. The road is thus open to persecution and corruption'.[5] An eminent economist, himself a small-islander, sketched a more graphic picture after his abortive attempt to federate the Windwards and Leewards:

In a small island of 50,000 . . . people, dominated by a single political party, it is very difficult to prevent political abuse. Everybody depends on the government for something, however small, so most are reluctant to offend it.

The civil servants live in fear; the police avoid unpleasantness; the trade unions are tied to the party; the newspaper depends on government advertisements; and so on.

---

[1] Aldwin Primus, Panther 'White Paper'. I am indebted to Frank J. McDonald for this reference.
[2] Singham, *The Hero and the Crowd in a Colonial Polity*, pp. 192–3.
[3] 'The Walter Rodney Issue', *Public Opinion*, 1 November 1968, p. 5.
[4] John Hoad, 'The Health of a Nation', ibid., p. 9.
[5] Mordecai, *The West Indies*, p. 461.

This is true even if the political leaders are absolutely honest. In cases where they are also corrupt, and playing with the public funds, the situation becomes intolerable.[1]

Small size thus intensifies the difficulties of Caribbean societies, released from colonial bondage only to suffer the tyranny of self-government. But West Indians manage somehow to survive these problems no worse than large states long accustomed to sovereignty. Countless observers have remarked on the poise, equanimity, and resilience West Indians habitually display in coping with everyday affairs, let alone with adversity.

The Caribbean, Trinidad's Prime Minister asserts, 'is one of the most unstable areas in our unstable world.' But the catalogue of instability he recites for 1969 hardly proves his point: Britain's invasion of Anguilla, anti-police rioting in Montserrat, labour disturbances in Curaçao, political crises in Surinam, labour unrest in Antigua, racial tension in Jamaica, the Rupununi rebellion in Guyana, separatism in Guadeloupe, Haitian dictatorship.[2] These hardly compare in violence with Vietnam, world-wide student unrest, or the domestic turmoil displayed in Poland, Northern Ireland, Quebec, or California. Few colonial areas gained self-rule with less disruption than the West Indies. Caribbean conflict may be endemic, and basic social problems are scarcely ameliorated; but destruction of life and property has been minimal there compared with social upheavals in other countries, developed or not. The toll of ethnic strife in Guyana fell far short of that in Cyprus or Nigeria. 'It is not the inherent instability that surprises; it is the relative stability. . . . What really seems necessary to explain is why every relatively poor country has not gone up in smoke long ago, with countless Papa Docs of all races in firm possession of power and Swiss bank accounts.'[3]

Measured against any of a hundred American riots of the past decade, Trinidad's 1970 black-power confrontation was a minor episode, posing a threat hardly commensurate with the offshore deployment of six United States aircraft carriers. Caribbean three-alarm fires show up in the American press, Jamaica's Prime Minister justly complains, as though whole cities were burning.[4] And by comparison with systematic

[1] Arthur Lewis, *The Agony of the Eight*, p. 16. See also K. W. Patchett, 'English Law in the West Indies', in *Law in the West Indies: Some Recent Trends*, 1966, pp. 3–53, ref. pp. 5 and 47.

[2] Eric Williams, *From Columbus to Castro: The History of the Caribbean, 1492–1969*, 1970, p. 498.

[3] Morris Cargill, 'What Makes Eric Run?' *CQ*, Vol. 15, Nos. 2 and 3, June–September 1969, pp. 122–7, ref. p. 127.

[4] 'What has occurred in the Caribbean is comparable to taking pictures of a three-alarm fire in some New York block . . . from several angles [to] create the impression the city was burning' (Hugh Shearer in 'U.S. Should Have a Particular Policy toward the Carib', *Jamaica Weekly Gleaner*, 26 August 1970, p. 5).

coercion in much of the world, Caribbean government book banning, anti-sedition acts, deportations, states of emergency, and curfews seem minor abridgements of liberty. Only Haiti bars political opposition; elsewhere, even in the smallest territories, criticism of parties in power is open and vigorous, and transfers of rule take place peaceably.

Smallness is so habitually deemed a handicap that West Indians themselves forget that it may have compensating benefits. 'Why must we always talk about the *problems* of small size?' a Barbadian student asked me recently. 'What about its advantages? What are its virtues? We need a positive approach to gain a sense of local worth.' Some West Indian territories, as we have seen, do achieve a sense of identity that transcends class division and economic privation. A rooted and passionate commitment to place is apparent in the novels of the Barbadian George Lamming, the prose poems of the Guyanese Wilson Harris, the stanzas and plays of the St. Lucian Derek Walcott. But most islanders have found no way, beyond boastful hyperbole or derivative poesy, to identify or convey the elements of this attachment, even to themselves. They none the less succeed in living together in a fashion which folk in greater nations often envy.

Ideological flexibility is a major component of West Indian ability to get along without necessarily agreeing and to contain strife within manageable limits. To those who condemn them for lack of faith or sincerity, a local scholar retorts that 'we ought to feel elated rather than depressed by knowing that we have the greatest gift a group of human beings can have, moral and psychological resilience.'[1] Flexibility stems from colonial circumstances but remains serviceable to West Indians who must adjust formal freedom to the exigencies of continuing dependence. In coping with external pressure and internal stress, West Indians retain 'the capacity to accommodate to anyone and everyone'.[2] They hedge their bets against grand enterprises, view lofty but impracticable aims with a healthy skepticism, and know when to stop fighting with folk who may tomorrow be allies in other enterprises.

Smallness also paradoxically enables West Indian societies to manage most of their own affairs. Strategically subordinate to American interests, economically dominated by international corporations and foreign investors, lacking a viable culture they can call their own, West Indians are self-condemned to be forever 'the Third World's third world.'[3] Yet they are less helpless than, say, the much larger black American minority *vis-à-vis* the majority society. West Indians, mostly

[1] William G. Demas, quoted in 'Creation of a New Caribbean Man', *News from Guyana*, No. 43/1970, 14 November 1970, p. 4.

[2] Singham, *The Hero and the Crowd in a Colonial Polity*, p. 95.

[3] V. S. Naipaul, 'Power to the Caribbean People', *New York Review of Books*, 3 September 1970, pp. 32–4, ref. p. 33.

black, by and large administer their own internal affairs, whereas black American efforts to develop community autonomy are nullified by an all-enveloping larger society. There are certain resemblances between Jamaica or Montserrat and such all-black American communities as Mound Bayou, Mississippi, or North Shreveport, Louisiana.[1] But Mound Bayou and North Shreveport are dependent communities in an impinging white world, whereas Jamaicans and Montserratians are largely masters in their own homes, however heavily mortgaged they may be.

This difference is an accident of geography no less than of history. Isolation and distinct boundaries give almost every West Indian territory a degree of self-government and a sense of its identity. Despite impoverishment and exploitation, West Indians feel to some extent in control of their own lives. In the United States, continentality and pervasive communications make local autonomy a chimera. Black capitalism, black political power, black culture are victims of the black minority position, and not even local concentration permits Harlemites, say, to take charge of their joint destiny even to the degree the 6,000 inhabitants of Anguilla enjoy.

Racial demography entails related differences. In the United States race relations have not until recently consciously touched most whites. Only today do black issues force themselves on the attention of all Americans, and even now few whites directly experience racial involvement. Much of white America remains cocooned against contact with the black ghetto. But in the Caribbean a different racial balance, and a smaller social field, required many people—and most whites—to be intimately involved in interracial relationships.

No West Indian is unaware, inexperienced, or unaffected by interracial contacts. Because colour, class, and personal identity are all intimately linked, racial awareness suffuses every aspect of West Indian life. Since such distinctions are by definition invidious, West Indian societies that describe themselves as 'multi-racial' are far removed from paradise. But West Indians have learned through experience how to deal with many distinctions, invidious or otherwise. In the smaller islands especially, propinquity and the need for local collaboration demand intimacy even among people who see themselves as racially different. A socio-racial continuum makes West Indians seem highly sophisticated by contrast with Americans, white or black, who are almost wholly cut off from the other 'race'. (One measure of this

[1] See Harold M. Rose, 'The All-Negro Town: Its Evolution and Function', *GR*, Vol. 55, 1965, pp. 362–81. As for the urban ghetto, all large-scale institutions—schools, police, welfare, health, mass transit, political machines, sources of credit—'are totally controlled from outside the community and generally not even susceptible to any influence from community members' (Charles A. Valentine, 'Blackston: Progress Report on a Community Study in Urban Afro-America', 1970, p. 73).

sophistication is the extraordinary preponderance of West Indian directors of black-studies programmes in American universities.)

Caribbean cultural connectivities also facilitate a range of interracial contacts that are rare in the United States. Black and white sub-cultures in North America are far more similar than those of elite and folk in the West Indies, which are marked, as has been shown, by profound pluralism. Yet despite great social distance, Caribbean classes believe that they share many significant cultural traits. Because almost all West Indian whites are in the company of non-whites from cradle to grave, Creole folklore and behaviour are integral parts of their lives. 'The elite child brought up in Grenada is cared for by black nursemaids from whom he learns some of the folk patois. . . . He will also learn about obeah or folk sorcery and magic; . . . folk cooperation in work, . . . about the "bamboo-tambou," . . . about "frien'ing" or extraresidential mating, keeping (concubinage) and its conditions, . . . family land, and so on'.[1] Relatively few white Southerners, let alone Northerners, participate to anything like the same extent in black folkways.

Most West Indians likewise share both the general concept and many specific elements of a 'classic' culture acquired by few Americans, black or white. 'A West Indian child grows up with . . . Bach through Episco-pal hymns, and Shakespeare as a living force. . . . West Indians know the Bible—chapter and verse . . . a tradition that was not the kind of thing even whites got' in the United States.[2] Shakespeare is not, to be sure, integral in the upbringing of most British West Indians, nor are French West Indians all familiar with Molière and Rousseau. But the classics are often a common expectation, if not a common experience, in West Indian life, permeating the schools, the legislatures, and a host of informal contacts. In the United States, by contrast, the cultural stage was a virtual *tabula rasa*; not even their mutual devotion to Biblical fundamentalism promotes black–white contact. Ways in which Ameri-can blacks and whites may resemble one another—speech, cuisine, sports—induce little sense of shared culture; whereas ways in which elite and folk West Indians differ seldom obliterate a sense of com-munality. Connectivities that cut across pluralism involve most West Indians in a dual vision of life, with some participation in one another's principal worlds, however different in their essentials those worlds may be.

The physical smallness of West Indian territories helps to bridge cultural chasms. In 'a small country personalities count for more than

---

[1] M. G. Smith, *Stratification in Grenada*, 1965, pp. 217–18. See also Frances P. Karner, *The Sephardics of Curaçao: A Study of Socio-Cultural Patterns in Flux*, 1969, p. 22. For the relative ignorance of whites in America, see Valentine, 'Blackston', p. 72.

[2] Elliott Skinner, quoted in C. Gerald Fraser, 'Neighborhoods: West Indies Flavor Bedford-Stuyvesant', *New York Times*, 28 October 1970, pp. 49, 57.

policies, and it is still possible for individual citizens to exercise considerable influence in the ordering of public affairs. . . . The centres of power are not only well known but also fairly easily accessible.'[1] And accessibility breeds intimacy. 'Familiarity need not bring contempt, but it will certainly wash away mystery, awe, and majesty. The judge looks less formidable in his wig and gown if we have often seen him in his shorts. There is consequently some compensating advantage in smallness. It can lead to straighter talking and to the substitution of earned respect for pomp and circumstance.'[2]

Intimacy can also humanize commerce and production. Employer and employee alike regard industry as much more than a merely economic enterprise. The effective businessman 'is not one *who gets the right things done*, but rather one . . . who thinks of his social obligations, is concerned about the country's affairs, as a whole'.[3]

West Indians are more conscious of internal differences than, say, most Americans or Britons. But they also more consciously seek modes of behaviour to diminish these differences and to reduce their impact. Distinction of race, colour, ethnicity, and class remain significant in many aspects of West Indian life, nor are West Indians committed to egalitarian principles. Yet for all their social and cultural pluralism, they are strong partisans of social unity.

West Indian black-power demonstrations and threats of violence are not racial conflicts in the American or British senses. The American civil-rights movement, black power, and white backlash are racial in programme, in focus, and in purpose. British minority problems are viewed by all participants as specifically racial, and the controversy over immigration hinges on this. But Caribbean conflicts are chiefly socio-economic in nature, and racial mainly in name. To be sure, these problems have their roots in slavery and in colonialism, both of which were racially organized. But these antecedents are not operationally significant today. Race and colour are rallying points for protest, not their essential ingredients or their major determinants.

From the current black American viewpoint, West Indian faith in multi-racialism seems self-deluding, especially among those 'confronted with the physicality of blackness, a fact so lasting, so incontrovertible'.[4] But West Indians do not simply seek to 'escape' the stigma of blackness, they mitigate it by defining colour in cultural terms. Black Americans reprehend West Indian middle-class striving as white emulation. But

---

[1] Cumper, 'In Search of a New Identity'.

[2] Hall, 'The Colonial Legacy in Jamaica', p. 21.

[3] Tony H. Bonaparte, 'The Influence of Culture on Business in a Pluralistic Society: A Study of Trinidad, West Indies', *American Journal of Economics and Sociology*, Vol. 28, 1969, pp. 285–301.

[4] Orde Coombs, 'West Indians in New York: Moving beyond the Limbo Pole', *New York Magazine*, Vol. 3, No. 28, 13 July 1970, pp. 28–32, ref. p. 32.

because interracial contacts are normal in small West Indian societies, 'racial exclusivity has never been able to win a strong central place in movements of national black assertion'[1]—Garvey's influence notwithstanding. The social diversity that West Indian flags and mottoes symbolize is partly a fiction, since it implies a simple federation of racial and ethnic groups based on equivalence of numbers and of opportunity. Yet West Indians almost everywhere are 'committed to a multiracial ethic, and even if people are not clear in their own minds what this is all about . . . it somehow seems to have a tremendous psychological effect on the populace at large.'[2]

This commitment distinguishes West Indian race relations from those in the United States as sharply as most Americans consider their own system to differ from the South African. In bald terms, South Africans believe in and practise apartheid; Americans believe in integration and practise apartheid; West Indians believe in and practise integration. Caribbean scholars recognize that 'the white colonists, the free people of colour and the Negro slaves [were all] joint participants in a human situation which shaped all their lives.'[3] However difficult it is to forge local pride into a steady common purpose, West Indian identity today entails a like sympathy. Never united, seldom co-operating, West Indians do not require unity to be uniquely themselves.

---

[1] Rex Nettleford, 'Poverty at the Root of Race Issue', in 'Jamaica: A Special Report', *The Times*, 14 September 1970, p. II.

[2] Ibid.

[3] Elsa V. Goveia, 'New Shibboleths for Old', *CQ*, Vol. 10, No. 2, June 1964, pp. 48–54, ref. p. 51.

Sources

The lists below are confined to materials cited in the footnotes or that were otherwise useful in the preparation of this book. Not included are items from newspapers, political broadsides, government press releases, and brief articles in ephemeral West Indian periodicals.

Abbreviations used in the bibliography:

AA	*American Anthropologist*
CERAG	*Cahiers du C.E.R.A.G.* (Centre d'Études Régionales Antilles-Guyane)
CO-M	*Cahiers d'Outre-Mer*
CQ	*Caribbean Quarterly*
CS	*Caribbean Studies*
GR	*Geographical Review*
ICS	Institute of Caribbean Studies (University of Puerto Rico)
ISER	Institute of Social and Economic Research (University of the West Indies)
JHR	*Jamaican Historical Review*
JJ	*Jamaica Journal*
NWQ	*New World Quarterly*
SES	*Social and Economic Studies*
WIE	*West Indian Economist*
UWI UCWI	University (College) of the West Indies

LIBRARY AND MANUSCRIPT SOURCES

Many materials used, published and unpublished, are not easily obtained. They were made available through the kindness of the staff at the following libraries, which have valuable specialized collections:

American Geographical Society, New York City
Barbados Museum, Bridgetown, Barbados
Department of Extra-Mural Studies, University of the West Indies, Jamaica
Department of History, University of the West Indies, Jamaica
Dominica Public Library, Roseau
Institute of International Relations, University of the West Indies, Trinidad

Institute of Jamaica, Kingston
Institute of Race Relations, London
Institute of Social and Economic Research, University of the West Indies, Jamaica, Trinidad, and Barbados
Research Institute for the Study of Man, New York City
University of the West Indies, Jamaica and Trinidad.

Most unpublished reports, theses, and other papers are separately listed by author under the alphabetical list of works below. The following special collections were of particular importance:

Edith Clarke Papers, Kingston, Jamaica
Dominica Archives, Roseau, Dominica
Montserrat Archives, Plymouth, Montserrat
Public Record Office, London (Colonial Office Records)

BIBLIOGRAPHIES

Abonnenc, E., Hurault, J., and Saban, R. *Bibliographie de la Guyane française*; Tome I: *Ouvrages et articles de langue française concernant la Guyane et les territoires avoisinants*, Paris, Éditions Larose, 1957. ca. 1600–1955. 3,664 refs.

Alcala, V. O., compiler. *A bibliography of education in the Caribbean*, Port-of-Spain, Caribbean Commission, 1959. 144 pp., 1,834 annotated items, topically arranged.

Baa, Enid M., compiler. *Theses on Caribbean topics, 1778–1968*, San Juan, ICS (Caribbean Bibliographic Series, No. 1), 1970. 1,242 items.

Canton, Berthe E. 'A bibliography of West Indian literature', *Current Caribbean Bibliography*, Vol. 7, 1957, pp. 1–56.

— 'The French Caribbean Departments: sources of information, 1946–1955', *Current Caribbean Bibliography*, Vol. 4, 1954, pp. 1–36.

Comitas, Lambros. *Caribbeana 1900–1965: a topical bibliography*, Seattle, University of Washington Press for the Research Institute for the Study of Man, 1968. The most comprehensive bibliography of the area, excluding Haiti. Focus on social science, history, humanities. Over 7,000 items.

Current 'Bibliography'. In *Caribbean Studies*, Río Piedras, Institute of Caribbean Studies. Quarterly listing by territory of books and periodical articles.

Current Caribbean Bibliography, Port-of-Spain, Caribbean Commission, Vols. 1–7, 1950–7.

Debien, Gabriel. 'Sources de l'histoire de l'esclavage aux Antilles', *Revue de la Société Haïtienne d'Histoire, de Géographie et de Géologie*, Vol. 34, No. 111, January–April 1967, pp. 12–48. Focuses especially but not exclusively on St. Domingue.

Easton, David K. 'A bibliography on the federation of the British West Indies', *Current Caribbean Bibliography*, Vol. 5, 1955, pp. 1–14.

Goveia, Elsa V. *A study on the historiography of the British West Indies to the end of the nineteenth century*, Mexico, D.F., Panamerican Institute of Geography and History, 1956. 183 pp. Analysis of the principal published sources.

Hills, Theo L., compiler. *Caribbean topics theses in Canadian university libraries*, Montreal, McGill University, Centre for Developing-Area Studies [1968]. 14 pp. Mainly 1940s–1960s. Supplements Baa.

Hiss, Philip Hanson. *A selective guide to the English literature on the Netherlands West Indies, with a supplement on British Guiana*, New York, Netherlands Information Bureau, 1943. 124 pp. Topically and geographically arranged.

Jahn, Janheinz. *A bibliography of neo-African literature from Africa, America, and the Caribbean*, London, Andre Deutsch, 1965. Antilles and Guiana section, pp. 132–95, 823 items. Twentieth century.

Jardel, Jean-Pierre, et al. 'Bibliographie de la Martinique', *CERAG*, Special Number 1969/3 (1st part). 231 pp., 3,000 items, topically arranged.

Lasserre, Guy. *La Guadeloupe: étude géographique*, 2 vols., Bordeaux, Union Française d'Impression, 1961, Vol. II, pp. 1069–112. 817 items.

Lowenthal, David. 'A selected West Indian reading list', in his *West Indies Federation: perspectives on a new nation*, New York, Columbia University Press with the American Geographical Society and Carleton University, 1961, pp. 101–35. Annotated. British Caribbean.

Miller, Elizabeth W., compiler. *The Negro in America: a bibliography*, Cambridge, Harvard University Press, 1966. 188 pp., topically arranged.

Mintz, Sidney W., and Carrol, Vern. 'A selective social science bibliography of the Republic of Haiti', *Revista Interamericana de Ciencias Sociales*, segunda epoca, Vol. 2, No. 3, 1963, pp. 405–16. Annotated list of major books and periodicals, 1940–61.

Mitchell, Harold. *Caribbean patterns: a political and economic study of the contemporary Caribbean*, Edinburgh, Chambers, 1967, pp. 408–51. About 1,000 items. Regionally organized.

Ragatz, Lowell Joseph, compiler. *A guide for the study of British Caribbean history, 1763–1834, including the abolition and emancipation movements*, Washington, D.C., Government Printing Office, 1932. 725 pp. Annotated.

Ramchand, Kenneth. *The West Indian novel and its background*, London, Faber and Faber, 1970, pp. 274–86. British Caribbean author bibliography, twentieth century.

Renselaar, H. C. van, and Speckmann, J. D., 'Social research on Surinam and the Netherlands Antilles', *Nieuwe West-Indische Gids*, Vol. 47, No. 1, September 1969, pp. 29–59. Analysis of 238 sources.

Sivanandan, A., compiler. *Coloured immigrants in Britain: a select bibliography*, 3rd ed., London, Institute of Race Relations, 1969. Works in the Institute library or British Museum. 1950–69. 110 pp., topically arranged.

Thompson, Edgar T. *The plantation: a bibliography*, Washington, D.C., Pan American Union, Social Science Monographs IV, 1957. 93 pp., 1,347 items, regionally organized.

Williams, Eric. *From Columbus to Castro: the history of the Caribbean, 1492–1969*, London, Andre Deutsch, 1970, pp. 516–68. The selected bibliography covers the entire Caribbean.

NEWSPAPERS AND PERIODICALS DEALING MAINLY WITH THE
WEST INDIES

Title and Publisher	Location	Frequency	Inclusive Dates of Publication [date of use]
Abeng (Abeng Publishing)	Kingston	weekly	1969
Action Radio Times (Guyana Broadcasting Co.)	Guyana	monthly	1969 —
Anguilla Beacon	Anguilla	weekly	1967 —
Annales des Antilles (Société d'Histoire de la (Martinique)	Fort-de-France	irregular	1955 —
Art and Man	Port-of-Spain	irregular	1968 —
Barbados Advocate	Bridgetown	daily	1895 —
Bim	Bridgetown, Barbados	semi-annual	1952 —
Bulletin de la Société d'Histoire de la Guadeloupe	Point-à-Pitre	semi-annual	1964 —
Cahiers du C.E.R.A.G. (Centre d'Études Régionales Antilles-Guyane)	Fort-de-France, Martinique	irregular (ca. 3 per year)	(?) 1966 —
Cahiers d'Outre-Mer (Institut de la France d'Outre-Mer de Bordeaux)	Bordeaux	quarterly	1948 —
Cahiers du CHISS (Centre Haïtien d'Investigation en Sciences Sociales)	Port-au-Prince, Haiti	3 times a year	(?) 1966 —
Cane Farmer	Trinidad	monthly	1959 —
Caribbean (Caribbean Commission)	Port-of-Spain	monthly	1947–1960
Caribbean Economic Review (Caribbean Commission)	Port-of-Spain	semi-annual and annual	1949–1954
Caribbean Historical Review (Historical Society of Trinidad and Tobago)	Trinidad	irregular	1950–1954
Caribbean Monthly Bulletin (ICS)	Río Piedras, Puerto Rico	monthly	1963–1969
Caribbean Quarterly (UWI, Extra-Mural Department)	Kingston/Port-of-Spain	quarterly	1949 —
Caribbean Review	Hato Rey, Puerto Rico	quarterly	1969 —
Caribbean Studies (ICS)	Río Piedras	quarterly	1961 —

Title and Publisher	Location	Frequency	Inclusive Dates of Publication [date of use]
Comment (UWI, Joint Policy Sub-Committee of the Academic Board)	Mona, Jamaica	irregular	[November 1968]
Conch Shell (Friends of Anguilla)	London	irregular (ca. 6 per year)	1968–1970
C.S.O. Research Papers (Central Statistical Office, Trinidad and Tobago)	Port-of-Spain	irregular	1963 —
Dawnlit (Dawbiney Literary Club)	Roseau, Dominica	irregular	1961 —
Dominica Chronicle	Roseau	weekly	1909 —
Dominica Colonist	Roseau	weekly	[1863]
Dominica Guardian	Roseau	weekly	[1894, 1896]
Dominica Herald	Roseau	weekly	1955 —
Dominica Star	Roseau	weekly	1965 —
The Dominican	Roseau	weekly	[1872]
Embryo (UWI, Guild of Under-graduates)	St. Augustine, Trinidad	irregular	[March 1970]
Flambeau (Kingstown Study Group)	Kingstown, St. Vincent	quarterly	1965–1967
Flamingo	London	monthly	[1962]
Georgetown Chronicle	Georgetown, Guyana	daily	1881 —
Guyana Graphic	Georgetown	daily	[1970]
Guyana Sun (The United Force)	Georgetown	weekly	[1970]
Jamaica Architect (Jamaican Society of Architects)	Kingston	annual, semi-annual	? 1967—
Jamaica Gleaner, Daily, Sunday, Weekly	Kingston		1834 —
Jamaica Journal (Institute of Jamaica)	Kingston	quarterly	1967 —
Jamaica Times	Kingston	weekly	1898 —
Jamaican Historical Review (Jamaican Historical Society)	Kingston	semi-annual or irregular	? 1949–1970
Journal of the Barbados Museum and Historical Society	Bridgetown	irregular	1933 —
Moko	Port-of-Spain	fortnightly	1968 —
Montserrat Herald	Plymouth	weekly	[1903]

Title and Publisher	Location	Frequency	Inclusive Dates of Publication [date of use]
New World (Fortnightly, Monthly, Quarterly, Pamphlets) (New World Associates)	Georgetown/ Kingston/Port-of-Spain		1963 —
Newday	Kingston	monthly	1957 —
News from Guyana (Guyana Ministry of Information)	Georgetown	weekly	[1970]
Nieuwe West Indische Gids (formerly *De West-Indische Gids*)	The Hague	3 per year	1919 —
Paralleles	Fort-de-France, Martinique	3 or 4 per year	? 1959 —
Pelican (UWI, Guild of Under-graduates)	Kingston	irregular	[March 1962]
Public Opinion	Kingston	weekly	1937 —
Revue de la Société Haïtienne d'Histoire, de Géographie, et de Géologie	Port-au-Prince, Haiti	quarterly	1925 —
Savacou (Caribbean Artists Movement)	Kingston and London	quarterly	1970 —
Scope (UWI, Guild of Under-graduates)	Mona, Jamaica	irregular	[November 1968]
Social and Economic Studies (ISER)	Kingston	quarterly	1953 —
Spotlight	Kingston	monthly	? 1939 —
St. Kitts Union-Messenger	Basseterre	weekly	[1960]
Tapia (Tapia House)	Tunapuna, Trinidad	irregular (ca. monthly)	1969 —
Tapia Pamphlets		irregular	
Timehri (Royal Agricultural and Commercial Society of British Guiana)	Georgetown	irregular	1882 —
The Torch (Democratic Labour Party, Trinidad)	Port-of-Spain	fortnightly	1970 —
Trinidad Express	Port-of-Spain	daily	[1969, 1970]
Trinidad Guardian	Port-of-Spain	daily	1918 —

Title and Publisher	Location	Frequency	Inclusive Dates of Publication [date of use]
Trinidad Nation (formerly P.N.M. Weekly)	Port-of-Spain	weekly	1958 —
Trinidad and Tobago Index	various	irregular	1965–1966
Tussle (UWI, Guild of Under-graduates)	Mona, Jamaica	irregular	[February 1970]
Vanguard (Oilfield Workers' Trade Union)	San Fernando, Trinidad	fortnightly	[March 1970]
Voices (Clifford Sealy, The Book Shop)	Port-of-Spain	3 per year	? 1967 —
Vox Guyanae	Paramaribo, Surinam	irregular	1954 —
West Indian Economist	Kingston	10 per year	1958–1962
West Indies Chronicle (West India Committee)	London	monthly	1886 —

BOOKS, ARTICLES, THESES, AND REPORTS

A

Abraham-van der Mark, Eva E. 'Yu'i mama: enkele facetten van gezins-structuur op Curaçao', Ph.D. thesis, University of Amsterdam, 1969.

Abrahams, Peter. *Jamaica: an island mosaic*, London, H.M.S.O., 1957.

— *This island now*, London, Faber and Faber, 1966.

— 'We can learn to be color-blind', *New York Times Magazine*, 11 April 1965, pp. 38, 102–6.

Abrahams, Roger D., 'Patterns of performance in the British West Indies', in Whitten and Szwed, op cit., pp. 163–78.

— 'The shaping of folklore traditions in the British West Indies', *Journal of Inter-American Studies*, Vol. IX, 1967, pp. 456–80.

Abrahams, Tony. 'Corner stones of Jamaica's tourism future', *Jamaica Architect*, Vol. 2, No. 2, 1969, p. 21.

Ackroyd, Elizabeth. 'Caribbean jaunt', *New Statesman*, 18 April 1969.

Adams, Nassau A., 'Internal migration in Jamaica: an economic analysis', *SES*, Vol. 18, 1969, pp. 137–51.

Adhin, Jan Hansdew. *Development planning in Surinam in historical perspective (with special reference to the 10 year plan)*, New York, W. S. Heinman, 1961.

Ahiram, E. 'Distribution of income in Trinidad-Tobago and comparison with distribution of income in Jamaica', *SES*, Vol. 15, 1966, pp. 103–20.

— 'Income distribution in Jamaica, 1958', *SES*, Vol. 13, 1964, pp. 333–69.

Alkire, William H. *Lamotrek Atoll and inter-island socioeconomic ties*, Urbana, University of Illinois Press, 1965.

Alland, Alexander. 'The Jews of the Virgin Islands', *American Hebrew* (New York), Vol. 146, Nos. 20–24, Vol. 147, No. 1, March–May 1940.

Allen, Grant. 'Ivan Greet's masterpiece', in his *The jaws of death*, New York, 1897, pp. 174–5.

Alleyne, Mervin C. 'Communication between the elite and the masses', in Andic and Mathews, op. cit., pp. 12–19.

— 'The cultural matrix of Caribbean dialects', in Hymes, op. cit.

— 'Language and society in St. Lucia', *CS*, Vol. 1, No. 1, April 1961, pp. 1–10.

Allsopp, S. R. R. 'British Honduras—the linguistic dilemma', *CQ*, Vol. 11, Nos. 3 and 4, September–December 1965, pp. 54–61.

Ammar, Nellie. 'They came from the Middle East', *JJ*, Vol. 4, No. 1, March 1970, pp. 2–6.

Andic, Fuat M., and Andic, Suphan. 'Government finance and planned development: fiscal surveys of Surinam and the Netherlands Antilles', *Caribbean Monograph Series*, No. 5, Río Piedras, ICS, 1968.

Andic, Fuat M., and Mathews, T. G., eds. *The Caribbean in transition: papers on social, political, and economic development*, Proceedings of the Second Caribbean Scholars' Conference, 1964, Río Piedras, ICS, 1965.

Andrade, Jacob A. P. M. *A record of the Jews in Jamaica from the English conquest to the present time*, Kingston, Jamaica Times, 1941.

The annexation of Chaguaramas. Historical Documents of Trinidad and Tobago, Series No. 1, Government Printing Office, 1963.

Anthony, Michael. *Green days by the river*, London, Andre Deutsch, 1967.

Aronoff, Joel. *Psychological needs and cultural systems: a case study*, Princeton, N.J., Van Nostrand, 1967.

Augelli, John P. 'The British Virgin Islands: a West Indian anomaly', *GR*, Vol. 46, 1956, pp. 43–58.

Augelli, John P., and Taylor, Harry W. 'Race and population patterns in Trinidad', *Annals Association of American Geographers*, Vol. 50, 1960, pp. 123–38.

Augier, F. Roy. 'The consequences of Morant Bay: before and after 1865', *NWQ*, Vol. 2, No. 2, Croptime 1966, pp. 21–42.

Augier, F. Roy, and Gordon, Shirley C. *Sources of West Indian history*, London, Longmans, Green, 1962.

B

Bacchus, M. K. 'Education and change', *NWQ*, Vol. 5, Nos. 1 and 2, Dead Season and Croptime 1969, pp. 63–73.

— *Education and socio-cultural integration in a 'plural' society*, Montreal, McGill University, Centre for Developing-Area Studies, Occasional Paper Series, No. 6, 1970.

— 'The ministerial system at work: a case study of Guyana', *SES*, Vol. 16, 1967, pp. 34–56.

Back, Kurt W., and Stycos, J. Mayone. *The survey under unusual conditions: methodological facets of the Jamaica human fertility investigation*, Ithaca, N.Y., Society for Applied Anthropology, 1959.

Bagley, Christopher. 'Migration, race and mental health: a review of some recent research', *Race*, Vol. IX, 1967–8, pp. 343–56.

Bagley, Christopher. 'The social aetiology of schizophrenia in immigrant groups', *Race Today*, Vol. 1, 1969, pp. 170–4.

Bahadoorsingh, Krishna. *Trinidad electoral politics: the persistence of the race factor*, London, Institute of Race Relations, 1968.

— 'What Trinidad's leaders believe about race and politics', *Trinidad and Tobago Index*, No. 4, September 1966, pp. 38–45.

Bangou, Henri. *La Guadeloupe, 1848–1939: ou les aspects de la colonisation après l'abolition de l'esclavage*, Aurillac, Éditions du Centre, 1963.

— *La Guadeloupe, 1492–1848: ou l'histoire de la colonisation de l'île liée à l'esclavage noir de ses débuts à sa disparition*, Aurillac, Éditions du Centre, 1962.

Banks, E. P. 'A Carib village in Dominica', *SES*, Vol. 5, 1956, pp. 74–86.

Banton, Michael. *Race relations*, London, Social Science Paperbacks, 1967.

— *White and coloured: the behaviour of British people towards coloured immigrants*, London, Jonathan Cape, 1959.

'Barbados independence issue'. *NWQ*, Vol. 3, Nos. 1 and 2, Dead Season 1966, and Croptime 1967.

Barbados Social Welfare Department. *Eighth annual report*, Bridgetown, 1958.

Bariteau, Claude. 'Organisation économique et organisation familiale dans une île antillaise: la Désirade', M.A. thesis in Anthropology, University of Montreal, 1968.

Barr, John. 'Carnival, cricket and The Mighty Sparrow', *New Society*, Vol. 11, 8 February 1968, p. 201.

Barrett, Leonard E. 'The Rastafarians: a study in messianic cultism in Jamaica', *Caribbean Monograph Series*, No. 6, Río Piedras, ICS, 1968.

Barrow, Errol. 'A role for Canada in the West Indies', *International Journal*, Vol. XIX, 1964, pp. 172–87.

Barzun, Jacques. *Race: a study in modern superstition*, New York, Harcourt, Brace, 1938.

Bastien, Elliott. 'The weary road to whiteness and the hasty retreat into nationalism', in Tajfel and Dawson, op. cit., pp. 38–54.

Bastien, Rémy. 'Vodoun and politics in Haiti', in Courlander and Bastien, op. cit., pp. 39–68.

Baudet, Henri. *Paradise on earth: some thoughts on European images of non-European man*, New Haven, Yale University Press, 1965.

Baugh, Edward. 'Towards a West Indian criticism', *CQ*, Vol. 14, Nos. 1 and 2, March–June 1968, pp. 140–4.

Bayer, A. E., *Surinaamse arbeiders in Nederland*, Assen, Neth., Van Gorcum, 1965.

Beachey, R. W. *The British West Indies sugar industry in the late 19th century*, Oxford, Basil Blackwell, 1957.

Beckford, G. L. 'Toward rationalization of West Indian agriculture', in *Papers presented at the regional conference on devaluation*, ISER, 1968, pp. 147–54.

Beckford, G. L., and Brown, E. A. 'Economic aspects of food availability in Jamaica', *CQ*, Vol. 14, No. 4, December 1968, pp. 61–5.

Beckwith, Martha Warren. *Black roadways: a study of Jamaican folk life*, Chapel Hill, University of North Carolina Press, 1929.

Beghin, I. D., Fougère, W., and King, Kendall W., *Food and nutrition in Haiti*, Paris, Presses Universitaires de France, 1968.

Bell, Henry Hesketh. *Glimpses of a governor's life*, London, Sampson, Low, Marston, 1946.

Bell, Kenneth N., and Morrell, W. P., eds. *Select documents on British colonial policy, 1830–1860*. Oxford, Clarendon Press, 1928.

Bell, Robert R. 'Marriage and family differences among lower-class Negro and East Indian women in Trinidad', *Race*, Vol. XII, 1970–1, pp. 59–73.

Bell, Wendell. *Jamaican leaders: political attitudes in a new nation*, Berkeley, University of California Press, 1964.

Bell, Wendell, ed. *The democratic revolution in the West Indies: studies in nationalism, leadership, and the belief in progress*, Cambridge, Mass., Schenkman, 1967.

Benedict, Burton. 'Pluralism and stratification', in Plotnicov and Tuden, op. cit., pp. 29–42.

— 'Sociological aspects of smallness', in Benedict, ed., *Problems of smaller territories*, pp. 45–66.

— 'Stratification in plural societies', *AA*, Vol. 64, 1962, pp. 1235–46.

Benedict, Burton, ed. *Problems of smaller territories*, London, Athlone Press for the Institute of Commonwealth Studies, 1967.

Bennett, J. Harry, Jr. *Bondsmen and bishops: slavery and apprenticeship on the Codrington plantations of Barbados, 1710–1838*, Berkeley, University of California Publications in History, Vol. 62, 1958.

Bennett, Louise. *Jamaica labrish*, Jamaica, Sangster's Book Stores, 1966.

Benoist, Jean. 'Anthropologie physique de la population de l'île de la Tortue (Haïti): contribution à l'étude de l'origine des noirs des Antilles', *Bulletins et Mémoires de la Société d'Anthropologie de Paris*, Ser. XI, Vol. 3, 1962, pp. 315–35.

— 'Les Martiniquais: anthropologie d'une population métissée', *Bulletins et Mémoires de la Société d'Anthropologie de Paris*, Ser. XI, Vol. 4, No. 2, 1963.

— 'Saint-Barthélemy: Physical anthropology of an isolate', *American Journal of Physical Anthropology*, Vol. 22, 1964, pp. 473–87.

— 'Du social au biologique: étude de quelques interactions', *L'Homme*, Vol. VI, No. 1, 1966, pp. 5–26.

Benoist, Jean, ed., *Les sociétés antillaises: études anthropoloqiques*, University of Montreal, Department of Anthropology, 1966.

Benson, Michael G. 'Social interaction on a Trinidad land development project' [Waller Field], M.A. thesis, Brandeis University, Waltham, Mass., 1968.

Bentley, Gerald, and Henry, Frances. 'Some preliminary observations on the Chinese in Trinidad', in Henry, op. cit., pp. 19–33.

Berghe, Pierre L. van den. 'The African diaspora in Mexico, Brazil, and the United States' [1970], mimeo.

— 'European languages and black mandarins', *Transition* (Kampala, Uganda), Vol. 7, No. 34, 1968, pp. 19–23.

— *Race and racism: a comparative perspective*, New York, John Wiley, 1967.

Beringuier, Ch. 'L'espace régional martiniquais', *CERAG*, No. 3 [1966], 2nd edn., 1969.

Berrian, Albert H., and Long, Richard A., eds. *Négritude: essays and studies*, Hampton, Va., Hampton Institute Press, 1967.

Berry, Paul. 'Literacy and the question of Creole', in Schaedel, op. cit., pp. 204–80.

Best, Lloyd. 'Black power and national reconstruction: proposals following the February Revolution', *Tapia Pamphlet* [1970].

— 'Chaguaramas to slavery?' *NWQ*, Vol. 2, No. 1, Dead Season 1965, pp. 43–70.

— 'Guest Editor's statement: the next round', *NWQ*, Vol. 4, No. 2, Croptime 1968, pp. 1–7.

— 'Independent thought and Caribbean freedom', *NWQ*, Vol. 3, No. 4, Cropover 1967, pp. 13–34.

Bickerton, Derek. *The murders of Boysie Singh*, London, Arthur Barker, 1962.

Biet, Antoine. *Voyage de la France équinoxiale en l'isle de Cayenne enterpris par les françois en l'année M.DC.LII*, Paris, 1664.

Bigelow, John. *Jamaica in 1850, or, the effects of sixteen years of freedom on a slave colony*, New York, George P. Putnam, 1851.

Billingsley, Andrew. *Black families in white America*, Englewood Cliffs, N.J., Prentice-Hall, 1968.

Blake, Evon. *The best of Evon Blake*, Kingston, Barbara Blake, n.d.

Blake, Judith, with Stycos, J. Mayone, and Davis, Kingsley. *Family structure in Jamaica: the social context of reproduction*, New York, Free Press, 1961.

Blanshard, Paul. *Democracy and empire in the Caribbean: a contemporary review*, New York, Macmillan, 1947.

Blassingame, John W. 'The press and American intervention in Haiti and the Dominican Republic, 1904–1920', *CS*, Vol. 9, No. 2, July 1969, pp. 27–43.

Blauner, Robert. 'Black culture: myth or reality?' in Whitten and Szwed, op. cit., pp. 347–66.

Blaut, James M., et al. 'A study of cultural determinants of soil erosion and conservation in the Blue Mountains of Jamaica: progress report', *SES*, Vol. 8, 1959, pp. 403–20.

Bogat, Raphaël. 'Dominique, terre de refuge', *Bulletin de la Société d'Histoire de la Guadeloupe*, No. 8, 1967, pp. 79–94.

Bois, Etienne P. *Les amerindiens de la Haute-Guyane française*, Paris, Collège de la Société de Pathologie Exotique, Monograph VII, 1967.

Bonaparte, Tony H. 'The influence of culture on business in a pluralistic society: a study of Trinidad, West Indies', *American Journal of Economics and Sociology*, Vol. 28, 1969, pp. 285–301.

Bone, Louis W. *Secondary education in the Guianas*, University of Chicago, Comparative Education Center, Monograph No. 2, 1962.

Borah, Woodrow, and Cook, Sherburne F. 'Marriage and legitimacy in Mexican culture: Mexico and California', *California Law Review*, Vol. LIV, No. 2, May 1966, pp. 946–1008.

Boromé, Joseph Alfred. 'George Charles Falconer', *CQ*, Vol. 6, No. 1, 1959–60, pp. 11–17.

— 'How crown colony government came to Dominica by 1898', *CS*, Vol. 9, No. 3, October 1969, pp. 26–67.

Bourguignon, Erika. 'Ritual dissociation and possession belief in Caribbean Negro religion', in Whitten and Szwed, op. cit., pp. 87–101.

Boxer, C. R. *The golden age of Brazil: 1695–1750. Growing pains of a colonial society*, Berkeley, University of California Press, 1963.
— *Race relations in the Portuguese colonial empire, 1415–1825*, Oxford, Clarendon Press, 1963.
Braithwaite, E. R. *A kind of homecoming*, London, Frederick Muller, 1963.
— *To sir, with love*, London, Bodley Head, 1959.
Braithwaite, Lloyd. 'The development of higher education in the British West Indies', *SES*, Vol. 7, 1958, pp. 1–64.
— 'The problem of cultural integration in Trinidad', *SES*, Vol. 3, No. 1, June 1954, pp. 82–96.
— 'Race relations and industrialisation in the Caribbean', in Hunter, ed., *Industrialisation and race relations*, q.v., pp. 30–45.
— 'Social and political aspects of rural development in the West Indies', *SES*, Vol. 17, 1968, pp. 264–75.
— 'Social stratification and cultural pluralism', *Annals New York Academy of Sciences*, Vol. 83, 1960, pp. 816–36.
— 'Social stratification in Trinidad: a preliminary analysis', *SES*, Vol. 2, Nos. 2 and 3, October 1953, pp. 5–175.
Brathwaite, Edward. 'Caribbean critics', *NWQ*, Vol. 5, Nos. 1 and 2, Dead Season and Croptime 1969, pp. 5–12.
— 'Creative literature of the British West Indies during the period of slavery', *Savacou*, Vol. 1, No. 1, June 1970, pp. 46–74.
— 'Jamaican slave society, a review', *Race*, Vol. IX, 1967–8, pp. 331–42.
— 'Jazz and the West Indian novel', *Bim*, Vol. 11, No. 44, January–June 1967, pp. 275–84.
— 'Negus', *CQ*, Vol. 15, Nos. 2 and 3, June–September 1969, pp. 130–2.
— *Rights of passage*, London, Oxford University Press, 1967.
Breton, André, with Masson, André. *Martinique charmeuse de serpents* [Paris], Éditions du Sagittaire, 1948.
Brewster, Havelock. 'The pattern of wages, prices and productivity in British Guyana, 1948 to 1962', *SES*, Vol. 18, 1969, pp. 107–36.
— 'Sugar—mechanizing our life or death', *NWQ*, Vol. 5, Nos. 1 and 2, Dead Season and Croptime 1969, pp. 55–7.
Broderick, Francis L., and Meier, August, eds., *Negro protest thought in the twentieth century*, Indianapolis, Bobbs-Merrill, 1965.
Brøndsted, Johannes, ed. *Vore gamle tropekolonier*, 2 vols., Copenhagen, Fremad, 1966–8.
Broom, Leonard. 'The social differentiation of Jamaica', *American Sociological Review*, Vol. 19, 1954, pp. 115–25.
Brougham, Henry. *A concise statement of the question regarding the abolition of the slave trade*, London, 1804.
Brown, G. Arthur. 'Sugar without emotion', *NWQ*, Vol. 5, Nos. 1 and 2, Dead Season and Croptime 1969, pp. 40–1.
Bruijne, G. A. de. 'Surinamers naar Nederland—een nieuwe vorm van urbanisatie', *Enig zicht op Suriname*, pp. VII-1–VII-5.
Bryans, Robin. *Trinidad and Tobago: isles of the immortelles*, London, Faber and Faber, 1967.

Bryce-Laporte, R. S. 'Crisis, contraculture, and religion among West Indians in the Panama Canal Zone', in Whitten and Szwed, op. cit., pp. 103–18.

Burn, W. L. *Emancipation and apprenticeship in the British West Indies*, London, Jonathan Cape, 1937.

Burnham, Linden Forbes Sampson. *A destiny to mould: selected discourses by the Prime Minister of Guyana*, Trinidad, Longman Caribbean, 1970.

Butt, Audrey J. 'The Guianas', *Bulletin of the international committee on urgent anthropological and ethnological research*, No. 7, 1965, pp. 69–90.

C

Cairns, H. Alan C. *Prelude to imperialism: British reactions to Central African society, 1840–1890*, London, Routledge and Kegan Paul, 1965.

Callender, David. 'The relationship between the social structure and public reaction to the sugar depression of 1884–1914 in Barbados and Trinidad', UWI, Department of History, Mona, Jamaica, n.d., mimeo.

Campbell, A. A. *St. Thomas Negroes: a study of personality and culture*, American Psychological Association, Psychological Monographs, Vol. 55, No. 5, Northwestern University, 1943.

Campbell, Carl. 'Towards an imperial policy for the education of Negroes in the West Indies after emancipation', *JHR*, Vol. VII, Nos. 1 and 2, 1967, pp. 68–102.

Capécia, Mayotte. *Je suis martiniquaise*, Paris, Corréa, 1948.

Carew, Jan. *Black Midas*, London, Secker and Warburg, 1958.

Cargill, Morris. 'What makes Eric run?' *CQ*, Vol. 15, Nos. 2 and 3, June–September 1969, pp. 122–7.

Carlozzi, Carl A., and Carlozzi, Alice A. *Conservation and Caribbean regional progress*, Yellow Springs, Ohio, Antioch Press for the Caribbean Research Institute, St. Thomas, U.S.V.I., 1968.

Carlyle, Thomas. 'Occasional discourse on the nigger question', *Fraser's*, Vol. XL, 1849, pp. 667–79.

Carpentier, Alejo. *Explosion in a cathedral*, Boston, Little, Brown, 1962.

Carr, W. I. 'Roger Mais: design from a legend', *CQ*, Vol. 13, No. 1, March 1967, pp. 3–28.

— 'The West Indian novelist: prelude and context', *CQ*, Vol. 11, Nos. 1 and 2, March–June 1965, pp. 71–84.

Carrington, Edwin. 'Industrialization in Trinidad and Tobago since 1950', *NWQ*, Vol. 4, No. 2, Croptime 1968, pp. 37–43.

Carrington, Lawrence D., 'St. Lucian Creole: a descriptive analysis of its phonology and morpho-syntax', Ph.D. thesis, UWI, Jamaica, 1967.

Carter, Martin. 'A question of self-contempt', *NWQ*, Guyana Independence Issue, Vol. 2, No. 3, High Season 1966, pp. 10–12.

'The case for law reform: return to the rule of law'. *WIE*, Vol. 2, No. 9, March 1960, pp. 7–8.

Cassidy, F. G. *Jamaica talk: three hundred years of the English language in Jamaica*, London, Macmillan, 1961.

Cassidy, F. G., and DeCamp, David. 'Names for an albino among Jamaican Negroes', *Names*, Vol. 14, 1966, pp. 129–33.

Cassidy, F. G., and Le Page, R. B. *Dictionary of Jamaican English*, Cambridge, University Press, 1967.

— 'Lexicographical problems of the *Dictionary of Jamaican English*', in *Proceedings of the conference on Creole language studies*, London, Macmillan, 1961, pp. 17–36.

Castles, Godula. 'Racial prejudice in France', *Race Today*, Vol. 2, 1970, pp. 10–13.

Césaire, Aimé. *Cahier d'un retour au pays natal* [1939], Paris, Présence Africaine, 1956.

— *Discours sur le colonialisme*, Paris, Présence Africaine, 1955.

Chamoiseau, Miguel. 'Les élèves des classes terminales de lycée', *CERAG*, No. 18, 1969, pp. 97–112.

Chan, V. O. 'The riots of 1856 in British Guiana', *CQ*, Vol. 16, No. 1, March 1970, pp. 39–50.

Chandler, A. D. 'The expansion of Barbados', *Journal of the Barbados Museum and Historical Society*, Vol. XIII, 1946, pp. 106–36.

Chapman, Edwin. 'Problems of tourism in Jamaica', in *Tourism in the Caribbean*, q.v., pp. 126–7.

Chartrand, Francine. 'Le choix du conjoint chez les blancs-Matignons de la Guadeloupe: critères économiques et critères raciaux', *Anthropologica*, New Series, Vol. 7, 1965, pp. 81–102.

— 'Au sujet des "blancs-Matignon"', *Bulletin de la Société d'Histoire de la Guadeloupe*, No. 2, 1964, pp. 8–11.

Chauleau, Liliane. *La société à la Martinique au XVIIᵉ siècle (1635–1713)*, Caen, Ozanne, 1966.

Christian, William A., Jr. *Divided island: faction and unity on Saint Pierre*, Cambridge, Harvard University Press, 1969.

Christopher, Bernard M. 'Middle-class and their European values', *Dawnlit*, Vol. V, 1965, pp. 22–6.

The Church and unemployment, Kingston, The Unmuzzled Ox, n.d.

Chutkin, Noelle. 'The administration of justice in Jamaica as a contributing factor to the Morant Bay riot of 1865', UWI, Department of History, Mona, Jamaica, 1969, mimeo.

Clark, Kenneth B. *Dark ghetto: dilemmas of social power* [1965], New York, Harper Torchbooks, 1967.

Clarke, Austin C. *The survivors of the crossing*, London, William Heinemann, 1964.

Clarke, Colin G. 'Aspects of the urban geography of Kingston, Jamaica', Ph.D. thesis, Jesus College, Oxford, 1967.

— 'Caste among Hindus in a town in Trinidad: San Fernando', in Schwartz, op. cit., pp. 165–99.

— 'Political fragmentation in the Caribbean: the case of Anguilla', *Canadian Geographer*, Vol. XV, 1971, pp. 13–29.

— 'Residential segregation and intermarriage in San Fernando, Trinidad', *GR*, Vol. 61, 1971, pp. 198–218.

— *Social structure and social change in Kingston, Jamaica*, Berkeley, University of California Press (in press).

Clarke, Edith. 'Land tenure and the family in four selected communities in Jamaica', *SES*, Vol. 1, No. 4, August 1953, pp. 81–118.

Clarke, Edith. *My mother who fathered me: a study of the family in three selected communities in Jamaica*, London, George Allen and Unwin, 1957; 2nd edn., 1966.

Clarke, John Henrik, ed. *William Styron's Nat Turner: ten black writers respond*, Boston, Beacon Press, 1968.

Clavier, Alex., compiler. *Report on the census of the island of Saint Lucia 1891*, Saint Lucia, Government Printing Office, 1892 (reprinted Central Statistical Office, Trinidad, 1964).

Clementi, Cecil. *The Chinese in British Guiana*, British Guiana, Argosy Press, 1915.

Cloak, F. T., Jr. *A natural order of cultural adoption and loss in Trinidad*, Chapel Hill, University of North Carolina Institute of Research in Social Science (Working Papers in Methodology No. 1), 1966.

Cohen, Yehudi A. 'Adolescent conflict in a Jamaican community' [1955], in his *Social structure and personality: a casebook*, New York, Holt, Rinehart and Winston, 1961, pp. 167–81.

— 'Character formation and social structure in a Jamaican community', *Psychiatry*, Vol. 18, 1955, pp. 275–96.

— 'Structure and function: family organization and socialization in a Jamaican community', *AA*, Vol. 58, 1956, pp. 664–86.

Coleridge, Henry Nelson. *Six months in the West Indies in 1825*, 3rd edn., London, John Murray, 1832.

Collins, B. A. N. 'The Public Service of Guyana: the report of the Commission of Inquiry', 1969, mimeo.

— 'Racial imbalance in public services and security forces', *Race*, Vol. VII, 1965–6, pp. 235–53.

Collins, Doreen. 'The Turks and Caicos Islands—some impressions of an English visitor', *CQ*, Vol. 7, No. 3, December 1961, pp. 163–7.

Collins, Wallace. *Jamaican migrant*, London, Routledge and Kegan Paul, 1965.

Collymore, Frank A. *Notes for a glossary of words and phrases of Barbadian dialect*, Bridgetown, Advocate Press, 1955.

— 'To meet her mother', *Bim*, Vol. 11, No. 44, January–June 1967, pp. 290–5.

'Color and race', *Daedalus*, Vol. 96, No. 2, 1967.

Comins, D. W. D. *Note on emigration from India to Trinidad*, Calcutta, Bengal Secretariat Press, 1893.

Comitas, Lambros. 'Occupational multiplicity in rural Jamaica', in Garfield and Friedl, op. cit., pp. 41–56.

Connor, Edric. *Songs from Trinidad*, London, Oxford University Press, 1958.

Coombs, Orde. 'West Indians in New York: moving beyond the limbo pole', *New York Magazine*, 13 July 1970, pp. 28–32.

Coore, David. 'Government and the community', in Cumper, *Report of the conference on social development*, q.v., pp. 108–10.

Corzani, Jack. *Splendeur et misère: l'exotisme littéraire aux Antilles*, Pointe-à-Pitre, Guadeloupe, Groupe Universitaire de Recherches Inter-Caraïbes, Études et Documents, No. 2, 1969.

Cosminsky, Sheila. 'Interethnic relations in Punta Gorda, British Honduras: a preliminary report', Brandeis University, Waltham, Mass., 1966, mimeo.

Coulthard, G. R. 'Négritude—reality and mystification', *CS*, Vol. 10, No. 1, April 1970, pp. 42–51.

Coulthard, G. R. *Race and colour in Caribbean literature*, London, Oxford University Press for the Institute of Race Relations, 1962.

Coulthard, G. R., ed. *Caribbean literature: an anthology*, London, University of London Press, 1966.

Coupland, Reginald. *The British anti-slavery movement* [1933], London, Frank Cass, 1964.

— *The Empire these days: an interpretation*, London, Macmillan, 1935.

— *Wilberforce* [1923], London, Collins, 1945.

Courlander, Harold. 'Vodoun in Haitian culture', in Courlander and Bastien, op. cit., pp. 1–26.

Courlander, Harold, and Bastien, Rémy. *Religion and politics in Haiti*, Washington, D.C., Institute for Cross-Cultural Research, 1966.

Craig, Hewan. *The Legislative Council of Trinidad and Tobago*, London, Faber and Faber, 1952.

Crane, Julia G., 'Concomitants of selected emigration on a Caribbean island: Saba', Ph.D. thesis in Anthropology, Columbia University, New York, 1966.

Cronon, Edmund David. *Black Moses: the story of Marcus Garvey and the Universal Negro Improvement Association*, Madison, University of Wisconsin Press, 1964.

Cross, Malcolm. 'Cultural pluralism and sociological theory: a critique and re-evaluation', *SES*, Vol. 17, 1968, pp. 381–97.

Cross, Malcolm, and Schwartzbaum, Allen M. 'Social mobility and secondary school selection in Trinidad and Tobago', *SES*, Vol. 18, 1969, pp. 189–207.

Crowley, Daniel J. 'Conservatism and change in Saint Lucia', *Actas del XXXIII Congreso Internacional de Americanistas, San José, 20–27 Julio 1958*, San José, Costa Rica, 1959, Vol. II, pp. 704–15.

— 'Plural and differential acculturation in Trinidad', *AA*, Vol. 59, 1957, pp. 817–24.

Cruikshank, J. Graham. *Black talk*, Demerara, British Guiana, Argosy Press, 1916.

Cruse, Harold. *The crisis of the Negro intellectual*, New York, William Morrow, 1967.

Cummings, Felix. 'Guyana before the United Nations', n.p., People's Progressive Party [1966].

Cumper, George E. 'Labour demand and supply in the Jamaican sugar industry, 1830–1950', *SES*, Vol. 2, No. 4, March 1954, pp. 37–86.

— 'Population movements in Jamaica, 1830–1950', *SES*, Vol. 5, 1956, pp. 261–80.

— 'Preliminary analysis of population growth and social characteristics in Jamaica, 1943–60', *SES*, Vol. 12, 1963, pp. 393–431.

Cumper, George E., ed. *The economy of the West Indies*, Kingston, ISER, 1960.

— *Report of the conference on social development held at the University College of the West Indies, 1961*, Kingston, Standing Committee on Social Services [1961].

— *The social structure of the British Caribbean (excluding Jamaica): Part I*, Jamaica, UCWI, Extra-Mural Department [1948].

Cumpston, I. M. *Indians overseas in British territories, 1834–1854*, London, Oxford University Press, 1953.

Curtin, Philip D. *The Atlantic slave trade: a census*, Madison, University of Wisconsin Press, 1969.

Curtin, Philip D. 'Epidemiology and the slave trade', *Political Science Quarterly*, Vol. LXXXIII, 1968, pp. 190–216.

— *The image of Africa: British ideas and action, 1780–1850*, Madison, University of Wisconsin Press, 1964.

— *Two Jamaicas: the role of ideas in a tropical colony, 1830–1865*, Cambridge, Harvard University Press, 1955.

D

Dallas, R. C. *The history of the Maroons* [1803], 2 vols., London, Frank Cass, 1968.

Dalton, Henry G. *The history of British Guiana*, 2 vols., London, Longmans, 1855.

Daly, P. H. *Revolution to Republic*, Georgetown, Daily Chronicle, 1970.

Damas, Léon-G. *Black-label*, Paris, Gallimard, 1956.

Darbois, Dominique. *Yanamale: village of the Amazon*, London, Collins, 1956.

Dathorne, O. R. 'Africa in West Indian literature', *Black Orpheus* (Ibadan, Nigeria), No. 16, October 1964, pp. 42–54.

— *Dumplings in the soup*, London, Cassell, 1963.

Davids, Leo. 'The East Indian family overseas', *SES*, Vol. 13, 1954, pp. 383–96.

Davie, Donald. 'Enjoy the African night', *New Statesman*, 10 December 1965, p. 936.

Davis, David Brion. 'The emergence of immediatism in British and American antislavery thought', *Mississippi Valley Historical Review*, Vol. XLIX, 1962–3, pp. 209–30.

— *The problem of slavery in western culture*, Ithaca, N.Y., Cornell University Press, 1966.

Davison, Betty. 'No place back home: a study of Jamaicans returning to Kingston, Jamaica', *Race*, Vol. IX, 1967–8, pp. 499–509.

Davison, R. B. *Black British: immigrants to England*, London, Oxford University Press for the Institute of Race Relations, 1966.

— 'W.I. Migration to Britain, 1955–61', *WIE*, Vol. 4, Nos. 1 and 2 (1961), pp. 14–30; No. 3, pp. 9–27; No. 4, pp. 6–16.

Day, Charles William. *Five years residence in the West Indies*, 2 vols., London, Colburn, 1852.

Debbasch, Yvan. *Couleur et liberté: le jeu du critère ethnique dans un ordre juridique esclavagiste, Vol. I.: l'affranchi dans les possessions françaises de la Caraïbe (1635–1833)*, Paris, Librairie Dalloz, 1967.

Debien, Gabriel. 'Le marronage aux Antilles françaises au XVIIe siècle', *CS*, Vol. 6, No. 3, October 1966, pp. 3–43.

— 'La nourriture des esclaves sur les plantations des Antilles françaises aux XVIIe et XVIIIe siècles', *CS*, Vol. 4, No. 2, July 1964, pp. 3–27.

Deerr, Noël. *The history of sugar*, 2 vols., London, Chapman and Hall, 1949.

Degler, Carl N. 'Slavery in Brazil and the United States: an essay in comparative history', *American Historical Review*, Vol. LXXV, 1970, pp. 1004–28.

Delaunay-Belleville, André. *Choses et gens de la Martinique*, 2nd edn., Paris, Nouvelles Éditions Debresse, 1964.

De Lisser, H. G. *Twentieth century Jamaica*, Kingston, Jamaica Times, 1913.

Demas, William G. *The economics of development in small countries with special reference to the Caribbean*, Montreal, McGill University Press for the Centre for Developing-Area Studies, 1965.

30 Mai 1969, Rapport van de Commissie tot onderzoek van de achtertgronden en oorzaken van de onlusten welke op 30 Mai 1969 op Curaçao hebben plaatsgehad. Aruba, De Wit, 1970.

De Rueck, Anthony, and Knight, Julie, eds. *Caste and race: comparative approaches*, Boston, Little, Brown, 1967.

Despres, Leo A. *Cultural pluralism and nationalist politics in British Guiana*, Chicago, Rand McNally, 1967.

— 'Differential adaptations and micro-cultural evolution in Guyana', *South-western Journal of Anthropology*, Vol. 25, 1969, pp. 14–44.

Dessarre, Ève. *Cauchemar Antillais*, Paris, François Maspero, 1965.

'Devaluation'. *New World Occasional Bulletin No. 3*, January 1968.

The development problem in St. Vincent: a report by a University of the West Indies development mission. Kingston, ISER [1969].

Developments towards self-government in the Caribbean: a symposium. The Hague, W. van Hoeve, 1955.

Diederich, Bernard, and Burt, Al. *Papa Doc: the truth about Haiti today*, New York, McGraw Hill, 1969.

Dodge, Peter. 'Ethnic fragmentation and politics: the case of Surinam', *Political Science Quarterly*, Vol. 81, 1966, pp. 593–601.

Donnan, E., ed. *Documents illustrative of the history of the slave trade to America*, 4 vols., Washington, D.C., Carnegie Institution, Publication No. 409, 1930–1, especially Vols. I and II.

Dookhan, I. 'A history of the British Virgin Islands: some notes on its writing and bibliography', Jamaica, UWI, Department of History, 1967, mimeo.

Doran, Edwin, Jr. 'The Caicos conch trade', *GR*, Vol. 48, 1958, pp. 388–401.

— 'Inbreeding in an isolated island community', *Journal of Heredity*, Vol. XLIII, 1952, pp. 263–6.

Douglass, Frederick. 'What the black man wants', in *The equality of all men before the law*, Boston, 1865.

Douyon, Emerson. 'La délinquence juvenile en Haïti', *Transcultural Psychiatric Research Review and Newsletter*, Vol. V, April 1968, pp. 75–7.

D'Oyley, Vincent Roy. *Jamaica: development of teacher training through the agency of the Lady Mico Charity from 1835 to 1914*. Toronto, Ontario College of Education, Department of Educational Research, Bulletin No. 21, 1964.

Drake, St. Clair. 'Reflections on the black diaspora', *NWQ*, Vol. 4, No. 4, Cropover 1968, pp. 73–8.

Drake, St. Clair, and Cayton, Horace. *Black metropolis: a study of Negro life in a northern city* [1945], 2 vols. New York, Harper Torchbooks, 1962.

Drayton, Kathleen. Review of James, Louis, *The islands in between*, in *CS*, Vol. 9, No. 2, July 1969, pp. 84–91.

Du Bois, Hazel. 'Working mothers and absent fathers: family organization in the Caribbean', paper presented at American Anthropological Association meeting, Detroit, Mich., 1964.

Du Bois, W. E. B. *Black reconstruction in America* [1935], Cleveland, World Publishing, 1962.

— 'Marcus Garvey', *The Crisis*, Vol. 21, No. 2, December 1920, p. 60.

Dubrueil, Guy. 'La famille martiniquaise: analyse et dynamique', *Anthropologica*, Vol. 7, No. 1, 1965, pp. 103–29.

Duncker, Sheila J. 'The free coloured and their fight for civil rights in Jamaica, 1800–1830', M.A. thesis, University of London, 1961.

Dupuis, Jacques. 'Les paradoxes de Curaçao: à travers les provinces de l'empire Shell', *CO-M*, Vol. 22, 1969, pp. 63–74.

E

Edel, Matthew. 'The Brazilian sugar cycle of the seventeenth century and the rise of West Indian competition', *CS*, Vol. 9, No. 1, April 1969, pp. 24–44.

Edwards, Bryan. *The history, civil and commercial, of the British colonies in the West Indies*, 2 vols., London, 1793.

Edwards, David T. 'An economic view of agricultural research in Jamaica', *SES*, Vol. 10, 1961, pp. 306–39.

— *Report on an economic study of small farming in Jamaica*, Kingston, ISER, 1961.

Efron, Edith. 'French and Creole patois in Haiti', *CQ*, Vol. 3, No. 4, August 1954, pp. 199–213.

Ehrlich, Allen S. 'East Indian cane workers in Jamaica', Ph.D. thesis in Anthropology, University of Michigan, Ann Arbor, 1969.

Eisner, Gisela. *Jamaica, 1830–1930: a study in economic growth*, Manchester, University Press, 1961.

Elkins, Stanley M. *Slavery: a problem in American institutional and intellectual life* [1959], Chicago, University of Chicago Press, 1968.

Elkins, Stanley M., and McKitrick, Eric. 'Institutions and the law of slavery: the dynamics of unopposed capitalism', *American Quarterly*, Vol. IX, 1957, pp. 3–21.

Elkins, W. F. 'Black power in the British West Indies: the Trinidad longshoremen's strike of 1919', *Science and Society*, Vol. XXXIII, No. 1, 1969, pp. 71–5.

Ellis, Robert A. 'Color and class in a Jamaican market town', *Sociology and Social Research*, Vol. 41, 1957, pp. 354–60.

Emmanuel, I. S. 'Joodse gemeenten in de Nederlandse Antillen: Curaçao', *Encyclopedie van de Nederlandse Antillen*, Amsterdam, Elsevier, 1969, pp. 313–16.

Enig zicht op Suriname. Geografisch Instituut, Vrije Universiteit, Amsterdam, 1969.

Equiano, Olaudah. *Equiano's travels* [1789] (edited by Paul Edwards), London, Heinemann, 1967.

Espinet, Adrian. 'Honours and *paquotille*', *NWQ*, Vol. 2, No. 1, Dead Season 1965, pp. 19–22.

Eyre, Alan. *Land and population in the sugar belt of Jamaica*, UWI, Department of Geology and Geography, Occasional Papers in Geography, No. 1 [1965].

F

Fanon, Frantz. *Black skin, white masks*, New York, Grove Press, 1967.

— *Toward the African revolution (political essays)*, New York, Grove Press, 1967.

Farley, Rawle. 'The rise of the peasantry in British Guiana', *SES*, Vol. 2, No. 4, 1954, pp. 76–103.

Farley, Rawle. 'The rise of the village settlements of British Guiana', *CQ*, Vol. 3, No. 2, September 1953, pp. 101–8.

'The federal principle'. *CQ*, Vol. 6, Nos. 3 and 4, May 1960 (special issue).

'Federation of the West Indies'. *SES*, Vol. 6, No. 2, June 1957 (special federation number).

Ferguson, J. Halcro. *Latin America: the balance of race redressed*, London, Oxford University Press for the Institute of Race Relations, 1961.

Fermor, Patrick Leigh. *The traveller's tree: a journey through the Caribbean islands*, New York, Harper, 1950.

Fernandes, Florestan. *The Negro in Brazilian society*, New York, Columbia University Press, 1969.

Figueroa, John J. 'Education for Jamaica's needs', *CQ*, Vol. 15, No. 1, March 1969, pp. 5–33.

Finkel, Herman J. 'Patterns of land tenure in the Leeward and Windward Islands and their relevance to problems of agricultural development in the West Indies', *Economic Geography*, Vol. 40, 1964, pp. 163–72.

Fischer, Roger A. 'Racial segregation in ante bellum New Orleans', *American Historical Review*, Vol. LXXIV, 1969, pp. 926–37.

FitzHerbert, Katrin. *West Indian children in London*, London, G. Bell, 1967.

Fitzhugh, George. *Cannibals all! or, slaves without masters* [1857], Cambridge, Harvard University Press, 1960.

Flagler, J. M. 'Well caught, Mr. Holder!' *New Yorker*, Vol. 30, 25 September 1954, pp. 65–85.

Foner, Laura, and Genovese, Eugene D., eds. *Slavery in the New World: a reader in comparative history*, Englewood Cliffs, N.J., Prentice-Hall, 1969.

Forbes, Urias. 'The West Indies Associated States: some aspects of the constitutional arrangements', *SES*, Vol. 19, 1970, pp. 57–88.

Frampton, A. de K. 'Land tenure in relation to the British West Indies', *Caribbean Economic Review*, Vol. IV, Nos. 1 and 2, December 1952, pp. 113–39.

Francis, O. C. *The population of modern Jamaica*, Kingston, Jamaica, Department of Statistics, 1963.

Frazier, E. Franklin. *Black bourgeoisie*, New York, Free Press, 1965.

— *The Negro family in the United States*, rev. edn., New York, Dryden Press, 1951.

Freeth, Zahra. *Run softly Demerara*, London, George Allen and Unwin, 1960.

Freilich, Morris. 'Sex, secrets, and systems', in Gerber, op. cit., pp. 47–62.

Freyre, Gilberto. *The racial factor in contemporary politics*, Brighton, University of Sussex Research Unit for the Study of Multi-Racial Societies, 1966.

Fried, Morton H. 'The Chinese in the British Caribbean', in idem, ed., *Colloquium on overseas Chinese*, New York, Institute of Pacific Relations, 1958, pp. 49–58.

— 'Some observations on the Chinese in British Guiana', *SES*, Vol. 5, 1956, pp. 54–73.

Froude, James Anthony. *The English in the West Indies, or, the bow of Ulysses*, London, Longmans, Green, 1888.

Frucht, Richard. 'Emigration, remittances and social change: aspects of the social field of Nevis, West Indies', *Anthropologica*, Vol. 10, No. 2, 1968, pp. 193–208.

Furness, A. E. 'George Hibbert and the defense of slavery in the West Indies', *JHR*, Vol. V, No. 1, May 1965, pp. 56–70.

— 'The Maroon War of 1795', *JHR*, Vol. V, No. 2, November 1965, pp. 30–49.

Furnivall, J. S. *Colonial policy and practice: a comparative study of Burma and Netherlands India*, Cambridge, University Press, 1948.

— *Netherlands India: a study of plural economy*, Cambridge, University Press, 1939.

Fyfe, Christopher, and Jones, Eldred, eds. *Freetown: a symposium*, Freetown, Sierra Leone University Press, 1968.

G

Garcia-Zamor, Jean-Claude. 'Social mobility of Negroes in Brazil', *Journal of Inter-American Studies and World Affairs*, Vol. XII, 1970, pp. 242–54.

Garfield, Viola, and Friedl, Ernestine, eds. *Proceedings of the American Ethnological Society, 1963*, Seattle, University of Washington Press, 1964.

Garvey, Amy Jacques. 'The source and course of black power in America', in her *Black power in America*, Kingston, privately published, 1968, pp. 4–12.

Garvey, Marcus. 'The Negro's greatest enemy', *Current History*, Vol. XVIII, 1923, pp. 951–7.

Gastmann, Albert L. 'The politics of Surinam and the Netherlands Antilles', *Caribbean Monograph Series*, No. 3, Río Piedras, ICS, 1968.

Gaston-Martin. *Histoire de l'esclavage dans les colonies françaises*, Paris, Presses Universitaires de France, 1948.

Genovese, Eugene D. 'American slaves and their history', *New York Review of Books*, 3 December 1970, pp. 34–43.

Gerber, Stanford N., ed. *The family in the Caribbean*, Proceedings of the First Conference . . ., Río Piedras, ICS, 1968.

Girwar, S. Norman. 'Economic diversification in the context of sugar production in some of the Caribbean Commonwealth territories', paper presented at the Eighth Annual Conference of the Caribbean Cane Farmers Association, 1969, mimeo.

Gisler, Antoine. *L'esclavage aux Antilles françaises (XVIIe–XIXe siècle): contribution au problème de l'esclavage*, Fribourg, Switzerland, Éditions Universitaires, 1965.

Gladwell, Joyce. *Brown face, big master*, London, Inter-Varsity Press, 1969.

Glissant, Édouard. *La Lézarde*, Paris, Éditions du Seuil, 1958.

González, Nancie L. Solien. *Black Carib household structure: a study of migration and modernization*, Seattle, University of Washington Press, 1969.

— 'Toward a definition of matrifocality', in Whitten and Szwed, op. cit., pp. 231–44.

— 'West Indian characteristics of the Black Carib', *Southwestern Journal of Anthropology*, Vol. 15, 1959, pp. 300–7.

Goode, William J. 'Illegitimacy in the Caribbean social structure', *American Sociological Review*, Vol. 25, 1960, pp. 21–30.

Gooding, E. G. B. 'Crop diversification in Barbados', *World Crops*, Vol. 20, March 1968, pp. 34–9.

— 'Diversification of agriculture in Barbados', in McKigney and Cook, op. cit., pp. 48–9.

Gordon, Shirley C. *A century of West Indian education: a source book*, London, Longmans, 1963.

— *Reports and repercussions in West Indian education, 1835–1933*, London, Ginn, 1968.

Goveia, Elsa V. 'Introduction', *Savacou*, Vol. 1, No. 1, June 1970, pp. 3–7.

— 'New shibboliths for old', *CQ*, Vol. 10, No. 2, June 1964, pp. 48–54.

— *Slave society in the British Leeward Islands at the end of the eighteenth century*, New Haven, Yale University Press, 1965.

— *A study on the historiography of the British West Indies to the end of the nineteenth century*, Mexico, D.F., Pan-American Institute of Geography and History, 1956.

— 'The West Indian slave laws of the eighteenth century', *Revista de Ciencias Sociales*, Vol. IV, 1960, pp. 75–105.

Graham, Sara, and Beckles, David. 'The prestige ranking of occupations: problems of method and interpretation suggested by a study in Guyana', *SES*, Vol. 17, 1968, pp. 367–80.

Grant, C. H. 'The civil service strike in British Honduras: a case study of politics and the civil service', *CQ*, Vol. 12, No. 3, September 1966, pp. 37–49.

Gratiant, Gilbert. *Île fédérée française de la Martinique*, Paris, Éditions Louis Soulanges, 1961.

Green, Helen Bagenstose. *Socialization values in the Negro and East Indian subcultures of Trinidad* (Ph.D. thesis, University of Connecticut), Ann Arbor, Mich., University Microfilms, 1963.

— 'Values of Negro and East Indian school children in Trinidad', *SES*, Vol. 14, 1965, pp. 204–16.

Green, William A., Jr. 'The apprenticeship in British Guiana, 1834–1838', *CS*, Vol. 9, No. 2, July 1969, pp. 44–66.

Greene, Hugh Carlton. 'On the track of Great Uncle Charles', *History Today*, Vol. XX, No. 1, January 1970, pp. 61–3.

Greenfield, Sidney M. *English rustics in black skin: a study of modern family forms in a pre-industrialized society*, New Haven, College and University Publishers, 1966.

Gresle, François. 'Les enseignants et l'école: une analyse socio-démographique des instituteurs et des professeurs de la Martinique', *CERAG*, No. 19, 1969.

Gresle, François, and Morel, Jean-Luc. 'Les touristes en Martinique', *CERAG*, No. 14, November 1968.

Griffith, J. A. G., et al. *Coloured immigrants in Britain*, London, Oxford University Press for the Institute of Race Relations, 1960.

Groot, Silvia W. de. *Djuka society and social change: history of an attempt to develop a Bush Negro community in Surinam, 1917–1926*, Assen, Neth., Van Gorcum, 1969.

— 'Migration movements of the Djuka tribe in Surinam from 1845 to 1863', *Nieuwe West-Indische Gids*, Vol. 44, 1965, pp. 133–50.

Grove, Gene. 'American scene: the West Indians', *Tuesday Magazine*, Vol. 2, No. 3, November 1966, pp. 12–15.

Guckian, Patrick. 'The balance of colour: a re-assessment of the work of Edgar Mittelholzer', *JJ*, Vol. 4, No. 1, March 1970, pp. 38–45.

Guérin, Daniel. *The West Indies and their future*, London, Dennis Dobson, 1961.

Guggenheim, Hans. *Social and political change in the art world of Trinidad during the period of transition from colony to new nation* (Ph.D. thesis, New York University), Ann Arbor, Mich., University Microfilms, 1968.

Guy, Henry A. *Men in prison*, Kingston, privately published, 1962.

'Guyana independence issue', *NWQ*, Vol. 2, No. 3, High Season 1966.

H

Hadley, C. V. D. 'Personality patterns, social class, and aggression in the British West Indies', *Human Relations*, Vol. II, 1949, pp. 349–62.

Hall, Douglas G. 'Absentee-proprietorship in the British West Indies to about 1850', *JHR*, Vol. IV, 1964, pp. 15–35.

— 'The colonial legacy in Jamaica', *NWQ*, Vol. 4, No. 3, High Season 1968, pp. 7–22.

— *Free Jamaica 1838–1865: an economic history*, New Haven, Yale University Press, 1959.

— 'Slaves and slavery in the British West Indies', *SES*, Vol. 11, 1962, pp. 305–18.

— 'The social and economic background to sugar in slave days (with special reference to Jamaica)', *Caribbean Historical Review*, Nos. III–IV, December 1954, pp. 149–69.

Hall, Robert A., Jr. *Pidgin and Creole languages*, Ithaca, N.Y., Cornell University Press, 1966.

Halperin, Ernst. 'Racism and communism in British Guiana', *Journal of Inter-American Studies*, Vol. VII, No. 1, January 1965, pp. 95–134.

Hamilton, B. L. St. John. *Problems of administration in an emergent nation: a case study of Jamaica*, New York, Frederick A. Praeger, 1964.

Hamilton, Bruce. *Barbados and the confederation question, 1871–1885*, London, Crown Agents, 1956.

Handler, Jerome S. 'The Amerindian slave population of Barbados in the seventeenth and early eighteenth centuries', *CS*, Vol. 8, No. 4, January 1969, pp. 38–64.

Hanke, Lewis. *Aristotle and the American Indians: a study of race prejudice in the modern world*, Chicago, Regnery, 1959.

Hare, Nathan. *The black Anglo-Saxons*, Collier Books, London, Collier-Macmillan, 1970.

Harlow, V. T. *Christopher Codrington, 1688–1710*, London, Oxford University Press, 1928.

— *A history of Barbados 1625–1685*, London, Oxford University Press, 1926.

Harris, Marvin. *Patterns of race in the Americas*, New York, Walker, 1964.

Harris, Wilson. 'History, fable and myth in the Caribbean and Guianas', *CQ*, Vol. 16, No. 2, June 1970, pp. 1–32.

— 'Impressions after seven years', *New World Fortnightly*, No. 44, 25 July 1966, pp. 17–20.

Hayot, E. 'Les gens de couleur libres du Fort-Royal, 1679–1823', *Revue Française d'Histoire d'Outre-Mer*, Vol. LVI, No. 203, 1969.

Hearne, John, and Nettleford, Rex. *Our heritage*, Public Affairs in Jamaica, No. 1, Mona, Jamaica, UWI, Department of Extra-Mural Studies, n.d.

Hendricks, Glenn. 'The British West Indian immigrant group of Puerto Plata', Teachers College of Columbia University, 1967, mimeo.

Hendriks, A. L. 'What colour is a kiss?' *Bim*, Vol. 13, No. 49, July–December 1969, p. 57.

Henriques, Fernando. *Family and colour in Jamaica*, London, Eyre and Spottiswoode, 1953; 2nd edn., London, MacGibbon and Kee, 1968.

Henry, Frances, ed. *McGill studies in Caribbean anthropology*, Montreal, McGill University, Centre for Developing-Area Studies, Occasional Paper Series, No. 5, 1969.

Herskovits, Melville J., *Life in Haitian valley*, New York, Alfred A. Knopf, 1937.

— *The myth of the Negro past* [1941], Boston, Beacon Press, 1958.

— 'Problem, method, and theory in Afroamerican studies' [1945], and 'The ahistorical approach to Afroamerican studies: a critique' [1960], in his *The New World Negro: selected papers in Afroamerican studies* (edited by Frances S. Herskovits), Bloomington, Indiana University Press, 1966, pp. 43–61 and 122–34, respectively.

Herskovits, Melville J., and Herskovits, Frances S. *Rebel destiny: among the Bush Negroes of Dutch Guiana*, New York, McGraw-Hill, 1934.

— *Trinidad village*, New York, Alfred A. Knopf, 1947.

Hilfman, P. A. 'Notes on the history of the Jews in Surinam', *Publications of the American Jewish Historical Society*, No. 18, 1909, pp. 179–207.

Hill, Errol, editor. *Caribbean plays*, Vol. II, St. Augustine, Trinidad, UWI, Extra-Mural Department, 1965.

Hill, Valdemar. *A golden jubilee: Virgin Islanders on the go under the American flag*, New York, Carlton, 1967.

Hinds, Donald. *Journey to an illusion: the West Indian in Britain*, London, Heinemann, 1966.

Hinton, John H. *Memoir of William Knibb, missionary in Jamaica*, London, Houlston and Stoneman, 1847.

Hiro, Dilip. 'The coloured man's view of the British', *New Society*, Vol. 11, 22 February 1968, pp. 263–6.

Hoetink, Harmannus. 'Curazao como sociedad segmentada', *Revista de Ciencias Sociales*, Vol. IV, 1960, pp. 179–92.

— 'Diferencias en relaciones raciales entre Curazao y Surinam', *Revista de Ciencias Sociales*, Vol. V, 1961, pp. 499–514.

— 'The Dominican Republic in the nineteenth century: some notes on stratification, immigration, and race', in Mörner, *Race and class in Latin America*, q.v., pp. 96–121.

— *The two variants in Caribbean race relations*, London, Oxford University Press for the Institute of Race Relations, 1967.

Holcomb, Beverly J. 'Colonialism, cooperation and cash in a West Indian society', Brandeis University, Waltham Mass., 1964, mimeo.

Hope, Colin. 'Gabrielle', *CQ*, Vol. 15, Nos. 2 and 3, June–September 1969, pp. 109–18.

Horowitz, Michael M. *Morne-Paysan: peasant village in Martinique*, New York, Holt, Rinehart and Winston, 1967.

Horowitz, Michael M., and Klass, Morton. 'The Martiniquan East Indian cult of Maldevidan', *SES*, Vol. 10, 1961, pp. 93–100.

Howard, Richard A. *The vegetation of the Grenadines, Windward Islands, British West Indies* (Contributions from the Gray Herbarium of Harvard University, No. CLXXIV), Cambridge, Mass., 1952.

Howes, Barbara, ed. *From the green Antilles: writings of the Caribbean*, New York, Macmillan, 1966.

Hoyos, F. A. *The rise of West Indian democracy: the life and times of Sir Grantley Adams*, Bridgetown, Advocate Press, 1963.

— *The road to responsible government*, Barbados, Letchworth Press, n.d.

Huggins, Molly Green. *Too much to tell*, London, Heinemann, 1967.

Hughes, Alister. 'Non-standard English of Grenada', *CQ*, Vol. 12, No. 4, December 1966, pp. 47–54.

Hughes, Langston. 'The Negro artist and the racial mountain', *Nation* (New York), Vol. CXXII, 23 June 1926, pp. 692–4.

Hughes, Marjorie, *The fairest island*, London, Victor Gollancz, 1962.

Hunter, Guy. *The new societies of tropical Africa: a selective study*, London, Oxford University Press for the Institute of Race Relations, 1962.

Hunter, Guy, ed. *Industrialisation and race relations: a symposium*, London, Oxford University Press for the Institute of Race Relations, 1965.

Hurault, Jean. 'Histoire des noirs réfugiés Boni de la Guyane française (d'après les documents de source française)', *Revue Française d'Histoire d'Outre-Mer*, Vol. 47, No. 166, 1960, pp. 76–137.

— *Les indiens Wayana de la Guyane française: structure sociale et coutume familiale*, Paris, Office de la Recherche Scientifique et Technique d'Outre-Mer, 1968.

— 'La population des indiens de Guyane française', *Population*, Vol. 20, 1965, pp. 603–32 and 801–28.

Hurault, Jean, and Frenay, P. 'Les indiens Emerillon de la Guyane française', *Journal de la Société des Américanistes*, Vol. 52, 1963, pp. 132–56.

Hurwitz, Samuel J., and Hurwitz, Edith. 'A beacon for Judaism: First Fruits of the West', *American Jewish Historical Quarterly*, Vol. 56, 1966, pp. 3–76.

— 'The New World sets an example for the Old: the Jews of Jamaica and political rights 1661–1831', *American Jewish Historical Quarterly*, Vol. 55, 1965, pp. 37–56.

Hyman, Herbert H, and Reed, John Shelton. '"Black matriarchy" reconsidered: evidence from secondary analysis of sample surveys', *Public Opinion Quarterly*, Vol. 33, 1969, pp. 346–54.

Hymans, Jacques Louis. 'French influences on Leopold Senghor's theory of négritude, 1928–48', *Race*, Vol. VII, 1965–6, pp. 365–70.

Hymes, Dell, ed. *Pidginization and creolization of language*, Proceedings of a Conference Held at UWI, April 1968, London, Cambridge University Press, 1971 (in press).

I

'Independence for Jamaica', *WIE*, Vol. 5, No. 1, July 1962, pp. 4–17.

'The intellectual tradition and social change in the Caribbean', *New World*

Pamphlet [1966] (reprinted from *New World Fortnightly*, Nos. 27 and 28, 12 November 1965).

International encyclopedia of the social sciences (edited by David Sills). New York, Macmillan and Free Press, 1968.

Isaacs, Harold R. *The new world of Negro Americans*, London, Phoenix House, 1963.

Ismael, Joseph. *De immigratie van Indonesiërs in Suriname*, Leiden, Luctor et Emergo, 1949.

J

Jackson, H. Merrill. 'Caribbean–West African field study: first report', Cambridge, Mass., Harvard Graduate School of Education, Center for Studies in Education and Development, 1969, mimeo.

Jagan, Cheddi. *Forbidden freedom: the story of British Guiana*, New York, International Publishers, 1954.

— *The west on trial: my fight for Guyana's freedom*, London, Michael Joseph, 1966.

Jahoda, Gustav. *White man: a study of the attitudes of Africans to Europeans in Ghana before independence*, London, Oxford University Press for the Institute of Race Relations, 1961.

Jamaica Central Planning Unit. *Economic survey Jamaica, 1968*, Kingston [1969].

Jamaica educational planning mission, September–November 1964. Paris, UNESCO, 1965.

Jamaica, Ministry of Development and Welfare, Central Planning Unit. *Five Year Independence Plan, 1963–68: a long term development programme for Jamaica*, Kingston, 1963.

Jamaica, Trinidad and Tobago, Leeward Islands, Windward Islands, Barbados, and British Guiana: projected levels of demand, supply and imports of agricultural products to 1975. U.S. Department of Agriculture, Economic Research Service, ERS Foreign 94 [1954].

James, C. L. R. *Beyond a boundary*, London, Hutchinson, 1963.

— *The Black Jacobins: Toussaint L'Ouverture and the San Domingo Revolution* [1938], New York, Vintage Books, 1963.

— '*The Black Scholar* interviews: C. L. R. James', *Black Scholar*, Vol. 2, No. 1, September 1970, pp. 35–43.

— 'The Caribbean confrontation begins', *Race Today*, Vol. 2, 1970, pp. 311–14.

— *The case for West-Indian self government*, London, Hogarth, 1933.

— 'Expatriate island', *New Society*, Vol. 13, 17 April 1969, p. 607.

— 'Introduction', in Hill, Errol, op. cit, pp. v–viii.

— *Party politics in the West Indies*, San Juan, Trinidad, privately published [1962].

— *West Indians of East Indian descent*, Port-of-Spain, Ibis Publications [1969].

James, Louis, ed. *The islands in between: essays on West Indian literature*, London, Oxford University Press, 1968.

Jane, Cecil, ed. *Select documents illustrating the four voyages of Columbus*, 2 vols., London, Hakluyt Society (Second Series, No. LXV), 1930.

Jayawardena, Chandra. *Conflict and solidarity in a Guianese plantation*, London, University of London, 1963.

— 'Ideology and conflict in lower class communities', *Comparative Studies in Society and History*, Vol. X, 1968, pp. 413–46.

Jayawardena, Chandra. 'Migration and social change: a survey of Indian communities overseas', *GR*, Vol. 58, 1968, pp. 426–49.

Jefferson, Owen. 'Some aspects of the post-war economic development of Jamaica', *NWQ*, Vol. 3, No. 3, High Season 1967, pp. 1–11.

John, K. R. V. 'Footnotes on slavery', *Flambeau*, No. 3, January 1966, pp. 10–14.

— 'Political crisis in St. Vincent', *NWQ*, Vol. 3, No. 3, High Season 1967, pp. 51–6.

Jones, David R. W. 'The Caribbean coast of Central America: a case of multiple fragmentation', *Professional Geographer*, Vol. XXII, 1970, pp. 260–6.

Jongh, Edward A. de. *E dia di mas historiko*, n.p., privately published, 1970.

Jordan, Winthrop D. 'American chiaroscuro: the status and definition of mulattoes in the British colonies', *William and Mary Quarterly*, 2nd ser., Vol. 19, 1962, pp. 183–200

— *White over black: American attitudes toward the Negro, 1550–1812*, Chapel Hill, University of North Carolina Press, 1968.

K

Kariel, Henry S. 'Pluralism', in *International Encyplopedia of the Social Sciences*, Vol. 12, pp. 164–9.

Karlins, Marvin, Coffman, Thomas L., and Walters, Gary. 'On the fading of social stereotypes: studies in three generations of college students', *Journal of Personality and Social Psychology*, Vol. 13, No. 1, 1969, pp. 1–16.

Karner, Frances P. *The Sephardics of Curaçao: a study of socio-cultural patterns in flux*, Assen, Neth., Van Gorcum, 1969.

Katznelson, Ira. 'White social science and the black man's world', *Race Today*, Vol. 2, 1970, pp. 47–8.

Kemble, Frances Anne. *A journal of a residence on a Georgian plantation, 1838–1839*, New York, Harper, 1863.

Kerr, Madeline. *Personality and conflict in Jamaica*, London, Collins, 1963.

Kesteloot, Lilyan. *Aimé Césaire*, Paris, Pierre Seghers, 1962.

— 'Naissance de la négritude: "l'étudiant noir"', in idem, *Les écrivains noirs de langue française: nuissance d'une littérature*, 2nd edn., Bruxelles, Université Libre, 1965, pp. 91–210.

Keur, Dorothy L. 'The nature of recent change in the Dutch Windward Islands', *International Journal of Comparative Sociology*, Vol. V, No. 1, March 1964, pp. 40–7.

Keur, John Y., and Keur, Dorothy L. *Windward children: a study in human ecology of the three Dutch Windward Islands in the Caribbean*, Assen. Neth., Royal Van Gorcum, 1960.

Khan, Ismith. *The Obeah man*, London, Hutchinson, 1964.

King, Grace. *New Orleans: the place and the people*, New York, Macmillan, 1896.

King, Kendall W., 'Nutrition research in Haiti', in Schaedel, op. cit., pp 347–70.

'King Sugar and the New World: the story of the great sugar debate'. *New World Pamphlet No. 5*, June 1968.

Kingsley, Charles. *At last: a Christmas in the West Indies*, 3rd edn., London, Macmillan, 1900.

Kirpalani, Murli J., et al. *Indian centenary review: one hundred years of progress*, Port-of-Spain, Guardian Commercial Printery, 1945.

Kitzinger, Sheila. 'The Rastafarian Brethren of Jamaica', *Comparative Studies in Society and History*, Vol. IX, 1966, pp. 33–9.

Klass, Morton. *East Indians in Trinidad: a study of cultural persistence*, New York, Columbia University Press, 1961.

Klein, Herbert S. *Slavery in the Americas: a comparative study of Virginia and Cuba*, Chicago, University of Chicago Press, 1967.

Klerk, C. J. M. de. *De immigratie der Hindostanen in Suriname*, Amsterdam, Urbi et Orbi, 1953.

Knox, A. D. 'Some economic problems of small countries', in Benedict, *Problems of smaller territories*, q.v., pp. 35–44.

Knox, John P., *A historical account of St. Thomas, W.I.*, New York, Charles Scribner, 1852.

Köbben, André J. F. 'Law at the village level: the Cottica Djuka of Surinam', in Nader, op. cit., pp. 117–40.

— 'Participation and quantification: field work among the Djuka (Bush Negroes of Surinam)', in Jongmans, D. G., and Gutkind, P. C. W., eds., *Anthropologists in the field*, New York, Humanities Press, 1967, pp. 35–55.

Kornhauser, William. *The politics of mass society*, Glencoe, Ill., Free Press, 1959.

Kovats-Beaudoux, Edith. 'Une minorité dominante: les blancs créoles de la Martinique', Doctoral thesis, University of Paris [1969].

Kroef, Justus M. van der. 'The Indonesian minority in Surinam', *American Sociological Review*, Vol. 16, 1951, pp. 672–9.

Kuczynski, R. R. *Demographic survey of the British colonial empire*, London, Oxford University Press for the Royal Institute of International Affairs, Vol. III, West Indian and American Territories, 1953.

Kuper, Hilda. *Indian people in Natal*, Natal, University Press, 1960.

Kuper, Leo, and Smith, M. G., eds. *Pluralism in Africa*, Berkeley, University of California Press, 1969.

L

Labat, Jean-Baptiste. *Voyage du Père Labat, aux isles de l'Amérique*, 6 vols., The Hague, P. Husson, 1724.

Lamming, George. 'Caribbean literature: the black rock of Africa', *African Forum* (American Society for African Culture, New York), Vol. 1, No. 4, Spring 1966, pp. 32–52.

— *In the castle of my skin*, London, Michael Joseph, 1963.

— *Of age and innocence*, London, Michael Joseph, 1958.

— *The pleasures of exile*, London, Michael Joseph, 1960.

— 'The pleasures of exile', *Tamarack Review*, No. 14, Winter 1960, pp. 32–56.

— *Season of adventure*, London, Michael Joseph, 1960.

— 'The West Indian people', *NWQ*, Vol. 2, No. 2, Croptime 1966, pp. 63–74.

Lamur, H. E. 'De levensomstandigheden van de in Paramaribo werkende Aukaner arbeiders', *Nieuwe West-Indische Gids*, Vol. 44, 1965, pp. 119–32.

Landes, Ruth. 'Biracialism in American society: a comparative view', *AA*, Vol. 57, pp. 1253–63.

— 'A preliminary statement of a survey of Negro–White relationships in Britain', *Man*, O.S., Vol. LII, September 1952, p. 133.

— 'Race and recognition', *Listener*, Vol. 48, 6 November 1952, pp. 751, 763.

Lanternari, Vittorio. *The religions of the oppressed: a study of modern messianic cults* [1960], New York, Mentor Books, 1965.

La Rose, John, editor. *New Beacon reviews: collection one*, London, New Beacon Books, 1968.

Lasserre, Guy. *La Guadeloupe: étude géographique*, Bordeaux, Union Française d'Impression, 1961.

— 'Les "Indiens" de Guadeloupe', *CO-M*, Vol. VI, 1953, pp. 128–58.

— 'Petite propriété et réforme foncière aux Antilles françaises', *Colloque Internationale Centre de la Recherche Scientifique*, Paris, 1965, pp. 109–24.

Latortue, François. 'Considerations sur la main-d'œuvre haïtienne', in Schaedel, op. cit., pp. 486–523.

Latortue, Gérard R., 'The European lands', in Szulc, op. cit., pp. 173–92.

— 'Political crisis in Haiti', *NWQ*, Vol. 3, No. 2, High Season 1967, pp. 45–50.

— 'Political status of the French Caribbean', in Mathews, *Politics and economics in the Caribbean*, q.v., pp. 148–83.

Lauber, Almon Wheeler. *Indian slavery in colonial times within the present limits of the United States*, New York, Columbia University, 1913.

Lauchmonen. *Old Thom's harvest*, London, Eyre and Spottiswoode, 1965.

Laurence, K. O. 'The development of medical services in British Guiana and Trinidad, 1841–1873', *JHR*, Vol. IV, 1964, pp. 59–67.

— 'The establishment of the Portuguese community in British Guiana', *JHR*, Vol. V, No. 2, November 1965, pp. 50–74.

Law in the West Indies: some recent trends. London, British Institute of International and Comparative Law, 1966.

Layne, Paul. 'Sunny Barbados', *Bim*, Vol. 13, No. 49, July–December 1969, pp. 46–51.

Le Page, R. B. *The national language question*, London, Oxford University Press for the Institute of Race Relations, 1964.

Le Page, R. B. and DeCamp, David, *Jamaican Creole*, London, Macmillan, 1960.

Lee, J. M. *Colonial development and good government: a study of the ideas expressed by the British official classes in planning decolonization, 1939–1964*, Oxford, Clarendon Press, 1967.

Leiris, Michel. *Contacts de civilisations en Martinique et en Guadeloupe*, Paris, UNESCO/Gallimard, 1955.

Leslie, Charles. *History of Jamaica*, London, 1740.

Lessinger, Johanna M. 'Produce vendors in the Princes Town Market', Brandeis University, Waltham, Mass., 1968, mimeo.

Levy, Jacqueline. 'The economic role of the Chinese in Jamaica: the grocery retail trade', UWI, Department of History, Mona, Jamaica, 1967, mimeo.

Lewis, Gordon K. *The growth of the modern West Indies*, New York, Monthly Review Press, 1968.

Lewis, Gordon K. 'An introductory note to the study of the Virgin Islands', *CS*, Vol. 8, No. 2, July 1968, pp. 5–21.
— 'The politics of the Caribbean', in Szulc, op. cit., pp. 5–35.
— 'Race relations in Britain: a view from the Caribbean', *Race Today*, Vol. 1, 1969, pp. 78–80.
Lewis, M. G. *Journal of a West India proprietor, 1815–17*, Boston, Houghton Mifflin, 1929.
Lewis, Oscar. *A study of slum culture: backgrounds for La Vida*, New York, Random House, 1968.
Lewis, S., and Mathews, T. G., eds. *Caribbean integration: papers on social, political, and economic integration*, Proceedings of the Third Caribbean Scholars' Conference, 1966, Río Piedras, ICS, 1967.
Lewis, W. Arthur. *The agony of the eight*, Barbados, Advocate Printery [1965].
— 'Epilogue', in Mordecai, op. cit., pp. 455–62.
Leyburn, James G. *The Haitian people*, rev. edn., New Haven, Yale University Press, 1966.
Lier, R. A. J. van. 'Negro slavery in Surinam', *Caribbean Historical Review*, Nos. III–IV, December 1954, pp. 108–48.
— *Samenleving in een grensgebied: een sociaal-historische studie van de maatschappij in Suriname*, The Hague, M. Nijhoff, 1949.
— 'Social and political conditions in Suriname and the Netherlands Antilles: introduction', in *Developments towards self-government in the Caribbean: a symposium*, q.v., pp. 125–33.
Lind, Andrew W. 'Adjustment patterns among the Jamaican Chinese', *SES*, Vol. 7, 1958, pp. 144–64.
Lindfors, Bernth. 'The African politician's changing image in African literature in English', *Journal of Developing Areas*, Vol. 4, 1969–70, pp. 13–28.
Linton, Neville. 'The role of the expatriate in developing countries', *International Development Review*, Vol. XII, No. 2, 1970, pp. 24–7.
Lipset, Seymour Martin, and Solari, Aldo, eds. *Elites in Latin America*, New York, Oxford University Press, 1967.
Little, Kenneth. 'Some aspects of color, class, and culture in Britain', in 'Color and race', q.v., pp. 512–26.
Littleton, Edward. *Groans of the plantations*, London, 1689.
Litwack, Leon F. *North of slavery: the Negro in the free states, 1790–1860*, Chicago, University of Chicago Press, 1961.
Long, Anton V. *Jamaica and the new order, 1827–1847*, Jamaica, ISER, Special Series, No. 1, 1956.
Long, Edward. *The History of Jamaica, or, general survey of the antient and modern state of that island*, 3 vols., London, T. Lowndes, 1754.
Lovelace, Earl. 'The wine of astonishment', *Voices*, Vol. 2, No. 1, September–December 1969, pp. 3–7.
Lowenthal, David. 'French Guiana: myths and realities', *Transactions New York Academy of Sciences*, Ser. II, Vol. 22, 1960, pp. 528–40.
— 'Levels of West Indian government', *SES*, Vol. 11, 1962, pp. 363–91.
— 'Montserrat: autonomy in microcosm', paper presented at the Conference on Political Sociology of the British Caribbean, December 1961, UCWI, Mona, Jamaica, mimeo.

Lowenthal, David. 'Population contrasts in the Guianas', *GR*, Vol. 50, 1960, pp. 41–58.
— 'The population of Barbados', *SES*, Vol. 6, 1957, pp. 445–501.
— 'Race and color in the West Indies', in 'Color and race', q.v., pp. 580–626.
— 'The range and variation of Caribbean societies', *Annals New York Academy of Sciences*, Vol. 83, 1960, pp. 786–95.
— 'The West Indies chooses a capital', *GR*, Vol. 48, 1958, pp. 336–64.
Lowenthal, David, ed. *The West Indies Federation: perspectives on a new nation*, New York, Columbia University Press for the American Geographical Society and Carleton University, 1961.
Lowenthal, David, and Comitas, Lambros. 'Emigration and depopulation: some neglected aspects of population geography', *GR*, Vol. 52, 1962, pp. 195–210.
Luckhoo, J. A. 'The East Indian in British Guiana', *Timehri*, Vol. 6, 1919.
Lynch, Hollis R. *Edward Wilmot Blyden: pan-Negro patriot, 1832–1912*, London, Oxford University Press, 1967.

M

MacInnes, Colin. *Westward to laughter*, London, MacGibbon and Kee, 1969.
Mack, Raymond W. 'Race, class, and power in Barbados', in Bell, *The democratic revolution in the West Indies*, q.v., pp. 140–64.
Madoo, Patricia. 'The transition from "light skinned" to "coloured"', in Tajfel and Dawson, op. cit., pp. 55–62.
Maharaj, Dayanand. 'The small farmer in the Trinidad sugar industry', paper presented at the Fifth Annual Conference on Agricultural Economics, Dominica, 1970, mimeo.
Maingot, Anthony P. 'From ethnocentric to national history writing in the plural society', *CS*, Vol. 9, No. 3, October 1969, pp. 68–86.
Malefijt, Annemarie de Waal. *The Javanese of Surinam: segment of a plural society*, Assen, Neth., Van Gorcum, 1963.
— 'Het sociaal-economisch vermogen van de Javanen in Suriname', *Tijdschrift van het Koninklijk Nederlandsch Aardrijkskundig Genootschap*, Vol. LXXX, 1963, pp. 467–73.
Malouet, V. P. *Collection de mémoires et correspondances officielles sur l'administration des colonies, et notamment sur la Guiane française et holandaise*, 5 vols., Paris, 1802.
Manley, Edna, ed. *Focus: an anthology of contemporary Jamaican writing*, Mona, Jamaica, UCWI, Extra-Mural Department, 1956.
Manners, Robert A. 'Tabara: subcultures of a tobacco and mixed crops municipality', in Steward, et al., op. cit., pp. 93–170.
Marino, Anthony. 'Family, fertility, and sex ratios in the British Caribbean', *Population Studies*, Vol. XXIV, 1970, pp. 159–72.
Mark, Francis. *The history of the Barbados Workers' Union*, Bridgetown, Barbados Workers' Union [1965].
Marshall, O. R. 'Legal education for the West Indies', in *Law in the West Indies*, q.v., pp. 137–52.
Marshall, Paule. *Brown girl, Brownstones*, New York, Random House, 1959.
— *The chosen place, the timeless people*, New York, Harcourt, Brace and World, 1969.
— *Soul clap hands and sing*, New York, Atheneum, 1961.

Marshall, Woodville K. 'Metayage in the sugar industry of the British Windward Islands, 1838–1865', *JHR*, Vol. V, No. 1, May 1965, pp. 28–55.

— 'Notes on peasant development in the West Indies since 1838', *SES*, Vol. 17, 1968, pp. 252–63.

— 'Social and economic problems in the Windward Islands 1838–65', in Andic and Mathews, op. cit., pp. 234–57.

Mason, Philip. *Patterns of dominance*, London, Oxford University Press for the Institute of Race Relations, 1970.

Mathews, T. G. 'Caribbean cooperation in the field of higher education', in Preiswerk, op. cit., pp. 151–6.

— 'Historical writing in the Caribbean', *Caribbean Review*, Vol. 2, No. 3, Fall 1970, pp. 4–6.

— 'Problems and leaders in the Caribbean', in Wilgus, op. cit., pp. 28–40.

— 'The three Guianas', *Current History*, Vol. 51, 1966, pp. 333–7, 365–6.

Mathews, T. G., et al. *Politics and economics in the Caribbean*, Río Piedras, ICS, Special Study No. 3, 1966.

Mathieson, William Law. *British slave emancipation, 1838–1849* [1932], New York, Octagon Books, 1967.

— *British slavery and its abolition, 1823–1838*, London, Longmans, Green, 1926.

Mathurin-Mair, Lucille. 'The student and the university's civilising role', *CQ*, Vol. 15, Nos. 2 and 3, 1969, pp. 8–19.

Mau, James A. *Social change and images of the future: a study of the pursuit of progress in Jamaica*, Cambridge, Mass., Schenkman, 1968.

— 'The threatening masses: myth or reality?' in Andic and Mathews, op. cit., pp. 258–70.

Maxwell, Neville. *The power of Negro action*, London, privately published, 1965.

Mayer, Adrian C. 'The Indian caste system', in *International encyclopedia of the social sciences*, Vol. 2, pp. 339–44.

Maynard, C. A. 'A carricature of a small society', *Dawnlit*, Vol. I, No. 2, March 1962, pp. 16–17.

Mazzarelli, Marcella. 'Intercommunity relations in British Honduras', *Human Organization*, Vol. 26, 1967, pp. 222–9.

M'Callum, Pierre F. *Travels in Trinidad, during the months of February, March, and April, 1803*, Liverpool, W. Jones, 1805.

McCloy, Shelby T. *The Negro in the French West Indies*, Lexington, University of Kentucky Press, 1966.

McIntyre, A., and Watson, B. *Studies in foreign investment in the Commonwealth Caribbean: No. 1, Trinidad and Tobago*, Jamaica, ISER, 1970.

McKigney, John I., and Cook, Robert, eds. *Protein foods for the Caribbean*, Kingston, Bolivar Press for the Caribbean Food and Nutrition Institute [1968].

McKoy, David L. *A memorable visit . . . by the Vincentian delegation to (Belize) British Honduras*, Belize, n.p., 1967.

McPherson, James M. *The struggle for equality: abolitionists and the Negro in the Civil War and reconstruction*, Princeton, N.J., Princeton University Press, 1964.

McPherson, James M. 'Was West Indian emancipation a success? the abolition argument during the American Civil War', *CS*, Vol. 4, No. 2, July 1964, pp. 28–34.

Meier, August. *Negro thought in America, 1880–1915: racial ideologies in the age of Booker T. Washington*, Ann Arbor, University of Michigan Press, 1964.

Memmi, Albert. *The colonizer and the colonized* [1957], Boston, Beacon Press, 1967.

Merrill, Gordon C. *The historical geography of St. Kitts and Nevis, the West Indies*, Mexico, D. F., Pan-American Institute of Geography and History, 1958.

— 'The role of Sephardic Jews in the British Caribbean area during the seventeenth century', *CS*, Vol. 4, No. 3, October 1964, pp. 32–49.

Metcalf, George. *Royal government and political conflict in Jamaica, 1729–1783*, London, Longmans for the Royal Commonwealth Society, 1965.

Métraux, Alfred. *Voodoo in Haiti* (Hugo Charteris transl.), New York, Oxford University Press, 1959.

Mikes, George. *Not by sun alone*, London, Andre Deutsch, 1967.

Miller, Errol L. 'Body image, physical beauty, and colour among Jamaican adolescents', *SES*, Vol. 18, 1969, pp. 72–89.

Millette, James. 'The Caribbean Free Trade Association: the West Indies at the crossroads', *NWQ*, Vol. 4, No. 4, Cropover 1968, pp. 30–48.

— 'The Civil Commission of 1802: an account and an explanation of an issue in the early constitutional and political history of Trinidad', *JHR*, Vol. VI, Nos. 1 and 2, pp. 29–111.

Millspaugh, Arthur C. *Haiti under American control, 1915–30*, Boston, World Peace Foundation, 1931.

Milner, T. H. *The present and future state of Jamaica considered*, London, H. Hooper, 1839.

Mintz, Sidney W. 'Cañamelar: The subculture of a rural sugar plantation proletariat', in Steward et al., op. cit., pp. 314–417.

— 'Caribbean nationhood in anthropological perspective', in Lewis and Mathews, op. cit., pp. 141–54.

— 'Historical sociology of the Jamaican church-founded free village system', *West-Indische Gids*, Vol. 38, 1958, pp. 46–70.

— 'The socio-historical background to pidginization and creolization', in Hymes, op. cit., pp. 154–68.

Mintz, Sidney W., and Davenport, William, eds. 'Caribbean social organization', *SES*, Vol. 10, No. 4, 1961 (special issue).

Mischel, Walter. 'Delay of gratification, need for achievement and acquiescence in another culture', *Journal of Abnormal and Social Psychology*, Vol. 62, 1961, pp. 543–52.

Mitchell, Harold Paton. *Caribbean patterns: a political and economic study of the contemporary Caribbean*, Edinburgh, Chambers, 1967.

— *Europe in the Caribbean: the policies of Great Britain, France, and the Netherlands towards their West Indian territories in the 20th century*, Edinburgh, Chambers, 1963.

Mitrasing, F. E. M. *Tien jaar Suriname, van afhankelijkheid tot gelijkgerechtigheid*, Leiden, Universitaire Pers, 1959.

Mittelholzer, Edgar. *Children of Kaywana*, London, Secker and Warburg, 1952.

— 'Color, class and letters', *Nation* (New York), 17 January 1959, p. 56.

Mittelholzer, Edgar. *The harrowing of Hubertus*, London, Secker and Warburg, 1954 (also issued as *Kaywana stock*, London, Ace Books, 1959).
— *Kaywana blood*, London, Secker and Warburg, 1958.
— *A morning at the office*, London, Hogarth Press, 1950
— *A swarthy boy*, London, Putnam, 1963.
— *With a Carib eye*, London, Secker and Warburg, 1958.
Mohammed, Kamaluddin. *Unifying our cosmopolitan community*, Port-of-Spain, P.N.M. Publishing Co., n.d.
Moisley, H. A. 'The deserted Hebrides', *Scottish Studies*, Vol. 10, Part 1, 1966, pp. 44–68.
Momsen, Janet D. 'Small scale farming in Barbados, St. Lucia and Martinique', paper presented at the Fifth Annual Conference on Agricultural Economics, Dominica, 1970, mimeo.
Montague, Ludwell Lee. *Haiti and the United States, 1714–1938*, Durham, Duke University Press, 1940.
Montserrat cotton industry enquiry (Beasley Report), n.p. [1953].
Moore, Garrie Ward. 'A study of a group of West Indian Negroes in New York City', M.A. thesis, Columbia University, New York, 1923.
Moore, Robert. 'Defeating the "come back home" call', *Action Radio Times*, Vol. 1, No. 1, October 1969, p. 23.
Moral, Paul. *Le paysan haïtien: étude sur la vie rurale en Haïti*, Paris, G. P. Maisonneuve and Larose, 1961.
Mordecai, John. *The West Indies: the federal negotiations*, London, George Allen and Unwin, 1968.
Moreau de Saint-Méry, Médéric-Louis-Élie. *Description topographique, physique, civile politique et historique de la partie française de l'isle Saint-Domingue* [1797], 3 vols., Paris, Société de l'Histoire des Colonies Françaises et Librairie Larose, 1958.
Morel, Jean-Luc. 'Jeunesse et emploi: de l'insertion des jeunes martiniquais dans le milieu social', *CERAG*, No. 13, 1968.
Morland, J. Kenneth. 'Race awareness among American and Hong Kong Chinese children', *American Journal of Sociology*, Vol. 75, 1969, pp. 360–74.
Mörner, Magnus. *Race mixture in the history of Latin American*, Boston, Little, Brown, 1967.
Mörner, Magnus, ed. *Race and class in Latin America*, New York, Columbia University Press, 1970.
Morrell, W. P. *British colonial policy in the mid-Victorian age: South Africa, New Zealand, the West Indies*, Oxford, Clarendon Press, 1969.
Morrill, Warren T., and Dyke, Bennett. 'A French community on St. Thomas', *CS*, Vol. 5, No. 4, January 1966, pp. 39–47.
Morris, H. S. 'Ethnic groups', in *International encyclopedia of the social sciences*, Vol. 5, pp. 167–72.
Morris, John. *Fever grass*, Jamaica, Collins and Sangster, 1969.
Morris, Mervyn. 'Feeling, affection, respect', in Tajfel and Dawson, op. cit., pp. 5–26.
— 'Some West Indian problems of audience', *English*, Vol. XVI, Spring 1967, pp. 127–31.
— 'To an expatriate friend', *JJ*, Vol. 3, No. 4, December 1969, p. 38.

Morris, Mervyn. 'Walcott and the audience for poetry', *CQ*, Vol. 14, Nos. 1 and 2, March–June 1968, pp. 7–24.

Morse, Richard M. 'The Caribbean: geopolitics and geohistory', in Lewis and Mathews, op. cit., pp. 155–73.

Moskos, Charles C., Jr. *The sociology of political independence: a study of nationalist attitudes among West Indian leaders*, Cambridge, Mass., Schenkman, 1967.

Munroe, Trevor. 'Nationalism and democracy in Jamaica', *NWQ*, Vol. 4, No. 4, Cropover 1968, pp. 24–9.

Murphy, H. B. M., and Sampath, H. M. 'Mental illness in a Caribbean community: a mental health study of St. Thomas, V.I.', Montreal, McGill University, Department of Psychiatry, 1967, mimeo.

Murray, D. J. *The West Indies and the development of colonial government, 1801–1834*, Oxford, Clarendon Press, 1965.

N

Nader, Laura, ed. *Law in culture and society*, Chicago, Aldine, 1969.

Naipaul, V. S. *An area of darkness*, London, Andre Deutsch, 1964.

—— *A flag on the island*, London, Andre Deutsch, 1967.

—— *A house for Mr. Biswas*, London, Andre Deutsch, 1961.

—— *The loss of El Dorado: a history*, London, Andre Deutsch, 1969.

—— *The middle passage*, London, Andre Deutsch, 1962.

—— *The mimic men*, London, Andre Deutsch, 1967.

—— *The mystic masseur*, London, Andre Deutsch, 1957.

—— 'Power to the Caribbean people', *New York Review of Books*, 3 September 1970, pp. 32–4.

—— 'St. Kitts: Papa and the power set', *New York Review of Books*, 8 May 1969, p. 23.

—— *The suffrage of Elvira*, London, Andre Deutsch, 1958.

Nascimento, Kit. 'Imported black power is hopelessly dangerously wrong', *Action Radio Times*, Vol. 1, No. 2, November 1969, p. 6.

Nath, Dwarka. *A history of Indians in British Guiana*, London, Nelson, 1950.

'Nationalism in the sixties'. *WIE*, Vol. 3, No. 7, January 1961, pp. 3–7.

Nederlandse Antillen Statistisch Jaarboek 1969. Willemstad, Curaçao, Bureau of Statistics, 1970.

Nègre, André. 'Les "Indiens" de la Guadeloupe et leurs rites religieux', *Bulletin de la Société d'Histoire de la Guadeloupe*, No. 1, 1964, pp. 33–43.

—— 'Origines et signification du mot "créole"', *Bulletin de la Société d'Histoire de la Guadeloupe*, Nos. 5–6, 1966, pp. 38–42.

Nettleford, Rex. 'The dance as an art form—its place in the West Indies', *CQ*, Vol. 14, Nos. 1 and 2, 1968, pp. 127–35.

—— 'National identity and attitudes to race in Jamaica', *Race*, Vol. VII, 1965–6, pp. 59–72.

——— 'Poverty at the root of race issue', in 'Jamaica: a special report', *The Times*, 14 September 1970. p. II.

Neumann, Peter. *Wirtschaft und materielle Kultur der Buschneger Surinames: ein Beitrag zur Erforschung afroamerikanischer Probleme*, Abhandlungen und Berichte des Staatlichen Museums für Völkerkunde Dresden, Band 26, Berlin, 1967.

Newton, Arthur Percival. *The European nations in the West Indies, 1493–1688* [1933], New York, Barnes and Noble, 1967.

Nicole, Christopher. *The self lovers*, London, Hutchinson, 1968.

— *White boy*, London, Hutchinson, 1966.

Niehoff, Arthur, and Niehoff, Juanita. *East Indians in the West Indies*, Milwaukee Public Museum, Publications in Anthropology, No. 6, 1960.

Nosel, José. 'Les étudiants à la Martinique', in 'Problèmes universitaires des Antilles-Guyane françaises', *CERAG*, No. 18, 1969, pp. 36–71.

Nugent, Maria. *Lady Nugent's journal* (edited by Philip Wright), Kingston, Institute of Jamaica, 1966.

O

Ober, Frederick A. *Camps in the Caribbees*, Boston, Lee and Shepard, 1886.

Olivier, Sydney. *The myth of Governor Eyre*, London, Hogarth Press, 1933.

— *White capital and coloured labour*, London, Independent Labour Party, 1910.

Olmsted, Frederick Law. *The slave states before the Civil War* (excerpted from various writings, 1856–1861, by Harvey Wish), New York, G. P. Putnam's Sons, Capricorn Books, 1959.

O'Loughlin, Carleen. *Economic and political change in the Leeward and Windward Islands*, New Haven, Yale University Press, 1968.

— 'The economy of Montserrat: a national accounts study', *SES*, Vol. 8, 1959, pp. 147–78.

Ong, Walter J. 'World as view and world as event', *AA*, Vol. 71, 1969, pp. 634–47.

Osofsky, Gilbert. *The burden of race: a documentary history of Negro–white relations in America*, New York, Harper and Row, 1967.

— *Harlem: the making of a ghetto: Negro New York, 1890–1930*, New York, Harper and Row, 1968.

Otterbein, Keith F. *The Andros Islanders: a study of family organization in the Bahamas*, Lawrence, University of Kansas Press, 1966.

Ottley, Carlton Robert. *A historical account of the Trinidad and Tobago police force from the earliest times*, Trinidad, privately published, 1964.

Oxaal, Ivar. *Black intellectuals come to power*, Cambridge, Mass., Schenkman, 1968.

— 'Race, pluralism and nationalism in the British Caribbean', *Journal of Biosocial Science*, Supplement No. 1, July 1969, pp. 153–62.

Oxtoby, F. E. 'The role of political factors in the Virgin Islands watch industry', *GR*, Vol. 60, 1970, pp. 463–74.

P

Paddock, John. 'The war of the myths: Spanish and English treatment of the native Americans', *America Indigena*, Vol. 18, 1958, pp. 281–92.

Paget, Hugh. 'The free village system in Jamaica', *CQ*, Vol. I, No. 4 [1954], pp. 7–19.

Palmer, B. M. *Slavery a divine trust: the duty of the South to preserve and perpetuate the institution*, New York, George F. Nesbitt, 1861.

Palmer, Ransford W. *The Jamaican economy*, New York, Frederick A. Praeger, 1968.

Panday, R. M. N. *Agriculture in Surinam 1650–1950: an inquiry into the causes of its decline*, Amsterdam, H. J. Paris, 1959.

Pares, Richard. 'Merchants and planters', *Economic History Review*, Supplement 4, 1960.

— *A West-India fortune*, London, Longmans, Green, 1950.

Park, Robert E. 'The nature of race relations', in Thompson, Edgar T., op. cit., pp. 3–45.

Parker, Seymour, and Kleiner, Robert J. 'The culture of poverty: an adjustive dimension', *AA*, Vol. 72, 1970, pp. 516–27.

Parry, J. H., and Sherlock, Philip M. *A short history of the West Indies*, London, Macmillan, 1956.

Parsons, James J. *San Andrés and Providencia: English-speaking islands in the Western Caribbean*, Berkeley, University of California Publications in Geography, Vol. 12, No. 1, 1956.

Parsons, Talcott. *The social system*, Glencoe, Illinois, Free Press, 1951.

Parsons, Talcott, and Shils, E. A., eds. *Toward a general theory of action*, Cambridge, Harvard University Press, 1951.

Pastner, Carroll McClure. 'A sociolinguistic study of a rural Trinidad community', Brandeis University, Waltham, Mass., 1967, mimeo.

Patchett, K. W. 'English law in the West Indies', in *Law in the West Indies: some recent trends*, q.v., pp. 1–53.

Patterson, H. Orlando. *An absence of ruins*, London, Hutchinson, 1967.

— 'A Jamaican dilemma', typescript, n.d.

— 'The ritual of cricket', *JJ*, Vol. 3, No. 1, March 1969, pp. 22–5.

— 'Social aspects of the sugar industry', *NWQ*, Vol. 5, Nos. 1 and 2, Dead Season and Croptime 1969, pp. 47–9.

— 'The social structure of a university hall of residence', *Pelican*, Vol. IX, No. 3, March 1962, pp. 22–39.

— *The sociology of slavery*, London, MacGibbon and Kee, 1967.

— 'West Indian migrants returning home: some observations', *Race*, Vol. X, 1968–9, pp. 69–77.

Patterson, Sheila. *Immigration and race relations in Britain, 1960–1967*, London, Oxford University Press for the Institute of Race Relations, 1969.

Payne, Millicent. 'The chink in his armour', *Bim*, Vol. 10, No. 41, June–December 1965, pp. 17–23.

Peach, Ceri. *West Indian migration to Britain: a social geography*, London, Oxford University Press for the Institute of Race Relations, 1968.

Pearse, Andrew C. 'Education in the British Caribbean: social and economic background', *Vox Guyanae*, Vol. II, No. 1, February 1956, pp. 9–24.

Persaud, B. 'Problems of the Commonwealth Caribbean sugar industry', *Cane Farmer*, Vol. 11, No. 2, February 1970, p. 30.

Peterson, John. 'Sierra Leone Creole: a reappraisal', in Fyfe and Jones, op. cit., pp. 100–17.

Petitjean-Roget, Jacques. 'Les juifs à la Martinique sous l'ancien régime', *Revue d'Histoire des Colonies*, 1956, pp. 138–58.

Phelps, O. W. 'Rise of the labour movement in Jamaica', *SES*, Vol. 9, 1960, pp. 417–68.

Phillips, Andrew Peter. 'The development of a modern labor force in Antigua',
Ph.D. thesis, University of California, Los Angeles, 1964.

Philpott, Stuart B. 'Remittance obligations, social networks and choice among
Monsterratian migrants in Britain', *Man*, N.S. Vol. 3, 1968, pp.
465–76.

Pierson, Donald. *Negroes in Brazil: a study of race contact at Bahia*, Carbondale,
Southern Illinois University Press, 1967.

Piquion, René. *Manuel de négritude*, Port-au-Prince, Haiti, Henri Duchamps
[1965].

Pitman, Frank Wesley. *The development of the British West Indies, 1700–1763*
[1917], Hamden, Conn., Archon Books, 1967.

Plank, John N. 'Neighborly relations in the Caribbean', in Wilgus, op. cit.,
pp. 161–70.

Plotnicov, Leonard, and Tuden, Arthur, eds. *Essays in comparative social stratification*, Pittsburgh, University of Pittsburgh Press, 1970.

Poinsett, Alex. 'Roy Innis: nation builder', *Ebony*, October 1969, p. 170.

Pompilus, Pradel. *La langue française en Haïti*, Paris, Institut des Hautes Études
de l'Amérique Latine, 1961.

Pope-Hennessy, James. *The Baths of Absalom: a footnote to Froude*, London, Allan
Wingate, 1954.

Porter, Arthur T. *Creoledom: a study of the development of Freetown society*, London,
Oxford University Press, 1963.

Post, K. W. J. 'The politics of protest in Jamaica, 1938: some problems of
analysis and conceptualization', *SES*, Vol. 18, 1969, pp. 374–90.

Powrie, Barbara E. 'The changing attitude of the coloured middle class
towards carnival', *CQ*, Vol. 4, Nos. 3 and 4, March–June 1956, pp.
224–32.

Preiswerk, Roy, ed. *Regionalism and the Commonwealth Caribbean*, St. Augustine,
Trinidad, UWI, Institute of International Relations, 1969.

Price, A. Grenfell. *White settlers in the tropics*, New York, American Geographical
Society Special Publication No. 23, 1939.

Price, Edward T. 'The Redlegs of Barbados', *Yearbook Association of Pacific
Coast Geographers*, Vol. 19, 1957, pp. 35–9.

Price, Thomas J. 'Ethnohistory and self-image in three New World Negro
societies', in Whitten and Szwed, op. cit., pp. 63–73.

Price-Mars, Jean. *Ainsi parla l'oncle: essais d'ethnographie* [1928], New York,
Parapsychology Foundation, 1954.

Prins, J. 'Twintig jaar praktijk van de aziatische huwelijkswetgeving in
Suriname', *Nieuwe West-Indische Gids*, Vol. 44, 1965, pp. 78–108.

'Problèmes universitaires des Antilles-Guyane françaises'. *CERAG*, No. 18,
1969.

Proceedings of the conference on Creole language studies. London, Macmillan, 1961.

Proctor, Jesse Harris, Jr. 'British West Indian society and government in
transition 1920–1960', *SES*, Vol. 11, 1962, pp. 273–304.

— 'East Indians and the federation of the British West Indies', *India Quarterly*,
Vol. XVII, 1961, pp. 370–95.

Proudfoot, Malcolm J. *Population movements in the Caribbean*, Port-of-Spain,
Caribbean Commission, 1950.

Proudfoot, Mary. *Britain and the United States in the Caribbean: a comparative study in methods of development*, London, Faber and Faber, 1954.

Pujadas, Leo. 'A note on education development in Trinidad and Tobago, 1956–1966', *Trinidad and Tobago C.S.O. Research Papers*, No. 6, 1969, pp. 1–46.

Punch, L. D. 'Lully'. *A journey to remember (39 years in the civil service)*, Trinidad, privately published [1967].

Q

Quarles, Benjamin. 'Frederick Douglass: letters from the Haitian legation', *CQ*, Vol. 4, No. 1, January 1955, pp. 75–81.

Quintus Bosz, A. J. A. *Drie eeuwen grondpolitiek in Suriname*, Assen, Neth., Van Gorcum, 1954.

R

Racial problems in the public service: Report of the British Guiana Commission of Inquiry. International Commission of Jurists, Geneva, 1965.

Rae, J. Stanley, and Armitage-Smith, Sidney A. *Conditions in the Carib Reserve and the disturbance of 18th September, 1930, Dominica: report of a commission appointed by the Governor of the Leeward Islands, July 1931*, London, Cmd. 3990.

Ragatz, Lowell Joseph. 'Absentee landlordism in the British Caribbean, 1750–1833', *Agricultural History*, Vol. V, 1931, pp. 7–24.

— *The fall of the planter class in the British Caribbean, 1763–1833: a study in social and economic history* [1928], New York, Octagon Books, 1963.

Rainwater, Lee, and Yancey, W. L. *The Moynihan Report and the politics of controversy*, Cambridge, Massachusetts Institute of Technology Press, 1967.

Ramchand, Kenneth. 'The artist in the balm-yard: "Season of adventure"', *NWQ*, Vol. 5, Nos. 1 and 2, Dead Season and Croptime 1969, pp. 13–21.

— 'The colour problem at the university: a West Indian's changing attitudes', in Tajfel and Dawson, op. cit., pp. 27–37.

— 'The Negro and the English language in the West Indies', *Savacou*, Vol. 1, No. 1, June 1970, pp. 33–44.

— *The West Indian novel and its background*, London, Faber and Faber, 1970.

Ramsahoye, Fenton H. W. *The development of land law in British Guiana*, Dobbs Ferry, N.Y., Oceana Publications, 1966.

Raphael, Lennox. 'West Indians and Afro-Americans', *Freedomways* (New York), Vol. 4, 1964, pp. 438–45.

Raspail, Jean. *Punch Caraïbe*, Paris, Robert Laffont, 1970.

— *Secouons le cocotier*, Paris, Robert Laffont, 1966.

Raveau, François H. M. 'Caste and race in the psychodynamics of acculturation', in De Rueck and Knight, op. cit., pp. 266–75.

— 'An outline of the role of color in adaptation phenomena', in 'Color and race', q.v., pp. 376–89.

Rawlins, Randolph. 'Black power', *Art and Man*, Act II, Scene II, June 1969, pp. 47–51.

Reed, T. Edward. 'Caucasian genes in American Negroes', *Science*, Vol. 165, 22 August 1969, pp. 762–7.

Reid, Ira de Augustine. *The Negro immigrant: his background, characteristics and social adjustment, 1899–1937*, New York, Columbia University Press, 1939.

Reisman, Karl. 'Cultural and linguistic ambiguity in a West Indian village', in Whitten and Szwed, op. cit., pp. 129–44.

Reno, Philip. 'The ordeal of British Guiana', *Monthly Review*, Vol. 16, Nos. 3 and 4, July–August 1964.

Rens, L. L. E. 'Analysis of annals relating to early Jewish settlement in Surinam', *Vox Guyanae*, Vol. I, No. 1, May 1954, pp. 19–38.

Report of the Amerindian Lands Commission, Georgetown, 1969.

Report of the Commission appointed by His Excellency the Governor-General to investigate allegations of discriminatory practices by the management of the Trinidad Country Club, Trinidad, Government Printery, 29 August 1969.

Report of the Commission appointed to enquire into the organization of the sugar industry of Antigua (Soulbury Report), London, 1949.

Report of the regional conference on the training of teachers in the British Caribbean, 1957, Development and Welfare in the West Indies, Bulletin No. 39 [1958].

Report of the tripartite economic survey of the Eastern Caribbean, January–April 1966, London, HMSO, 1967.

Report on the UNESCO educational survey mission to British Guiana, 1962–3, WS/0663.22.

Reuter, Edward Byron. *The mulatto in the United States* [1918], New York, Negro Universities Press, 1969.

Revert, Eugène. *La Martinique: étude géographique*, Paris, Nouvelles Éditions Latines, 1949.

Revista de Ciencias Sociales (Río Piedras, UPR), Vol. IV, No. 1, March 1960 (special number on the Caribbean).

Rex, John. *Race relations in sociological theory*, London, Weidenfeld and Nicolson, 1970.

Ribeiro, Orlando. *L'île de Madère: étude géographique*, Lisbon, 1949, Union Géographique Internationale, Congrès International de Géographie.

Richards, Novelle H. *The struggle and the conquest: twentyfive years of social democracy in Antigua*, Antigua, Workers Voice [1964].

Rivière, P. G. *Marriage among the Trio: a principle of social organisation*, Oxford, Clarendon Press, 1969.

— 'A policy for the Trio Indians of Surinam', *Nieuwe West-Indische Gids*, Vol. 45, 1966, pp. 95–120.

Roback, Judith. 'Bases of social differentiation in a Guyana mining town', M.A. thesis, McGill University, Montreal, 1968.

Robequain, Charles. 'Saint-Barthélemy: terre française', *CO-M*, Vol. II, No. 5, 1949, pp. 14–37.

Roberts, George W. 'Emigration from the island of Barbados', *SES*, Vol. 4, 1955, pp. 242–88.

— 'A life table for a West Indian slave population', *Population Studies*, Vol. V, 1951–2, pp. 238–43.

— 'A note on school enrolment in Trinidad and Tobago, 1960', *SES*, Vol. 16, 1967, pp. 113–26.

Roberts, George W. *The population of Jamaica*, Cambridge, University Press for the Conservation Foundation, 1957.

Roberts, George W., and Abdulah, N. 'Some observations on the educational position of the British Caribbean', *SES*, Vol. 14, 1965, pp. 144–54.

Roberts, George W., and Byrne, J. A. 'Summary statistics on indenture and associated migration affecting the West Indies, 1834–1918', *Population Studies*, Vol. XX, 1966–7, pp. 125–34.

Roberts, George W., with Byrne, J. A. 'Memorandum on the racial composition of British Guiana's public service', in *Racial problems in the public service*, q.v., pp. 139–61.

Rodman, Hyman. 'Marital relationships in a Trinidad village', *Marriage and Family Living*, Vol. 23, 1961, pp. 166–70.

— 'On understanding lower-class behaviour', *SES*, Vol. 8, 1959, pp. 441–50.

Rogler, Charles C. 'The role of semantics in the study of race distance in Puerto Rico', *Social Forces*, Vol. 22, 1943–4, pp. 448–53.

Rohlehr, Gordon. 'Character and rebellion in "A house for Mr. Biswas" by V. S. Naipaul', *NWQ*, Vol. 4, No. 4, Cropover 1968, pp. 66–72.

— 'The ironic approach: the novels of V. S. Naipaul', in James, Louis, op. cit., pp. 121–39.

Ronceray, Hubert de. 'Le changement social dans les familles haïtiennes: première partie: familles urbaines', *Les Cahiers du CHISS*, Vol. 3, No. 4, May 1969, pp. 1–34.

Rose, E. J. B., et al. *Colour and citizenship: a report on British race relations*, London, Oxford University Press for the Institute of Race Relations, 1969.

Rose, Harold M. 'The all-Negro town: its evolution and function', *GR*, Vol. 55, 1965, pp. 362–81.

Rottenberg, Simon. 'Entrepreneurship and economic progress in Jamaica', *Inter-American Economic Affairs*, Vol. 7, No. 2, Autumn 1953, pp. 74–9.

Rubin, Vera. 'Approaches to the study of national characteristics in a multi-cultural society', *International Journal of Social Psychiatry*, Vol. V, No. 1, Summer 1969, pp. 20–6.

Rubin, Vera, ed. *Caribbean studies: a symposium*, Jamaica, ISER, 1957.

— 'Social and cultural pluralism in the Caribbean', *Annals New York Academy of Sciences*, Vol. 83, Article 5, 1960.

Rubin, Vera, and Zavalloni, Marisa. *We wish to be looked upon: a study of the aspirations of youth in a developing society*, New York, Teachers College Press, 1969.

Ruhomon, Peter. *Centenary history of the East Indians in British Guiana, 1838–1938*, Georgetown, Daily Chronicle [1946].

Russell, Richard J., and McIntire, William G. *Barbuda reconnaissance*, Baton Rouge, Louisiana State University Press, 1966.

Russell-Wood, A. J. R. 'Class, creed and colour in colonial Bahia: a study in prejudice', *Race*, Vol. IX, 1967–8, pp. 133–57.

Russett, Bruce M. *International regions and the international system: a study in political ecology*, Chicago, Rand McNally, 1967.

Ryan, Selwyn Douglas. 'Decolonization in a multi-racial society: a case study of Trinidad and Tobago', Ph.D. thesis, York University [1967].

Ryan, Selwyn Douglas. 'Restructuring the Trinidad economy', *NWQ*, Vol. 4, No. 4, Cropover 1968, pp. 7–23.

— 'Rise and fall of the barefooted man', *Trinidad and Tobago Index*, No. 3, Winter 1966, pp. 4–15.

— 'The struggle for Afro-Indian solidarity in Trinidad and Tobago', *Trinidad and Tobago Index*, No. 4, September 1966, pp. 3–28.

S

Sablé, Victor. *La transformation des isles d'Amérique en départements français*, Paris, Édition Larose, 1955.

St. John, Spenser. *Hayti, or, the black republic*, New York, Scribner and Welford, 1889.

St. Omer, Garth. *Shades of grey*, London, Faber and Faber, 1968.

St. Pierre, Maurice. 'Industrial unrest in Mackenzie, Guyana', in Henry, op. cit., pp. 65–92.

Salisbury, Richard F. 'Ethnographic notes on Wapishana agriculture', in Salisbury, Richard F., et al., *Ethnographic notes on Amerindian agriculture*, Montreal, McGill University Savanna Research Series No. 9, 1968, pp. 7–20.

Salkey, Andrew. *The late emancipation of Jerry Stover*, London, Hutchinson, 1968.

— *A quality of violence*, London, New Authors, 1959.

'Sans humanité: violence in Jamaica'. *Moko*, Nos. 13 (pp. 4–3), 14 (pp. 3–4), and 15 (pp. 3–4), April and May 1969.

Sartre, Jean-Paul. *Black Orpheus* (S. W. Allen, transl.), n.p., Présence Africaine [1963].

Sauer, Carl Ortwin. *The early Spanish Main*, Berkeley, University of California Press, 1966.

Saul, S. B. 'The British West Indies in depression 1880–1914', *Inter-American Economic Affairs*, Vol. 12, No. 3, Winter 1958, pp. 3–25.

Sausse, André, 'Pathologie comparée des populations primitives noirs et indiennes de la Guyane française', *Bulletin de la Société de Pathologie Exotique*, Vol. 44, 1951, pp. 455–60.

— *Populations primitives du Maroni (Guyane française)*, Paris, Institut Géographique National, 1951.

'Saving and development'. *WIE*, Vol. 5, No. 2, August–September 1962, pp. 10–21.

Saxe, Allen. 'Urban squatters in Trinidad: the poor in a mass society', M.A. thesis, Brandeis University, Waltham, Mass., 1968, mimeo.

Schaad, J. D. G. 'Epidemiological observations in Bush Negroes and Amerindians in Surinam', *Tropical and Geographical Medicine*, Vol. 12, 1960, pp. 38–46.

Schaedel, Richard P., ed. *Papers of the conference on research and resources of Haiti*, New York, Research Institute for the Study of Man, 1969.

Schlesinger, Arthur, Jr. *A thousand days: John F. Kennedy in the White House*, Boston, Houghton Mifflin, 1965.

Schlesinger, Benjamin. 'The Jews of Jamaica: a historical view', *CQ*, Vol. 13, No. 1, March 1967, pp. 46–53.

Schoelcher, Victor. *Esclavage et colonisation*, Paris, Presses Universitaires de France, 1948.

Schuler, Monica. 'Akan slave rebellions in the British Caribbean', *Savacou*, Vol. 1, No. 1, June 1970, pp. 8–31.

Schwartz, Barton M., ed. *Caste in overseas Indian communities*, San Francisco, Chandler, 1967.

Scott, Dennis. 'Bennett on Bennett', *CQ*, No. 14, Nos. 1 and 2, March–June 1968, pp. 97–101.

Seaga, Edward P. G. 'Parent-teacher relationships in a Jamaican village', *SES*, Vol. 4, 1955, pp. 289–302.

— 'Revival cults in Jamaica', *JJ*, Vol. 3, No. 2, June 1969, pp. 3–13.

Sealy, Clifford. 'The professor', in Hill, Errol, op. cit., pp. 119–48.

Seditious and undesirable publications. Dominica Act No. 16, 1968.

Seers, Dudley. 'A step towards a political economy of development (illustrated by the case of Trinidad/Tobago)', *SES*, Vol. 18, 1969, pp. 218–53.

Segal, Aaron. *The politics of Caribbean economic integration*, Río Piedras, ICS, Special Study No. 6, 1968.

Segal, Aaron, with Earnhardt, Kent C. *Politics and population in the Caribbean*, Río Piedras, ICS, Special Study No. 7, 1969.

Selvon, Samuel. 'Calypsonian', in Coulthard, *Caribbean literature: an anthology*, q.v., pp. 72–83.

— *An island is a world*, London, MacGibbon and Kee, 1955.

Semmel, Bernard. *The Governor Eyre controversy*, London, MacGibbon and Kee, 1962.

— 'The issue of "race" in the British reaction to the Morant Bay uprising of 1865', *CS*, Vol. 2, No. 3, October 1962, pp. 3–15.

Senghor, Léopold S.-, ed. *Anthologie de la nouvelle poésie nègre et malgache de langue française*, Paris, Presses Universitaires de France, 1948.

'The 7 year itch . . . and 7 members of the Theatre Workshop give reasons why'. *Art and Man*, Act II, Scene II, June 1969, pp. 34–8, 61, 64.

Sewell, William Grant. *The ordeal of free labour in the West Indies*, New York, 1861.

Seymour, A. J. 'The novel in the British Caribbean—III', *Bim*, Vol. 11, No. 44, January–June 1967, pp. 238–42.

Shapiro, Norman R. 'Negro poets of the French Caribbean: a sampler', *Antioch Review*, Vol. XXVII, 1967, pp. 211–28.

Sheridan, R. B. 'The wealth of Jamaica in the eighteenth century', *Economic History Review*, Vol. 18, 1965, pp. 292–311.

Sherlock, Philip. *West Indies*, London, Thames and Hudson, 1966.

Shibutani, Tamotsu, and Kwan, Kian M. *Ethnic stratification: a comparative approach*, London, Macmillan, 1965.

Shils, Edward. 'Color, the universal intellectual community and the Afro-Asian intellectual', in 'Color and race', q.v., pp. 279–95.

— 'The theories of mass society', *Diogenes*, No. 39, 1962, pp. 45–66.

Sibley, Inez Knibb. *The Baptists of Jamaica*, Kingston, Jamaica Baptist Union, 1965.

Simey, T. S. *Welfare and planning in the West Indies*, Oxford, Clarendon Press, 1946.

Simms, Peter. *Trouble in Guyana*, London, George Allen and Unwin, 1966.

Simpson, George Eaton. 'Baptismal, "mourning", and "building" ceremonies of the Shouters in Trinidad', *Journal of American Folklore*, Vol. 79, 1966, pp. 537–50.

— 'Jamaican revivalist cults', *SES*, Vol. 5, No. 4, 1956.

— 'Political cultism in West Kingston, Jamaica', *SES*, Vol. 4, 1955, pp. 133–49.

— 'The Shango cult in Trinidad', *Caribbean Monograph Series*, No. 2, Río Piedras, ICS, 1965.

Singh, H. P. *The Indian enigma*, Port-of-Spain, privately published, 1965.

Singham, A. W. *The hero and the crowd in a colonial polity*, New Haven, Yale University Press, 1968.

Sio, Arnold A. 'Interpretations of slavery: the slave status in the Americas', *Comparative Studies in Society and History*, Vol. VII, 1965, pp. 289–308.

Sires, Ronald V. 'The Jamaica constitution of 1884', *SES*, Vol. 3, No. 1, June 1954, pp. 64–81.

Slater, Mary. *The Caribbean islands*, London, B. T. Batsford, 1968.

Sluisdom, E. E. 'Het aantal Surinamers in Nederland', *Enig zicht op Suriname*, pp. VII-6–VII-7.

Smith, Adam. *An inquiry into the nature and causes of the wealth of nations*, 3 vols., 7th edn., London, A. Strahan and T. Cadell, 1793.

Smith, Arthur F. 'The Spanish abolition law of 1870: a study in legislative reluctance', *Revista de Ciencias Sociales*, Vol. IV, 1960, pp. 215–35.

Smith, M. G. *Dark Puritan*, Kingston, UWI, Department of Extra-Mural Studies, 1963.

— 'A framework for Caribbean studies' [1955], in his *The plural society in the British West Indies*, q.v., pp. 18–74.

— *Kinship and community in Carriacou*, New Haven, Yale University Press, 1962.

— 'Introduction', to Clarke, Edith, *My mother who fathered me*, 2nd edn., q.v., pp. i–xliv.

— *The plural society in the British West Indies*, Berkeley, University of California Press, 1965.

— *Stratification in Grenada*, Berkeley, University of California Press, 1965.

— 'A study of West Indian development trends and their relation to the future development of the U.W.I.', Kingston, UWI, 1965, mimeo.

— 'The transformation of land rights by transmission in Carriacou', *SES*, Vol. 5, 1956, pp. 103–38.

— *West Indian family structure*, Seattle, University of Washington Press, 1962.

Smith, M. G., Augier, Roy, and Nettleford, Rex. *The Ras Tafari movement in Kingston, Jamaica*, Kingston, ISER, 1960.

Smith, M. G., and Kruijer, G. J. *A sociological manual for extension workers in the Caribbean*, Kingston, UWI, Department of Extra-Mural Studies, 1957.

Smith, Raymond T. *British Guiana*, London, Oxford University Press for the Royal Institute of International Affairs, 1962.

— *The Negro family in British Guiana*, London, Routledge and Kegan Paul, 1956.

— 'Social stratification, cultural pluralism and integration in West Indian societies', in Lewis and Mathews, op. cit., pp. 226–58.

Smith, Raymond T. 'Social stratification in the Caribbean', in Plotnicov and Tuden, op. cit., pp. 43–76.
— 'Some social characteristics of Indian immigrants to British Guiana', *Population Studies*, Vol. XIII, 1959, pp. 34–9.
Smith, Raymond T., and Jayawardena, Chandra. 'Caste and social status among the Indians of Guyana', in Schwartz, op. cit., pp. 43–92.
— 'Marriage and the family amongst East Indians in British Guiana', *SES*, Vol. 8, 1959, pp. 321–76.
Sobers, Garfield, and Barker, J. S., eds. *Cricket in the sun: a history of West Indies cricket*, London, Arthur Barker, 1967.
Solien, Nancie L. *See* González, Nancie L. Solien.
Spackman, Ann. 'The Senate of Trinidad and Tobago', *SES*, Vol. 16, 1967, pp. 77–100.
Sparer, Joyce L. 'Attitudes towards "race" in Guyanese literature', *CS*, Vol. 8, No. 2, July 1968, pp. 23–63.
Spear, Brian. 'Family planning in Barbados', *New Society*, Vol. 14, 4 September 1969, p. 357.
Speckmann, Johan D. 'The caste system and the Hindustani group in Surinam', in Schwartz, op. cit., pp. 201–12.
— 'The Indian group in the segmented society of Surinam', *CS*, Vol. 3, No. 1, April 1963, pp. 3–17.
— *Marriage and kinship among the Indians in Surinam*, Assen, Neth., Van Gorcum, 1965.
Springer, Hugh W. 'Barbados as a sovereign state', *Journal of the Royal Society of Arts*, Vol. CXV, 1967, pp. 627–41.
— *Reflections on the failure of the first West Indian Federation*, Occasional Papers in International Affairs No. 4, Harvard University, Cambridge, Mass., 1962.
Spurling, John Jasper. *Social relationships between American Negroes and West Indian Negroes in a Long Island community: an exploratory examination of intragroup relationships in the Addisleigh Park neighbourhood of St. Albans, Long Island, N.Y.* (Ph.D. thesis, New York University, 1962), Ann Arbor, Mich., University Microfilms, 1969.
Srinivas, M. N. *Religion and society among the Coorgs of South India*, Oxford, Clarendon Press, 1952.
Star, Jack. 'Virgin Islands: shame in the U.S. tropics', *Look*, 10 March 1970, p. 18.
Starkey, Otis P. *The economic geography of Barbados: a study of the relationships between environmental variations and economic development*, New York, Columbia University Press, 1939.
The state of the nation: Trinidad and Tobago in the later 1960's. Port-of-Spain, Civicus, n.d.
Stedman, J. G. *Narrative, of a five years' expedition, against the revolted Negroes of Surinam, in Guiana, in the wild coast of South America; from the year 1772 to 1777: elucidating the history of that country, and describing its productions*, 2 vols., London, J. Johnson, 1806.
Stein, Stanley. *Vassouras: a Brazilian coffee county, 1850–1900*, Cambridge, Harvard University Press, 1957.

Steward, Julian H., et al. *The people of Puerto Rico: a study in social anthropology*, Urbana, University of Illinois Press, 1956.

Stewart, J. *A view of the past and present state of the island of Jamaica; with remarks on the physical and moral condition of the slaves, and on the abolition of slavery in the colonies*, Edinburgh, Oliver and Boyd, 1823.

Storm van 's Gravesande, Laurens. *The rise of British Guiana* (C. A. Harris and J. A. J. Villiers, comps.), 2 vols., London, The Hakluyt Society, 2nd Series, No. 26, 1911.

Sturge, Joseph, and Harvey, Thomas. *The West Indies in 1837, being the journal of a visit to Antigua, Montserrat, Dominica, St. Lucia, Barbados, and Jamaica, undertaken for the purpose of ascertaining the actual condition of the Negro population of those islands*, London, 1838.

Stycos, J. Mayone, and Back, Kurt W. *The control of human fertility in Jamaica*, Ithaca, N.Y., Cornell University Press, 1964.

'The sugar industry: our life or death?' *New World Pamphlet No. 4*, December 1967.

Suttles, Gerald D. *The social order of the slum: ethnicity and territory in the inner city*, Chicago, University of Chicago Press, 1968.

Swan, Michael. *The marches of El Dorado: British Guiana, Brazil, Venezuela*, Boston, Beacon Press, 1958.

Sydnor, Charles S. *Slavery in Mississippi*, Baton Rouge, Louisiana State University Press, 1966.

Szulc, Tad, ed. *The United States and the Caribbean*, Englewood Cliffs, N.J., Prentice-Hall, 1971.

T

Tajfel, Henri, and Dawson, John L., eds. *Disappointed guests: essays by African, Asian, and West Indian Students*, London, Oxford University Press for the Institute of Race Relations, 1965.

Tannenbaum, Frank. *Slave and citizen: the Negro in the Americas* [1946], New York, Vintage Books, 1963.

Taper, Bernard. 'Letter from Port of Spain', *New Yorker*, 23 October 1965, pp. 203–26.

Tawney, R. H. *Equality* [1931], New York, Capricorn Books, 1961.

Taylor, Douglas MacRae. *The Black Carib of British Honduras*, New York, Viking Fund Publications in Anthropology No. 17, 1951.

— 'The Caribs of Dominica', in *Smithsonian Institution Bulletin 119: anthropological papers*, 1938, pp. 103–60.

Thelwell, Arthur. *Report on squatter problem and land use, island of Dominica*, Kingston, Jamaica Lands Department, 1950.

Tholenaar–Van Raalte, J. 'De integratie van Westindische immigraten in Groot-Brittannië en in Nederland', *Nieuwe West-Indische Gids*, Vol. 46, 1968, pp. 150–63.

Thomas, Clive Y. 'British Guiana', *NWQ*, Vol. 1, No. 1, March 1963, pp. 87–96.

— 'Diversification and the burden of sugar to Jamaica', *NWQ*, Vol. 5, Nos. 1 and 2, Dead Season and Croptime 1969, pp. 41–7.

Thomas, J. J. *Froudacity* [1889], London, New Beacon Books, 1969.

Thompson, Edgar T., ed. *Race relations and the race problem: a definition and an analysis* [1939], New York, Greenwood Press, 1968.

Thompson, Era Bell. 'Saba's youngest ruler', *Ebony*, October 1969, pp. 116–22.

Thompson, Wally. 'Creoles and pidgins, east and west', *NWQ*, Vol. 2, No. 4, Cropover 1966, pp. 11–16.

Thorne, Alfred P. 'An economic phenomenon (study of an apparent psychological trait and its probable effect on regional economic development)', *CQ*, Vol. 6, No. 4, 1960, pp. 270–8.

Thornton, A. P. 'Aspects of West Indian society', *International Journal*, Vol. XV, 1960, pp. 113–21.

Thorpe, Marjorie. '"The mimic men": a study of isolation', *NWQ*, Vol. 4, No. 4, Cropover 1968, pp. 55–9.

Tidrick, Gene. 'Some aspects of Jamaican emigration to the United Kingdom, 1953–1962', *SES*, Vol. 15, 1966, pp. 22–39.

Tourism in the Caribbean: essays on problems in connection with its promotion. Assen, Neth., n.p., 1964.

'Tourisme et développement en Martinique', *CERAG*, No. 16, 1969.

'Trinidad Carnival issue', *CQ*, Vol. 4, Nos. 3 and 4, March–June 1956.

Trinidad and Tobago. *Third five-year plan, 1969–1973*, Trinidad, Government Printery, 1970.

Trippett, Frank. 'Grenada: the nowhere island', *Look*, 10 March 1970, p. 28.

Trollope, Anthony. *The West Indies and the Spanish Main*, London, Chapman and Hall, 1860.

Tyson, J. D. *Report on the condition of Indians in Jamaica, British Guiana and Trinidad, 1938–39*, Simla, Government of India Press, 1939.

U

Ucko, E. *La fusión de los Sefardíes con los Dominicanos*, Ciudad Trujillo, Dominican Republic, 1944.

'Unemployment'. *New World Pamphlet*, September 1967.

'The United Congregation of Israelites, Duke Street', Kingston (pamphlet, n.d.).

Updike, John. 'Letter from Anguilla', *New Yorker*, 22 June 1968, pp. 70–80.

UWI Institute of Education. 'Textbook survey draft', 1969, mimeo.

V

Valdman, Albert. 'The language situation in Haiti', in Schaedel, op. cit., pp. 155–203.

Valentine, Charles A. 'Blackston: progress report on a community study in urban Afro-America' [New York], 1970, mimeo.

— *Culture and poverty: critique and counter-proposals*, Chicago, University of Chicago Press, 1968.

Vaissière, Pierre de. *Saint-Domingue (1629–1789): la société et la vie créoles sous l'ancien régime*, Paris, 1909.

Vatuk, Ved Prakash. *British Guiana*, New York, Monthly Review Press, 1963.

Vérin, Pierre. 'Notes sur la vie sociale du village de la Pointe Caraïbe (Sainte-Lucie, Antilles), *Annales de l'Université de Madagascar*, Série Lettres et Sciences Humaines, No. 6, 1967, pp. 139–64.

Vérin, Pierre. 'The rivalry of Creole and English in the West Indies', *West-Indische Gids*, Vol. 38, 1958, pp. 163–7.

— 'Sainte-Lucie et ses derniers Caraïbes', *CO-M*, Vol. XII, 1959, pp. 349–61.

Viau, Alfred. *Noirs, mulâtres, blancs ou rien que du sang*, Ciudad Trujillo, Dominican Republic, Montalvo, 1955.

Viélot, Klébert. 'L'enseignement primaire en Haïti', in Schaedel, op. cit., pp. 281–346.

Vignon, R. 'French Guiana—looking ahead', *Caribbean Commission Monthly Bulletin*, Vol. 7, 1954, p. 254.

Vincent, Sténio. *En posant les jalons*, Port-au-Prince, Haiti, 1939.

W

Waddell, D. A. G. *The West Indies and the Guianas*, Englewood Cliffs, N.J. Prentice-Hall, 1967.

Wade, Richard C. *Slavery in the cities: the South 1820–1860*, New York, Oxford University Press, 1964.

Wagley, Charles. *Amazon town: a study of man in the tropics*, New York, Macmillan, 1953.

Wagley, Charles, ed. *Race and class in rural Brazil*, Paris, UNESCO, 1962.

Wagley, Charles, and Harris, Marvin. *Minorities in the New World: six case studies*, New York, Columbia University Press, 1958.

Walcott, Derek. *The castaway and other poems*, London, Jonathan Cape, 1965.

— 'The dream on Monkey Mountain', *CQ*, Vol. 14, Nos. 1 and 2, March–June 1968, pp. 110–26.

Walker, Della M. 'Family and social structure in Anguilla', in Gerber, op. cit., pp. 111–16.

Waller, John Augustine. *A voyage in the West Indies*, London, Richard Phillips, 1820.

Walmsley, Anne. 'Second C.A.M. conference', *Bim*, Vol. 12, No. 48, January–June 1969, pp. 233–6.

Ward, R. G. 'The consequences of smallness in Polynesia', in Benedict, *Problems of smaller territories*, q.v., pp. 81–96.

Waters, Ivor. *The unfortunate Valentine Morris*, Chepstow, Mon., The Chepstow Society, 1964.

Weller, Judith Ann. 'The East Indian indenture in Trinidad', *Caribbean Monograph Series*, No. 4, Río Piedras, ICS, 1968.

Wesley, Charles H. 'The free colored population in the British Empire', *Journal of Negro History*, Vol. XIX, 1934, pp. 137–70.

West India Royal Commission Report, London, Cmd. 6607, 1945.

West, Robert C. and Augelli, John P. *Middle America: its lands and peoples*, Englewood Cliffs, N.J., Prentice-Hall, 1966.

Westergaard, W. *The Danish West Indies under Company rule (1671–1754) with supplementary chapter, 1755–1917* [1917], New York, Macmillan, 1957.

Whitbeck, R. H. 'The Lesser Antilles—past and present', *Annals Association of American Geographers*, Vol. 23, 1933, pp. 21–6.

White, Landeg E. 'Steelbands: a personal record', *CQ*, Vol. 15, No. 4, December 1969, pp. 32–9.

Whitten, Norman E., Jr., and Szwed, John F., eds. *Afro-American anthropology: contemporary perspectives*, New York, Free Press, 1970.

Wickham, John. 'West Indian writing', *Bim*, Vol. 13, No. 50, January–June 1970, pp. 68–80.

Wilgus, A. Curtis, ed. *The Caribbean: its hemispheric role*, Gainesville, University of Florida Press, 1967.

Willeford, Mary Jo. 'Negro New World religions and witchcraft', *Bim*, Vol. 12, No. 48, January–June 1969, pp. 216–22.

Williams, Eric. *Britain and the West Indies: historical and contemporary aspects of the relationship between Britain and the West Indies* (Fifth Noel Buxton Lecture of the University of Essex), London, Longmans, Green, 1969.

— *British historians and the West Indies*, London, Andre Deutsch, 1964.

— *Capitalism and slavery*, Chapel Hill, University of North Carolina Press, 1944.

— *From Columbus to Castro: the history of the Caribbean, 1492–1969*, London, Andre Deutsch, 1970.

— *The historical background of race relations in the Caribbean*, Teachers Economic and Cultural Association Public Affairs Pamphlet No. 3, Port-of-Spain, 1955.

— *History of the people of Trinidad and Tobago*, Port-of-Spain, P.N.M. Publishing Co., 1962.

— *Inward hunger: the education of a Prime Minister*, London, Andre Deutsch, 1969.

— *Massa day done: a masterpiece of political and sociological analysis*, Port-of-Spain, P.N.M. Publishing Co., 1961.

— *The Negro in the Caribbean*, Washington, D.C., Associates in Negro Folk Education, 1942.

— *Reflections on the Caribbean economic community*, Port-of-Spain, P.N.M. Publishing Co., 1965.

— *Slavery to Chaguaramas*, Port-of-Spain, P.N.M. Publishing Co., 1959.

Willis, J. C. *Agriculture in the tropics*, Cambridge, University Press, 1914.

Willis, William S. 'Divide and rule: red, white, and black in the Southeast', *Journal of Negro History*, Vol. XLVIII, No. 3, July 1963, pp. 157–76.

Wilson, Edmund. *Red, black, blonde and olive: studies in four civilizations: Zuñi, Haiti, Soviet Russia, Israel*, New York, Oxford University Press, 1956.

Wilson, Peter J. 'Caribbean crews: some unconsidered aspects of social structure', paper presented at American Anthropological Association meeting, Washington, D.C., 1967, mimeo.

— 'The possibilities of Caribbean social organization' [1968], mimeo.

— 'Reputation and respectability: a suggestion for Caribbean ethnology', *Man*, N.S. Vol. 4, No. 1, March 1969, pp. 70–84.

Wingfield, Roland, and Parenton, Vernon J. 'Class structure and class conflict in Haitian society', *Social Forces*, Vol. 43, 1965, pp. 338–48.

Wood, Donald. *Trinidad in transition: the years after slavery*, London, Oxford University Press for the Institute of Race Relations, 1968.

Wooding, H. O. B. 'The constitutional history of Trinidad and Tobago', *CQ*, Vol. 6, Nos. 2 and 3, May 1960, pp. 143–59.

Wooding, Hugh. 'Foreword', in *Law in the West Indies*, q.v., pp. vii-viii.

Woodson, Carter G. *The Negro professional man and the community: with special emphasis on the physician and the lawyer*, Washington, D.C., Association for the Study of Negro Life and History, 1934.

Wrong, Hume. *Government of the West Indies*, Oxford, Clarendon Press, 1923.

Wyndham, H. A. *The Atlantic and emancipation*, London, Oxford University Press for the Royal Institute of International Affairs, 1937.

Wynter, Sylvia. *The hills of Hebron: a Jamaican novel*, London, Jonathan Cape, 1962.

Y

Yawney, Carole D. 'Drinking patterns and alcoholism among East Indians and Negroes in Trinidad', M.A. thesis, McGill University, Montreal, 1968.

— 'Drinking patterns and alcoholism in Trinidad', in Henry, op. cit., pp. 34–48.

Yearwood, Trevor. 'Maureen', *Bim*, Vol. 13, No. 50, January–June 1970, pp. 96–109.

Young, Allan. *Approaches to local self-government in British Guiana*, London, Longmans, Green, 1958.

Young, Virginia Heyer. 'Family and childhood in a Southern Negro community', *AA*, Vol. 72, 1970, pp. 269–88.

Z

Zavalloni, Marisa. *Adolescents' values in a changing society: a study of Trinidad youth*, Paris, Mouton, 1968.

Zeitlin, Maurice. 'Economic insecurity and political attitudes of Cuban workers', *American Sociological Review*, Vol. 31, No. 1, February 1966, pp. 35–51.

Zolberg, Aristide R. 'Frantz Fanon: a gospel for the damned', *Encounter*, No. 27, November 1966, pp. 56–63.

Zylberberg, Jacques. 'Outline of the sociology of la Guadeloupe', *Civilisations*, Vol. 16, No. 4, 1966, pp. 478–99.

Index